The Sociology of Rural Life

HARPER'S SOCIAL SCIENCE SERIES

UNDER THE EDITORSHIP OF

F. Stuart Chapin

Single Farmstead of a Middle-Class
Farm Family in Chester County,
Pennsylvania, Illustrating the Im-
proved Farm Practices (Terracing,
Contour Plowing, and Strip Cropping)
Now Diffusing Rapidly Throughout
the United States. (*Courtesy of the*
U.S. SOIL CONSERVATION SERVICE.)

THE SOCIOLOGY
OF RURAL LIFE

THIRD EDITION

T. Lynn Smith

PROFESSOR OF SOCIOLOGY
UNIVERSITY OF FLORIDA

HARPER & BROTHERS   *Publishers*   NEW YORK

TO

My Wife

CONTENTS

ix

PART IV.   Social Processes in Rural Society

PART V.   Conclusion

ILLUSTRATIONS

EDITOR'S INTRODUCTION

The sociology of rural life is a study of the rural population, rural social organization, and the social processes operative in rural society. To the treatment of this task the author brings a vigorous new approach that has grown out of the experience of extensive research and wide travel. He attempts to correct some current misconceptions about rural living; he elaborates aspects of the subject hitherto given scanty attention; and he utilizes a large number of well-selected illustrations, maps and diagrams, that serve to clarify such fundamental factors as settlement patterns, land division, land tenure, and the size of agricultural holdings. His interpretation of rural social relationships in terms of such sociological processes as competition, conflict, coöperation, accommodation, assimilation, acculturation and social mobility, is carried out with both scientific insight and practical realism. This combination of case history data, graphic illustrations and sound theoretical orientation, makes a textbook with balanced content consisting of intrinsically interesting materials. Bibliographies and aids to teachers in the form of carefully prepared questions for each chapter will be a great convenience for those who do not have access to large libraries. In these various ways the author has produced a treatment of rural living that meets the criteria of a good teaching text.

F. STUART CHAPIN

PREFACE TO THE FIRST EDITION

This book was written for students of rural sociology; but it is also addressed to all workers engaged in activities designed to increase the welfare of the people on the land, and especially to those public servants who are responsible for planning, guiding, and carrying out the agricultural policies of the nation.

The last decade has seen the multiplication of detailed analytical studies of this and that part of the sociology of rural life, but there has been no recent attempt to offer a perspective of the entire field. The general objective of the present work has been to give due consideration to all scientific approaches and to assemble from the most reliable sources pertinent facts, significant tested hypotheses, and demonstrated illuminating theories relative to the social relations among the rural population. In this way it is hoped that the present volume will contribute to systematization in a field where synthesis at present is lagging far behind analysis.

In my attempt to see the field as a whole, I have thought it necessary to develop in some detail portions hitherto omitted from systematic treatment in any of the general works. Nearly all of Part IV comes in this category. The pioneering nature of these efforts should partially excuse some of the mistakes that undoubtedly have been made in the process.

For analytical purposes the chart or diagram is a step in advance of the frequency distribution table. Charts and graphs are also very effective in the presentation of findings. For these reasons this book contains few tables, whereas illustrations are used freely.

To the persons who have contributed in one way or another to the production of this book my obligations are great. Authors and publishers have generously allowed me to quote their materials. It has been a pleasure to make proper acknowledgment in footnotes to those fellow workers who have contributed most directly.

But the book has been facilitated in many other ways. Director C. T. Dowell of the Louisiana Agricultural Experiment Station has been most generous in providing clerical and stenographic assistance. Dean Fred C. Frey of the College of Arts and Sciences of Louisiana State University, while still head of the department of sociology, established instruction in rural sociology on a firm basis at the university, and this book grew out of those courses.

To five men I am greatly indebted for orientation and instruction in the sociology of rural life: Lowry Nelson, John C. Swenson, P. A. Sorokin, Carle C. Zimmerman, and Fred C. Frey. The first four are my former teachers. Through ten years of intimate association, first when we were graduate students together and later as colleagues in the same department, Frey has contributed greatly to my point of view and approach in the study of social relationships.

I alone am responsible for all errors of fact and interpretation which the book may contain, but these would have been much more numerous had it not been for the generous assistance of my colleagues and assistants. Professors Rudolf Heberle, E. H. Lott, Edgar A. Schuler, and Marion B. Smith read portions of the manuscript and made helpful suggestions. Professor H. C. Hoffsommer permitted me to use unpublished materials and photographs. Contributions by my research assistants and graduate students, Vernon J. Parenton, Homer L. Hitt, and Reed Bradford, include the assembling of data, drafting of charts and maps, checking of references, and the most stimulating discussions of hypotheses and methodology. Other students, both graduate and undergraduate, furnished inspiration for the work, and several of them contributed in term papers specific facts for which I gratefully give credit at the proper place. Miss Marjory Stephens assisted in preparing the final manuscript for publication, and Mrs. Margery McCall assisted with the index. In addition to checking innumerable details my secretary, Miss Mabel Cleary, typed the manuscript several times and assumed most of the responsibility in the preparation of the index.

                                                    T. LYNN SMITH

PREFACE TO THE THIRD EDITION

The task of revising and bringing up to date this third edition of *The Sociology of Rural Life* has not been a simple one. Since 1945, when the text of the revised edition was completed, the development of a science of rural society has been pushed forward vigorously. It has not been easy to incorporate all of the more significant new contributions that have been made; and some of the treatments have had to be completely redone. The inclusion of the materials from the 1950 censuses of agriculture and population in the United States, for which definitive results began appearing late in 1952, also has demanded a great deal of care and attention. Nevertheless to the best of his ability the author has sought to produce a new edition that, like its predecessors, would be based upon the tested results of research studies in all sections of the United States. In addition he has sought to make more adequate use of the valuable studies which American rural sociologists and their co-workers in other lands are producing for many heretofore sociologically unknown parts of the world.

Chapter 14 is entirely new, as are various parts of other chapters throughout the book. It also was thought advisable to transfer the treatments of marital status, educational status, and religious affiliations from the chapter on the Composition of Population to those dealing with domestic institutions, educational institutions, and religious institutions, respectively.

The author is deeply indebted to many persons for assistance in connection with the preparation of the present text. The greatest thanks are due those from all parts of the nation, and from several foreign countries as well, who have used the previous editions or the translation as texts and have made specific suggestions as to ways in which the book might be improved. Many others assisted in the procurement of the materials for the illustrations, and to them likewise the author desires to express his appreciation.

Students in the author's courses in rural sociology at Louisiana State University, Vanderbilt University, and the University of Florida, including large numbers of public school teachers from the various states, deserve considerable credit for their sincere efforts in helping the writer to produce a better text. Mr. Joseph Sardo, a graduate assistant in the department of sociology and anthropology at the University of Florida, assisted with part of the tabulations and in the drafting of some of the charts. My son Jackson, as a sophomore student in the same University, read and criticized the new chapter on "Systems of Agriculture" from the standpoint of the ultimate consumer. Miss Louetta Young typed parts of the manuscript. My colleagues and administrative superiors at the University of Florida offered much friendly counsel and encouragement; and my wife, to whom the volume is dedicated, as ever shared in the division of family labor which alone makes possible this and my other volumes. None of these persons is responsible for any errors of fact or interpretation which the book may contain, but to all of them I am very grateful.

T. LYNN SMITH

Gainesville, Florida
January 15, 1953

PART ONE

Introduction

Anything worth writing deserves an introduction. Chapter 1 outlines the features of science in general, presents the essentials of the scientific method, states the nature of sociology, and explains the relationship of rural sociology to the more general science of society. It also sets forth the need for the present work. The second chapter, "The Rural World," sets forth the particular ways in which the rural environment differs from the urban—the factors that make society and people in the country different from those in the city.

1

INTRODUCTION

This book is an attempt to assemble in a single volume the essential facts and the basic principles that have been derived from the application of the scientific method in the study of rural social relationships. An endeavor is made to present these in a manner that can be understood by college students of sophomore standing.

Science

Science is a term used to denote an organized body of knowledge, including both fact and theory. As Wolf has stated, "Science as such is a species of theoretical knowledge," and as such it differs from all active skills and practical wisdom.[1] Science is the accumulation, arranged in orderly fashion, of facts and principles which have been derived from the application of the scientific method. Thus the questions of what is and what is not science resolve themselves into the question of whether or not the scientific method has been employed. Science also is used as a collective noun to embrace the various sciences such as physics, chemistry, botany, and astronomy, or it may also refer to one of these separately. The lesser lights in these disciplines frequently attempt to monopolize the term "science" for their own specialties. To the extent that the scientific method is applied to the study of human relationships, the resulting body of fact and inference entitles sociology and the various social sciences to be classed with the other sciences. Because of this it is desirable to consider, first, the principal characteristics of science itself, and, second, the essentials of the scientific method.

[1] A. Wolf, *Essentials of the Scientific Method*, New York, The Macmillan Company, 1930, pp. 10–11.

3

Science possesses certain characteristics in common with other species of knowledge such as philosophy and history, but it differs from them in fundamental ways. All sound knowledge is dependent upon critical discrimination, "the ability to get at the naked facts" and not to be misled by mere appearances, generally accepted ideas, or one's own desires. Although science has no monopoly on critical discrimination, an inquiring state of mind is the basic element in all scientific endeavor. It alone can command the necessarily careful making of observations, can keep the observer from being included with the observed, can guarantee that all pertinent evidence both for and against a specific hypothesis will be recorded. Generality and system are also essential to all science. Science seeks to discover order in nature, to ascertain common and repeated characteristics. For science the most important facts are those which occur many times, those which are constant or repeated in time or space.[2] For this reason science is concerned with types and classes; it seeks general principles or uniformities. The unique is of little scientific value. Individual objects and particular events are of interest merely as specimens. Other disciplines, such as history, differ from science in this respect by being primarily interested in particular nations, objects, persons, institutions, etc. As Wolf has so clearly stated: "History is concerned with *particular* nations, or institutions, discoveries, or inventions, not with laws relating to nations and institutions, etc., generally. Such general laws would belong to ethnology, or anthropology, or sociology, or psychology, which are sciences, not to history."[3]

But the most fundamental characteristic of science, and the one which most clearly differentiates it from philosophy, is empirical verification. Sensory stimuli are all-important in scientific endeavor; science begins with observation, but it does not end there. After the mind has reflected upon these observations, it tends to run forward into the unknown, to penetrate the realm of supposition. Propositions are developed that may be true. But in

---

[2] Cf. H. Poincaré, *The Foundation of Science* (translated by G. B. Halsted), New York, The Science Press, 1929, p. 363; and Robert E. Park, "Sociology," in Wilson Gee's *Research in the Social Sciences*, New York, The Macmillan Company, 1929, p. 4.

[3] Wolf, *op. cit.*, p. 13. Frederick J. Teggart has stated the difference between history and science as follows: "Science deals with objects, entities, things, and their relations; history concerns itself with events." *Theory of History*, New Haven, Yale University Press, 1925, p. 71.

science all tentative hypotheses and explanations must be thoroughly checked by further observation. Mere internal consistency is not a sufficient test of scientific validity. A well-disciplined scientific mind is one capable of formulating significant hypotheses. For scientific purposes hypotheses which cannot be tested are useless, regardless of how consistent they may be with other hypotheses.[4] In philosophy, on the other hand, the chief criterion of usefulness and value is that a hypothesis or proposition be consistent with previous assertions. Unlike philosophy, science insists that all hypotheses be tested empirically, and it retains only those which are confirmed by further observation. So in common with other species of theoretical knowledge, science is based upon critical discrimination, generality, and system. Unlike other systems of knowledge such as history, science is interested in the ordinary, usual, and commonplace; unlike philosophy, science demands the empirical verification of all hypotheses.

A word is necessary pertaining to the interrelationships of the various fields of science. As indicated above, science is the product of the application of the scientific method. Hence the difference between sciences derives from the differences in the fields or areas to which scientific methods are applied. Astronomy results from the scientific study of the heavenly bodies, geology from the application of the scientific method in the study of the earth, botany from the scientific study of plant life. Since the claim that sociology should be numbered among the sciences is based upon the insistence that it is the result of applying the scientific method to the study of social relationships, it is pertinent to inquire concerning the essentials of the scientific method.

The Scientific Method

The mental activities necessary to acquire scientific knowledge are of two main types: (1) *observation,* and (2) *inference;* and the essence of the scientific method consists of skill in securing unbiased, pertinent observations and accuracy in making logical inferences from these observations. Wolf has defined observation as "the act of apprehending things and events, their attributes and their concrete relationships, also the direct awareness of our mental experiences."[5] He also defined inference as "the formation

[4] Wolf, *op. cit.,* p. 14.
[5] *Ibid.,* p. 17.

of judgments (beliefs or opinions) on the strength of, or as a consequence of, other judgments already formed, it may be, on the ground of observation, or only entertained provisionally either for further consideration, or for sake of argument."[6] Observation is of two types: (1) *bare observation* of uncontrolled phenomena, and (2) *experiment*. Bare observation is so commonplace that its basic importance in scientific endeavors is frequently overlooked. In sharp contrast to the neglect of bare observation, experiment has been in many of the sciences so important in setting the stage for fruitful observation that it is frequently asserted to be all-important. Science is often referred to as "experimentally verified knowledge." It is upon this ground that the social sciences are most frequently excluded from the family of sciences. The untenability of this position is amply demonstrated by the fact that the mere mention of astronomy is sufficient to upset such a hasty generalization. In addition to experimentation, or the control of extraneous factors so that only one circumstance is varied at a time, there are many other aids to observation. The astronomer has his telescope, the botanist his microscope, and the chemist his test tubes and retorts. In the social sciences, where experiment is rarely possible, the carefully designed schedule and the well-kept record have proved useful aids to observation.

Inference, too, may be divided into two chief types, namely, *induction* and *deduction*. Induction is the process of ascertaining some general uniformity or regularity among the phenomena under observation. It consists of reasoning from the particular to the general. It is the process by which a conclusion is reached through the observation of facts; as Westaway has said, it is "the legitimate inference of the general from the particular, or of the more general from the less general."[7] Deductive reasoning consists of applying general conclusions expressed in concepts to particular classes or cases. It involves postulating attributes of the specific from a knowledge of the general. Both induction and deduction are indispensable elements in the scientific method. Induction plays a most useful role in the formulation of hypotheses or generalizations concerning uniformities or principles which may be valid. In inductive reasoning the individual cases suggest broader

[6] *Ibid.*, pp. 17–18.

[7] F. W. Westaway, *Scientific Method*, New York, Hillman-Curl, Inc., 1937, p. 178.

generalizations which *may* be true. Deduction then comes into play to see what consequences would follow if the induction were valid. Providing the hypothesis itself is of significance, if some of these results or consequences can be tested empirically the hypothesis is a good one, and the testing of it will contribute to the sum total of human knowledge. Thus through induction comes hypothesis, and through deduction the stage is set for testing the hypothesis. The testing of significant and meaningful hypotheses is all-important in the advance of scientific knowledge. The great scientist is the one who can conceive the most important hypotheses, and who can devise ways and means of testing them with empirical data. The good hypothesis is the one which permits, through the application of deduction, the inference of consequences which may be tested empirically, which does not conflict with any established uniformity, and whose inferred consequences do not conflict with the facts of observation.[8]

Observations and inferences would be of very little value of meaning unless arranged in an orderly system. For this reason *classification* and *description* are of paramount importance in the scientific method. Observations, or sensory experiences, are so diverse that all would be chaos unless some arrangement of them were possible. Classification was one of the earliest and simplest ways of determining order in nature; it remains today one of the most important. From the most remote times the human mind has had a tendency to note similarities between different things, and this process has constituted a beginning in classification. Things possessing common attributes have been placed together in a class and given a name. Language would be impossible without names, yet "every name expresses the recognition of a class of objects."[9] At the present time many of these groupings seem superficial indeed, and will not do for scientific purposes. Nevertheless, popular classification in language is the usual starting point for scientific classification.

Of necessity, classification for scientific purposes must be more exacting than that for practical purposes. For classification to assist in the study of a particular phenomenon, all the things which show evidence of that phenomenon must be brought into one

---

[8] *Ibid.*, pp. 245–246.
[9] Wolf, *op. cit.*, p. 29.

category, and then they must be arranged in a series according to the degree to which they exhibit it.[10] In classification the rules of logical division must be kept in mind. As Westaway has stated them: "(1) There must be only one basis of division (and the sub-classes will therefore be mutually exclusive); (2) the division must be exhaustive; (3) in continued division, each step must be a proximate one; and (4) the division must be appropriate."[11]

Description is also of primary importance in the scientific method. When objects or traits are recognized as constituting a class, the next scientific task is to name and describe the group. The description may consist of a mere statement giving the easily recognized parts, qualities, and processes. But very frequently in scientific classifications the predicating of attributes is not sufficient—exact quantitative measures are generally essential. Some sciences have developed elaborate systems of nomenclatures and terminologies as means of obtaining short but adequate descriptions. This procedure (taxonomy) has been especially important in the biological sciences. In sociology the work of LePlay is the most important contribution yet made,[12] although Eubank's efforts[13] are deserving of mention. In all probability this is a fertile field awaiting cultivation by the sociologist.

Most of the social sciences, and particularly economics and sociology, rely greatly upon statistical devices as convenient and quantitative ways of describing their data. Most of the simpler statistical devices are important aids to description, and the "economic description of the things in a class constitutes the definition of the name of the class."[14] Description of the class necessarily involves enumerating the most important attributes, i.e., those which are most likely to be correlated with the remaining characteristics. It also involves consideration of differences. In sociology the *frequency table* is of fundamental importance for summarizing and showing the outstanding characteristics of mass data; measures of the average, whether it be the arithmetic average or *mean*, the most frequent or the *mode*, or the middle value or the *median*, are of great assistance in sensing the magnitude of the typical class

[10] Westaway, *op. cit.*, p. 219.

[11] *Ibid.*, p. 222.

[12] See a summary of LePlay's "Nomenclature" in P. A. Sorokin, *Contemporary Sociological Theories*, New York, Harper & Brothers, 1928, pp. 70–72.

[13] Cf. E. E. Eubank, *The Concepts of Sociology*, Boston, D. C. Heath & Co., 1932.

[14] Wolf, *op. cit.*, p. 35.

member; and the *standard deviation* or σ is of great assistance in visualizing the extent to which the series is clustered about or departs from the average of the group.

It should be apparent that definition is closely associated with classification, being to a considerable extent merely the statement of the principles involved in the particular classification. An object or thing is adequately defined when it is (1) referred to its proper class, and (2) differentiated through the enumeration of its unique characteristics from the remainder of the objects in that class.

The scientific roles of perspective and insight also need some clarification. To see clearly the position and relative importance of phenomena in time and space is to have perspective. To understand the relationship between facts, to evaluate properly the results and importance of the various relevant factors is to have insight. Perspective and insight are the indelible marks of the learned person. In most cases, if not all, both perspective and insight probably come through intense practice and experience in grappling mentally with carefully selected sensory impressions. This is to say that not all impressions or experiences contribute to the growth of perspective and insight: many sensory impressions add little if anything to knowledge; they merely contribute to blurring still further an already confused intellect. But carefully selected observations, and especially those to which the attention is directed for the purpose of interrogating nature concerning the validity of a specific hypothesis, are the warp and woof of the learning process.

Sociology and Rural Sociology

In the preceding pages sociology has been referred to as the body of fact and principle, the systematized knowledge, which has been developed through the application of the scientific method in the study of human social relationships. At this point it is pertinent to inquire, Is there also a rural sociology? And if so, How does rural sociology differ from sociology in general?

The point of view represented in this book holds that all sociology is a unity. Its fundamental facts and principles must apply generally within the limits of carefully stated reservations or else be abandoned. Some investigators study social phenomena that are present only in, or largely confined to, the rural environment, to persons engaged in the agricultural occupation. Such sociologi-

cal facts and principles as are derived from the study of rural social relationships may be referred to as rural sociology. Probably it
is more logical, however, to refer to the systematized knowledge of
rural social relationships under the heading *sociology of rural life.*
Because of its close association with the work of the agricultural
colleges, it is customary to think of this discipline as embracing
research, teaching, and extension activities.

The Development of Rural Sociology

Rural sociology grew out of the humanitarian philosophy
which had become a potent force in the United States in the closing half of the nineteenth century. The decline of the open-country church, soil exhaustion and depopulation in many long-settled
rural areas in the eastern states, and the rapid differentiation of the
rural and urban patterns of living probably were among the developments which helped call attention to the rural problem and
stimulate a humanitarian interest in rural affairs. In any case such
an interest became widespread, especially among the clergymen
of the day. It was characterized by pity, sympathy, and a burning
desire to improve rural conditions by applying means already at
hand. Since the new subject of sociology was just then being introduced in various colleges and universities, this rural interest
gained concrete expression in college courses dealing with rural
institutions and rural social problems. Pioneers in the field included Charles R. Henderson at the University of Chicago, Kenyon L. Butterfield at the University of Michigan, Ernest Burnham
at Michigan State College, John Morris Gillette at the University
of North Dakota, Franklin H. Giddings at Columbia University,
Thomas Nixon Carver at Harvard, and Henry C. Taylor at the
University of Wisconsin. Early in the twentieth century the publication of the *Report of the Country Life Commission*[15] gave great
impetus to the new discipline of rural sociology. This commission
sounded a call for better living on the farms and recommended
conferences, the federation of all forces striving for rural improvement, and rural social surveys as means for accomplishing the objective. The publication of this report ushered in a decade of conferences and social surveys which made up the fundamental part
of what has been called the Country Life Movement. Largely be-

[15] Sixtieth Congress, 2nd Session, Senate Document 705, Washington, 1909.
The report, with a foreword by Theodore Roosevelt, was reissued by the Sturgis
& Walton Company of New York in 1911.

cause of the surveys undertaken at about the time of the First World War, enough sociologists had become interested in rural society so that in 1917 they grouped together to establish the Section on Rural Sociology in the American Sociological Society.

Following the close of the First World War the economic and social welfare of the farmers came even more into the field of national consciousness, and rural sociology entered a period of rapid development. In 1919 the Bureau of Agricultural Economics was organized in the United States Department of Agriculture. One of its divisions, the unit called Farm Life Studies (now the Division of Farm Population and Rural Life), headed by Dr. Charles J. Galpin, represented the federal government's entry into the field of rural sociological research. But the states, the territorial units which were close to the problems, were in a less fortunate position. The limited budgets of their agricultural experiment stations were all earmarked for experiments in technical agriculture. Sensitive to the pleas from the states for more federal funds in order that the agricultural experiment stations could extend their research work into the social science fields (home economics, agricultural economics, marketing, and rural sociology), Congress in 1925 passed the Purnell Act, which provided financial support for such work.

In some ways it is to be regretted that research funds for use in this field became suddenly available at many of the agricultural experiment stations with the passage of the Purnell Act, before there were sufficient competently trained personnel to conduct genuine scientific investigations. As a result, a motley array of projects appeared, and publications multiplied. It soon became apparent that the intentions were much better than the product. In this way, rural sociology received a setback from which it was some time in recovering.

Happily at this juncture the Social Science Research Council stepped in and inaugurated a program for developing a well-trained personnel in rural sociology. Carefully selecting its candidates, providing them with excellent fellowships for study at the best institutions, and fitting them to work into the research programs of the various state agricultural colleges, the council deserves great credit for the changes it has wrought in rural sociology. Today it might be contended with justification that the intensive studies of rural phenomena and rural problems by the sociologists of the agricultural experiment stations are the most important contributions of social facts made recently in the field of sociology. These investigators, working under the watchful eyes of men trained in the other sciences, and under the constant necessity of satisfying other careful scientists on the validity of their methods and results, have done much to remove sociology from its unenviable position of being the science with the fewest facts and the most theories. It is the results of their studies which most generally are known as rural sociology. But just as Dr. Galpin's *Social Anatomy of the Agricultural Community* was the inspiration for the ecological studies of the Chicago group, the fructifying influences of recent quantitative studies at the various agricultural experiment stations are rapidly being felt throughout the entire field of sociology.[16]

The efforts of the Social Science Research Council came none too soon, for in the early 1930's the severe depression and the efforts to cope with its paralyzing effects made great demands upon the professional training and experience of scores of the nation's rural sociologists. Through their efforts were supplied many of the facts needed by Congress and the administration for the guidance of the various emergency programs; and the experience they gained in empirical studies contributed greatly to the growth of rural sociology as a discipline.

Another important event in the development of rural sociology was the establishment of the quarterly journal, *Rural Sociology,* in 1936. This review, "Devoted to the Scientific Study of Rural Life," gave those interested in the objective and impartial study and analysis of rural social relationships the professional journal of which they were so badly in need. Almost immediately it gained a respected position among the nation's social science periodicals; and its launching was followed shortly, in December, 1937, by the organization of the Rural Sociological Society, the national professional association of those interested in the sociology of rural life.

The years of the Second World War and the period of ferment and tension which followed it also made heavy demands upon the

---

[16] For brief historical treatments of the developments of rural sociology, see Charles J. Galpin, "The Development of the Science and Philosophy of American Rural Society," *Agricultural History,* XII (1938), 195–208, and Paul H. Landis, "The Development of Rural Sociology in the United States," *Sociology and Social Research,* XXII (1938); see also Charles J. Galpin, *My Drift into Rural Sociology,* University, Louisiana State University Press, 1938.

time and the skills of the nation's trained rural sociologists, and they, too, have contributed to the growth and development of the field. Since Pearl Harbor specialists in the sociology of rural life have been engaged in all parts of the world in various activities undertaken by the government of the United States and the many agencies established by the United Nations. Carrying on fundamental background studies of the people and their relationships to the land in several countries, serving as advisers on colonization and settlement to the governments of South American republics, directing or otherwise participating in programs of technical agricultural assistance to other nations, aiding with the planning and execution of programs of land reform in Japan and Italy, participating in the reform and further development of agricultural education in Greece, and teaching in the universities of various countries—these are some of the functions that have been filled by American rural sociologists in recent years. Already the literature of rural sociology has been considerably enriched by the publications that have resulted from these efforts;[17] and they have also done much to bring sociology a deserved recognition in the new and rapidly developing field of world area studies. The flow of reports on observations and analyses may be expected to continue

[17] Some of the publications growing out of recent activities of American rural sociologists in other countries are as follows: John Biesanz, "Social Forces Retarding Development of Panama's Agricultural Resources," *Rural Sociology*, XV (1950); Olen E. Leonard, *Pichilingue: A Study of Rural Life in Coastal Ecuador*, Foreign Agriculture Report 17, Washington, Office of Foreign Agricultural Relations, 1947; Olen E. Leonard, *Canton Chullpas: A Socioeconomic Study in the Cochabamba Valley of Bolivia*, Foreign Agriculture Report 27, Washington, Office of Foreign Agricultural Relations, 1948; Olen E. Leonard, *Santa Cruz: A Socioeconomic Study of an Area in Bolivia*, Foreign Agriculture Report 31, Washington, Office of Foreign Agricultural Relations, 1948; Charles P. Loomis, "Trial Use of Public Opinion Survey Procedures in Determining Immigration and Colonization Policies for Bolivia, Ecuador, and Peru," *Social Forces*, XXVI (1947); Charles P. Loomis, *Studies in Rural Social Organization*, East Lansing, Michigan State College Book Store, 1945; Lowry Nelson, *Rural Cuba*, Minneapolis, University of Minnesota Press, 1950; Arthur Raper, "Some Recent Changes in Japanese Village Life," *Rural Sociology*, XVI (1951); Arthur Raper, *The Japanese Village in Transition*, Tokyo, General Headquarters Supreme Commander for the Allied Powers, Natural Resources Section Report 136, 1950; Bruce Ryan, "Socio-Cultural Regions of Ceylon," *Rural Sociology*, XV (1950); T. Lynn Smith, *Brazil: People and Institutions*, Baton Rouge, Louisiana State University, 1946; T. Lynn Smith, Justo Diaz Rodriguez, and Luis Roberto Garcia, *Tabio: A Study in Rural Social Organization*, Washington, Office of Foreign Agricultural Relations, 1945; Carl C. Taylor, *Rural Life in Argentina*, Baton Rouge, Louisiana State University Press, 1948; and Nathan L. Whetten, *Rural Mexico*, Chicago, University of Chicago Press, 1948. See also the contributions by Biesanz, Loomis and Powell, Nelson, Smith, and Whetten in *Materiales para el Estudio de la Classe Media en la America Latina*, Washington, Pan-American Union, 1950–1951, I–VI.

for years, and indeed it is likely to increase. With the development of the Point Four programs for helping raise the levels of living in the less-developed parts of the world, the services of well-trained and experienced rural sociologists are in even greater demand. For better or worse the impact of the indigenous American discipline of rural sociology is being felt to the ends of the earth.

2

THE RURAL WORLD

Farm folk differ from urban people, and rural society differs from urban society, principally because of the different environments impinging upon the two populations. In this chapter an attempt is made to outline and briefly characterize the principal features of the rural world, i.e., the surroundings amid which the farming population resides. Particular attention will be given to the aspects in which the surroundings of rural people differ markedly from those of urban dwellers, i.e., to rural-urban differences. Logically and methodologically this is a sound procedure. Undoubtedly the environmental factors and conditions are the influences that are chiefly responsible for the contrasting patterns of behavior to be found in the two populations; and a knowledge of the fundamental characteristics of the rural situation should contribute much to an understanding of the structure of rural society, the way it functions, the operation of social controls in the rural group, and the manner in which social change proceeds in the rural districts.

The City and the Country

At first thought nothing seems more apparent than the difference between the city and the country. The contrasts between the two are so sharp! But one who attempts to set forth the specific differences between the city and the country, to distinguish accurately between rural and urban, is immediately confronted with some serious difficulties, obstacles which are not immediately perceptible.[1] Even in scholarly treatises it usually has been thought

[1] Cf. A. F. Weber, *The Growth of Cities in the Nineteenth Century,* New York, Columbia University Press, 1899.

sufficient to utilize a simple dichotomy, setting forth only two classes—the rural and the urban, the country and the city—as though these two were readily distinguishable and described by mutually discriminating categories. This is the practice followed in the official population statistics of most countries. But regardless of the basis selected for the differentiation, usually some inconsistencies or weakness in the scheme will appear if it is subjected to much analytical study. Consider, for example, size of community, the criterion most frequently used and the basis the United States Census utilizes in differentiating rural from urban. In America incorporated centers range in size from hamlets with less than 100 inhabitants to great metropolitan centers having millions of residents. Is a village rural or urban? How shall a town be classified? When does a given center cease to be a village and become a town or city? Similar questions might be raised about any other attempt to distinguish between rural and urban on the basis of a single characteristic. Is a manufacturing center with 2000 inhabitants as rural as an agricultural trade center of 3000 population? or a Mormon village community in which 5000 farm people reside? or a Mexican city of 20,000 population most of whom are engaged in agriculture?

Or, let us suppose that the enjoyment of administrative and governmental functions or titles is the basis for distinguishing urban centers from rural territory, as is largely the case in many countries.[2] Is the sleepy little agricultural village of less than 1000 inhabitants, although enjoying the distinction of being the seat of a local governmental unit, more entitled to be classed as urban than a bustling mining or manufacturing center several times larger which lacks such administrative functions? Is a decadent old town necessarily entitled to be considered a city today, even though it is in possession of a charter from some medieval monarch attesting to the fact that the rank of "city" had once been conferred upon it?

For statistical purposes some simple criterion obviously is necessary. But the distinctions made on such a basis as the size of the community, legal incorporation or the lack of it, the possession of a

---

[2] Cf. *Data on Urban and Rural Population in Recent Censuses*, United Nations Population Studies 8, Lake Success, United Nations, 1950; the United Nations *Demographic Yearbook, 1948*, Lake Success, United Nations, 1949, pp. 213–218; and T. Lynn Smith, *Population Analysis*, New York, McGraw-Hill Book Company, 1948, pp. 27–30.

charter or title conferred by some ancient king may be quite inadequate for sociological purposes. What may be very useful statistically may leave a great deal to be desired from the standpoint of deeper sociological analysis.

Probably two things are chiefly responsible for the unsatisfactory nature of these simple distinctions. (1) Rural and urban do not exist of themselves in a vacuum, as it were, but the principal characteristics of each may be found shading into, blending, or mixing with the essential characteristics of the other. Thousands of crossroads corners have grown into hamlets, villages, towns, and some even into cities. All these categories shade into one another by almost imperceptible degrees, whether the question be regarded from the historical or the cross-sectional point of view. Rather than consisting of mutually exclusive categories, rural and urban, the general society seems to resemble a spectrum in which the most remote backwoods, subrural settlements blend imperceptibly into the rural and then gradually through all degrees of rural and suburban into the most urban and hyper-urban ways of living. If such be the case, a scale, rather than a dichotomy, would provide the most satisfactory device for classifying the population or group according to rural or urban characteristics. Instead of being purely rural or purely urban, one community merely has *more* urban or *more* rural characteristics than another. (2) The difference between the rural and urban modes of living is not the product of one simple characteristic or factor but the result of a number of closely integrated and functionally related attributes. As Sorokin and Zimmerman have indicated so clearly,[3] size, density, occupational differences, etc., each strikingly different in city and country, individually are inadequate bases for distinguishing between rural and urban agglomerations. Sorokin and Zimmerman have also shown that the choice of any single basis for classification will inevitably lead to many inconsistencies, contradictions, uncertainties, and mistakes, not to mention fallacious conclusions and interpretations. An adequate distinction between rural and urban can be secured only if it is based upon a series of mutually dependent and functionally related characteristics.

The following attempt at formulating and discussing the principal difference between the rural and urban worlds follows to a

[3] P. A. Sorokin and Carle C. Zimmerman, *Principles of Rural-Urban Sociology*, New York, Henry Holt & Company, 1929, pp. 13–58.

considerable extent the excellent treatments of this subject by Sorokin and Zimmerman,[4] and by the Urbanism Committee of the National Resources Committee.

Characteristics of the Rural World

1. *Occupation*

Among all the differences which have been noted between the rural and urban portions of society, the occupational difference seems to be the one having the most fundamental importance. Agriculture and the collecting enterprises are the basis of the rural economy; "farmer" and "countryman" are almost synonymous terms. "Rural non-farm," one of the United States Census categories, is almost a contradiction in terms; in addition to the residents of villages and hamlets it includes a hodgepodge of everything urban—from roadhouses, night clubs, and tourist camps to boarding schools, summer resorts, and canning factories—which is to be found outside the corporation limits of towns and cities.

One of the fundamental characteristics of farming is that those who engage in it shall deal with living, growing things, either plants or animals, or both. This is in very sharp contrast with urban occupations, which determine that those following such callings shall handle lifeless or mechanical things and instruments. The nature of agriculture also prescribes that the farmer shall work in a natural environment amid the fresh air and sunshine of the open country, but subject to the vicissitudes of changing seasons and weather, instead of in the artificial environment of the city, where the heat of the summer, the cold of the winter, and the dryness and dampness of the weather are all moderated by man's ingenuity. Few who study the personalities of farm and city folk will deny the importance of these factors as basic influences in molding the characters of the persons concerned.[5]

The foregoing should not be interpreted to mean that there are not important variations within the agricultural occupation. Size of the farm business, system of farming, type of farming, and many other factors contribute to make farmers differ from one

---

[4] *Ibid.*

[5] James M. Williams has contributed one of the most penetrating analyses of the effects of climatic factors upon the social psychology of the agriculturist. See especially his *Our Rural Heritage*, New York, Alfred A. Knopf, Inc., 1925, pp. 25–31.

another. Consider type of farming, for example. Although as compared with urban occupations farm tasks are multitudinous and
call for the exercise of innumerable skills and techniques, some
specialization takes place. There is division of labor between the
cotton belt, the wheat belt, the corn belt, etc. Cotton farming is
not the same thing as farming in the corn belt. Both are fundamentally different from dairying, truck farming, tobacco raising,
and fruit growing. Ranching is still more different, as are other
highly specialized enterprises such as the growing of rice and
sugar cane.

Within the general agricultural occupation, each of these types
of farming gives rise to distinct rhythms of daily, weekly, monthly,
and seasonal activities. The dairy farmer must be on the job at
definitely specified hours every day of the week, year in and year
out, although he may have a great deal of leisure time at other
hours of the day. Other types of farming, such as wheat growing,
are characterized by peak loads of labor at certain seasons. Almost
continuous work day and night during harvest may be followed
by a long period of relative inactivity. Such a distribution of working periods exerts a profound influence upon the personalities of
the individuals concerned.

The amount and nature of the rewards from the various types
of farming also make for fundamental differences among farmers.
It is one thing to count on the small, steady, frequent, and relatively sure amounts received by the dairy farmer and quite another to gamble on the small fortune to be made or the great losses
to be incurred in the large-scale commercial production of a crop
like potatoes. A slight variation in temperature is of little consequence to the producer of corn and hogs; it may be the difference
between success and failure to the citrus grower.

In general, the care of livestock calls for skills and aptitudes
different from those involved in the growing of plants. General
farming calls for a fusion of the two. All of the variations make for
special activities, distinctive family time-budgets, and different
attitudes toward the work. Each in turn serves as a mold in which
the personalities of the participants are given a distinctive turn.

2. Size of Community

The limitations or conditions imposed by the agricultural mode
of gaining a subsistence in turn give rise to other fundamental fea-

tures of rural life, aspects which are frequently seized upon as the elemental and distinctive traits of rurality. For example, the nature of the farming occupation demands a considerable area of land per person—a high land-to-man ratio—a fact which makes large communities almost impossible and brings about a low density of population per square mile. In other words, the size of the community and the density of population both are directly dependent upon the nature of the agricultural occupation. For convenience these two, and especially the size of the community, are most frequently taken as the bases for distinguishing between the rural and urban portions of a society. Small community and rural community become synonymous, and urban center and large community also have the same connotations. In statistical compilations the size of community has come to be the criterion of rurality most frequently used. This is the practice followed in the censuses taken by various countries, including the United States, where all incorporated centers with 2500 or more inhabitants are now classed as urban. This criterion, the size of the community, has proved to be a useful yardstick only because the nature of the agricultural occupation makes large farming communities almost impossible.

3. *Density of Population*

Low density of population is another feature of rural society that is imposed by the nature of the agricultural occupation and frequently accepted as the basic difference between the rural and urban modes of living. Since a considerable area is necessary for the successful pursuit of farming as an occupation—whether it consist of growing plants, grazing livestock, or both—agriculture inevitably results in a low man-to-land ratio. It is obvious that the farmer must reside either on the land he tills or in close proximity to it; this requirement not only effectively prevents large aggregations of rural people but means that those who live through agriculture will be widely scattered over the arable lands. This proposition is true of even the most densely populated agricultural countries. If it were otherwise, no land would be left on which to grow crops or graze livestock. Even the most intensive agricultural systems fail to bring about a density of population remotely approaching that of the spacious suburbs which constitute the residential areas for the elite classes of urban centers. Far more striking are the contrasts of the open country with the apartment house, tenement, and slum districts of modern cities.

Some quantitative data are useful in helping to bring out the great extent of the differences referred to. Thus in 1950, in the continental United States as a whole, there were 50.6 persons per square mile. At this time the density of population in rural United States was less than 19 per square mile, and of the rural farm population approximately 8 persons per square mile. Meanwhile in typical urban centers people were crowded together, hundreds and even thousands of persons residing within a single city block an acre or so in extent. In 1950 almost 84,000,000 persons, 55 percent of all the people in the United States, lived in the nation's 168 standard metropolitan areas. Furthermore, the congestion in a few selected portions of the national territory was increasing rapidly, for in the decade 1940 to 1950 over four-fifths of the nation's increase in population took place in these 168 metropolitan areas.[6]

These differences in the density of population are instrumental in giving the general cast to many important features of rural and urban life. For the city person they mean, on the one hand, congestion, noise, racket, lack of privacy, high rents, difficulty in finding parking places, impersonal relations, smoke, soot, impure air to breathe, constant exposure to disease germs, psychosocial isolation, nervous strains, and numerous other disadvantageous environmental influences. But, on the other hand, a high density of population also means numerous social contacts, availability of all conceivable specialists and services, opportunity to specialize, possibility of being selective of associates, freedom from trying inquisitiveness and gossip of primary group members, superior schools, well-supported churches, opportunity to participate in the cultural advantages of the city, availability of modern household conveniences, safe water supply, greater variety in diet, etc.

For the country the low density of population has many advantages. It offers the opportunity for quiet and solitude; it means that fresh air is abundant, air which has not been contaminated by being breathed over and over again, having soot and smoke poured into it, and being thoroughly mixed with the fumes from

[6] U.S. Bureau of the Census, "Population of Standard Metropolitan Areas: April 1, 1950," *1950 Census of Population, Preliminary Counts,* Series PC-3, No. 3, Washington, November 5, 1950.

the exhausts of automobiles. Low density of population is favorable to abundance of green grass, trees, flowers, birds, and other natural beauties; it is also favorable to the intimate social relationships, those forms of social interaction possible only in small primary groups which shield the farmer from psychosocial isolation; and it frees the countryman from the city's noise, racket, frictions, and nervous strain. But the low density of population also has its negative aspects for the rural person. It means, to some extent, geographical isolation (this, however, is a result which is rapidly being overcome by the automobile, good roads, the radio, telephone, etc.). With low density of population comes constant exposure to the prying eyes and busy wagging tongues of local neighborhood gossips. A few people cannot support up-to-date schools and hire the best teachers, and consolidation of rural schools has many limiting factors as well as several severe disadvantages. The same limitation is true of churches. Where population is sparse, cultural advantages are rare and expensive, and modern conveniences are scarce and costly. The most skillful professional men, such as physicians and dentists, seek the more thickly populated districts where their own advantages are greater. Both city and country have strong points and weak points; but all in all, density of population effectively works to make the life of the city person differ greatly from that of the countryman.

Density of population is also related to the number of social contacts, as will be pointed out below. Some urban groups, notably the white-collar workers, are dealing constantly with other human beings. These individuals are thus placed under tremendous mental strain; people come to be regarded as pawns to be manipulated for personal ends, rather than as neighbors, as in the country.

4. *Environment*

That agriculture is the primary occupation of the rural population has been indicated. Several other important rural characteristics such as small communities and low density of population have also been identified. Although such features as size of community and density of population are commonly used as the basic criteria for differentiating the rural from the urban portions of society, a little analytical thinking reveals that they both are dependent upon the nature of the occupation, which is the primary factor.

The nature of the agricultural occupation also limits rural life in many other ways and serves as a causal factor determining many of the channels in which the processes of rural life must move. By determining the principal nature of the environmental influences amid which rural people must live, agriculture wields an all-important influence upon all aspects of rural life, for environmental factors operating upon organic bases give rise to all the multifarious behavior patterns of human life.

The concept of environment is of itself so broad that it must be broken down or analyzed into its constituent elements before it can serve any specific purpose of sociological analysis. Bernard has attempted such an analysis and classification.[7] According to his system, there are four principal classes of environments: (1) the physical or inorganic environments; (2) the biological or organic environments; (3) the social environments; and (4) composite or institutionalized derivative control environments.

Bernard includes in the physical environments all cosmic and physiographic forces, soil, climate, inorganic resources, natural forces like winds and tides, combustion, radiation, and gravity. Attention has already been directed to the fact that the rural person is exposed to the direct action of these, while the urbanite's cultural surroundings place a thick man-made shield between him and these natural phenomena.

In the second class, the biological environments, Bernard places all microörganisms, insects, parasites, undomesticated plants and animals, together with the relationships between these, both ecological and symbiotic. He also includes in this class the prenatal environment of man and the natural biological processes such as reproduction, growth, decomposition, circulation, etc. (Parenthetically it should be pointed out that this last category seems to include much of the environed with the environment.)

The social environment, according to Bernard, is composed of three parts: (a) the physiosocial, (b) the biosocial, and (c) the psychosocial. Physiosocial is used to include those portions of our material culture whose objective expressions are constructed out of inorganic materials, i.e., tools, weapons, machines, roads, etc. The biosocial may be further divided into the nonhuman and the human. Domesticated plants and animals and all materials used

[7] L. L. Bernard, *Introduction to Social Psychology*, New York, Henry Holt & Company, 1926, pp. 75–76.

by man which are derived from organic sources make up the non-human portion. The human part of the biosocial environment consists of human beings in their service relationships to one another. The third part of the social environment, the psychosocial, designates the inner behavior (the attitudes, ideas, desires, etc.) of the human population. Customs, folkways, mores, and external symbols, such as language, make up the outward expressions of this category.

Bernard's fourth class of environments, the composite or institutionalized derivative control environment, consists of elements from the other three integrated into definite working systems. This is the environment which actually operates in our social organization. These systems may be general in character, represented by such systems as the economic, political, racial, educational, etc.; or they may be special in character like the American, Italian, Catholic, Democratic, feminine, conservative. For immediate purposes in accounting for human behavior this environment far outweighs the others in importance.

Owing to the nature of the agricultural occupation, the farmer lives amid an environment which is radically different from that of the urbanite. In the first place, great importance should be attached to the fact that practically all aspects of rural life are conditioned directly by the physical environment. Agricultural activities necessitate outdoor work. This means that the agriculturist is directly exposed to the weather. The farmer basks in the beneficial influences of abundant sunlight, he breathes the pure air of the countryside, and he is cooled by the fresh breezes. He is in direct contact with nature in all its friendly aspects. But the countryman lacks the protective social environment—exemplified by steam heat, air conditioning, and paving—which stands between him and the inclemencies of the weather. When nature shows its malignant aspects, the farmer is also directly exposed to them.

Agriculture is merely the process of facilitating or directing the creative forces of nature. For this reason the rural person is much more influenced by the organic environment than is the city person. Sorokin and Zimmerman have described this contrast, in some detail, as follows:

Further he [the farmer] is in a much greater proximity to, and in a more direct relation with, "nature,"—soil, flora, fauna, water, river, the sun, the moon, the sky, the wind, the rain, and so on—than an urbanite. The urban dweller is separated from all this by thick walls of vast and huge city buildings and the artificial city environment predominantly of stone and iron. Whether an urbanite is "indoors"—in his factory, shop, office, church, library, theater, school, home,—or "out-of-doors" amidst the city streets and squares—he rarely is in contact with nature. He is, so to speak, "wrapped in a thick blanket of artificial culture." In his dwelling-room, apartment, or house, he is separated from nature by a long row of walls and other buildings. Sometimes he has to travel miles before he reaches out of the city circle to the country. Not a free wind refreshes him but a draft of the electrical fan; not the sunlight but the artificial gas or electric light greets his eyes; not a soil but a pavement is found under his feet; in place of the river or stream he has a channel, usually imprisoned in stone and iron and diluted with sewage, oil, and other products of the urban industry and population. Huge and tall buildings built out of stone and iron hover over his head, and together with a thick layer of smoke, steal the brightness of the sky and hide any view of the natural environment. The bits of his flora and fauna in the form of parks and zoological gardens are rarely seen and even then they are artificially "bobbed," and polished. The miracles and mysteries of nature are seen primarily in movies, theaters, from pictures in his papers and only once in a while on a picnic. Brick, stone, iron, and for modern times, particularly paper-books, magazines, newspapers, manuscripts, and so on—such are [the] principal components of the artificial environment of the city man. Quite different is the environment of a cultivator. If he lives on an open farm he is nearly all the time in the bosom of nature. If he lives in a small village or hamlet, he is in a similar condition. Only the thin walls of his farm house or hut separate him from nature when he is indoors. While he is outdoors he is at all times amidst nature, whatever it may be.[8]

It should be stressed that the farmer, who deals constantly with living things, usually sees the organic aspects in the guise of a friend to man. The same is not so true of the city person. Shut off from the great bulk of natural phenomena, to him the organic environment is all too frequently displayed through the medium of contaminated milk or water supplies or through the spread of a contagious disease. More and more, as the city walls shut him in, the urbanite sees only the menacing aspects of the organic en-

[8] P. A. Sorokin and Carle C. Zimmerman, *Principles of Rural-Urban Sociology*, New York, Henry Holt & Company, 1929, p. 17; cf. Warren H. Wilson, *The Farmer's Church*, New York, D. Appleton-Century Company, 1925, p. 5.

vironment. That his life, too, is dependent upon the workings of natural organic forces is seldom called to his attention.[9]

There are likewise great differences in the social environments of rural and urban peoples. Thus the physiosocial environment (the material culture) of the city greatly exceeds that of the country, in both quantity and complexity. Buildings, machines, pavement, etc., are the basic elements out of which the city is constructed. The richest accomplishments of the country in these respects pale before the overwhelming display of the city. The biosocial environment of the country also differs from that of the urban area. In no respect is this more striking than by contrasting the seething mass of humanity, a mass composed of all races and nationalities, with the dispersed but more homogeneous group of the typical rural district. Later on, considerable attention will be given to analyzing the nature of the psychosocial aspects of rural society. Here it is sufficient to state that in this respect, too, the urban environment is much more complex than the rural.

Finally, all of these traits in combination make what Bernard terms the composite or institutionalized derivative control environment of the city very different from that of the country. The institutional patterns of the city and the country are vastly dissimilar. The truth of this assertion will be amply demonstrated throughout the remainder of this book.

5. Social Differentiation

The social differentiation of the rural world differs in several fundamental respects from that of urban society. In the first place, the city's social groups are much more numerous and complex than those of the country. This difference is intimately associated with the differing origins of rural and urban populations. That urban districts almost never produce enough children to replenish their population is now well known; practically all urban growth, and a good portion of replacement needs as well, is brought about by migration to the city from the rural districts or from other lands. As a consequence of this migration, the city numbers among its inhabitants members of all races—the native races being most heavily represented, of course, but the population including a

[9] It is interesting to note the descriptive adjectives applied to bacteria in a popular work: ferocious, deadly, small assassins, beasts, silent assassins, etc. See Paul de Kruif, *Microbe Hunters,* New York, Harcourt, Brace & Company, 1926.

sprinkling of peoples from all corners of the earth. Culturally, too, the city is a babel of all religious, political, occupational, educational, national, and linguistic groups. As Sorokin and Zimmerman[10] have indicated so clearly, the city is characteristically heterogeneous, a hodgepodge of racial and cultural elements, a true "melting pot." The city person lives amid this tremendous diversity, constantly in contact with people having the most widely divergent ideas, beliefs, mores, languages, economic positions, occupations, religious traditions, morals, etc. And this is particularly true of American urbanites. Says the Urbanism Committee of the National Resources Committee:

> Never before in the history of the world have great groups of people so diverse in social backgrounds been thrown together into such close contacts as in the cities of America. The typical American city, therefore, does not consist of a homogeneous body of citizens, but of human beings, with the most diverse cultural backgrounds, often speaking different languages, following a great variety of customs, habituated to different modes and standards of living, and sharing only in varying degrees the tastes, the beliefs, and the ideals of their native fellow city dwellers. In short, far from presenting a picture of a single unified body of human beings, the American city is a motley of peoples and cultures forming a mosaic of little worlds which in part blend with one another, but in part and for a time, remain segregated or come into conflict with one another.[11]

Yet in spite of all its heterogeneity and all its complexity, the city possesses a high degree of integration and coördination. Through division of labor and specialization, every part has become mutually interdependent with every other part. The downtown business area, the industrial, wholesale, shipping, and storage districts, the slums, the middle-class residential portions, the better residential sections, and even the suburban fringes are all part of a functioning whole.[12]

In the country the situation is strikingly different. Social differentiation has not proceeded as far as in the cities. Rural districts are essentially homogeneous, even in a country like the United

---

[10] *Op. cit.*, pp. 23–28; cf. National Resources Committee, *Our Cities: Their Rôle in the National Economy*, Washington, Government Printing Office, 1937, p. ix.

[11] *Op. cit.*, p. 10.

[12] It is true of course that urban society is a delicate organism which can undergo swift disorganization and demoralization.

States whose tremendous rural area embraces almost all the racial
and cultural groups which are found in the cities.[13] The reason is
that there is an essential difference between the social structures
of rural and of urban districts. Rural society may be said to be
segmented; it does not function as an integral unit. Instead it is
made up of thousands of small, relatively independent and unrelated units—families, neighborhoods, and communities. Unlike
the situation in urban communities, the actual portion of rural
society with which a given individual or family comes into contact
exhibits little heterogeneity. The rural person's contacts are mainly
with other farmers, who in turn are the sons of farmers. His associates generally are also members of his own religious group,
neighbors of much the same economic and educational attainments, persons whose mores, traditional beliefs, language, and
general behavior patterns are very similar to his own. The countryman's contacts are mostly with those who live in close proximity to him. It matters little that elsewhere in the nation there are
other farmers with radically different cultural traits. For practical
purposes the important thing is that each segment of rural society
is highly homogeneous, or very slightly differentiated.

But, as we have pointed out, rural society does not function as
a unit. It lacks the integration of the more highly differentiated
urban society. Such unity as it has is based mainly on similarities
and not on the mutual interdependence brought about by specialization and the division of social labor. As a consequence, it is very
difficult to secure concerted action on the part of the rural population. Rural society remains merely the product of numerous
small, relatively independent and unrelated segments. Its structure is greatly different from that of the city.

6. Social Stratification

The principles of class and caste operate differently in rural
societies from the way they work in urban. There seem to be at
least four major general differences between the social pyramids
of rural and urban areas. (1) The number of social classes is less
in rural society than in urban society, although the rural is far from
being classless. (2) The extremes of the social pyramid are not so
far apart in rural societies as in urban. To quote again the report of

[13] Cf. J. M. Gillette, *Rural Sociology*, New York, The Macmillan Company,
1936, p. 263.

the Urbanism Committee of the National Resources Committee: "The most drastic inequalities of income and wealth are found within the urban community. Relatively to their rich fellow citizens, the poor are poorer in the city than they are elsewhere despite an increasing standard of living for the city worker. Widespread poverty and cyclical unemployment and insecurity threaten purchasing power, and without continuous mass purchasing power our urban industry and mass-production economy cannot continue to function properly."[14] These urban districts, and especially the largest cities, have at the same time much higher average incomes and much higher proportions of their populations on relief than the rural areas.[15] Although very large incomes from rural enterprises are almost always diverted to urban residents, it is the national govenment "that has had to assume the major burdens of providing emergency relief for the city as well as the farm, of stimulating public works in the Nation's urban centers, and even of reviving insolvent municipal finances."[16] (3) It is not only that the range of social classes is less in rural society, but that rural classes tend to be intermediate or "middle classes." The rural social pyramid as a whole neither sinks so low nor rises so high as the urban pyramid. Despite considerable range in the social status of rural people, rural society in general lacks the extreme of wealth and poverty, of authority and disfranchisement, of privilege and lack of privilege to be found in the city. The city is the home not only of the millionaire but of the pauper, and "the poor are poorer in the city than they are elsewhere."[17] (4) The caste principle is not so rigid in urban as in rural societies. Although there are more classes, their membership is not so fixed. Movement from one class to another is easier than in rural society, where intimate social contacts make a person's antecedents well known to all members of the community and cause one's position to be more largely determined by the status of his immediate ancestors than is the case in the city.

7. *Social Mobility*

"The rural community is similar to calm water in a pail, and the urban community to boiling watter in a kettle. In the rural

[14] *Op. cit.,* p. viii.
[15] *Ibid.,* pp. 9, 18.
[16] *Ibid.,* p. v.
[17] *Ibid.,* p. 55.

areas, the members are more strongly attached to their social status; in the urban they are shifted from one status to another more often and more easily. Stability is the typical trait for the one; mobility is the typical for the other."[18] With this suggestive analogy and terse generalization, Sorokin and Zimmerman conclude their comparison of mobility in the rural and urban worlds. Certain it is that the social dynamics of the rural world differ fundamentally in nature and tempo from those of the urban. Most noticeable are the quantitative differences, but there are qualitative differences as well. Despite great variation within the agricultural group, rural people as a whole are not so mobile as the members of urban groups. This statement applies to shiftings on a horizontal plane from one social group to another, to vertical changes both up and down from one social class to another, and to changes in space (territorial mobility) from one place to another.[19] These generalizations apply equally well to culture traits and population. They are true in a highly mobile society like the United States and also in the longer-established and less mobile societies of the Old World.

That there is more horizontal mobility, shifting from one social group to another, in the city than in the country is demonstrated by many types of data. Sorokin, Zimmerman, and Galpin have assembled a considerable body of facts which demonstrate that change of occupation is less frequent among farmers than any other significant occupational group.[20] They show that despite the "rural exodus," farm children more frequently inherit their fathers' occupation than is the case in other groups. Farmers are primarily sons of farmers, but members of urban occupations are recruited from many other occupational groups than their own. Sorokin and Zimmerman[21] quote the following data from a study of the changes of occupations in Austria from 1907 to 1910. During this three-year period 9.31 percent of the actively employed population changed its occupation. In the principal industries the percentage of change was as follows: agriculture and forestry, 8.64; manufacture and handicrafts, 19.68; trade and transport, 13.74;

[18] Sorokin and Zimmerman, *op. cit.*, p. 44.

[19] For a discussion of the forms of mobility, see P. A. Sorokin, *Social Mobility*, New York, Harper & Brothers, 1927, pp. 133–163.

[20] P. A. Sorokin, Carle C. Zimmerman, and Charles J. Galpin, *A Systematic Source Book in Rural Sociology*, Minneapolis, University of Minnesota Press, 1930, I, 226–228.

[21] *Op. cit.*, p. 40.

public service and professions, 14.56; military, 84.25; and domestic service, 15.43. Anderson's data on the families of students at Cornell University reveal the same situation. In the grandfather's generation sons followed their father's occupation 50 percent of the time among farmers and only 19 percent among non-farmers. In the father's generation the corresponding percentages were 31 and 15.[22]

Another important variety of horizontal mobility is the shifting from one family group to another. In this connection the data on broken homes and remarriage are relevant. The most thoroughgoing study of this question shows that in 1930 broken homes were more than twice as prevalent in the city as in the country.[23] According to size of community, the data were as follows: metropolitan area, 19.0 percent of the homes broken; cities of 100,000 population, 16.7 percent; villages, 14.7 percent; and rural area, 8.1 percent. Ogburn adds that the importance of broken homes as an indicator of interfamily mobility is sustained by the fact that most estimates place the proportion of divorced persons remarrying as around one-third.[24]

Any thoroughgoing study of shifting from one religious group to another is unknown to the writer. However, a survey made of 109 students (63 urban and 46 rural) at the University of Minnesota indicated that 42.9 percent of the urban students' parents had changed religions since marriage, as compared with 33.3 percent among rural.[25]

"From shirt sleeves to shirt sleeves in three generations" is the picturesque American expression for characterizing the intensive vertical social mobility taking place in urban United States. Intensive vertical social circulation, the passing up and down from class to class of individuals and culture traits, such as is present in cities and especially American cities, is unthinkable in connection with rural society. So also is the great social insecurity resulting from this excessive mobility.[26] Sorokin and Zimmerman, after

[22] W. A. Anderson, *The Transmission of Farming as an Occupation,* Cornell AES Bulletin 768, Ithaca, New York, 1941.

[23] W. F. Ogburn, "The Family and Its Functions," in *Recent Social Trends,* New York, McGraw-Hill Book Company, 1933, I, 690. Data for other countries are given by Sorokin in his *Social Mobility,* pp. 397–399, although unfortunately comparisons of the rural and urban populations are lacking.

[24] *Op. cit.,* p. 696.

[25] Sorokin, Zimmerman, and Galpin, *op. cit.,* II, 24. Cf. Sorokin, *op. cit.,* pp. 402–405, for a general discussion of interreligious circulation.

[26] National Resources Committee, *op. cit.,* p. 11.

indicating that intensive vertical mobility is associated with urbanization, present a penetrating analysis of the factors which are
responsible for this state of affairs. According to them, there are
five principal factors involved: (1) Churches, army headquarters,
political headquarters, parliaments, universities, most of the important institutions which serve as channels of vertical circulation,
the ladders for ascending and descending the social scale, are
concentrated in the cities. In order to use these avenues for social
climbing, one must leave the country and go to the city. These
authors recognize that the country may have social ladders of its
own, but contend that *"climbing the urban social ladder automatically gives one a position on the rural social ladder.* The reverse is not so true or general." (2) Since social stratification is not
so great in rural districts, country people have less chance to rise
or fall from class to class. (3) Differential fertility, which results in
the dying out of the urban upper classes, leaves vacancies in the
top positions of the social pyramid and thus serves as a vacuum
which creates a vertical current. This factor operates very little
or not at all in rural areas, where differential fertility is not so
great or is entirely lacking. (4) Parents and children are dissimilar
in their biological and psychosocial traits, and this condition is
more pronounced in the city's heterogeneous population than in
the country's homogeneous population. Since those children who
lack capacities as great as their parents' frequently are unable to
maintain themselves at the level they are born to, and children
possessing greater abilities than their parents are likely to ascend
to a higher social level, this becomes an important factor in vertical mobility. It also helps to explain the greater vertical mobility
of the city. And (5) every change of social or cultural environment fosters vertical mobility. Changes are particularly great in
urban districts.[27] To this set of five factors as listed by Sorokin and
Zimmerman might be added (6) the fact that the caste principle
seems to be stronger in rural than in urban areas. Where inheritance counts more in determining social status, the amount of
moving from one class to another will be less.

Finally there is the question of territorial mobility. Obviously
where society is highly segmented, as in the case with rural societies, migration will be comparatively slight. On the basis of the

[27] *Op. cit.,* pp. 41–44; cf. Sorokin, *op. cit.,* pp. 346–376.

data and conclusions of Sorokin and Zimmerman[28] and the Urbanism Committee of the National Resources Committee,[29] it seems certain that urban people change residence more often within a given community, move from community to community more frequently, cover much more mileage, and are in many more communities in the course of their daily work than is true of rural people. In this respect urban communities may be said to resemble a swiftly moving river where the water churns about incessantly, rural communities a quiet pond with tiny streams meandering into and out of it.

8. *Social Interaction*

Frequently the farmer's scarcity or lack of social contacts is asserted to be one of the chief disadvantages of rural life.[30] Usually the proponents of this hypothesis fail to recognize that there are qualitative as well as quantitative differences in the social contacts of rural and urban people, and that it may be impossible to gain by increasing the number of contacts without losing by lowering the quality of the contacts. In any case these discussions bring out clearly that the country's system of social interaction differs from that of the city.

The number of social contacts is of course much greater in the city than in the country. The nature of urban occupations makes it necessary for the urban dweller to mingle with throngs, to see, hear, and speak with hundreds of people each day. Recreation, too, in the city must be found where thousands of others are present. Solitude is practically impossible. Within the home, which is hardly separated from the dwellings of others, the newspaper, the telephone, and the radio bring a multitude of secondary contacts.

The situation is quite different in rural areas. Even today, unless the farmer lives on a trunk highway, visitors except peddlers and salesmen are rare enough to be a treat. In many of the more isolated farm sections, strangers are a curiosity and may be the object of considerable suspicion. Only at church, at farm gather-

[28] *Op. cit.*, pp. 28–36.

[29] *Op. cit.*, pp. 7–8.

[30] H. B. Hawthorne's *The Sociology of Rural Life* (New York, D. Appleton-Century Company, 1926) is the most detailed exposition of this thesis, although it will be found in a majority of the works on rural sociology. Cf. Carl C. Taylor, *Rural Sociology*, New York, Harper & Brothers, 1933, p. 18.

ings, or at the movies in the neighboring village does the farmer meet with large groups, and these are assemblies of neighbors for the most part. Rare shopping expeditions to towns and cities are almost the only occasions for mingling in crowds. The bulk of the contacts of the farmer is with members of his family and with the immediate neighbors. In many ways the general store is the most important rural social center, and its informal contacts loom large in the rural system of social interaction.[31] The farmer's secondary contacts through the same devices as the city man's are increasing greatly, but they are still far less numerous than those of the urbanite. On the whole, the farmer has relatively few social contacts.

But Sorokin and Zimmerman have shown[32] that there are important qualitative differences between the rural and urban systems of social interaction. (1) The area of contact of the rural person is narrower and more limited than that of the urban person. The people and institutions with which the farmer is in contact are located in a relatively small area; those of the urban people are much more widely disseminated and may be scattered throughout the world. (2) The totality of contacts by the ruralite is composed more largely of direct or face-to-face relations than are those of the urbanite. The farmer is in direct interaction with the others in his small world. The city person has many more contacts, but they are largely of an indirect and secondary nature. Instead of neighbors, he deals with names, numbers, addresses, clients, inspectors, collectors, customers, employees, officials, creditors, etc. Only a few of the people with whom he is in interaction are known personally to him. He has little direct information about them. Contacts through the telephone, letters, telegrams, and radios are still more indirect and secondary in nature. Yet this kind of social interaction occupies a large portion of the city man's time and attention. (3) Rural contacts are largely personal in nature, whereas urban contacts tend toward the impersonal. The city man knows very little about the thousands of people he sees or meets in the course of a day's work. The majority of them he may never see again. Ofter the urban dweller does not even know the name of his next-door neighbor. He does not deal with John Smith or Henry Jones, but with the milkman, the postman,

[31] Cf. A. W. Small and George E. Vincent, *An Introduction to the Study of Society*, New York, American Book Company, 1894, pp. 118–119; James M. Williams, *The Expansion of Rural Life*, New York, Alfred A. Knopf, Inc., 1926, p. 32.

[32] *Op. cit.*, pp. 49–56.

the streetcar conductor, the auto mechanic, the radio repairman, the doctor, the dentist, etc. "His attitude regarding them is almost the same as to the mechanisms, automatic telephones, automatic restaurants, and automatic frigidaires, which tend more and more to replace these human mechanisms."[33] All is very different in rural society. The personality of the individual is well known to everyone in the neighborhood. If a person has many idiosyncrasies, he becomes a "character." All forms of social interaction in rural communities are greatly affected by this intimate acquaintanceship of the parties. The social contacts are intimate, personal, and tend to be lasting. (4) Of the total number of social contacts, a much larger proportion of the farmer's are those of a permanent, strong, and durable nature. The bulk of the city person's contacts are casual, superficial, and short lived.

The interaction system of an urbanite, in this respect, may be compared to telephone contacts with a multitude of people: the connection is made, a few words are exchanged, and a few moments later the totality is disconnected and forgotten. The whole network of telephone lines in a city station changes every minute and is composed, at any moment, of a multitude of short-lived connections. The rural "social telephone system" is composed of permanent "private" lines which go directly from farmer to farmer, and often without the mediation of a central station, are used by each individual, so to speak, permanently. Lines are few but permanent and direct.[34]

(5) Because of these differences the rural system of social interaction is less differentiated and complex, less plastic and at the same time less superficial, less standardized, and less mechanized than the urban system.

9. *Social Solidarity*

Finally, in addition to all the differences in the rural and urban social worlds which have been discussed in the preceding pages, there is a basic difference in the social solidarity or cohesion of rural and urban societies. The forces making for unity in the two are quite different. To use the distinctions made by Durkheim, who has analyzed this aspect of social organization with great brilliance, the rural world is characterized by a different type of

[33] *Ibid.*, p. 52.
[34] *Ibid.*, p. 54.

social solidarity from the urban solidarity.[35] The former has a unity based on similarities, the union which results from common traits, objectives, and sameness of experience, the type of cohesion Giddings had in mind when he coined the term "consciousness of kind." In essence it is based upon very informal and non-contractual relationships.[36] Urban solidarity, on the other hand, is a type of unity based on differences, dissimilarities which arise out of the division of labor, specialization, and the mutual interdependence which arises from the normal or non-pathological expression of these. This type of solidarity is founded upon strictly formal and contractual kinds of relationships.

The solidarity possessed by homogeneous, segmented groups, such as rural society has been seen to be, is found in many of James M. Williams' descriptions of rural life. Note the expression of rural solidarity in the following quotation from one of his best-known works:

The farmer's day at its fullest and best was one in which the family all were in action early under the suggestion of the most positive characters, then at the close of the day, were at rest and in sympathetic intercourse, under the suggestion of the most sympathetic. The family liked harmony in these its two fundamental moods. The girl idling around during work hours was told: "For heaven's sake, Ann, get to work! I don't care what you do, but do something!" Then Ann, scolded during the working period, might at the close of the day be the most prized member of the family circle because of her restful and sympathetic qualities, and the leader in the work, still clattering in the kitchen, might be told, "For mercy's sake, Bess, come and sit down and be quiet!" The neighbourhood, as well as the family, satisfied the rhythm somewhat as a unit. An industrious farmer's family was annoyed by a neighbouring family that lacked the customary industry, and was pleased by an industrious one. And a family was immensely pleased with a neighbouring family that was "good company" after the day's work was done. The tendency throughout the neighbourhood

[35] Cf. George Simpson, *Emile Durkheim on the Division of Labor in Society*, New York, The Macmillan Company, 1933, pp. 129–132, *passim*.

[36] Durkheim's term to describe rural solidarity is, curiously enough, the word "mechanistic." Since current usage in America is to identify this word with mechanical contrivances and machine culture, evidently a quite different connotation from that which Durkheim intended, we have departed from his categorical usage but have given the essential idea he had in mind in nontechnical language. The same has been done for urban solidarity to avoid the confusion introduced by Durkheim's term "organic" in this connection.

was to be industrious during the day and good company in the evening.[37]

Durkheim also concluded that, as culture develops and society becomes more complex, rural solidarity is gradually replaced by that based upon division of labor. For this reason, in complex urban groups solidarity is primarily of the organic type, although the segmental type does not entirely disappear.

As we advance in the evolutionary scale, the ties which bind the individual to his family, to his native soil, to traditions which the past has given to him, to collective group usages, become loose. More mobile, he changes his environment more easily, leaves his people to go elsewhere to live a more autonomous existence, to a greater extent forms his own ideas and sentiments. Of course, the whole common conscience does not, on this account, pass out of existence. At least there will always remain this cult of personality, of individual dignity of which we have just been speaking, and which, today, is the rallying-point of so many people. But how little a thing it is when one contemplates the ever-increasing extent of social life, and, consequently, of individual consciences![38]

The analysis by this noted French scholar does much to clarify the fundamental differences in the rural and urban worlds. These two types of social solidarity will be found at the base of the fundamental differences in rural and urban attitudes. In particular with regard to law enforcement, they explain the country's rigid insistence on the strict letter of law, whereas in urban society crime and punishment becomes more of a struggle of individual or group against individual or group, with society as the referee. In fact, in an urban environment it is not at all unusual to find the majority of the population on the side of the lawbreaker. Corresponding situations arise in rural communities mainly in connection with the infringement of laws which have been forced upon the local groups by the general society, as, for example, the attitude of Appalachian mountaineers toward the enforcement of the revenue laws.

[37] James M. Williams, *Our Rural Heritage*, New York, Alfred A. Knopf, Inc., 1924, p. 201.
[38] Simpson, *op. cit.*, p. 400.

PART TWO

The Rural Population

The study of rural population is one of the most advanced phases of the entire field of sociology. For this reason it deserves detailed treatment, and Part II contains seven of the twenty-five chapters that make up this book. The number, origin, distribution, and importance of the rural population are first outlined. A detailed exposition of the composition of this population follows. Two companion chapters then summarize what is known concerning the physical and psychological characteristics and the physical and mental health of rural people. The knowledge concerning the all-important vital processes, the rate of reproduction, and the rapidity with which people die is outlined in another pair of chapters. A treatment of the spatial movements of the rural population completes Part Two.

3

THE NUMBER, ORIGIN, DISTRIBUTION, AND IMPORTANCE OF THE RURAL POPULATION

Rural Demography

In a treatise on the sociology of rural life it is essential to give a prominent place to a discussion of the rural population, because any thoroughgoing understanding of rural society and rural life is largely dependent upon a rather full knowledge of the characteristics of the rural people themselves. It is pretty generally known that rural people differ from the general population in many ways; but, as a rule, no great stress is placed on this knowledge, even though the differentiating characteristics of the rural population may be precisely the factors which would do most to facilitate an understanding of the outstanding phenomena of rural life. For example, it is frequently asserted that rural society is complacent, that it lacks dynamics, that it is content to follow along traditional grooves—in short, that rural folk are ultraconservative. Perhaps this is true; and if so, it seems important to note that elderly people occupy a position of relative importance in rural society. People of advanced age, as will be shown later, are relatively more numerous in the rural than in the general population, and, despite a few exceptions, aged people are notoriously conservative. But this point should not be stressed as much as a second one, namely, that in rural society these elderly people retain control of the property much longer, and they continue actively to direct the affairs of rural communities to a much larger extent than is true of urban people in the same age groups. All of this is important if one would really understand rural life.

The unwillingness of the rural portions of a society to change

41

the traditional ways of doing things is also widely recognized and commented upon. It forms an important theme in literature and song and is frequently the basis for urban disparagements of rural life. Here again the demographic basis of the phenomena should not be overlooked. Especially should it be remembered that the rural population is composed more largely of native elements than is true of the general population. It is a demographic truism that the foreign-born elements in a population will always be found concentrated in the cities. Thus much greater proportions of rural New Yorkers are the sons and daughters of people born in the state of New York than is true of the population of New York City; rural Southerners are more generally the sons and daughters of Southerners than are the people who reside in southern cities. Thus the rural population contains large proportions of those particular ethnic elements which have given to a society's culture its particular mold or cast. The traditional ways of doing things, the accepted national folkways and mores, are very largely the creations of rural folk and their ancestors. They represent the cultural heritage into which rural people have been born and amid which they have been reared. The most intimate associations and sentiments of rural people are firmly bound up with the traditional culture patterns. Urban folk, on the other hand, are more cosmopolitan, less limited in their perspectives to the cultural horizon of any single national group. In view of this fact, it is not surprising that the country people insist on preserving the cultural values of the group much more than do the city people. Since these cultural values belong to the rural folk, quite naturally they have a stronger appeal to the rural population than to urban people.[1] Such are but examples of the importance of beginning this study of rural life with an analysis of the make-up of the rural population.

The Rural Population of the World

There can be no doubt that the bulk of the world's population is rural and derives its livelihood from agriculture. Merely the overwhelmingly rural nature of both China and India would make

[1] In this connection the conclusion of Le Bon is pertinent: "A preponderating influence of foreigners is a sure solvent of the existence of states. It takes away from a people its most precious possession—its soul." Quoted in H. P. Fairchild, *Immigration*, New York, The Macmillan Company, 1925, p. 110.

that statement true even though all other parts of the earth were far more urban than they are. However, it is no easy task to determine, even approximately, the numbers and proportions of rural people throughout the various countries. In many parts of the globe, such as China, some other parts of Asia, and Africa, there has been little in the way of a modern census of the population. In some of the other countries little attention has been paid to any rural and urban classification of the inhabitants. And even where a rural-urban division of the population has been made, there has been little uniformity in the criteria employed or the tabulations completed. Some countries, such as the United States and France, have relied heavily upon the size of the community as measured by the number of inhabitants as the basis for separating the population into the rural and urban categories. Others, including Canada, Scotland, Sweden, and the Soviet Union, have depended to a much greater extent on the nature of the title or charter a place has received from the central government in determining whether its people were to be classified as rural or urban.[2] For these reasons, the percentages of rural and urban reported for one country may be difficult or impossible to compare fairly with those for another.

The need for comparable data with respect to the rural and urban populations of the various countries of the earth is one of the things to which the population commission of the United Nations early gave attention. As a result, the first issue of its monumental *Demographic Yearbook* is to be found by far the most comprehensive tabulation of rural and urban population data that has ever been assembled in any one volume. Along with the figures themselves are given brief indications of the criteria employed in the various countries for separating the urban residents from the rural. In order that the essential materials may be readily available for study and comparison, a summary of some of the more important items from this United Nations compilation is presented in Table 1.

Growth of Population in the United States

In the three centuries since the colonization of North America the population of the continental United States has grown at an

[2] Cf. T. Lynn Smith, *Population Analysis,* New York, McGraw-Hill Book Company, 1948, pp. 28–29.

TABLE 1. The Absolute and Relative Importance of the Rural Population of Each Country for Which the Data Are Available

Country	Year	Total Population	Rural Population	Percent Rural	Definition of Urban Areas
AFRICA					
Egypt[a]	1937	15,920,694	11,918,288	74.9	Governorates and chief towns of provinces and districts.
Union of South Africa	1946	11,391,949	7,246,966	63.6	All towns and villages having some form of urban local government, e.g., municipal councils, village management boards, or health committees.
OTHER AREAS					
Belgian Congo[b]	1947	10,804,761	9,099,590	84.2	Agglomerations containing 100 or more non-indigenous inhabitants and all indigenous population living outside the regular districts.
South-West Africa[c]	1946	37,858	19,793	52.3	Administrative areas having some form of urban local government, e.g., municipalities, village management boards, or health committees.
Eritrea[d]	1947	1,067,700	876,992	82.1	
Somalia[d]	1948	940,347	770,347	81.9	
AMERICA, NORTH					
Canada	1941	11,506,655	5,254,239	45.7	Incorporated cities, towns, and villages of all sizes.
Cuba	1943	4,778,583	2,171,093	45.4	Populated centers (*poblaciones*) of all sizes.
Dominican Republic	1935	1,479,417	1,212,852	82.0	Seats and capitals of districts, some of which include suburban zones of a rural character.
El Salvador	1930	1,434,361	885,640	61.7	Populated centers (*poblaciones*).
Guatemala	1940	3,283,209	2,405,374	73.3	Cities, towns, and villages. (Rural population is that of hamlets, small settlements, and farms.)
Honduras	1945	1,200,542	852,499	71.0	Seats of municipalities.

	Year	Population	Urban	Percent	Definition
Mexico	1940	19,653,552	12,756,883	64.9	Populated centers (*localidades*) of more than 2500 inhabitants.
Panama^e	1940	566,589	356,064	62.8	Populated centers (*poblaciones*) of 1500 or more inhabitants which have essentially urban living conditions. A few places of less than 1500 that are essentially urban are included and some places of more than 1500 that are essentially rural are excluded.
United States	1940	131,669,275	57,245,573	43.5	Incorporated places of 2500 or more inhabitants, and certain additional unincorporated but thickly settled areas that were designated as urban for purposes of the census.
OTHER AREAS					
Curaçao	1930	45,191	26,372	58.4	Cities of St. John's (Antigua) and of Basseterre (St. Kitts).
Leeward Islands	1946	108,838	85,679	78.7	Towns of Roseau and Portsmouth (Dominica); Castries, Vieux Fort, and Soufrière (St. Lucia); and towns of 1000 or more inhabitants on other islands.
Windward Islands	1946	251,771	208,598	82.9	
Puerto Rico	1940	1,869,255	1,302,898	69.7	Cities, towns, and villages of 2500 or more inhabitants.
Virgin Islands	1940	24,889	8,095	32.5	Cities of Charlotte Amalie, Christiansted, and Frederiksted, the smallest of which has a population of slightly less than 2500.
AMERICA, SOUTH					
Argentina	1947	16,108,573	6,213,622	38.6	Cities, towns, or villages of 2000 or more inhabitants.
Bolivia	1900	1,633,610	1,194,605	73.1	The 22 cities of the Republic.
Brazil	1940	41,236,315	28,356,133	68.8	The principal towns of "districts" and their suburbs. A "district" may not be established until the chief center contains at least 30 households and the urban and suburban limits have been determined.
Chile	1940	5,023,539	2,390,060	47.6	
Columbia	1938	8,701,816	6,168,136	70.9	Centers of more than 1500 inhabitants which are seats of municipalities (*municipios*) or districts (*corregimientos*).

TABLE 1. The Absolute and Relative Importance of the Rural Population (*Continued*)

Country	Year	Total Population	Rural Population	Percent Rural	Definition of Urban Areas
Peru[f]	1940	6,207,967	4,010,834	64.6	Capitals of departments, provinces and districts, and other populated centers (*centros poblados*) the number of whose inhabitants exceeds the average for the capital, provided such centers do not have typically rural characteristics.
Venezuela[e]	1941	3,850,771	2,684,861	69.7	Places (*lugares*) of 2500 or more inhabitants.
ASIA					
Ceylon[g]	1946	6,657,339	5,634,297	84.6	Towns of 5000 or more inhabitants, possessing definite urban characteristics. A few places of less than 5000 are also included.
India[h]	1941	388,997,955	339,301,902	87.2	
Japan	1948	80,216,896	40,851,444	50.9	Areas under municipal administration (*shi*) corresponding roughly to cities of 30,000 or more inhabitants.
Korea	1944	25,900,142	23,948,576	92.5	The 12 incorporated cities.
EUROPE					
Austria[i]	1946	6,818,593	2,434,490	35.7	Self-governing units (*Ortsgemeinden*) of more than 2000 inhabitants.
Belgium	1930	8,092,004	3,198,321	39.5	Administrative subdivisions (*communes*) of 5000 or more inhabitants.
Czechoslovakia	1947	12,164,095	6,228,662	51.2	Administrative districts of 2000 or more inhabitants.
Denmark[j]	1945	4,045,232	1,411,045	34.9	Towns and agglomerations, including suburbs of the capital and of provincial cities.

Country	Year				Definition
Finland[k]	1947	3,849,097	2,892,795	75.2	Communes having more than 2000 inhabitants in the chief town (*chef-lieu*).
France[l]	1946	40,502,513	18,951,093	46.8	Townships or adminstrative subdivisions (*Gemeinden*) with more than 2000 inhabitants.
Germany[m]					
British Zone	1946	21,894,099	4,718,915	21.6	
French Zone	1946	5,029,342	2,470,938	49.1	
U.S. Zone[n]	1946	8,738,412	3,984,844	45.6	
Greece[o]	1940	7,344,860	4,726,785[p]	64.4	Municipalities and communes having 5000 or more inhabitants in the largest center of population.
Hungary[q]	1941	9,316,613	5,944,101	63.8	Agglomerations qualified as towns from the administrative point of view, regardless of the number of inhabitants.
Iceland	1940	121,474	46,984	38.7	Towns or places of more than 300 inhabitants.
Ireland	1946	2,953,452	1,842,985	62.4	Towns of 1500 or more inhabitants.
Italy[r]	1936	42,993,602	23,809,250	55.4	Communes with less than 50 percent of the active population engaged in agriculture.
Luxembourg	1947	286,786	120,115	41.9	Communes having more than 2000 inhabitants in the chief town (*chef-lieu*).
Monaco	1946	19,242	—	—	Entire principality.
Netherlands[s]	1946	9,494,214	4,355,914[t]	45.9	Administrative subdivisions (municipalities) of 20,000 or more inhabitants.
Norway	1946	3,123,338	2,246,579	71.9	Cities or towns (*Kjøpsteder, Ladesteder*) officially designated as urban.
Poland[u]	1946	23,625,435	16,200,846	68.6	Communities having an urban administrative organization.
Portugal	1940	7,722,152	5,323,380	68.9	Places (*aglomerados urbanes*) of 5000 or more inhabitants.
Rumania[q]	1948	15,872,624	12,159,485	76.6	Cities and towns under urban administration.
Sweden	1945	6,673,749	3,851,262	57.7	Cities or towns (*Stader*) with an urban administration.
Switzerland	1941	4,265,703	2,863,368	67.1	Communes (*communes politiques*) of more than 10,00 inhabitants.

TABLE 1. The Absolute and Relative Importance of the Rural Population (*Continued*)

Country	Year	Total Population	Rural Population	Percent Rural	Definition of Urban Areas
EUROPE (*Cont.*)					
United Kingdom[v]					
England and Wales	1931	46,075,102	9,565,703	20.8	The following administrative areas: county boroughs, mu-
	1931	39,952,377	8,000,459	20.0	nicipal boroughs, urban districts, London Administra-
					tive County.
Northern Ireland	1937	1,279,745	602,200	47.1	The following administrative areas: cities, municipal bor-
					oughs, and urban districts.
Scotland	1931	4,842,980	963,044	19.9	Burghs, special lighting districts, and special scavenging
					districts of 1000 or more inhabitants.
Yugoslavia	1948	15,751,935	13,196,297	83.8	Administrative units that are governed by City People's
					Committees.
OTHER AREAS					
Trieste[w]	1936	343,100	60,808	17.7	Communes with less than 50 percent of the active popula-
					tion engaged in agriculture.
OCEANIA					
Australia[z]	1947	7,560,755	2,354,248	31.1	Capital cities of states and territories, other cities which are
					separately incorporated, and some additional areas within
					boundaries determined for census purposes and classified
					as urban.
New Zealand[v]	1945	1,699,113	671,198	39.5	Cities, boroughs, and town of 1000 or more inhabitants.
OTHER AREAS					
Campbell, Cook, Niue, Kermadec and Tokelau Islands (N.Z.)	1945	19,761	19,761	100.0	No urban areas.

a Excluding nomadic population.

b Excluding 897 Asiatics.

c European population only.

d Estimates.

e Excluding tribal Indians.

f Excluding jungle population.

g Excluding military and shipping personnel.

h Area as of 1 March 1941.

i Estimates based on ration card registrations.

j Excluding Faeroes.

k Based on tax lists of 1 January 1947.

l Habitually resident population, excluding enemy prisoners of war, military and naval personnel.

m Excluding prisoners of war, enternees, etc. as follows:

British Zone—male: 122,251; female: 2,855
French Zone—male: 23,486; female: 350
U.S. Zone (Bavaria only)—male: 51,130; female: 108

n Bavaria only.

o Excluding Dodecanese.

p The rural population may be subdivided to distinguish the population of communes with less than 2000 inhabitants in the largest center, as follow: total, 3,876,030; males, 1,916,119; females, 1,959,911.

q Present territory.

r Territory of 21 April 1936. Resident population.

s Estimates, excluding persons listed in the Central Register of Population (26,926 males; 21,519 females).

t The rural population may be subdivided to distinguish the population in municipalities of less than 5000 inhabitants, as follows: total, 1,500,041; males, 768,886; females, 731,155.

u Present territory. Excluding 286,999 males and 17,323 females not classified by urban and rural residence.

v Figures for Northern Ireland included in the totals relate to the census of 1937.

w Resident population.

x Excluding migratory population (16,408 males; 2195 females).

y Excluding migratory population (3151 males; 34 females).

Adapted from the United Nations, *Demographic Yearbook, 1948*, Lake Success, New York, 1949, Table 8.

unprecedented rate. No other large nation has ever increased at anything like a comparable speed.[3] Exclusive of Indians, there were in this territory approximately 50,000 people in 1650. By 1700 the number had increased to around 275,000. The first census of the United States (1790) placed the total population at approximately four million (3,929,214). By 1850 this number had increased nearly five times (23,191,876), and the 1850 population was more than tripled by 1900 (75,994,575). The last count, in 1950, placed the population of the nation at 150,697,361.[4] From 4 to 151 millions in 160 years is truly a phenomenal increase.

Other changes in the nation's population are also of great import. For our purposes the shift from a population overwhelmingly agricultural and rural to one largely industrial and urban is of paramount importance. All this has been accomplished in the short span of a century. When the United States set out on its career as a new nation, it contained no city with 50,000 inhabitants. When the first census was taken, in 1790, only six cities contained over 8000 inhabitants and thus qualified to be counted as urban. Over 96 percent of the population lived either in the open country or in towns of less than 8000 and were classed as rural. It was 1820 before the first city of 100,000 inhabitants was recorded, but thereafter urbanization proceeded very rapidly. By 1850, there were 85 cities containing 8000 or more people, and 12.5 percent of the nation's population lived in these centers. In the next fifty years urban growth proceeded at an amazing pace, the Census of 1900 enumerating 546 places of 8000 or more inhabitants; these centers contained 25,018,335 persons, or 32.9 percent of the total population.[5] If 2500, which was selected in 1900 as the point of separating rural from urban, is taken as the criterion, at the beginning of the twentieth century the urban population totaled 30,380,433 and made up 40 percent of the total population. The urban population also continued greatly to outgain the rural population during the next fifty years. In 1920, for the first time, less than half of the population was classed as rural, the urban part making up 51.4 percent of the total. This trend con-

[3] W. S. Thompson and P. K. Whelpton, *Population Trends in the United States,* New York, McGraw-Hill Book Company, 1933, p. 1.

[4] U.S. Bureau of the Census, *1950 Census of Population, Preliminary Reports,* "General Characteristics of the Population of the United States: April 1, 1950," Series PC-7, No. 1, Washington, February 25, 1951.

[5] *Abstract of the Fifteenth Census of the United States.* Washington, Government Printing Office, 1933, p. 20.

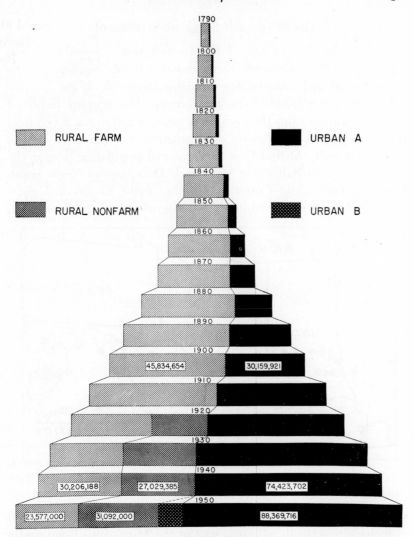

RURAL FARM

URBAN A

RURAL NONFARM

URBAN B

1790
1800
1810
1820
1830
1840
1850
1860
1870
1880
1890
1900
45,834,654   30,159,921
1910
1920
1930
1940
30,206,188   27,029,385   74,423,702
1950
23,577,000   31,092,000   88,369,716

FIGURE 1.   The Growth of Population in the United States, 1790 to 1950, by Residence.

tinued to 1950, when, of the 150,697,361 people in the United States, only about 54,669,000 persons, 36.3 percent of the total,[6] were classified as rural. The 160 years of population growth in the United States classified according to residence is graphically portrayed in Figure 1.

[6] U.S. Bureau of the Census, *1950 Census of Population, Preliminary Reports,* "Population of the United States, Urban and Rural, by States, April 1, 1950," Series PC-3, No. 10, Washington, February 16, 1951. As a result of the changes

The Westward Surge of Settlement

When the first census of the United States' population was taken in 1790, settlements were almost entirely confined to the eastern seaboard, constituting a narrow fringe along the Atlantic plain extending from Maine to Georgia. The average depth of the settled area from the coast was around 250 miles. Even over this limited area the density of population was very low, sixteen per square mile. At that time the center of population[7] was in the neighborhood of Baltimore, Maryland,[8] the center of Negro population in Dinwiddie County, Virginia, about twenty-five miles west-southwest of Petersburg.[9] (See Figure 2.) By 1850, so rapid

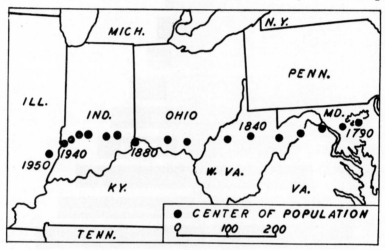

FIGURE 2. The Westward March of the Center of Population, 1790 to 1950.

was the growth of the nation, the band of settlement had widened to include practically all areas east of the Mississippi River and a tier of states to the west of it. Also included in the settled areas were large portions of California and Texas. At this time the aver-

---

in the rural and urban definitions described in this report, the rural population in 1950 was about 7,522,000 smaller than it would have been had the 1940 definitions been retained.

[7] If all the people of the nation were to collect together in one spot, the center of population would be the point they could reach with the minimum of air-line travel.

[8] *Report of the Population of the United States at the Eleventh Census: 1890,* Washington, Government Printing Office, 1895, Part I, pp. xix–xx.

[9] *Statistical Atlas of the United States,* Washington, Government Printing Office, 1925, p. 18.

age density of population was around twenty-four persons per square mile, and the center of population had moved westward into what is now West Virginia.[10] By 1900 the westward surge of population across the continent was almost complete, and much had been done to fill in the open spaces on the map which had been passed by in the rapid rush of settlement. The density of population at this time was twenty-six per square mile, and the center of population had moved westward to south-central Indiana,[11] the center of Negro population west to DeKalb County, Alabama.[12] In 1950 there was no longer a western frontier, nor were there many unsettled areas which had been overlooked in the westward surge that were suitable for settlement. The density of population was 50 per square mile, and the center of population was in east south-central Illinois and was moving in a southwesterly direction.

The Rural Farm, Rural Nonfarm, and Urban Populations

The classification of the population into the rural and urban categories, with the former subdivided into the rural farm and the rural nonfarm segments, respectively, is one of the most important sets of tabulations in the United States Census of population. For many years, however, there has been considerable dissatisfaction with the criteria employed, and the results have been subject to serious criticism. The rural nonfarm class was particularly unsatisfactory, since by 1940 it included many millions of persons who lived in the highly urban areas just outside the corporation limits of our great cities.[13]

In response to requests from many sources, between 1940 and 1950 the U.S. Bureau of Census attempted fundamental improvements in its residential classification. The new definitions of rural and urban introduced in the 1950 Census are the result.

According to the new definition, the urban population comprises all persons living in (a) places of 2,500 inhabitants or more incorporated as cities, boroughs, and villages; (b) the densely settled suburban area, or urban fringe, incorporated or unincorporated, around

---

[10] *Eleventh Census*, p. xxiv.

[11] *Abstract of the Fifteenth Census*, p. 13; Robert Tudor Hill, *The Public Domain and Democracy*, New York: Columbia University Press, 1910, chap. 1.

[12] *Statistical Atlas of the United States*, p. 19.

[13] Cf. T. Lynn Smith, *Population Analysis*, New York, McGraw-Hill Book Company, 1948, pp. 33–37.

cities of 50,000 or more; (c) unincorporated places of 2,500 inhabitants or more outside of any urban fringe; and (d) places of 2,500 inhabitants or more incorporated as towns except in New England, New York, and Wisconsin, where "towns" are simply minor civil divisions of counties. The remaining population is classified as rural.[14]

In the 1920, 1930, and 1940 censuses the rural farm population was secured by classifying as farms all tracts of land which met certain specfied requirements and counting everyone residing on those tracts as belonging to the category. In 1950 this practice was substantially changed for the better. In the latest enumeration "the rural population is subdivided into the rural-farm population, which comprises all rural residents living on farms, and the rural-nonfarm population, which comprises the remaining rural population." However, in 1950 "persons on 'farms' who were paying cash rent for their house and yard only were classified as nonfarm; furthermore, persons in institutions, summer camps, 'motels,' and tourist camps were classified as nonfarm."[15]

At the time of our latest enumeration only 23,577,000 persons were included in the rural farm population, a considerable decrease from the figure of more than 30,000,000 that prevailed from about 1890 until the outbreak of the Second World War. Only a small part of the decrease may fairly be attributed to the change in the definition of the rural farm population. Since 1940 there has been an actual decrease of some 6,000,000, perhaps slightly more, in the bona-fide farm population of the United States. On a percentage basis the 30,216,188 persons in the rural farm population at the time of the 1940 census made up 22.9 percent of the national population, while the 23,577,000 persons classified as rural farm in 1950 constituted only 15.6 percent of the people in the United States.

As noted above, almost eight million persons were classified as urban in the 1950 census who would have figured as part of the rural nonfarm population under the definitions used in 1940. Nevertheless, in spite of this tremendous loss by definition, in 1950 the rural nonfarm population substantially outnumbered the rural farm population. According to the results available, this segment of the rural population numbers 31,092,000 and makes up 20.6

[14] "General Characteristics of the Population of the United States: April 1, 1950," p. 3.
[15] *Ibid.*

percent of the nation's total. This upward surge of the part of our population that is neither urban nor farm is one of the most significant population and social trends in the nation. It is likely to continue for some time to come.

Origin of the Rural Population

Other than the American Indians, rural Americans derive from (1) the North American colonists and (2) immigrants. For purposes of this chapter, colonists refer to those Europeans who had established themselves within the present limits of the United States prior to 1787, immigrants to all those coming after the formation of the new nation. The population which established the original colonies in America was not exceedingly heterogeneous in origin. The first settlers in the original colonies came very largely from the British Isles, the first comers including the Puritans of New England, the Quakers of Pennsylvania, and the Cavaliers of Virginia. The Dutch of New York, the Germans and Swedes of Pennsylvania, Maryland, and New Jersey, and the French Huguenots who distributed themselves throughout all the colonies constituted the principal non-British elements. But the settlers were drawn from widely separated social classes. New England drew mainly from the middle and lower classes, and the colonists established themselves on the new continent as small farmers or yeomen. New York, under the Dutch, and the tidewater areas of the South, on the other hand, were selected as sections into which the manorial systems of the mother countries might be transplanted. New York was soon taken over by the English; and although many large estates have survived upon the Hudson, the Revolutionary War and the expulsion of the Tories gave the small holders possession of many of the former estates and presented the aristocratic system from being widely perpetuated or carried westward to any great extent. In the South many large estates were granted and a considerable number of the aristocracy laid the foundations for the plantation system which played such a conspicuous role in the history of southern society. At first manual labor on these *latifundia* was done by indentured servants, white and black. Later the importation of Negro slaves added great numbers of Negroes to the plantation and established the close association between good land, the plantation, the Negro, and the rigid social stratification which has persisted to the present day.

So prominent has the plantation been in the South that it is common to think of the North as colonized by yeomen and the South by landed proprietors and their Negro slaves. However, this conception overlooks one of the most important elements in the American population—the small-farming white class of the South.

The story of the southern farmer, as distinguished from the planter, is one of the most interesting chapters in American history. Although this group has not figured so prominently in literature, its role in American agriculture has been and remains one of first-rate importance. Perhaps the characterization of the two types of agriculturists in the South can best be given in the words of Dr. Daniel Drake, written in 1850. He says:

In the slave states, from the Appalachian Mountains to the Rio del Norte, there are, in reference to agricultural labor, two classes of white men: *First.* Those who own a sufficient number of slaves to perform the required work of the plantation, as it is there called; and, therefore, do not labor with their own hands, but lead lives of superintendence, recreation, or idleness; spending, it is true, much of their time in the open air, but often without adequate provision against all its inclemencies; and without taking systematic exercise, for the sake of hygienic effects. The further we go south, the greater is the proportional number of this class. *Second.* Those who either own no slaves, or so few, as to be under the necessity of participating in the labors of the field. No portion of the slaveholding states is without this class; but they are most numerous in western Virginia, east Tennessee, Kentucky, and Missouri; that is, above the cotton zone, in the latitudes which produce wheat, hemp, tobacco, horned cattle, horses, and sheep. The hardest and heaviest labors of this class consist in cutting down the forests, and opening the farm. In the south, they do not work much among the sugar and cotton; but in miscellaneous agriculture—they are farmers, not planters, in the discriminating vocabulary of the country.[16]

Long before the Revolutionary War, thousands of Ulster Presbyterians (or Scotch-Irish), English, and Germans were entering the colonies.[17] Using Philadelphia as their port of entry and moving at once into western Pennsylvania, they spread up and

[16] Daniel Drake, *Principal Diseases of the Interior Valley of North America,* Cincinnati, 1850, pp. 684–685.
[17] Constance Lindsay Skinner, *Pioneers of the Old Southwest,* New Haven, Yale University Press, 1921, pp. 1–2.

down the valleys of the Appalachians. Says John R. Commons of the Scotch-Irish and their role in American civilization:

It has long been recognized that among the most virile and aggressive people who came to America in colonial times, and who have contributed a peculiar share to the American character, are the Scotch-Irish. . . . Yet until recent years it has been the misfortune of the Scotch-Irish to have escaped historical investigation; for American history has been written chiefly in New England, whose colonial Puritans forbade them in their midst. In fact, from the earliest settlement, the Scotch-Irish have been pioneers and men of action. . . .

A paradoxical fact regarding the Scotch-Irish is that they are very little Scotch and much less Irish . . . they are the most composite of all people in the British Isles. They are called Scots because they lived in Scotia, and they are called Irish because they moved to Ireland. . . . They are a mixed race through whose veins run the Celtic blood of the primitive Scott and Pict, the primitive Briton, the primitive Irish, but with a larger admixture of the later Norwegian, Dane, Saxon and Angle.[18]

By 1726 they were well established in the counties back of Philadelphia where they had been allowed to settle in order to provide a bulwark between the older settlements and the Indians; and ten years later they had begun their great trek south into the Shenandoah Valley of Virginia, the migration which eventually furnished the great bulk of settlers to the southern portion of the nation. In Yadkin Valley of North Carolina they were met by another migratory current similar in composition which had entered the new country through the port of Charleston and had pushed its way up the rivers to the "back country."[19] The numerical importance of this influx of settlers may be partially judged by the estimate that 20,000 Ulstermen left Ireland for America between 1700 and 1730, by the known fact that more than 6000 of them entered Philadelphia in thé single year 1729, and that they comprised one-fourth of the total population of Pennsylvania in 1750.[20] U. B. Phillips has summarized concisely the nature and direction of this important trend of settlement:

. . . But Philadelphia was preeminently the port of entry for the American frontiersmen, and Pennsylvania the first halting place of the

[18] *Races and Immigrants in America*, New York, The Macmillan Company, 1907, pp. 31–32.
[19] Skinner, *op. cit.*, p. 2.
[20] *Ibid.*, p. 6.

horde which furnished the main population of the Southern Piedmont.

The tide of emigrants from Pennsylvania, mostly Scotch-Irishmen and Germans, began to pour across Maryland into the Shenandoah Valley, about 1730. It ascended the valley in a fairly rapid movement, and between 1740 and 1750 began to flow out upon the rolling plateau of middle Carolina. It mingled there with a stream of emigrating Virginians, and with them flowed farther southwestward. Braddock's defeat in 1775, by creating uneasiness on the frontier of the middle colonies, increased the volume of this movement.

By this tide of migration a thin population of pioneer farmers was established in all of the districts to which it spread. The farther extension southwestward was checked in the uplands of eastern Georgia, about 1760, by the resistance of the Indian tribes. The next few decades witnessed a gradual thickening of settlement in the region through reinforcements from the same northward sources, aided now also by straggling Irish, English, and other recruits from across the barrens from Charleston and Savannah.

The country invited the farming class. The roving huntsmen, whether redskin or white, had their game driven away by the farming invasion, and as a class disappeared from the region. The straggling cattle drovers who for a period in the middle of the century pastured their herds in some parts of the Piedmont were likewise gradually driven out by the entrance of the farmers. . . . This conquest of the Piedmont was the work of backwoodsmen, in a movement entirely spontaneous. The settlement was made by individual families with the primary intention of producing each of the articles which it needed to consume. The people were squatters, without encouragement or even recognition from any government, establishing a self-sufficing economy in isolation from the rest of the world. The conditions were in salient contrast with those of the lowland planters.[21]

[21] U. B. Phillips, *A History of Transportation in the Eastern Cotton Belt to 1860*, New York, Columbia University Press, 1918, pp. 48–50. Cf. the same author's *American Negro Slavery*, New York, D. Appleton-Century Company, 1918, pp. 172–173, 180, and 333–334; W. E. Dodd, *The Cotton Kingdom*, New Haven, Yale University Press, 1920, pp. 19–20; Theodore Roosevelt, *The Winning of the West*, New York, The Current Literature Publishing Company, 1905, Part I, *passim;* Ellen Churchill Semple, *American History and Its Geographic Conditions*, Boston, Houghton Mifflin Company, 1903, p. 62; W. H. Yarbrough, *Economic Aspects of Slavery in Relation to Southern and Southwestern Migration*, Nashville, George Peabody College for Teachers, 1932, pp. 96–97; Wesley M. Gewehr, *The Great Awakening in Virginia, 1740–1790*, Durham, Duke University Press, 1930, pp. 19–39; Robert Preston Brooks, *The Agrarian Revolution in Georgia, 1865–1912*, University of Wisconsin Historical Series, III (1914), 74–76; and Skinner, *op. cit.*, pp. 1–2. See also the *Proceedings of the Congress of the Scotch-Irish Society of America*, particularly the reports of the first congress held at Columbia, Tennessee, 1889; the fourth congress at Atlanta, Georgia, 1892; the sixth congress at Des Moines, Iowa, 1894; and the eighth congress at Harrisburg, Pennsylvania, 1896.

Through their persistent habit of squatting upon desired lands, these small farmers set the pattern which was later legalized in the Homestead Acts. The numerous progeny of these small farmers and backwoodsmen spread down through the upland parts of western Maryland, Virginia, North Carolina, South Carolina, and Georgia, pushed through the passes of the Appalachians, and, spilling over the mountains, furnished Ohio, Kentucky, and Tennessee with settlers. Then they spread westward, populating those parts of the South and Southwest that were hilly in topography. It is interesting to observe them in various parts of the South, as far west as Oklahoma and Texas. Throughout the entire region, a description similar to the following is applicable:

The inhabitants of North Louisiana are different in many respects from those of the low country. They are generally of English, Scotch or Irish descent, immigrants from the older and more eastern States, or the offspring of such immigrants. Georgia, Alabama, the two Carolinas and Virginia, have all furnished their quota towards making up the population of this part of Louisiana.[22]

The inhabitants of the piny woods are proverbially poor, but honest, moral, virtuous, simple-hearted and hospitable. In some [woods] that I passed through I found little communities banded together by kinship or long friendships, with many of the evidences of thrift, comfort, and prosperity around them.[23]

The pine hills, flats and prairies were left to yeomanry who came into the country. Those pioneers who settled the pine hills "pitched their tents" in the thousand creek bottoms which divide the hills, and with their own hands worked their way to wealth—their sons and daughters learned to work, and when they married entered lands either "up" or "down the creek."[24]

Powers described the formation of new settlements in these upland areas as follows:

When you chop off a place for it to stand upon, you have nearly logs enough to build a Mississippi cabin. The immigrant's family can live ten days in a wagon, while he chops goodly trunks, and flattens them on two sides. On the eleventh there come to him men out of the

---

[22] Daniel Dennett, *Louisiana as It Is*, New Orleans, Eureka Press, 1876, p. 30.
[23] *Ibid.*, p. 31.
[24] William H. Harris, *Louisiana Products, Resources and Attractions, With a Sketch of the Parishes*, New Orleans, New Orleans *Democrat*, printer, 1881, p. 8. Cf. T. Lynn Smith and Martha Ray Fry, *The Population of a Selected "Cut-Over" Area in Louisiana*, Louisiana AES Bulletin 268, Baton Rouge, 1936, pp. 6–7.

pathless depths of the woods, summoned by some mysterious telegraphy, and they "raise." In five days more he mortises a bedstead into the corner, and knits a chimney with sticks.[25]

Other cabins, a saloon, a grocery store, a meetinghouse follow, and "at last there is a village, but it is only an auger-hole in the woods."[26]

Throughout the great West and Southwest the Scotch-Irish exemplified those pioneer qualities essential for the "winning of the West." John R. Commons is authority for the statement that more than any other stock "they served as the amalgam to produce, out of divergent races, a new race, the American."[27] Frederick Jackson Turner elaborated upon this thesis in his monumental work, *The Frontier in American History.*[28]

Heavy immigration has been one of the distinguishing characteristics of American national life. The nineteenth century was the great period when all manner of racial and national stocks were incorporated into the American population. Early in the century the migration began, rather slowly at first, and was drawn largely from the northern European countries. During the first half of the nineteenth century the immigrants were primarily of Teutonic and Celtic stock; and these Germans and Irish, coming at a time when the nation was dominantly agricultural, were taken up largely by the demands of agriculture and distributed upon our farms.[29] This was especially the case with those of German descent, who migrated mostly in family groups, including a large number of children; not so true of the Irish immigration, which consisted largely of unmarried youth of both sexes, and which from the very first expressed a preference for the cities.[30] This influx from Germany and Ireland was followed during the latter portion of the century by a heavy tide from southern and southeastern Europe, the so-called "new immigration."

[25] Stephen Powers, *Afoot and Alone: A Walk from Sea to Sea by the Southern Route,* Hartford, Connecticut, Columbia Book Co., 1872, p. 80.

[26] *Ibid.,* p. 81; for excellent descriptions of life in early southwestern settlements, see Carl Coke Rister, *Southern Plainsmen,* Norman, University of Oklahoma Press, 1938.

[27] Commons, *op. cit.,* p. 37.

[28] New York, Henry Holt & Company, 1921.

[29] Cf. Frank Julian Warne, *The Tide of Immigration,* New York, D. Appleton-Century Company, 1916, p. 225.

[30] Richmond Mayo Smith, *Emigration and Immigration,* New York, Charles Scribner's Sons, 1890, p. 51.

Much light is thrown upon the question of our rural population by soundings into the birthplace of foreign-born residents, first in 1850 before the threat of war was too disturbing, and again in 1910 after the high tide of immigration had passed. It would be most lamentable that data for rural and urban areas were not separated in the Census of 1850, were it not for the fact that at that time the population of the entire country was largely rural, only 12.5 percent living in places of 8000 or more. Even as late as 1850 the urban elements in our national population were of minor importance.

Despite the newness of the nation in 1850, of a white population totaling 19,553,068, only 2,240,581, or 11.5 percent, were born in foreign countries.[31] This is just slightly under the proportion in 1930, when 12.4 percent of the white population was foreign-born. But at this early date the constitution of the immigrant population was very different from that of the present. In 1850 the great bulk of the foreign elements had originated in the British Isles. In fact, nearly one-half of them (961,719), or 43 percent, came from Ireland alone, another 278,675 (12.5 percent) came from England, while Scotland and Wales contributed 70,550 (3.2 percent) and 29,868 (1.3 percent), respectively; combining these figures makes a total of 1,340,812 from the British Isles, 60 percent of the whole number of foreign-born whites. To these might be added another 147,711 (6.6 percent) who came from British America.

Next to Ireland, Germany was the largest single contributor, having sent over a total of 583,774 (26 percent of all), followed by France (54,069 or 2.5 percent). Prior to the Civil War practically no Scandinavians had entered the United States, although by 1850 the stream which later became so important was just beginning to flow; in the seventh census Norwegians numbered 12,678, Swedes 3559, and Danes 1838. Foreign-born Dutch totaled 9848. Although individuals and small groups of Italians had made notable contributions to American life prior to the Civil War,[32] natives of Italy were very slightly represented in the Census of 1850, numbering only 3645. Natives of Spain were only 3113. Other streams, soon to be swollen with thousands of migrants, were, so far, tiny rivulets.

[31] J. D. B. De Bow, *Statistical View of the United States: A Compendium of the Seventh Census*, Washington, A. O. P. Nicholson, 1854, p. 61.

[32] See Giovanni Schiavo, *The Italians in America Before the Civil War*, New York, The Vigo Press, 1934, pp. 203–227.

Russians were 1414 in number, the Portuguese only 1274, and there were in 1850 a total of but 86 Greeks in the United States.[33]

Some data also may be derived from the *Compendium of the Seventh Census,* which indicates the residential preferences of the newcomers. Of the total foreign-born white population, 705,-498 (31.5 percent) were residents of what De Bow called the twenty-nine leading cities. The basis of his classification is not entirely clear, and it is evident that some places with more than 40,000 persons were not included in the list. But in any case the data are sufficient to show that, even in 1850, there was a pronounced tendency for the foreign-born to congregate in the cities. As suggested above, this trait was most pronounced among the Irish, 37.4 percent of them being in these twenty-nine cities. Much the same thing is indicated by the fact that the great bulk of the Irish were in New York (343,111), Pennsylvania (151,111), and Massachusetts (115,917), although considerable contingents of people from the Emerald Isle resided in Ohio, New Jersey, Illinois, and Connecticut. Germans were more widely dispersed through the various states than the Irish, and they were not confined to the cities to such a great extent, only 26.2 percent of them residing in the above-mentioned twenty-nine cities. It is particularly significant that the members of this group moved into the more rural western states, where they have made large permanent contributions to the national stock and culture, the rural environment being much more favorable to such contribution than the urban. New York, with 120,609, contained more Germans than any other state, but Ohio (112,022) ranked second, and Pennsylvania (79,005) third. Then came four western states, Missouri (45,049), Illinois, Wisconsin, and Indiana. The Germans also turned south

---

[33] De Bow, *op. cit.,* pp. 117–118. Some data on immigration into the United States are of interest for comparative purposes. Between 1811 and 1855, the entry into the country of 4,212,624 persons of foreign birth was reported. Of these the largest contingent, 2,343,455, or 55.5 percent, were born in the United Kingdom; the next largest number, 1,242,082, or 29.5 percent, in Germany and Prussia; and the third largest number, 188,725, or 4.5 percent, in France. Other European countries had contributed the following numbers: Switzerland, 31,071; Norway and Sweden, 29,441; Holland, 17,583; Spain, 11,251; Italy, 7185 (388 more came from Sicily, 706 from Sardinia, 9 from Corsica, and 116 from Malta); Belgium, 6991; Portugal, 6049; and Denmark, 3059. Other American countries had sent considerable numbers, including 91,699 from British America (many of whom had not remained), 35,317 from the West Indies, 15,969 from Mexico, 5440 from South American countries, and 640 from the various parts of Central America. During the period under consideration, 16,714 Chinese entered the United States. See William J. Bromwell, *History of Immigration to the United States,* New York, Redfield, 1856, pp. 16–17.

to some extent, 27,124 of them being enumerated in Maryland. Also widely distributed at this time were the English and Welsh. They were even less concentrated in the cities than the Germans, only 22.9 percent of them being enumerated as residents of the twenty-nine cities referred to above.

Foreign-born white persons reached their maximum in the rural United States in the Census of 1910, when 3,770,189 were enumerated in the rural parts of the nation.[34] But during the sixty-year period from 1850 many new streams of migration had entered the United States, giving a quite different appearance to the character of the rural immigrants. Among the foreigners who were rural residents, those born in Germany headed the list; and these Germans were widely diffused throughout the farming sections of the country. Of the 832,018 German-born residents of rural communities, the largest number (111,582) was in Wisconsin; but Illinois contained 78,591, Iowa 71,875, Minnesota 69,919, and Michigan 52,257. The rural parts of New York, Nebraska, and Pennsylvania each furnished homes for over 40,000, those of Texas for 30,365, and those of Missouri for 26,392.

The Scandinavian countries had furnished the second largest contingent of foreigners to rural America (589,551), and like the Germans most of these had settled on the farms of the Northwest. Of the various Scandinavian stocks, rural Danes were the most numerous in the states of North Dakota (16,577), Minnesota, and Nebraska; rural Norwegians in Minnesota (69,845), North Dakota, and Wisconsin; and rural Swedes in Minnesota (65,198), Illinois, and Nebraska.

A total of 436,778 natives of Austria-Hungary were residing in rural United States in 1910. The bulk of the rural Austrians (112,240) lived in Pennsylvania, although the populations of Minnesota, Texas, Wisconsin, Nebraska, New York, Ohio, Illinois, and Michigan each contained between ten and twenty thousand rural Austrians. Hungarians, too, were largely confined to Pennsylvania (51,624), the only other states containing as many as 10,000 being Ohio and New Jersey. Foreign-born persons from England, totaling 340,614 in the rural districts of the United States, were widely scattered. Only Pennsylvania (27,373) contained more than 25,000 of these, although more than 10,000 were counted in

[34] The high-water mark in total immigration was reached in 1907, when almost 1,300,000 immigrants entered the United States. Cf. Julius Drachsler, *Democracy and Assimilation*, New York, The Macmillan Company, 1920, p. 3.

the rural populations of each of the following states: New York, Michigan, Illinois, and Ohio. Canada had contributed a total of 324,282 whites to our 1910 immigrant residents of rural areas. Michigan (13,124), New York, and New Hampshire received the bulk of those from French Canada; Michigan (65,627), New York, North Dakota, Maine, Washington, California, and Minnesota the most significant numbers of those from the other parts of Canada.

Late in the nineteenth and early in the twentieth century there was a tremendous influx of Italians into the United States; although most of them stopped in the eastern cities, 293,735 were enumerated in rural communities by the Census of 1910. Pennsylvania had the largest number (72,994) of foreign-born Italians in its rural population, but New York and California also had large representations. Another new source of immigrants was Russia (including Finland), the land of birth of 273,687 of the rural foreign-born white population of the United States in 1910. Pennsylvania (41,155), North Dakota, and New York contained the largest numbers of these.[35] Although the Irish have consistently avoided the agricultural regions of the country, the rural foreign-born white population of 1910 included 207,254 of them. They remained close to the cities, however, largely in New York (39,-276), Pennsylvania, and Illinois.

Mexicans represent one of the most recent groups to enter the United States in any great numbers. Although essentially agriculturists in their homeland, they too flock to cities when they enter the United States. The rural population of 1910 included only 145,968 persons born in Mexico, and of these the bulk were in the Southwest, Texas (84,320), Arizona, and California having the greatest numbers.

Distribution of the Rural Population

The absolute numbers of persons in the rural population are the basic figures upon which all discussions of distribution must be founded. It is, of course, not practicable in a volume like this to give such data for units smaller than the states, although for many purposes the county figures are the most important of all. In Table 2 are presented the pertinent materials from the latest

[35] However, less than one-tenth of the immigrants born in Russia were Russians, most of them being Poles, Lithuanians, Finns, Germans, and Jews. See Fairchild, *op. cit.*, p. 143.

TABLE 2. The 48 States Arrayed According to the Sizes
of Their Rural Farm Populations, 1950

State	Rank	Rural Farm Population
North Carolina	1	1,376,664
Texas	2	1,292,267
Mississippi	3	1,097,207
Tennessee	4	1,061,204
Kentucky	5	974,210
Georgia	6	962,435
Alabama	7	960,846
Missouri	8	863,496
Ohio	9	853,088
Arkansas	10	801,827
Iowa	11	782,606
Illinois	12	763,196
Minnesota	13	739,795
Virginia	14	731,947
Wisconsin	15	725,550
Pennsylvania	16	705,207
South Carolina	17	700,611
Michigan	18	694,742
Indiana	19	667,154
New York	20	577,654
California	21	568,231
Louisiana	22	567,455
Oklahoma	23	553,039
Kansas	24	443,739
West Virginia	25	410,922
Nebraska	26	391,435
Washington	27	273,771
North Dakota	28	254,448
South Dakota	29	253,545
Florida	30	232,806
Oregon	31	228,235
Colorado	32	198,181
Maryland	33	184,482
Idaho	34	164,960
Montana	35	135,939
New Mexico	36	131,823
Maine	37	121,828
New Jersey	38	105,300
Vermont	39	81,132

State	Rank	Rural Farm Population
Utah	40	80,620
Massachusetts	41	79,796
Arizona	42	76,914
Connecticut	43	62,656
Wyoming	44	56,705
New Hampshire	45	47,170
Delaware	46	34,225
Nevada	47	13,461
Rhode Island	48	10,338

These data are from the various state reports in Series P-B, "General Characteristics," *1950 United States Census of Population*, Washington, Government Printing Office, 1952; and from pre-publication materials supplied by the U.S. Bureau of the Census for the nine states (California, Illinois, Massachusetts, Michigan, Missouri, New Jersey, New York, Ohio, Pennsylvania, and Texas) for which the reports had not appeared prior to November 10, 1952. These materials are from the final figures and do not give exactly the same total as that in the preliminary reports used earlier in this chapter.

(the 1950) census. The facts presented in this compilation are the basic ones relating to the present distribution of the farm population of the United States.

North Carolina is the state with the largest farm population, although Texas is a close rival; Mississippi and Tennessee, each with more than one million inhabitants on the farms, also are not far behind. Together the four account for more than one fifth (21 percent) of the national total. Either North Carolina or Texas has more people living on its farms than are found on those in the fifteen states of Rhode Island, Nevada, Delaware, New Hampshire, Wyoming, Connecticut, Arizona, Massachusetts, Utah, Vermont, New Jersey, Maine, New Mexico, Montana, and Idaho taken collectively. In fact North Carolina has almost as large a rural farm population along with the State of Maryland taken for good measure. Together the eight states with the largest numbers of persons on farms account for 37.3 percent of the national total, the ten with the largest numbers for 44.5 percent, and the twelve with the biggest totals for more than 51 percent of all the farm people in the United States.

Importance of the Rural Population

The rural population is of fundamental importance to the nation and national welfare in a number of ways:

1. Because it makes up more than one-third of the total population, even in a highly industrialized nation like the United States.

2. Because it is the seedbed of national population for the future, the source from which the depleted human resources of the urban centers are replenished, and, now that immigration is largely shut off, practically the only source of urban growth.

3. Because the institutions maintained by the rural population, and especially the rural family, the rural school, and the rural church, are those in which the oncoming population of the nation are nourished and trained.

4. Because the farming population constitutes an immense national balance wheel, a stabilizing influence which is necessary to keep the rapidly changing social life of the cities from running amuck and plunging the nation too deeply into the mire of disorders, strikes, revolutions, and other upheavals. A strong and intelligent rural citizenry is the best guarantee that these will never succeed in entering their most extreme stages where civilization itself may be destroyed.

5. Because in times of national peril the rural population constitutes a huge reservoir of national patriotism and man power, a citizenry largely unaffected by varieties of internationalism and pacifism which flourish amid the heterogeneous ethnic and cultural hodgepodge that is the city, and which frequently come to be the greatest menace to international good will and peace.

6. Because the natural resistance of rural culture to change serves as a life preserver for many distinctively national cultural traits and complexes which otherwise might be lost in the city's mad rush for the new.

7. Because in the rural enterprises of farming there still remains the opportunity to combine the skills of entrepreneur, manager, and laborer in the one individual, thus giving rise to a well-developed type of personality, a citizen fully attuned to the interests of all classes in the society and capable of participating in the democratic process with the least possible class discrimination.

4

COMPOSITION OF THE POPULATION

Urban attitudes of superiority, growing out of the farmer's apparent awkwardness in city situations and widely diffused by means of the city's excellent communication systems, are matched by the countryman's knowledge of his own excellence in all tests involving rural situations. To the average city dweller, whose knowledge of country folk has been gleaned mainly from conversing with and reading the writings of other city people, this may sound very strange. It must be admitted that rural people seldom express themselves in books and articles for the purpose of counterbalancing statements such as the following: "In New England there are rural counties which have been losing their best for three or four generations, leaving the coarse, dull, and hidebound. The number of loafers in some slackwater villages of the middle states indicates that the natural pacemakers of the locality have gone elsewhere to create prosperity. In parts of southern Michigan, Illinois, Wisconsin, and even as far west as Missouri, there are communities which remind one of fished-out ponds populated chiefly by bull-heads and suckers."[1] Nevertheless, the rural population generally regards itself as superior to the urban, and much rural humor is based upon the gullibility and discomfiture of the city "dude," "slicker," or "greenhorn."

The important facts are that there are fundamental differences in the make-up of the rural and urban populations and that these differences are not well known. Even where there is an awareness of the differences, they seldom receive the attention they deserve in the formation of adequate public policies. For example, the fact

[1] E. A. Ross, *The Outlines of Sociology*, New York, D. Appleton-Century Company, 1924, pp. 23–24. Cf. Carter Goodrich and others, *Migration and Economic Opportunity*, Philadelphia, University of Pennsylvania Press, 1936, p. 662.

that the country has a disproportionately large share of children, many of whom will spend their adult lives in the city, seldom receives adequate attention in the financing of public schools.[2] Race and nativity, age, and sex are the characteristics of population to receive attention in this chapter. Other aspects of the general subject of the composition of population which might legitimately be included will be found as follows: marital status in the chapter on "Marriage and the Family"; educational status in the chapter on "Rural Education and Educational Institutions"; and religious affiliations in the chapter on "Religion and the Rural Church."

Race and Nativity

Of all the traits that distinguish one population from another, race and nativity are among the most obvious and important. Race, a biological concept, is based upon physical traits such as texture of the hair, cephalic index, pigmentation, etc., whereas national origins, although somewhat correlated with race, are an index of the cultural heritage of a people, of the background of folkways, mores, and other customs characterizing particular locality groups. The United States Census, however, uses a classification which is a curious mixture of the two, making it necessary to consider them together.

Rural America might well be styled the home of the "Old Americans."[3] This characterization is doubly true if the term is used to include Negroes as well as whites. Thompson and Whelpton have been impressed by the fact that the native white stock of the United States is and always has been primarily a rural (small-town and open-country) population[4]—a fact that is even more pronounced for Negroes, although it was not singled out for specific attention by these authors.[5]

It has been demonstrated frequently that the "native" elements in a population constitute high proportions of the rural people, while "foreign" elements are concentrated in the cities.[6] This

---

[2] Cf. Roland R. Renne, "Rural Educational Institutions and Social Lag," *Rural Sociology,* I (1936), 306–321.

[3] Cf. T. Lynn Smith, *Population Analysis,* New York, McGraw-Hill Book Company, 1948, pp. 51–52.

[4] W. S. Thompson and P. K. Whelpton, *Population Trends in the United States,* New York, McGraw-Hill Book Company, 1933, p. 45.

[5] *Ibid.,* p. 46.

[6] Cf. P. A. Sorokin and Carle C. Zimmerman, *Principles of Rural-Urban Sociology,* New York, Henry Holt & Company, 1929, p. 23.

principle is excellently illustrated by the situation in the United States. Data from the 1950 Census show that for the country as a whole the proportion of foreign-born among the rural farm population was only 2.4 percent, as compared with 3.5 percent among the rural nonfarm and 8.9 percent among the urban populations, respectively. In 1930, when the foreign-born white population of the United States was at its maximum (13,336,407), 80.3 percent of the total lived in cities, 11.6 percent in rural nonfarm territory, and only 8.1 percent on rural farms. The same census showed the proportions of foreign-born population to be highest in the most industrialized sections of the country, amounting to 22.6 percent of the population in New England and 20.4 percent in the Middle Atlantic States. On the other hand, foreign-born persons constituted only 3.6 percent of the population in the West South Central States, 2.0 percent in the South Atlantic States, and 0.6 of 1 percent in the East South Central States. As might be expected, three of the most highly urbanized states in the Union (New York, Massachusetts, and Rhode Island) led the list in the proportion of foreign-born, the percentages in 1930 being 25.9, 25.1, and 25.0, respectively. At the other extreme, North and South Carolina and Mississippi contained the smallest proportions of foreign-born, the percentages being 0.3, 0.3, and 0.4, respectively, for these three states in the rural South. Several other states in the southern regions contained less than 1 percent of foreigners, namely, Alabama, Oklahoma, Georgia, and Tennessee. No southern state, except Texas with its large Mexican population, and Florida, contained as high as 2 percent of foreign-born in its population. Thus the South, which contains the bulk of the nation's rural population, and which itself is predominantly rural, has received but little of the tremendous influx of foreign-born people who have migrated to the United States in the last century. (See Figure 3.)

Not only are foreign elements much scarcer in the rural population than in the urban, but those foreigners who do reside on farms have been in the United States longer and have had more time to become acculturated than the foreign-born residents of cities.[7] Thus, in 1930, when the immigrant population was greatest, of the foreign-born whites who resided on rural farms, 51.4 percent of the males and 49.2 percent of the females had entered

[7] Cf. Smith, *op. cit.*, pp. 79–87.

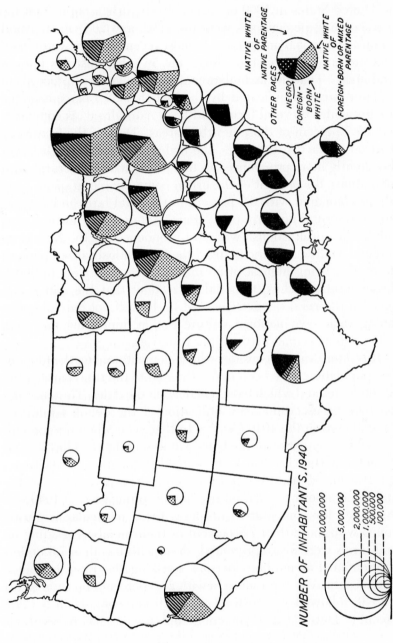

FIGURE 3.   Race and Nativity of the Population in 1940, by States.

the United States in 1900 or earlier. In the urban population the corresponding percentages were only 29.8 and 26.1; in the rural nonfarm, only 38.6 and 40.5. The most recent comers were about three times more numerous, relatively, in urban districts than in rural areas.[8] That the assimilation of the foreign-born proceeds in the rural areas is indicated by the fact that 68.8 percent of the foreign whites on rural farms had been naturalized, as compared with 57.7 percent of those in urban areas.[9] Despite the frequency of social contact in the cities, the inability to speak English was also slightly more pronounced in the urban than in the rural farm populations, 6.7 percent of the urban being unable to speak English, as compared with 6.2 percent in the rural farm and 5.9 percent in the rural nonfarm population.[10] Interestingly enough, this inability to speak English was most pronounced in the New England and Middle Atlantic States,[11] the most industrialized parts of the nation, being highest of all in Fall River and New Bedford, Massachusetts.[12] Thus it should be evident that the native elements in the rural districts succeed fairly well not only in maintaining their own national culture but in impressing the same traits upon newcomers from other countries.

It is interesting to consider which elements among the foreign-born population have been most attracted to the rural parts of the United States and which have remained in the cities. This information may be ascertained by utilization of the detailed information gathered in the 1940 Census. In that year, when the foreign-born white population of the United States totaled 11,419,138, 22.6 percent reported English as their mother tongue, 14.3 German, 14.1 Italian, 8.3 Yiddish, and 7.2 Polish. The percentage of the total foreign-born population residing on rural farms in 1940 was 7.8; hence for comparative purposes those particular linguistic groups with more than 7.8 percent of their members residing on rural farms were overrepresented, those with less than 7.8 under-represented. Foreign-born persons speaking the Finnish tongue were most heavily represented (with 28.8 percent) on rural farms in 1940, followed by Norwegians (24.9 percent), Danish (22.7 percent), Dutch (22.0 percent), and Czechs (17.5 percent).

[8] Cf. *Abstract of the Fifteenth Census of the United States*, Washington, Government Printing Office, 1933, Table 88, p. 173.

[9] *Ibid.*, Table 80, p. 164.

[10] *Ibid.*, Table 148, p. 292.

[11] *Ibid.*, Table 151, p. 297.

[12] *Ibid.*, Table 152, p. 298.

More than 15 percent of the foreigners whose mother tongue was Portuguese, Swedish, or Flemish also resided on farms; and the Spanish, German, Ukrainian, Slovak, and Slovenian language groups were slightly overrepresented in the rural farm population. All the other foreign-language groups were concentrated in the cities, the most extreme cases being the Yiddish group, of whose members only 0.35 of 1 percent resided on farms. They were followed by the Greeks, Arabs, Italians, Rumanians, Serbians, Russians, English, Croatians, Lithuanians, Armenians, Magyars, French, and Polish in the order named, none of whom had as many as 7 percent on rural farms. Persons speaking Yiddish tongues, of whom there were 924,440 in 1940, were most highly concentrated in the cities, 98.2 percent of all these residing in urban centers. Other groups most highly concentrated in cities (over 85 percent) are as follows: Greeks, Armenians, Arabs, Rumanians, Russians, and Italians. The rural nonfarm population, on the other hand, has received disproportionately large shares of Slovenians, Magyars, Spanish, Finns, Norwegians, Croatians, Slovaks, Dutch, and Danes. Among all groups the Yiddish has avoided rural nonfarm territory to the greatest extent, only 1.4 percent of this group being so classed, as compared with 12.0 percent of the total foreign-born white population.[13]

Negroes, of course, are concentrated in the South, where they are one of the "native" elements. Similar to other native elements in the South, they, too, are primarily residents of the country. This fact is easily demonstrated by a few pertinent data. Of the 9,904,-619 Negroes residing in the three southern Census Divisions, 45 percent were classed as rural farm, 19 percent as rural nonfarm, and 36 percent as urban. Among the urban population of these states, Negroes made up only 24 percent of the total, as compared with 27 percent of the total rural farm population. Thus it is evident that in the South, Negroes, a native element, are disproportionately rural. But when one examines the situation in other regions where Negroes are relatively newcomers, a great difference appears.

For example, the majority of Negroes in the Northeastern States (New England along with New York, New Jersey, and Pennsylvania) are not native to that part of the country. In these states,

---

[13] The data in this section were drawn from the *Sixteenth Census of the United States: 1940,* "Population, Nativity and Parentage of the White Population, Mother Tongue," Washington, Government Printing Office, 1943, Table 1, pp. 7–10.

as might be expected, they are almost entirely confined to the cities. In this highly industrialized area nearly nine out of every ten Negroes resided in urban centers. Thus of a total of 1,369,875 Negroes in this geographic division in 1940, 1,234,211 (90 percent) were classed as urban and only 10 percent as rural. But even these figures do not correctly depict the situation. Most of the rural Negroes in this area were included in the rural nonfarm population, of which the suburban fringe has been shown to constitute such an important element. Only 1.4 percent (19,175) of the Negroes in this division were classed among the rural farm population, the great bulk of the so-called rural Negroes coming in that ill-defined and heterogeneous category which is designated as rural nonfarm. Thus the native elements are seen to be residents of rural areas, and rural America may well be considered the great reservoir of native population stocks.

The fact that foreign-born persons are concentrated in the cities must be taken into account if rural-urban comparisons are to be made of many other social characteristics. For example, the foreign-born persons in a given country have a distinctive age and sex distribution, males being very heavily represented, the younger age groups practically unrepresented, etc. (See Figure 4.) The

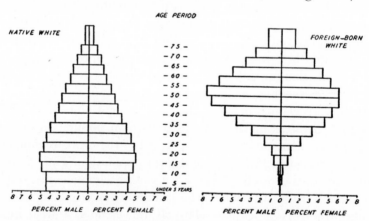

FIGURE 4.   Age and Sex Pyramids for the Native White and Foreign-Born White Populations of the United States, 1940.

presence of foreign-born in the cities assists in giving the urban age distribution its distinctive shape.

The situation with regard to sex is even more interesting and, in many ways, more significant than that pertaining to age. The concentration of foreign-born groups in the cities means that large numbers of foreign-born males at the marriageable ages are to be found in urban centers, for such long-distance migrants are predominantly males. Were it not for the presence of those men from other countries, the urban sex ratio would be much lower than it is because large numbers of native women gravitate to the cities from the country. As will be shown in another place, females between the ages of fifteen and twenty-five predominate among rural-urban migrants. Thus the factors involved in migration and the selectivity of migration operate in such a manner that large numbers of native females are thrown into immediate proximity to the unmarried immigrant males coming from other countries. At the same time they are removed from practically all social contacts with the native white males in the country. The net result is a great excess of females in the city, a scarcity of women in the country. Thus the dynamics of our population movements operate in a manner that gives the male person of foreign birth a comparative advantage over his native-born farmer rival in securing a mate from among the native women.[14] The immigrant woman also is placed in a very keen competitive situation with regard to attentions from the members of the male sex. Perhaps the presence of social barriers between the immigrant men and native women is an important factor in lowering the marriage rate of cities. It may also have much to do with the low fertility of the urban population, and the tremendous increase in the homogeneity of the American urban population which has taken place since 1935 may be one of the principal causes of the substantial rise in the birth rate in the last fifteen years. It also would be interesting to know if large percentages of the children of these parents of mixed ancestry do not carry the father's foreign name while at the same time they are rather thoroughly acculturated through the mother's influence. In any event it is certain that the concentration of foreigners in the cities, their relative scarcity in the country, is fraught with much social significance for the nation.

But before leaving this subject it is important to call attention to a very important trend that is now under way. In recent years immigration has been almost entirely shut off, with the result that we can expect a rapid change in the composition of our popula-

[14] Niles Carpenter, *Immigrants and Their Children: 1920*, Census Monographs VII, Washington, 1927, pp. 232–235, has shown that the bulk of mixed marriages are between native women and foreign men.

tion, especially in that of the cities of the nation. No longer drawn from abroad, replacements for our urban population are now coming almost exclusively from the rural parts of our own nation, largely from the rural South, and most largely from the stocks which were present in America when the first census was taken in 1790.

Age

In a great variety of ways, some of them very subtle, age exerts a tremendous influence upon social phenomena. Much sociological interest is attached to the fact that the age constitution is one of the most obvious, uniform, and persistent ways in which the make-up of the rural population differs from that of the urban. The principal differences may be summarized as follows: (1) The country population includes large proportions of children; (2) the rural population has low percentages of its population in the ages fifteen to forty-five, i.e., the "productive" years of life; (3) the country contains a disproportionately large share of aged persons.[15] The city, on the other hand, has a great scarcity of children, high proportions in the productive ages, and relatively few aged people. If the rural population is divided into the rural farm and rural nonfarm segments, the differences between the age structures of the various residential groups stand out even more clearly. Then it becomes obvious that the nation's children are concentrated on the farms, its persons of productive ages in the cities, and its elderly folk in the villages, small towns, and suburban areas. (See Figures 5 and 6.) The proportions of elderly persons, especially of aged females, have been particularly high in the villages.[16] However, in the decades which lie ahead it is likely that disproportionately large shares of the aged population will be found in the urban category. The forces bringing about the change are two: (1) the new definition of urban which now includes the

[15] It should be noted that in 1940 there was no excess of aged persons in the South. The explanation should be clear to demographers. It can be demonstrated easily that the scarcity of births due to the ravages of the Civil War is just now being reflected in the number of aged persons. The generation born between 1860 and 1870 were aged 60 to 70 in 1930, and the smallness of the war-period age group is obvious in every census from 1870 to the present. See T. Lynn Smith, "The Demographic Basis of Old Age Assistance in the South," *Social Forces*, XVII (1939), 356–361.

[16] Cf. T. Lynn Smith, "Some Aspects of Village Demography," *Social Forces*, XX (1941), 16–23; see also T. Lynn Smith, "The Role of the Village in American Rural Society," *Rural Sociology*, VII (1942), 18–19.

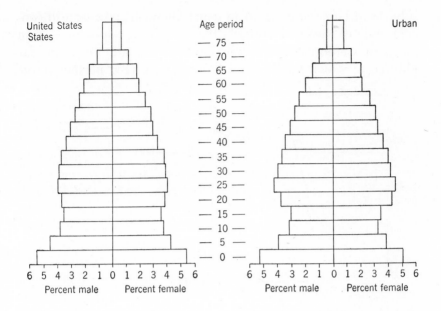

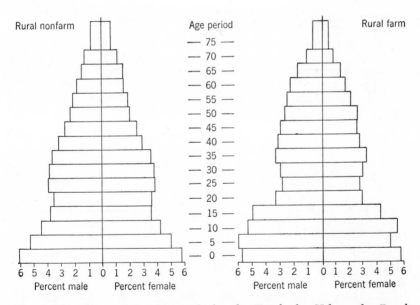

FIGURE 5. Age and Sex Pyramids for the Total, the Urban, the Rural Nonfarm, and the Rural Farm Populations of the United States, 1950.

suburbs of large cities, areas in which there is a pronounced concentration of the aged, and (2) the rise of "retirement towns" in
southern California, along the Gulf Coast, and in peninsular
Florida, to which hundreds of thousands of aged persons resort

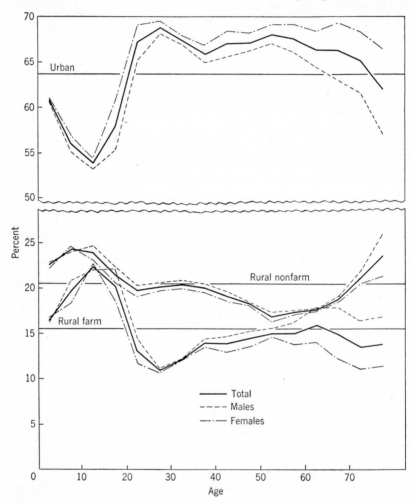

FIGURE 6.   Percentages of the Population of the United States in the Urban, Rural Nonfarm, and Rural Farm Categories, by Age and Sex, 1950.

to spend their declining years of life.[17] Of course an atomic war
and the destruction of the principal cities could bring about even

[17] Cf. T. Lynn Smith, "The Migration of the Aged," in T. Lynn Smith (ed.),
Problems of America's Aging Population, Gainesville, University of Florida Press,
1951, pp. 15–28.

more drastic changes in the distribution of the various age groups in the population.

From an economic standpoint the chief significance of these data is this: The country with low proportions of its population in the productive ages of life must care for high proportions of the dependent persons, i.e., the very young and the very old. From an educational standpoint it is that an excessive burden is placed upon the few to provide facilities for children, many of whom, as will be shown in the following pages, are to migrate and spend their productive years in urban centers. From an institutional point of view it is that there will be a scarcity of energetic young adults to take the leadership in community, civic, and religious affairs. Furthermore, the fact that the country is traditionally conservative may be influenced greatly by its age composition as well as by its wide distribution of ownership in real property.

The differences in the age composition of rural and urban populations seem to be the result of several factors. In the first place, the differential birth rate of country and city gives the rural districts excessive proportions of children. In the second place, there is always a strong movement of young able-bodied persons from the farms to the city. Part of this arises out of the specialization and division of labor in the cities, which creates varied economic activities and opportunities that attract young and vigorous persons from the country. It is well known that for unskilled laborers, so commonly recruited from the country, urban employers desire and, unless the supply of labor is scarce, accept only the youthful and active. Indeed, even during periods of severe depression when employees are being laid off by the thousands, many industrial firms add new employees who are young and vigorous to their pay rolls. Educational institutions, which annually ingest thousands of young people, after a few years place these same young people in urban professions, occupations, and industries. Thus the agencies which induct country people into city life concentrate their efforts upon the young. In the third place, if the rural person is to migrate to the city it must be while he is young, energetic, capable of making adjustments, and before residence in the country has developed ties such as family obligations, sentimental attachments, community responsibilities, deep-rooted habits, and property ownership. After the age of twenty-five or thirty, few persons leave the country for the city. In the fourth place, after farm people attain the age of forty-five or fifty, a great many of them, especially the widows of farmers, take up residence in the nearby village or small town. Finally, many a person in the older age groups who has spent the productive years of his life in the cities moves to the country or to a small town to spend the twilight of his life. For some such a transfer represents the attainment of a lifelong objective, the goal of long-continued work and struggle; for others this landward migration represents an attempt to make slender resources go as far as possible in a place where living costs are low, after their earning power has been seriously curtailed or shut off entirely. But in either case this backwash of elderly people toward the land helps swell the numbers of the aged in the villages and the open country. Combined with the greater expectancy of life in the country, it accounts for the high proportion of oldsters in the rural population.

Thus the combined influences of the differential birth rate, the cityward migration of young adults, the backwash of aged persons toward the land, and the greater expectancy of life in the country are sufficient to account for the major differences in the age constitution or make-up of the rural and urban populations.

Perhaps the social significance of this information is demonstrated most clearly by comparisons such as the following. Broadly speaking, persons of less than fifteen years of age and those who are sixty-five or over are dependent upon those aged fifteen to sixty-four. Therefore the ratio of the former to the latter, of dependents to contributors, is an important index.[18] In 1950 the urban population of the United States contained only 486 persons in these dependent ages for every 1000 persons between the ages of fifteen and sixty-four, inclusive; in the rural farm population the corresponding ratio was 688 per 1000.

Sex

Next to being born, the most important single fact concerning a person's existence is whether one is male or female. The sex of the offspring is probably the first question in the minds of prospective parents; and "It's a boy!" or "It's a girl!" is the phrase which ordinarily relieves the tension at one of the greatest crises of life.

[18] Alfred H. Stone in his article, "Some Problems of Southern Economic History," *American Historical Review*, XII (1908), 779–797, made use of this index. Cf. T. Lynn Smith, *The Population of Louisiana: Its Composition and Changes*, Lousiana AES Bulletin 293, Baton Rouge, 1937, pp. 38–39.

The proportion of the sexes in a given population is also a very important characteristic in its make-up. When males greatly outnumber females, or vice versa, the unequal sex ratio reacts in a significant manner upon the marriage rate, the birth rate, the death rate, etc. It also affects the tempo of practically all social activities. Scarcity of women is largely responsible for the unique characteristics and reckless abandon of life on the frontier, in the mining camp or lumber camp, or in the steel towns. On the other hand, the lack of men is felt keenly in textile centers; some residential cities are overcrowded with women; and in many rural villages women, especially widowed females, are the principal element in the population.[19]

Significant variations in the proportions of the sexes is another characteristic difference between the rural and urban populations. Records in the United States go back to 1820, and they indicate that males have always outnumbered females on the farms, while women have been more numerous than men in the cities.[20] Agriculture is a man's occupation, a fact which is reflected in the high proportion of males in the farm and rural populations. On the other hand, residential cities and industrial centers, other than those in which heavy industries, such as steel, are concentrated, number large proportions of females among their inhabitants. A few data[21] will bring this point out clearly.

In the United States as a whole there were 98.1 males to every 100 females in 1950; but among the urban population this ratio was only 94.1 and in the rural nonfarm population only 102.7, whereas among the rural farm population (which is the closest approximation to the agricultural population) it was 109.8. Comparisons based on the total population are not entirely valid, however, for the reason that the foreign-born are concentrated in the cities and that males are greatly in excess among these immigrant groups, as is the case for all long-distance migrants. Therefore, more significance is to be attached to observations of the rural-urban differences among the native white and Negro populations. Among native whites the differences are very pronounced, there

[19] See the penetrating analysis in Ross, *op. cit.*, pp. 3–7. For villages, see C. Luther Fry, *American Villagers*, New York, Doubleday, Doran & Company, 1926, pp. 105, 109.

[20] Thompson and Whelpton, *op. cit.*, pp. 186–187.

[21] Computed from materials in *1950 Census of Population, Preliminary Reports*, "General Characteristics of the Population of the United States: April 1, 1950," Series PC-7, No. 1, Washington, 1951.

being in 1950 only 93.5 males per 100 females in urban areas and only 101.9 in the rural nonfarm population, as compared with 110.2 in the rural farm group. For Negroes the differences were also great, urban districts having a sex ratio of only 91.2 and the rural nonfarm population one of 107.1, while in the rural farm population there were 102.5 males for every 100 females. Thus there can be no doubt that the farms contain high proportions of males, the cities high proportions of females. Farmers face keen

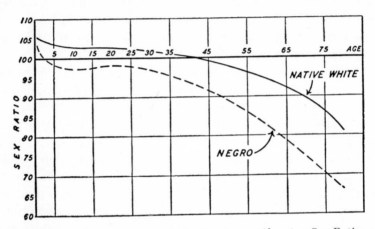

FIGURE 7.   Expected Variations in the Curves Showing Sex Ratios by Age, by Race.

competition for wives, whereas in the cities there are not enough husbands to go around.

Unfortunately the data are not sufficiently accurate to permit a detailed analysis and comparison of the sex ratios by age for rural and urban population groups. It seems likely that the scarcity of women on farms is greatest at precisely the ages at which mating is most frequently consummated. The nature of the errors in these data is not well known, and persons using them rarely take proper precautions. Hence it is important to indicate the nature of the discrepancies. The pertinent demographic data being taken into account, simple norms for studying sex ratios by age have been developed and are presented in Figure 7. These norms were secured in the following manner: (1) Assumed were infant populations of 206,100 whites and 203,300 Negroes, of whom 100,000 of each race were females. These ratios are exactly in proportion to the sex ratios at birth during the period 1915 to 1933. (2) Specific death rates for the white and Negro populations of the registration area in 1910 were applied to these infant groups, and, successively, to each group of survivors, from 1–4 to 75-over. Finally, (3) for each race the sex ratios of each age group were computed, plotted, and all the points connected to make the curves shown on the chart.

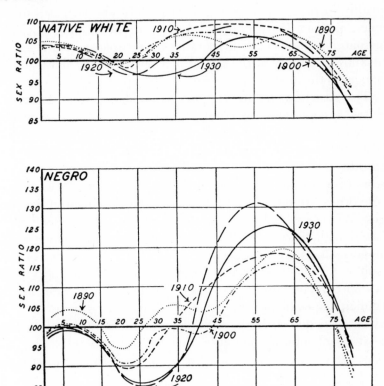

FIGURE 8. Curves Showing the Reported Variations in the Sex Ratios by Age for the Native White and Negro Populations of the United States, 1890, 1900, 1910, 1920, and 1930. (Source: *The United States Census*.)

When data for actual populations are compared with these norms, wide discrepancies are evident. In order to eliminate influences due to emigration and immigration it is best to confine the discussion to two race and nativity groups; native whites and Negroes. Obviously the native whites cannot gain by immigration, and relatively few members of this group leave the United States. Negroes, too, rarely emigrate, and the immigration of Negroes is negligible.[22] For both native whites and Negroes the curves depicting sex ratios by age have a characteristic shape—that of a long-drawn-out S or sine curve. Thus among native whites the curve begins at 103.5, falls slightly for the age groups 1–4, 5–9, and 10–14. After this it declines rapidly to a low point of 97.5 per 100 females for the age group 20–24. Then it reverses itself, rises steadily to 107.5 for the group 55–64, and then decreases to 91.0 among persons 75 years of age and over. (See Figure 8.) These fluctuations in the curve of sex ratios by age reflect sharply against the known stability of the sex ratio at birth and the slow, gradual changes in the death rate.

The situation among Negroes is similar to that for native whites, except that the gyrations are much more pronounced. Furthermore, for both whites and Negroes, the curves for 1920, 1910, 1900, and 1890 are similar in shape to those for 1930. This indicates that the cause of these fluctuations is errors in the data, errors of a constantly recurring nature. The writer believes that these errors are introduced through the misstatement of women's ages. Women who belong in the age goup 25–29 come to be classed with the group 20–24, some of those who belong in the category 30–34 are included with those aged 25–29, etc. The net result is too many women reported for ages 15–34, too few for ages 35–54. This discrepancy seems sufficient to account for the peculiar shapes of the curves representing sex ratios by age.[23] In any case the defects in the data greatly reduce their usefulness in the study of internal migration, health, and mortality.

[22] Ira De A. Reid, "Negro Immigration to the United States," *Social Forces,* XVI (1938), 411–417.

[23] Cf. T. Lynn Smith and Homer L. Hitt, "The Misstatement of Women's Ages and the Vital Indices," *Metron,* XVIII (1939), 95–108.

5

PHYSICAL CHARACTERISTICS AND HEALTH

Physical Characteristics

A study of the physical characteristics or traits of the rural population has considerable social significance for a number of reasons. (1) Physical traits, such as stature, pigmentation, the cephalic index, texture of the hair, etc., are the criteria upon which racial groupings are based; and the concept of race, in one form or another, permeates all social phenomena and colors the thinking about almost every aspect of human relationships.[1] Frequently racial questions become so deeply embodied in a program of action that all other social phenomena are subordinated to them. (2) In the popular mind physical features are commonly associated with mental and social traits such as intelligence and social satus. Lombroso and his disciples,[2] who attempted to set forth a definite relationship between physical characteristics and criminal tendencies, have had numerous followers. In this case, as in many others, there is some scientific evidence in support of these associations, a fact of no little social significance. If stature, or pigmentation, or the shape of the head, or configuration of the face, is associated with social status, or intelligence, or mobility, or crime, it is important for the student of rural society and the rural-life worker to know of such relationships. But there are other important phases to the problem. For example, as will be demonstrated below, the

[1] There are cases, of course, in which racial differences are ignored, with the result that little or no validity can be attached to the findings of the study. Any comparison of the northern with the southern states which does not correct for race differences is sadly deficient in its methodology. An otherwise excellent study by J. F. Thaden of the Michigan State College, "Characteristics of Persons Listed in *Rus*," *Rural Sociology* II (1937), 429–443, illustrates this point.

[2] Cf. Cesare Lombroso, *Crime, Its Causes and Remedies,* Boston, H. P. Horton, 1911.

rural population is the seedbed of all population, both urban and rural. Recognition of this fact, together with the point to be discussed next, makes readily understandable the importance of securing the basic facts on these questions. (3) Allegations of dysgenic selection favoring the cities in the exchange of population between rural and urban areas are very prevalent in sociological literature. This contention has been widely circulated and has gained credence extensively in intellectual circles. Data on physical characteristics would seem to be the most satisfactory basis for determining the validity of such hypotheses. (4) A comparison of the physical traits of rural and urban populations is one of the most satisfactory means of measuring the relative advantages and disadvantages of the rural and urban environments.

Stature

Studies of the physical traits of rural populations have been numerous. Large quantities of data bearing on this topic have been collected in connection with the physical examinations of army recruits.[3] This type of information has frequently been utilized for comparing the stature of rural and urban populations. Sorokin and Zimmerman, in an important volume, have included a section giving an exhaustive survey of the literature in this field.[4]

Since stature seems to be positively correlated with social status, it would be very much worth while to demonstrate that there is a uniform difference in stature of rural and urban populations. Sorokin, assembling evidence from many investigations, has shown that there is a definite relationship between stature and social class. The upper classes in society are taller than the lower classes, a uniformity which holds true in most present-day societies as well as in those of the past.[5] Partisans of the doctrine of Nordic

---

[3] For the Civil War these data are presented by B. A. Gould, *Investigations in the Military and Anthropological Statistics of American Soldiers*, Boston, Hurd and Houghton, 1869; and in J. H. Baxter, *Medical and Anthropological Statistics of the Provost-Marshal General's Bureau*, Washington, Government Printing Office, 1875; comprehensive data for World War I recruits are given by Charles B. Davenport and A. G. Love in "Army Anthropology," *The Medical Department of the United States Army in the World War*, XV, Washington, 1921. Data for World War II should be particularly important when they become available.

[4] See P. A. Sorokin and Carle C. Zimmerman, *Principles of Rural-Urban Sociology*, New York, Henry Holt & Company, 1929, pp. 104–105; cf. P. A. Sorokin, Carle C. Zimmerman, and C. J. Galpin, *A Systematic Source Book in Rural Sociology*, Minneapolis, University of Minnesota Press, 1932, III, 4–22.

[5] P. A. Sorokin, *Social Mobility*, New York, Harper & Brothers, 1927, pp. 217–224.

superiority doubtless would also be interested in such an association between residence and stature. In fact, several advocates of this theory have concluded that such differences actually exist, the rural population usually being designated as the taller. Other scholars, however, have secured contradictory results.[6] At the present time it seems to be impossible to discover any uniform difference in stature between rural and urban populations. In many countries the city population appears to be taller than the country population; in other countries the reverse is true.[7] R. Livi, an Italian scholar, has formulated a principle which seems adequate to explain all the known facts on the subject.[8] Two things need to be kept in mind to grasp his explanation: (1) that hereditary biological factors are of primary importance in determining stature; and (2) that urban populations are heterogeneous, recruited from far-distant places, while rural populations are homogeneous, recruited mainly from the immediate vicinity. Therefore, in a country where the native population is short, as in Italy, the average stature of the city's hodgepodge population will exceed that of the rural area's homogeneous group, while in a country where the native population belongs to a tall race, as in Norway, the urban population, which includes many foreign elements, will not be equal in average stature to the rural population, a group recruited mainly from the native stock. Livi's principle adequately refutes all contentions of a uniform rural-urban difference in stature. It utilizes the facts presented by such investigators as Ammon and Lapouge to substantiate a much broader and more workable principle or uniformity than any developed by them. With regard to stature, the one uniform difference between city and country populations is greater variability in the urban districts.

Head Form or Cephalic Index

The shape of the head is one of the most fundamental criteria of race.[9] Its importance and usefulness are enhanced by the fact that

[6] See the excellent summary in Sorokin, Zimmerman, and Galpin, *op. cit.* I, 4–15. F. H. Hankins, *The Racial Basis of Civilization*, New York, Alfred A. Knopf, Inc., 1926, does much to show the inadequacies of the hypotheses of Ammon, Lapouge, and others.

[7] Sorokin and Zimmerman, *op. cit.* pp. 106–107.

[8] For a statement and discussion of Livi's contribution, see *ibid.*, pp. 108–109, 142.

[9] Cf. R. B. Dixon, *The Racial History of Mankind*, New York, Charles Scribner's Sons, 1923, p. 5.

the skull of man often remains long after almost every other remnant has disappeared. The cephalic index is extensively used as a measure of head form. It is, perhaps, the most reliable of all racial indexes. This index is derived as follows: $\dfrac{\text{width of cranium}}{\text{length of cranium}} \times 100$. Longheaded persons or races, i.e., those with cephalic indexes of less than 75, are termed dolichocephals. Persons or races with indexes of 80 or more are termed roundheads or brachycephals. Intermediate between these two are the mesocephalic persons or races. These are cranial indexes; an allowance of approximately 2 percent should be added to the indexes of living persons in order to offset the effect of the flesh which covers the skull.

The shape of the head, or cephalic index, has figured prominently in many discussions of the physical characteristics of the rural population. Since it has been a basic element in the Nordic theory, whenever Nordicists expounded or explained rural-urban differences the cephalic index has always received major consideration. For example, Ammon and Lapouge found that urban people were more dolichocephalic than the rural people within the same country. In the principles or "laws" formulated by these scholars, rural-urban differences occupied an important position. Sorokin and Zimmerman have presented the following statements of the Ammon-Lapouge "laws" in their well-known work:

The cephalic index of an urban population is lower than that of the country population around the city.

In regions where the brachycephalic type exists, it tends to concentrate in the country, while the dolichocephals tend more to the city.

The cephalic index of the emigrants from a given country to the city or another country is generally lower than that of the stay-at-home people.

Urban life tends to perform a selection in favor of the dolichocephals, and destroys or eliminates the most brachycephalic elements.[10]

Fortunately it is not necessary to resort to such mysticism in order adequately to explain all the pertinent facts. The principle of Livi, given above in connection with stature, is applicable in this case as well. This generalization seems sufficient to summarize adequately all the data, and leaves no room for any principle im-

[10] *Op. cit.*, p. 125.

plying a uniform difference in head form between rural and urban populations. A more widespread acquaintance with Livi's law should do much to inhibit rash generalizations about rural-urban physical differences.

Pigmentation

Pigmentation not only is the fundamental characteristic differentiating the Negroid from the Caucasoid group of races, but is of primary importance in distinguishing among the different groups of Caucasoids. Thus although the Nordic is blond, both the Alpine and Mediterranean races are brunet. Proponents of the Nordic theory have loudly maintained that blonds have always constituted the bulk of the mental and social aristocracy of Western civilization. Such one-sided treatments as the following are, of course, entitled to slight consideration:

The Alpine race is always and everywhere a race of peasants, an agricultural and never a maritime race. In fact, they only extend to salt water at the head of the Adriatic. . . .

The Nordics are, all over the world, a race of soldiers, sailors, adventurers, and explorers, but above all, of rulers, organizers, and aristocrats in sharp contrast to the essentially peasant character of the Alpines. Chivalry and knighthood, and their still surviving but greatly impaired counterparts, are peculiarly Nordic traits, and feudalism, class distinctions, and race pride among Europeans are traceable for the most part to the north. . . .

The wars of the last two thousand years in Europe have been almost exclusively wars between the various nations of this race, or between rulers of Nordic blood.[11]

But even so careful a student as W. Z. Ripley has written as follows: "Were there space we might adduce abundant evidence to prove that the upper classes in France, Germany, Austria, and the British Isles are distinctly lighter in hair and eyes than the peasantry."[12]

Thus it should be evident that there is genuine value in understanding Livi's principle. Regardless of the question involved, whether referring to stature, cephalic index, pigmentation, or any

[11] Madison Grant, *The Passing of the Great Race*, New York, Charles Scribner's Sons, 1916, pp. 198–200.

[12] W. Z. Ripley, *The Races of Europe*, New York, D. Appleton and Company, 1894, p. 469.

other physical characteristic, Livi's law is sufficient to explain all rural-urban differences discovered to date. It should be well known to every student of rural society because of its usefulness in assisting in the proper interpretation of fragmentary results from scattered studies.

Health

The health problems of the rural community are of national concern. Sickness is one of the best-known and most common things of life; its control and reduction are of fundamental importance. The need for factual data on rural health should be obvious. The following quotation from Sanderson emphasizes the salient points of the question:

What is the effect of sickness on the life of the farm family? To what extent does it limit the social life and the education of the family? How frequently does the sickness of the father cause a reduced farm income? Is medical service adequate for farm families? Is there more sickness on the farm or in the village? Is it true, as has frequently been asserted, that health conditions are worse in the country than in the city, and that the difficulty of obtaining medical aid on isolated farms is one of the reasons why women desire to leave the farm for the town?[13]

It is evident that health is of vital concern for all phases of social organization and participation from the aesthetic to the economic. As O. D. Duncan has stated so clearly, poor health in a community is part of a vicious circle which involves inability to work, low income and poverty, undernourishment and anemia, spread of infections and fostering of endemic diseases. Every repetition of this cycle saps the human resources of the community.[14]

The Incidence of Sickness in the General Population

When one searches for facts about the health situation, he is likely to be seriously disappointed by the nature of the information available, especially with regard to rural areas.[15] A widespread practice among writers on this subject has been to substi-

[13] Dwight Sanderson, *A Survey of Sickness in Rural Areas in Cortland County, New York*, Cornell AES Memoir 112, Ithaca, 1928, p. 3.

[14] Cf. O. D. Duncan, *Some Social and Economic Aspects of the Problem of Rural Health in Oklahoma*, Oklahoma AES Circular 78, Stillwater, 1931, p. 3.

[15] Sanderson, *loc. cit.*

tute data on mortality for data on morbidity, although it has been pointed out repeatedly that the pictures resulting from the two types of data are by no means identical.[16] Accordingly, data on mortality will be presented in another chapter, and this section will be devoted entirely to materials dealing with health itself.

As yet there is no census of sickness.[17] In 1928 the Committee on the Cost of Medical Care could secure only fragmentary studies in response to the query: "What data are now available showing the incidence of disease and disability requiring medical services . . . ?"[18] And the same is generally true today. There seems to be no thoroughgoing survey in existence of the problem as a whole, not to mention adequate study of the rural aspects.

Some years ago Dr. Frankel and Dr. Dublin summarized the data about the health of one-half million Metropolitan Life Insurance Company policyholders. They found that 2 percent of these insured people were sick constantly, i.e., so ill that they required medical service of one kind or another. Converting their data into economic terms, they estimated that sickness results in a loss of 2 percent in the current production, a conclusion which may not be entirely justified. They also pointed out that great expense is incurred for medical care, hospitalization, drugs, medicines, etc.[19] Later, in 1928, Dr. Dublin estimated that the cost of sickness in the United States aggregated over $2,000,000,000 per year.[20]

The studies of Sydenstricker and his associates in twenty-four South Carolina mill villages at about the time of World War I, and later in Hagerstown, Maryland, constitute another important sounding into the incidence of sickness. According to their findings, disabling sickness varied from eighteen to thirty-six per 1000 population in the course of a year, averaged about nine days per person per year, reached a peak in February with another high point later on in the spring, was positively associated with low in-

[16] Cf. Selwyn D. Collins, "The Incidence and Causes of Illness at Specific Ages," *Milbank Memorial Fund Quarterly*, XIII (1935).

[17] Cf. Sir Arthur Newsholme, *The Elements of Vital Statistics*, New York, D. Appleton-Century Company, 1924, pp. 120–131.

[18] *The Five Year Program of the Committee on the Cost of Medical Care*, Washington, 1928, pp. 15–18. Cf. Frederick D. Mott and Milton I. Roemer, *Rural Health and Medical Care*, New York, McGraw-Hill Book Company, 1948, p. 76.

[19] Louis I. Dublin, *Health and Wealth*, New York, Harper & Brothers, 1928, p. 8.

[20] *Ibid.*, p. 21.

come, was highest in childhood, lowest in youth, and then increased gradually with age.[21]

More recently the National Health Survey of the United States Public Health Service attempted to determine the amount of disabling illness which was present among the population of the United States on an average winter day. Although the methods of sampling employed, which have not been completely divulged, may leave much to be desired, and although the published estimates are based entirely on urban areas, it is important to consider some of the findings of this study. It was discovered that 4.5 percent of the 2,300,000 persons surveyed were disabled on the day of the canvass, a winter day during the months of November to March. The highest proportion of sickness was found in the age group 65 and over, 12.1 percent; the lowest among youths 15–24, 2.5 percent; and the proportions among children under 15 and persons 25–64 were nearly equal, 4.2 and 4.4 percent, respectively. The incidence of sickness seems to have been slightly lower in towns of 5000 than in the larger centers, although the statement of findings is not very clear in this respect. On the basis of data secured from 2,300,000 persons in eighty-one cities, it was estimated that "six million people in the United States are unable to work, attend school, or pursue other usual activities each day during the winter months on account of illness, injury or gross physical impairment resulting from disease or accident."[22] The study does not indicate why the data secured from twenty-three rural areas were not reported and were not used even in making the estimate of total sickness. A breakdown by disease indicated that approximately one-fourth of these people were ill with acute respiratory diseases (influenza, grippe, pneumonia, colds, etc.); two-fifths were suffering from chronic diseases (rheumatism, diseases of the heart, cancer, asthma, tuberculosis, nervous diseases, etc.) or permanent impairments resulting from previous diseases or accident; and injuries incurred in accidents accounted for the disability of one-twelfth of those interviewed. Approximately one in twenty-five, mostly children, were ill with infectious diseases

[21] See *United States Public Health Reports*, XXXIX (1924), 1417–1443, 1723–1738; *ibid.*, XXXIII (1918), 2038–2051; and Edgar Sydenstricker, *Health and Environment*, New York, McGraw-Hill Book Company, 1933, pp. 31–39.

[22] *An Estimate of the Amount of Disabling Illness in the Country as a Whole*, National Health Survey, United States Public Health Service, Sickness and Medical Care Series Bulletin 1, Washington (mimeographed), 1938, p. 1.

of some kind; the same proportion with diseases of the stomach, liver, and appendix; and other acute diseases accounted for the disability of the remainder.[23]

The survey indicated further that illnesses lasting a week or more had occurred at the rate of 172 per 1000 population during the period of twelve months preceding; and that the annual days of disability per person averaged 9.8, being 6.0 for those aged under 15, 9.1 for those aged 15–64, and 32.6 for persons of 65 years of age or over.[24] Of the 172 disabling illnesses per 1000 persons, 29 were diagnosed as due to infections, 49 to respiratory troubles, 9 to digestive ailments, 15 to diseases of the puerperal state, 16 to accidents, 46 to chronic diseases, and 10 to all other causes.[25]

The relationships between incidence of disabling illness and economic status revealed by this study are very interesting. As stated above, disabling illness occurred with a frequency of 172 per 1000 population; of these, 124 were classed as acute and 48 were classed as chronic. For the population on relief the corresponding rate was much higher, amounting to 234, of whom 163 were classed as acute and 71 as chronic. Non-relief families had rates as follows: those with annual incomes of less than $1000 per family, 174; $1000 to $2000, 155; $2000 to $3000, 150; and $3000 and over, 149.[26] Chronic disability prevented 5.2 percent of the heads of relief households from seeking work, 2.4 percent of the heads of non-relief families with incomes of less than $1000, and less than 1 percent of those with incomes of more than $1000 per year.[27] Relief and other low-income families also received relatively few calls by physicians, although hospital cases averaged 62.8 per 1000 population among relief families, as compared with 46.7 per 1000 in the entire sample. The visiting nurse was also much in evidence among the relief cases.[28]

Because the data are so revealing and of such fundamental importance, it is most unfortunate that the comparable data for the twenty-three rural areas have not been made public.

[23] *Ibid.*, p. 2.
[24] *Ibid.*, p. 4.
[25] *Ibid.*, p. 5.
[26] *Illness and Medical Care in Relation to Economic Status,* National Health Survey, United States Public Health Service, Sickness and Medical Care Series Bulletin 2, Washington (mimeographed), 1938, p. 2.
[27] *Ibid.*, p. 3.
[28] *Ibid.*, pp. 6–7.

Rural-Urban Comparisons

Popular ideas about rural health are of two principal but rather contradictory types. As Taylor has pointed out, it is commonly assumed that rural people are a hardy lot who can endure a hard life and strenuous labor. Probably the fact that rural people work long hours and that fresh air, fresh food, sunshine, and good water are readily available in the country contributes much to this belief. At the same time the popular mind, knowing that dirt is everywhere present on the farm, concludes that the farm is teeming with disease germs, a proposition which Taylor holds to imply the spontaneous generation of bacteria![29] In addition, the southern agriculturist, who, as has been indicated, belongs to the modal group and is the farmer most entitled to be called the typical American farmer, is frequently thought of as undernourished, anemic, and beset with all manner of ailments from hookworm to malaria and pellagra.

As mentioned above, it is very unfortunate that the Public Health Survey has completely ignored its rural data and that in the official publications no attempt was made to present a comparison of rural and urban districts with respect to the incidence and duration of illness. However, after a lapse of more than a decade some of the principal results of the survey, as done in what was said to be representative rural areas of Michigan and Missouri, were incorporated in Mott and Roemer's comprehensive study of rural health.[30] The data for rural Georgia were omitted, since they had been taken in ways that were not comparable to the methods employed elsewhere. These authors attempted to compare the rural materials for the two states mentioned with those secured in the eighty-three cities reported upon in the National Health Survey. To facilitate those comparisons they classified the rural areas involved into three categories, not mutually exculsive, as follows: (1) towns and cities with between 5000 and 2500 inhabitants; (2) villages of less than 2500 population and open-country districts; and (3) the open country. The second of these classes is, of course, the familar total rural one employed for most census purposes. The procedure of establishing rural-urban differences by comparing the results secured in selected rural areas of two

---

[29] Carl C. Taylor, *Rural Sociology*, New York, Harper & Brothers, 1928, p. 415.
[30] *Op. cit.*, pp. 79–82.

states with those obtained in eighty-three cities scattered through-out the nation is hardly to be commended. Nevertheless, the re-sults may be given in order that the individual student may have readily at hand such data as are available.

Seemingly the data indicate a tendency for disabling sickness to be most prevalent in the small villages and hamlets and least prevalent in the small towns and cities, with the open country and the eighty-three cities in intermediate positions and approximately equal. Thus on the day of the survey there were in places of from 2500 to 5000 inhabitants 41 cases of disabling illness per 1000 population, compared with 45 in the 83 cities, 46 in the open-country areas, and 49 in the villages and open-country districts combined. It is highly probable that the age differences in the composition of the various segments of the population alone are sufficient to account for all of the observed differences. Thus the concentration in the villages of elderly persons, among whom the illness rates are high, probably is sufficient to explain the greater incidence of sickness in the small population centers.

The evidence, such at it is, also suggests that rural people, and particularly those living in villages and hamlets, may suffer more from enduring acute and chronic illnesses than is true of urban people generally. Thus 25 percent of the cases reported for the general rural category lasted for more than six days, and in the open country the percentage (24.6) was almost as high. In the places of from 2500 to 5000 inhabitants, on the other hand, the cor-responding figure was only 23.3 and in the eighty-three cities it was far lower, 17.1. Again it should be indicated that the re-ported differences probably are largely, or entirely, a reflection of the age differences between the populations being compared.

The late Dr. Edgar Sydenstricker, scientific director of the Mil-bank Foundation, writing in 1933, said there had been only one study of the gross illness rate. This was made by the United States Public Health Service in a special tabulation of data from 9000 families interviewed for the Committee on the Costs of Medical Care. Unfortunately this tabulation combines town and rural. There can be little disagreement with Sydenstricker's conclusion that, based on these data, "the gross illness rate seems to be ap-proximately the same in the country as in the city."[31]

Soundings into the extent of illness in various parts of the

[31] *Op. cit.*, p. 66.

nation are of great importance, and fortunately several excellent ones have been made in various parts of the United States. One such study of 883 families, made in Ross County, Ohio, in 1925, indicated that 43 percent of the population had been ill in the previous twelve-month period.[32] Another study of the amount of sickness in a rural area was made in 1923 and 1924 by Professor Dwight Sanderson of Cornell University. The area surveyed consisted of three townships in Cortland County, New York; a total of 2060 persons were included; and the situation in villages was compared with that in the open country. Country people on the average were sick 5.17 days per year, village people 7.37 days. Most of the difference was accounted for by the presence of more old people in the village. Nearly one-half (46.5 percent) of the families reported some sickness during the year.[33] An important addition to knowledge in this field is the study of Madison County, Arkansas. During the period of one year, 2292 people reported a total of 1065 illnesses, 3.3 per family. Per capita loss of time amounted to 12.3 days, of which 4.5 days were spent in bed.[34] More recently a more comprehensive study has been made in Missouri, and the results indicate that the rural people of that state are subject to an extremely large amount of chronic illness. Thus in the course of the year for which data were taken, one person out of six had been ill for three months or more. One person in nine had been ill throughout the entire twelve-month period. It was also found that chronic illnesses were most prevalent among the aged and those on the lower income levels. Four-fifths of all these chronic illnesses occurred among one-third of the families.[35]

Michigan is another state in which there has been an attempt made to inventory illness among the rural population. In this case Charles R. Hoffer used the "Symptoms Approach" devised in the U.S. Department of Agriculture[36] for a study of 1219 persons in a

[32] C. E. Lively and P. G. Beck, *The Rural Health Facilities of Ross County, Ohio*, Ohio AES Bulletin 412, Columbus, 1927, p. 31.

[33] Dwight Sanderson, *op. cit.*, pp. 4, 7–8.

[34] Isabella C. Wilson and William H. Metzler, *Sickness and Medical Care in an Ozark Area in Arkansas*, Arkansas AES Bulletin 353, Fayetteville, 1938, p. 5.

[35] See Harold F. Kaufman and Warren W. Morse, *Illness in Rural Missouri*, Missouri AES Research Bulletin 391, Columbia, 1945, pp. 3–4. See also Ronald B. Almack, *The Rural Health Facilities of Lewis County, Missouri*, Missouri AES Research Bulletin 365, Columbia, 1943, p. 15.

[36] For a description of this method see Edgar A. Schuler, Selz C. Mayo, and Henry B. Makover, M.D., "Measuring Needs for Medical Care: An Experiment in Method," *Rural Sociology*, XI (June, 1946), pp. 152–158.

sample of 306 farm families in "typical areas of Michigan." Of them almost one-half "reported one or more of a selected list of 27 symptoms which were judged by medical doctors to indicate need of medical attention."[37] Of those having one or more of such symptoms nearly one-third had used only home remedies or had neglected the ailment entirely. The proportion of those needing medical attention, as revealed by the procedures used, was positively correlated with the age of the persons involved and it also increased as the gross income of the family decreased.

Despite their many deficiencies, the army medical examinations given to recruits and soldiers probably more nearly approximate a health census than any other body of information in existence. Fortunately a large and probably fairly representative sample of the data secured in the physical examinations of the men called up for service in World War II has now been analyzed and published. On the whole these materials show that the selective service registrants from rural areas were rejected in slightly lower proportions than were those from the urban districts. Thus, among the whites 54.7 percent of those from urban areas were found acceptable for general service whereas among those from the rural sections of the nation the corresponding percentage was 57.3. For Negroes, on the other hand, the difference was slightly in favor of the urban, the general acceptance rates being 48.6 and 47.7 for those from urban and rural areas, respectively. In the case of the whites the higher acceptance rates among the rural registrants prevailed in all four of the regional divisions used (East, South, Midwest, and Far West), but among the Negroes the rural registrants had fewer defects than the urban registrants only in the South and the Far West. Interestingly enough, within rural territory the white registrants occupationally engaged in farming showed slightly higher rejection rates on account of physical defects than was true of the non-farmers, and this difference prevailed in all of the regions except the Midwest.[38]

Earlier there were the studies of Gould and Baxter for the Civil War period and of Davenport and Love for the period of World War I. These have been summarized by Sorokin and Zim-

[37] Charles R. Hoffer, *Health and Health Services for Michigan Farm Families,* Michigan AES Special Bulletin 352, East Lansing, 1948, p. 6.

[38] Selective Service System, *Physical Examination of Selective Service Registrants,* Special Monograph 15, Washington, Government Printing Office, 1948, I, 181.

merman,[39] and by Sorokin, Zimmerman, and Galpin.[40] Data from both of these immense compilations indicate that physical defects were more prevalent among urban than among rural recruits. Thus Davenport and Love reported that in rural districts there were 528 defects per 1000 men, as compared with 609 in the urban. Part of this excess they attributed to more critical examinations in urban districts.[41]

Similar studies in England yield comparable results. Between 1915 and 1918, 2,425,184 conscripts from eighteen to forty-two years of age were given medical examinations. In nonindustrial areas 70 percent of the recruits were classed as fit for all branches of military service, and 20 percent more as fit for certain branches of service, making a total of 90 percent in sound health. On the other hand, only 19 percent of the recruits from industrial areas were classed as fit for all branches of service and 27 percent for certain branches, or a total of 46 percent in sound health.[42]

Data from Germany, Great Britain, Holland, and Switzerland also indicate fewer defects among agriculturists and rural recruits than among those from the cities.[43] There can be little doubt that, on the whole, the evidence from army examinations indicates that the health of the rural population is superior to that of the urban.

This conclusion is in accord with that derived from other types of data. Sorokin, Zimmerman, and Galpin present an exhaustive analysis of all studies bearing on the relative incidence of specific diseases in rural and urban areas. They conclude that the urban population has a greater prevalence of the following constitutional diseases and ailments: tuberculosis, diseases of the lungs, syphilis and other venereal diseases, alcoholism and drug addiction, tabes dorsalis, progressive paralysis, organic heart diseases, arteriosclerosis, cancer and malignant tumors, nephritis, Bright's disease, dental defects, obesity, underweight, errors of refraction or disorders of the digestive organs, and diabetes mellitus. On the other hand, pellagra and a few other relatively unimportant diseases are more prevalent in rural areas.[44]

[39] *Op. cit.*, pp. 149–155.

[40] *Op. cit.*, III, 66–69.

[41] Albert G. Love and Charles B. Davenport, *Defects Found in Drafted Men*, Washington, Government Printing Office, 1920, p. 348. Cf. Sorokin, Zimmerman, and Galpin, *op. cit.*, III, 68.

[42] René Sand, *Health and Human Progress*, New York, The Macmillan Company, 1936, pp. 148–149.

[43] Sorokin, Zimmerman, and Galpin, *op. cit.*, III, 68–69.

[44] *Ibid.*, III, 70–94, and especially 95–96.

It is interesting to compare the conclusions of the *Source Book's* authors with those of Sydenstricker based upon his observation of data gathered from white male holders of insurance policies. According to this study of 100,000 males, agriculturists had much lower proportions of defective vision, nose and throat ailments, and constipation than did urban groups. On the other hand, the agriculturists had high proportions of dental troubles, gall bladder ailments, and genitourinary complaints.[45] Sydenstricker concludes that the rural man makes a good showing on medical examinations as compared with urban residents, or, to quote his original study: "For most conditions, the agricultural group would seem to have rates definitely below the average for all examined, but there are important exceptions, notably for teeth, stomach and abdominal conditions, and the genito-urinary system."[46] He also indicates that the city man's impairments are serious ones affecting the heart and circulatory system and the nervous system.[47]

Even more revealing in many ways is the prevalence of the various defects which lead to the rejection from military service of such a large proportion of the nation's men. From the tremendous mass of materials assembled in World War II, those providing a basis for comparing the men from agricultural occupations with those from nonagricultural pursuits have been analyzed and set forth in some detail by Marcus S. Goldstein.[48] Figures 9 and 10, for whites and Negroes, respectively, present some of the more striking parts of this analysis, and they deserve detailed observation and study. Among the whites it will be observed that the agriculturists were much less frequently rejected because of poor eyes, poor teeth, nose ailments, skin trouble, deficient ears, ailments of the abdominal viscera, varicose veins, hemorrhoids, tuberculosis, syphilis, neoplasms, kidney and urinary troubles, gonorrhea and other venereal diseases, the miscellaneous category of medical ailments, and the nonmedical and unstated causes for rejection. On the other hand they were rejected in much larger proportions than the non-farmers on account of illiteracy and mental deficiency and troubles involving the mouth and gums; and in slightly larger percentages because of poor feet, mental

[45] Sydenstricker, *op. cit.*, p. 63.

[46] Edgar Sydenstricker, "Physical Impairments and Occupational Class," *United States Health Reports*, XLV (1930), 1959.

[47] Sydenstricker, *Health and Environment*, p. 64.

[48] "Physical Status of Men Examined Through Selective Service in World War II," *Public Health Reports*, LXVI (May 11, 1951), pp. 587–609.

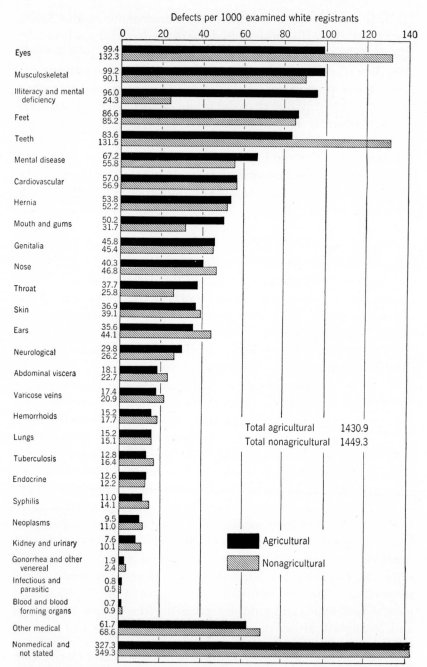

Defects per 1000 examined white registrants

	Agricultural	Nonagricultural
Eyes	99.4	132.3
Musculoskeletal	99.2	90.1
Illiteracy and mental deficiency	96.0	24.3
Feet	86.6	85.2
Teeth	83.6	131.5
Mental disease	67.2	55.8
Cardiovascular	57.0	56.9
Hernia	53.8	52.2
Mouth and gums	50.2	31.7
Genitalia	45.8	45.4
Nose	40.3	46.8
Throat	37.7	25.8
Skin	36.9	39.1
Ears	35.6	44.1
Neurological	29.8	26.2
Abdominal viscera	18.1	22.7
Varicose veins	17.4	20.9
Hemorrhoids	15.2	17.7
Lungs	15.2	15.1
Tuberculosis	12.8	16.4
Endocrine	12.6	12.2
Syphilis	11.0	14.1
Neoplasms	9.5	11.0
Kidney and urinary	7.6	10.1
Gonorrhea and other venereal	1.9	2.4
Infectious and parasitic	0.8	0.5
Blood and blood forming organs	0.7	0.9
Other medical	61.7	68.6
Nonmedical and not stated	327.3	349.3

Total agricultural 1430.9
Total nonagricultural 1449.3

Agricultural
Nonagricultural

FIGURE 9. Defects per 1000 White Registrants in Agricultural and Nonagricultural Employment Examined Through Selective Service, November,
1940, to December, 1943. (Illustration from the Selective Service System.)

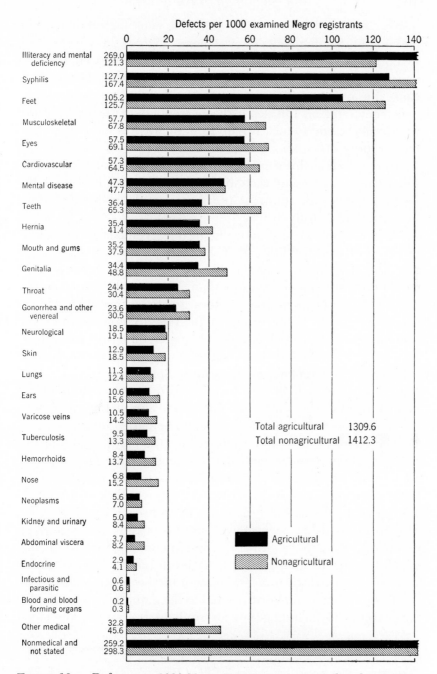

FIGURE 10.   Defects per 1000 Negro Registrants in Agricultural and Non-agricultural Employment Examined Through Selective Service, November, 1940, to December, 1943. (Illustration from the Selective Service System.)

disease, hernia, disorders of the genitalia, neurological difficulties, and malfunctioning endocrines. Among Negroes there is only one exception to the general rule that the agriculturists were rejected in smaller proportions than the non-agriculturists. The leading cause for rejecting Negro registrants was illiteracy and mental deficiency, and on this score the percentage of the agricultural registrants failing to measure up to standard was more than double the proportion among the non-farmers.

In concluding this summary of the factual information on the subject it should be said that, although the data are far from satisfactory, the health status of the rural population seems rather superior to that of the urban.

A serious defect in practically all these comparisons of rural-urban health and vitality is that the racial factor nearly always is neglected by the investigators. The incidence of sickness commonly is greater among Negroes than among whites, and Negroes are concentrated in rural areas to a greater extent than whites. Comparisons which fail to adjust for race differences therefore overemphasize the rural disabilities, underemphasize the urban. This point is illustrated very clearly by means of data on the distribution of tuberculosis in the United States. (See Figure 11.) Note the relatively high incidence of tuberculosis among the total population of the Southeastern States. Note also that it is relatively low among both the white and colored populations of this area.

The factors which are responsible for the better health of the rural population are not immediately recognizable. That superior medical attention on the part of physicians, nurses, hospitals, etc., is not the explanation is easily shown, because all these are much more prevalent in the city than in the country. Furthermore, by demonstration it has been shown that it is possible to effect great improvements in the health of the rural population by introducing modern health techniques and facilities in rural counties.[49] Probably the most satisfactory explanation of the superior health of rural communities can be attributed to the natural environment of the countryside, including pure air, sunlight, fresh water and food,

[49] The expansion of public health work in selected rural counties which were aided by the Commonwealth Fund is reported in Estella Ford Warner and Geddes Smith, Children of the Covered Wagon, New York, The Commonwealth Fund, 1930; Harry S. Mustard, Cross-Sections of Rural Health Progress, New York, The Commonwealth Fund, 1930; and A Chapter of Child Health, New York, The Commonwealth Fund, 1930. Cf. R. M. Atwater, Public Health in Cattaraugus County, Olean, New York, The Commonwealth Fund, 1929.

etc., and to the rural person's more complete adaptation to his environment. The lack of the former in the city, coupled with an unnatural sedentary life, may very well contribute to the appearance of endemic disorders. Infectious diseases, on the other hand,

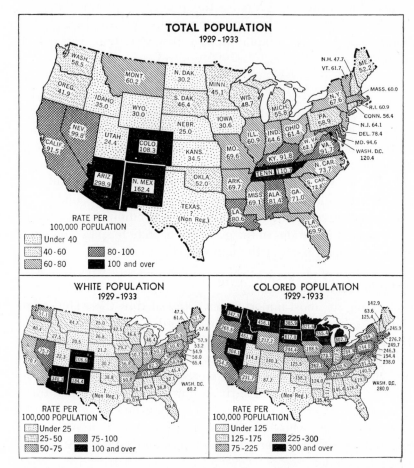

FIGURE 11.   Death Rates from Tuberculosis—All Forms—in the Total, White, and Colored Populations, 1929–1933. (Reproduced from *U.S. Public Health Bulletin No. 225*, Washington, 1936, Maps 1, 2, 3; pp. 5–8.)

thrive in cities, where the density of population facilitates their rapid spread. Thus the most important factor would seem to be that modern men still possess the cave man's physical make-up. Those living in cities frequently attempt to retain good health and still live a most unnatural life; many think that if they can just find the correct pill or the right doctor all will be well. Residence in the country compels, to a much greater extent, habits and modes of living more in accordance with those to which the human organism is adapted. Natural selection operates very slowly. It may take a million years for this process to produce a species capable of properly driving automobiles! What, then, are the hopes that physical adaptation to urban conditions can ever be attained?

Medical Services and Hospitals

The extent to which the services of physicians and other medical personnel, hospitals, and other health facilities are available in the rural communities is another aspect of the general health situation to which rural sociologists have given careful study during the last two decades. Thanks to their efforts a considerable amount of well-tested facts and theory is already available; and the systematized knowledge they have accumulated has found important applications in the guidance of state hospital and health plans in several parts of the nation.[50]

The Supply of Rural Physicians

Among the most important facts revealed by these studies and those of a few medical men is the marked scarcity of physicians in the rural districts of the nation. To begin with, there are many more people per physician in the rural areas than in the urban, and this situation is made even more disadvantageous to the rural population by the distances the country practitioner must travel. In addition the rural communities contain much higher proportions of doctors who already have passed the prime of life, and this unfavorable fact becomes more pronounced with the passage of each decade.

[50] Three excellent examples of this kind of applied rural sociology are Leland B. Tate, *The Health and Medical-Care Situation in Rural Virginia*, Virginia AES Bulletin 363, Blacksburg, 1944; C. Horace Hamilton, S. H. Hobbs, and R. T. Stimson, M.D., *Medical Care Services in North Carolina: A Statistical and Graphic Summary Prepared for the Governor's Commission on Hospital and Medical Care*, Raleigh, Department of Rural Sociology, North Carolina Agricultural Experiment Station, 1944; and Homer L. Hitt and Alvin L. Bertrand, *Social Aspects of Hospital Planning in Louisiana*, Baton Rouge, Department of Rural Sociology, Louisiana Agricultural Experiment Station and the Health and Hospital Division, Office of the Governor, 1947.

Consider a few of the data. In succinct summary a publication of the U.S. Department of Agriculture pictures the national scene in the following words:

When we consider all the time it takes for a rural doctor to travel about the countryside seeing patients, a ratio of about one physician to 1,000 people, or even fewer, is probably necessary, if rural people are to enjoy a true parity of physicians' services with city people. Yet, in the thousand most rural and isolated counties just before the war, there were so few doctors that each one had to serve 1,700 people, while in the big city area, there was a doctor for each 650 people. What's more, many country doctors are getting well along in years and often through no fault of their own find it hard to keep up with advances in medical science.[51]

More detailed materials for the nation and each of the states have been assembled by Mott and Roemer in their volume *Rural Health and Medical Care*, the most complete treatment of the subject in the literature. Among the most revealing of their computations are those of the number of persons per effective physician for the counties in the various states classified according to their degree of urbanity. In 1940 this index was 876 for all counties in the United States, but it was only 674 in those counties classed as metropolitan. In the counties bordering on the metropolitan districts there were 1221 persons per effective physician, and in those not bordering upon them the corresponding index varied with degree of urbanity as follows: counties containing cities of 10,000 or more inhabitants, 1054; counties whose largest centers varied from 5000 to 9999 in population, 1383; counties whose largest centers varied from 2500 to 4999 in population, 1607; and counties containing no urban centers, 1409.[52] (See also a slightly different compilation of similar data in Figure 12.) More recent materials for Missouri in 1950 show that the number of persons per physician was only 544 in the counties containing the four

[51] Interbureau Committee on Post-War Problems, *Better Health for Rural America: Plans of Action for Farm Communities*, Washington, Government Printing Office, 1945, p. 3.

[52] Mott and Roemer, *op. cit.*, p. 158. See also Tate, *op. cit.*, p. 19; Robert L. McNamara, "Changes in the Characteristics and Number of Practicing Physicians in Rural Ohio in 1923–1942," *Rural Sociology*, IX (March, 1944), p. 13; Hamilton, Hobbs, and Stimson, *op. cit.*, p. 74; and John M. Maclachlan and Forbes R. de Tamble, "Florida's Medical Care Resources," University of Florida *Economic Leaflets*, III, No. 6 (May, 1944).

largest cities whereas it was 1405 in the remainder of the state;[53] and in Louisiana, also for 1950, the corresponding ratio was 2549 in the twenty-three parishes (counties) lacking urban centers altogether and only 596 in the eight parishes which were 40 percent or more urban in 1940.[54]

Mott and Roemer indicate that the country's disadvantageous

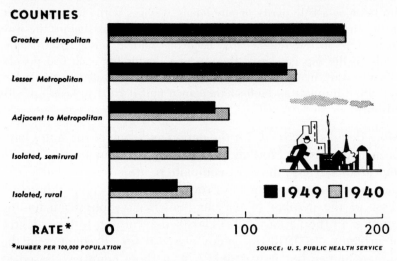

COUNTIES

Greater Metropolitan

Lesser Metropolitan

Adjacent to Metropolitan

Isolated, semirural

Isolated, rural

■1949 ☐1940

RATE*   0   100   200

*NUMBER PER 100,000 POPULATION   SOURCE: U. S. PUBLIC HEALTH SERVICE

FIGURE 12. The Relative Scarcity of Physicians in Rural Areas. (Illustration from the Bureau of Human Nutrition and Home Economics.)

position in relation to the city with respect to the supply of physicians has been becoming more acute in the course of the twentieth century. The data they present indicates that as early as 1906 the rural areas of the United States, with 56 percent of the nation's population, had only 41 percent of the physicians. After that, however, the tendency of young graduates of the medical schools to locate in cities was so strong that by 1940 the rural districts, with 43.5 percent of the population, contained only 20 percent of the medical practitioners.[55] This tendency, in turn, brought about a situation in which those physicians who are practicing in the rural districts, and who must spend an estimated 25 percent of their time in travel, are of an average age considerably above

[53] Robert L. McNamara and John B. Mitchell, *Supply of Physicians in Selected Rural Areas*, Columbia, Department of Rural Sociology, University of Missouri, (mimeographed), 1951, p. 5.

[54] Paul H. Price and Homer L. Hitt, *The Availability of Medical Personnel in Rural Louisiana*, Louisiana AES Bulletin 459, Baton Rouge, 1951, p. 7.

[55] *Op. cit.*, pp. 163 and 167.

that of those located in towns and cities. On this point the most comprehensive data are those for 1938, when the proportion of practicing physicians who were aged fifty-seven years or over varied from 22.6 percent in counties containing cities of 50,000 or more inhabitants to 34.6 percent in counties whose largest urban centers were less than 50,000 in population, and 45.7 in counties containing no urban centers (places of 2500 or more).[56]

The basic causes for the concentration of physicians in urban areas seem to be rather obvious, and they are largely economic. In 1941, according to the most reliable comprehensive data, the private practitioner in the rural districts of the United States (up to 2500 inhabitants) "does less than half as well financially as the practitioner in large cities of between 100,000 and 500,000 population."[57] There is little reason to suppose the disparity of incomes has become any less pronounced since that time.

The Lack of Hospitals

Although the rural health facilities and conditions in the United States are hardly equaled in any other large country on the face of the earth, our rural population is far from enjoying parity with urban people in this respect. Only a few years ago a committee of governmental employees could generalize correctly as follows: "Widespread rural areas are very poorly served by hospital facilities. Over 1,250 of the 3,070 counties in our Nation are without a single satisfactory general hospital. Over 700 of these counties have populations exceeding 10,000 people."[58] According to the data considered by this group, the people of a state need 4.5 general hospital beds for each 1000 population if its people are to have adequate hospital facilities. Since many cases of illness among rural people are referred to city hospitals, this ratio should be as high as 5.0 in the urban districts, whereas 3.5 might suffice for the rural areas. Nevertheless, "the fact is that today most rural areas do not have even 2.0 beds per 1,000. Besides the hundreds of counties with no satisfactory hospital at all,

[56] J. W. Mountin, E. H. Pennell, and Virginia Nicolay, "Location and Movement of Physicians, 1923 and 1938; Age Distribution in Relation to County Characteristics," *Public Health Reports*, LVIII (1943), 488. Cf. John F. Thaden, *Distribution of Doctors of Medicine and Osteopaths in Michigan Communities*, Michigan AES Special Bulletin 370, East Lansing, 1951, pp. 31–32.

[57] Mott and Roemer, *op. cit.*, p. 176.

[58] U.S. Department of Agriculture, Interbureau Committee on Post-War Problems, *op. cit.*, p. 3.

there are 450 counties in which the only general hospital is a proprietary institution (operated for profit) and in these counties the average ratio is only 1.5 beds per 1,000 people."[59] Since the committee reported in 1945 there undoubtedly have been improvements in many parts of the nation, but it will be many years before the hospital facilities readily available for use by rural people will be roughly equal to the standard proposed.

The Use of Medical Facilities

There can be little doubt that rural people make far less use of the services of physicians and other medical personnel and of the facilities of hospitals and other health facilities than do the inhabitants of towns and cities. However, it is not easy to supply adequate documentation of this fact with comprehensive and recent data from all parts of the United States. Several years ago the "working group" of the Interbureau Committee on Post-War Problems of the United States Department of Agriculture, which had Dr. F. D. Mott of the U.S. Public Health Service as its chairman, no doubt had most of the available facts at its disposition when the important report (*Better Health for Rural America*) quoted from above was under preparation. In any case, since this "working group" undoubtedly made by far the most thorough study of rural health ever done in this country, it is well to present some of its more significant conclusions and generalizations: Directly after the sections in the report entitled "Too Few Doctors and Dentists and Other Health Workers," "The Lack of Hospitals and Other Facilities," "Poor Sanitation," and "Weak Public Health and Public Welfare Programs" comes the one headed "Fewer Health Services Received." "With this lean supply of professional people and facilities in the rural areas, it is obvious that farm people must receive far less than their due share of medical services" are its opening words and the following statements among its more important conclusions:

1. ". . . For every 1,000 people in cities of 100,000 or over, 3,003 physicians' calls in the home or office are received per year; in communities of 5,000 to 100,000 population, 2,679 calls are received; but in towns under 5,000 and in the open country only 2,240 physicians' calls are received per year."

---

[59] *Ibid.*, p. 3; see also, for more detailed data, Mott and Roemer, *op. cit.*, pp. 226–227.

2. "As for dental care, far less is received by rural than by city people and thousands of farmers have lost teeth that could have been saved by early care. . . . It is not only their teeth that suffer but sometimes their entire system and, because of appearances, even their self-respect."

3. "Hospitalization, too, is far less in rural areas. In cities of over 100,000 there have been 68 hospital cases per 1,000 population each year to every 42 cases in the rural areas. . . . It is not that country people *need* this much less hospitalization, but rather that they *get* this much less."

4. "Rural people manage to obtain only slightly fewer emergency operations than city people. But for so-called elective conditions—that is, chronic disorders that need surgical attention but are not immediate matters of life and death—rural people get far less surgical care than city people."

5. "About the only health items that farm people obtain relatively more of than city people are patent medicines—most of which are of very doubtful value."

6. "Whatever type of needed health service is considered, less of it is received in the country than in the cities. Even for people of the same income, those in the country appear to get fewer services than those in the city, simply because the doctors and the facilities are not at hand. More important, however, most people in the rural areas are of a far lower income level than city people. This we find is the main reason why rural health services are so poor."[60]

Since the time (largely during the "depression years") health and economic data were gathered on which the Interbureau Committee based its conclusions, and even since the committee reported in 1945, momentous changes in the United States probably make the stated conclusions much less valid than they once were. However, comprehensive data to serve as a secure basis for evaluating the changes are largely lacking. Nevertheless, a few significant indicators are to be had.

Consider the important materials gathered annually relative to the place of occurrence of births and the persons in attendance upon mothers at the time of childbirth. (See Figures 13 and 14.)

[60] Interbureau Committee on Post-War Problems, *op. cit.*, p. 6. Much of the data available to the "working group," of which, unfortunately, a large proportion already was rather antiquated, and some of the results of a few more recent studies are summarized in Mott and Roemer, *op. cit.*, chap. 17.

Since 1935 the proportion of births taking place in hospitals with physicians in attendance has more than doubled, with the increase in the rural districts (32.3 in 1940 and 75.8 in 1949) much more pronounced than that in the urban areas (76.0 in 1940 and 94.3 in 1949). Of course the rural had farther to go. Births not in hospitals but attended by physicians decreased sharply from 50.6 percent

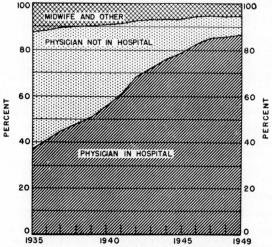

FIGURE 13. The Increase in the Use of Hospital Facilities and Physicians in the Delivery of Babies. (Illustration from the National Office of Vital Statistics.)

in 1935 to only 8.1 percent in 1949. In this case the rural-urban division, which can be made satisfactorily only after 1940, when more adequate precautions taken to report births by place of residence of mothers were in effect, indicates that the decrease was from 51.3 to 14.7 percent in the rural sections and from 20.9 to 3.6 percent in the urban places. Thus the percentage of births in which no physicians were in attendance, with only midwives or other nonmedical personnel assisting the mothers at the time of delivery, decreased from 9.3 percent in 1940 to 5.1 percent in 1949; and in the rural districts the change during the decade was from 16.4 percent to 9.5 percent, whereas in the urban the drop was from 3.1 percent to 2.1 percent.[61]

[61] The data given are from National Office of Vital Statistics, "Births by Person in Attendance: United States, Each Division and State, 1949," *Vital Statistics— Special Reports*, XXXVI (1951).

Figure 14 makes it evident that the United States has almost attained the point at which every urban white mother is, as a matter of course, delivered of her child in a hospital with a physician in attendance; and it also shows that the rural white mothers

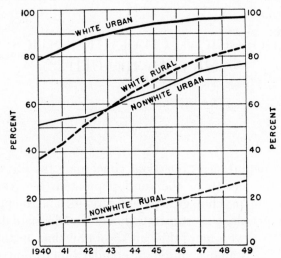

FIGURE 14. Racial and Residential Differences in the Use of Hospitals at the Time of Childbirth. (Illustration from the National Office of Vital Statistics.)

rapidly are attaining a similar position. Colored mothers, too, in the urban districts already are in hospitals for the most part when their children are born; but the nonwhite (largely Negro) mothers in the rural districts still rank very low in this respect. It is upon them that the heavy hand of traditionalism in the reliance upon midwives, the lack of medical personnel and hospital facilities in the rural districts, low incomes, and the difficulties of transportation weigh most heavily.[62]

[62] For a few recent studies of the extent to which rural families make use of medical facilities in specific localities, see Selz C. Mayo and Kie Sebastian Fullerton, *Medical Care in Green County*, North Carolina AES Bulletin 363, Raleigh, 1948, pp. 11–23; Hoffer, *op. cit.*, pp. 26–27 and 31–35; Harold F. Kaufman, *Use of Medical Services in Rural Missouri*, Missouri AES Research Bulletin 400, Columbia, 1946; Robert E. Galloway and Harold F. Kaufman, *Health Practices of Rural People in Lee County*, Mississippi State College Sociology and Rural Life Series, No. 1, State College (mimeographed), 1950; Robert E. Galloway and Harold F. Kaufman, *Health Practices in Choctaw County*, Mississippi State College Sociology and Rural Life Series, No. 2, State College (mimeographed), 1950; and Robert E. Galloway and Marion T. Loftin, *Health Practices of Rural Negroes in Bolivar County*, Mississippi State College Sociology and Rural Life Series, No. 3, State College (mimeographed), 1951.

6

PSYCHOLOGICAL CHARACTERISTICS AND MENTAL HEALTH

Fully as important as questions concerning the physical characteristics and health of the rural population is a comparable analysis of the psychological characteristics and mental health of the rural people. Unfortunately, however, adequate data in the latter field are even more difficult to obtain than in the former, although there is an oversupply of popular supposition and fancy in connection with these vitally important topics. Perhaps the most vicious of these is the widespread assumption by urban people that rural folk are in some way the mental inferiors of their city cousins. In this chapter are summarized the most trustworthy findings in the fields of comparative rural-urban intelligence and mental health. Some attention is also given to the specific psychological traits of farmers.

Rural-Urban Intelligence

Intelligence has been given a working definition by Sorokin and Zimmerman as follows: "Intelligence is that combination of mental factors which the individual is supposed to use in achieving some aim or goal in life or the ability to adjust itself adequately to a new situation."[1] Kolb and Brunner, who quote this definition with approval, also call attention to the fact that intelligence involves both innate and acquired elements, and that in essence intelligence "is the ability to learn."[2] Intelligence testing, sometimes by well-qualified psychologists and educators, and all too fre-

[1] P. A. Sorokin and Carle C. Zimmerman, *Principles of Rural-Urban Sociology*, New York, Henry Holt & Company, 1929, p. 234.

[2] J. H. Kolb and E. deS. Brunner, *A Study of Rural Society*, Boston, Houghton Mifflin Company, 1952, p. 47.

quently by novices, has been epidemic in the United States for a good many years. Intelligence is tested by exposing the individual to a battery of questions or a series of activities and rating his performance upon these exercises in comparison with the norm or average for persons of his age group. For example, a person whose score is the average for individuals of his own age is given a rating of 100; that is to say, his intelligence quotient (I.Q.), derived by dividing his "mental age" by his chronological age, is 100. The individual who falls below average receives an I.Q. of less than 100; a person rating above the average is said to have an intelligence quotient of more than 100.

Intelligence Tests

The psychologists are to be complimented for their efforts to devise measures of individual capacity. They are making much progress in this line. Unfortunately, however, some persons have been all too prone to use the data gathered from these tests for purposes other than those for which they are suited. For example, it is doubtful indeed, since admittedly the tests measure acquired skills as well as innate capacities, if there is any valid basis for thinking that they are an instrument by which the relative intelligence of rural and urban populations may be determined. Yet in spite of this limitation, Sorokin, Zimmerman, and Galpin in 1929 analyzed sixty-five studies in which these tests had been used to compare rural-urban intelligence, and these authors considered only the most important ones.[3] Since that time dozens of new ones have been added to the list.[4] As might be expected, with hardly an exception these tests reveal rural persons and agriculturists to have lower I.Q.'s than urban persons and nonagricultural occupational groups.

Such findings immediately raise questions concerning the fairness of the intelligence tests as a measure of comparative rural-urban intelligence. Sorokin and Zimmerman have offered six criticisms of the use of intelligence tests for such purposes, of which their contention that the tests are biased seems to be the

[3] P. A. Sorokin, Carle C. Zimmerman, and Charles J. Galpin, *A Systematic Source Book in Rural Sociology*, Minneapolis, University of Minnesota Press, 1932, III, 266–281.

[4] Cf. C. A. McMahan, "Personality and the Urban Environment," in T. Lynn Smith and C. A. McMahan, *The Sociology of Urban Life: A Textbook with Readings*, New York, The Dryden Press, Inc., 1951, pp. 748–760.

most important. They offer the following analysis in support of
their contention that the tests are biased in favor of urban groups:
(1) The tests measure the direct experience which falls within
the experience world of the urbanite more than the ruralite. This
is to say that they deal with concrete situations such as tennis
games, in which the urban population participates, more than with
plowing, or milking cows, etc., the everyday activities of rural folk.
(2) The tests are based upon indirect experience more than upon
direct experience. The urban person has acquired a larger share of
his mental luggage through reading, conversation, and in other
indirect ways than through direct, firsthand experience, whereas
the opposite is the case with the man in the country. For this reason, the tests which measure "book learning" obviously are unfair
to the farm population. (3) The tests are administered by means
of certain activities which fall within the everyday work and recreation of city people, such as reading, writing, and calculating;
not by means of the activities which are customary doings of rural
people. In no small part, high scores on most intelligence tests demand ready facility in the manipulation of tools and concepts that
fall within the customary routine of city people, skills quite outside
the ordinary activities of the farm population. Such general criticisms are sufficient to warn that evidence from the tests alone is
an insufficient basis for branding rural people as inferior to urban
folk in intelligence.

Special criticisms may also be leveled against particular tests.
Thus World War I army tests, most of which are included in the
analysis of Sorokin, Zimmerman, and Galpin, have often been
used as a yardstick for making comparisons of rural and urban
intelligence; frequently, so low have been the scores of farmers
on these tests that such data have been used as justification for
branding a high proportion of rural folk as feeble-minded. Kolb
and Brunner indicate correctly that these tests have been misused
ever since their publication. They point out that the army tests
were designed to assist in the search for prospective officers, not as
criteria for comparing rural and urban intelligence. Farmers rated
a low average on them, while officers of the engineering corps, as
might be expected, were the ones of "superior intelligence."[5]

The conclusion that the tests are heavily biased in favor of
urban experience is strongly supported by the results of some
studies in which tests have been constructed that were weighted

[5] *Op. cit.,* p. 51.

with information from the rural experience world in the same degree as the conventional tests are weighted with urban materials. One of the most interesting and important of these is that by Myra E. Shimberg.[6] Her study posited the hypothesis that the failure of rural children to score as high on intelligence tests as urban children is "due not to any innate intellectual difference between the two groups, but to the tools used in measuring them." Two tests were constructed, one consisting of typical questions based upon information freely available to city people. This test has been used daily for clinical purposes in the Judge Baker Foundation in Boston, and has been found adequate as a test of "practical common-sense information. . . ." In similar manner and with the same methods of standardization that had been used in constructing the first test, a second one was made that was based upon experiences common to the rural world. "Test B is no more specialized in favor of rural children than Test A (or any standard test) is specialized in favor of the urban children." Both tests were then given to nearly 10,000 school children, of whom about half were rural and half urban. On the first test rural children were retarded a full year as compared with the urban; on the second the situation was exactly reversed. This investigator concluded that the so-called mental differences revealed by the tests were more a function of the tools of measurement than of innate intellectual differences.

The more recent comparative studies of rural-urban intelligence have been concerned less with blanket comparisons and more with the specific differences in the psychosocial traits and characteristics of rural and urban people. The methods, the age and sex of the groups compared, and the degree to which other related factors actually were under control vary widely fom one study to another, and the results secured to date should hardly be thought of as conclusive. Nevertheless, they are suggestive of the kind of differences that eventually may be established. As given by McMahan in a recent survey of the principal differences found by one or more of the investigators, the results may be summarized briefly. Thus in comparison with their rural counterparts the city persons in the respective studies were found to be: (1) better adjusted emotionally, (2) less neurotic, (3) more likely to exhibit symptoms of nervousness, (4) less introverted, (5) possessed of

⁶ *An Investigation into the Validity of Norms with Special Reference to Urban and Rural Groups*, Archives of Psychology No. 104, 1929. Extracts from this study are reproduced in Sorokin, Zimmerman, and Galpin, *op. cit.*, III, 282–286.

more withdrawing tendencies, (6) better adjusted personally, (7) more independent, (8) more dominant, (9) higher in resourcefulness, (10) less self-reliant, (11) lower in feeling of personal worth, (12) low in the sense of belonging, (13) higher in rationality, (14) less practical-minded, (15) more "unfavorable" in their attitudes toward work, (16) higher in verbal ability, (17) lower in mechanical ability, (18) more speedy in performance, and (19) inferior in musical ability.[7]

The work of Mangus and his associates at the Ohio State University is among the best that has been done in the field of comparative rural and urban mental health. Now available are the results of two of their recent studies not included in the McMahan summary. In one of these, the California Test of Personality, Elementary Series, Form A, was administered to 1638 fourth-, fifth-, and sixth-grade children in the public schools of Butler County, Ohio, of whom 1161 were urban and 477 rural. The results indicated that the children from the farms had a greater sense of personal worth and were less likely to exhibit withdrawing tendencies. They also were more free of nervous symptoms and they "differed favorably in school relations." However, they rated lower than the urban children in the sense of personal freedom.[8] The second of the studies also was made in Butler County, but in this case the Mental Health Analysis, Secondary Series, Form A, tests were given to students in the tenth grade. Included were 415 boys

[7] McMahan, *op. cit.*, pp. 759–760. The specific studies from which he drew his materials are as follows: Evelyn Millis Duval and Annabelle Bender Motz, "Are Country Girls So Different?" *Rural Sociology*, X (1945), 263–274; Paul H. Landis, "Personality Differences of Girls from Farm, Town, and City," *Rural Sociology*, XIV (1949), 10–20; A. R. Mangus, "Personality Adjustment of Rural and Urban Children," *American Sociological Review*, XIII (1948), 566–575; Charles W. Nelson, "Testing the Influence of Rural and Urban Environment on A.C.E. Intelligence Test Scores," *American Sociological Review*, VII (1942), 743–751; Cecil H. Patterson, "The Relationship of Bernreuter Scores to Parent Behavior, Child Behavior, Urban-Rural Residence, and Other Background Factors in 100 Normal Adult Parents," *Journal of Social Psychology*, XXIV (1946), 3–49; Eugene L. Shepard, "Measurements of Certain Nonverbal Abilities of Urban and Rural Children," *Journal of Educational Psychology*, XXXIII (1942), 458–462; Leland H. Stott, "Parental Attitudes of Farm, Town, and City Parents in Relation to Certain Personality Adjustments in Their Children," *Journal of Social Psychology*, XI (1940), 325–339; and the White House Conference on Child Health and Protection, *The Adolescent in the Family*, New York, D. Appleton-Century Company, 1936.

[8] A. R. Mangus and R. H. Woodward, *An Analysis of the Mental Health of Elementary School Children*, Hamilton, Ohio State Department of Public Welfare, The Ohio State University, and the Ohio Agricultural Experiment Station, in coöperation with the Butler County Mental Hygiene Association (processed), 1949, p. 23.

and 390 girls, of whom 328 were urban, and 118 lived on farms, and the other 359 were from rural nonfarm territory. It was found that the "rural students differed favorably from those living in city homes in several ways." They scored higher in emotional maturity, the sense of personal security, emotional stability, social participation, and lack of mannerisms denoting nervousness.[9]

Other Tests of Intelligence

School achievement and retardation, and the attainment of eminence are other yardsticks sometimes used to measure the comparative intelligence of rural and urban groups. Numerous complicating factors, such as differences in educational facilities and their accessibility, rural-urban migration, and absence of institutional framework for giving recognition to rural leadership, render very dubious any interpretations regarding relative native ability. Attempts at such inference accordingly deserve little mention. For example, studies of the origins of the persons listed in *Who's Who* prove little more than that this work is a compliation of the names of urban leaders, and offer few data of significance in judging the comparative intelligence of rural and urban populations.

Mental Health

Mental abnormalities may be grouped into three principal classes: (1) feeble-mindedness or mental defect, (2) insanity, and (3) epilepsy. Each of the three, in turn, may be subdivided into many different kinds of varieties. Of the three, mental defect refers to a lack of mental ability, insanity to the loss or derangement of mental faculties which were once possessed, and epilepsy to recurrent paroxysms commonly attributed to nervous, cerebral, and hereditary venereal disorders. Thus it would see proper to call the first a deficiency; insanity and epilepsy, mental diseases. By all odds mental defect is the most prevalent of the three.

Mental Defects

Criteria of feeble-mindedness are not well developed. Scores on intelligence tests seem to be distributed rather generally accord-

[9] A. R. Mangus and R. H. Woodward, *An Analysis of the Mental Health of High School Students*, Hamilton, Ohio State Department of Public Welfare, The Ohio State University, and the Ohio Agricultural Experiment Station, in coöperation with the Butler County Mental Hygiene Association (processed), 1949, p. 20.

ing to the normal or bell-shaped curve; those in the upper ranges are classed as geniuses, those in the lower ranges as feeble-minded. Just where to make the distinction between mental defectives and the least intelligent of the normal individuals is a perplexing problem. In any case, to a considerable extent feeble-mindedness is a matter of definition, the category including all falling below a certain score on the tests. Consequently the number of feeble-minded is entirely dependent upon the point chosen for drawing the line. The classification of mental defectives currently in use is one prepared by the American Association on Mental Deficiency in coöperation with the National Association for Mental Health, Inc. According to its criteria the principal categories of mental defectives are as follows: (1) idiot, a mentally defective person whose mental age is less than three years, or, if a child, whose intelligence quotient is less than 20; (2) imbecile, a mentally defective person whose mental age is from three to seven, inclusive, or, if a child, whose intelligence quotient is from 20 to 49, inclusive; and (3) moron, a mentally defective person whose mental age is from eight to eleven years, inclusive, or, if a child, whose intelligence quotient is 50 or more.[10]

The incidence of feeble-mindedness in the entire United States is unknown; it would in any case depend upon the criteria used. In 1910 H. H. Goddard proposed that the dividing line be placed at the mental age of twelve. Using this criterion in the army intelligence scores during the First World War, we find that 47.3 percent of the white recruits and 89 percent of the Negro recruits fell in the feeble-minded group. About 2 percent of the white and 17 percent of the Negro recruits were below the mental age of eight; 5 percent of the white and 32 percent of the Negro were below the mental age of nine. Since feeble-mindedness is thought to be carried as a recessive trait in inheritance, Hankins has estimated that between 7 and 14 percent of the population either are feeble-minded themselves or are the potential progenitors of feeble-minded descendants.[11] This rightfully is considered to be a terrific "load of defective genes."

Probably the official data are much more complete for idiots and imbeciles than for morons. According to the official statistics,

[10] National Institute of Mental Health, *Patients in Mental Institutions, 1948*, Washington, Government Printing Office, 1951, p. 113.

[11] Frank H. Hankins, *Introduction to the Study of Society*, New York, The Macmillan Company, 1930, pp. 248, 250.

there were in the United States at the beginning of 1948 nearly 145,000 patients on the books of public and private institutions for mental defectives and epileptics. Of these, 124,673 were in institutions, 916 in family care, and 18,132 in extramural care.[12]

Such data as are available seem to indicate that the incidence of feeble-mindedness is somewhat more frequent in the city than in the country.[13] However, it is probable that the differences are of little significance. Very likely they merely indicate a somewhat greater tendency to institutionalize mental defectives in the city.[14] All recent reports of the Bureau of the Census and the Federal Security Agency on this subject have not included tabulations showing the rural and urban incidence of feeble-mindedness. They also warn that the data are not a safe guide to the numbers of mental defectives in the various states.[15] Sorokin and Zimmerman,[16] and Sorokin, Zimmerman, and Galpin,[17] after summarizing an immense quantity of data, concluded that there is probably little difference in the incidence of feeble-mindedness in the country and city, and that the non-institutionalized cases are probably disproportionately large in rural areas, institutionalized cases somewhat more prevalent in the urban districts. If there have been any selective drains upon rural intelligence exercised by rural-urban migration, the cities should show a marked relative under-representation with respect to the incidence of feeble-mindedness. The fact that they fail to do so augurs well for the future of the nation's population.

Insanity

Mental illness or derangements of the mind are called insanity. In our society the insane are chronic mental cases, persons whose mental behavior has become far out of the ordinary and who have been taken into court where they have been pronounced legally insane and committed to some institution. Many "mild" cases are never institutionalized. Therefore the statistics of mental diseases

---

[12] *Patients in Mental Institutions, 1948*, p. 68.

[13] *Feeble-minded and Epileptics in Institutions: 1923*, Washington, Government Printing Office, 1926, pp. 56–57.

[14] Frederick D. Mott and Milton I. Roemer, *Rural Health and Medical Care*, New York, McGraw-Hill Book Company, 1948, pp. 140–143.

[15] See, for example, Bureau of the Census, *Mental Defectives and Epileptics in Institutions: 1935*, Washington, Government Printing Office, 1937.

[16] *Op. cit.*, pp. 267–268.

[17] *Op. cit.*, III, 240.

are not a direct measure of the prevalence of the various types of insanity, but only of the extent to which the mentally ill receive hospital treatment.

There are many types of mental diseases or psychoses. The most widely used classification is that approved by the American Psychiatric Association and the National Committee for Mental Hygiene, adopted for use in the 1923 census of mental patients. It divides mental ailments into twenty-two classes, including twenty different groups of psychoses, one class for undertermined psychoses, and a category for patients without psychosis.[18]

According to the results of the 1948 survey, there were 568,762 patients on the books of the hospitals for mental disease in the United States. Of these, 494,580 were in the hospitals, 2237 in "family care," and 71,945 "in other extramural care."[19]

The data from the early tabulations show that insanity is much more prevalent in urban than in rural areas, but the rural-urban classification is not carried in the recent reports. In 1933 the rates per 100,000 were 79.5 for urban males compared with 41.3 among rural males, and 57.3 among urban females compared with 27.3 among rural females.[20] These figures may mean merely that there is a greater tendency to hospitalize urban cases, but it is unlikely that such is the full explanation. The indication probably is that a higher rate of insanity is a result of urbanization.

Psychosocial Traits

The result of the rural environment upon the farmer's psychology has been the cause of endless speculation and some scientific study.[21] The particular brand of psychological thinking to which a writer subscribes has, of course, a great deal to do with the sort of characteristics he will attribute to farmer folk. Some, like Galpin, have written under the influence of an extreme form of behavior-

[18] See *Patients in Hospitals for Mental Disease: 1933*, Washington, Government Printing Office, 1935, p. 18.

[19] *Patients in Mental Institutions: 1948*, p. 22.

[20] *Patients in Hospitals for Mental Disease: 1933*, p. 49. Incidentally, this information concerning the low incidence of insanity among rural females is of considerable interest in connection with the old and oft-repeated myth that isolation of the farm causes a great deal of insanity among farm women. Many excellent "explanations" have been offered to account for the "fact" that farm women go insane so commonly; not a few works of fiction have taken this as their motif.

[21] For a brief summary of some of the principal problems and approaches in this field, see C. Arnold Anderson and T. Lynn Smith, *Research in the Social Psychology of Rural Life*, Bulletin 17, Social Science Research Council, New York, 1933.

ism, with the result that the psychological behavior of the rural people is interpreted solely as a function of the muscles utilized in the manual labor of the farm, and the "hoe farmer" and the "machine farmer" are set forth as rural types. The hoe farmer is the "primitive muscular type." He utilizes mostly the large muscles of the legs, thighs, trunk, and shoulders, achieving a high development of these and, indirectly, of the viscera, lungs, and heart. Since these are largely controlled by the spinal cord, the brain and remaining portions of the nervous system are not highly developed, and the fine adjustment and coördination of the other muscles are not achieved. The machine farmer is the new cerebral type. The muscles most exercised by the hoe farmer fall into disuse; and the smaller, finer muscles, controlled through the cortex of the brain, are called into play. Connective tissues are perfected through use, with the end result that there is an "infinite coordination and precision of movement of these little muscles," and the logical outcome of a "large range of intellectual intercourse, a constant enticement to a change in ideas."[22] Leaving this rather extreme behavioristic characterization of rural types by Dr. Galpin, we may consider those specific psychosocial traits said to be distinctive of the farmer class. The psychosocial traits of farmers are not well known despite the great volume of material that has been written on the subject.

The number of psychosocial traits alleged by various writers to be characteristic of farmers is legion. Only a few of the lists presented by the best-known writers in the field will be given here. Long ago Butterfield gave the following as mental characteristics of farmers: (1) individualism; (2) conservatism; (3) intense radicalism on occasion; (4) deep-seated prejudices; (5) a tendency to brood over more or less imaginary injuries; and (6) a tendency to be moody, pessimistic, fatalistic, and resigned[23] Gillette early took over Butterfield's list;[24] later revised it to include "Puritanism," repressed desires, and susceptibility of the farmer to mass hysteria;[25] and more recently has concluded that the characteristic psychosocial traits of the farmer are individualism,

[22] Charles J. Galpin, *Rural Life*, New York, D. Appleton-Century Company, 1920, pp. 32–36.

[23] Kenyon L. Butterfield, *Chapters in Rural Progress*, Chicago, University of Chicago Press, 1907, pp. 17–20.

[24] John M. Gillette, *Constructive Rural Sociology*, New York, Sturgis and Walton Company, 1913, p. 75.

[25] *Rural Sociology*, New York, The Macmillan Company, 1928, pp. 50–54.

aloofness to other classes, parsimoniousness or thrift, and extreme familism.[26] Bernard has named individualism, conservatism, orthodoxy, suggestibility, mysticism, shyness, suspiciousness, introvert personality, personal democracy, and sentimentality as the mental characteristics of farmers.[27] Sims gives the following as characteristic mental attitudes of the farmer: extreme individualism, conservatism, the magical mind, emotional intensity and high degree of suggestibility, thriftiness and frugality, suspiciousness, and frankness.[28] Hayes has catalogued the thought processes of the farmer as follows: The farmer is a direct thinker and speaker, is fatalistic, superstitious, has deep convictions, is conservative, is filled with "fogyism," dwells upon past experiences, is resourceful, and is inclined to be temperamental.[29]

Taylor has assembled all of these and added to them the generalizations of Sorokin and Zimmerman, who indicate that: (1) the experience world of the farmer is limited in extent; (2) the city population has a greater volume of indirect experience; (3) because of the limited indirect experience of the farmer, he is often misled, imbued with fallacious opinions, subject to superstition and prejudice in the fields outside his realm of direct experience; (4) the direct experience of the farmer is so wide that he is frequently highly resistant to inadequate and misleading theories which may find a large following in the city; (5) the farmer's direct experience is in such a large volume, compared with his indirect experience, that his mental luggage is more stable and less fluctuating than the attitudes and convictions of the urbanite, whose conclusions are based upon a rapidly changing series of indirect experiences; (6) in perception, sensation, attention, imagination, etc., the farmer is highly sensitive to the impressions from the immediate environment, not so sensitive as the city man to urban stimuli; (7) the farmer is more stern and "Puritanic," less soft and feminized than the city person; (8) virility, sternness, austerity, patience, endurance, and perseverance are conspicuous in the farmer; (9) rural imagination and fantasy differ as to topics,

[26] *Rural Sociology*, 3rd ed., p. 77.

[27] L. L. Bernard, "A Theory of Rural Attitudes," *American Journal of Sociology*, XXII (1917), 648; and "Research Problems in the Psychology of Rural Life," *Journal of Social Forces*, III (1925), 446.

[28] N. L. Sims, *Elements of Rural Sociology*, New York, Thomas Y. Crowell Company, 1928, pp. 226–238.

[29] A. W. Hayes, *Rural Sociology*, New York, Longmans, Green & Company, 1929, pp. 167–174.

images, associations, and combinations from the urban; and (10) within the realm of the direct experience, the logic of farmers is likely to be sound, while outside the realm of their direct experience it is likely to be very faulty.[30] Taylor concludes that there is considerable agreement as to the most distinctive psychosocial traits characterizing the farmer-peasant class, and, that after duplication is eliminated, the total is between fifteen and twenty.[31]

Several limitations of these lists, and others of a similar nature, should be indicated. (1) Many of these terms or traits are so loosely defined, or so ambiguous, that they have little value for scientific purposes. For example, it is hard to reconcile Gillette's alleged extreme individualism and familism, or Sims' extreme individualism and conservatism, or Butterfield's conservatism and intense radicalism, as being at one and the same time characteristic of farmers. At least in some of their connotations, each of these pairs of concepts is contradictory. (2) Although the majority of the lists include "individualism" as one of the traits of farmers, it is by no means demonstrated that the farmer is more individualistic than his city relative in the most widely accepted senses of the term; in fact, much of the evidence would seem to indicate that the farmers are the least individualistic of all social classes. Probably, however, the controversy over whether the farmer is individualistic or the opposite does no more than focus attention upon the highly ambiguous meaning of this term. In the sense in which it is used by Frederick Jackson Turner and those who have followed him, "individualistic" is practically synonymous with "independent." In the sense that the farmer is highly independent, assumes that he and his family must provide for their own support and welfare, is an entrepreneur or job maker instead of a job seeker, resists strenuously all efforts to do away with private ownership and use of the land, he is highly individualistic. But in the sense that he is unwilling to coöperate with or assist his fellows, the overwhelming importance of informal mutual-aid practices in rural areas and even, in recent years, the rapid strides made in formal contractual coöperative ventures cry out the inadequacy of the contention that the farmer in this sense is individualistic.[32]

[30] Carl C. Taylor, *Rural Sociology*, New York, Harper & Brothers, 1933, pp. 137–141; Sorokin and Zimmerman, *op. cit.*, pp. 282–301.

[31] *Op. cit.*, p. 141.

[32] See excellent summaries of the data on this point in Sorokin and Zimmerman, *op. cit.*, pp. 511–514; and Sorokin, Zimmerman, and Galpin, *op. cit.*, III, 264–266;

In the sense that individualism denotes the possession of unique characteristics of personality, it can hardly be contended that the farmer is individualistic. In fact, almost all the authors seem agreed that the farmer is bound by custom and tradition and that the personality of the rural person is rather completely submerged in the family group. Folk music, folk medicine, folklore, in fact almost all the cultural products for which no one individual receives the credit of discovery, invention, or creation, are produced only in rural areas.[33] As Sorokin and Zimmerman have shown so clearly, impersonality—the very antithesis of individualism in many of its connotations—is the outstanding characteristic of rural arts.[34] Individualism certainly should be used to designate the condition in which social solidarity is achieved through specialization and division of labor, in which each individual's personality takes on unique features because of the peculiar combination of functions which are his alone. It should not be used to designate the condition in which social solidarity is achieved because of the numerous things that individuals have in common. Durkheim and Toennies and many others have shown that the solidarity based upon homogeneity is typical of rural districts, that based upon division of labor characteristic of urban aggregates.[35] Thus the "individualism" of the farmer would seem to reduce itself to the state of affairs in which self-reliant, independent men personally assume the responsibility for their own welfare, combine with others (sometimes on a contractual basis, more frequently informally through mutual aid and "neighboring") to achieve ends which cannot be secured by working alone, at the same time that their own personalities are submerged in the family, neighborhood, and community groups more completely than is true of any other segment of society.

In essence it would seem that the rural sociologists of America

---

cf. Dwight Sanderson, *The Rural Community*, Boston, Ginn and Company, 1932, p. 541; and for excellent examples of coöperation among rural folk see T. Lynn Smith and Lauren C. Post, "The Country Butchery: A Co-operative Institution," *Rural Sociology*, II (1937), 335–337; and C. R. Hoffer, "Co-operation as a Culture Pattern Within a Community," *Rural Sociology*, III (1938), 153–158.

[33] Cf. R. E. Park's introduction to *Shadow of the Plantation* by Charles S. Johnson, Chicago, University of Chicago Press, 1934.

[34] *Op. cit.*, pp. 514–516.

[35] Cf. George Simpson, *Emile Durkheim on the Division of Labor in Society*, New York, The Macmillan Company, 1933, pp. 174–181; F. Toennies, *Gemeinschaft und Gesellschaft*, Leipzig, Hans Bushe, 3rd ed., 1935, *passim*; and Sorokin and Zimmerman, *op. cit.*, pp. 516–518.

are most agreed that the farmer is: (1) conservative and orthodox —that he tends to accept rural culture as it came to him and to preserve its values; this being the case, it is not surprising that at certain times and places traits such as the magical mind, suggestibility, "fogyism," etc., have been assigned to him; (2) thrifty and frugal, traits necessary to survival when dealing with nature, which may exhibit unfriendly aspects for years at a time; (3) fatalistic, in the sense that he has no mechanistic explanation of the universe, thinks the vagaries of the weather and the seasons cannot be accurately predicted, and resigns himself to make the best of what the future may bring; (4) possibly actuated by the tendency to be suspicious of strangers, who are not frequent enough so that he becomes accustomed to them; and (5) more outspoken and frank than city people, many of whom might lose their jobs, meet economic boycott or political reprisals if they spoke their minds too freely.

7

FERTILITY

Birth, death, and marriage make up the three great crises in the lives of individuals. From the standpoint of society the fertility of the population, the mortality of the population, and the marital condition of the people are among the most important items in a system of national or state bookkeeping. It is not surprising that the collection of demographic data concerning these vital processes began at a very early date. The English pattern of registration, from which our own practices have been derived, dates back to 1538, to the time of Henry VIII, when the clergy were charged with the responsibility of making weekly records of all baptisms, marriages, and deaths, and were also made responsible for the care of the register in all the parishes.[1] Marriage can best be indexed with data on marital conditions, given in a succeeding chapter. In this chapter are discussed the questions of human fertility. Mortality is treated in the one to follow.

Indexes for Measuring Fertility

Students of demography have long been concerned with objective methods for measuring and comparing the fertility of human populations. At the present time two methods are commonly used. One of these is the birth rate. It expresses the ratio of the number of births during an interval of time (one year) to the total number of the population. Usually the births per 1000 persons in the population is given. Thus for the United States during 1950 the following formula gives the birth rate:

[1] Sir Arthur Newsholme, *The Elements of Vital Statistics*, New York, D. Appleton-Century Company, 1924, p. 71.

$$\frac{\text{Number of births during 1950}}{\text{Population April 1, 1950}} \times 1000 = \frac{3,548,000}{150,697,361} \times 1000 = 23.5$$

Birth rates fall into a number of rather distinct groups, depending upon the particular population which is used as a base. Ordinarily the number of births per 1000 people living is the expression used, such an index being termed the *crude* birth rate. For most valid comparisons some refinements of this crude expression are necessary. When allowances are made for differences in the age and sex composition of a population so as to make its rate strictly comparable with the rates for other populations, the index is referred to as a *standardized* birth rate. It is customary to use the "standard million," or the population of England and Wales as it was in 1901, as the standard to which other populations are equated. However, any normally composed population would serve the purpose. There might be some value in using the population of a "life table" as a base. For some purposes the number of births is related to the number of married women; a rate computed for this population is referred to as a *nuptial* birth rate. For other purposes rates for various age groups are necessary. These are referred to as *specific* birth rates.

It is important to note that birth rates are always based on data secured by registration, i.e., on facts observed and recorded as they occur. Obviously, for groups that lack machinery for recording these vital phenomena, it is impossible to secure reliable birth rates. Furthermore, the rates for any group will be useful only to the extent that registration is accurately, consistently, and completely carried on.

The second index used in measuring the fertility of a population may be styled the *fertility ratio*. It differs from a birth rate in that it is not based on information secured by registration. Instead, all the data needed for this index are secured by an enumeration, or census of the population under consideration. This makes it especially useful for gauging the fertility of a population that lacks the machinery for registering vital phenomena. It also limits its use in a country such as ours to the census years, or to special groups that are enumerated for one purpose or another. If there is any question concerning the accuracy of registration at any time or place, this is an important device for use in checking the results given by computation of the birth rates.

The computation of the *fertility ratio* is very simple. It consists in relating the number of children in a population to the number of women in the childbearing ages in the population. Ordinarily, the ratio of children under five years of age to women fifteen to forty-four (or twenty to forty-four) is secured. Expressing this as the number of children per 100 women gives a simple and useful method of measuring the fertility of a particular group and comparing the fertility of various populations.[2] Unfortunately, the fertility ratio can be used only in connection and with a census. But the birth rate, too, requires the total population for its calculation, and this number must be either enumerated or estimated.

Increasingly useful in population study is an index called the *net reproduction rate,* which balances fertility against mortality and indicates the degree to which a given population is either increasing or failing to reproduce itself. As defined by the Bureau of the Census, "the net reproduction rate represents the number of daughters a cohort of 1000 female infants beginning life together would have during the course of their lives if the cohort were subject to both the birth rates and death rates at each age level which prevailed at the time specified."[3] Hence, for replacement each cohort of females must in the course of their lifetime give birth to 1000 daughters. More than this will make for population increase; fewer than 1000 will not meet replacement needs and will eventually result in population decrease.

Fallacies in Comparison of Rural and Urban Birth Rates

In gauging the fertility of a given population at a particular time, in estimating the trend in fertility of a population, and in comparing the fertility of one population with another it has been customary to use a birth rate, usually the crude birth rate. For example, practically all writers in this country who have made comparisons of rural and urban fertility have used the birth rate as their index. Many have been content to use the crude birth

[2] It has been the practice to express the fertility ratio as the number of children under five per 1000 women of childbearing ages. The author contends that the resulting figure, which always has three or four digits, is unnecessarily cumbersome, and that the use of 1000 as a multiplier is merely an example of cultural lag, growing out of its use in the formula for the birth rate. In the interests of simplicity and economy of space he uses 100.

[3] Bureau of the Census, *Sixteenth Census of the United States: 1940,* "Population: Differential Fertility 1940 and 1910, Standardized Fertility Rates and Reproduction Rates," Washington, Government Printing Office, 1944, p. 3.

rate as a basis for making comparisons. A few have seen the necessity of correcting for age and sex differences in the composition of the two populations before proceeding with the comparisons.[4]

Those presenting the census materials at their face value seem to have been unaware of the fact that at least three serious fallacies were nullifying the validity of their comparisons. In eliminating one of them, the students who standardized the rates before presenting them made a good start. It is obvious that differences in the sex composition affect the fertility of various populations. The scarcity of women in a mining territory such as Alaska is certain to make the crude birth rate there very low. On the other hand, a community or state which functions as a place for aged people to spend their declining years necessarily has its crude birth rate lowered by the inclusion of this non-childbearing population in the computations. The birth rates of many rural villages, and even of states such as California or Florida, are undoubtedly affected by this factor. As has already been indicated, the rural population has high proportions of males, of children, and of aged persons; the urban population has high proportions of females and of people in the productive ages. Consequently the students of rural-urban fertility who first standardized the birth rates made a good start.

But there are two other serious errors in the data, defects far more important than age and sex differences, which make fallacious the results of many comparisons of rural and urban fertility in the United States. One of these is the difference in the accuracy or completeness of registration. The second is the practice, in vogue in the United States until 1935, of counting births as belonging to the registration districts in which the births took place.

Consider first the underregistration of births. In this connection it is interesting to compare the number of children under one, reported by the 1930 Census, with the number of births recorded in 1929. In many counties, especially in rural areas such as the South and West, it will be found that many more children under one year of age were enumerated in the Census of 1930 than were reported as having been born during the preceding year. Sometimes the number living exceeds by twice the number of births registered. Thus in Evangeline Parish, Louisiana, the Census of

[4] Cf. P. A. Sorokin and C. C. Zimmerman, *Principles of Rural-Urban Sociology,* New York, Henry Holt & Company, 1929, pp. 205–206.

1930 reported 638 children of less than one year of age on April 1, 1930, although the number of births registered in the parish during the year of 1929 was only 216. In Cimarron County in the Panhandle of Oklahoma, the difference was even more pronounced, the census reporting 125 children under one year of age, whereas the births registered totaled only 26; and in Choctaw County in southeastern Oklahoma, only 115 births were recorded in 1929, although the census enumeration reported 575 children under one as of April 1, 1930. Of course where large numbers of deliveries are attended only by midwives, many of whom are illiterate, we can hardly expect a complete registration of births. This situation is prevalent in large sections of the country, and is especially so in the rural South where the bulk of the rural population of the nation resides.

In a study[5] of the forty-six states in the 1929 registration area, the author estimated that only about 91 percent of the births occurring during 1929 were registered. Registration was far more adequate in urban than in rural areas, the urban districts registering 102 births for every 100 births occurring, the rural districts registering only 83 out of every 100 births. (Failure to allocate births according to residence is sufficient reason to explain the excessive registration in urban districts.) In the rural areas of Arizona, Colorado, Connecticut, Louisiana, Nevada, New Jersey, Oklahoma, and Tennessee, less than 75 percent of the births were registered. Obviously it is unfair to compare rural fertility with urban fertility on the basis of the birth rates unless allowances are made for the differences in the completeness of registration.

The years since 1930 have been marked by strenuous efforts to secure a more complete registration of births. Although data are by no means perfect as yet, considerable improvement has been shown. For example, according to official tests made by the Bureau of the Census, in 1926 only ten of Mississippi's counties succeeded in registering as many as 90 percent of the births actually occurring in the county. In 1939 the tests showed that sixty of the counties registered as high as 90 percent of the births occurring in the county. However, even in 1939 there were twenty-two counties in Mississippi in which more than one birth out of nine was

[5] T. Lynn Smith, "Rural-Urban Differences in the Completeness of Birth Registration," *Social Forces*, XIV (1936), 368–372; cf. P. K. Whelpton, "The Completeness of Birth Registration in the United States," *Journal of the American Statistical Association*, XXIX (1934), 125–136.

unrecorded. The official report recognized that there was a close association between rurality and incompleteness of registration.[6]

A comprehensive study by the Bureau of the Census based on 1939 and 1940 experience proves that the author was thoroughly conservative in his earlier estimates of the proportion of births going unregistered in the United States. This census investigation revealed that, for the period December 1, 1939, to March 31, 1940, only 92.5 percent of the births actually occurring were registered. In urban areas 96.0 percent of all births were registered, in rural areas only 86.5 percent. South Carolina, where only 82.8 percent were recorded, had the poorest record of any state, and Minnesota (99.6 percent complete) had the best. In four states less than 75 percent of all births occurring in rural areas were registered, Arizona with only 68.6 percent making the poorest showing, followed by Arkansas, Tennessee, and South Carolina in the order named. Minnesota, which registed 98.9 percent of all births in rural areas, made the best showing, its nearest rivals being New York and Vermont.[7]

The latest test, from which preliminary data were released on January 15, 1952,[8] indicates that by 1950 birth registration in the United States was 97.8 percent complete. There had been a 5.7 percent gain in coverage between 1940 and 1950. At the time of this most recent check only 1.5 percent of the white births went unrecorded, while 6.0 percent of the nonwhites were not registered. Only two states, Arkansas and South Carolina, both highly rural, failed to attain a mark of 90 percent completeness. Connecticut scored 100, and Minnesota and Rhode Island each failed by only 0.1 percent to attain the perfect mark. California, Delaware, the District of Columbia, Iowa, Kansas, Massachusetts, Montana, New Hampshire, New Jersey, New York, North Dakota, Oregon, Pennsylvania, Vermont, Washington, and Wisconsin all registered above 99 percent complete. The preliminary report does not give the data separately for the rural and urban segments of the population.

[6] See Bureau of the Census, "Birth and Death Registration in Mississippi with Special Reference to the County Registrar," *Vital Statistics—Special Reports*, IX (1940), 41, 52–53.

[7] Bureau of the Census, "Completeness of Birth Registration in Urban and Rural Areas, United States and Each State, December 1, 1939, to March 31, 1940," *Vital Statistics—Special Reports*, XXIII (1945), 101–103.

[8] National Office of Vital Statistics, *Preliminary Results of the 1950 Birth Registration Test*, Washington, Federal Security Agency (mimeographed), 1952.

The failure to allocate births according to the residence of the mother has introduced another significant error into the vital statistics of the United States. Prior to 1935, if a mother from a rural district were delivered in an urban hospital, the birth was credited to the city. Fortunately, the procedure has been corrected.

It has been a demographic truism to say that the country is the producer of population, the city the consumer. This was the case when the new science of "political arithmetic" gave us our first glimpse of rural-urban differentials in fertility in England in the middle of the seventeenth century,[9] and it has remained generally valid since that time. In the United States the rural population of the South and West has produced the bulk of the population of the nation, while the cities of the North and East have failed by considerable margins to produce enough children to take the place of their older citizens as they passed away. Only since the close of the Second World War, owing to the very low level to which the death rate has fallen coupled with a rise in fertility that has been more rapid in the urban than in the rural areas, as is shown below, is the city beginning to share more equally in the production of the nation's future population.

The birth data are now sufficiently good for the United States so that the rural-urban differential in fertility may be demonstrated easily by using them. Thus in 1949 the crude birth rates computed from the data as reported were as follows: 24.2 in the urban parts of the United States and 24.1 in the rural. Correcting these for underregistration raises the urban birth rate to 24.6 and the rural to 26.1. Eliminating part of the distortions due to the differing age and sex compositions of the urban and rural populations by computing the rates per 1000 women aged fifteen to forty-four years, and using the data as corrected for underregistration, gives rates of 102.4 for the urban population and 122.8 for the rural.[10] In short, in 1949 the rate of reproduction in the rural parts of the United States was nearly one-fifth higher than that in the urban portions of the country.

The results obtained by basing the comparisons upon the

[9] Cf. Walter F. Willcox (ed.), *Natural and Political Observations Made upon the Bills of Mortality by John Graunt*, Baltimore, Johns Hopkins University Press, 1939, pp. 52–56.

[10] These materials are from "Births by Race and by Urban and Rural Areas: United States, Each Division and State, 1949," *Vital Statistics—Special Reports*, XXXVI (1951), 54.

fertility ratios are essentially similar. These measures have the advantage, however, that the rural population may be divided into the farm and nonfarm segments for purposes of the comparisons. In 1950 the fertility ratio of the urban population stood at 44 children of less than five years of age for each 100 women in the ages fifteen to forty-four, inclusive. This was considerably below the fertility ratio of 55 for the rural nonfarm population, and much below that of 60 for the rural farm segment of the nation's people.[11]

Similar are the rural-urban differentials in fertility revealed by earlier compilations of data. For example, Thompson and Whelpton estimated that the 1929 birth rate among native white women aged fifteen to forty-four was 103 per 1000 in the rural parts of the United States and 59 in the urban.[12] Only a little later, according to a report by the National Resources Committee, when all proper allowances were made, the fertility ratio in the United States stood at 50 for native women, 55 for foreign-born white women, and 55 for Negro women. Without exception, fertility decreased as the size of the city increased, the ratio for native whites dropping from 75 in the rural farm and 68 in the total rural population to 46 in places of between 2500 and 10,000 inhabitants, and to only 34 in cities of 100,000 or over. Similar was the situation among the foreign-born white and the Negro groups, the ratio of 34 among Negroes in cities of 100,000 and over being the lowest recorded. Expressed as percentages of the ratio necessary to maintain a stationary population, in 1930 the urban native white population met only 86 percent of replacement needs, the rural population 154 percent, and the rural farm 170 percent.[13]

In connection with the Census of 1940 the Bureau of the Census published net reproduction rates for the United States and for the urban, rural nonfarm, and rural farm populations, subdivided according to race for each of the states. Since children under five were used in computing the indexes of fertility, the rates are for the period 1935 to 1940. According to these highly refined data,

[11] These computations are based upon data given by the Bureau of the Census, *1950 Census of Population: Preliminary Reports*, "General Characteristics of the Population of the United States: April 1, 1950," Series PC-7, No. 1, Washington, February 25, 1951.

[12] Warren S. Thompson and P. K. Whelpton, *Population Trends in the United States*, New York, McGraw-Hill Book Company, 1933, p. 274.

[13] National Resources Committee, "Urban Data," *Population Statistics*, Washington, Government Printing Office, 1937, pp. 21, 23–24.

in 1935 to 1940 the adjusted net reproduction rate in the United States was 978, or slightly below that necessary to maintain the population. As was to be expected, the urban rates were far below reproduction levels, being only 731 for the whites and 702 for the nonwhites. The rural nonfarm population, with rates of 1146 for its white and 1210 for its nonwhite elements, was reproducing rapidly enough to make up part of the urban deficit. However, the rural farm districts continued to be the seedbed of the nation's population, having a net reproduction rate of 1572 among whites and of 2058 among nonwhites.[14]

Naturally, there are great regional differences in the rate at which the population is reproducing. These are at a minimum among the urban population and most pronounced among rural farm people. Following the 1940 Census, maps were prepared to show how the fertility varies throughout the nation. (See Figures 15 and 16.) The data are for the farm population; but of course the area of urban districts is slight, so that most of the attention in studying such a fertility map would in any case be directed to the situation in the rural districts. Several outstanding associations are revealed by observation of these figures. In the first place, attention should again be called to the low fertility of the rural population residing near cities. Almost without exception, the lowest fertility ratios in the United States will be found in those counties containing large cities. On these maps of human fertility, the cities of the United States represent the "Death Valleys" and the "Dead Seas."

The peaks of human fertility, on the other hand, are found in the most remote rural sections of the country. Observe the high fertility ratios in the Appalachian Mountains of eastern Kentucky and Tennessee, western Virginia and North Carolina, southern West Virginia, and Alabama; in several of the most isolated parts of Louisiana, Arkansas, Missouri, and Texas; in the central Rocky Mountain area generally, and in the most inaccessible parts of Utah, Colorado, Arizona, and Nevada particularly; and in the Indian areas of North Dakota and South Dakota.

The low fertility of certain rural areas calls for some comment. The most evident examples of this are in areas immediately adjacent to large metropolitan centers, as is very apparent in parts of

[14] Bureau of the Census, *Sixteenth Census of the United States: 1940,* "Population, Differential Fertility 1940 and 1910, Standardized Fertility Rates and Reproduction Rates," Washington, Government Printing Office, 1944, Table 7, p. 20.

RURAL FARM WHITE POPULATION 1940

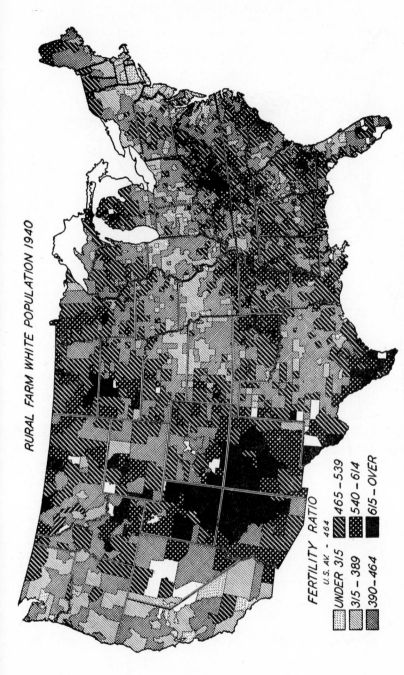

FERTILITY RATIO

U.S. AV. - 464

UNDER 315
315 - 389
390 - 464
465 - 539
540 - 614
615 - OVER

FIGURE 15. Fertility Ratios of the White Rural Farm Population, 1940. (Reproduced from J. Allan Beegle and T. Lynn Smith, *Differential Fertility in Louisiana*, Louisiana AES Bulletin 403, Baton Rouge, 1946.)

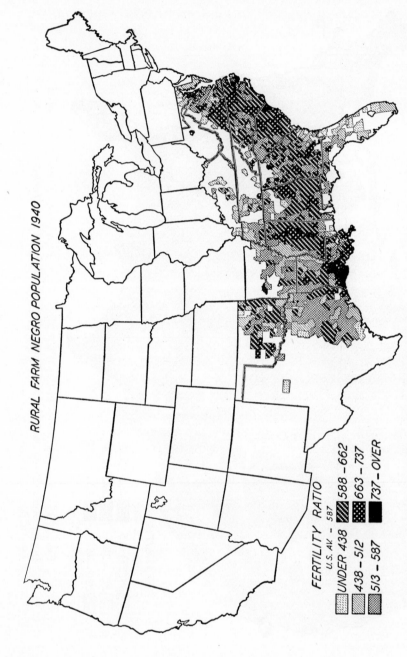

RURAL FARM NEGRO POPULATION 1940

FERTILITY RATIO
U.S. AV. – 587

UNDER 438
438 – 512
513 – 587
588 – 662
663 – 737
737 – OVER

FIGURE 16. Fertility Ratios of the Negro Rural Farm Population, 1940. (Reproduced from J. Allan Beegle and T. Lynn Smith, *Differential Fertility in Louisiana*, Louisiana AES Bulletin 403, Baton Rouge, 1946.)

New York, New Jersey, Delaware, Connecticut, Massachusetts, and California; or in parts which have been treated with large doses of the most superficial aspects of urban life via the resort business or the divorce mills (portions of Florida and Nevada).

. Particularly important is a comparison of human fertility in the corn belt and the cotton belt, the habitations of the greatest portion of America's farmers. One can almost trace the line between them by the sudden change in fertility ratios. In this respect the cotton belt resembles a young plateau on which the leveling forces of erosion have only lately begun their operations; the corn belt resembles an ancient peneplain, mostly reduced to a very low level, with only here and there some highly resistant formation breaking the monotony with a slight elevation. Within the cotton belt there is one association revealed by this map which calls for some elaboration. Compare Figures 15 and 16 with Figures 76 and 77, and the fact is at once apparent that the cotton-plantation areas of the South are characterized by a very low fertility of population. And this raises a host of questions, many of which cannot be answered in the present state of our sociological knowledge but which suggest, at least, that the factory system of agriculture may depress the birth rate in much the same way as the factory system does in industry. In any case it should help to check a once widespread tendency to attribute the high birth rate in the South to the demand for workers on the cotton plantation.[15]

Among rural farm Negroes, the eastern portions of Virginia, North and South Carolina, and the French portion of Louisiana have the highest fertility ratios of any areas where the Negro population is dense. On the other hand, the plantation areas and particularly the Mississippi and Yazoo valley deltas are characterized by low fertility ratios.

The same fundamental relationship is measured in those studies which show an inverse association between fertility and size of the community. One of the best of these is that by Notestein; Figure 17 is reproduced from his valuable contribution.[16]

[15] See, for example, T. J. Woofter, Jr., and others, *Landlord and Tenant on the Cotton Plantation*, Works Progress Administration Research Monograph V, Washington, 1936, pp. xx, 6, and *passim*. For an early challenge to this assumption, see the writer's review of the Woofter monograph in the *American Sociological Review*, II (1937), 441–443.

[16] Frank W. Notestein, "Differential Fertility in the East North Central States," *Milbank Memorial Fund Quarterly*, XVI (1938), 179. See also, for results that

The data presented above suggest another important relationship: Not only is there a much lower rate of reproduction among the population of the cities than among that on the farms, but in the rural districts the fertility of the population seems to decline in proportion to the extent that urban influences are felt. That there

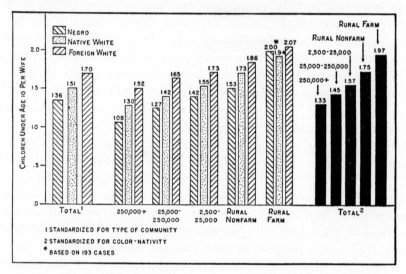

FIGURE 17. Fertility in Relation to Race and Nativity and Residence, East North Central States, 1930. (Reproduced from Frank W. Notestein, "Differential Fertility in the East North Central States," *The Milbank Memorial Fund Quarterly, XVI* [1938], 179.)

is such a relationship between the importance of urban influences as measured by proximity to urban centers and the decrease in the fertility of population is clearly shown by Figure 18. According to these computations presented by the National Resources Committee, seven cities largely of American stock are failing by one-third to replenish the population; all cities of 100,000 or over are doing but slightly better; and all the increase of population, as well as the population to balance the urban deficit, comes from the rural districts, particularly the rural farm population, and most especially the more remotely located segments of the rural farm group.

are essentially similar, Clyde V. Kiser and P. K. Whelpton, "Social and Psychological Factors Affecting Fertility, IX. Fertility Planning and Fertility Rates by Socio-Economic Status," *Milbank Memorial Fund Quarterly,* XXVII (1949), 189; and J. Allan Beegle, *Differential Birth Rates in Michigan,* Michigan AES Special Bulletin 346, East Lansing, 1948, pp. 9–16.

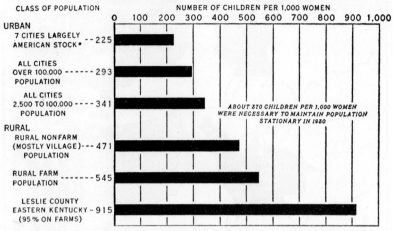

NUMBER OF CHILDREN UNDER 5 YEARS OF AGE PER 1,000 WOMEN
15 TO 45 YEARS OF AGE IN UNITED STATES, APRIL 1, 1930

CLASS OF POPULATION

NUMBER OF CHILDREN PER 1,000 WOMEN

ABOUT 370 CHILDREN PER 1,000 WOMEN WERE NECESSARY TO MAINTAIN POPULATION STATIONARY IN 1930

URBAN
7 CITIES LARGELY AMERICAN STOCK* --225

ALL CITIES OVER 100,000 ------293 POPULATION

ALL CITIES 2,500 TO 100,000 ----341 POPULATION

RURAL
RURAL NONFARM (MOSTLY VILLAGE)---471 POPULATION

RURAL FARM -------545 POPULATION

LESLIE COUNTY EASTERN KENTUCKY -915 (95% ON FARMS)

* PORTLAND (OREGON), SAN FRANCISCO, LOS ANGELES, KANSAS CITY, ST. LOUIS, NASHVILLE, AND ATLANTA

FIGURE 18. Fertility Ratios of the Population in Selected Residential Groups, 1930. (Reproduced from O. E. Baker, "The Effect of Recent Public Policies on the Future Population Prospect," *Rural Sociology*, II [1937], 129.)

The diffusion of the fall in the birth rate also exemplifies this relationship. Settling in the northeastern section of the country about 1800, it has gradually overspread the nation, until now a comparatively low birth rate is characteristic of practically all sections of the country, except a few of the most isolated rural parts of the nation. (See Figure 19.) A study by the Scripps Foundation for Population Research is also of importance in this connection. In an analysis of the areas of sixteen cities, the distance from cities was found to be highly significant in modifying fertility in five areas, significant in four others, and of little or no significance in seven areas. As finally reported, *isolation* and *economic status* were the social and economic factors principally responsible for variations in rural fertility.[17] It should be indicated, however, that such a study suggests that in some areas distance from the city is a fairly reliable index of the strength or weakness of city influences in the countryside; in other areas this is not the case.

There also seems to be an inverse relationship between economic status and the birth rate: as the economic status increases, the fertility of the population decreases. (See Figure 20, based on

[17] Warren S. Thompson and Nelle E. Jackson, "Fertility in Rural Areas in Relation to Their Distance from Cities, 1930," *Rural Sociology*, V (1940), 162.

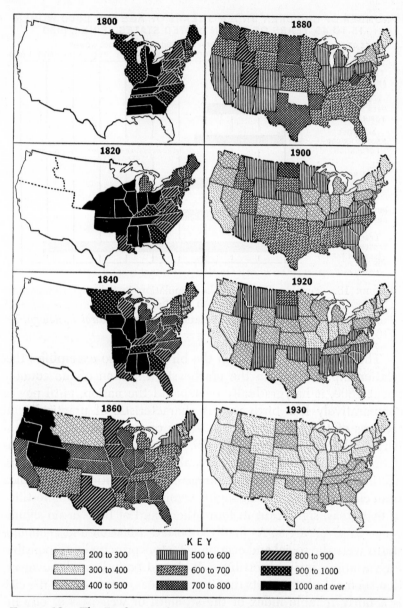

FIGURE 19. The Decline in the Fertility of the White Population of the United States, 1800 to 1930, Showing the Number of White Children Under 5 Years of Age to 1000 White Women 15 to 49 Years of Age. (After O. E. Baker, "The Effect of Recent Public Policies on the Future Population Prospect," *Rural Sociology*, II [1937], 124.)

data from the Census of 1910.) This relationship is particularly striking in the cities.

Among the most thorough of recent studies of the relationships of economic status and fertility is one of Butler County, Ohio, by Warren S. Thompson. With full coöperation from the Bureau of the Census, data from the census files were secured and tabulated in some ingenious ways that brought forth many significant facts relative to differential fertility. Previously it had been almost im-

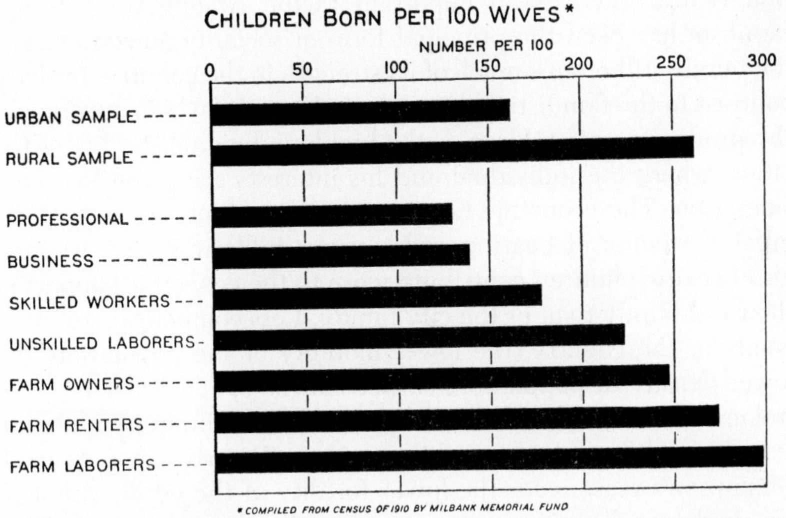

CHILDREN BORN PER 100 WIVES*

NUMBER PER 100

| | 0 | 50 | 100 | 150 | 200 | 250 | 300 |

URBAN SAMPLE -----

RURAL SAMPLE -----

PROFESSIONAL -----

BUSINESS --------

SKILLED WORKERS ---

UNSKILLED LABORERS-

FARM OWNERS------

FARM RENTERS-----

FARM LABORERS ----

* COMPILED FROM CENSUS OF 1910 BY MILBANK MEMORIAL FUND

FIGURE 20. Fertility in Relation to Occupational and Tenure Status, 1910. (Illustration from the Bureau of Agricultural Economics.)

possible to utilize census data bearing on these questions. Thompson's analysis carefully examined the relationship between economic status and fertility in both the rural and the urban portions of the county. Furthermore, it examined this relationship when each of the residential categories had been further subdivided so as to classify the women of the county into "north born" and "south born." A concise statement of results is given in the following quotation: "The findings of this study on the relation of economic status, as measured by family rentals, to average number of children can be summed up very briefly by saying that there was a very close and consistent inverse relation between them— the higher the economic status the lower the average number of children."[18]

[18] Warren S. Thompson, *Average Number of Children per Woman in Butler County, Ohio: 1930—A Study in Differential Fertility*, Washington, Bureau of the Census, 1941, p. 9.

Factors

Sorokin, Zimmerman, and Galpin attribute the higher birth rate of the country to a series of factors, including religion and the traditional mores, especially as exemplified in the Biblical injunction "multiply and replenish the earth," etc. According to these writers, cities have freed themselves to a considerable extent of such an attitude, while the country has not. The family organization is also cited as an important factor. Among rural groups familism has been the principal form of social organization, and the family still retains much of its strength in the country. In sharp contrast to the familistic nature of rural society, which encourages the production of children, is the highly individualistic life of the cities, where the individual and his interests are given first consideration. The economic factor is also important, because of the greater expense of bearing and rearing children in the city, and also because children contribute more to the economic support of the rural family than of the city family. Less competition of other wants in the country, the lower mobility of the population, the lower density of population, earlier marriage, and less birth control are also listed as factors to explain why the country population is more prolific in bearing children than the urban population.[19] Thompson's reasons for the lower fertility of the cities, although couched in different terms, are essentially the same as those of Sorokin, Zimmerman, and Galpin. He does stress, with much justification, the matter of ideals, i.e., standards of success; and he maintains that city folk measure these largely in terms of levels of consumption, that children may be nothing but a hindrance to the attaining of urban success. In the country much the same standards exist, but they do "not militate so strongly against raising a family of fair size as in the city."[20]

Before leaving this subject attention should be called to the findings of two other important studies. One by McKain and Whetten shows definitely that the size of family is positively related to the homogeneity of the individuals making up the married pair. Likeness of the mates with respect to fundamental social

[19] P. A. Sorokin, Carle C. Zimmerman, and Charles J. Galpin, *A Systematic Source Book in Rural Sociology*, Minneapolis, University of Minnesota Press, 1932, III, 141–144; cf. Sorokin and Zimmerman, *op. cit.*, pp. 216–220.

[20] Warren S. Thompson, *Ratio of Women to Children, 1920*, Census Monograph XI, Washington, Government Printing Office, 1931, pp. 131–132.

traits makes for larger families, a fact of no little significance in interpreting the higher fertility of rural areas.[21] Another study by Clyde V. Kiser shows that fertility within northern cities was about the same for recent migrants, both white and Negro, from the rural areas of the South as for city-born of corresponding race. This indicates definitely that the low fertility is a function of urban life and not, as sometimes asserted, of migration.[22]

The tremendous fall in the birth rate in the United States which took place between 1800 and 1936 certainly was among the greatest forces shaping our society; and the recent upswing in the rate of reproduction must be reckoned as among the most significant developments in our atomic age. Every recess of our social structure and every detail of our social processes is influenced by the fact that the number of births in this country has been well above 3,500,000 every year from 1947 through 1952, and not less than 2,100,000, as was the case every year from 1932 through 1937.

Although only recently have the data on births in the United States become sufficiently good to make their use advisable, by means of the fertility ratio it is possible to trace the course of the rate of reproduction in this country from 1810 to 1950. (See Figure 21.) This index fell from 98 children under five to 100 women sixteen to forty-four in 1810, to 34 in 1940. This decline of the fertility of the population to some 38 percent of its 1810 level was brought about by an almost continuous reduction from decade to decade. By 1950, however, the trend definitely had been reversed and the fertility ratio had risen to a level of 50. That is, the birth rate between 1945 and 1950 was back to about its 1915–1920 level.

It is important to note that in the first forty years of the twentieth century the fall in the rural birth rate was much less precipitous than the decline in the urban rate. Thus in 1910 the ratio of children under five to white women fifteen to forty-nine stood at 55 in the rural farm districts, as compared with 34 in the urban areas; but in 1940 the corresponding ratios were 22 and 40, respec-

[21] Walter C. McKain and N. L. Whetten, "Size of Family in Relation to Homogeneity of Parental Traits," *Rural Sociology*, I (1936), 26; and William H. Sewell and Robert L. Fisher, "Size of Farm Family in Relation to Homogeneity of Parental Traits," *Rural Sociology*, VIII (1943), 73–76.

[22] See "Birth Rates Among Rural Migrants in Cities," *Milbank Memorial Fund Quarterly*, XVI (1938), 369–381. But these findings should not cause the relationship between residential shifting and fertility to be overlooked. Within a homogeneous rural environment a tendency for fertility to vary directly with residential instability has been observed. Cf. Homer L. Hitt and Reed H. Bradford, "The Relation of Residential Instability to Fertility," *Rural Sociology*, V (1940), 88–92.

tively,[23] the changes representing a fall of only 28 percent in the rural districts as compared with 34 percent in the urban. However, from 1940 to 1950 the recovery was more pronounced in the urban areas than in the rural districts. Thus increase from an index of 48 children under five to 100 women aged fifteen to forty-four in

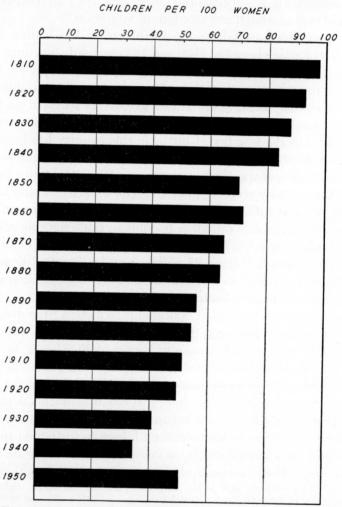

FIGURE 21. Trends in the Number of Children Under Five per 1000 Women Sixteen to Forty-Four in the United States, 1810–1950.

[23] See Bureau of the Census, *Sixteenth Census of the United States: 1940,* "Population, Differential Fertility 1940 and 1910, Fertility for States and Large Cities," Washington, Government Printing Office, 1943, Tables 7 and 8, pp. 21–22.

the rural farm population in 1940 to one of 60 in 1950 was a gain of only 25 percent, whereas the corresponding change from 26 to 44 in the urban population was a 69 percent increase. Similarly, a comparison of birth rates per 1000 women aged fifteen to forty-four in 1940 with those in 1949 shows that the urban rate rose from 67.8 to 102.4, a gain of 51 percent in the nine years, whereas the rural rate increased from 98.7 to 122.8, a change of only 24 percent in the corresponding period.[24]

When the birth rate in the United States first began to move upward, about 1940, many persons attributed this rise entirely to young people's rushing into marriage before the boys were inducted into the armed forces. It should not be forgotten, however, that the small crop of babies during World War I was in the most fertile ages during the middle thirties, while the large crop which followed demobilization began entering the stage of high age-specific birth rates along about 1940. In other words, the small proportion of persons aged twenty to twenty-four (women aged twenty to twenty-four give birth to about 32 percent of all babies born in the United States) depressed the birth rate about 1937–1938, whereas the high percentage in these ages following 1940 caused it to soar.[25] After the men returned from service in World War II the number of babies born in a single year in this country reached the all-time high of 3,876,000 in 1947.

[24] "Births by Race and by Rural and Urban Areas," p. 54.
[25] For the data, see Bureau of the Census, *Vital Statistics—Special Reports,* XXII (1945), 5–7.

8

MORTALITY

Mortality is the second of the all-important vital processes of society to receive attention in this book. Measures of mortality are the principal indexes available for indicating progress in the application of medical and sanatory science to the welfare of mankind. Registration of deaths began in the United States in 1900, somewhat earlier than the registration of births, probably because more people, and especially the life insurance companies, were interested in having complete and reliable information on deaths. Even so the United States was far behind other nations of the Western world in this important item of national bookkeeping; the registration of deaths in England dates back to 1836, when reports of the cause of deaths as well as the occurrence of the fatality were first required.[1] Registration of deaths in the United States was first enforced by the states of Massachusetts and New Jersey. Out of the experiences of these two states came the first death registration area in the nation, established in 1880 and comprising in addition to the states of Massachusetts and New Jersey certain cities in several other states.[2]

In spite of this early training, national registration began in earnest with the establishment of the original death registration

[1] Sir Arthur Newsholme, *The Elements of Vital Statistics*, New York, D. Appleton-Century Company, 1924, p. 156.

[2] See John W. Trask, *Vital Statistics*, Supplement 12 to *The Public Health Reports*, Washington, 1914, p. 53. It should also be mentioned that during the colonial period a beginning was made in securing vital statistics, i.e., records of births and deaths. In 1632 the Grand Assembly of Virginia passed a law requiring a minister or warden from every parish to present at court on June 1 of every year a register of all burials, christenings, and marriages. The Massachusetts Bay Colony adopted an ordinance in 1639 requiring the recording of births, deaths, and marriages, and the Plymouth Colony enacted much the same requirement in the recording of data on birth, deaths, and marriages. *Ibid.*, p. 18.

area embracing ten states—Maine, New Hampshire, Vermont, Massachusetts, Rhode Island, Connecticut, New York, New Jersey, Michigan, and Indiana—and the District of Columbia. In these states the registration of deaths began before work was commenced on the Census of 1900. To this original area state after state has been added until by 1933, with the addition of Texas, all the states in the Union were regularly reporting both deaths and births to the Bureau of Public Health.

So important are these data that strenuous attempts are made to secure complete registration of deaths. The model law prepared by the federal authorities and enacted in the various states of the registration area provides that no corpse may be disposed of, or held for "more than 72 hours after death unless a permit for burial, removal, or other disposition thereof shall have been properly issued by the local registrar of the registration district in which the death occurred or the body was found. And no such burial or removal permit shall be issued by any registrar until, wherever practicable, a complete and satisfactory certificate of death has been filed with him."[3] Despite all this, demographers are handicapped by the lack of reliable data concerning the mortality of the population.[4] Just as is the case with births, there are the fundamental difficulties (1) of underregistration, especially in the rural areas, and (2) of failure to allocate deaths according to residence. Willcox seems to have demonstrated conclusively that a good proportion of the deaths have not been recorded in some of the more sparsely populated states such as North Dakota and Arizona.[5] Formerly the failure in most instances to allocate deaths, especially those occurring in institutions, to the areas where the deceased persons formerly resided gave rise to much misunderstanding. For example, the city of New Orleans showed a crude death rate of 16.2 per 1000 in 1930; but when nonresident deaths were omitted (New Orleans contains a large state-supported hospital and several private hospitals) the rate was reduced to 13.4.[6] For

[3] See *ibid.;* cf. Walter F. Willcox, *Introduction to the Vital Statistics of the United States, 1900–1930,* Washington, Government Printing Office, 1933, p 14.

[4] For a careful analysis of the reliability of death data in the United States, see Willcox, *op. cit.,* pp. 16–25.

[5] *Ibid.,* pp. 16, 19, 97.

[6] See Mary Byrd, *"Factors Influencing the Death Rates in Louisiana,"* M. A. thesis (unpublished), Louisiana State University, 1934, p. 24. Similarly, 14.4 percent of all deaths occurring in Syracuse, New York, during the years 1924–1929 were those of nonresidents. See Elliot H. Pennell, "Death of Non-residents in Syracuse," *Milbank Memorial Fund Quarterly,* X (1932), 215.

the state of Ohio, Harold F. Dorn studied the effects upon the rural and urban mortality rates of allocating the nonresident deaths. According to his results, in 1930 the rural rate in Ohio would have been considerably increased and the urban rate significantly decreased had the statistics been tabulated on the basis of residence rather than place of death.[7] The National Office of Vital Statistics has now recognized the necessity of tabulating births and deaths by place of residence as well as by place of occurrence, thereby adding greatly to the value of the data.[8]

In addition to such errors in the death data themselves, there is also the necessity of carefully standardizing the populations for age and sex as well as race, before one can make valid comparisons of rural and urban mortality rates. In this respect, however, comparisons of mortality are not likely to miss the mark as far as do comparisons of fertility. For births the under-enumeration in the rural areas combines with an abnormal age and sex distribution to make the fertility of the rural population appear to be much below the actual rate of reproduction. Failure to recognize these shortcomings in the data has vitiated the results of practically all the rural and urban comparisons that have been made. But for mortality the effects of the under-enumeration of deaths in rural areas are offset by the consequences of the same abnormal age and sex distribution. The reason, of course, is that the ages which are most favorable to the production of children, and which are overrepresented in the urban population, are also the ages of low mortality, whereas the ages unfavorable to reproduction, the ages overrepresented in the country, are the ages of high mortality. Because the city has an excess and the country a deficiency of middle-aged persons, comparisons of rural-urban death rates, based upon the crude data, are much more reliable than comparisons of rural-urban fertility, based upon the crude birth rates. However, the great differential between the mortality rates of whites and Negroes, and the concentration of the latter in the rural portions of the South make necessary added precautions on that account. It

[7] Harold F. Dorn, "The Effect of Allocation of Non-Resident Deaths upon Official Mortality Statistics," *Journal of the American Statistical Association,* XXVII (1932), 401–412.

[8] See the excellent discussion in Forest E. Linder and Robert D. Grove, *Vital Statistics Rates in the United States, 1900–1940,* Washington, Government Printing Office, 1943, pp. 15–18.

is not valid to compare rural and urban mortality without making the comparisons separately for the two major races. Rarely does one find a research report which has made proper corrections or allowances for these differences.

In spite of the fact that death rates are more reliable than birth rates, the study of mortality is probably not so fully developed as the study of fertility. So far no index of mortality has been derived from the decennial census data which serves the purpose in the study of mortality that is filled by the fertility ratio in the study of fertility.

Turning now to the indexes used in measuring mortality, we mention the two principal ones: (1) the death rate and (2) the life table. The concept of a death rate is exactly comparable to the birth rate and requires no elaboration. Because mortality is particularly heavy among babies and old folks, and because both of these are more important in the rural than in the urban population, standardized rates are necessary for accurate comparisons of rural-urban mortality. And, as suggested above, if reliable rural and urban comparisons are to be made, it is absolutely essential to correct the data further for differences in race. This correction is necessary because there is such a striking difference in the mortality of whites and Negroes, the crude rate in 1949 being 9.5 and 11.1 for whites and nonwhites (mostly Negroes), respectively,[9] and because the Negroes are concentrated in the rural districts of the South. As in most other fields of study, detailed information is essential and specific death rates are of great usefulness in the field of demography.

All in all, the life expectation table is probably the most useful yardstick available for the study of mortality. Theoretically, life tables indicate the duration of life of persons born at the same time. The life table irons out differences due to the various conditioning factors that influence the death rate, applies the facts of mortality for the whole life span, and supplies the resulting expected average longevity for the individual members of the group. Unlike the death rate, the life table does not tempt the novice to invalid comparisons, for it is based upon all the specific death rates of the population. Life tables show merely the average number of

[9] "Deaths by Race and by Urban and Rural Areas: United States, Each Division and State, 1949," *Vital Statistics—Special Reports*, XXXVI (1952), 176.

years that the individuals of any given age from birth on up may expect to live; they constitute an easily understood and accurate measure of mortality.

In a stationary population, i.e., one in which the number of births just equals the number of deaths and in which the age distribution is solely dependent upon mortality rates, the death rate is the reciprocal of the expectation of life. For example, an expectation of life of sixty years would mean a death rate of 16.7 per 1000. In such a stationary population every child born would have to live an average of eighty years in order for the death rate to be as low as 12.5 per 1000. Thus the 1949 rate of 9.7 in the United States was possible only because the population is growing rapidly and this growth concentrates persons in the younger and in the middle age groups, in which specific death rates are low.

Since the mortality of males and females differs considerably it is customary to construct separate life tables for each of the sexes. If the factors of race and residence are also taken into account and tables constructed for rural white males, urban white males, rural colored males, urban colored males, etc., the data are sufficiently refined to make for a higher degree of dependability and usefulness. Of course the discrepancies in the original data will be reflected in the final results; but given accurate data, the life expectation is the most satisfactory method of comparing the mortality of different populations or of the same population at different times.

Rural-Urban Mortality

Some of the most suggestive early work on the mortality rates in rural and urban districts was done in Germany by the scholars Ammon and Hansen. Ammon early reached the conclusion that the rate at which a city population disappears is much more rapid than might be popularly supposed. Carefully studying two small German cities (Karlsruhe and Freiburg), he found that descendants of a given population in these cities constituted only 29 percent of the second generation and only 15 percent of the third generation. He came to the conclusion that, on the average, families moving from the country to the city die out in the course of two generations.[10] Hansen found that approximately one-half of a

[10] Otto Ammon, *Die natürliche Auslese beim Menschen*, Jena, G. Fisher, 1893, p. 300.

given city's population was born in the country, and concluded that the city population renews itself in two generations.[11] The results of both these investigations indicate that only through the constant supply of migrants which the city attracts from the country is it able to offset its own high mortality rate and keep up its population.

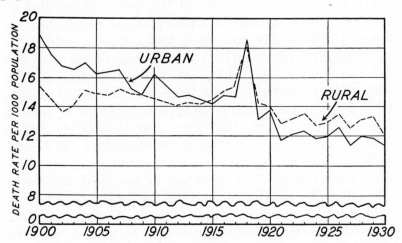

FIGURE 22.   Death Rates in Urban (10,000-over) and Rural Districts of the Death Registration States of 1900, 1900–1930. (After Walter F. Willcox, *Introduction to the Vital Statistics of the United States 1900–1930*, Washington, Government Printing Office, 1933, p. 25.)

For the United States it is well to begin with mortality statistics from the registration area. The crude death rates for the rural (under 10,000 inhabitants) and urban portions of the original death registration states for the period 1900 to 1930 are presented in Figure 22. Making no allowances for differences in the age and sex make-up of the populations, we see that, whereas the rural rate was considerably below the urban rate in 1900, by 1930 the situation was reversed and the urban rate was slightly below the rural. In interpreting these rates and changes, it should again be emphasized that the age and sex composition of the populations tends to overrate the rural index and underrate the urban, but that, on the other hand, incompleteness of registration may have slightly underrated the rural figure, even though this is not so likely to be the case in the states having the longest experience in registration. But no allowance has been made for race differences, and it is un-

[11] Georg Hansen, *Die drei Bevölkerungstuffen*, Munich, Lindauer, 1889, p. 27.

safe to generalize too quickly and conclude that urban districts have lower mortality of population than rural districts. Furthermore, the author has encountered so many pitfalls in his efforts to compare rural and urban mortality over a period of time that he believes it almost impossible to make a fair comparison of such trends until our statistical data are greatly improved.

The findings of Thompson and Whelpton indicate that the death rate is lower in rural areas than in urban. Basing their conclusions largely on life expectation tables, they assert that "the more rural the division and the more dependent upon agriculture the longer the expectation of life."[12] Unfortunately, there are as yet no life tables for 1950 that enable us to check the current accuracy of this generalization, and it is not likely that any will be available in the near future. But for 1901, 1910, 1930, and 1939 the data are sufficiently detailed to permit significant comparisons. "Sufficiently detailed," in this case, means separate tables for females and males, further subdivided according to race, and still further broken down by residential categories. In Table 3 have been assembled data illustrative in general of the rural-urban differentials in mortality, to the extent that these can be gauged by the life expectation tables. Such materials would seem to be the most satisfactory data for comparing rural and urban mortality, and they certainly favor the conclusion of Thompson and Whelpton. The same is true of the somewhat more detailed 1939 materials, which give a life expectation at birth of 61.6 for white males in cities of 100,000 or more, 61.4 in other urban places, and 64.1 in rural areas; the corresponding values for females are 66.3, 66.2, and 67.7 in the cities of 100,000 or more, other urban places, and rural territory, respectively.[13]

The most satisfactory mortality data are those compiled by the National Resources Committee in their inclusive study of population problems. For the year 1930 they prepared life tables for both males and females for each state in the Union except Texas. In order to get an overall view of the fluctuations of mortality in the United States, the data of these tables have been utilized in the preparation of Figures 23 and 24. These charts show the variations

[12] Warren S. Thompson and P. K. Whelpton, *Population Trends in the United States,* New York, McGraw-Hill Book Company, 1933, p. 241.
[13] National Office of Vital Statistics, "United States Abridged Life Tables, 1939: Urban and Rural by Regions, Color, and Sex," *Vital Statistics—Special Reports,* XXIII (1947), 314.

in life expectancy throughout the nation; they are prepared in a manner that easily permits the comparison of the situation in any state with the national average.

From the standpoint of rural-urban mortality and longevity, several pertinent observations can be made from these charts.

TABLE 3. Expectation of Life of the White Population of the Original Registration Area, by Residence and Sex, 1901, 1910, and 1930

		Expectation of Life (Years)	
Year	Sex	Cities	Rural Parts
At Birth			
1901	Males	43.97	54.03
	Females	47.90	55.41
1910	Males	47.32	55.06
	Females	51.39	57.35
1930	Males	56.73	62.09
	Females	61.05	65.09
At Age 20			
1901	Males	39.13	45.95
	Female	41.86	46.09
1910	Males	36.54	42.06
	Females	39.46	42.95
1930	Males	44.20	48.32
	Females	47.35	50.37
At Age 40			
1901	Males	25.32	30.52
	Females	27.30	31.23
1910	Males	25.32	30.20
	Females	27.88	31.15
1930	Males	27.33	31.47
	Females	30.34	33.19
At Age 60			
1901	Males	12.80	15.54
	Females	14.05	16.30
1910	Males	12.68	15.23
	Females	14.04	15.93
1930	Males	13.44	15.98
	Females	15.37	16.98

Data from James W. Glover, *United States Life Tables 1890, 1901, 1910, and 1901–1910* (Washington, 1921); and *Statistical Bulletin of the Metropolitan Life Insurance Company*, XVI (1935), 2. Cities in 1901 refers to municipalities containing 8000 or more inhabitants, in 1910 and 1930 to those with 10,000 or more residents. The states included in the original registration area are: Maine, New Hampshire, Vermont, Massachusetts, Rhode Island, Connecticut, New York, New Jersey, Indiana, and Michigan. The District of Columbia is also included.

First, the expectation of life among both males and females in the most highly industrialized and urbanized states is consistently below the national average, whereas the rural sections, on the whole, make a very good showing. Second, the southern Rocky Mountain area has the lowest expectation of life. This condition immediately

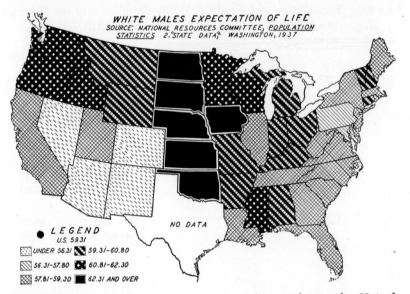

FIGURE 23.   Expectation of Life Among White Males in the United States, 1930.

suggests the necessity of the utmost caution in the interpretation of life tables as well as death rates. To these areas annually come thousands in quest of health, which artificially reduces life expectation in these sections and increases it in the states of origin. From intimate acquaintance of this area the writer knows that a good share of the health seekers are from the cities of the Northeast.[14] Third, expectation of life is highest in the great Mississippi Valley and the northern Pacific Coast. Perhaps the superiority of the "Plains" states from North Dakota to Oklahoma is partially due to the movement of ailing persons from the area, but this migration would have to be very large indeed to account for all the difference. All factors taken into consideration, these charts reveal that mortality in rural areas compares favorably with that in urban districts.

The South generally makes the least favorable showing of any

[14] Cf. Louis I. Dublin and Alfred J. Lotka, *Length of Life*, New York, The Ronald Press Company, 1936, pp. 90–93.

rural portion. Studies in limited areas which indicate a tendency for the mortality of whites to correlate positively with the percentage of Negroes in the population suggest that the presence of large numbers of Negroes in the rural South has a very unfavora-

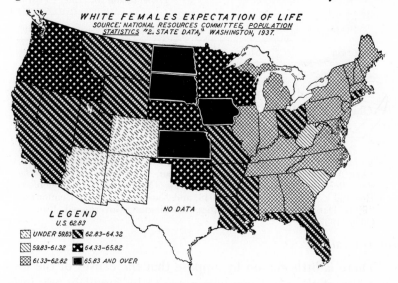

FIGURE 24. Expectation of Life Among White Females in the United States, 1930.

ble influence upon the mortality of whites in the region. And if this proposition is valid, then the maintaining of better health and living conditions for Negroes is of vital importance to the South's white population.

Particularly important in the study of rural-urban differentials in mortality are the life tables for three states in which the computations were prepared in sufficient detail to enable valid comparisons to be made. The states are Georgia, Mississippi, and Ohio, and the necessary detail mentioned is the materials subdivided according to sex for both the rural and urban populations further classified according to race. From these three important compilations some of the more significant values are presented in Table 4. As is the case with the national data, they all indicate that the expectation of life in rural areas is somewhat higher than that in urban centers.[15]

[15] See also C. A. McMahan, "Rural-Urban Differentials in Longevity," in T. Lynn Smith and C. A. McMahan, *The Sociology of Urban Life: A Textbook with Readings*, New York, The Dryden Press, Inc., 1951, pp. 280–289; J. Lambert Molyneaux, "Differential Mortality in Texas," *American Sociological Review*, X (1945), 17–25; J. Lambert Molyneaux, *Differential Mortality in Virginia*, Char-

TABLE 4.   Expectation of Life at Birth Among the White Population of Georgia and Mississippi in 1940–1941 and Ohio in 1930

		Expectation of Life (Years)	
State	Sex	Rural	Urban
Georgia	Males	64.1	58.1
	Females	69.4	65.9
Mississippi	Males	64.0	57.2
	Females	67.7	65.1
Ohio	Males	62.8	60.1
	Females	64.1	63.6

Data from C. A. McMahan, *Georgia Life Tables by Sex, Race, and Residence*, Atlanta, Georgia Department of Public Health (mimeograped), 1950; Vernon Davies and John C. Belcher, *Mississippi Life Tables by Sex, Race and Residence, 1940*, Jackson, Mississippi Commission on Hospital Care, (mimeograped), 1948; and National Resources Committee, "State Data," *Population Statistics*, Washington, Government Printing Office, 1937.

Interpretation

There is little reason to suppose that the causes of the lower mortality of the rural population are to be found in any innate factors differentiating the rural from the urban population. No evidence so far brought forth supports such a contention, and such biological interpretations, which someone has referred to as "the lazy man's explanation," should not be resorted to unless there are undisputable evidences favoring them. Neither will economic factors, the prevalence of medical care or hygienic facilities be of any assistance, for their operation is all in favor of the urban groups. Furthermore, the size of the birth rate, which has a high positive correlation with the magnitude of the death rate, would by itself make the mortality of the country outstrip that of the city. For these reasons, in explaining the lower mortality of the country it is necessary to seek other factors in the rural world, factors which are not only potent enough to account for the observed differences in rural and urban mortality but also strong enough to

lottesville, University of Virginia, 1947, pp. 9–24; Louise Kemp and T. Lynn Smith, *Health and Mortality in Louisiana*, Louisiana AES Bulletin 390, Baton Rouge, 1945; Homer L. Hitt and Alvin L. Bertrand, *Social Aspects of Hospital Planning*, Baton Rouge, Louisiana Agricultural Experiment Station and the Office of the Governor, 1947, pp. 2–4; John N. Burrus, *Life Opportunities*, Oxford, University of Mississippi, 1951, pp. 15–18; and John C. Belcher and Morton B. King, Jr., *Mississippi's People*, Oxford, University of Mississippi, 1950, pp. 30–32.

offset the effects of the influences mentioned above which operate in a manner favoring low mortality in urban areas, high mortality in rural districts. Sorokin and Zimmerman gave this problem careful consideration and enumerated the following important factors in the situation: (1) low density of population in the country, which is especially important in connection with mortality from infectious diseases; (2) the greater integrity of the rural family, and especially the influence of maternal care of the child which is exercised in the rural family; (3) the outdoor work of the rural population, which enables rural people to secure an abundance of fresh air and sunshine and plenty of physical exercise in the performance of farm tasks; (4) the peace of mind associated with rural life; and (5) the better adaptation of the human organism to the rural surroundings in which it has evolved, as contrasted with the artificial surroundings of the city, to which the human species is a comparative stranger.[16]

Infant Mortality

Infant mortality deserves attention apart from the general consideration which has been given to the subject of mortality: (1) It is by itself such a large factor in the magnitude of the death rate; (2) the saving of infant lives is largely responsible for the recent great decrease in the death rate or the prolongation of life; (3) so much still remains to be done, especially in rural areas, to reduce still further the proportion of deaths among very young children; and (4) as Sir Arthur Newsholme has stated, "infant mortality is the most sensitive index of social welfare and sanitary improvements which we possess."[17] Or, as Whipple has said, "People who will not take care of their offspring will not take care of themselves."[18]

The mortality rates of infants are calculated differently from the way in which other death rates are secured. In computing the infant mortality rate, the number of deaths of children less than one year of age forms the dividend; the number of live births registered in the period of one year, the divisor. For a group in

[16] P. A. Sorokin and Carle C. Zimmerman, *Principles of Rural-Urban Sociology,* New York, Henry Holt & Company, 1929, p. 204; cf. P. A. Sorokin, Carle C. Zimmerman, and Charles J. Galpin, *A Systematic Source Book in Rural Sociology,* Minneapolis, University of Minnesota Press, 1932, III, 134–135.

[17] Quoted in George C. Whipple, *Vital Statistics,* New York, John Wiley & Sons, Inc., 1923, p. 393.

[18] *Ibid.*

which any large proportion of the births go unregistered, as has been shown to be the case in rural America or Negro America, this procedure will make the resulting ratio too high. For the same reason, any marked improvement in registration will make the infant mortality rate appear to fall even though there is no change in the actual rate of mortality. Both of these possibilities must be kept in mind in interpreting the data for the United States. Especially should it be remembered that the reported rates in rural districts and the rates for Negroes in general are too high, while at the same time, because births were not allocated according to the residence of the mother prior to 1935, some urban rates are likely to have been underestimated.[19] Trustworthy infant mortality statistics in the United States are a recent development.

In modern times infant mortality has fallen rapidly in the Western world. Swedish data going back to 1750 reveal a rate of over 200, compared with 20.5 for the year 1950.[20] Data for the United States do not go back very far. However, since they have become available, there has been a significant decline in the infant mortality rate, this ratio falling in the registration area from 94 in 1917 to 29.2 in 1950.[21] The rates for whites and other races, respectively, were 91 and 151 in 1917, and 30 and 47 in 1950. In 1917 the urban rate was 100, considerably higher than the rate of 88 that was recorded in the rural parts of the registration area. As time has passed, great improvements have been made, especially in the urban areas; and in 1948 the urban rate stood at 31.2, the rural at 33.1. The differential may be purely a fictitious one brought about by the underregistration of rural births.[22]

Although the official data indicate that the infant mortality rates of both whites and nonwhites are now slightly higher in rural than in urban areas, it is unlikely that such is actually the case. The differences reported are slight, with the 1948 rates being as

[19] See the importance of this factor in Dorothy G. Wiehl, "The Correction of Infant Mortality Rates for Residence," *American Journal of Public Health*, XIX (1929), 495–510.

[20] See the data in Whipple, *op. cit.*, p. 400; and United Nations, *Demographic Yearbook, 1951*, New York, United Nations, 1952, p. 335.

[21] See Linder and Grove, *op. cit.*, Table 26, pp. 572–573; and United Nations, *op. cit.*, p. 329.

[22] For the period 1920 to 1930 some estimate of the importance of this factor is possible. The writer and C. L. Folse have estimated that 14 percent of the reported decline in infant mortality between 1920 and 1930 was due to better registration of births.

follows: 30.8 for rural whites, 29.3 for urban whites; 47.6 for rural nonwhites, and 45.6 for urban nonwhites.[23] However, the poorer registration of births in the rural districts, which has the effect of inflating the infant mortality rates, is probably the entire explanation of the differences.

[23] National Office of Vital Statistics, "Infant Mortality by Race and by Urban and Rural Areas," *Vital Statistics—Special Reports*, XXXV (1950), 305.

9

MIGRATION

Migration, or the movement of people from one place to another, is of great social significance. This is especially true of present-day migrations. In preagricultural times, for the most part, migrations were by groups, and the movement from one place to another did not bring about wholesale disruption of social relationships. But among sedentary people the shifting of residence from one locality to another means the disruption of almost all other social ties.

Most advanced peoples and cultures take for granted permanent residence and a settled mode of living. But it should not be forgotten that there are other modes of life than the sedentary, and that they have played important roles in world history. The student of rural society can learn much from the fascinating study of nomadic and pastoral societies and the great migrations of ancient times, when surges of barbarians poured into areas where the sedentary habits of the people had induced great advancement in culture or civilization. The repeated overrunning of the highly developed cultures of the "Fertile Crescent" between the Tigris and the Euphrates by the more barbaric tribes from the deserts has a peculiar interest for us because of its intricate relation to our own cultural heritage. Old Testament stories tell much about the subjection of the sedentary and agricultural Canaanites in the western portion of the "Fertile Crescent" by the Hebrews, a group of half-savage nomads who followed a pastoral life, driving their flocks from one oasis to another.[1] A thousand years later the Roman possessions were overrun by barbarians from the north, and

[1] Cf. Lewis Browne, *This Believing World,* New York, The Macmillan Company, 1926, pp. 223–225.

the chronicles of this mass migration still hold a prominent place in the minds of the people. With the emergence of national states and a rather general adoption of fixed abodes, the nature of migration has been changed, but it has not lost its importance as one of the significant forces in social life.[2]

The subject of migration is a large one, and its many subdivisions are not of equal concern to the student of rural society. For example, emigration and immigration are large questions calling for specialized treatment by themselves. For rural sociology four phases of migration seem to be especially significant: (1) the interchange of population between rural and urban areas, including both the movement from farms to cities and the back-to-the-land migrations; (2) interstate migrations and especially the migratory currents which carry populations to the rural portions; (3) farm-to-farm movements; and (4) the constant stream of migratory agricultural laborers flowing in many well-defined currents from one section of the country to another.[3] We shall discuss only these four aspects in this chapter, although in their ramifications they involve many other phases of the general subject.[4]

The interchange of population between rural and urban areas includes both the rural-urban migrations and the movement from cities to farms. These seem to be among the most basic processes in our social metabolism. Migration from the farms to cities is probably an indispensable concomitant to urban life. It has been well said that cities are "kinds of colonies that the country districts are obliged to repeople every year. . . ."[5]

[2] Rupert B. Vance, in his *Research Memorandum on Population Redistribution in the United States,* Social Science Research Council Bulletin 42, New York, 1938, pp. 85–134, has given a penetrating analysis of the present social significance of migration within the United States. One of the better analyses of the types of migrations and their causes is to be found in O. D. Duncan, *The Theory and Consequences of Mobility of Farm Population,* Oklahoma AES Circular 88, Stillwater, 1940.

[3] Cf. Carl C. Taylor, Helen W. Wheeler, and E. L. Kirkpatrick, *Disadvantaged Classes in American Agriculture,* Social Research Report VIII, Washington, 1938, pp. 71–76.

[4] No consideration will be given here to annual migrations of herdsmen in well-defined routes in search of water and grass for their flocks, although in several western states these are of considerable significance. We lack studies of these movements comparable to Julius Klein's *The Mesta: A Study in Spanish Economic History, 1273–1836,* Cambridge, Harvard University Press, 1920.

[5] "Population," *L'encyclopédie,* quoted in P. A. Sorokin, Carle C. Zimmerman, and Charles J. Galpin, *A Systematic Source Book in Rural Sociology,* Minneapolis, University of Minnesota Press, 1932, III, 545. Early in the seventeenth century John Graunt observed that burials exceeded christenings in the City of London and reasoned as follows: "From this single Observation it will follow, That London

The movement from cities to farms, whether it be a "back-to-the-land movement" or a backwash of disabled and superannuated employees sloughed off by urban industries and trades seeking a haven of refuge in the land, is also fraught with much social significance. The interchange of farm population between the states

FIGURE 25.   An Important Chapter in the Story of Migratory Agricultural Labor in the United States. (From *Harper's Weekly*, 1890.)

is of considerable importance, more so historically than at the present moment, although recent developments are again bringing this into the limelight. The movement stage by stage in early days of farmers from the hills of the Carolinas, Georgia, and Alabama to the upland portions of Mississippi, Arkansas, Louisiana, Texas, and Oklahoma must be understood for a correct interpretation of the culture and problems of the present-day South. Likewise the settlement of the river bottoms and deltas by large-scale operators from the eastern seaboard with their retinues of slaves must be

---

should have decreased its people; the contrary whereof we see by its daily increase of Buildings upon new Foundations, and by the turning of great palacious Houses into small Tenements. It is therefore certain that London is supplied with people from out of the country, whereby not only to supply the overplus or difference of burials above-mentioned, but likewise to increase its Inhabitants, according to the said increase of housing." *Natural and Political Observations Made upon Bills of Mortality* (4th impression), Oxford, 1665, p. 84.

known for the proper evaluation of state, regional, and even county contrasts in much of the South. During the 1930's the infiltration of agriculturists from the South into the neighboring midwestern and western states awakened anxiety in certain quarters.[6] Whether the movement took place far in the past or is oc-

Figure 26.   Migratory Laborers in the Wheat Fields of the Great Plains. (From *Harper's Weekly*.)

curring at the present time, the source from which the rural population is derived is basic to all attempts to understand the social organization and structure, the social processes, or the social and cultural evolution of rural society. Facts regarding the backgrounds of the population are elemental in all special surveys of rural areas. The fourth general type of migration, the movement of seasonal or migratory farm laborers, has only recently begun to receive the attention it deserves. Long important in the production of fruits and truck crops, sugar (both beet and cane), and wheat (Figures 25 and 26), migratory labor now bids to become an essential element in the cotton culture complex.

[6] Cf. O. E. Baker, "The Effect of Recent Public Policies on the Future Population Prospect," *Rural Sociology*, II (1937), 140; and Paul H. Landis' discussion of it, p. 142.

Rural-Urban Migration

The annual estimates made by the Division of Farm Population and Rural Life of the United States Department of Agriculture are the most important comprehensive data available on the interchange of population between rural and urban areas. Beginning in 1920 this division has attempted to determine the extent of the flow of population from farms to the cities, towns, and villages of the nation, and also the magnitude of the reverse current. Figure 27 gives the results of these estimates.

During the period from 1922 to 1929 inclusive, more than two million persons annually left the farms of the United States for the cities of the nation. In 1926, when the urbanward tide crested, more than 2,300,000 persons left the farms for the cities. But this is only part of the picture. During the same period millions of people abandoned residence in the cities and moved to farms. However, the outward flow, great as it was, failed to equal the inward tide, and the net gain for the cities amounted to about 700,000 per year. With the onslaught of the great depression, a sharp rise in the movement to farms (1930 to 1932), coupled with a precipitous decline in the number leaving the farms for the cities, reversed the net movement and resulted in a slight excess in favor of the farms during the years 1931 and 1932. Migration from farms to towns and cities remained at a low ebb throughout the 1930's and then, following Pearl Harbor, shot up to the all-time high of nearly two and three-quarter millions during 1942. After this the number fell sharply to a low in 1945 that was below the level for any year following 1920, then recovered somewhat in 1946–1948. Meanwhile the movement to farms from nonfarm territory remained low except for a rather spectacular spurt in 1945, accompanying victory in Europe and the surrender of Japan.

Although the cities which attracted the migrants are located mostly in the North and East, most of the migrants came from the farms of the rural South. (See Figures 28, 29, and 30.) From 1920 to 1930 the farms of Texas alone contributed more than half a million people to urban areas, and in the next five years they gave up 138,000 more. Georgia, in the fifteen-year period, made a net contribution of more than 600,000. South Carolina, Georgia, and Utah delivered the largest percentages of their farm populations to the cities. All through the area north and east of Tennessee (also

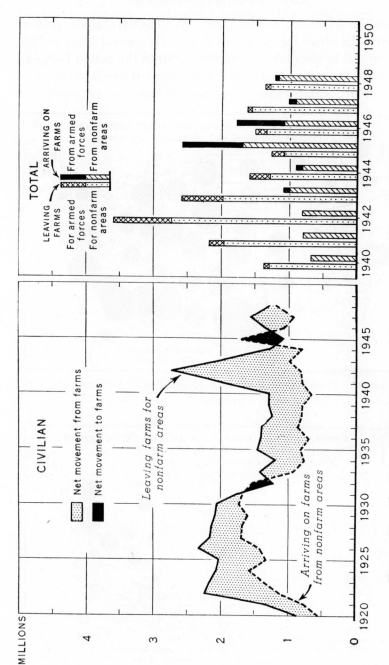

FIGURE 27. The Volume of Migration to and from Farms, 1920 to 1948 (Births and Deaths not Taken into Account). (Data from the Bureau of Agricultural Economics.)

in Florida, Missouri, Oregon, and Washington), more persons deserted the cities for the farms during the period 1930 to 1934 than moved in the opposite direction; but in the cotton belt, and in most of the states west of the Mississippi, the trek to the cities went on in great numbers. The tremendous flow of population

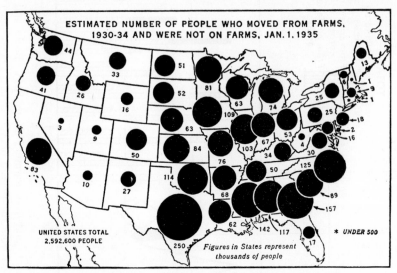

FIGURE 28. Distribution of Movement from Farms, 1930 to 1934. (Illustration from the Bureau of Agricultural Economics.)

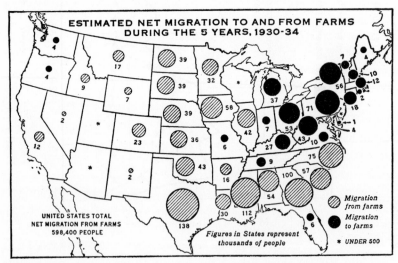

FIGURE 29. Net Flow of Population to and from Farms, 1930 to 1934. (Illustration from the Bureau of Agricultural Economics.)

from the farms of the South, even in a period of great stress (1930–1934), is indicated in Figures 28 and 30.

The charts, particularly Figures 29 and 31, indicate that most of the net movement from cities to farms has been confined to the northeastern portion of the nation. The distribution of all persons who moved from cities to farms between 1935 and 1940 is clearly portrayed in Figure 31.

On the basis of present information concerning migration it is probably valid to generalize somewhat as follows concerning the rural-urban exchange of population. In normal times, i.e., periods similar to the years immediately preceding World War I, when remuneration in agriculture and industry is fairly well balanced, the cityward flow of population carries away the excess natural increase from the rural areas, leaving just about enough to maintain the populations of the various rural areas, taking enough to make up the vital deficit in the cities and to bring about urban growth. In abnormal times, when rural areas are greatly disadvantaged, such as the 1920's in the United States, the appeal of the cities' high industrial wages combines with other lures to attract all the country's natural increase of population and to cut into its reserves as well. In such periods urban growth and rural depopulation go hand in hand. On the other hand, in times of great disorder, distress, upheaval, famine, and disease, people flee the cities. In such periods great alarm is felt for the future of the city; security seems to be found only on the land. In the United States the latest expression of this type of movement occurred during the depth of the great depression in the years 1931–1933, a development which was checked only by strenuous governmental efforts through the Civil Works Administration, the Federal Emergency Relief Administration, and other government agencies.

To interpret properly the rural-urban exchange of population, several rather well-established facts and principles should be kept in mind and related to one another. In the first place, it is necessary to recall that the natural increase of population (excess of births over deaths) is as a rule negative in the cities, positive in the rural areas; that it probably increases in direct proportion to the distance from the urban center; and that it reaches its maximum in the most rural areas, where the forces of urbanism strike last of all and then only weakly. Thus the more remote the area from urban centers the greater the surplus of population over replace-

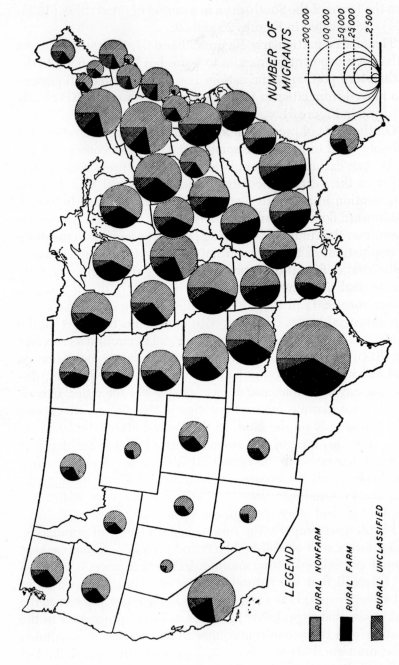

FIGURE 30. Migration from Rural Areas to Urban Districts, 1935 to 1940.

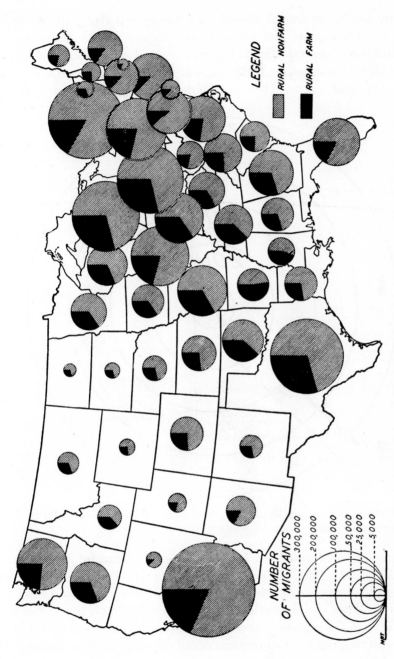

FIGURE 31. Migration from Urban Districts to Rural Areas, 1935 to 1940.

ment needs. Second, it should be remembered that part of the city's replacements and all of its growth are due to migration, primarily to the tide flowing from the rural areas and to a less extent to immigration from abroad. Finally, it is necessary to have in mind several of the most thoroughly established principles

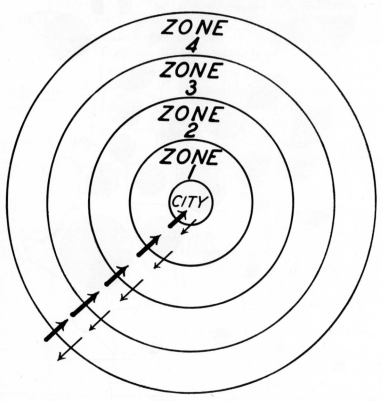

FIGURE 32.   Chart Illustrating the Process of Absorption and Dispersion of Rural-Urban Migrants.

of migration. Formulated by Ravenstein after careful studies in Great Britain, the Continent, and America, and supported by the subsequent studies of a long list of careful students, these principles or "laws" have considerable significance. With some slight changes in the phrasing, several of these principles most useful in interpreting rural-urban movements of population are as follows: (1) Most migrants move only a short distance; (2) the process of absorption is like this: inhabitants of the immediately surrounding area flock to the city, creating gaps in the rural population which are filled by persons from more remote districts, which removal in turn creates other gaps, until the attractive force of the city makes itself felt step by step in the most remote corners of the nation; (3) each main current of migration sets up a compensating countercurrent, and the process of dispersion is the reverse of the process of absorption; and (4) long-distance migrants go immediately to great centers of trade and industry.[7] Figure 32 illustrates the process of absorption and dispersion.

To generalize again: in normal times migration and differential natural increase of population seem to combine in the following manner: natural increase resembles a huge saucer with the city, a "dead sea" area, at the center; the most remote and isolated sections, the areas of high natural increase, make up the rim. Migration operates like a great steam shovel, reaching out to the outermost limits, cutting down population increase to replacement levels, leveling off the rate of growth in the rural districts, and heaping population up in the cities of the middle. Here it either is "consumed" or contributes to urban growth. During periods of prosperity, in spite of the rapid reproduction of the people in such sections,[8] the population of poor land areas does not mount. Movement out of the areas is large, movement into them slight if any. To change the figure: in normal times isolated sections are on the giving end of the migratory current, the cities on the receiving end. In times of distress, all is changed. Migration from the areas is immediately blocked; movement into the areas either commences or becomes more intense; the damming up of youth in these remote areas, supplemented by the backwash from the cities, causes the population to mount at a dizzy pace.[9]

[7] See E. G. Ravenstein, "On the Laws of Migration," *Journal of the Royal Statistical Society*, XLVIII (1885), 167–235; *ibid.*, LII (1889), 241–305; cf. Sorokin and Zimmerman, *Principles of Rural-Urban Sociology*, New York, Henry Holt & Company, 1929, pp. 584–585; Conrad Taeuber, "A Registration System as a Source of Data Concerning Internal Migration," *Rural Sociology*, I (1936), 441–451; Sorokin, Zimmerman, and Galpin, *op. cit.*, III, 611–620; A. F. Weber, *The Growth of Cities in the Nineteenth Century*, New York, Columbia University Press, 1899, p. 255; and C. E. Lively, "Spatial Mobility of the Rural Population with Respect to Local Areas," *American Journal of Sociology*, XLIII (1937), 89–102.

[8] Bushrod Allin and K. H. Parsons, "Changes in the School Census Since 1920," *Land Policy Review*, I (1935), 7.

[9] Cf. *ibid.* for data on the changes during the depression. The immense depopulation which occurred in rural areas during World War II is still waiting to be mapped and studied.

Selectivity of Rural-Urban Migration

Since cities are a kind of colony which the farms repopulate each year, it is a matter of the highest social importance to know what types or kinds of people leave the land for the urban centers. The well-known tendency for like to beget like presages serious consequences for any nation in which rural-urban migration consistently carries away the "cream" of the population from the land. It is not necessary here to attend to all the popular theories on this subject, most of which assume that persons leaving the farms are innately superior to their brethren who remain. Instead we may turn immediately to the best-established principles developed by those who have given serious objective study to the phenomenon.

It is well established by numerous studies that the movement from rural areas to urban centers is mostly a phenomenon of youth, that the majority of the migrants are between the ages of fifteen and twenty-five. In fact, the researches of Hornell Hart for the period 1890 to 1910 indicated that over one-half of the migrants were less than twenty years of age and that migration to cities "is a phenomenon of the adolescent period."[10] For the period 1920 to 1930, C. Warren Thornthwaite estimated that the net loss of farm population to the cities equaled eight million, that more than 50 percent of this was made up of persons between ten and twenty years of age, and that only 10 percent were persons over forty-five years of age.[11] Perhaps the most unique methodology which has been applied in the study of rural-urban migration is that developed by C. Horace Hamilton. Although his study is confined to the single state of North Carolina during the decade 1920 to 1930, the conclusions are highly significant. His findings indicate that heavy migration from farms to cities begins as low as seventeen years of age and that the modal age at migration is about twenty years.[12]

[10] Hornell N. Hart, *Selective Migration as a Factor in Child Welfare in the United States, with Special Reference to Iowa,* University of Iowa Studies in Child Welfare, Iowa City, 1921, p. 32.

[11] C. Warren Thornthwaite, *Internal Migration in the United States,* Philadelphia, University of Pennsylvania Press, 1934, p. 32.

[12] C. Horace Hamilton, *Rural-Urban Migration in North Carolina, 1920 to 1930,* North Carolina AES Bulletin 295, Raleigh, 1934, p. 39. Hamilton has also devised a very useful technique for measuring the rate at which rural youths leave their homes. See his article, "The Annual Rate of Departure of Rural Youths from Their Parental Homes," *Rural Sociology,* I (1936), 164–179.

Sorokin, Zimmerman, and Galpin, in the most comprehensive study of the subject, which examined "an enormous amount of relevant data," came to an identical conclusion, setting forth that most migrations to the cities take place during early adulthood, which includes the years of greatest physical activity, that females migrate at somewhat younger ages than males,[13] that migration occurs at the time that non-migrants are establishing homes for themselves, and that the influx of this youthful population exerts a tremendous influence upon the social and economic life of the city.[14] It can be set down as one of the most thoroughly established principles in sociology that cityward migration selects persons just on the threshold of adulthood.

Migration from farms to cities is selective also with respect to sex. With some exceptions, notably the movement of Negroes from the South to the North, females outnumber males in the flight from the land. This exception merely emphasizes the fact that the northward migration of Negroes is more than a rural-urban movement and possesses many of the characteristics of an emigration. Within the South, the movement of the Negro population to the city takes more females than males, as is indicated clearly by Hamilton, who found that males outnumbered females in North Carolina's loss of population to other states, but that females of both races were attracted to North Carolina cities "in much larger numbers than males."[15] There is an overwhelming evidence that short-distance

[13] Also confirmed by Hamilton, *Rural-Urban Migration in North Carolina, 1920 to 1930*, p. 44; and more recently by Joe M. Bohlen and Ray E. Wakeley, "Intentions to Migrate and Actual Migration of Rural High School Graduates," *Rural Sociology*, XV (1950), 328–334.

[14] See Sorokin, Zimmerman, and Galpin, *op. cit.*, III, 479–481; cf. Sorokin and Zimmerman, *op. cit.*, pp. 540–546. These authors cite a large number of studies from all over the world. Cf. A. F. Weber, *op. cit.*, pp. 280–283. The field has also been surveyed thoroughly by Dorothy Swaine Thomas in her *Research Memorandum on Migration Differentials*, Social Science Research Council Bulletin 43, New York, 1938. Utilizing more refined concepts and techniques, and the more adequate Swedish data, her conclusions are in full accord with those of her predecessors; see especially pp. 11–54. See also T. Lynn Smith, "Characteristics of Migrants," *Southwestern Social Science Quarterly*, XXI (1941), 335–350; and Jane Moore, *Cityward Migration: Swedish Data*, Chicago, University of Chicago Press, 1938, pp. 65–67. C. A. McMahan, "Selectivity of Rural-to-Urban Migration," in T. Lynn Smith and C. A. McMahan, *The Sociology of Urban Life: A Textbook with Readings*, New York, The Dryden Press, Inc., 1951, pp. 336–337, is the most adequate recent survey of pertinent data and studies.

[15] Hamilton, *Rural-Urban Migration to North Carolina, 1920 to 1930*, pp. 33, 43–44; cf. T. J. Woofter, Jr., *Negro Migration*, New York, W. D. Gray, 1920, p. 149.

migration, including the movement from farms to cities, is selective for sex.[16]

For traits other than age and sex it is difficult to prove that rural-urban migration is selective. Many writers who have observed the great tendency for university-educated sons of farmers to remain in urban callings after the completion of their formal education have concluded at once that the best elements, physically, morally, intellectually, and economically, were leaving the country for the city. But such a position overlooks large masses of rural-born persons who enter city occupations through other avenues than the schools and colleges. Handicapped by their lack of training for positions of responsibility in trade and industry and poorly equipped to oust urban-reared persons from their vested positions, large numbers of the unskilled laborers from the country districts annually accept employment at the cities' most menial tasks. In addition, the city frequently is a place of refuge for economic failures from the country, for criminal elements from the rural districts, and for prostitutes from the open country. Zimmerman, after a thoroughgoing study of all available materials, formulated a principle which is of tremendous assistance to one who would attempt to understand the selectivity of rural-urban migration. He came to the conclusion that the city attracts the extremes, while the country retains the means. In physical traits, economic and social status, and intelligence, it is probable that the city secures the most desirable and also the least desirable elements in the population while the country retains the great middle group.[17] The net result, according to this author, is neither advantageous

[16] See Sorokin and Zimmerman, *op. cit.*, pp. 546–555; Sorokin, Zimmerman, and Galpin, *op. cit.*, III, 481–485; Weber, *op. cit.*, pp. 276–280; Thomas, *op. cit.*, pp. 55–69; Moore, *op. cit.*, pp. 55–68; McMahan, *op. cit.*, pp. 337–338; and Ray E. Wakeley, *Differential Mobility Within the Rural Population in 18 Iowa Townships, 1928 to 1935*, Iowa AES Bulletin 249, Ames, 1938, p. 285. Long-distance migration, on the other hand, carries away more males than females. See Robert T. McMillan, *Migration of Population in Five Oklahoma Townships*. Oklahoma AES Bulletin B–271, Stillwater, 1943, p. 3.

[17] This conclusion finds some support in Gee's study of a rural township in South Carolina. The population was grouped into three economic classes (upper, middle, and lower) and the incidence of migration was observed. Over the period 1900 to 1930, migration to cities depleted the upper classes, the middle classes increased 15 percent, and the heaviest losses were among the lower classes whose members moved to nearby textile mill towns. Wilson Gee, "A Qualitative Study of Rural Depopulation in a Single Township, 1900–1930," *American Journal of Sociology*, XXXIX (1933), 210–221. See also Ronald Freedman and Amos H. Hawley, "Education and Occupation of Migrants in the Depression," *American Journal of Sociology*, LVI (1950), 161–166.

to the city nor disadvantageous to the country; i.e., there is no evidence that the eugenic selection occurs. He and Sorokin used this principle in interpreting the well-established fact that the city is much more heterogeneous than the country with respect to economic status, composition of the population, profile of the cultural pattern, or any other social index which might be chosen for comparison.[18]

Limited studies would seem to indicate that there is some tendency for first-born children, particularly males, to remain on the farm. No doubt this disposition is related to a tradition of long standing that the oldest boy shall inherit and perpetuate the family homestead. This finding has a definite relationship to the uniformity developed by Young on the basis of his New York studies; he concluded that persons are most likely to leave the farm in the following order: (1) the hired man, (2) the farmer's son (3) the share tenant, (4) the cash tenant, and (5) last of all, the owner.[19] It also seems pretty well established that the migrants receive more educational training than the stay-at-homes, although the extent to which this is a function of migration instead of a cause of migration is probably impossible to determine.[20] This evidence should not be used, as so frequently is the case, to support allegations that the better elements are leaving the country. The school is the most urban influence in the rural community or neighborhood. To an amazing degree it fails to prepare students for life

[18] Sorokin and Zimmerman, *op. cit.*, pp. 570–571, 582; and Sorokin, Zimmerman, and Galpin, *op. cit.*, III, 498. Thomas, *op. cit.*, pp. 70–167, surveys the existing literature on differentials with particular reference to family status, physical health, intelligence, and occupation. Any conclusions as to differences are, at best, only tentative. Assertions are widespread that the cities attract the intellectual cream from the country, but existing intelligence tests cannot supply facts for testing this inference. See above, pp. 113–115.

In the writer's opinion the following criteria must be satisfied before any differences in the scores on the tests will be satisfactory evidence of selectivity in migration: (1) The test must be weighted with indirect experience ("book learning") and direct experience in the same proportions as these are represented in the totality of the farm family's activities. (2) The test must give as much opportunity for the child who uses his leisure time in the fields and woods swimming, hunting, fishing, etc., to make a high score as it affords opportunity for a high score on the part of the child who secures his recreation at the "movies" and in other forms of commercialized activities. And (3) the test must be administered by such skills as reading, writing, etc., which are not among the customary run of farm activities, to no greater degree than they are conducted by means of skills that form part of the daily round of farm living.

[19] E. C. Young, *The Movement of Farm Population*, Cornell AES Bulletin 426, Ithaca, 1924, p. 88.

[20] Sorokin, Zimmerman, and Galpin, *op. cit.*, III, 501–507, 510–515.

in the rural community, where the majority of them are certain to spend their lives.[21] The present division of labor among rural institutions allocates the training in urban lore to the schools and forces the oncoming generation of farmers to rely upon the family for instruction in the elements basic to rural living. The probability is high that those most interested in school studies are also those who are most dissatisfied with and ill adjusted to farm life. Before asserting that the superior educational attainments of the migrants are evidence of dysgenic selection, extreme care should be taken to determine whether the children who early grow dissatisfied with farm life and indisposed to become agriculturists do not specialize in formal education, while their brothers and sisters who plan to remain on the farm spend correspondingly more time and effort in acquiring, through the family apprentice system, the skills and techniques needed in the life of the countryside.

Several of these principles find additional support through the fact that they were tested with data for 10,672 Negroes in the state of Louisiana, a group radically different in race and culture from the samples upon which the original studies were made. In particular this study of Negro migration indicated that the flow of population to the cities is much more important than the countercurrent to the land, that the migrants received more educational training than their brothers and sisters who remained on the farms, and that, on the whole, the migrants were drawn most heavily from the upper and lower economic classes. Owing to the fact that the independent Negro farm owner is a negligible element in the Negro farm population, it is not surprising that there was no tendency for the oldest Negro male child to stay on the farm; and because Negroes left the South for northern cities—a long-distance migration—it is not unusual that there were more male than female migrants.[22] Furthermore, to a considerable extent the villages, towns, and cities of the South served as stepping stones in the northward trek of Negroes, disproportionate shares of the migrants coming from these centers of population.[23]

[21] Cf. M. B. Smith, *A Sociological Analysis of Rural Education in Louisiana,* University, Louisiana State University Press, 1938; and T. Lynn Smith, "Characteristics of Migrants."

[22] See Fred C. Frey, "Factors Conditioning the Incidence of Migration Among Louisiana Negroes," *Southwestern Social Science Quarterly,* XV (1934), 210–217.

[23] See the United States Department of Labor, *Negro Migration in 1916–17,* Washington, Government Printing Office, 1919, pp. 19, 55–56.

One special phase of the rural-urban migration in the United States is the flight of the Negroes from the lands of the South to the cities of the North and East. Although this is largely a movement from the farms to the cities of the nation, it has many of the aspects of an immigration. Thornthwaite's data show this movement getting under way between 1890 and 1900, when the net movement out of the thirteen southern states approximated 113,-000, decreasing slightly to 97,000 during the next decade, then swelling to 364,000 between 1910 and 1920, and finally mounting to 614,000 from 1920 to 1930. In forty years more than a million Negroes abandoned the South, the overwhelming majority of them moving to northern cities. His analysis also indicates that the northward drag cut deeper and more consistently into the cotton states of the lower South than into the remainder of the region. Thus the net movement of Negroes from the five states of South Carolina, Georgia, Alabama, Mississippi, and Louisiana closely approximated the entire net movement out of the South, being 107, 125, 296, and 553 thousand for the four decades 1890–1900 to 1920–1930, respectively. The movement from Mississippi and Alabama crested in the decade 1910 to 1920; that for the other three states, between 1920 and 1930.[24] Negroes who had migrated to New York City and Philadelphia and were living there in 1930 came mainly from the eastern seaboard states. To New York City, Virginia had contributed 44,500, South Carolina 33,800, Georgia 19,500, and North Carolina 26,100. Philadelphia received 41,300 Negroes from Virginia, 27,900 from South Carolina, 22,900 from Georgia, and 18,700 from North Carolina. Detroit and Cleveland have drawn most heavily from Georgia and Alabama. Negro migrants totaling 38,400, born in Mississippi, were living in Chicago in 1930; the same city had received over 20,000 Negroes from the states of Tennessee, Georgia, and Alabama, and over 10,000 from Louisiana and Kentucky. St. Louis had drawn most heavily from Mississippi, Tennessee, and Arkansas. On the other hand, New Orleans Negroes were nearly all born in Louisiana, Birmingham Negroes in Alabama, and Atlanta Negroes in Georgia. During World War II a tremendous migration of Negroes from the South to the Pacific coast took place.

[24] Carter Goodrich and others, *Migration and Economic Opportunity: The Report of the Study of Population on Redistribution*, Philadelphia, University of Pennsylvania Press, 1936, Plate IIIa, facing p. 680.

Migration from Cities to Farms

The volume of migration from cities to farms is very large, amounting in a single year to nearly one and three-quarter million people and averaging well over one million annually for the period 1920 to 1935. (See Figure 33.) But in spite of the magnitude of this movement, little is known concerning the attributes or quali-

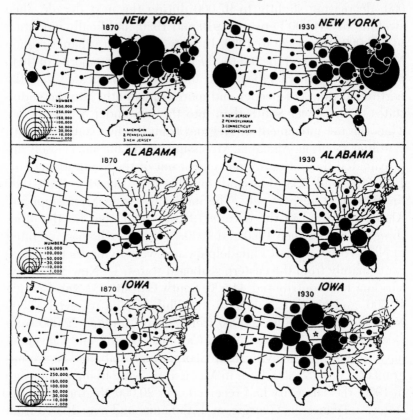

Figure 33. Native White Migrants Born in New York, Alabama, and Iowa, Living Elsewhere.

ties of those who flee the city for the land. Galpin's limited study of 1167 persons who moved from cities to farms during 1926 and 1927 is one of the most revealing investigations of the situation in predepression times. If we can generalize from these results: (1) The landward movement is composed almost entirely of persons with previous farm experience (only 13 percent had not lived on farms), of whom more than one-half had previously been farm operators; and (2) over 40 percent are between the ages thirty and fifty years, indicating that landward migrants are much older than those going to the city and are "men in the prime of life."[25]

A study of retirement in rural Connecticut is one of the few others that throws some light upon the subject of urban to rural migration. The location for the study was East Haddam, a summer resort community in Middlesex County, and a total of 220 elderly persons were included in the inquiry. Here it was found that "practically all of the retired men who operate part-time farms had previous agricultural experience although about one-half of them held non-farm jobs just before their retirement." Only forty-three persons in the sample had been born in East Haddam whereas sixty-one of them gave New York City as their place of previous residence.[26]

Interstate Migration

Strictly speaking, interstate migrations are either farm-to-farm movements or part of the rural-urban exchange of population. They are treated separately here for the simple reason that this is the type of migration which supplied the various agricultural sections of the nation with their original settlers. Much of this took place within the memory of persons now living. Its factors are those responsible for the surge across the continent; its results are American rural life in all its variety and complexity. There is available in the various census reports, and fairly well analyzed in several special studies, a mass of material on state-to-state migration which cannot be separated into the farm-to-farm or rural-urban categories, but which contributes a great deal to our understanding of both rural-urban and farm-to-farm movements of population. Beginning in 1870 the census began securing and tabulating data showing the state of birth and the state of residence of the population. Galpin and Manny thoroughly charted these data in an ingenious way that adds much to our understanding of the flow of population across the continent. Figures 33 and 34, presenting the data for Alabama, which is fairly well representative of the rural South, for Iowa as representative of the agricultural Mid-

[25] Galpin's study is summarized in Sorokin, Zimmerman, and Galpin, *op. cit.*, III, 625–627.

[26] Walter C. McKain, Jr., and Elmer D. Baldwin, *Old Age and Retirement in Rural Connecticut*, Storrs AES Bulletin 278, Storrs, 1951, pp. 5, 22. See also H. Otto Dahlke and Harvey V. Stonecipher," A Wartime Back-to-Land Movement of Old Age Groups," *Rural Sociology*, XI (1946), 148–152.

west, and for New York, representing the urban East, have been reproduced from their excellent study.[27]

Before 1910, as these charts and others in the series indicate, the prevailing direction of migration was to the West. This was the era of settlement of the great agricultural frontiers of the West and

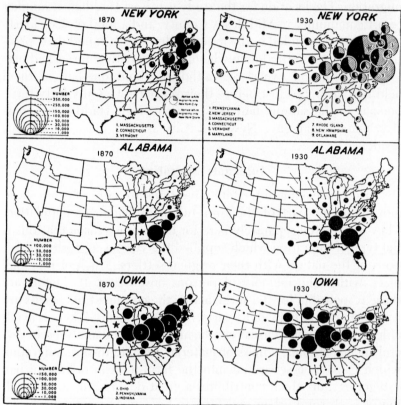

FIGURE 34.   Native White Migrants into New York, Alabama, and Iowa, from State of Birth.

Southwest. (See Figure 35.) Following 1910, the stream of population turned increasingly in the direction of urban centers and the pattern prevailing during the preceding decades was greatly modified. In particular, the West-East and the South-North currents of migration have recently resembled swollen tides.[28] New York State

[27] Charles J. Galpin and T. B. Manny, *Interstate Migrations Among the Native White Population as Indicated by Differences Between State of Birth and State of Residence*, Washington, United States Department of Agriculture, 1934.

[28] Cf. Warren S. Thompson, *Research Memorandum on Internal Migration in the Depression*, Social Science Research Council Bulletin 30, New York, 1937, pp. 14–18.

has exerted a heavy drag on the neighboring states, but New York City has recruited population from all over the nation.

During the 1930's the flight of persons from the drought-ridden areas of the Great Plains to the Mountain and Pacific Coast States added a new chapter to our history of state-to-state movements of farm population.[29] Some studies indicate that many of these migrants possessed agricultural skills and thrifty habits which are making them an asset to the communities to which they moved.[30] On the other hand, recent arrivals, a "crowded-out section of the population—people who do not belong anywhere," who are drawn most heavily from the neighboring states of Oregon, Washington, and Arizona, and from Texas, Oklahoma, Missouri, Illinois, and New York, created serious problems in California.[31] It is regrettable that comparable analyses are not available for the tremendous migration to the west coast that took place during and following World War II.

Movement from Farm to Farm

Not all significant rural migrations involve the crossing of state lines or the passing from farm to city or from city to farm. Annually there occurs a great mass movement of farm families from one farm to another.

Conspicuous in this respect has been the annual movement of southern croppers and "tenants" from one plantation to another. Some comprehension of the amount of this movement can be gained from the following data from the 1935 *Census of Agriculture.* In 1935 nearly one-fifth (18 percent) of the farm operators had been on their farms for less than one year, a figure only slightly larger than that (17 percent) reported in the 1930 Census. More than one-fourth (26 percent) of all farm operators in 1935 had been on their farms less than two years, and only 28 percent had been on their farms as long as ten years. It should be remembered, on the one hand, that this movement is swelled by the inclusion of the large mass of croppers, who are but laborers in

[29] See, for example, V. B. Stanberry, *Migration into Oregon, 1930–1937,* Oregon State Planning Board, 1938; and Varden Fuller and E. D. Tetreau, *Volume and Characteristics of Migration to Arizona,* Arizona AES Bulletin 176, Tucson, 1941.

[30] Cf. Charles S. Hoffman, "Drought and Depression Migration into Oregon, 1930 to 1936," *Monthly Labor Review* (January, 1938), pp. 1–9; Richard Wakefield and Paul H. Landis, "Types of Migratory Farm Laborers and Their Movement into the Yakima Valley, Washington," *Rural Sociology,* III (1938), 133–144.

[31] Cf. William T. and Dorothy E. Cross, *Newcomers and Nomads in California,* Stanford University, Stanford University Press, 1937, pp. 9, 128, *passim.*

reality, among the farm operators, a fact which must be kept in mind in comparing the sections of the country with each other and the tenure classes with one another. But it should also be remembered that the excessive movement of the population, such as that among croppers in the South, is one of the social correlatives of large-scale agriculture that does most to emphasize the social and

FIGURE 35.   Migration, Vertical Social Mobility, and Improving Agricultural Techniques in the American Dream. (From a print in the collection at the Library of Congress.)

economic wastes which are inherent in the concentration of land ownership. (See Figure 36.) Among agricultural laborers, constant shifting is even more pronounced than among farm operators. Outside the South (with which the census includes Delaware, Maryland, and West Virginia), only 11 percent of the farm operators had been on their farms less than one year, and 35 percent had occupied their places for fifteen years or longer. In the West the corresponding percentages were 13 and 23, respectively; in the South 25 and 23 percent, respectively. Among owners the period of farm occupancy is much longer than among tenants; 59 percent of

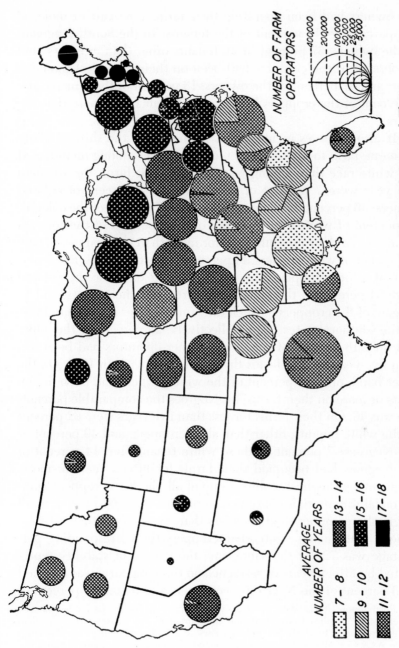

FIGURE 36. Variations in the Amount of Time Farm Operators Had Occupied Their Farms, 1940. (Starting at 12:00 o'clock on the circles and reading clockwise, the segments represent the nonwhite and white operators, respectively.)

the owners had been operating their farms ten years or more, as compared with 14 percent of the tenants. In the South 7 percent of the owners, 37 percent of all tenants other than croppers, and 44 percent of the croppers had been on their farms less than one year; and 57 percent of the owners, 13 percent of the tenants, and 8 percent of the croppers had occupied their farms more than ten years.[32]

It also deserves mention that in the South the shifting about from one farm to another was more prevalent among members of the white race than among Negroes. On their farms for less than one year were 7 percent of white owners, 3 percent of colored owners; 40 percent of white tenants, and 27 percent of the colored; 49 percent of white croppers, and only 38 percent of the colored. Similarly, on their present farms for more than ten years were only 56 percent of white owners, 11 percent of white tenants, and 5 percent of white croppers; the corresponding data for the colored were 64 percent of the owners, 22 percent of the tenants, and 11 percent of the croppers.[33] Much the same was the situation in 1940. In the southern states taken collectively, 22 percent of the white and only 18 percent of the Negro owner-operators had been less than five years on the farms they were occupying in 1940. On the other hand, only 41 percent of the white owners had been fifteen years or more on their farms; for Negroes the comparable percentage was 46. On their farms for less than five years were 62 percent of the white tenants, other than sharecroppers, and 49 percent of the Negroes; 7 percent of these white tenants and 14 percent of the Negroes had occupied their farms for fifteen years or more. Even among the most mobile group of all, the sharecroppers, similar racial differentials continued to prevail. Thus 64 percent of all Negro sharecroppers had been less than five years in their 1940 locations, but among white sharecroppers the corresponding percentage was 72. At the same time the degree of stability represented by fifteen years of residence on the same farm was attained by 5 percent of the Negro sharecroppers and by only 3 percent of

[32] Furthermore, these data are for 1935, when it is highly probable that the movement of families from plantation to plantation was considerably less than in the years prior to 1933. See Fred C. Frey and T. Lynn Smith, "The Influence of the AAA Cotton Program upon the Tenant, Cropper, and Laborer," *Rural Sociology*, I (1936), 504–505.

[33] These data were taken from the *United States Census of Agriculture: 1935*, "Period of Farm Occupancy," a special report issued October 28, 1936.

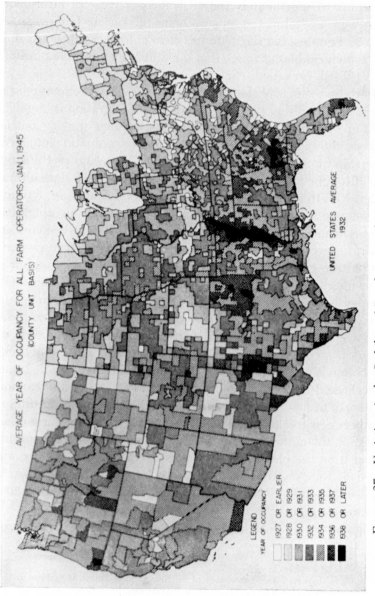

FIGURE 37. Variations in the Stability of Residence on the Farms of the United States, 1945. (Illustration from the Bureau of the Census.)

the white.[34] Unfortunately the 1945 data on year of farm occupancy were not tabulated separately for the various tenure classes and racial groups; but the materials were mapped on a county unit basis which enables us to see that the differences observed in 1935 and 1940 still prevailed. (See Figure 37.)

In those sections of the United States in which the family-farm system of agriculture prevails, farm-to-farm migration is largely a function of the agricultural ladder. Young men starting out as laborers, climbing rung after rung, and finally graduating into farm ownership from the tenant class, are rarely able to stay on the same farm throughout the entire process of climbing the agricultural ladder, with the consequence that a considerable amount of transfer from one farm to another takes place. Thus while an individual is in the tenant class he is more mobile than when he becomes an owner, and tenants as a group are more migratory than owners. This pattern gives rise to a definite age cycle of migration, but it also confines the movements to an area of very slight radius.[35] On the other hand, in those parts of the United States where the plantation system has been the dominant agricultural institution, the share-wage labor system has generated a tremendous amount of shifting from one plantation to another. Dr. Park has pointed out how closely this is related to the heritage from slavery, a fact that is overlooked by most students of the subject. According to him, the liberty to move was, for the Negro, the one significant difference between freedom and slavery. The right to move from one plantation to another became the Negro's way of securing consideration from the planter.[36] More recently the right to move is reported as the Negro's test of whether he or the planter owns a mule—if, when the "tenant" moves, the planter allows him to take the mule along, it is *his* mule.

Plantation farming and share-of-the-crop wages also seem to set

[34] Cf. T. Lynn Smith, "A Demographic Study of the American Negro," *Social Forces*, XXIII (1945), 379–387.

[35] Cf. C. E. Lively, "The Development of Research in Rural Migration in the United States," *Congrès International de la Population*, IV (1938), 93–107; C. E. Lively and Frances Foott, *Population Mobility in Selected Areas of Rural Ohio, 1928–1935*, Ohio AES Bulletin 582, Columbus, 1937, pp. 18–22; and W. A. Anderson and Charles P. Loomis, *Migration of Sons and Daughters of White Farmers in Wake County, 1929*, North Carolina AES Bulletin 275, Raleigh, 1930, in which it was found that 30 percent of the farmers' children settled within ten miles of the parental home.

[36] Robert E. Park, "Racial Assimilation in Secondary Groups," *American Journal of Sociology*, XIX (1913–1914), 615–616.

up a current of migration from the plantation section, which usually monopolizes the good lands, to small farms in the poorest sections, and then back to the plantations.[37] Finally, those crops other
than cotton which have a pronounced seasonal demand for labor,
and especially such of them as are produced on a large scale, generate a great deal of seasonal movement from one agricultural area
to another. This migration is of such a volume and is fraught with
so many serious social consequences that it deserves attention by
itself.

Migratory Agricultural Labor

Migratory labor is a class apart from the settled farm population amid which it moves. Forced to till the soil of others, poorly
paid, forever on the move, its members are never an accepted part
of any community.[38] Working in one crop today, another tomor-
row, this rural proletariat alone makes possible the seeming "efficiency" of certain large agricultural operations and accounts for
the most serious relief problems of many towns and cities. In the
words of the President's Commission on Migratory Labor:

Migratory farm laborers move restlessly over the face of the land,
but they neither belong to the land nor does the land belong to them.
They pass through community after community, but they neither claim
the community as home nor does the community claim them. Under
the law, the domestic migrants are citizens of the United States but
they are scarcely more a part of the land of their birth than the alien
migrants working beside them.

The migratory workers engage in a common occupation, but their
cohesion is scarcely greater than that of pebbles on the seashore. Each
harvest collects and regroups them. They live under a common condition, but create no techniques for meeting common problems. The
public acknowledges the existence of migrants, yet declines to accept
them as full members of the community. As crops ripen, farmers
anxiously await their coming; as the harvest closes, the community,
with equal anxiety, awaits their going.

. . . .

Migrants generally are easily identified as outsiders. Their faces are
those of strangers and, for many of them, differences of color and other

[37] For a thorough study of some phases of this interchange of population between plantation and other areas, and for data on the circulation of families from
one place to another within the plantation section, see Homer L. Hitt, *Recent
Migration into and Within the Upper Mississippi Delta of Louisiana*, Louisiana
AES Bulletin 364, Baton Rouge, 1943.

[38] Cf. Paul S. Taylor, "Migratory Farm Labor in the United States," *Monthly
Labor Review*, XLIV (1937), p. 1.

physical characteristics serve as badges of identification. Their heavily laden cars or trucks, packed with beds, cooking utensils, and furniture are easily distinguished from those of campers on vacation. Even their work clothes by material, style, or cut seem to indicate an outside origin. All along the way are those who take advantage of the migratory worker's helplessness. Professional gamblers, prostitutes, and peddlers of dope follow the work routes to obtain, each in his own way, a share of the migrant's money.

Residents tend to separate migrants from themselves in domicile and law, in thought and feeling. They assign special places to migrants seeking shelter, or leave them to go where their poverty and condition force them. Here they encamp in tents or simply under canvas supported by a rope strung between two trees or from the side of the car to the ground. They sleep on pallets, or on bedsprings or folding cots which some of them carry. Where rains are frequent during work season they find shelter in crude shacks. On farms they use what shelter their employers may provide.

The lines of segregation are further sharpened, particularly for Negroes, Mexicans, and Puerto Ricans by differences of skin color, stature, and language. For several years the Mexican Government declined to allow its citizens to go to Texas under the Mexican-United States International Agreement because of the flagrant social discriminations under which they had to live.[39]

The exact number of migratory farm laborers in the United States is not known. The results of any attempt to inventory the people who "follow the crops" would depend largely upon the definition of migrant used in the inquiry. There are many persons resident in small towns and cities who move to the rural parts of the same county or adjoining counties to assist with the harvest. Usually these people are not regarded as migrants by the localities in which they labor. There are others who move hundreds of miles for a long season before returning to their abodes. And there are some who follow regular routes across the nation and back year after year, following the crops. Defining migrants "as those field workers . . . who follow crops in periodic movement, in groups or as part of a well-defined movement commonly recognized as a movement of migrants, so that for a few months, if not the full year, migratory labor becomes a way of life," in 1936 Paul S. Taylor estimated that there were between 200,000 and 350,000

[39] President's Commission on Migratory Labor, *Migratory Labor in American Agriculture,* Washington, Government Printing Office, 1951, pp. 3–4.

migratory agricultural laborers in the United States.[40] More recently the President's Commission on Migratory Labor has set the figure at one million. "However, of this total number, domestic migrants represent only about one-half. The other half is made up of approximately 100,000 Mexicans legally under contract, a relatively small number of British West Indians and Puerto Ricans, and, by far the most important, illegal Mexican workers who in

DEPORTATIONS AND VOLUNTARY DEPARTURES
OF ILLEGAL MEXICAN ALIENS

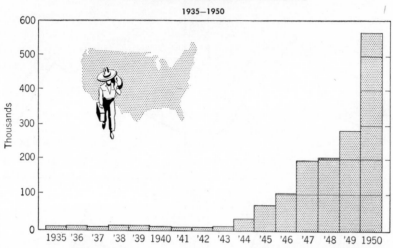

FIGURE 38. The Increasing Importance of the "Wetback" Problem. (Reproduced from *Migratory Labor in American Agriculture*, Washington, Government Printing Office, 1951, p. 70.)

recent years have amounted to an estimated 400,000."[41] The tremendous increase in the importance of these workers from across the Rio Grande, commonly and somewhat derisively called "wetbacks," is shown in Figure 38.[42] They help greatly to swell the numbers of agricultural laborers in this country, but the basic causes of the increase in migratory agricultural labor as a way of life are due to changes in our methods of extracting a living from the soil. In the southern region the decline of the system of sharecropping is intimately linked to the increasing demand for workers

[40] *Op. cit.*
[41] *Op. cit.*, p. 3.
[42] See also Lyle Saunders and Olen E. Leonard, *The Wetback in the Lower Rio Grande Valley of Texas*, Inter-American Education Occasional Papers VII, Austin, University of Texas, 1951.

Changes in Seasonal Employment of
HIRED FARM WORKERS
Month by Month 1931 and 1949
Four Regions

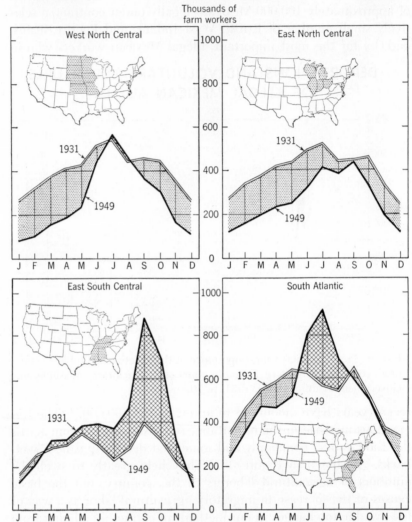

FIGURE 39. A Basic Cause of the Increase in Migratory Agricultural Laborers. (Reproduced from *Migratory Labor in American Agriculture,* Washington, Government Printing Office, 1951, p. 11.)

from off the plantations; and throughout the United States the growing tendency for seasonality in the need for agricultural labor is a basic factor in the rapidly rising numbers of migratory agricultural workers. (See Figure 39.)

Taylor deserves much credit for his excellent work in identify-

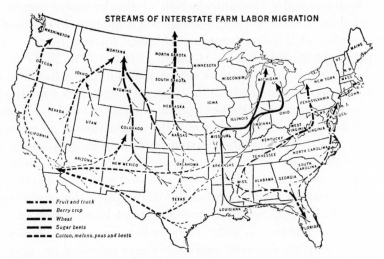

FIGURE 40. Principal Currents of Migratory Agricultural Laborers in the United States. (Illustration from the Bureau of Agricultural Economics.

ing the chief currents of migration among these migratory farm workers, indicating the routes of travel, the succession of crops in which they work, and making some preliminary attempts at gauging the relative strength of each stream. Figure 40 is based upon his data. There is the wheat belt migration, which played a significant role in the Middle West and Great Plains during the entire period from 1900 until the 1920's. In this area a small number of workers with the machines were sufficient for all phases of the production of wheat except the harvest. To shock and thresh the grain required as many as 250,000 men, and these were annually on the move, keeping pace with the ripening grain. Beginning in Texas around the first of June, the harvest season ends in the Dakotas in August, and in Canada even later. Some migrants followed the crop all the way beginning in Texas, ending in Canada in the fall. Also much of the work of gathering the wheat was performed by workers from various states, following restricted routes within each. Every city in the region and especially centers like

Minneapolis were ports of entry for laborers passing into the wheat belt to assist in the harvest. It was among these migratory workers that radical movements such as the I.W.W. gained such headway that it was not safe to ride the freights unless in possession of a "red card." A rapid mechanization of the harvesting process, and especially the introduction of the harvester combine, sounded the death knell of this wheat belt migration. In Oklahoma the number of laborers furnished to wheat farmers by the state employment offices fell from 11,296 in 1921 to 165 in 1932.[43]

In the western portions of the cotton belt, and especially in Arizona and California where the growing of cotton is a relatively new introduction, a second current of migratory labor has manifested itself. In the old cotton belt the production of cotton was dominated by the plantation system. Although mechanization of some of the processes has long been feasible, its progress has been relatively slow. Planters have been obsessed with the idea that it was necessary to maintain a family on the place the year round in order to have its members available to pick the cotton grown on each fifteen to twenty acres. Hence when slavery was abolished by the federal government, and cash wages provided an unsatisfactory method of securing a permanent labor supply, a share-wage system, which has come to be known as cropping, was adopted for the purpose. In the spread of cotton culture toward the west, many elements of the plantation system have been abandoned, and, most important of all, its system of labor contract has been given up. In western Texas, New Mexico, Arizona, and California, the "share-crop system, which binds the laborers to the soil throughout the year, is practically unknown." Laborers are drawn from far and near to chop and pick the cotton; until 1929, when restrictions were introduced, many of them came from the *tierra templada* of Mexico. In 1937 Taylor estimated that there were 50,000 mobile cotton pickers (whites, Negroes, and Mexicans) in Texas and Oklahoma alone, and indicated that many of them journeyed annually from 600 to 900 miles, gathering the opening cotton bolls as they went.

Small fruits such as the berry crops require large numbers of pickers and generate a great deal of migration on the part of agricultural laborers. "In the years of good crops a thin stream of migrant families works its way northward with the berry crops

[43] Taylor, *op. cit.*, pp. 2–3.

from the Gulf to Lake Michigan, a few following the whole way from the strawberry harvest of northern Florida in the spring to Tangipahoa Parish in Louisiana, next to Judsonia in central Arkansas, thence to Paducah, Ky., Vermillion or Farina, Ill., and Benton Harbor, Mich. After the berry harvest they pick grapes and peaches in northern Michigan."[44] The volume of the migration depends of course upon the size of the harvest and general economic conditions. In 1934 it was estimated that 20,000 people, most of them from outside the community, worked in the Arkansas harvest, while in a year of small crop there may be almost no migration.[45] Before World War II the citrus, berry, and truck crops of Florida attracted a large number of migratory workers (10,000 to 20,000), many of whom were from outside the state, some being dislodged sharecroppers from Georgia, Mississippi, and even faraway Arkansas. In the spring these workers floated northward into the peach orchards of Georgia, or to the strawberry, potato, and trucking areas along the Carolina and Virginia coasts, and thence along the eastern shore into Maryland, Delaware, and New Jersey, returning to Florida in the fall. Some proceeded to the vicinity of Crystal Springs, Mississippi, where they worked in the tomato harvest, then to Humbolt, Tennessee, for the tomato harvest. From there they dispersed in all directions, some going to the Shenandoah Valley of Virginia, a few to the fruit and vegetable harvests of northwestern New York, others to the lower part of the Rio Grande Valley of Texas, and some even to the melon-producing areas around Rocky Ford, Colorado, and then to Oregon and Washington.[46]

The production of sugar, both beet and cane, is also characterized by extreme peak labor loads at certain limited seasons, a factor which makes migratory labor of considerable importance in both the middle- and far-western beet sugar sections and in the Louisiana "sugar bowl." But the variations in the demand for seasonal laborers are also very great. In Utah beets are produced largely upon family-sized units by the farmer and the members of his own family, migratory labor being of little importance. A comparable situation exists in parts of Louisiana, where small French Acadian farmers of the bayous have retained possession of their

[44] *Ibid.*, p. 5; cf. John N. Webb, *The Migratory Casual Worker*, Research Monograph VII, Works Progress Administration, Washington, 1937.
[45] Taylor, *loc. cit.*
[46] *Ibid.*, pp. 6–7.

little ribbonlike farms and find family labor practically sufficient to care for and harvest their small acreages of sugar cane. But in much of the sugar beet country, and in much of Louisiana's "sugar bowl," large-scale operations demand the influx of an annual supply of floating agricultural workers to assist with the harvest of the crops. Taylor has indicated that the beet fields of the Mountain States are a meeting place for German-Russians, Mexicans, Spanish-Americans from the valleys of New Mexico, and even Japanese. In the Middle West the beet fields of Minnesota and the Dakotas depend to some extent for hoeing, thinning, and digging operations upon Mexicans, Belgians, Poles, and even Filipinos. The number of persons whose mode of life is migratory labor in the beet fields is difficult to estimate, but may run as high as 30,000 in peak years.[47] Sugar cane workers, in great demand during the season from October to January when the cane is being cut, are recruited largely from the cotton plantations to the north of the "sugar bowl," from the towns and villages of the sugar-producing section. In sugar production, both cane and beet, the migration is mostly from the worker's place of residence to one farm or plantation, where the laborer works for the duration of the harvest season. "Following the crop" is hardly possible in sugar production.

Finally there is much migrant labor utilized in connection with California's fruit and truck crops. This factor is largely responsible for the fact that "today the greatest seasonal migrations of farm labor in the United States take place on the Pacific coast. The main whirlpool of migratory labor is in California, but the high mobility of workers makes all the western areas parts of a common labor market. Seeking to dovetail brief seasons of employment,"[48] prior to World War II workers made their way from the Imperial Valley on the Mexican border to the Willamette and Yakima valleys of Washington,[49] and some even got as far east as the beet fields of Montana or the mellon harvests east of the Rockies in Colorado. The volume of this movement was tremendous. In 1935, for exam-

[47] *Ibid.*, pp. 7–8.

[48] *Ibid.* See also William H. Metzler and Afife F. Sagin, *The Agricultural Labor Force in the San Joaquin Valley, California, 1948*, Washington, U.S. Department of Agriculture coöperating with University of California, Institute of Industrial Relations (mimeographed), 1950.

[49] For a careful study of their composition, movements, mode of living, etc., see Paul H. Landis and Melvin Brooks, *Farm Labor in the Yakima Valley*, Washington AES Bulletin 343, Pullman, 1936; cf. Wakefield and Landis, *loc. cit.*

ple, it was estimated that 188,000 laborers were needed during the peak harvest in California's thirty-three agricultural counties, 50,-000 of whom had to come from outside the counties. Taylor adds that since labor distribution is far from perfect, the number of migrants would exceed this figure. "The number of persons—men, women, and children—who follow the California crops away from home at some time during the year, may well have reached 150,-000 in recent years, as some estimate."[50]

Of all migratory movements of rural people, the floating about of migratory laborers from one seasonal crop to another is fraught with the most serious social consequences. Earnings are low, expenditures for transportation high, and there is little possibility of accumulating any reserve to tide the workers or family over periods of unemployment or adversity. Housing of such workers is mostly a makeshift affair, with little or no care given to sanitation. To quote Taylor: "In California the ragged camps of migrants squatting in filth by the roadside, in open fields, along ditch banks, or on garbage dumps fairly beggar description."[51]

Attachment to or participation in the activities of social institutions such as churches and schools is almost out of the question for the migrant laborer or the members of his family.[52] Even the whites are not accepted by the communities in which they work for a spell, and workers of other races are even more discriminated against. A system of agriculture based upon migratory labor breeds social results among the most demoralizing that can be contemplated. Such a pattern of life does not make for acceptable citizenship and cannot hope to produce good citizenship.[53]

[50] *Op. cit.*, pp. 9–10; cf. Webb, *op. cit.*, Fig. 6, p. 36.

[51] *Op. cit.*, pp. 10–11. See also Paul S. Taylor, "Perspective on Housing Migratory Agricultural Laborers," *Land Economics*, XXVII (1951), 193–204; and President's Commission on Migratory Labor, *op. cit.*, pp. 137–151.

[52] In April, 1927, the California Department of Education enumerated 37,000 migratory children. Paul S. Taylor and Tom Vasey, "Contemporary Background of California Farm Labor," *Rural Sociology*, I (1936), 418.

[53] Unfavorable community attitudes toward migratory agricultural workers, as well as the disorganization of personality brought about by such a wandering existence in the midst of a settled society, are reflected in the present connotations of the terms "rogue" and "vagabond." These came into the language as innocuous terms to designate the farm workers set adrift by the decay of the English manorial system. Sorokin, Zimmerman, and Galpin, *op. cit.*, I, 359.

PART THREE

Rural Social Organization

*Social organization is used in this book to refer
to the structural or anatomical aspects of society. Next to population, this is the most
highly developed portion of sociology and
rural sociology. Part Three falls logically into
three divisions: (1) relations of the people to
the land, (2) relations of person to person, and
(3) the institutional aspects. The five important
relationships between the population and the
land are as follows: (1) the manner in which
the population is distributed on the land, or
settlement patterns; (2) the way in which the
land is divided for purposes of surveying and
recording; (3) the nature of property rights in
the land; (4) the distribution of ownership and
control of the land; and (5) the ways of extracting a living from the soil, designated in
this volume as the "systems of agriculture."
Two aspects of the person-to-person relationships are analyzed, the discussion of social differentiation setting forth the nature of the social units or groupings, and that of social stratification describing the class and caste elements
in rural social organization. Finally, a discussion of the functioning of the more fundamental social groups—the family, the school, the
church, and political bodies—through the established institutional forms through which
they work, completes Part Three.*

10

FORM OF SETTLEMENT

The manner in which the rural population is arranged on the land is one of the most important aspects of rural social organization. The terms "form of settlement," "type of settlement," and "settlement patterns" are used by various authors to refer to the spatial relationships of farm dwellings to one another and to the cultivated land. As is well known, the nature of the agricultural process requires that each farmer have a relatively large acreage of land; and this inevitably makes the density of an agricultural population slight. Therefore, in the location of farm residences a choice must be made between placing the homes near one another and at a distance from the fields, or placing the dwellings amid the fields and away from one another. If the first alternative is chosen, one mode of settlement arises; if the second is selected, the arrangement is quite different.

To the average American the "natural" type of settlement is one in which the homes of the farm families are scattered over the landscape, each in the midst of the fields cultivated by the operator and all at some distance from one another. In other words, dispersed settlement patterns are common and nucleated patterns rare in rural America. Agricultural villages there are in America, to be sure; but from early times these have been merely trade and service centers for the farm population.[1] They are not genuine farm villages. In them reside professional and business classes, laborers of various kinds, many retired farmers, and large propor-

[1] Cf. Timothy Dwight, *Travels in New England and New York*, London, W. Baynes and Son, 1823, IV, 4–5; T. Maxwell Morrison, *Coopersburg Survey: Being a Study of the Community Around Coopersburg, Lehigh County, Pennsylvania*, Easton, Moravian Country Church Commission, 1914, p. 11; and Morris Birkbeck, *Notes on a Journey in America*, Philadelphia, Caleb Richardson, 1817, pp. 90–91.

tions of widows. Only to a minor degree do they serve as locations for homes of farmers. Throughout most of the world, however, the hamlet or village with the residences of farmers grouped together in clusters is most common. Surrounding the village at some distance are the lands tilled by the agriculturists whose homes make up the village. Most of the landscape is devoid of farm buildings.

A pattern of settlement there must be, but diverse circumstances cause the patterns to differ. The manner in which the population is spaced on the land is a conditioning factor which vitally affects all other aspects of social organization and the social processes; it is one of the most persistent elements of the cultural heritage. Its great importance reflects but little credit upon the cursory manner in which it has been dismissed in treatises dealing with the social organization of rural society.

Although most sociologists have failed to sense the significance of this aspect of rural organization, fortunately this cannot be said concerning the workers in all disciplines. Cultural geographers have long been aware of the importance of the mode of settlement, and most monographic studies in the field of cultural geography have given some attention to the settlement patterns of the area under consideration. Furthermore, great colonizers of the past, such as William Penn and Lord Selkirk, realized the importance of selecting the right type of settlement pattern. They even experimented on a considerable scale with various possibilities. Today if social planning in and for rural areas is to amount to more than pure verbosity, it must start with the types or patterns of settlement that might be utilized in the areas undergoing reconstruction.

Like other aspects of the cultural heritage, a form of settlement once established becomes the "natural" pattern and is accepted as a matter of course. Innovations and changes can be effected only in the face of great resistance. That old established settlements should perpetuate traditional patterns is to be expected and should not be disquieting. But every effort should be made in the establishment of new colonies, even in so-called experimental settlements, not to allow cultural inertia to result in the unconscious transfer of the customary pattern of settlement to the new communities. A comparative study of various possibilities, the advantages and disadvantages of each, is the sound approach in social planning.

Types of Settlement

The possibilities offered in the distribution of the farm population on the land are definitely limited. All the existing forms of settlement may be grouped into three principal types.

The Village Form of Settlement

From the standpoinnt of the number of farm people affected, the village form of settlement is by far the most important. In Europe, Asia, much of Latin America (Figures 41 and 42), and Africa (Figure 43), it is the principal mode of settling on the land. It is not unknown in the United States. In this type of settlement the homes of the farmers are grouped together to form a village or hamlet, leaving the cultivated fields, pastures, and woodlands in the surrounding area quite devoid of dwellings, except for the "crop-watching cottages" to be found in some countries. A generalized picture of such a settlement usually consists of five parts: (1) Forming the core is the village proper, made up of the homes, barns, and other farm buildings; (2) nearest the village are small garden plots; (3) more remote are the cultivated lands; (4) sometimes competing with the cultivated plots for land adjacent to the village and sometimes beyond the arable lands are pastures; and (5) most remote from the village at the outer limits of the community's domain usually are to be found waste lands and woods.[2] Where density of population is not great, there may be an indeterminate area between communities, and the property of one village may shade indiscriminately into that of another. The essential element in the village pattern is the clustering of farm homes in a

---

[2] For an excellent brief description of the English village settlement, see Edward P. Cheyney, *An Introduction to the Industrial and Social History of England*, New York, The Macmillan Company, 1916, chap. 2. The classic work on the English village is Frederic Seebohm, *The English Village Community*, New York, Longmans, Green & Company, 1926. However, the interested student should also consult George Laurence Gomme, *The Village Community, with Special Reference to the Origin and Form of Its Survivals in Britain*, London, Walter Scott, Ltd., 1890; F. W. Maitland, *Domesday Book and Beyond*, Cambridge, University Press, 1897; N. S. B. Gras and E. C. Gras, *The Economic and Social History of an English Village*, Cambridge, Harvard University Press, 1930; Sir Henry Sumner Maine, *Village-Communities in the East and West*, New York, Henry Holt & Company, 1889; Emile de Laveleye, *Primitive Property*, London, The Macmillan Company, 1878; Harold Peake, *The English Village*, London, Benn Brothers, Ltd., 1922; Paul Vinogradoff, *The Growth of the Manor*, New York, The Macmillan Company, 1905; and N. Neilson, *Medieval Agrarian Economy*, New York, Henry Holt & Company, 1936.

FIGURE 41. Village Settlement in Peru, Surrounded by Fields on the Remnants of the
Old Inca Terraces. (Courtesy of M. Kuczynski-Godard.)

FIGURE 42. A Coffee Fazenda in São Paulo, Brazil. Note the Workers' Village, or Colony, at the Upper Right. (Courtesy of Carlos Borges Schmidt.)

FIGURE 43. Village Type of Settlement Used by the Natives of Senegal, Africa. (From *Vollstandige Völkergallerie*, Meissen, F. W. Goedsche, n.d., II Abtheilung.)

FIGURE 44. German Village of the *Runddörfer* Type and the Surrounding Fields. (Courtesy of Plan und Karte, B. m. b. H., through Katherina Elisseieff.)

village and the separation of the dwellings from the fields which lie about the core of the settlement.

The village nucleus itself shows a great many variations. In Europe, for example, there are pronounced differences between the settlements established by the Germans and those made by the Slavs. The great work of Meitzen has shown clearly that the genuine German village was merely a compact group of houses

Figure 45.   German Village of the *Strassendörfer* Type and the Adjacent Fields. (Courtesy of Plan und Karte, B. m. b. H., through Katherina Elisseieff.)

arranged with no definite plan.[3] Slavic villages, on the other hand, were constructed in a distinctive and orderly fashion. They are of two principal types, "round" villages (*Runddörfer*) and "long" villages (*Strassendörfer*). (See Figures 44 and 45 for examples of these types.) The distinctive culture patterns carried by each ethnic group and given material expression in the type of village constructed have enabled scholars to throw a great deal of light upon the migrations of the various stocks in prehistoric times.[4]

[3] A. Meitzen, *Siedlung und Agrarwesen der Westgermanen und Ostgermanen, der Kelten, Finnen, und Slaven*, Berlin, Besser, 1895, 4 vols. Cf. A. W. Ashley, "Meitzen's Siedelung und Agrarwesen der Germanen," *Political Science Quarterly*, XIII (1898), 143–145.

[4] Cf. W. Z. Ripley, *The Races of Europe*, New York, The Century Company, 1894, pp. 240–242. Ripley is indebted to Meitzen for his materials.

FIGURE 46.   The Village Pattern of Settlement: Map of Escalante, Utah, Showing the Village and a Part of the Fields. (Reproduced from Lowry Nelson, *The Mormon Village*, Brigham Young University Studies 3, Provo, Utah, 1930, p. 28.)

Village settlements in the United States are no less distinctive in character. A feature of the New England "plantations" was the village common or green at the center of the settlement. In the

FIGURE 47. The Village Pattern of Settlement: A Typical Mormon Village from the Air. (Photo by the Western Division Laboratory of the Agricultural Adjustment Division.)

Southwest the Spanish colonizers were first concerned with the location of the plaza, which in inland towns was a rectangle in the center of the pueblo, in river or coastal locations was placed facing the water front.[5] And the Mormon settlements in the Rocky

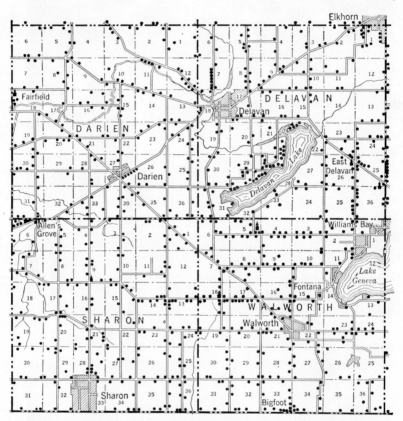

Figure 48. The Scattered Farmsteads Type of Settlement: Map of a Portion of Walworth County, Wisconsin. (Reproduced from C. J. Galpin, *The Social Anatomy of an Agricultural Community*, Wisconsin AES Bulletin 34, 1915.)

Mountain region conformed closely to the plan for the "City of Zion" which was formulated as early as 1833. The essential elements of the Mormon plan called for a rectangle one mile square

[5] Cf. Frank W. Blackmar, *Spanish Institutions of the Southwest*, Baltimore, Johns Hopkins University Press, 1891, pp. 164–183; Herbert I. Priestley, *The Coming of the White Man, 1492–1848*, New York, The Macmillan Company, 1929, p. 37; and Herbert Howe Bancroft, *History of California*, San Francisco, The History Company, 1886, I, 345 n.

to be divided into blocks of ten acres; these were then cut into lots of one-half acre, allowing twenty houses to the block; streets were eight rods wide, intersected at right angles, and ran north and south.[6] (See Figures 46 and 47.)

Single Farmsteads

In sharp contrast with village patterns of settlement is that in which each farm home is located among the fields worked by the family. Whereas the village settlement is characterized by close and intimate relations between the homes of the farmers, in the scattered or isolated farmsteads mode of settlement the homes of the farmers are widely separated from one another. (See Figures 48 and 49.) Just as the village pattern of settlement makes the relationships between the family and the land remote and intermittent, scattered farmsteads make for close and constant contacts between the family and the land but more distant relations with other farm homes.

There are varying degrees of remoteness between the dwellings under a system of single farmsteads. If density of population is slight and holdings are large, the houses will be more dispersed than in areas of denser population and smaller farms. Cultural and natural factors also affect the dispersion of the homesteads. If situations are chosen in valleys and the surrounding ridges are used for boundaries, as is reported from the early trans-Appalachian settlements,[7] each farm home will be nearer the center of the holding and more remote from neighbors. And the more the tracts of land are held in the form of squares, other things being equal, the more impossible it will be for farmers to construct their homes in close proximity to one another. The checkerboard pattern of land division that prevails in the United States, if combined with the scattered farmsteads type of settlement, nears the maximum possible in separation or isolation of farm homes.[8] But in Brazil, Colombia, and many other countries the use of metes and bounds

[6] Cf. Lowry Nelson, *The Mormon Village: A Study in Social Origins*, Brigham Young University Studies 3, Provo, Utah, 1930, pp. 18–19.

[7] Cf. Dr. Joseph Doddridge, *Settlement of Western Country*, Bowling Green, Ohio, Historical Publications Company, 1923, pp. 11–12; and John W. Monette, *History of the Discovery and Settlement of the Valley of the Mississippi*, New York, Harper & Brothers, 1846, II, 6.

[8] Cf. T. Lynn Smith, "The Social Effects of Land Division in Relationship to a Program of Land Utilization," *Journal of Farm Economics*, XVII (1935), 703–704.

FIGURE 49. The Scattered Farmsteads Type of Settlement: The Iowa Design for Farming, from the Air. (Photo by The Register and Tribune Company of Des Moines, Iowa.)

FIGURE 50. Bayou Lafourche from the Air. Note the extensive line village settlements. Observe the plantation with its nucleated settlement in the lower right-hand corner. (Photo by the Davis Aerial Photographic Service, Houma, La.)

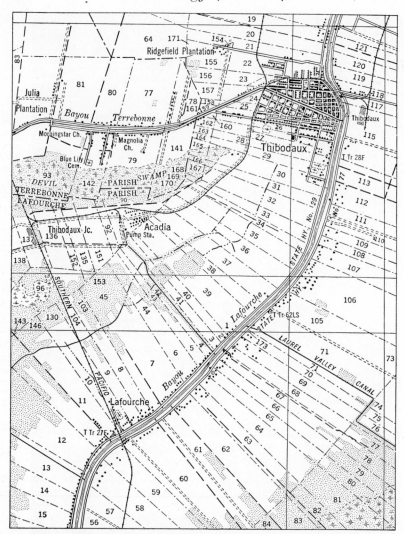

FIGURE 51.   The Line Village Settlement Pattern: Map of a Portion of Lafourche Parish, Louisiana, Showing the River-Front Land Division and the Typical Arrangement of Farm Homes.

in dividing the land also has brought about extreme dispersion of farm homes.[9]

[9] Cf. T. Lynn Smith, "The Locality Group Structure of Brazil," *American Sociological Review,* IX (1944), 41–42; T. Lynn Smith, *Brazil: People and Institutions,* Baton Rouge, Louisiana State University Press, 1946, chap. 13; and T. Lynn Smith, Justo Diaz Rodriguez, and Luis Roberto Garcia, *Tabio: Estudio de la Organizacion Social Rural,* Bogotá, Ministerio de la Economía Nacional, 1944, pp. 34–40. See also Peter A. Munch, "Gard: The Norwegian Farm," *Rural Sociology,* XII (1947), 356–363.

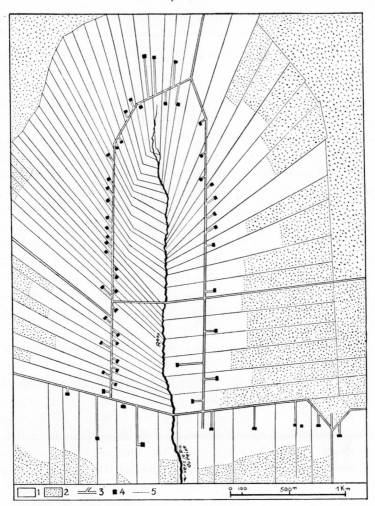

1. Area Cleared by 1936.
2. Area Wooded in 1936 (Since Cleared).
3. Road.
4. House.
5. Property Line.

FIGURE 52. Plan of a Modified Form of the Line Village Settlement Pattern Used by Japanese Colonists in the State of São Paulo, Brazil. (Reproduced by courtesy of the author and publisher from Pierre Monbeig, *Pionniers et Planteurs de São Paulo,* Paris, Librairie Armand Colin, 1952, p. 211.)

The Line Village

If some common base of departure is employed in laying out the land, if the length of the holdings is great in comparison with

the width, and if the farm families rather consistently locate their
dwellings at the same end of their ribbonlike farms, a considerable
aggregation of dwellings can occur without sacrificing residence
on the farmstead. Such a settlement has the appearance of a long,
one-streeted village winding its way across the landscape.[10] (See
Figures 50 and 51.) By most students it has been classed with villages proper in which the farmers reside apart from the land, in
the group of nucleated settlements or grouped habitats.[11] The fact
that under such a pattern farmers reside on their lands is sufficient
reason, however, for differentiating it from other agglomerated
types. It is more properly placed in a separate category.

Two highly rationalized varieties of the line village pattern
of settlement are deserving of special mention. One of these has
been employed by native Brazilians and Japanese immigrants
alike in parts of the state of São Paulo, Brazil. (See Figure 52.)
Note that the river-front system of land division employed gives
all of the farms access to the stream; that the road encircles the
valley in which such a settlement is located; and that the line
village arrangement of the houses, all of them on the land and on
the road, results in fairly compact settlement. The second has been
employed to some extent in the modern colonization of an ancient
land—in the laying out of some of the new agricultural communities the Jews have built in what is now the new nation of Israel.
(See Figure 53.) In this case the farms and homes all front on a
circular street, and the wedge-shaped holdings become wider as
their depth increases. Were it not for the fact that each of the
farm homes is located on the tract of land which makes up the
farm, this compact arrangement would properly be classified in
the true village category rather than as one of the varieties of the
line village type of settlement.

Line village settlements are widespread throughout the world,
apparently in many cases arising spontaneously along the banks
of rivers. However, this mode of arranging the population on the

[10] Cf. T. Lynn Smith, *Farm Trade Centers in Louisiana, 1901–1931,* Louisiana
AES Bulletin 234, Baton Rouge, 1933, p. 3; and T. Lynn Smith, "An Analysis of
Rural Social Organization Among the French-Speaking People of Southern
Louisiana," *Journal of Farm Economics,* XVI (1934), 680–688.

[11] Cf. A. Demangeon, "La géographie de l'habitat rural," *Annales de géographie,*
XXXVI (1927), 1–23, 97–114; P. A. Sorokin, Carle C. Zimmerman, and Charles J.
Galpin, *A Systematic Source Book in Rural Sociology,* Minneapolis, University of
Minnesota Press, 1930, I, 266–304; N. S. B. Gras, *An Introduction to Economic
History,* New York, Harper & Brothers, 1922, pp. 56–58; and Paul H. Landis,
Rural Life in Process, New York, McGraw-Hill Book Company, 1940, pp. 26–27.

FIGURE 53. The New Settlement of Nahalal, Israel, Depicting a Highly Rationalized Settlement Pattern of the Line Village Type. (Courtesy United Israel Appeal.)

land early became set in the cultural patterns of the French and has been carried by them to many countries, including parts of Canada and the United States. Interestingly enough, the line village seems to have developed independently in south Brazil and has come to be the dominant settlement pattern in the important small farming areas of that country.[12]

Advantages and Disadvantages of the Various Settlement Patterns

The comparative desirability of the various patterns of settlement is greatly dependent upon the point of view. If economic considerations are great, and especially if the farm management aspects are the primary elements considered, the village pattern is highly undesirable. Village residence makes the proper care of livestock a great problem. To keep horses and cattle in the village, which is usually done, entails the transportation of feed to the village and of the manure back to the fields. To secure pasture the stock must be driven out from the village and back again daily. If they are kept in the fields, someone must go frequently to see that feed and water are available. A good farmer cannot "rest easy" if his work stock and cattle are left to themselves several miles from his dwelling. In any case much time is lost driving to and from the fields, not to mention the fact that the daily commuting to and from work is hard on the work stock. Under the village pattern of settlement it is more difficult to utilize by-products from the farming enterprise for the feeding of chickens, pigs, etc.

There is also the matter of fragmentation of holdings. This is an almost inevitable concomitant of the village type of settlement. The ancient Hebrews, the Russians, and others arrested the development of extremes along this line with legal provision for community ownership of land, periodic redistribution of holdings, etc. But private property in land and a system of inheritance that does not provide for transmitting landed properties intact to one heir bring about a rapid pulverization of landholdings. For example, in Newton, Massachusetts, on May 1, 1635, the holdings of John White consisted of the following elements: (1) Two small tracts of about three rods each in "cowyard row." On one of these was located his dwelling, farm buildings, and garden. (2) Three separate tracts in "old field," one containing two and one-half

---

[12] See T. Lynn Smith, *Brazil: People and Institutions*, chap. 13; and T. Lynn Smith, "Brazilian Land Surveys, Land Division, and Land Titles," *Rural Sociology*, IX (1944), 269–270.

acres, and two of one acre and one rod each. (3) One acre on
"long marsh hill" and another tract of three acres in "long marsh";
13½ acres in the "neck of land"; 11 acres in the "great marsh"; and
one acre in "ox marsh."[13] In the Mormon villages of the present

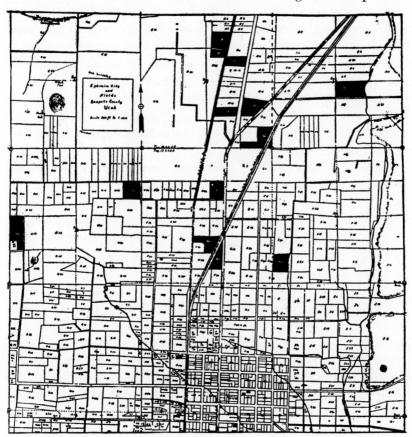

FIGURE 54. The Village Settlement Pattern is Accompanied by Fragmentation of Holdings. Map of a portion of Ephraim, Utah, showing the
location of the fields owned and cultivated by one man. (Reproduced from
Lowry Nelson, *The Utah Farm Village of Ephraim,* Brigham Young University Studies 2, Provo, Utah, 1928, p. 12.)

day, fragmentation or divided holdings continue as a source of
inconvenience and vexation to the inhabitants. In one village

[13] Cf. Herbert L. Osgood, *The American Colonies in the Seventeenth Century,*
New York, The Macmillan Company, 1904, I, 449–451; for examples in other
communities, see Anne B. MacLear, *Early New England Towns,* Columbia
University Studies in Economics, History, and Public Law, New York, 1908, XXIX,
86.

(Ephraim), Nelson discovered the extreme case of a man with a farm of twelve pieces, no two of which were adjacent.[14] (See Figure 54.) Acute as is the problem in this village, it is minor in comparison with the situation in the older countries of Europe. From Germany comes a description of a farm of twenty hectares that is split up into sixty-seven separate plots. For the owner to go from his village residence to each of these and back would necessitate traveling eighty-one miles.[15] It should not be supposed that this case is not matched by hundreds of others in various countries. For example, the 1939 census in Switzerland revealed that there was an average of ten plots per farm in the nation as a whole; and there was a total of 1234 holdings each of which consisted of 100 or more fragments.[16]

From the standpoint of farm management the village system obviously is greatly inferior to both the line village pattern and the single farmstead type of settlement. Undoubtedly this is the factor that has caused the diffusion of the single farmstead type of settlement throughout the world as one of the direct results of the employment of American agricultural engineers as technical experts in various foreign countries.[17]

But if one approaches the question of settlement patterns from the standpoint of social efficiency, as many have done, then the advantages of the village system are readily apparent. Close and intimate contact with neighbors, proximity to social institutions, availability of playmates for children, facilitation of mutual aid, and, in brief, a rich social life are made possible when the homes of farmers are congregated in the true village community. Terpenning's study of European villages convinced Dr. Ross that a satisfactory farm life was impossible as long as American farmers live

[14] Cf. Lowry Nelson, *The Utah Farm Village of Ephraim*, Brigham Young University Studies 2, Provo, Utah, 1928, p. 11; and Lowry Nelson, *Some Social and Economic Features of American Fork, Utah*, Brigham Young University Studies 4, Provo, 1933, p. 28.

[15] H. Richter, "Consolidation of Scattered Farm Holdings in Germany," *Foreign Agriculture*, II (1938), 235–242.

[16] Bernard O. Binns, *The Consolidation of Fragmented Agricultural Holdings*, FAO Agricultural Studies 11, Washington, Food and Agricultural Organization of the United Nations, 1950, p. 78.

[17] For example, see R. B. Hall, "Some Rural Settlement Forms in Japan," *Geographical Review*, XXI (1931), 93–123, where a miniature likeness to our system of land division and scattered farmsteads is described and attributed to American agricultural experts; and G. M. McBride, "The Agrarian Problem in Chile," *Geographical Review*, XX (1930), 574–586.

apart from one another as they now do.[18] Dr. Branson came to much the same conclusion on the basis of his European travels.[19] More recently H. C. Nixon has stated the case for "villages for villagers" in the South, and has urged a transition to village settlements.[20] But the case for the village type of settlement has never been stated better than it was set forth by Timothy Dwight more than one hundred years ago.

It is a remarkable fact, that New-England was colonized in a manner widely different from that which prevailed in the other British colonies. All the ancient, and a great part of the modern townships, were settled in what may be called the village manner; the inhabitants having originally planted themselves in small towns. In many other parts of this country the planters have almost universally fixed themselves on their several farms, each placing his house where his own convenience dictated. In this manner, it is evident the farmer can more advantageously manage his own property, can oversee it more readily, and labour on it with fewer interruptions, than when it is dispersed in fields at some distance from each other.

But scattered plantations are subject to many serious disadvantages. Neither schools nor churches can, without difficulty, be either built by the planters or supported. The children must be too remote from the school, and the families from the church, not to discourage all strenuous efforts to provide these interesting accommodations. Whenever it is proposed to erect either of them, the thought that one's self, and one's family, are too distant from the spot to derive any material benefit, will check the feeble relentings of avarice, the more liberal dispositions of frugality, and even the noble designs of a generous disposition. Should all the first difficulties be overcome, trifling infirmities, foul weather, and the ill state of roads, will prevent a regular attendance. But the family, or the children, who do not go with some good degree of regularity to the church or the school, will in the end scarcely go at all. The education of the one, and the religion of both, will therefore in many cases be prevented.

[18] See the Editor's Introduction in Walter A. Terpenning, *Village and Open-Country Neighborhoods,* New York, D. Appleton-Century Company, 1931, p. vii; Terpenning's own conclusions, indicating a marked superiority of the European village form of settlement over our own scattered farmsteads, are found on pp. 384–408. Especially does he stress the advantages of the village from the standpoint of working together, mutual-aid activities, education, and recreation.

[19] E. C. Branson, *Farm Life Abroad,* Chapel Hill, University of North Carolina Press, 1924, pp. 43–44.

[20] *Forty Acres and Steel Mules,* Chapel Hill, University of North Carolina Press, 1938, pp. 61–70.

At the same time, persons who live on scattered plantations are in a great measure cut off from that daily intercourse which softens and polishes man. When we live at a distance from every neighbour, a call demands an effort, and a visit becomes a formal enterprise. A family, thus situated, must in a great measure be confined to its own little circle of domestic objects, and wrought insensibly into an insulated character. At the sight of a stranger the children, having been unaccustomed to such an object, are abashed, and the parents awkward and uneasy. That which generally gives pain will be regarded with apprehension, and repeated only from necessity. Social intercourse, therefore, exercised too little to begin to be pleasant, will be considered as an incumbrance; and the affections which cherish it, and which it cherishes and refines in its turn, will either sleep or expire. The gentle and pleasing manners, naturally growing out of it, can never be formed here. On the contrary, that rough and forbidding deportment, which springs from intercourse with oxen and horses, or with those who converse only to make bargains about oxen and horses, a rustic sheepishness, or a more awkward and provoking impudence, take possession of the man, and manifest their dominion in his conduct. The state of the manners, and that of the mind, are mutually causes and effects. The mind, like the manners, will be distant, rough, forbidding, gross, solitary, and universally disagreeable. A nation, planted in this manner, can scarcely be more than half civilized; and to refinement of character and life must necessarily be a stranger.

In such settlements schools are accordingly few and solitary; and a great multitude of the inhabitants, of both sexes, are unable either to write or read. Churches are still more rare; and the number of persons is usually not small, who have hardly ever been present either at a prayer or a sermon. Unaccustomed to objects of this nature, they neither wish for them, nor know what they are. The preachers whom they hear are, at the same time, very frequently uneducated itinerants, started into the desk by the spirit of propagandism; recommended by nothing but enthusiasm and zeal; unable to teach, and often even to learn. In such a situation, what can the character and manners become, unless such as have been described?

A New-Englander, passing through such settlements, is irresistibly struck with a wide difference between their inhabitants and those of his own country. The scene is changed at once. That intelligence and sociality, that softness and refinement, which prevail among even the plain people of New-England, disappear. That repulsive character, which, as Lord Kaimes has remarked, is an original feature of savage man; intelligence bounded by the farm, the market, and the road which leads to it; affections so rarely moved as scarcely to be capable of being moved at all, unless when roused to resentment; conversation confined to the properties and price of a horse, or the sale of a load of wheat; ignorance, at fifty years of age, of what is familiarly known by every New-England school-boy; wonder, excited by mere common homespun things, because they are novelties; a stagnant indifference about other things, equally common, and of high importance, because they are unknown; an entire vacancy of sentiment, and a sterility of mind, out of which sentiment can never spring; all spread over a great proportion of the inhabitants, make him feel as if he were transported to a distant climate, and as if he were travelling in a foreign country.

New-England presents a direct contrast to this picture. Almost the whole country is covered with villages; and every village has its church and its suit of schools. Nearly every child, even those of beggars and blacks in considerable numbers, can read, write, and keep accounts. Every child is carried to the church from the cradle, nor leaves the church but for the grave. All the people are neighbours; social beings; converse; feel; sympathize; mingle minds; cherish sentiments; and are subjects of at least some degree of refinement. More than six hundred youths, natives of New-England, are always in the colleges erected here. In almost every village are found literary men, and social libraries. A great number of men also, not liberally educated, addict themselves to reading, and acquire extensive information. Of all these advantages the mode of settlement has been one, and, it is believed, a powerful cause.[21]

Thus, much depends upon the point of view. In a relatively self-sufficing economy the choice between villages and the isolated farmsteads, if made in a rational manner, would involve weighing the social advantages of the village against the farm management advantages of the scattered farmsteads. But as society becomes more complex and interdependent, the significance of other economic factors is greatly increased. These factors are all those involved in the relationships, communication, and exchange with the great society. Today electricity, paved roads, telephones, radios, daily access to fresh meats, fruits, and vegetables, transportation for school children, etc., have become basic necessities of life. Thus in addition to the economics of farm management the economics of transportation and communication with the outside world must be considered. Great indeed must be the economies of farm management to pay for the increased expenditures for

[21] *Op. cit.*, I, 300–302.

paved roads, automobiles, gasoline, school buses, electric lines, telephone lines, etc.

But fortunately the choice is not limited to two settlement types. The line village type of settlement offers a convenient way of attaining most of the social advantages of compact settlement without sacrificing the farm management advantages that come from residence on the land. In addition such a pattern of settlement offers great economies in the provision of all the avenues for contact with the great society such as are exemplified in good roads, electric lines, minimum distances for school buses, etc. Without doubt in rural America the line village type of settlement would prove an economic and social boon to a large part of the rural farm population.

But it is difficult to change the fundamental pattern of settlement, once it has been established, even in those rare cases in which cultural inertia is overcome through popular education to the extent that the mass of the people are aware that other possibilities than the traditional pattern exist. Everyone knows that it is a cumbersome task to move farm buildings from one site to another; and the inconvenience involved in such transfers is probably a small matter in comparison with the difficulties inherent in rearranging the boundaries of lands. One who suggests that changes are desirable and possible is likely to be considered an extreme visionary. Nevertheless, granted that it is possible to make the farm population thoroughly aware of the advantages and disadvantages of the several types of settlement, the author believes that rather thoroughgoing changes could be brought about in the course of a couple of generations.[22]

In the first place, much might be accomplished through a careful planning of farmers' roads. The blueprint that is now being followed, if carried through to completion, will eventually place a paved road around every 640 acres in the nation or those parts of the nation that were surveyed following 1785. Of course it will be many years before this program can be completed—perhaps fortunately, since its desirability is open to question. With either the village or the line village form of settlement it would not be necessary to build a road around every section of land.

The paving of a farm road places a premium upon the land

[22] A very thought-provoking study of this subject is Walter R. Goldschmidt, "Some Evidence on the Future Pattern of Rural Settlement," *Rural Sociology*, VIII (1943), 386–395.

next to the pavement and makes it more desirable than land of a comparable quality not adjacent to the highway. When a new paved road passes through a farming territory there is a tendency for farm dwellings, barns, etc., to appear next to it. Part of this is due to the fact that old buildings back in the fields are gradually being destroyed and replaced by new ones located on the highway. Part of it is also due to the moving of the farm buildings out to the road. If, for the time being, paved roads were placed no nearer than two miles to each other, the mileage of projected roads in the United States would be reduced by approximately two-thirds; also, in the manner indicated in the next paragraph, there would be a gradual change in the basic pattern of settlement in the nation.

Farms do not remain of a given size year after year. Some are growing, others diminishing in extent. Farm estates are constantly being accumulated by some operators, only to be divided later among the heirs. Consider the simple case of dividing equally between two heirs one half section, 320 acres of land, a situation by no means rare in America. In the past each has been satisfied to have his 160 acres in a square, a quarter section. Now suppose a paved road passes along the end but not the side of the original holding. With this new factor in the situation the chances are that each would desire his 160-acre allotment in a plot fronting on the highway. Instead of quarter sections each would seek a plot consisting of four "forties" laid end to end. Therefore, in subdividing lands of any size the road would be a factor of genuine significance demanding consideration. Because of this, careful planning of roads in rural districts would in all probability effect a great change in rural settlement patterns during the course of two or three generations. Already in the neighborhood of large cities, where great concentrations of rural population are occurring, this factor is operating to make for settlements of the line village type.

Settlement Patterns in the United States

In the territory now occupied by the United States, practically every form of settlement has been utilized. The settlers who spread from the Atlantic to the Pacific at one time or another, in one place or another, tried out almost every possibility in the way of arranging the population on the land. Of course the single farmstead has been and remains the principal American pattern of settlement, but village forms have played their part in the colonization of the country, and the line village settlements have not been entirely lacking.

Village Settlements

Cultural influences are so potent as social determinants that, almost inevitably, the first English colonists transferred the traditional English village form of settlement to the New World. In New England practically all the early settlements were established according to the village pattern.[23] With practically no modification, group settlement, or the "swarming"[24] of established communities carried the village pattern of settlement throughout New England and to some extent into New York and New Jersey as well.[25] The settlement types were so little changed from the villages of England, and the villages of England from those of Germany, that the New England village of Puritan days has been described as an exact counterpart of the German village in the time of Tacitus.[26] The location, general appearance, and composition of these villages of New England have been set forth concisely by Timothy Dwight as follows:

> New England villages . . . are built in the following manner.
> The local situation is pitched on as a place in itself desirable; as a

[23] The literature on this subject is voluminous. Bradford's *History of Plymouth Plantation, 1606–1646*, is an indispensable source concerning the first settlement. A convenient edition is the one edited by William T. Davis, New York, Charles Scribner's Sons, 1908. Among the best monographic studies are: Herbert B. Adams, *Village Communities of Cape Anne and Salem*, Johns Hopkins University Studies in Historical and Political Science, First Series, IX–X, Baltimore, 1883; Herbert B. Adams, *The Germanic Origin of New England Towns*, Johns Hopkins University Studies in Historical and Political Science, First Series, II, Baltimore, 1882; McLear, *op. cit.;* Charles M. Andrews, *The River Towns of Connecticut*, Johns Hopkins University Studies in Historical and Political Science, Seventh Series, VII–IX, Baltimore, 1889; and Melville Egleston, *The Land System of the New England Colonies*, Johns Hopkins University Studies in Historical and Political Science, Fourth Series, XI–XII, Baltimore, 1886. An invaluable but much neglected source is the four-volume work by Timothy Dwight, already cited.

[24] Cf. *Report of the Commissioner of Agriculture for the Year 1866*, Washington, Government Printing Office, 1867, p. 502; and Edward Channing, *Town and County Government in the English Colonies of North America*, Johns Hopkins University Studies in Historical and Political Science, Second Series, X, Baltimore, 1884, pp. 459–460.

[25] Cf. Andrews, *op. cit.*, pp. 42–46, 61, 75–78; Egleston, *op. cit.*, pp. 572–599; Dwight, *op. cit.*, III, 167; and Percy W. Bidwell and John I. Falconer, *History of Agriculture in the Northern United States, 1620–1860*, Washington, The Carnegie Institution of Washington, 1925, pp. 64–66.

[26] Adams, *The Germanic Origin of New England Towns*, p. 12. The English manorial system had important effects upon land tenure but probably did little to change settlement patterns.

place, where life may be passed through more pleasantly than in most others; as a place, not where trade compels, but where happiness invites to settle. Accordingly the position of these towns is usually beautiful. The mode of settlement is such as greatly to enhance the pleasure intended. The body of inhabitants is composed of farmers; and farmers nowhere, within my knowledge, of a superior character for intelligence and good manners. . . .

To this character of the inhabitants the manner of locating and building these towns is happily suited. The town-plat is originally distributed into lots, containing from two to ten acres. In a convenient spot, on each of these, a house is erected at the bottom of the court-yard (often neatly enclosed); and is furnished universally with a barn, and other convenient outbuildings. Near the house there is always a garden, replenished with culinary vegetables, flowers, and fruits, and very often, also, prettily enclosed. The lot, on which the house stands, universally styled the home lot, is almost of course a meadow, richly cultivated, covered during the pleasant season with verdure, and containing generally a thrifty orchard. It is hardly necessary to observe, that these appendages spread a singular cheerfulness and beauty over a New-England village, or that they contribute largely to render the house a delightful residence.[27]

Very early there arose among some of the inhabitants of New England a desire to leave the village and establish homes on the land. Innovations in this field were not welcomed. Bradford mentions that for the first seven years each person was given only one acre of land "as nere the towne as might be" so that the inhabitants might be kept close together "both for more saftie and defense. . . ."[28] Weeden refers to a decree of the General Court in 1635 ordering that no dwelling in any of the new settlements should be established at a distance of more than half a mile from the meetinghouse. He also cites a case from Ipswich in 1661 where because a certain man and his wife had absented themselves from public worship, the Court authorized "seven men" to sell his farm and thus compel him to live nearer the church.[29] Some of the settlements also found it necessary to place restrictions upon the establishment of new plantations because in scattered settlements "the posterity of such, most of them, are endangered to degenerate

---

[27] *Op. cit.*, II, 317.
[28] Davis, *op. cit.*, p. 175.
[29] William B. Weeden, *Economic and Social History of New England, 1620–1789*, Boston, Houghton Mifflin Company, 1891, I, 73; cf. Channing, *op. cit.*, p. 464.

to heathenish ignorance and barbarisme," unless they were built in "such neerness together" as to afford protection and facilitate social interaction.[30]

Thus cultural forces supplemented by law enabled this type of settlement to maintain its importance in the older parts of New England for more than two hundred years. As late as 1820, Timothy Dwight, the president of Yale University, gave the following indignant reply to Volney's assertion that scattered farmsteads were frequently to be found in New England: ". . . The representation of M. Volney is merely a flight of the imagination. It will appear also that a great part of the ancient settlements in New England, instead of being scattered farmhouses, are composed chiefly of villages. . . ."[31] Dwight, who had traveled on horseback through practically every township in New England, undoubtedly had good evidence to support his contention. In his notes concerning a township he nearly always made mention of the mode of settlement. Such entries as the following are numerous throughout the four volumes of his work:

The town [Deerfield] is built on an elevation, spreading out from the foot of the mountain. The principal street, on which stand three-fourths of the houses, runs from north to south. The buildings are generally neat; and exhibit everywhere a tidy, thrifty appearance. The inhabitants are generally farmers, and of the first class in this country.[32]

Immediately above Watertown lies South-Farms; the southern parish of Litchfield . . . the houses good farmers' dwellings, of which a little village is formed around the church.[33]

Pomfret contains a pretty village, lying partly on this road, and partly on the Norwich road, which joins it at right angles. The inhabitants are principally a collection of sober, industrious farmers.[34]

Milford . . . was purchased by the Rev. Peter Prudden and others, principally from Wethersfield, in 1639. Forty-four planters settled themselves here immediately; but they found the Indians so numerous, that they surrounded the town plat, nearly a mile square, with a strong palisade.[35]

[30] Weeden, *op. cit.*, pp. 269–270.
[31] *Op. cit.*, IV, 207.
[32] *Ibid.*, II, 54–55.
[33] *Ibid.*, II, 351.
[34] *Ibid.*, III, 127.
[35] *Ibid.*, III, 501.

And a few of the settlements such as Old Hadley, Old Deerfield, and Sunderland, Massachusetts, have preserved their patterns pretty much intact until the present day.[36]

In New York, where the original settlers were Dutch, single farmsteads constituted the prevailing pattern of settlement. Neither on the large estates nor in the areas of small farms was the village type of early importance. Later on, comparisons of the lot of the Dutch settlers with that of the English in New England convinced the authorities, including Stuyvesant, of the superiority of the village form of settlement. They made definite efforts to remold the settlement pattern through pressure from above. For example, when the settlers of Pavonia petitioned for special favors, Stuyvesant granted their requests on condition that they concentrate their homes into a village.[37] Such efforts were successful only to a minor degree; and although a few settlements of the village form persisted for many years,[38] the bulk of the state was colonized with single farmsteads. New York also served as a powerful center in diffusing the scattered farmsteads type of settlement westward.

Under the influence of Penn much experimentation with settlement patterns took place in Pennsylvania, but those of the village form prevailed in the beginning. Penn himself described the type of settlement utilized in the colony as follows:

We do settle in the way of Townships or Villages, each of which contains 5,000 acres, in square, and at least Ten Families; the regulation of the Country being a family to each five hundred Acres. . . .

Our Townships lie square; generally the Village in the Center; the Houses either opposit, or else opposit to the middle, betwist two houses over the way, for near neighborhood.[39]

---

[36] Cf. N. L. Sims, *Elements of Rural Sociology*, New York, Thomas Y. Crowell Company, 1928, pp. 537–545.

[37] See Clarence White Rife, "Land Tenure in New Netherland," in *Essays in Colonial History* (presented to Charles McLean Andrews by his students), New Haven, Yale University Press, 1931, p. 63.

[38] Cf. Irving Elting, *Dutch Village Communities on the Hudson River*, Johns Hopkins University Studies in Historical and Political Science, Fourth Series, I, Baltimore, 1886.

[39] William Penn, "A Further Account of the Province of Pennsylvania, 1685," in *Narratives of Early Pennsylvania, West New Jersey and Delaware, 1630–1707*, New York, Charles Scribner's Sons, 1912, p. 263; cf. Albert Bernhardt Faust, *The German Element in the United States*, Boston, Houghton Mifflin Company, 1909, I, 37–39; James Curtis Ballagh, "Southern Economic History: Tariff and Public Lands," *Annual Report of the American Historical Association, 1898*, Washington, 1899, p. 237.

In the Middle Colonies of New Jersey and Delaware early efforts were devoted to establishing the village form of settlement.[40] Much the same was the case in Maryland.[41] Jamestown, the first settlement in Virginia, was of the village type; and later, when a modified form of the manorial system became the dominant institution of Virginia, one of the characteristic features of each plantation was a slave "village" or "quarters" for the Negroes. The slave village was the Negro's world. Miss Bremer observed these villages in the Carolinas and Georgia and outlined their essential characteristics as follows:

I range about in the neighborhood, through the rice fields and Negro villages, which amuses me greatly. The slave villages consist of small, white-washed wooden houses, for the most part built in two rows, forming a street, each house standing detached in its little yard or garden, and generally with two or three trees about it.[42]

Miss Butler gave a more detailed description:

At the rear of the house about twelve yards, is what is called the colony, where are situated the kitchen, servants' sitting-room and bedrooms, the laundry and dairy, and in a corner of the yard is a turkeyhouse, full of prime Christmas fowl. Behind the colony is Settlement No. 1, where the coloured people (I believe this also is the correct term) reside. It consists of an avenue of orange trees, on each side of which are rows of wooden houses, and at the end of which, facing the avenue, is what was the old hospital, but which is half of it the church and the other half the residence of our English labourers, eight in number.[43]

[40] Ballagh, "Introduction to Southern Economic History—The Land System," *Annual Report of the American Historical Association, 1897*, Washington, 1898, pp. 114–115.

[41] Cf. L. C. Gray, *History of Agriculture in the Southern United States to 1860*, Washington, The Carnegie Institution of Washington, 1933, I, 377.

[42] Fredrika Bremer, *The Homes of the New World; Impressions of America*, New York, Harper & Brothers, 1854, I, 288–289.

[43] Frances Butler Leigh, *Ten Years on a Georgia Plantation Since the War*, London, R. Bentley & Son, 1883, pp. 243–244; cf. Frederick Law Olmsted, *A Journey in the Seaboard Slave States*, New York, G. P. Putnam's Sons, 1904, I, 123–124; John Johnson, *Old Maryland Manors, with the Records of a Court Leet and a Court Baron*, Johns Hopkins University Studies in Historical and Political Science, First Series, VII, Baltimore, 1883, pp. 9–10; Charles Sackett Sydnor, *Slavery in Mississippi*, New York, D. Appleton-Century Company, 1933, pp. 39, 42; U. B. Phillips, *American Negro Slavery*, New York, D. Appleton-Century Company, 1918, pp. 309–310; Marshall Hall, *Two-Fold Slavery of the United States*, London, A. Scott, 1854, pp. 34–35, 155; and Phillip A. Bruce, *Economic History of Virginia in the Seventeenth Century*, New York, The Macmillan Company, 1895, II, 161.

FIGURE 55. A Louisiana Sugar Plantation, Showing the Mill, the Homes of the Planter and His Skilled Employees, the "Quarters," and the Surrounding Fields. (Photo by Davis Aerial Photographic Service, Houma, La.)

Throughout the entire South wherever the planter class settled, the three-way association between large landholdings, good
land, and the Negro supported the ante-bellum plantation with
its village form of settlement. Even the planters concentrated their
homes to a considerable extent into towns and villages, from which
they commuted to their plantations at distances of ten, fifteen,
and even thirty miles.[44] In the sugar-producing sections of south
Louisiana the plantation system has retained the nucleated settlement pattern until the present. (See Figure 55.)

Although the plantation and the dispersed farmsteads settlements eventually gained the upper hand, settlements of freeholders arranged on the village plan were attempted in North Carolina,[45] South Carolina,[46] and Georgia.[47]

The cultural heritage is a persistent thing; and even though
the practice of squatting had spread the isolated farmstead
throughout the back settlements from Maine to Georgia, attempts
were made to develop village settlements beyond the Alleghenies.
A clear case of this was the first settlement (Manchester) in the
Virginia Military District, established by General Massie from
Kentucky. Massie gave notice of his intentions to the settlers of
Kentucky in the winter of 1790, offering to the first twenty-five
families to join him a donation of one in-lot and one out-lot of
100 acres on condition that they would settle in the village he
proposed to establish. Instead of twenty-five, thirty families accompanied him; and by the middle of March, 1791, the village
was planted and surrounded with strong pickets.[48]

More usual, however, in the settlement of the western country

[44] Cf. Thomas Perkins Abernethy, "Social Relations and Political Control in the
Old Southwest," *The Mississippi Valley Historical Review*, XVI (1929–1930),
529–530; and Herdman F. Cleland, "The Black Belt of Alabama," *Geographical
Review*, X (1920), 375–387.

[45] Cf. Adelaide L. Fries (ed.), *Records of the Moravians in North Carolina*,
Raleigh, Edwards and Broughton, 1922, I, 211, 220, 253, 271–272, 415, 435, 439.

[46] Alexander Gregg, *History of the Old Cheraws*, Columbia, S.C., The State
Company, 1905, p. 45; Verner W. Crane, *The Southern Frontier, 1670–1732*,
Durham, N.C., Duke University Press, 1928, p. 283; Peter Purry, "Proposals," in
Historical Collections of South Carolina, New York, 1836, II, 124–125; and Ed-
ward McCrady, *The History of South Carolina Under the Proprietary Government,
1670–1719*, New York, The Macmillan Company, 1897, pp. 145–146.

[47] Ballagh, "Introduction to Southern Economic History—The Land System,"
pp. 119–120; and Gray, *op. cit.*, I, 97.

[48] Cf. *The Pioneer* (a monthly periodical devoted to the objects of the Logan
Historical Society), Cincinnati, 1842, pp. 71–72; and Henry Howe, *Historical
Collections of Ohio*, Cincinnati, E. Morgan, 1856, pp. 21–22. For other instances
of village settlements in the West, see Gray, *op. cit.*, I, 93.

was a combination of the village and the scattered farmsteads type of settlement. That is, each settler located a cabin on his claim, but he also assisted others in the construction of a fort or station into which all the families in a neighborhood could retire in time of danger. Monette describes the typical fort or station as follows:

. . . A station, in most cases, was constructed for the protection of a large number of families, as a safe retreat in time of danger. It consisted of an inclosure of cabins, stockades, and block-houses, embracing about two acres or more, in the shape of a parallelogram or square; the inclosure being formed generally by cabins on two sides and by stockades on two sides. A large station sometimes presented three sides inclosed with cabins, the windows and doors all on the inner side. The outside wall of the cabin was generally ten or twelve feet high, without external openings, and perfectly bulletproof, with the roof sloping downward to the inside. The cabins otherwise were finished in the usual manner, for the residence of families. The gate or entrance was a strong puncheon door between the parallel walls of adjoining cabins, and protected by a platform and sentry-box above. The remainder of the inclosure was completed by strong palisades set in the ground, with their sharpened points standing ten feet above ground. The whole inclosure, cabins and stockades, was provided with port-holes for defensive firing. In time of danger the gate was closed, and securely barricaded each day at sunset. During the day, if no immediate danger threatened, the inmates dispersed to their several homes or employments, until nightfall again approached.

. . . .

In the absence of Indian alarms and "signs," the people left the station and dispersed upon their respective farms and improvements, and resided in their own individual residences. But so soon as any alarm was given, or any "Indian sign" was found, they again retired into the station for security.[49]

One interesting feature of the settlement of the West is the part played by various communistic or coöperative colonies. There have been many of these and all have utilized the village patterns in the establishment of their settlements. The Shakers, New Harmony, the Amana colony, the "Little Landers," Bishop Hill, New

[49] *Op. cit.*, II, 9–11; Doddridge, *op. cit.*, pp. 43–44; Timothy Flint, *The First White Man of the West, or the Life and Exploits of Col. Dan'l Boone,* Cincinnati, Applegate and Company, 1856, pp. 13, 83–84, and 108–111; and Thomas P. Abernethy, *From Frontier to Plantation in Tennessee,* Chapel Hill, University of North Carolina Press, 1932, pp. 12–13.

Llano—wherever one of these "experiments" has been tried, the village mode of settlement has been utilized.[50]

Greatly influenced by these communistic and socialistic attempts, especially those of Owen, and also strongly motivated by the ideal of founding in America the New Jerusalem, were the Latter-day Saints or Mormons under the leadership of Joseph Smith. In Ohio, Missouri, Illinois, and later on in the Great Basin, settlements were established by this group according to the village pattern. Today in Utah, Idaho, Arizona, Wyoming, Montana, Colorado, New Mexico, Nevada, Montana, and in Alberta, Canada, and Chihuahua, Mexico, are to be found village communities in which reside some 300,000 of these people.[51] For many years the origin of this particular variety of the village community was facilely attributed to borrowing from New England,[52] or the need for protection.[53] But detailed study has shown these "guesses" to be quite wide of the mark. This settlement form is a cultural complex whose origins are to be found in the communistic "United Order" doctrines of Mormonism and the repeated efforts of the Latter-day Saints to build the New Jerusalem on this continent.[54]

With the penetration of Spanish culture into what is now the United States came another variety of village settlement into this country. This element has been especially important in the Southwest. Many cities of the present time such as Los Angeles, San Jose, and San Francisco in California, and El Paso and San Antonio in Texas, were established according to the village pattern either as missions or as colonial municipalities.[55] Throughout much of Texas, New Mexico, Arizona, California, and in southern Colorado, the village pattern so introduced continues to exert an

[50] See, for examples, Michael A. Mikkelsen, *The Bishop Hill Colony*, Johns Hopkins Studies in Historical and Political Science, Tenth Series, I, Baltimore, 1892, pp. 37, 52, 54; Albert Shaw, *Co-operation in the Northwest*, Johns Hopkins Studies in Historical and Political Science, Sixth Series, IV–VI, Baltimore, 1888, pp. 352–354; Henry S. Anderson, "The Little Landers' Land Colonies: A Unique Agricultural Experiment in California," *Agricultural History*, V (1931), 139; and the map appended to the "Report of the Committee of the Association for the Relief of the Manufacturing and Labouring Poor," in Robert Owen, *A New View of Society*, London, 4th ed., 1818.

[51] See Lowry Nelson, "Bauerndörfer im westen der Vereinigten Staaten," *Internationale Agrar-Rundschau*, II (1939), 38.

[52] Sims, *op. cit.*, p. 547.

[53] John M. Gillette, *Rural Sociology*, New York, The Macmillan Company, 1928, p. 73.

[54] On this point consult Nelson, *The Mormon Village*.

[55] Cf. Blackmar, *op. cit.*, pp. 112–191.

important influence upon the behavior of the rural inhabitants of the region.[56] Analysis is showing that life in these village settlements in the southwestern United States still bears strong resemblances to that in similar settlements in Colombia, Chile, and other Latin American countries.[57]

Finally, before leaving the matter of village settlements in the United States, mention should be made of two recent developments making toward compact settlements for farming people. One of these is the rise of "suitcase farming" in the Great Plains. A person residing in a city such as Denver may go for a few weeks during the planting season to eastern Colorado or western Kansas, and with the use of a tractor and other equipment prepare the soil and plant a crop. Then he will return to his home in the city until harvest season, when another short visit to the fields is of sufficient duration to gather the grain. The use of tractors and combines may make these visits extremely brief. The net result is town or city residences for many persons engaged in agricultural production. A similar phenomenon is to be observed in western fruit-growing sections. With the assistance of the automobile many owners of orchards are enabled to reside in a town or city and to commute to and from the orchards as necessity arises. These developments, particularly important at the present time in the western states, may eventually come to have an important bearing on the settlement patterns of the United States. Already there are substantial areas in the nation in which more than one-fifth of the farm operators do not live on the land. See Figure 56.

The Line Village

Line villages are known throughout the world. Their origins seem to lie in peculiar geographic features of the landscape which

[56] For a description of village settlements established in Missouri during the Spanish domination, see H. M. Brackenridge, *Views of Louisiana Together with a Journal of a Voyage up the Missouri River in 1811*, Pittsburgh, Cramer, Spear, and Eichbaum, 1814, pp. 119–132. For recent literature relative to the village settlements in New Mexico, see George I. Sanchez, *Forgotten People: A Study of New Mexicans*, Albuquerque, University of New Mexico Press, 1940, pp. 4–5, 62.

[57] Compare, for example, the text and photographs in Olen Leonard and C. P. Loomis, *Culture of a Contemporary Rural Community: El Cerrito, New Mexico*, Rural Life Studies 1, Washington, United States Department of Agriculture, 1941, and in Irving Rusinow, *A Camera Report on El Cerrito, a Typical Spanish American Community in New Mexico*, Miscellaneous Publication 479, Washington, United States Department of Agriculture, 1942, with those in T. Lynn Smith, Justo Diaz Rodriguez, and Luis Roberto Garcia, *Tabio: Estudio de la Organizacion Social Rural*, Bogotá, Ministerio de la Economía Nacional, 1944.

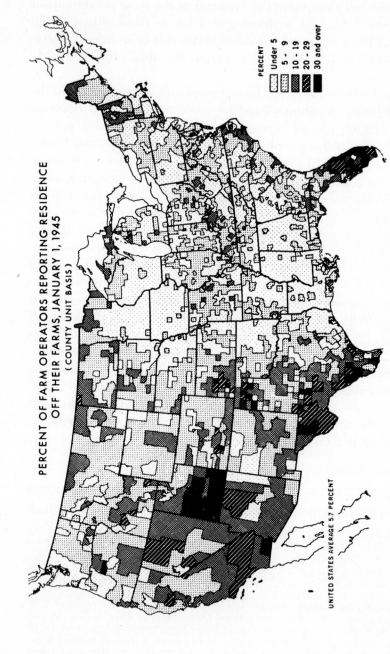

FIGURE 56. Variations in the Proportions of Farm Operators Not Living on Their Farms, 1945. (Illustration from the Bureau of Agricultural Economics.)

combine with cultural needs and practices in a way to place a premium upon river frontages, alluvial fans at the foot of sharp escarpments, intervals along the beds of streams that flow through narrow mountain valleys, "dry points" along ancient dunes and levees of a marshy country, etc.[58]

For the most part the line village form of settlement in the United States is a result of French cultural influences. From early times the line village has been an important settlement form in France. Well established by the ninth century was the practice of dividing land into rectangles 30 rods wide by 720 rods long, known as the *mansus regalis*. This was widely associated with line villages in the Frankish realm. The diffusion of this pattern seems to have followed the fortunes of the Carolingians (751–987). Soon it was known and used in Holland, where both marsh and moor *Hufen* were surveyed in this manner, and the practice was also adopted in forest settlements or *Waldhufen*. Dutch migrants seem to have carried the pattern to Germany, where it was widely used in the colonization of Weser, Holstein, Mecklenberg, and Brandenberg. Later it played a most important role in the spread of German cultural influences to the East.[59]

---

[58] The association between the river front and the line village is too common to need documentation. For the settlements on alluvial fans, see Glenn T. Trewartha, "The Suwa Basin: A Specialized Sericulture District in the Japanese Alps," *Geographical Review*, XX (1930), 229; the line villages in the valleys of San Luis Potosí and Hildalgo, Mexico, and those along the São Francisco and Amazon rivers in Brazil have been observed by the writer; and "dry point" settlements are described in R. B. Hall, *op. cit.*, p. 110, and Raoul Blanchard, "Flanders," *Geographical Review*, IV (1917), 426. This is not to say that these topographical circumstances will always give rise to this particular form of settlement. Once a settlement pattern is established, it becomes "set" in the culture of the group and may be carried by them into very different geographic surroundings. The failure of the Mormons to develop line village settlements along the front of the Wasatch escarpment, where obviously they are much more practicable than the village system that is in use, is an excellent case in point. Sometimes line villages appear as a transitional stage in the change from village settlements to single farmsteads. Cf. Edna Scofield, "The Origin of Settlement Patterns in Rural New England," *Geographical Review*, XXVIII (1938), 661–663.

[59] Cf. James W. Thompson, "East German Colonization in the Middle Ages," *Annual Report of the American Historical Association, 1915*, Washington, 1917, p. 145. See also the contribution of Herman Aubin, "The Lands East of the Elbe and German Colonization Eastwards," in *The Agrarian Life of the Middle Ages*, edited by J. H. Clapham and Eileen Power, which constitutes the first volume of *The Cambridge Economic History*, Cambridge, The University Press, 1941, p. 377. This author indicates that such a type of settlement was "extraordinarily widespread" in the German colonial area, that the *Hufen* lay side by side facing on a brook or street, and that each holding contained everything necessary in farming— meadowland, arable land, pasture, and forest. He also adds that this type of settlement was principally used in the forests, or "in connection with dyking."

French colonists also brought the pattern to America, where it was widely used in Canada[60] and in Louisiana.[61] The line village form of settlement was utilized also in the other French settlements throughout the New World. At Old Kaskaskia, Prairie du Rocher, Cahokia, and Prairie du Chien on the Upper Mississippi; in and about St. Louis, Fort Chartres, St. Genevieve, and St. Charles, Missouri; Vincennes, Indiana; Green Bay, Wisconsin; and Detroit, Michigan, are still to be found traces of the old French line villages and river-front land division in the land system.[62]

Line villages in the United States, however, have not been due entirely to French influences. Grouped settlements approximating the line village have appeared in several parts of the United States quite independent of French cultural contacts. For example, Dwight in his travels through New York passed through "long continued lines of farm houses, distant from each other an eighth, a fourth, a half, and sometimes three-quarters of a mile."[63] And another New York settlement was described as "almost a continual village."[64] Even in Connecticut and elsewhere he found settlements where houses were "built everywhere on the road, at little distances, so as to form one continual village. . . . Windsor, therefore, as a town, lies seven miles in one continued settlement on the road."[65] Other writers have also described line villages in New England, where the unequal desirability of the lands in the intervals along the river and on the terraces above may have

[60] For good descriptions of the Canadian settlements, see Ellen Churchill Semple, "The Influence of Geographic Environment on the Lower St. Lawrence," *Bulletin of the American Geographical Society*, XXXVI (1904), 449, 453–466; Roderick Peattie, "The Isolation of the Lower St. Lawrence Valley," *Geographical Review*, V (1918), 102–118; William Bennett Munro, *The Seigneurs of Old Canada*, Toronto, Brook and Company, 1922, pp. 90–94, 105–107; and S. H. Scudder, *The Winnipeg Country, or Roughing It with an Eclipse Party*, New York, N. D. C. Hodges, 1890, pp. 109–112.

[61] The line village is the principal settlement type in south Louisiana, where French cultural influences have always been dominant. In addition to the author's own studies cited above, see William H. Harris, *Louisiana Products, Resources and Attractions, with a Sketch of the Parishes*, New Orleans, 1881, pp. 174–175; and Monette, *op. cit.*, I, 182–191.

[62] Cf. Monette, *op. cit.*, I, 183; B. H. Hibbard, *A History of the Public Land Policies*, New York, The Macmillan Company, 1924, p. 23; Priestley, *op. cit.*, pp. 281–282; and Thomas M. Cooley, *Michigan: A History of Governments*, Boston, Houghton Mifflin Company, 1905, pp. 190–191, 233.

[63] *Op. cit.*, IV, 26.

[64] *Ibid.*, III, 224.

[65] *Ibid.*, I, 263; see also II, 107, 268, 278, 336, 358, 360, 367, and 390.

played a part in giving rise to this form of settlement.[66] In general these villages of New England were established in the years following 1713, when land speculators obtained large tracts and offered inducements to the first settlers to establish residence on their holdings. The proprietors usually laid out the township beforehand into long narrow strips from 30 to 120 acres in size, and the resulting settlements were necessarily of a line village type.[67] In North Carolina ten families of Moravians who moved from New England and located in Wachovia so laid out their farms of 200 acres each as "to form a long village."[68] And in South Carolina in the Marion District the settlers built their homes immediately on the river in close proximity to one another, for convenience of transportation, social intercourse, and better protection.[69]

Single Farmsteads

The typical settlement in the United States is composed of single or isolated farmsteads; and of all the countries in the world, the dispersed form of settlement is most important here. Probably for this reason there is a tendency among American scholars to regard this as the most advanced settlement pattern (the "modern community") and one that has developed through a series of stages from other less progressive modes of settlement.[70] But scattered farmsteads are an old phenomenon and ethnocentrism a widespread attitude.

Scattered farmsteads have existed in America from early times. In and about Boston, Samuel Maverick (who settled on Noddells Island in what is now East Boston and who owned the "Antientist house in the Massachusetts Government"), David Thompson, William Blaxton, and other "old planters" did not reside in the limits of the village settlements later established, and were not always on friendly terms with the residents of the Massachusetts vil-

[66] See Martha Krug Genthe, "Valley Towns of Connecticut," *Bulletin of the American Geographical Society of New York*, XXXIX (1907), 522–525; and M. Aurousseau, "The Distribution of the Population: A Constructive Problem," *Geographical Review*, XI (1921), 576.

[67] See Scofield, *op. cit.*, p. 661.

[68] Fries, *op. cit.*, I, 436.

[69] Gregg, *op. cit.*, p. 70.

[70] See N. L. Sims, *The Rural Community; Ancient and Modern*, New York, Charles Scribner's Sons, 1920, pp. 113–129; cf. Dwight Sanderson, *The Rural Community*, Boston, Ginn and Company, 1932, p. 461.

lages.[71] In spite of strong pressure from the religious community, centrifugal forces were always operating to bring about disperse-ment of homes. The operation of some of these forces at Water-town is reported as early as 1631, where there were "pleasant Springs, and small Rivulets, running like veines throughout her Body, which hath caused her inhabitants to scatter in such a man-ner, that their Sabbath-Assemblies prove very thin if the season favour not. . . ."[72] At Lynn, also, the people feeling inclined to husbandry built "many farms remote there"; and a similar pro-cedure is reported from Newberry.[73] Following 1713, after the General Court had ceased to guide settlement, and the establish-ment of new communities was in the hands of land speculators, the line village came into use. But it was a transitional form, and during the last part of the colonial period new settlements were definitely of the scattered farmstead type.[74] In the report of his travels through the western and northern portions of New Eng-land Dwight repeatedly mentioned the scattered nature of the settlements, and commented upon the "usual inconveniences, both moral and physical, of such settlements."[75]

In New York, despite the efforts of the authorities to the con-trary, the isolated farm pattern of settlement prevailed, both on the manors and in the areas of small farms.[76] At the time of Dwight's visits, only scattered farmsteads were to be observed.[77] In fact, throughout all the back settlements from Maine to Georgia scattered farmsteads became the prevailing mode of settlement and, with the exceptions noted in the discussion of village and line village settlements, came to blanket all the United States.

[71] J. Franklin Jameson, *Johnson's Wonder-Working Providence, 1628–1651*, New York, Charles Scribner's Sons, 1910, pp. 63–64.

[72] *Ibid.*, p. 74.

[73] *Ibid.*, pp. 73–99.

[74] Scofield, *op. cit.*, pp. 661–663.

[75] *Op. cit.*, IV, 3, *passim.*

[76] Instructions sent the Director and Council at New Amsterdam on July 7, 1645, contained the following provision:

"They shall endeavor as much as possible, that the colonists settle themselves with a certain number of families in some of the most suitable places, in the manner of villages, towns and hamlets, *as the English are in the habit of doing, who thereby live more securely.*" Quoted by A. E. McKinley, "The English and the Dutch Towns of New Netherlands," *American Historical Review*, VI (1901), 5. Cf. Maud Wilder Goodwin, *Dutch and English on the Hudson*, New Haven, Yale University Press, 1919, pp. 40–41.

[77] *Op. cit.*, III, 160–161.

The Transition from Village Settlements to Scattered Farmsteads

Probably no development in American agriculture has been more significant than the transition from the early pattern of village settlement to the typical American isolated farm of the present day. Had America been covered with village communities of the pattern established in the original colonies and preserved in full force for generations, the cultural landscape of the nation would be very different, the characteristics and problems of the farming communities quite unlike those that we know. But one can search hundreds of historical treatises and documents without finding any real attempt to answer the questions as to why and how this transition occurred.

In the preceding pages it has been show that village settlements were the established modes of settling on the land in early New England, in Pennsylvania and the other Middle Colonies, and in the first settlements of Virginia, South Carolina, and Georgia. It has also been indicated that the ante-bellum plantation throughout all the richer portions of the South employed this manner of arranging the population on the land. The English form of settlement was envied by the Dutch in New York, who attempted to copy it. As late as 1820 its virtues in New England were highly extolled by the president of Yale University. In some parts of New England it persists to this day. Therefore the question logically arises as to why this pattern of settlement was abandoned in favor of single farmsteads as the tide of settlement left the seaboard and forged its way to the Pacific. Did not the village settlement pattern have every advantage and stand every chance of blanketing rural America?

Culturally, old forms persist unless great disturbing forces intervene. Consider the factors asserted to be responsible for the variations in settlement forms. Was the physical environment responsible? What was there in the physical environment of western and upper New England and the western portions of the other colonies that caused the village to give way to single farmsteads in those areas? The need for protection is frequently cited as a factor making for compact village settlements. Why did the colonists who settled among the peaceful and even helpful Indians of

New England utilize the village pattern, while their descendants and the later immigrants resorted to the single farmstead when they moved among the savage Iroquois? What about soils? The isolated farm type of settlement that came into being in the back portions of the original colonies spread from the Atlantic to the Pacific and came to be the method of settling on soils of almost every conceivable type. Availability of water, wood, pasture, etc. —can any of them adequately explain why village settlements gave way to scattered farmsteads, and why with few exceptions these were allowed to prevail throughout the entire United States?

An explanation of the transition from the village form of settlement to one based on single farmsteads must necessarily be very tentative. Nevertheless, some of the factors that were associated with the process may be enumerated. Probably among the most important are the following: (1) the difficulties of caring for livestock in the village; (2) the decrease of religious homogeneity and solidarity; (3) the shift from governmental to proprietorial responsibility for organizing new settlements; (4) the decline of group settlement; (5) speculation in lands; (6) the production in the new environment of a personality type not afraid of the wilderness and equipped to cope with its hardships; (7) the practice of "squatting" on unoccupied land; and (8) the establishment of isolated farmsteads as a defense measure.

The importance of caring for livestock is not to be underestimated. Bradford's first complaints about the dispersion of homesteads during the early years of Plymouth specify the cause as the increase of the livestock. "And no man now thought he could live, except he had catle and a great deale of ground to keep them; all striving to increase their stocks. By which means they were scatered all over the bay, quickly, and the towne, in which they lived compactly till now, was left very thine, and in a short time allmost desolate."[78] Granting lands to trusted farmers who agreed to use servants to care for the livestock and themselves promised to live in Plymouth did not solve the problem. After a few years the favored ones "rente themselves away, partly by force, and partly by wearing the rest with importunitie and pleas of necessity, so as they must either suffer them to goe, or live in continual opposition and contention." Bradford feared that this would "be

[78] Davis, *op. cit.*, p. 293.

the ruin of New-England, at least of the church of God ther, and will provoke the Lords displeasure against them."[79]

Obviously such dissensions in the church were an expression of some differentiation of belief. Bradford complains that "the church must also be divided, and those that had lived so long together in Christian and comfortable fellowship must now part and suffer many divissions."[80]

The transfer of authority for new settlements from the government, where the rules pertaining to the establishment and functioning of new settlements were laid down by the General Court, to a group of private proprietors is an important factor. Under the old system only group settlement was sanctioned, and the colonial government superintended the settlement. The authorities proceeded on the principal of intensive settlement—one township or group of townships being granted at a time and these to actual settlers, the lands surveyed in advance, and the tenure fee simple. The establishment of a new settlement under such cirumstances was literally a "swarming" from an old one. Later the participation of the government was greatly lessened and that of private individuals greatly increased. A group interested in a new settlement would petition the General Court, or legislature, for a grant. That body would appoint a committee to lay off the grant, which frequently was a tract six miles square, and this land was transferred to the quasi-corporation of proprietors. The proprietors were charged with the responsibility of laying out the town, constructing roads, providing for defense, and arranging for a schoolhouse and a resident minister. As the religious bonds weakened and the controls of the General Court became less strict, such grants came to be secured on a strictly commercial basis and by persons who had no intention of settling personally in the new settlements.[81] Massachusetts laid out townships to be granted to soldiers who had served in the Indian wars, and after 1735 both Massachusetts and Connecticut sold entire townships to speculators who resold at higher prices.[82] By 1762 Massachusetts, New

[79] *Ibid.*, p. 294.
[80] *Ibid.*, p. 293.
[81] Stella H. Sutherland, *Population Distribution in Colonial America*, New York, Columbia University Press, 1936, pp. 40–41.
[82] Edward C. Kirkland, *A History of American Economic Life*, New York, Appleton-Century-Crofts, Inc., 1932, pp. 27–28; cf. Shaw Livermore, *Early Land Companies: Their Influence on Corporate Development*, New York, The Commonwealth Fund, 1939, pp. 27–29.

Hampshire, and Connecticut were auctioning land to the highest bidders.[83] And a little later western lands were purchased by land jobbers hoping to gain through increased land values, land speculation became a fever, and salesmen peddled proprietors' rights through New England and even England.[84] Frequently a town proprietor owned land in several towns; John Nelson, a wealthy West Indies trader residing in Portsmouth, owned proprietorships in forty-six townships scattered throughout Vermont and New Hampshire.[85] Thus in less than a century the traffic in lands changed from a governmental monopoly, rigidly controlled in the interest of close group settlement on the village plan, to a wild speculation. The change exerted a tremendous influence upon settlement patterns.[86]

The influence of squatting must not be minimized. Official attempts at limiting settlement to the seaboard met an insurmountable obstacle in the abundance of land in the West. But in these extralegal settlements a man could be sure of his land only by "sitting down" or "squatting" upon it. This practice inevitably meant scattered farmsteads in the numerous settlements so established.[87]

Contrary to popular opinion on the subject, isolated farmsteads were resorted to as a defense measure. In this case, however, it was the "powers that be" in the older settlements near the coast who offered lands to newcomers on condition of actual settlement for ten months out of the year, in order to erect a barrier between themselves and the Indians.[88]

[83] Marcus W. Jernegan, *The American Colonies, 1492–1750*, New York, Longmans, Green & Company, 1929, pp. 359–360.

[84] Kirkland, *loc. cit.*

[85] *Ibid.*

[86] The author is indebted to V. L. Bedsole, a former graduate student, for part of the material used in this paragraph.

[87] Cf. Dwight, *op. cit.*, II, 207.

[88] Cf. Crane, *op. cit.*, pp. 214–215.

11

LAND DIVISION

When Daniel Boone and his contemporaries pushed through the passes of the Appalachian Mountains and established themselves in the rich valleys of the West, each person selected the land that best suited him, seated himself upon it, and set forth the limits of his claim with convenient trees, stones, creeks, and other natural phenomena. Seldom has the world seen an example of more complete freedom of location, or more absolute lack of system in the surveying and recording of lands; rarely has it seen more confusion and litigation over land titles resulting therefrom. The French and Spanish, in allocating lands to settlers in America, regularly selected as a base some river or creek and granted to the settler or concessionnaire lands fronting on the stream and extending back a specified distance. The bank of the stream and the boundaries of neighboring holdings set rather definite limits upon a given land patent. Only in cases where a stream changed its course did this system give rise to serious trouble over land titles. After 1785 lands patented in the United States were allocated as parts of regularly surveyed blocks or sections containing 640 acres each. Astronomical observations and not surface phenomena were used in setting the limits of these surveys, thus making determinate and permanent the boundaries of any given tract of land. This system has reduced to a minimum disputes concerning boundaries and titles. Represented in these three examples are the principal ways in which it is possible to divide the lands among the farming population. To the system or lack of system followed in thus subdividing the land we give the name *land division*.

Social Significance of Land Division

The manner in which lands are divided is one of the most all-pervasive determinants in rural life. Stable farm life is facilitated when the boundaries of farm lands are easily determined, well known, and subject to little litigation. At all times systems of surveying farm lands and of recording the titles to these lands are of great social significance to the individual farm family. In case of litigation they frequently have been of overwhelming importance.

Nevertheless, it is with much justification that Miss Semple has complained that "most systems of sociology treat man as if he were in some way detached from the earth's surface; they ignore the land basis of society."[1] Whenever a society has adopted both the sedentary agricultural mode of life and the trait of private property in land, the manner in which the lands are divided among the population has become of paramount importance.

Geographers have demonstrated very clearly the effects of the divisions of land upon the cultural landscape.[2] But it should be insisted that the importance of this factor is much greater in the social than in the geographic sphere. Practically every aspect of the social system is conditioned by the mode of land division employed. Consider the effect upon communication and transportation. Roads, highways, hedges, fences, and terraces are a few of the agencies utilized whose location and direction are affected by the manner in which the lands are subdivided. Or again, consider the effects upon the legal aspects of agriculture and rural life. Only a well-ordered, determinate, and permanent system of surveying makes possible a simple and accurate recording of titles and the easy transfer of property rights. Such a system also makes possible quick and certain resurveys of disputed boundaries. In these and many other ways a determinate mode of dividing lands makes for harmonious personal relationships and contributes to the smooth, efficient operation of private and governmental controls.

---

[1] Ellen Churchill Semple, *Influence of the Geographic Environment on the Basis of Ratzel's System of Anthropo-Geography*, New York, Henry Holt & Company, 1911, p. 53.

[2] The practice of plowing so that the furrow is always turned downhill, if long continued, creates a series of terraces at the boundaries of the fields.

Endless unproductive and destructive litigation accompanies the lack of such a system. The original American colonies were without a systematic pattern of land division. The cultural heritage from Europe passed on a haphazard system of land division that had come down from the earliest times. It is true that through the centuries the metes and bounds of these indeterminate and indefinite systems had become crystallized in the minds of the peasants; so static were conditions that only occasional quarrels over the removal of landmarks troubled the small village communities. It is also true that most of the early American settlements were subject to some regulation as to locations, but this was lacking in system and regularity.[3]

In the westward surge of settlement, especially in the illegal squatting on unoccupied lands and particularly in the settlement of the trans-Appalachian counties, all semblance of order disappeared. Throughout the Appalachian valleys and westward to the 1785 fringe of settlement, haphazard surveys and freedom of location resulted in hopeless confusion, ceaseless litigation, and finally in thousands of blasted hopes. Because of a faulty system of surveying and recording land titles, Daniel Boone in his failing years was ousted from the homestead he first established in Kentucky and was forced to make a new start in the West[4]—eloquent testimony of the importance of these matters, of the havoc wrought by clumsy systems of surveying and recording lands.

In 1785 the adoption of the checkerboard system of land surveys overcame most of the difficulties due to faulty surveying and recording, and introduced a system almost perfect from these standpoints.[5] But the checkerboard pattern of surveys, adopted to facilitate the ready sale of public land, introduced other social consequences which are hardly of less importance. Today the typical American farm family is isolated from its neighbors to nearly the nth degree, forced to make the maximum outlay to obtain such modern necessities as roads, public utilities, etc., barred from many social contacts with other families and with

---

[3] Cf. Amelia Clewley Ford, *Colonial Precedents of Our National Land System as It Existed in 1800*, Bulletin of the University of Wisconsin 352 (1910), *passim*.

[4] Timothy Flint, *The First White Man of the West, or The Life and Exploits of Col. Dan'l Boone*, Cincinnati, Applegate and Company, 1856, pp. 235–238.

[5] See S. V. Proudfit, *The Public Land System of the United States*, U.S. Department of Interior, Washington, 1923.

social institutions, all because of a socially and economically short-sighted and inefficient manner of dividing the lands.[6]

Systems of Land Division

Man's ingenuity has created numerous modes of dividing the lands among the population. For convenience they may be grouped into three principal types: (1) indiscriminate location with metes and bounds as boundaries; (2) river-front patterns wherein the point of departure is relatively stable; and (3) rectangular systems founded upon astronomical observations. In addition several other varieties of land division may be placed together in a miscellaneous category.

Indiscriminate Location

Men have not always sensed the importance of system when they have settled on land and divided it among the respective families. In most instances, even in modern times, practically no system whatsoever has been followed. This has been especially the case in America, where the supply of land seemed to be inexhaustible and men soon came to think they were entitled to plenty of good land wherever they wanted it.[7] The history of the United States is filled with instances of almost complete freedom of location. Thousands of individuals and communities have seated themselves upon lands, established claims, and outlined boundaries without making the slightest pretense at system or order.

Prior to the American Revolution each colony disposed of lands in its own way. The southern colonies particularly, where individual settlement was the rule, allowed almost complete freedom of location. The settler was permitted to locate his land warrants upon any unappropriated soil. The surveys were supposed to be made by public surveyors, but many of these were inexperienced, and there were many opportunities for error. Furthermore, records were poorly kept. Individual initiative played an important role. Anyone could select unappropriated land and have the county surveyor lay it off under his own direction. He

[6] T. Lynn Smith, "The Social Effects of Land Division in Relationship to a Program of Land Utilization," *Journal of Farm Economics*, XVII (1935), 703–709.

[7] Similar were the developments in Australia and Chile, where much the same conditions prevailed. Cf. H. Stephen Roberts, *History of Australian Land Settlement (1788–1920)*, Melbourne, Macmillan & Co., Ltd., 1924, pp. 166–168; and G. M. McBride, "The Agrarian Problem in Chile," *Geographical Review*, XX (1930), 581–582.

was not required to consider the situation of other properties or
their relation to his own. Great overlapping and litigation resulted.
Some men got a virtual monopoly on the best lands. Treat has
called this lack of system "indiscriminate location."[8]

New England gradually evolved a system of surveying townships, many of which were six miles square.[9] However, even in
New England, where group settlement was general, many communities established the limits of their claims through a system of
metes and bounds. Consider the case of Dorchester, Massachusetts, where in 1636 the General Court fixed the bounds

> . . . to run from the outside of Mr. Rossiters farm, next the sea to
> the foot of ye great hill, from a marked tree to a second marked tree,
> in a straight line to the top of the Blue Hills, nexte Naponsett south-
> west and by west, half a point westerly, & all the marsh ground from
> the southeast side of Mr. Newberrys house along Naponsett River, to
> Mr. Stoughtons mill, to lie to Dorchester & all the rest of the upland &
> marsh from Mr. Rossiters farm to the sea, & so to the mouth of the
> river beyond Minotiquid River, running into the country southwest &
> to the west, to lie to Boston onely excepting such land as they have
> right to by grand of the court formerly. . . .[10]

Many similar cases demonstrate that as between communities
even the New England pattern was very irregular, but the practice
of group settlement reduced the irregularity within the community, made for compactness, and placed the responsibility for
accurate surveys upon the entire community.[11]

Irregularity of holdings, indefiniteness of boundaries, and confusion of land titles probably reached their maximum in the trans-
Appalachian settlements. Among the pioneers no one was more
adept at squatting on unoccupied government or private land
than the German and Scotch-Irish immigrants who settled the
frontiers. It has been estimated that as early as 1726, 100,000 of

[8] Payson Jackson Treat, *The National Land System, 1785–1820*, New York,
E. B. Treat and Company, 1910, pp. 24–25; cf. Benjamin Horace Hibbard, *A
History of the Public Land Policies*, New York, The Macmillan Company, 1924,
p. 37; and James Curtis Ballagh, "Introduction to Southern Economic History—
The Land System," *American Historical Association Annual Report for the Year
1897*, Washington, 1898, p. 115.

[9] P. J. Treat, "Surveys of Land," *Cyclopedia of American Government*, New
York, 1914, III, 463.

[10] *Records of the Governor and Company of the Massachusetts Bay*, Boston, The
Commonwealth of Massachusetts, 1854, I, 162–163.

[11] Treat, *The National Land System*, pp. 25–26.

them had settled in Pennsylvania "without a shadow of a right."[12]
The Ulstermen, particularly, settled on any unoccupied land as
they pleased and were in constant trouble with the state government as well as with the Indians.[13] Even the lands of George Washington were not free from the inroads of these squatters. Fourteen
families established themselves in 1773 upon 2813 acres he had
patented in western Pennsylvania, drove away his caretaker, and
constructed twelve houses and nine barns.[14]

In many cases the form and shape of the tracts claimed have
been governed almost entirely by the objective of securing the
most desirable lands; such plots were extremely irregular in
shape, and for boundaries recourse was had to natural objects
such as trees, stones, mountains or hills, watercourses, etc. Such
metes and bounds show the greatest irregularity of holdings, not
to mention the fact that they foster clouded titles, misunderstandings, and untold legal proceedings. Consider the following example, typical of thousands of surveys in the years prior to 1785:

Surveyed for Ann Garrett, 130 acres of land on part of Military
Warrant No. 5901, on Upper Twin Creek, a branch of Paint Creek.

Beginning at two beeches, west corner of Abraham Shepherd's survey No. 4710; thence N. 73° E. 170 poles, crossing the creek to a poplar,
east corner to said survey; thence N. 89° W. 93 poles to two beeches;
thence S. 55° W. 40 poles to a sugar tree, hornbeam, and white oak;
thence West 110 poles, crossing the creek at 95 poles to two buckeyes
and an elm.[15]

Even more indefinite and confusing is the following description of
lands in Livingston's Manor, New York:

. . . another tract of land called Tachkanick lyeing and being adjacent unto the aforrecited tract of land beginning behind Pattkook on
a certaine creeke and runns into the East side of Hudsons River and is
known by the name of Roeloffe Johnson's kill beginning on the North
west side of the said kill that runns along the flatt or plaine land at a
place called by the native Minissichtanock where two black Oake trees
are marked with L and from thence along a small hill to a valley that
leads to a small creeke called by the Indians Quissicheook and over the

[12] William R. Shepherd, "The Land System of Provincial Pennsylvania," *Annual
Report of the American Historical Association*, Washington, 1895, p. 123.

[13] Cf. Sidney G. Fisher, *The Quaker Colonies*, New Haven, Yale University
Press, 1920, p. 49.

[14] Cf. Archer B. Hulbert, *Washington and the West*, Cleveland, Arthur H. Clark
Company, 1911, pp. 49–55, 147–150, 152–153.

[15] W. E. Peters, *Ohio Lands and Their Subdivisions*, Athens, 1918, pp. 22–23.

said creeke to a high place to the westward of a high mountaine where
two black oake trees are marked L and is called by the natives Kach-
kawanick from thence westward to a small kill on the side of a creeke
called Skannpook where two white oake trees are marked L and soe
runns a long the eastside of the said creeke which a little lower is
called the name of Twastawekah and is the westerly bounds the
southerly bounds beginning on the other side of the creeke that runnes
along the flatt or plaine over against Minissichtanock where two trees
are marked and runnes along the foot of the high mountains to the path
that goes to Wawijchtanok to a hill called by the Indians Mananosick
where two trees are marked L on the south west side of the path from
thence westward to a creeke called by the natives Nachawawachkano
where two white oake trees are marked L which creeke comes into the
other creeke called Twantawekak which is the west bounds and soe in-
closes all the land above recited the place where the two creekes meet
being called Mawichnanck the flatt or Plaine land lying on both sides
of Mawichnanck the flatt or plaine land lying on both sides of the
said creeke containing about three hundred morgan or six hundred
acres. . . .[16]

In Figure 57 is presented a map of a rather typical farm surveyed
according to metes and bounds.

Persons whose lands adjoined usually selected the division
lines between their holdings long before any surveys were actually
made. Tops of ridges and watercourses were most often relied
upon as guides. Doddridge asserts that for this reason most of the
farms in western Pennsylvania and Virginia resemble an amphi-
theater—the buildings occupy a low position and the farm is
bounded by the surrounding hills. He also contends that the fore-
fathers liked farms of this sort because "everything comes to the
house down hill."[17] Monette describes this method of dividing
land, and adds: "Thus they consulted their own convenience in
obtaining a constant supply of water, and also, considering that
everything coming to the house from abroad is more easily carried
'down hill' than up, the house was seldom placed upon an eminence. In all the first locations the bottoms were selected, and the
contiguous ridges formed the boundaries of the tract."[18] As a con-

[16] Thomas Dongan, "Gov. Dongan's Patent for the Manor of Livingston," *Documentary History of the State of New York*, Albany, 1850, III, 623–624.

[17] Dr. Joseph Doddridge, *Settlement of Western Country*, Bowling Green, Ohio,
Historical Publications Company, 1923, pp. 11–12.

[18] John W. Monette, *History of the Discovery and Settlement of the Valley of
the Mississippi*, New York, Harper & Brothers, 1846, II, 6.

sequence of such practices holdings were frequently extremely irregular, entirely unrelated to one another, and part of no system. Frequently—in Kentucky, for example—such vague inaccurate entries were made in the land office that later settlers were unable to determine the location and extent of the patented lands. "It thus happened that the whole or a part of almost every tract was covered with different and conflicting titles—forming what have

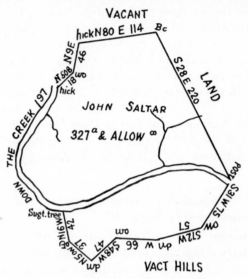

FIGURE 57. Diagram of the Holdings Surveyed to John Saltar on May 22, 1776, and Returned to the Surveyor-General of Pennsylvania, Showing the Usual Manner of Marking the Limits of a Patent. (After Thomas Donaldson, *The Public Domain,* Washington, Government Printing Office, 1884, p. 472.)

been aptly called 'shingle titles'—overlaying and lapping upon each other, as shingles do upon the roof of a building."[19] The following entry illustrates about the limit to which claims can go in vagueness of lines: "George Smith enters nine hundred acres of land on a treasury warrant, lying on the north side of Kentucky river, a mile below a creek; beginning about twenty poles below a lick; and running down the river westwardly, and northwestwardly for quantity."[20]

[19] Flint, *op. cit.,* pp. 230–231.
[20] *Ibid.,* p. 231.

Inaccuracies introduced by use of poor instruments, careless surveyors, and the presence of tremendous natural handicaps tended to make the situation even more confusing. Wrote Governor Sharp of Maryland to Lord Baltimore:

> The method always followed here of locating Land Warrants by selecting the most rich and fertile Land without regarding any regularity of its Area, or making one of its courses to coincide with the Boundary of the adjacent prior patented Tract has left the Land hitherto remaining vacant and uncultivated, in such irregular, small, and incommodious parcels that it is thought scarcely worth any one's While but those on whose possession it joins to take it up even at the common rate.[21]

The situation in Maryland became even more complicated by the fact that, prior to the middle of the seventeenth century, no record was kept of the grants, and "loose practices of all kinds prevailed."[22] And for the western settlements Theodore Roosevelt illustrated the looseness of the systems of surveys by pointing out that the title to lands which were entered and paid for might be shifted elsewhere if it were discovered that the first entry had already been claimed by another.[23]

Finally, the indefiniteness of the indeterminate surveys has made possible the swindling operations of thousands of land sharks. Henry George has described the situation in California, where the vague Mexican grants delimited by natural boundaries and other grants made for such rascality that they were a curse to the state. George says:

> As soon as settlers began to cultivate farms and make improvements, the grants began to float. The grant-holders watched the farmers coming into their neighbourhood, much as a robber chief of the Middle Ages might have watched a rich Jew taking up his abode within striking distance of his castle. The settler may have been absolutely certain that he was on Government land, and may even have been so assured by the grant-holder himself; but so soon as he had built his house and fenced his land and planted his orchard, he would wake up some morning to find that the grant had been floated upon him, and that his land and improvements were claimed by some land

[21] Quoted in Ford, *op. cit.*, p. 15.
[22] Ballagh, *op. cit.*, p. 117.
[23] "The Indian Wars, 1784–1787," in *The Winning of the West*, New York, The Current Literature Publishing Company, 1905, IV, 18.

shark who had gouged a native Californian out of his claim to a cattle-run, or wanting an opportunity to do this, had set up a fraudulent grant, supported by forged papers and suborned witnesses. Then he must either pay the blackmailer's price, abandon the results of his hard labour, or fight the claim before surveyor-general, courts, commissioner, secretary, and Congress itself, while his own property, parcelled out into contingent fees, furnished the means for carrying the case from one tribunal to another, for buying witnesses and bribing corrupt officials. And then, frequently, after one set of settlers had been thus robbed, new testimony would be discovered, a new survey would be ordered, and the grant would stretch out in another direction over another body of settlers, who would then suffer in the same way, while in many cases, as soon as one grant had been bought off or beaten away, another grant would come, and there are pieces of land in California for which four or five different titles have been purchased.[24]

Indiscriminate location and river-front patterns of location vied with each other in early America. Because of group settlements in New England which did much to regulate the outlines of holdings within the community, surveys in the area exhibited more regularity than those in the South, where almost complete individual freedom of location prevailed. However, the river-front pattern played a significant role in the history of southern settlement. Indiscriminate location and freedom of settlement attained their greatest importance in the settlement of the Appalachian valleys and the territories west of the mountains, south of the Ohio, and east of the Mississippi. Throughout much of this area the "shingle titles" thus created long disturbed the economic and social development of the settlements.

River-Front Patterns

In many parts of the world the river front, the seacoast, or the lake shore has served as a basis for systems of land surveys. From West Florida during the period of English domination, for example, it is reported that the governor was instructed to grant each settler proportional parts of the most desirable and the least desirable land, to limit the breadth of the holding to one-third of its length, and to see that the length did not extend along the banks of any stream, "but into the mainland, that thereby the said

[24] Henry George, *Our Land and Land Policy*, New York, Doubleday, Doran & Company, 1911, pp. 39–40.

grantees may have each a convenient share of what accommodation the said river may afford for navigation or otherwise."[25] This second system may well be styled the *river-front pattern*.

America was colonized and much of it settled while water routes were all-important for purposes of communication and transportation. In those early days streams were an aid to social interaction, rather than a factor contributing to social isolation. Particularly in the southern colonies were locations on the banks of navigable streams valued at a high premium. As late as the end of the seventeenth century practically all land grants in Virginia were situated upon the larger rivers. In laying off the estates the surveyors adopted the bank of the stream as a base and ran their lines at right angles to the river for a distance of one mile. Patents were arranged side by side in the same manner so that the holdings made up a series of parallelograms fronting on the river and extending into the interior for the necessary distance. This arrangement brought considerable regularity and system into the distribution of lands, and from the standpoint of surveying and recording of titles represented a marked improvement over indiscriminate location.

In Maryland a pattern similar to that of Virginia was followed, except that this colony regulated the amount of river front to fifty poles for every fifty acres of land patented.[26]

But even with the river front as a base many irregularities appeared. Some of these were, of course, introduced by the meanderings of the streams. Consider the following description, typical of many Spanish grants in Louisiana:

Charles Triche and Edmond Rogrigue—claim a tract of land in the parish of Assumption, on the left bank of Bayou Lafourche, containing three arpents, more or less, front, with convergent lines and a depth of forty arpents, now bounded on the upper side by land of Francis Nicholls, and on the lower by that of Honoré Folse.

The land claimed is the lower half of a tract surveyed in 1790, by order of Governor Miro, in favor of Jean Nicholas Bertrand, the upper half having been confirmed to George Mather by Old Board, certificate No. 149.[27]

[25] Instruction 52, quoted in Cecil Johnson, "The Distribution of Land in British West Florida," *Louisiana Historical Quarterly*, XVI (1933), 545–546.

[26] Ford, *op. cit.*, pp. 16–18.

[27] *Documents of the First Session of the Sixth Legislature of the State of Louisiana*, Baton Rouge, 1862, p. 27.

Other irregularities resulted from the inaccuracy of instruments. Frequently useless acreages were left out of account entirely. Not uncommonly side lines were lengthened or shortened to correspond to natural phenomena. And finally the difficulties of surveying plus general carelessness added much to the irregularity of the pattern.

In New England, which attained the greatest regularity of colonial landholdings, many surveys were made largely according to the river-front pattern. Says Ford of the New England fields:

> . . . one is at once struck by the extreme regularity of arrangement. The small oblong strips are, in nearly every case, grouped together in a few long rows or tiers. These tiers are often parallel, but sometimes one tier will be at right angles to another. The cause of this regularity is that the strips or lots are laid off from one or two (sometimes more, according to the size of the field), main base lines, usually a river or highway; each field is thus a parallelogram divided into tiers of small, usually equal, parallelograms. So early were the common lands thus laid out by men who had up to that time been familiar with the irregular method, that it seems as if the plan must have been one of the first products of the new American environment. Under the stimulus of unlimited area and an untouched soil, the newcomers at once improved the old system of dividing land. The new colonial idea of orderly arrangement was adopted, with the result that instead of many very small holdings, irregularly grouped, there were long stretches of lots laid out at right angles from a very few straight lines or bases. In this arrangement one sees in miniature the great base lines of the future national system, with the tiers of rectangular townships erected upon them.[28]

The river-front pattern of surveys owes its greatest development in America to the French. River fronts were at a premium and a frontage of five arpents commonly accompanied a depth of forty, making holdings eight times as long as they were wide. In both Canada and Louisiana this river-front type was used as a basic system of surveys, and the pattern so early established persists to affect the social activities of the present-day population. Furthermore, the French left an indelible stamp upon the American land system at every place they settled in the great West: at Detroit; on Green Bay; around Vincennes, Indiana; in the neighborhood

[28] Ford, *op. cit.*, pp. 12–13.

of Kaskaskia, Illinois; in and about St. Louis, Missouri, etc. (See Figure 58 for an example of French river-front surveys.)

Although the founding fathers were little concerned with the system of surveys, the selection of the river front as a base did much to bring order and system into the manner of dividing lands among the settlers. Freedom of location under such a system was

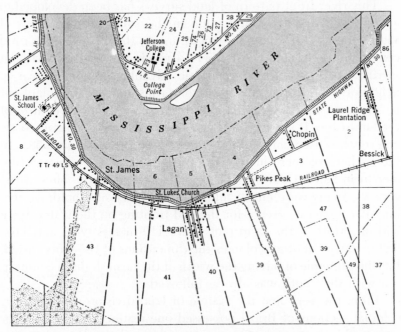

FIGURE 58. Map of a Selected Area on the Mississippi River in South Louisiana. Note the outlines of the French concessions granted according to a river-front system of dividing lands, and the official retangular system that has been superimposed. Observe how changes in the bed of the river have disrupted the old surveys. The arrangement of homes on the sugar plantations, in the "lanes," and in line villages may also be seen.

considerably restricted, holdings were much more determinate, and on the whole the boundaries were much more permanent. It is true, to be sure, that the course of a river is not fixed in the sense that the position of a star is. Sudden changes in the courses of rivers have disorganized land titles and caused endless litigation. Furthermore, most rivers are gradually changing their courses, cutting the outsides of curves, filling in on the inside; and this deviation has sometimes been a fruitful source of confusion. But on the whole the adoption of a river as the base of departure for land surveys is vastly superior to the selection of trees which may soon disappear, stones which may be moved, or even divides which may be difficult to locate exactly. When watercourses became the determining factor in land surveys, as they did in many of the colonies, it represented a decided advance over the system of indiscriminate location with metes and bounds as boundaries.

This river-front pattern of land surveys has been developed to a very high degree of perfection in the small farming areas of south Brazil. The system in general use in these prosperous rural communities permits the farmer to reside on the land without sacrificing the social and economic advantage of being near to neighbors, and at the same time the farms and roads are laid out in a manner that is best adapted to the topographical features of the landscape. It is a modified version of the type so characteristic of French settlements throughout the world. (See Figure 59.) In the earlier colonies such as the settlement of Germans at Blumenau in Santa Catarina, the river was taken as the base of the surveys; roads were cut to follow the streams; and holdings rectangular in shape, except for the end fronting on the water, were laid off. Most of the farm plots were 110 meters wide and 1100 meters deep. In other colonies the dimensions of the plots varied, but the principle of having the width of the farm slight in comparison with the depth was always followed.

From the very first the system of land division used in these colonial sections of Brazil possessed one distinct advantage over comparable systems in France, Canada, and the United States. Meanders in the streams did not lead to the use of nonparallel lines for bounding the sides of the holdings, so that the width of the holding was uniform throughout its length. In the early colonies the rear boundaries of the contiguous concessions made up a jagged line which created serious problems in the settlement of the lands back from the rivers and also prevented the fullest adaptation of settlement patterns to topographical features. But

. . . gradually, as experience was secured, practices were modified, and the systems of land division perfected to higher degrees. This important feature of the relationship of men to the land seems to have attained its highest stage of development in the colonization projects of the North Paraná Land Company, and in those of the Government on the former *fazendas* of the State of Santa Catarina. [See Figure 60.] Today the procedures used in dividing the land are fairly well defined.

When a new settlement project is undertaken, the land is first surveyed in order to determine the course of all streams and to delineate the lines followed by the divides of all the principal watersheds. A detailed

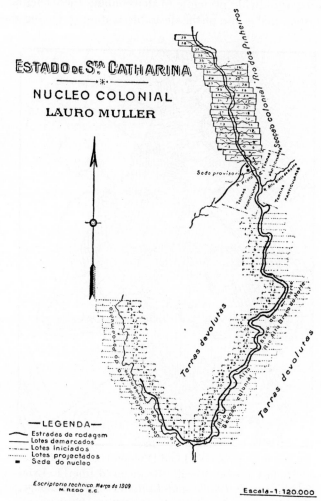

FIGURE 59. System of Land Division Used in the Early Brazilian Colonization Projects. (Reproduced from *Relatorio, Serviço de Povomento em 1908,* Rio de Janeiro, Imprensa Nacional, 1909, p. 123.)

map of the area is made in which all of these are plotted. In the northern Paraná project roads are laid out along the top of the divide; in Santa Catarina they usually follow the stream. But in both states the tract of land cut off for a prospective purchaser or colonist is bounded on one end by the stream and on the other by the ridge or road. Variations in the sizes of the farming plots sold or allotted are secured by increasing or decreasing the width of the holding, and never by modifying the stream-to-divide principle of determining their length.

This system makes use of the desirable feature of having the hold-

FIGURE 60.   System of Land Division Used by the State of Santa Catarina, Brazil. (Reproduced from T. Lynn Smith, *Brazil: People and Institutions*, Baton Rouge, Louisiana State University Press, 1946, p. 439.)

ings much less in width than in length, the long-lot farm, thus allowing the settlers to capitalize on the social and economic advantages of line village settlements. At the same time it permits a high degree of adaptation to topographical and other natural features of the landscape. Every settler has access to water. All have some bottom land and some hillside. If the natural covering is varied, as frequently is the case, all have some of the types of timber that grow in the lowlands as well as the upland varieties. In short, every settler participates in both the advantageous and disadvantageous features of the location.[29]

Rectangular Systems

For purposes of surveying and recording, the ultimate in simplicity of land surveys is attained when all survey lines run parallel or at right angles to one another and the lands are divided into rectangles of a uniform size. The surveys are most determinate and the divisions most permanent when they are based upon astronomical observations and are independent of surface phenomena. The official land system of the United States, called for convenience the "checkerboard pattern," excellently meets these conditions. From the standpoint of surveying and recording, it represents the acme of simplicity, determinateness, and permanency, and no more adequate mode of land division has been devised. It provides definite bounds free from overlapping claims; insures against loss of landmarks, since each point may be redetermined with great accuracy; and, of great importance, it renders possible the simplest kind of deed.[30] Enthusiastically wrote the traveler James Flint in 1819 soon after its adoption:

The land system now adopted in the United States is admirable in regard [to] ingenuity, simplicity, and liberality. A slight attention to the map of a district, will enable any one to know at once the relative situation of any section that he may afterwards hear mentioned, and its direct distance in measured miles. There can be no necessity for giving names to farms or estates, as the designation of the particular township, and the number of the section is sufficient, and has, besides, the singular convenience of conveying accurate information as to where it is situated. By the new arrangement the boundaries of possessions are most securely fixed, and freed alike from the inconvenience of rivers changing their course, and complexity of curved lines. Litigation amongst neighbours as to their landmarks, is in a great measure excluded.[31]

[29] T. Lynn Smith, "Brazilian Land Surveys, Land Division, and Land Titles," *Rural Sociology*, IX (1944), 270.

[30] Treat, *The National Land System*, p. 179. Says Shosuke Sato of the checkerboard system: "Indeed, the value of the rectangular system of surveys can hardly be overestimated. Not only does it afford positive advantages to the settlement, but, negatively, it prevents litigations, which are in ineviable consequence of irregular surveys and settlements." *History of the Land Question in the United States*, Johns Hopkins University Studies in Historical and Political Science, Fourth Series, VII–IX, Baltimore, 1886, p. 393.

[31] Reuben Gold Thwaites, "Flint's Letters from America, 1818–1820," in *Early Western Travels, 1748–1846*, Cleveland, Arthur H. Clark Company, 1904, IX, 179.

The backgrounds of the rectangular system of the United States are fairly well known. It came into existence at the birth of the public domain, when the states ceded their western lands to the United States. The system is largely the work of Thomas Jefferson. The bill creating this pattern of land surveys was reported from a Congressional committee (Jefferson, chairman) on May 7, 1784. As first drawn, the bill provided that lands should be divided into townships ten miles square and subdivided into 100 sections of 640 acres each. It was debated, amended to make the townships six miles square with thirty-six sections of 640 acres, and the ordinance was passed on May 20, 1785.[32] An important feature of the new law forbade the sale of unsurveyed public lands. The first surveys made according to the new national system were in the territory northwest of the Ohio in the range of townships in the state of Ohio that adjoin the state of Pennsylvania.[33]

The American checkerboard system of land surveys utilizes the principal meridians as the bases of the divisions. Starting from these measurements of longitude and latitude, the lands are first surveyed into rectangular tracts six miles square which are called townships. "Any series of contiguous townships, north or south of each other, constitutes a range; the townships counting from the base, either north or south, and the ranges from the principal meridian, either east or west. Each township is subdivided into thirty-six sections of one mile square, or 640 acres, in all 23,040 acres." The section was the smallest unit whose out-boundaries were required by law to be surveyed. However, the law created imaginary lines which formed four squares of 160 acres each. Each of these was in turn broken down into four squares of forty acres each. Thus each section of 640 divided into its legal subdivisions affords 40 descriptions, easily determined, permitting blocks of 640 and 40 acres to be readily described and patented. Any surveyor in the various states and territories, assisted by the field notes from the original survey, could lay out the definite lines of subdivision if they were required.[34] Figure 61 shows a typical section of such checkerboard surveys.

As mentioned above, the ordinance of 1785 required that public lands be surveyed according to the checkerboard pattern

[32] Thomas Donaldson, *The Public Domain*, House Misc. Doc. 45, 47th Congress, Washington, 1884, XIX, 178.
[33] *Ibid.*, p. 188.
[34] *Ibid.*, pp. 183–184.

before they could be patented. Accordingly this pattern of survey has been utilized in all parts of the United States settled after that date, except those later territorial acquisitions where lands had previously been laid off in some other manner. With minor exceptions the system has been spread over the entire states of Ohio, Indiana, Illinois, Michigan, Alabama, Mississippi, Arkansas, Mis-

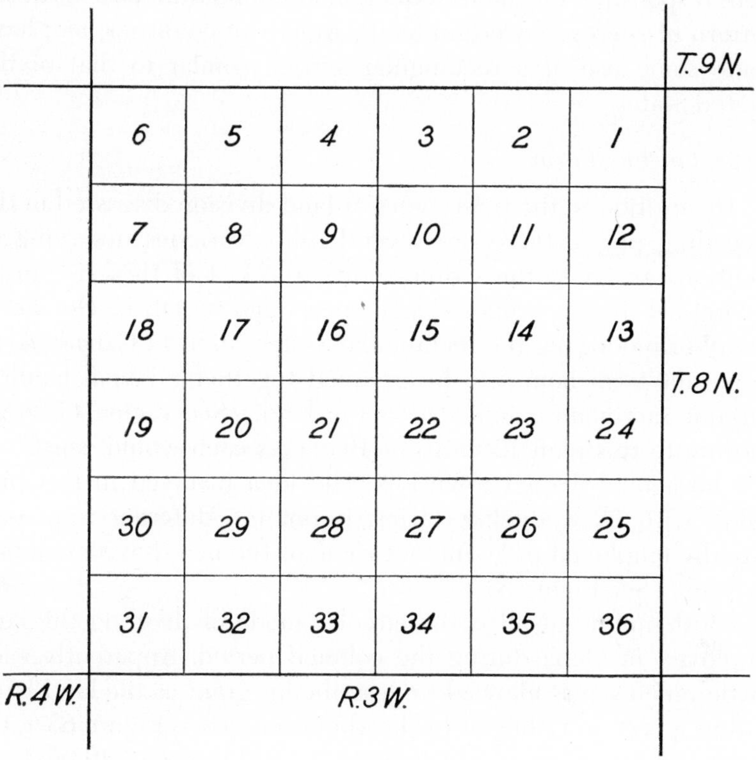

						T. 9 N.
6	5	4	3	2	1	
7	8	9	10	11	12	
18	17	16	15	14	13	*T. 8 N.*
19	20	21	22	23	24	
30	29	28	27	26	25	
31	32	33	34	35	36	
R.4 W.			*R.3 W.*			

FIGURE 61. The Official Checkerboard Pattern of Land Division in the United States. Note the arrangement of the thirty-six sections in the township.

souri, Iowa, Wisconsin, Minnesota, North Dakota, South Dakota, Nebraska, Kansas, Oklahoma, Colorado, Wyoming, Montana, Idaho, Utah, Arizona, Nevada, Washington, and Oregon. It has also been used in parts of California, New Mexico, Texas, Louisiana, and Florida.[35] The areas embraced in these thirty states constitute the great bulk of the land in the nation, every variety of climate, temperature, and rainfall, and topographic variations

[35] *Ibid.*, p. 188.

from the swamp and plain to the most rugged mountain ranges on the continent.

But the influences of the American system of land surveys have not been confined to the United States. The land system of Canada was patterned upon that of the United States, with some "beneficial additions."[36] In faraway Japan American agricultural experts were responsible for the introduction of a miniature checkerboard pattern of surveys.[37] Certain South American countries, too, have made some use of a rectangular system similar to that of the United States.[38]

Miscellaneous Forms

In addition to the three types of land division discussed in the preceding pages, there are several other varieties deserving of mention. As far as the writer knows, the first of these is purely theoretical. It was proposed some years ago by Dr. E. Deville as a way of modifying the rectangular system used in Canada so as to permit farm homes to be grouped together in small hamlets without sacrificing residence on the land. (See Figure 62.) According to this plan 12 farms of 160 acres each would constitute one hexagonal-shaped township. The idea involved in this proposal, with its wedgelike farms, is not too different from that actually employed in laying out some of the new Jewish colonies in Israel. (See Figure 53.)

Most unique of all is the circular mode of dividing the land employed in Cuba during the colonial period. Apparently each cattle rancher was allowed to describe his grant as the land lying within a certain radius of his headquarters. (See Figure 63.) Today hundreds of these old boundaries still survive, although, of course, they have since been overlaid by the metes and bounds pattern so commonly employed in Spanish America.[39]

[36] *Ibid.*, p. 477.

[37] Cf. R. B. Hall, "Some Rural Settlement Forms in Japan," *Geographical Review*, XXI (1931), 120–121.

[38] Cf. Mark Jefferson, *Peopling the Argentine Pampa*, New York, American Geographical Society, 1926, pp. 66, 94, 114.

[39] For maps of the various Cuban *municipios*, or counties, showing the extent to which these circular surveys prevail throughout the island, see the "Atlas" prepared as part of the *Censo de la Republica de Cuba, 1943*, Havana, Editorial Guerrero, 1946. These surveys are also referred to and described briefly in Robert S. Platt, *Latin America: Countrysides and United Regions*, New York, McGraw-Hill Book Company, 1943, pp. 126–128, and Lowry Nelson, *Rural Cuba*, Minneapolis, University of Minnesota Press, 1950, pp. 84–90.

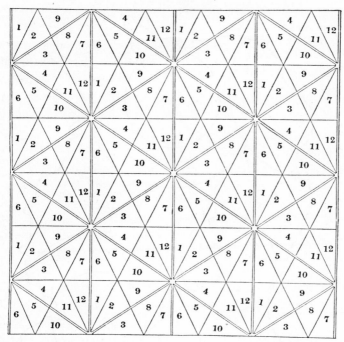

FIGURE 62. Diagram of a Hexagonal System of Laying Out a Township with Twelve Farms of 160 Acres Each Radiating from the Center. (From a design by Dr. E. Deville, in Thomas Adams, *Rural Planning and Development*, Ottawa, Commission of Conservation, 1917, facing p. 259.)

Advantages and Disadvantages of the Various Systems of Land Division

The evolution of the American land system has employed almost every possibility in the manner of dividing land among the population. Indeterminate location and haphazard surveys were widely used in the group settlement of New England as well as in the individualistic settlements of the middle and southern colonies. On the frontier among the trans-Appalachian settlements it may be said to have run riot. The river-front pattern in various degrees of intensity, or with frontages varying from one-fortieth of their depth, has been widely scattered in the United States. In the French and Spanish colonies, especially French Canada, Louisiana, and Texas, this was the prevailing mode of dividing lands. And in 1785 a thoroughly determinate rectangular system was adopted and became the national pattern for subdividing

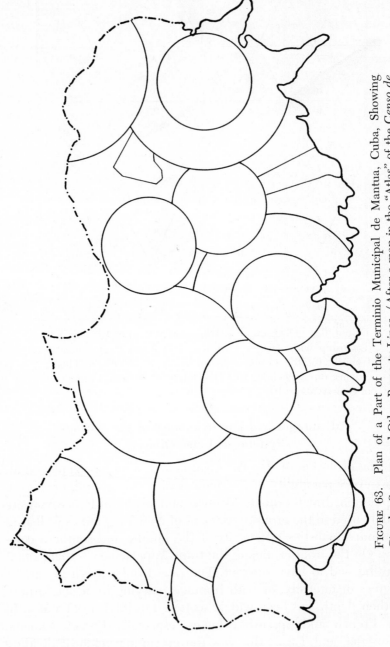

Figure 63. Plan of a Part of the Término Municipal de Mantua, Cuba, Showing Circular Surveys and Other Property Lines. (After a map in the "Atlas" of the *Censo de la Republica de Cuba, 1943*.)

public lands. It is well to ask, What are the relative merits and weaknesses of these various systems? What general considerations should be taken into account in judging the efficiency and merit of any system for subdividing agricultural lands? What are the strong points and the weaknesses of the present American system? How can weaknesses, once established in the land system, be overcome? And particularly, What immediate steps may be taken to improve the American pattern?

Two general principles relative to equitable and efficient modes of subdividing lands may be set forth. (1) For purposes of surveying and recording,[40] it is essential that the system of surveys be simple, determinate, and permanent. They should be based not upon mere surface phenomena, which are relatively short-lived and changeable, but upon astronomical observations. They must provide for quick, easy redetermination of boundaries, and above all make possible a short and simple deed. (2) Unless the village form of settlement is utilized, the social welfare of the agricultural population requires that the holdings be considerably less in width than in length. This is the principle of the long-lot survey. Only this provision allows the individual families to satisfy their desires with respect to neighbors. Unless landholdings are relatively narrow as compared to their length, it becomes impossible for farmers to avoid having excessive distances between their houses. And this circumstance in turn makes prohibitive the cost of securing roads, telephones, electricity, school buses, and many of the other advantages of modern living. Conversely, only if this principle is adhered to can the hermit (if there be such) enjoy the greatest opportunity for avoiding his fellows. The extent to which this principle is followed determines the extent to which farmers are allowed to arrange their homes in proximity to others.

Judged by these standards, indiscriminate location has little to recommend it as a system of land division. It fails entirely to meet the first condition, since it makes surveying and recording as difficult as possible, is based upon short-lived surface phenomena, and generally gives rise to endless quarrels, lawsuits, and social conflict. Such a haphazard system is absolutely unsatisfactory from the standpoint of governmental controls. Usually

[40] The evolution of the American recording system and its distinctive characteristics are treated in Richard B. Morris, *Studies in the History of American Law,* New York, Columbia University Press, 1930, pp. 69–73.

evolved under conditions where possession is all-important, indiscriminate location has seldom been associated with the village form of settlement; in its extreme form it is incompatible with any kind of group settlement. Highly individualistic in background, it appears never to have given rise to line villages. By and large, it has been almost as ruthless in isolating farm houses from one another as the checkerboard rectangular system, which, as we shall see, attains almost the nth degree in the spatial isolation of farm homes. Indeed, indiscriminate location, after the initial advantage of allowing each person to gerrymander his claim to include any unoccupied land he desires and only that, appears to have only one thing in its favor: It possesses the doubtful advantage of allowing farmers located in hilly districts to arrange their fields and build their houses so that everything "comes down hill to the house."

The river-front pattern of land division meets our first condition much better than indiscriminate location, but not nearly so well as a rectangular system. In any given case the amount of uniformity in the river-front pattern is dependent upon the nature of the river, lake front, or coast upon which it is based. Of course the limits of holdings defined on one side by the bank of the stream and running back inland a specified distance are much more fixed and easily determined or resurveyed than those patents whose boundaries are marked with trees, stones, and other perishable and readily movable features of the landscape. To the extent that the shores of the lake or stream remain fixed, the system offers determinateness and permanency. However, it is well known that rivers are constantly cutting away from the bank on the outside of curves and building up sand bars on the inside. In the course of time this makes for confusion. And occasionally a river suddenly changes its course. Where such a stream is the base for land surveys this shift causes great confusion in the land titles. Further discussion is not necessary in order to demonstrate that the river-front pattern is vastly inferior to rectangular patterns for the purposes of surveying and recording.

It is, however, in relation to the second condition that the river-front land division gains its chief recommendation. The conservation of river frontages seems to have been a major determination wherever this pattern has been used. It has usually been specified that holdings may not lie with the long side on the river, and frequently the amount of frontage granted has been only a fraction of the length of the holding. Out of these conditions has been developed the close association that exists between the river-front pattern of land division and the line village form of settlement; the line village makes for ready contact between farm families and the economical provision of such modern conveniences as roads, telephones, electricity, etc. In the southern colonies, where freedom of location was limited to some extent by regulations concerning the amount of river frontage that could accompany acreages of a given amount, the relationship between this form of settlement and the manner of dividing lands was in a rudimentary form. Closer was the association in the Spanish settlements such as those of southern Texas. It reached the acme of perfection in the French settlements of Canada and Louisiana and in Lord Selkirk's colonies on the Red River of the North.[41]

Some of the advantages of this mode of land division are apparent from the following data pertaining to a rather typical settlement in Louisiana. One four-mile stretch along Bayou Lafourche contained ninety-five homes all placed at the front of ninety-five ribbonlike farms averaging approximately forty acres in size, although only 220 feet in width. In this settlement four miles of paved road passes directly in front of the ninety-five farm homes. Contrast this with the situation in an agricultural area corresponding in size and divided into 96 squares of 40 acres each, where 15½ miles of pavement would be required in order to reach each home. Similar savings are present in the procuring of electricity, telephone, etc., and in the transportation of school children, collection of farm products, delivery of dry goods and groceries, not to mention the extent to which such a system of land division fosters contacts among the population.

[41] For a description of the Canadian settlements, see Ellen Churchill Semple, "The Influence of the Geographic Environment on the Lower St. Lawrence," *Bulletin of the American Geographical Society*, XXXVI (1904), 449–466; for material dealing with the line village and river-front land division, see the author's articles, "An Analysis of Rural Social Organization Among the French-Speaking People of Southern Louisiana," *Journal of Farm Economics*, XVI (1934), 680–688, and "The Social Effects of Land Division," *loc. cit.*; and for an account and description of Selkirk's Manitoba colonies, consult John M'Greagor, *British America*, Edinburgh, W. Blackwood Publishing Company, 2nd ed., 1833, I, 505, 525, W. H. Smith, *Canada: Past, Present and Future*, Toronto, Thomas Maclear, 1851, I, 2, and *A Handbook to Winnipeg and the Province of Manitoba*, prepared for the 79th Annual Meeting of the British Association for the Advancement of Science, 1909, pp. 67–68.

The checkerboard variety of the rectangular surveys which has been utilized in the land system of the United States is one of the simplest, most determinate, and most permanent ways of dividing lands ever devised by man. From the standpoint of surveying and recording it approaches perfection. But from the standpoint of the social and economic welfare of the population on the land it is one of the most vicious modes ever devised for dividing lands. Combined with the scattered or isolated farmsteads mode of settlement, it has greatly handicapped the rural population of the United States for the past century and a half. As the writer has pointed out elsewhere:

> Suppose one were assigned the distasteful task of designing a system of land division that would contribute most to the social and physical isolation of the farm population. The system aimed at would disperse agricultural families as widely as possible; make neighboring, co-operation, and mutual aid possible only with the utmost difficulty; make the securing of roads, telephone lines, electric power and lights, etc., the most expensive; make participation in the activities of schools, churches, etc., the most difficult; make marketing of produce, or purchase of supplies the most burdensome; even make the hindrances to the innocent association of children as great as possible. In brief, from the standpoint of the farm family, suppose one were to devise the most vicious system of land division possible. He should then be graded 100 per cent or A plus when he had developed the familiar checkerboard system and placed the dwelling of each farm family at the middle of its holding.[42]

The social inefficiency of the dominant mode of dividing American farm lands is the more to be regretted because it is possible to have a system just as simple, just as determinate, and just as permanent as the checkerboard pattern without setting obstacles in the way of social contacts among the population and making the cost of roads, electricity, etc., prohibitive. Utilization of rectangles instead of squares would make practicable the formation of line village settlements without detracting at all from the system for surveying and recording purposes.

For illustrative purposes consider two areas in which 160-acre farms are arranged as in Figures 64 and 65. In the one, farms are

---

[42] T. Lynn Smith, "Social Effects of Land Division," pp. 703–704; cf. Thomas Adams, *Rural Planning and Development*, Commission of Conservation, Ottawa, Canada, 1917, p. 53.

uniformly quarter sections; in the other, they consist of rectangles one mile long and one-quarter of a mile wide. In the area utilizing rectangles, one mile of road would reach as many homes as four miles would serve in the area divided into squares. Similar saving

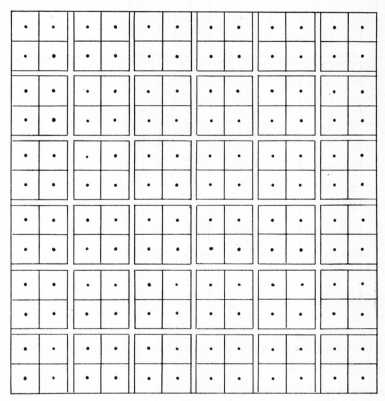

FIGURE 64. A Township Divided into 144 Tracts of 160 Acres Each, Illustrating the Extreme Dispersion of Farm Homes Resulting from the Checkerboard Pattern of Land Division.

in lines for electricity, telephones, etc., would be attained. In every respect making the width of the holdings only one-fourth their length would contribute to the social and economic welfare of the population. Even from the standpoint of technical agriculture and farm management such a system probably has more advantages than disadvantages.[43]

Recently, in connection with his work in South America, the writer has proposed a similar system for use in the vast unsettled

[43] See C. P. Barnes, "Economies of the Long-Lot Farm," *Geographical Review,* XXV (1935), 298–301.

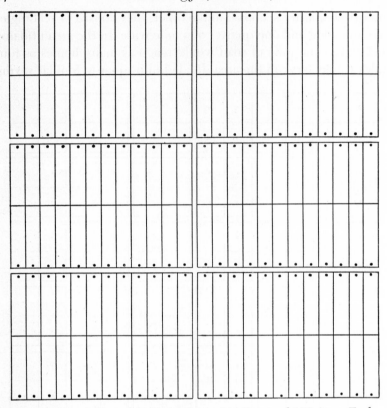

FIGURE 65. A Township Divided into 144 Tracts of 160 Acres Each, Illustrating the Grouping of Farm Homes Made Possible by a Slight Revision in the Customary Pattern of Land Division.

portions of Colombia and Brazil. This system provides for laying off an entire country into square degrees by projecting all the degrees of latitude and longitude across its territory. Each of the squares formed in this manner is given a number on a base map. The actual survey lines would be run as needed and only a little in advance of actual settlement. In the surveys each square degree would be divided into square sections and lots, as in Figure 66. The lots, including 100 hectares or 247 acres, would frequently be small enough for family farms without further subdivision, but the plan allows for dividing each of them into 25-hectare tracts if it is deemed advisable. To deed a given acreage of land according to this system, it is necessary only to indicate the parcels, lot, section, square, and degree involved. For example, if degree No. 75 fell in the Amazon Valley near Leticia, the title to 50 hectares

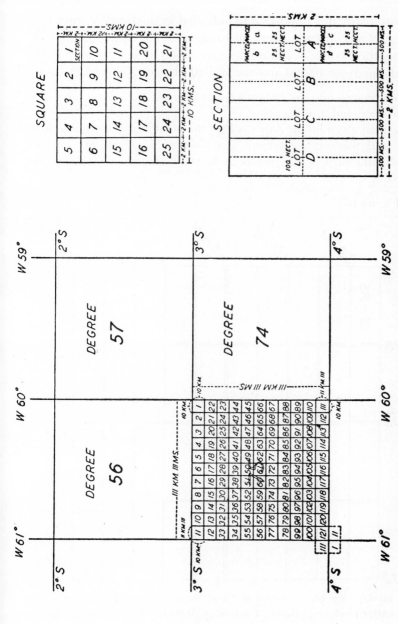

FIGURE 66. System of Land Surveys Recommended for Use in the Unsettled Parts of South America. (Reproduced from T. Lynn Smith, *Brazil: People and Institutions*, Baton Rouge, Louisiana State University Press, 1946.)

might read "parcels a and b of lot B, section 17, square 9, degree 75."

Historically it is important to note that in the third century B.C. the Egyptians already were utilizing a comparable manner of dividing their lands. Seebohm describes their manner of laying out a great square of 10,000 arouras into 40 plots of 250 arouras each.

The divisions into the 40 lots were to be made by 3 dykes across in one direction and 9 in the other.

The plan given on the papyrus fixes the point that it was to be in a square and the text accordingly describes its circumference as 400 schoinia, and each of the 40 lots as 10 x 25 schoinia, i.e. 250 square schoinia.[44]

(See Figure 67.)

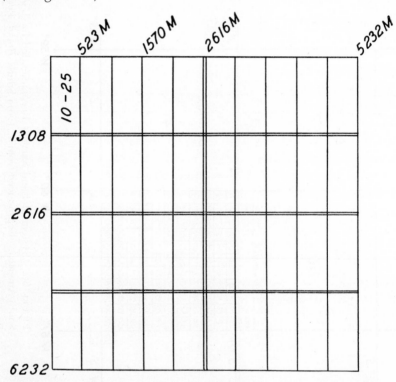

FIGURE 67. Egyptian System of Land Surveys of the Third Century B.C. (After Frederic Seebohm, *Customary Acres and Their Historical Importance*, New York, Longmans, Green & Company, 1914, p. 209.)

[44] Frederic Seebohm, *Customary Acres and Their Historical Importance*, New York, Longmans, Green & Company, 1914, p. 209.

Finally there is the question of what to do in order to modify our present checkerboard system of land division so as to obtain the economies and social advantages of the long-lot system. Two suggestions may be offered. Concentration of lands in the hands of the most successful farmers is always going on in the United States, and just as constant is the redivision of these lands among the various heirs of the farmer who has made the accumulation. Widespread consciousness of the merits of the oblong-rectangular system as compared with the checkerboard pattern could, in a few generations, completely change the pattern of land division in the nation, merely through the manner of subdivision of inherited estates. The state highway commissions are also in strategic positions for improving the manner of dividing lands. Today the paved highway is rapidly remolding rural America. It is already decidedly advantageous to have a farm home located on a paved highway. No sooner is a new highway completed through a farming section than farmers begin relocating their houses and barns in order to be on it. Already on the outskirts of towns and cities frontages on the highways are at a premium, with the result that ribbonlike holdings line these highways for many miles. State highway commissions working in coöperation with state planning commissions should adopt the policy of projecting roads no closer than two miles apart. Roads in rural areas should not be built along each section line, as the present blueprint calls for, but only along every other section line. This procedure would rapidly have a pronounced effect on the shape of the farms in the United States. The need and desire for situations on the highways would set about transforming farmsteads of 160 acres of square quarter sections into oblong rectangles one-quarter of a mile wide and one mile long. The ultimate results, gauged by the social and economic welfare of the population, would do much to establish the efficiency of long-range social planning.

12

LAND TENURE

Land tenure denotes a social relationship between the population and the land. It refers to the way of holding land, to the property rights of the individual to the land. Questions about land tenure are as old as civilization itself. Because the rural population is directly dependent for its sustenance upon the soil and because the amount of productive land readily available to any sedentary group is definitely limited, the social regulations regarding the use of land always constitute an important part of the culture pattern of any agricultural group. Therefore the subject of land tenure deserves a prominent place in all treatises on the sociology of rural life.

Practically every primitive group has placed some restrictions upon the use of the land.[1] Provisions regulating the use of land are part of the earliest literature known to mankind. A study of the early law codes reveals that much attention was given to matters relating to the use of land. One of the earliest codes, and one that served as a pattern for many that followed, is that of Hammurabi. This compilation was written on clay tablets some four thousand years ago. It was made at a time when agriculturists living within the town walls cultivated the irrigated areas surrounding the settlement, and it is rather explicit in its rules concerning the social relationships between the people and the land. No less than seventeen of its 247 sections pertain to the use of land, and of these at least thirteen (numbers 42–47, 52, and 60–65) deal with land tenure, defining specifically the accepted relations of the landlord and

[1] See Richard Thurnwald, *Economics in Primitive Communities*, New York, Oxford University Press, 1932, pp. 186–194; and Robert H. Lowie, *Primitive Society*, New York, Boni & Liveright, 1920, pp. 210–233.

the tenant. Typical of the provisions contained in the code is section 253, which reads as follows: "If a man hire a man to oversee his farm and furnish him the seed-grain and intrust him with oxen and contract with him to cultivate the field, and that man steal either the seed or the crop and it be found in his possession, they shall cut off his fingers."[2] In the codes, as at the present time, many might find reason to complain that the regulations are drawn up in the interest of the landlord and not the tenant.

Although the Hebrews inherited a nomadic culture, provisions regulating land tenure are of considerable importance in their ancient regulations.[3] Even more important are the statutes regulating property rights in land that are found in the law codes of the Hindus, the Chinese, and other ancient peoples. The problems of land tenure are as old as civilization based upon agriculture.

Land problems are also very pressing in the modern world. Following World War I, practically every nation was troubled with problems of land tenure. The "Green Rising" in Europe brought fundamental changes in the land systems of nearly every country of central Europe and the Near East.[4] The cry of "land for the peasants" was one of the most powerful stimuli in the early phases of the Russian Revolution. Germany and Italy made sweeping changes in their land systems. Land reforms in Spain made up one stage in the development of the deep-cutting Spanish Civil War. Land reform is the core of the present-day Mexican revolution, and fundamental changes in the land system are being attempted in Brazil, Chile, Colombia, and other Latin American republics.[5] Programs designed to bring about a wider distribution

[2] A later, slightly different translation is readily available in J. M. Powis Smith, *The Origin and History of Hebrew Law*, Chicago, University of Chicago Press, 1931.

[3] Cf. Leviticus 25.

[4] Cf. William B. Bizzell, *The Green Rising*, New York, The Macmillan Company, 1926.

[5] N. S. Timasheff, in his article "Structural Changes in Rural Russia," *Rural Sociology*, II (1937), 10–28, gives an excellent summary of recent Russian developments and policy; a useful summary of German attempts and experience will be found in John B. Holt, "Recent Changes in German Rural Life," *Rural Sociology*, II (1937), 266–277; and his book, *German Agricultural Policy, 1918–1934*, Chapel Hill, University of North Carolina Press, 1936, is a painstaking review of legislation under the Third Reich. The agrarian aspects of the upheaval in Spain await adequate treatment. Eyler Simpson, *The Ejido: Mexico's Way Out*, Chapel Hill, University of North Carolina Press, 1937, long was the most comprehensive work on the Mexican agrarian revolution; and Nathan L. Whetten, *Rural Mexico*, Chicago, University of Chicago Press, 1948, has carried the story through the all-important Cárdenas regime. Land tenure in Brazil occupies a prominent place in

of landownership in Europe and Asia also are much in evidence following the close of World War II.[6]

The United States has never faced questions of land distribution and land tenure in the serious manner that has been forced upon other countries. Because of the seemingly inexhaustible supply of good lands to be had for the taking (from the Indians), this nation has been enabled to postpone facing the fundamental questions of land tenure and land distribution with which all civilized peoples are eventually called upon to deal. This is not to say that no attention has been given to the problem. The ceding of state lands to the federal government created the bond that did most to bring about a strong union among the original states; the revenue from the sale of these lands was the money that paid for the operation of the governmental machinery; and the ready outlet to the West was the factor which quieted most of the difficulties in the East. Led by riots and bloodshed the new government early evolved a system, or lack of it, whereby settlers could get possession of unoccupied lands. Customary procedures for obtaining land without leave, such as sitting down or "squatting" on the land, "cabin" rights, and "tomahawk" rights, eventually came to be thoroughly legalized in the homestead laws.[7] And as long as free land was in abundance, the problem required little more attention. With more good land available, the questions of land-grabbing by the privileged, large grants to railroads, etc., did not come in for great consideration, or at least they did not lead to fundamental reforms.

Tenure Classes

Land tenure is an exceedingly complicated and complex subject. Depending upon the particular purpose in mind, several im-

T. Lynn Smith, *Brazil: People and Institutions,* Baton Rouge, Louisiana State University Press, 1946. For Chile, see G. M. McBride, *Chile: Land and Society,* American Geographical Society Research Series 19, New York, 1936. A little information about Colombia is presented in T. Lynn Smith, "The Cultural Setting of Agricultural Extension Work in Colombia," *Rural Sociology,* X (1945), 235–246; and the stirrings in Argentina are summarized in Carl C. Taylor, *Rural Life in Argentina,* Baton Rouge, Louisiana State University Press, 1948, pp. 383–392.

[6] Among the most important studies available to date on developments in Asia are Arthur F. Raper, *The Japanese Village in Transition,* Tokyo, General Headquarters, Supreme Commander for the Allied Powers, 1950, and Lawrence I. Hewes, Jr., *Japanese Land Reform Program,* Tokyo, General Headquarters, Supreme Commander for the Allied Powers, 1950.

[7] Cf. Thomas Donaldson, *The Public Domain,* House Misc. Doc. 45, IV, 47th Congress, Washington, 1884, XIX, 156–167.

portant classifications of the property rights in land are possible.

The Nature of Grants from the King or the State

Theoretically all land belongs to the king, or, in a democracy, to the state. The conditions or qualifications imposed in granting lands to subjects or citizens are many. At the time of the discovery of America the feudal system was still in full practice in England. Under feudalism the sovereign allocated lands to his trusted followers in return for specific services, especially services of a military nature. This practice is known as *knight-service*. The lord of the manor, in turn, let out portions of his estate to various serfs and tenants in exchange for services rendered and portions of the crops and livestock produced. Usually the common people were bound to the land, and the services and obligations they owed to the lord were legion and specified in minute detail.[8] Before the colonization of America became successful, a bitter struggle brought about the substitution of *socage* (i.e., the holding of lands by a fixed and determined service not of a military nature, and not subject to variation at the will of the sovereign) for knight-service. The charter given by Elizabeth to Sir Walter Raleigh in 1584 granted him and his heirs and assigns the right to dispose of lands in *fee simple* (i.e., pure inheritance, free of conditions or qualifications of alienation). This was a tremendous step toward liberation of landholding.[9]

In the United States all land granted or patented within the English colonies before the Revolution was held in socage tenure. In theory all landholders, whether in fee, for life, or for years, were obligated to render service to the lord when required to do so. However, for the most part in the English colonies this was a mere form. But in the Dutch colony of New York this was not the case. For example, it is reported from Rensselaerswyck that the patroon reserved for himself one-tenth of all grains, fruits, and other products raised in the bouwerie. In addition the tenant paid a rent of two hundred dollars, kept up the roads, repaired the buildings, cut ten pieces of oak for firewood and transported it to

[8] Cf. N. S. B. Gras and Ethel C. Gras, *The Economic and Social History of an English Village,* Cambridge, Harvard University Press, 1930, pp. 53–58, *passim.*
[9] Donaldson, *op. cit.,* pp. 156–158; cf. Shosuke Sato, *History of the Land Question in the United States,* Johns Hopkins University Studies in Historical and Political Science, Fourth Series, VII–IX, Baltimore, 1886, pp. 273–276.

the shore of the river, each year gave three days' service with team and wagon to the patroon, furnished two fathoms of firewood annually, and paid quitrent of two bushels of wheat, twenty-five pounds of butter, and two pairs of fowls.[10]

Although the attempts to transfer the feudal system to America were many, socage tenure was about all that was accomplished, and even this was for the most part only a form. By the ordinance of 1787, the first general legislation by Congress on the subject of real property, all the leading features of feudalism were specifically repealed. This ordinance made the individual absolutely independent of the state, and the sole owner of his land. It provided for the establishment of thousands of free and independent holdings out of the public domain. Thus in America it became a fundamental maxim that the state is the source of the title to land. All titles, to be valid, must derive from the grants from or under the authority of England, Sweden, Holland, France, Spain, Russia, Mexico, the colonies, the federal government, or the governments of the several states. All treaties defining boundaries, purchases, cessions, or relating to territory now in the United States specifically guard the individual property rights in land.[11] The one right retained by the government is that of eminent domain.

Property Rights Under Fee Simple

In spite of the uniform method by which the government of the United States has granted lands to its citizens or confirmed them and their heirs in rights previously obtained, there are great variations as among individuals in the way lands are held and the period for which they are secure. The individual's property rights in land may be said to reach their maximum in a system of ownership in fee simple, or absolute right to use and dispose of the land. At the other end of the scale is serfdom, where the person's only right in the land is the security he obtains because of the fact that he cannot be parted from it. Between the two there are many shades of difference. Furthermore, in addition to tenure rights there is the absence of such rights. A goodly portion of the agricultural population, slaves and agricultural laborers, lack any property rights whatsoever in the land.

[10] Cf. Maud Wilder Goodwin, *Dutch and English on the Hudson*, New Haven, Yale University Press, 1919, pp. 43–44.
[11] Donaldson, *op. cit.*, pp. 156–157.

The United States Census Classification

For many purposes it is necessary to classify the agricultural population according to tenure. In America the most widely used and accepted classification is the one given by the United States Bureau of the Census. The census begins by drawing a fundamental distinction between farm laborers and farm operators. Little further attention is given to farm laborers except to group them into two categories separating unpaid family laborers from the other laborers. For the most part, however, laborers are ignored. Farm operators are subdivided into the categories of owners, managers, and tenants. Tenants in turn are classed as cash tenants, standing renters, share tenants, croppers, and other tenants. The classification may be presented in summary form as follows:

    I. Farm operators
        A. Owners
        B. Managers
        C. Tenants
            1. Cash tenants
            2. Standing renters
            3. Share tenants
            4. Sharecroppers
            5. Other tenants
    II. Farm laborers
        A. Unpaid family laborers
        B. All others

This classification is basically unsound.[12] Its use destroys the validity of practically all the agricultural statistics in the South— statistics that have been gathered and tabulated at a tremendous cost. So long as the Bureau of the Census persists in the use of its erroneous and misleading distinctions and terminology it will be impossible to know the total number of farms in the southern region, the percentages of them operated by owners or renters, the

[12] This fact was pointed out long ago by Alfred H. Stone, "The Negro and Agricultural Development," *Annals of the American Academy of Political and Social Science,* XXXV (1910), 15. For a more recent analysis, see T. Lynn Smith, "The Significance of Reported Trends in Louisiana Agriculture," *The Southwestern Social Science Quarterly,* XXII (1941), 233–241. The unsoundness of the classification also is implicit, if not explicit, in one of the recent publications issued by the Bureau of the Census itself. See "Multiple-Unit Operations," *United States Census of Agriculture, 1945,* Washington, Government Printing Office, 1947, p. vii.

average income per farm, trends in the number of farms or in farm tenancy, the average size of farms in the area and trends in this respect, and practically all the other data that are of vital importance in the development of modern agricultural policy.[13] So long as our official agricultural statistics are handled in an unrealistic and fallacious manner, most comparisons of the southern region with others will continue to deceive writer and reader alike. Furthermore, owing to the rapid decline of the sharecropping system, the data on number of farms, average size of farms, percentage of tenancy, and so on, secured in one census will be largely lacking in comparability with those gathered in another enumeration.

What, then, it may well be asked, are the basic fallacies in the census terminology and classifications? The answer is that a proper distinction is not made between farm operators and farm laborers. The census classifies sharecroppers with farm operators, when in sociological and economic reality they (and some of the "share tenants" as well) belong with the farm laborers.

Probably this fundamental difficulty has arisen from the fact that the term "tenant" has various connotations in different sections of the country. In the North and West *farm tenant* and *farm renter* are synonymous terms. But this is by no means the case in the South. Following the Civil War and the trial period of operation with free labor paid a cash wage, the system of sharecropping was developed in the South. Basically, it seems to have arisen as a method of tying the laborer more securely to the soil and thus assuring many hands to pick cotton.[14] From ancient times similar systems of share wages have prevailed in other countries. In some way, perhaps for want of a better term, and perhaps because the Negro sharecroppers were allowed the use of a cabin on the place, the practice arose of referring to the families working on the plantations as "tenants."[15] As some of the workers accumulated property and came to own a mule and a little equipment, obviously

---

[13] Cf. Karl Brandt, "Fallacious Census Terminology and Its Consequences in Agriculture," *Social Research*, V (1938), 31.

[14] Cf. Ulrich B. Phillips and James David Glunt, *Florida Plantation Records*, St. Louis, Historical Society, 1927, pp. 37–38, 191–193; Henry Latham, *Black and White*, London, Macmillan & Co., Ltd., 1867, pp. 271–272; and Charles H. Otken, *The Ills of the South*, New York, G. P. Putnam's Sons, 1894, pp. 35–37.

[15] However, southern writers recognized this class not as tenants but as share laborers. See William H. Harris, *Louisiana Products, Resources and Attractions, with a Sketch of the Parishes*, New Orleans, 1881, pp. 125–126.

they were entitled to a larger portion of the crop. Whereas share-croppers or "half-hands" were customarily paid one-half of the cotton, those who owned mules were given a larger portion and came to be known as "three-fourths hands" or "share tenants." Somehow there arose early in the Bureau of the Census the practice of counting these "half-hands" and "three-fourths hands" as farm operators. Apparently the term *tenant* was received and interpreted as though it were synonymous with *renter*.[16] But in the discriminating vocabulary of the region, the connotations of the two were entirely different.[17] Furthermore, when specifically tested in a legal manner the precise sociological connotations of the term have been explicitly set forth. This fact has been brought out so clearly by Robert Preston Brooks that one can hardly do better than to quote extensively his evidence and excellent analysis:

When it is once realized that the share system finds place only on plantations under close supervision, that the share tenant is really a day laborer, and that his holding is not a farm but a section of a well-ordered unit, it should be manifest that there is little cause for alarm on account of the decline in the percentage of farms operated by owners, and the growth of tenancy in Georgia. . . .

The law of Georgia sustains the position that the share tenant is only a day laborer and not a real tenant. Of course, the law simply crystallizes the actual economic facts as they have worked out. In 1872, the Supreme Court in the case of Appling vs. Odum (46 *Georgia Reports*, pp. 584–585) held:

"There is an obvious distinction between a cropper and a tenant. One has a possession of the premises, exclusive of the landlord, the other has not. The one has a right for a fixed time, the other has only a right to go on the land to plant, work and gather the crop. The possession of the land is with the owner as against the cropper. The case made in the record is not the case of a tenant. The owner of the land furnished the land and the supplies. The share of the cropper was to remain on the land and to be subject to the advances of the owner for supplies. *The case of the cropper is rather a mode of paying wages than a tenancy.* The title to the crop subject to the wages is in the owner of the land."

[16] The result is that one who works with agricultural statistics for the South finds himself "floundering in a tangle of figures which may mean much or nothing. . . ." Cf. Stone, *loc. cit.*

[17] Thus the Arkansas State Policy Committee in its Published Paper No. 1, *Agricultural Labor Problems in Arkansas*, Little Rock, 1936, p. 1, refers to the *renter* as the highest type of tenant.

The important words have been italicized, in which the court expressed the opinion that a share hand is a wage earner, not a tenant, or renter. This decision has been the basis of all subsequent rulings as to the relations of landlords and tenants in Georgia. The view was reiterated in 1878 (61 *Georgia Reports,* p. 488) when the court held that "Where one is employed to work for part of the crop, the relation of landlord and tenant does not rise." Ten years later the court defined with great clearness the position of the share hand: (80 *Georgia Reports,* p. 95).

"Where an owner of land furnishes it with supplies and other like necessaries, keeping general supervision over the farm, and agrees to pay a certain portion of the crop to the laborer for his work, the laborer is a cropper, and judgments or liens cannot sell his part of the crop until the landlord is fully paid, but where there is a renting, and the relation of landlord and tenant exists, an older judgment will subject the renter's crop . . . (both parties) swore that Plunkett (the tenant) rented the land from Almand for a specified rent. The land, therefore, was in possession of Plunkett, the tenant, and not in Almand, the owner. The work was not done under Almand's superintendence and direction. Almand had no control over the land, and the crop made on the land was not to go in payment to Plunkett for his labor in making the crop. He was therefore not a cropper as defined in 46 Ga. 583 (Appling vs. Odum)."

It should now be clear that in economic significance, and in their practical and legal aspects, renting and share tenancy are as wide apart as the poles. The cropper is a day laborer, works under constant direction, has no exclusive right to the premises or title to the crop he produces. The renter, on the other hand, is a real tenant. The court has explicitly held (75 *Georgia Reports,* p. 274) that the landlord has no right to enter on the tenant's farm against his will to interfere with the crops. The tenant has exclusive possession of the premises for the time being and entire control over his crops. It is scarcely necessary to point out that the reason underlying this distinction is that, in case of the cropper, the landlord is the sole capitalist and entrepreneur. Everything necessary to make the crop is supplied by him; while, in the case of the tenant, a fixed rental per acre is paid the landlord, and the landlord's connection with the tenant's farm ceases there.[18]

In another place the author has tried to clarify the differences between croppers and real tenants or renters in the following manner:

[18] *The Agrarian Revolution in Georgia,* University of Wisconsin Historical Series, III (1914), 67–68; cf. T. Lynn Smith, "Discussion," *Journal of Farm Economics,* XIX (1937), 143–147.

. . . The typical cropper works under an arrangement whereby the plantation operator agrees to give him a specified share of the crop from a designated acreage of ground, and the cropper agrees to perform the manual labor needed to produce and pick the crop. The landlord may allow him certain privileges on the plot of land assigned to him, i.e., he may be permitted to use some of it for a garden, to keep a pig, etc. But if any question arises concerning the use being made of the land by the cropper, it will be found that all the rights not specified in the agreement remain with the planter. The cropper has no rights in the land other than those specifically transferred to him by the landlord. For this reason there is no logical basis, whatsoever, for considering the cropper a tenant and a farm operator. A tenant is one who secures the right to use land for a specified period of time through the payment of rent to the owner. If the owner desires to retain certain rights in the land for the period of the contract, these must be specified in the lease. Then the tenant has the right to use the land subject to the terms of the lease. If no limitations are made in the contract, he has all the rights of the owner for the period of the lease. The tenant is strictly within his rights as long as he uses the land in ways not forbidden by the contract or by the law of the land. To summarize this point, the cropper has no rights in the land except those specifically transferred by the owner, while the tenant has all the rights in the land except those specifically withheld by the contract.[19]

A Proposed Classification

The simplest and most practicable cure for the misunderstandings would be for the Census Bureau to eliminate the word "tenant" from its definitions, instructions, and tabulations and use the word "renter" in its place. For the northern and western states this would not be different from present procedures. For the southern states it would have the advantages of eliminating the source of the fallacies, making the agricultural statistics comparable with those of other areas, and best of all making possible the collection of meaningful agricultural statistics for the South.[20]

[19] T. Lynn Smith, "Discussion," *Journal of Farm Economics*, XX (1938), 161. Clarification of terminology would dissipate many of the most perplexing problems confronting the student of rural social problems. For example, the curious fact that the South has a very high proportion of persons who become "tenants" without passing through the wage-earner stage (cf. L. C. Gray, Charles L. Stewart, Howard A. Turner, J. T. Sanders, and W. J. Spillman, "Farm Ownership and Tenancy," *Yearbook of the Department of Agriculture, 1923*, Washington, 1924, p. 554) means little more than that the southern cropper is not a genuine tenant or renter.

[20] Such a procedure is recommended by the American Farm Economics Association. See the condensed report of the Agricultural Census Committee in *Journal of Farm Economics*, XXI (1939), 404–408.

Were this practice adopted, the following classification of farmers according to tenure might well be used:

    I. Farm operators
        A. Owners and part owners
        B. Managers
        C. Renters
            1. Cash
            2. Standing
            3. Share
    II. Farm laborers
        A. "Share tenants"
        B. Sharecroppers
        C. Wage hands
        D. Unpaid family laborers

There is also justification for distinguishing between those unpaid family laborers who belong to the families of the farm operators and those who belong to the families of the laborers.

Except for a small class of absentee landlords this classification includes all the agriculturists of the present-day United States. Historically there have been two other important groups, i.e., indentured servants and slaves; but the former were important only during early colonial days, and slavery was abolished during the Civil War.

The fundamental division in the above classification separates farm operators and farm laborers. Farm operators include those who assume the functions of the entrepreneur, those who make the actual decisions for running the farm, including decisions regarding the crops to be planted, the time for cultivation, fertilization, and all similar matters relative to the culture of crops. Obviously the owner-operator, the entrepreneur who has title to the land he tills, is of primary importance in this group. A second group of farm operators includes those farm managers who are employed for the job of running the farm enterprises. Absentee landlords, whether persons, banks, insurance companies, or estates, utilize the services of such specialists. A third class of entrepreneurs does not own land but bargains with those who do for the use of a farmstead, paying a specified rent per acre or a given sum for a definite tract of land. In return for this cash the renter is entitled to the use of the land for a given period of time. The landlord frequently makes certain reservations as to how the land shall be used, and these are ordinarily recorded in the lease; but by and large the tenant exchanges cash in return for the right to use the land as he wishes. A fourth type of operator, the standing renter, is one who pays a fixed amount of produce (bales of cotton, bushels of wheat, etc.) for the use of the land. Usually his lease differs from the cash tenant's primarily in the kind of payment, but it is obvious that the landlord assumes part of the risk, i.e., his rent varies with the price of the product. Finally, the share renter is the entrepreneur who secures the right to the use of the land in return for a specified share of the crop. Under a share-renting arrangement there is the greatest division of the risks of production and chances of profit between the landlord and the renter. The landlord shares in the chances inherent in both price fluctuations and crop failure.[21]

In the labor classes are included, in addition to unpaid family workers and wage hands, the categories of sharecroppers and a special class of "share tenants." Some croppers come to own a little livestock and some equipment. In payment for their services in the production of cotton they are given a larger share than the half-hands. These persons, who are really in the category of the-cropper-who-has-a-mule, are properly classified with the farm laborers.

Tenure Classes in the United States

Despite the lack of satisfactory statistical data, it is nevertheless true that, viewed from the standpoint of tenure relationships to the land, the agricultural population of the United States falls into four principal categories. First, there are those who own, fully or partially, the land that they use in farming operations. The owner-operator is generally supposed to be the typical American farmer, and has long been singled out as the chief support of the nation. Second, there is a small class of managers who operate for others. These have become increasingly important as banks and insurance companies have sought to protect their equities in farm lands by operating a chain of farms. Third, there are those who secure the right to use land for a specified period of time through the payment of rent to the owner of the land. And finally, there are

[21] For an analysis of the relative merits of these several types of leases and the way they operate in one western state, see E. D. Tetreau, *Arizona Farm Leases*, Arizona AES Bulletin 179, Tucson, 1942.

the great masses of agricultural laborers, a group that is practically lacking in rights to the land, and whose members earn a scanty livelihood by working on the farms of others, selling their labor for wages.

The unsatisfactory nature of our statistical data makes it difficult to arrive at a close approximation of the number of families in the United States dependent upon agriculture as their chief means of support, much less to determine the proportion of those owning farms. The reason is that residence, not occupation, is taken as the chief basis for classification, and that an extremely unrealistic definition of a farm is used for census purposes. In addition to the fact that part of the farm laborers (sharecroppers and "share tenants") are confused with farm operators, comprehensive and accurate data are lacking pertaining to the agricultural wage hands of the nation.

The basic difficulties confronting the student are clearly revealed in the studies of Karl Brandt. In an attempt to determine roughly how many farms there were in the United States, Brandt corrected the published figures by subtracting 90 percent of the croppers from the number of farm operators and the number of farm tenants, and by allowing for the ratio of plantation operators to croppers that was found in the 1910 special enumeration of plantations. He reasoned that it was not valid to eliminate all the croppers, since some plantations were cultivated entirely by cropper labor. Brandt was probably unduly conservative in his procedure since, without doubt, the large group of laborers called "share tenants," who are merely croppers in possession of mules, would much more than offset the discrepancy he allowed for. In any case his data illustrate the difficulty and are probably much more reliable than any other in existence at the present time. His estimates for 1935 reduce the number of farms in the United States by 9.5 percent, or from 6,812,000 to 6,168,000; and in eleven southern states by 21.8 percent, or from 2,771,000 to 2,166,000. They place the number of owner-operated farms in the United States at 4,019,-000 instead of 3,947,000 (a gain of 1.8 percent), and the number in the eleven southern states at 1,275,000 instead of 1,208,000 (an increase of 5.6 percent). His corrections reduce the number of tenant-operated farms in the United States from 2,865,000 to 2,149,000, or 25 percent, and the percentage of tenancy from 42.1 to 34.8. Similarly in the southern states the number of tenant-operated farms is reduced by his corrections from 1,563,000 to 890,000, or 43 percent, and the percentage of tenancy from 56.4 to 41.1. He also estimated the average size of all farms, the average size of owner- and tenant-operated farms, the average values of farms, and the average values of both owner- and tenant-operated farms. In all cases, of course, the figures are radically changed by allowing for the common-sense corrections he has applied. Brandt's study reveals clearly the great need for a thorough revision in census practices.[22]

Because "the promotion of home ownership on individual farms has been a great tradition in American history," and because "individual farm ownership was always recognized as the cornerstone of a free democratic society,"[23] it is important to know the extent of farm ownership among American agriculturists. It must be stressed, however, that the customary procedure of determining the percentage of farm owners among those enumerated as farm operators does not show this.

A useful simple index of value in comparing the systems of land tenure in the various states and regions would be the percentage of all families directly dependent upon agriculture who were the owners of the farms they worked. This index would show the prevalence of the security associated with ownership, and also the degree to which the rural population of the various states and regions were enjoying the authority and assuming the responsibility that go with the ownership and operation of land. Such an index would also indicate in a fairly reliable manner the strength or weakness of the family farm institution, which itself is an important guide to the desirability of the tenure systems in practice. One should not deny the possibility that large-scale coöperative agricultural undertakings may eventually be developed that can combine security for the workers with opportunities for growth and development that come from the exercise of authority and the assumption of responsibility. But thus far in the history of the world, the widespread distribution of landownership has been the most successful method of attaining security for the agricultural population, accompanied by the production of an able, self-reliant citizenry. For these reasons the proportion of all the families di-

[22] *Op. cit.*, pp. 29–30.
[23] Henry A. Wallace, "Farm Tenancy," an address delivered over the Columbia Broadcasting System, January 22, 1937.

rectly dependent upon agriculture who own the land that they till is a very important index.

Unfortunately the present condition of our agricultural statistics makes it impossible to do more than make a rough estimate of the number of families directly dependent upon agriculture, and of the proportion of these who own their farms. The census tabulations are based upon residence rather than occupation, and the population enumerated as the "farm" population is by no means synonymous with the agricultural population.[24] An approximation to the number of families engaged in agriculture may be had by increasing the number of farm operators by the number of male wage hands. Such a tabulation for each of the states is the basis for Figure 68. Much more clearly and certainly than any index of tenancy now available, this chart shows the important variations in the security of land tenure throughout the United States. One would not be overrash in concluding that the desirability of tenure conditions closely parallels the proportions of farm owners among agricultural families. The factors responsible for the principal variations may also be indicated. In the Midwest, centering in Iowa, farm tenancy makes the proportion low. From California to South Carolina, including Colorado, the prevalence of large-scale agriculture is responsible for the low proportions of farm owners.

Farm Tenancy

The word *tenant* has been used to dramatize the plight of America's underprivileged farm classes. To keep the record straight it should be pointed out that many of the ills ordinarily attributed to tenancy are in reality the results of large-scale agriculture, the concentration of landownership and management, and not the mode of leasing lands. For this reason most of the ill effects often attributed to tenancy will be reserved for discussion in the following chapter.

There are many systems of leasing farm lands, but tenancy itself is not an unmitigated evil. Provided a sound and equitable basis for renting land is utilized, there is much to recommend tenancy, both to the young farmer struggling to advance on the agricultural ladder and to the commercial farmer whose capital

[24] Cf. T. Lynn Smith, "The Agricultural Population: Realism vs. Nominalism in the Census of Agriculture," *Journal of Farm Economics*, XX (1938), 679–687.

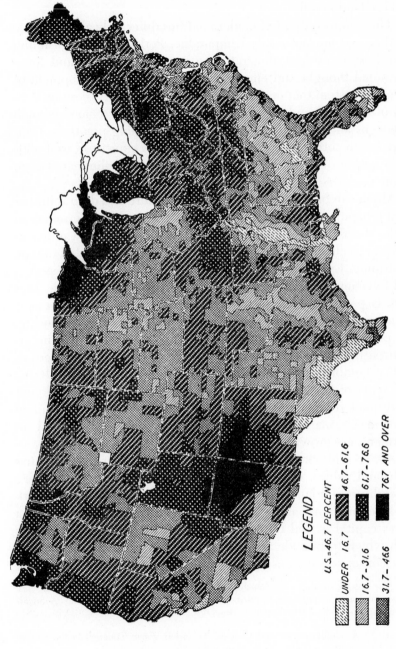

LEGEND

U.S.=46.7 PERCENT

UNDER 16.7

16.7 - 31.6

31.7 - 46.6

46.7 - 61.6

61.7 - 76.6

76.7 AND OVER

FIGURE 68.   Percentage of Farm Owners Among All Families (Estimated) Engaged in Agriculture, 1940.

may not allow him to own both sufficient livestock and equipment and the land he tills.

The tenure systems of modern nations differ radically from one another and are not easily comparable. Perhaps the English and Danish systems best illustrate the extremes. In England long-continued thought and effort have gone into the development of a leasing system that enables the landed proprietors to retain control of the land and at the same time gives the tenants enough privileges and security to promote good farming practices. Denmark, on the other hand, has concentrated its efforts toward building a nation of farm owners and has practically eliminated farm tenancy.

Much can be learned concerning the nature and desirability of farm tenancy as a system of land tenure through a determination of the social and economic situations associated with it either as cause or as effect.[25] Tenancy, for example, is closely related to type of farming. Except in cotton farming, where the plantation system and fallacious census terminology make the data impossible, tenancy is positively correlated with the production of cash crops. An informative table from the 1900 Census shows this relationship, the percentages of tenancy in various types of farming being as follows: tobacco, 47.9; rice, 45.7; hay and grain, 39.3; sugar crops, 35.1; vegetables, 30.4; dairy, 23.3; livestock, 20.3; and fruits, 16.5.[26] The types of farming which require large investments and do not yield quick results are associated with ownership, whereas annual crops, easily marketed and requiring relatively little capital investment, are grown extensively by tenants.

Another important association is that between tenancy and high land values. From the economic point of view the farmer's expenditures for land must compete with his expenditures for work stock, equipment, and other operating expenses. If much of a man's capital is tied up in land, he may have inadequate funds with which to provide adequate work stock and equipment, and as a consequence farm operations may suffer.[27] On this account

[25] The nature of these relationships still awaits detailed analysis. For a very suggestive list of hypotheses requiring verification, see O. D. Duncan, "A Sociological Approach to Farm Tenancy Research," *Rural Sociology*, V (1940), 287–289.

[26] See E. A. Goldenweiser and Leon E. Truesdell, *Farm Tenancy in the United States*, Census Monographs IV, Washington, 1924, p. 33.

[27] Henry C. Taylor, *The Decline of Landowning Farmers in England*, University of Wisconsin Economic and Political Science Series, I, 1904–1906, Madison, 1906,

there is a close relationship between the extent of farm tenancy and the degree to which farming is commercialized; where tenancy is highest the average value of farms is highest. This relationship is true, of course, only in areas where "tenant" is synonymous with "renter," and not in the South where several types of farm laborers are indiscriminately mixed in with tenants.[28]

When leases are for a short time, as in the United States, tenancy is associated with a rapid destruction of the fertility of the soil. The tenant's interest is best served if he mines as much as possible from the landlord's farm during his brief stay. To plant soil-building crops is for the tenant to sacrifice his own welfare for that of his successor. To practice contour plowing and strip cropping is a burden and not a benefit to the tenant with a short lease. His immediate interests may be served much better by plowing across terraces than along them. Fertilizers cannot be profitably applied unless their contribution can be harvested during the period of the lease. In brief, the system of farming practiced under a short-term tenant lease is one of the significant causes of rapid soil erosion.[29]

For the sociologist one of the most important associations is that between farm tenancy and poor, ill-kept homes and farm buildings. Where tenancy is high, semipermanent and movable farm property is also poor. The reason was set forth long ago by one of Cromwell's officers who had studied firsthand the disastrous results of farm tenancy in Ireland.

. . . If a tenant be at ever so great pains or cost for the improvement of his land, he doth thereby but occasion a greater rack-rent upon himself, or else invests his landlord with his cost and labour *gratis,* or at least lies at his landlord's mercy for requital; which occasions a neglect of all good husbandry, to his own, the land, the landlord, and the commonwealth's suffering.[30]

p. 58, gives a discussion of this; see also Theodore W. Schultz's chapter, "What Has Happened to the Agricultural Ladder?" in *Farm Tenure in Iowa,* Part III, Iowa AES Bulletin 357, Ames, 1937, pp. 305–308.

[28] Cf. Bureau of the Census and Bureau of Agricultural Economics, *Graphic Summary of Farm Tenure in the United States,* Washington, Government Printing Office, 1948, pp. 29–31.

[29] Cf. Rainer Schickele, *Farm Tenure in Iowa,* Iowa AES Bulletin 356, Ames, 1937, p. 262.

[30] Quoted in James Godkin, *The Land-War in Ireland,* London, Macmillan & Co., Ltd., 1870, pp. 257–258.

As in the days of Cromwell, so at the present time the tenant who makes improvements on the landlord's farm runs the risk of having his rent raised thereby. And as in Cromwell's day, this ". . . might be removed, if there were a law enacted, by which every landlord should be obliged either to give him reasonable allowance for his clear improvement, or else suffer him *or his* to enjoy it so much longer or till he hath had a proportionable requital."[31]

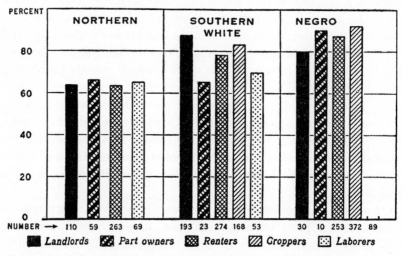

FIGURE 69. Percentages of Farmers Who Have One-Year Rental Agreements. (Reproduced from E. A. Schuler, *Social Status and Farm Tenure,* U.S. Department of Agriculture, Washington, 1938, p. 166.)

Where leases are of the short-term variety, as is the case in the United States (see Figure 69), poorly supported and scantily attended social institutions are one of the results. The children of farm tenants are enrolled in smaller proportions in the schools than the children of owners, and their attendance is more sporadic. The tenant's children frequently must change schools in the middle of the term. Where tenancy is high, the rural church suffers in membership and attendance.[32] And tenants rarely participate in civic and govermental affairs. In short, tenancy is closely associated

[31] *Ibid.*, p. 258.

[32] See, for example, O. D. Duncan's "Relation of Tenure and Economic Status of Farmers to Church Membership," *Social Forces,* XI (1933), 541–547. See also O. D. Duncan and J. T. Sanders, *A Study of Certain Economic Factors in Relation to Social Life Among Oklahoma Cotton Farmers,* Oklahoma AES Bulletin 211, Stillwater, 1933, pp. 18–22; and J. L. Charlton, *Social Aspects of Farm Ownership and Tenancy in the Arkansas Ozarks,* Arkansas AES Bulletin 471, Fayetteville, 1947, pp. 76–80.

with poorly attended and ill-supported social and civic institutions˙ and agencies.[33]

If surrounded by the legal protections recommended by the Special Committee on Farm Tenancy, renting as a method of acquiring the use of land for productive farming enterprises would have few unfavorable aspects. The recommendations of this committee, which to be effective must be embodied in state legislation, are as follows:

1. Agricultural leases shall be written.
2. All improvements made by the tenant and capable of removal shall be removable by him at the termination of the lease.
3. The landlord shall compensate the tenant for specified unexhausted improvements which he does not remove at the time of quitting the holding, provided that for certain types of improvements the prior consent of the landlord be obtained.
4. The tenant shall compensate the landlord for any deterioration or damage due to factors over which the tenant has control, and the landlord shall be empowered to prevent continuance of serious wastage.
5. Adequate records shall be kept of outlays for which either party will claim compensation.
6. Agricultural leases shall be terminable by either party only after due notice given at least 6 months in advance.
7. After the first year payment shall be made for inconvenience or loss sustained by the other party by reason of termination of the lease without due cause.
8. The landlord's lien shall be limited during emergencies such as serious crop falure or sudden fall of prices where rental payments are not based upon a sliding scale.
9. Renting a farm on which the dwelling does not meet certain minimum housing and sanitary standards shall be a misdemeanor, though such requirements should be extremely moderate and limited to things primarily connected with health and sanitation, such as sanitary outside toilets, screens, tight roofs, and other reasonable stipulations.
10. Landlord and tenant differences shall be settled by local boards of

[33] The most thoroughgoing recent study, E. A. Schuler's *Social Status and Farm Tenure: Attitudes and Social Conditions of Corn Belt and Cotton Belt Farmers,* United States Department of Agriculture, Social Research Report IV, Washington, 1938, pp. 214–215, reports the following participation of northern tenants in formally organized groups in comparison with owner participation regarded as 100: religious, 88.8; occupational, 92.6; economic, 47.0; and fraternal, 118.7. Likewise renters voted and paid taxes less frequently than owners.

arbitration, composed of reasonable representatives of both landlords and tenants, whose decisions shall be subject to court review when considerable sums of money or problems of legal
interpretation are involved.[34]

Trends in Land Tenure

From around 1880 until about 1935, American farmers were
gradually losing possession of the soil. Especially in the years following 1920 the rise of farm mortgage indebtedness was pronounced; and throughout the fifty-five-year period the proportion
of farm tenancy was rising continuously. Says the Report of the
Special Committee on Farm Tenancy:

For the past 55 years, the entire period for which we have statistics
on land tenure, there has been a continuous and marked decrease in
the proportion of operating owners and an accompanying increase in
the proportion of tenants. Tenancy has increased from 25 per cent of
all farmers in 1880 to 42 per cent in 1935. Because of debt the actual
equity of operating owners is far less than these figures indicate. In
some of our States, among them a number settled under the homestead system little more than a generation ago, it is estimated that the
equity of operating farmers in their lands is little more than one-fifth;
nearly four-fifths is in the hands of landlords and mortgage holders.

Thus, hundreds of thousands of farm families have attained only a
semblance of ownership. Especially in times of depression they have
witnessed their hard-won equities steadily decline and finally disappear. After years of effort to retain their foothold as farm owners, they
find themselves poorer for the struggle. At the same time, hundreds of
thousands of tenant farmers, in spite of years of scrimping, have not
been able to accumulate enough to make a first payment on a farm of
their own. And a further large segment of the farm population has
never reached a stage of economic advancement where its members
could even aspire to farm ownership.[35]

Had croppers been properly classified as farm laborers, these
trends would have appeared even more pronounced, for only the

[34] *Farm Tenancy,* Message from the President of the United States Transmitting
the Report of the Special Committee on Farm Tenancy, 75th Congress, 1st Session,
House Document 149, Washington, 1937, p. 20. For analysis of the English system
of land tenure where stability in social relations has been achieved under a system
of tenancy, see Marshall Harris, *Agricultural Landlord-Tenant Relations in England
and Wales,* Land Use Planning Publication 4, Resettlement Administration, Washington, 1936; and Karl Brandt, "The English System of Regulating Landlord-
Tenant Relations," *Journal of the American Society of Farm Managers and Rural
Appraisers,* II (1938), 3–14.

[35] *Farm Tenancy,* p. 2.

decrease in croppers (because many of them were shifted from share wages to cash wages) brought about a decrease in the number and percentage of tenants between 1930 and 1935. Over most of the nation tenancy gained rapidly during this period.

Following 1935, however, there was an abrupt change in the situation and with the passage of each year the farmers obtained a larger equity in the land they operated. In part this change was due to the reduced importance of mortgage indebtedness (see Figure 70); but in a large measure it was accomplished by a sharp decrease in the proportion of farm tenancy throughout the nation.

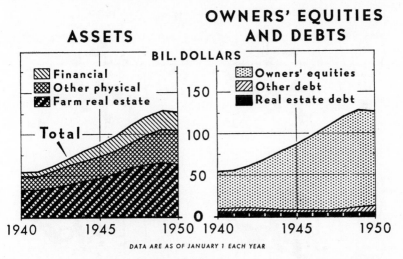

FIGURE 70. The Farmers' Increasing Equity in the Land. (Illustration from the Bureau of Agricultural Economics.)

(See Figure 71.) Whereas in 1935 42 percent of all farms in the United States were classified as tenant operated (census definition), by 1945 the corresponding proportion had fallen to 32 percent and by 1950 it was only 27 percent. As might be expected, in the South, where the decline of sharecropping make the decreases seem fictitiously great, the reported percentages fell off from 48 percent in 1940 to 34 percent in 1950. However, in other sections of the country in which the figures for the one year are more comparable with those for the other the decreases were from 31 percent in 1940 to 21 percent in 1950 in the North, and from 21 percent to 13 percent for the corresponding years in the West.[36]

[36] For the recent data see Bureau of the Census, *1950 Census of Agriculture,* Series AC50–3, No. 00, Washington, November 25, 1951.

**COUNTIES IN WHICH AT LEAST HALF THE FARMS WERE OPERATED
BY TENANTS, 1880, 1900, 1920, 1930, 1940, AND 1945**

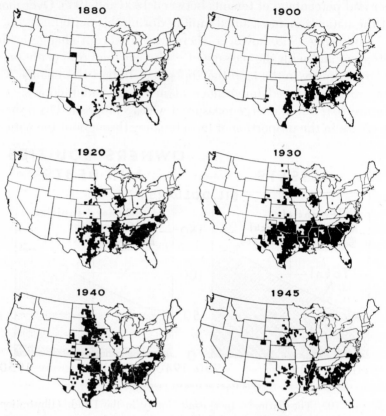

FIGURE 71.   Regional Aspects of the Rise and Decline of Farm Tenancy.
(Illustration from the Bureau of Agricultural Economics.)

13

THE SIZE OF HOLDINGS

The extent to which the ownership and control of the land is concentrated in a few hands or widely distributed among those who live from farming is probably the most important single determinant of the welfare of the people on the land. Throughout the world wherever there is a widespread distribution of land ownership and control one also observes (1) the strongest propulsions to steady work and the maximum of thrift; (2) the highest average levels and standards of living; (3) the least development of social stratification, the fewest class distinctions, the relative absence of caste, and very little class conflict and class struggle; (4) a high degree of vertical social mobility so that the individual comes nearest to occupying the social position commensurate with his natural abilities and the amount of effort he personally is willing and able to put forth; (5) general intelligence that is at a high level and a minimum in range; and (6) a rural population possessed of well-rounded and highly developed personalities. The opposite of this system, the concentration of control in the hands of a few and the consequent reduction of the masses of the population to the category of landless agricultural workers, appears to result always and everywhere in (1) a very low average level of living, and an equally low standard, although the members of the landowning elite may live in fantastic luxury; (2) tremendous class distinctions between the favored few at the apex of the social pyramid and the toiling masses who lack rights to the soil; (3) relatively little vertical social mobility because caste is strong and because the chasm which separates the upper classes from the masses is so great that the offspring of those of low estate, even those who are endowed with rare abilities, find it almost impossible to ascend in the social scale; (4) low average intelligence because the great attainments of the select members of the small upper class are far more than offset by the meager development of the personal qualities of those who belong to the lower classes; (5) people skilled only in the performance, under the closest of supervision, of a limited number of manual tasks, and lacking almost entirely in the ability to carry on the self-directed activities involved in managerial and entrepreneurial work; and (6) a society in which a premium is placed upon routine, regulation, and order, rather than upon innovation, progress, and change.[1]

Stimulated by numerous popular assertions concerning the advantages of large-scale agriculture, one searches history in vain for a case in which the concentration of landownership has resulted in an elevated plane of living for the masses of agriculturists. Resorting to geography, the search is conducted with no better results. Indeed, it can be stated with some degree of certainty that concentration of landownership and large-scale agriculture inevitably result in the production of a small, highly cultured class of the elite, on the one hand, and the reduction of the masses dependent upon agriculture to a state of ignorance and poverty, on the other. The Biblical threat, "woe to them that join house to house, that lay field to field, till there be no place, that they may be placed alone in the midst of the earth,"[2] was an attempt to stay the proletarizing of the rural workers that accompanies a concentration of landownership.

If large-scale agriculture actually were efficient, the rural South would today be characterized by enlightenment and a high plane of living instead of ignorance and poverty. But whether one considers the *latifundia* of the Romans, the estates of the Junkers in eastern Germany, the *haciendas* of the Latin Americas, the sugar *centrals* of Cuba and the West Indies, the extensive ranches of the western states, or the plantations of the South, one seeks in vain for a case in which the large-scale organization of agriculture has produced among the masses a prosperous, sturdy, independent, self-reliant, and well-informed citizenry. In fact, in addition to those disadvantages imposed upon rural classes as a result of state and national policies—such as the present disabilities affecting

[1] Consult on this score T. Lynn Smith, *Brazil: People and Institutions*, Baton Rouge, Louisiana State University Press, 1946, chap. 16. See also Henry Grady, "Cotton and the South," *Harper's Magazine*, LXIII (1881), 719–720.
[2] Isaiah 5:8.

rural Americans because of state reliance upon the general property tax and the national tariff policy—close inspection will show maldistribution of lands to be at the core of practically every rural problem, whether it be popularly diagnosed as a problem of agricultural labor, of tenancy and tenantry, low standards of living, excessive territorial mobility, ignorance and illiteracy, poverty, or any other of the current ills besetting the people on the land. It follows that the diagnoses made and the prescriptions frequently given are dealing with symptoms rather than causes.

But scholars are slow to recognize this point. The plantation system has plagued the South for centuries, but early scholars attributed the region's ills to the system of slavery.[3] More recently others diagnosed the troubles of the region in terms of tenancy.[4] The term "tenant" has been used to dramatize the ills of America's underprivileged agricultural classes, and in this respect has played a beneficial role; but in order to keep the records straight it should be indicated that most of these ills are properly attributed to the plantation system and not to the methods of leasing lands.

Classifications of Landholdings

Classification in this field is not an easy task, and almost any categories established are sure to lack precision. The size of a farm is not easy to determine because the elements of production are all variable and may be combined in smaller or larger proportions one with another. Lands are not similar in productivity and are not equally situated with respect to markets. For these and other reasons, a measure of area is a very unsatisfactory measure of size.[5] Holdings vary all the way from the small plot of land controlled and utilized by the part-time farmer and his family in an effort to supply part of the foodstuffs they consume to the extensive hold-

[3] Cf. George M. Weston, *Progress of Slavery in the United States*, Washington, 1857, p. 44, *passim*, who attributed the one-crop system, inefficient labor, low returns per worker, soil exhaustion, etc., to the institution of slavery. Hinton Rowan Helper, *The Impending Crisis of the South: How to Meet It*, New York, Burdick Brothers, 1857, p. 60, *passim*, vociferously upheld the same thesis.

[4] See, for example, Charles S. Johnson, Edwin R. Embree, and W. W. Alexander, *The Collapse of Cotton Tenancy*, Chapel Hill, University of North Carolina Press, 1935; H. C. Nixon, *Forty Acres and Steel Mules*, Chapel Hill, University of North Carolina Press, 1938; T. J. Woofter, Jr., and others, *Landlord and Tenant on the Cotton Plantation*, Works Progress Administration Research Monograph V, Washington, 1936; and Rupert B. Vance, *Regional Reconstruction: A Way Out for the South*, Chapel Hill, University of North Carolina Press, 1935.

[5] Cf. John D. Black, *Introduction to Production Economics*, New York, Henry Holt & Company, 1926, p. 584.

ings of the land baron whose subjects may number hundreds of thousands. Some agricultural families are entirely landless, others have insufficient lands to support them and must find a supplementary income at nonagricultural employment, still others have portions well adjusted to their demands, and a few own and control acreages greatly over their own necessities and on which they utilize the labor of the landless classes.

The essential distinction seems to be one that separates the farming unit in which the farm operator and the members of his family supply the capital, perform the managerial functions, and themselves supply the greater part of the manual labor required for the farm tasks, from the one in which the labor supplied by the operator and his family is only incidental, operations are greater than a single-family scale, and a force of laborers is maintained to perform the manual labor on the farm. For purposes of analysis landholdings may be divided into the following three categories: (1) *minifundia,* (2) family-sized farms, and (3) large holdings.

Minifundia

This term comes from the Andean countries of South America where it is applied to the hundreds of thousands of small, pocket-handkerchief-sized farms which blanket the mountainsides of Ecuador, Colombia, and Venezuela. Only an acre or two in extent, these little tracts of ground are far too small to support a humble family of peasants even at the pitifully low levels of living to which they are accustomed. That many Latin American countries suffer severely from the blighting effects of the *hacienda* system, as the system of large estates frequently is called, is well known, but that several of the countries are plagued with the problem of the minifundia has received practically no mention beyond the borders of the countries themselves.[6] In any case the term "minifundia" is an excellent one and much more expressive than "small holdings," which is another designation that might be used for the small subsistence plots whose operators, along with other able-bodied members of their families, are forced to seek other work in order to eke out a bare livelihood.

Minifundia are not as yet of major importance in the United States, although there are many sections of the country in which the farms are too small to provide an adequate living for the fami-

---

[6] For some discussion of the problems of the minifundia and the great estates, or latifundia, in Colombia, see T. Lynn Smith, "The Cultural Setting of Agricultural Extension Work in Colombia," *Rural Sociology,* X (1945), 241–242.

lies on the basis of the standards prevailing in the second half of the twentieth century. Those farms which border on the class of minifundia are especially prevalent throughout the Appalachian Mountains, in the Ozarks, and in the "hill" sections of the South generally.[7]

Family-Sized Farms

The family-sized farm has long been the American ideal. It is generally thought to be the design of American agriculture.[8] Although the general connotations of the term are clear, one searches the abundant literature in vain for a precise definition. Certainly it refers to the condition in which each farm family has sufficient land to occupy its members fully at agricultural pursuits, but not enough land to necessitate the steady employment of a great deal of supplementary labor. If labor is employed it is of the "farm hand" type and not the "industrialized masses of hand laborers."[9] Tractors, trucks, combines, and all other modern machinery and equipment might well add to the production per member without destroying the family-farm concept; but similarly increased production attained by the utilization of adding laboring forces from outside the family would just as certainly cause a given farming unit to fall outside the family-farm category. Historically in the United States, the yeoman of the North is representative of the family farmer, as contrasted with the large Tory landholders, many of whom were forced to flee the country at the close of the Revolution; and in the South family farms have long been exemplified by the small holdings in the "hills" as contrasted with the plantations of the lowlands and deltas. Historically, too, the driving out of the Tories,[10] the practice of squatting eventually legal-

---

[7] Cf. Bureau of the Census and Bureau of Agricultural Economics, *Graphic Summary of Farm Tenure in the United States*, Washington, Government Printing Office, 1948, p. 27.

[8] Cf. Paul S. Taylor and Tom Vasey, "Contemporary Background of California Farm Labor," *Rural Sociology*, I (1936), 419. For evidence that this ideal was nurtured in colonial America, see Richard B. Morris, *Studies in the History of American Law*, New York, Columbia University Press, 1930, pp. 74–76. See also Carle C. Zimmerman, "The Family Farm," *Rural Sociology*, XV (1950), 211–221.

[9] Taylor and Vasey, *op. cit.*, p. 401.

[10] For example, at the time of the Revolution, Philipse Manor in Westchester County, New York, contained 92,160 acres, extending twenty-four miles along the Hudson River. Following the Revolution this estate was confiscated and sold in over 300 conveyances, former tenants coming into possession of much of it and establishing themselves as freeholders. Harry B. Yoshpe, *The Disposition of Loyalist Estates in the Southern District of the State of New York*, New York, Columbia University Press, 1939, pp. 52–53, 139–147.

FIGURE 72. Single Farmstead of a Middle-Class Farm Family in North Dakota. (Photo by Marion Post Wolcott in the Farm Security Administration Collection at the Library of Congress.)

FIGURE 73. The Farmstead of a Middle-Class Iowa Farm Family in the Winter. (Photo by Arthur Rothstein in the Farm Security Administration Collection at the Library of Congress.)

ized through the Homestead Acts, and the influx of a constant
stream of land-hungry peasants from Europe fixed firmly a family-
farm pattern on much of the northern and western parts of the nation. (See Figures 72 and 73.) But in the South many of the large
landholders were patriots, and the Revolution had little effect
upon the distribution of land. Later on, land speculation and land-
grabbing, the institution of slavery, and the more rapid spread of
settlement firmly established a system of large-scale agriculture
upon the good land areas of the region. In the Southwest, too, the
Spanish practice of allocating large grants of land resulted in a distribution of ownership essentially different from the family-farm
pattern. The distribution of family farming in the nation is fairly
well indexed by the data in Figure 68. The more important the
owner-operator, the stronger the family-farm system.

Large Holdings

This term refers to the situation in which the ownership and
operation of the land are in the hands of a few people, while the
majority of the rural people are forced to gain their livelihood by
working on the estates of the few. Largeness is of course a matter
of degree. Where the operator works at manual labor only incidentally if at all, while as many as half the people must gain their livelihood by working as laborers on the lands of others, certainly the
family-farm pattern is not predominant and the system may be
classed as one of large holdings. The plantation of the South, the
estates on the Hudson, the western ranch, and the bonanza farms
of the Northwest are the best examples of large holdings in the
United States.[11] Of these, by far the most important is the southern
plantation. (See Figures 74 and 75.)

The southern plantation was borrowed from the West Indies.
Introduced into the states on the eastern seaboard, it served first
as a system for the production of tobacco with slave labor. In Louisiana the first large concessions were granted for the production of
sugar cane and tobacco. As early as 1730 the realistic social planning of the day resulted in a plan to settle on the Mississippi "325
white families and 19,000 blacks, in the cultivation of sugar cane
and tobacco."[12] On the eastern seaboard the system of large holdings early dominated rice growing, and later it became the con-

[11] For an indication of the distribution of large holdings throughout the world
and a discussion of the responsible factors, see Edgar T. Thompson, "The Climatic
Theory of the Plantation," *Agricultural History*, XV (1941), 49–60.

[12] E. J. Forstall, "French Colonial Records—Louisiana," *DeBow's Review*, I
(1846), 367.

FIGURE 74. "Air View" of Model Cotton Plantation. (Illustration by courtesy of T. J. Woofter, Jr., and the Works Progress Administration.)

FIGURE 75. A Large Estate in the Deep South. (From a Library of Congress copy of a Currier & Ives print of a painting by W. A. Walker, 1884.)

trolling element in the cotton complex. In the spread westward of cotton culture, the plantation and the Negro nearly always were successful in displacing the yeoman from the best lands, crowding him farther westward or into the less fertile areas. The distribution of the plantation in 1860 corresponds closely with its distribution today.[13] As Woofter has written, "*Ante bellum* plantations have persisted as units to a remarkable degree . . . in the area characterized by plantations in 1860 large-scale operations persist to a remarkable extent today."[14] (See Figures 76 and 77.) For the United States as a whole the distribution of large-scale agriculture is best indicated by a map showing the importance of laborers (hired hands and croppers) among all those gainfully employed in agriculture. (See Figure 78.) From California eastward throughout the South to Virginia, large-scale agriculture is of fundamental importance in the nation's agricultural design.

Large-scale agriculture is in reality the factory system in agriculture. This point is most clearly demonstrated in the bonanza farming of the Northwest but manifests its greatest effects in the plantation system of the South.[15] Concentration of landownership, centralized control of a large force of laborers, specialization by enterprises or the "one-crop system," rigid supervision, and specialization by tasks (managers, overseers, foremen, hostlers, blacksmiths, cooks, nurses, plow hands, and, more recently, tractor drivers and mechanics) are some of the elements of the system. The essentials of the system are evidenced by the extent of supervision exercised by the plantation operator. In 215 southern plantations studied by Brannen in 1920–1921 all but two reported supervision of the employees, and 68 percent reported "close supervision." The essential elements in close supervision as found in Brannen's study were as follows:

1. There is a bell system. In the morning a bell is rung as a signal for rising; later (in the summer at sunrise and in the winter before

[13] The census data, based on faulty definitions of farm and farm operator, conceal the distribution of large holdings in the United States. The difficulties thus placed on the social scientist are well illustrated by two reports, both written in 1936. Taylor and Vasey report that one-third of all large-scale farms are in California, where 2892 farms reported annual products with a value of $30,000 or more, as compared with only twenty-nine in Mississippi. *Op. cit.*, p. 403. T. J. Woofter, Jr., et al., the same year inform us that along both banks of the Mississippi and its tributary the Yazoo "large-scale, highly organized plantations persist and are predominant in the rural economy." *Op. cit.*, p. 5.

[14] Woofter, and others, *op. cit.*, p. 1.

[15] Cf. Vance, *op. cit.*, p. 3.

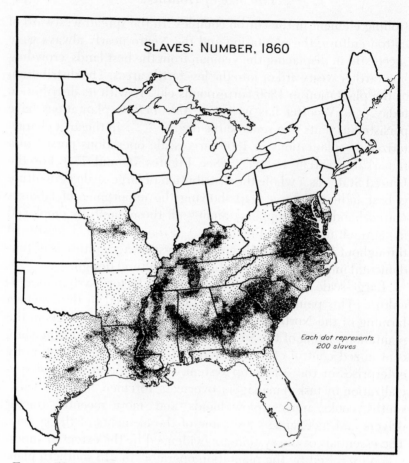

FIGURE 76. Distribution of Slaves in the United States, 1860. (Illustration from the Bureau of Agricultural Economics.)

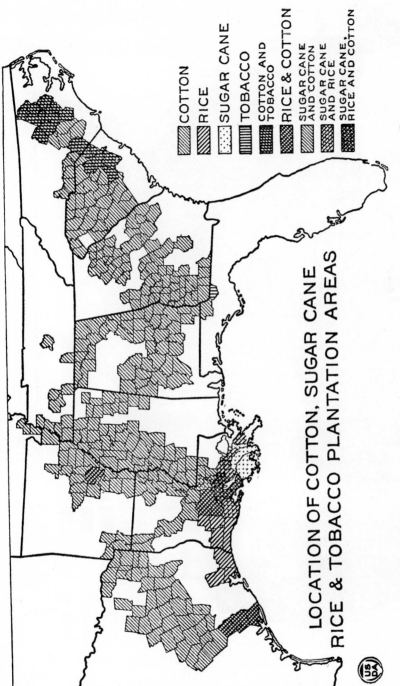

COTTON

RICE

SUGAR CANE

TOBACCO

COTTON AND
TOBACCO

RICE & COTTON

SUGAR CANE
AND COTTON

SUGAR CANE
AND RICE

SUGAR CANE,
RICE AND COTTON

LOCATION OF COTTON, SUGAR CANE
RICE & TOBACCO PLANTATION AREAS

FIGURE 77. The Plantation Areas of the South. (Reproduced from C. O. Brannen, *Relation of Land Tenure to Plantation Organization*, U. S. Department of Agriculture Bulletin 1269, Washington, 1924, p. 3.)

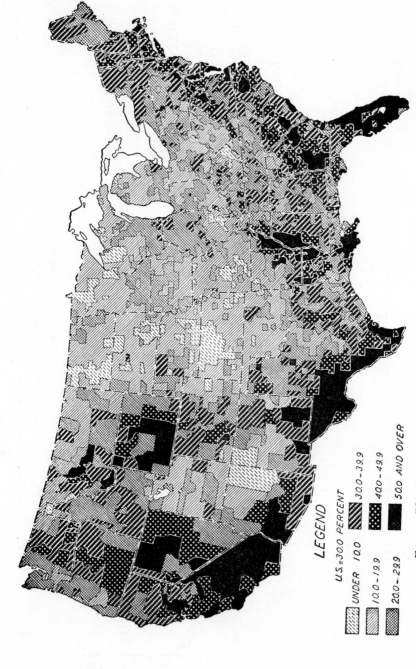

LEGEND

U.S.=30.0 PERCENT

UNDER 10.0

10.0 – 19.9

20.0 – 29.9

30.0 – 39.9

40.0 – 49.9

50.0 AND OVER

FIGURE 78. Percentages of Agricultural Laborers (Including Sharecroppers) Among All Males Fourteen Years of Age and Over Gainfully Employed in Agriculture, 1940.

sunrise) it is rung as a signal to begin work; and in the evening it is rung to indicate the close of the day's labors. "The worker who fails to respond promptly to the bell, or the one who leaves the field before the bell sounds, is questioned and unless reasonable excuse is given he is usually reprimanded."

2. The landlord or planter determines the holidays. These are, as a rule, in addition to Saturday afternoons, June 19th (Emancipation day), July 4th, and Christmas. Funerals are occasions for partial holidays.

3. The management controls the work stock. As a rule each cropper is assigned a mule, but sometimes all stock are kept in a "pool" and distributed weekly. About two-thirds of the plantations studied by Brannen allowed the laborers some personal use of the work stock, for use either in going to town or in doing work for themselves.

4. Implements are assigned for the season. One wagon usually serves from three to six croppers.

5. For the most part the planter assigns the plots of land to the various families. Croppers are given those nearest headquarters. If any renters are allowed on the plantation, as may be the case if labor is scarce, they are given the most remote fields.

6. The manner of handling field work varies from time to time. Immediately following the Civil War all field workers were organized into "gangs" in charge of an overseer. At the time of Brannen's study, this system was in an eclipse. But it is again appearing. Many croppers now work in gangs at the tasks assigned by the operator.[16] (See Figure 79.) In any case the manager makes his rounds constantly, inspecting the work and giving instructions on details.

7. The manager, the overseer, and the "gang" leader are an indispensable portion of the labor organization. The manager plans and directs the enterprises; the overseer, at the present time, is reduced to a labor boss in charge of a gang of laborers, usually wage hands; the "gang" leader is one of the workers, who by outdoing the others receives slightly higher wages.[17]

Large-scale agriculture favors agricultural operations on the part of merchants, bankers, and professional men who make up the "best families" of villages, towns, and small cities in the South. In this way it fosters a system of part-time farming quite different from that desired by the advocates of subsistence homesteads.

[16] Cf. S. Earl Grigsby and Harold Hoffsommer, *Cotton Plantation Laborers,* Louisiana AES Bulletin 328, Baton Rouge, 1941.

[17] See C. O. Brannen, *Relation of Land Tenure to Plantation Organization,* United States Department of Agriculture Bulletin 1269, Washington, 1924, pp. 42–44.

FIGURE 79. A Gang of Laborers on a Cotton Plantation. (Photo by H. C. Hoffsommer.)

Note the following observations from a study of her home community by a student in the writer's class in rural sociology:

> Mansfield is predominantly agricultural, for even though some members of the city spend a great part of their time in some business in the "city proper," they have a farm which they go out to in the afternoon. The principal occupation could be called a combination of the "merchant-farmer." There are eight large department-grocery-hardware stores in Mansfield, owned by Mansfield's "leading citizens." These merchants all have large farms near Mansfield. Some of these farms are large enough to have six or eight families working on them. . . . Every large business owner in Mansfield owns some acres of land. . . . Even the owners of two [small] manufacturing plants have a small amount of acreage near the city, which is farmed by hired laborers
>
> . . . The "merchant-farmer" usually has inherited a huge tract of land and the large store from his father and grandfather. In every instance, the business and the land of the present owner have been given to him by his ancestors.[18]

This situation is not unique. Throughout much of the South a great part of the best agricultural land is controlled and operated directly by business and professional men living in the towns and villages. "Merchant and planter" is a designation commonly applied to the leading citizens of the communities in the South.

Social Effects of Large-Scale Agriculture

The social effects of large-scale agriculture are to be observed in the multiplicity of ills that infest a region in which there is any considerable amount of concentration of land ownership.[19] As Alfred H. Stone has said, there is "something inherently vicious in the whole [plantation] system and methods, from an economic standpoint,—from the beginning to the present time."[20] In con-

[18] From a term paper by Viola Griffith, May, 1938.

[19] In the ancient world systems of *latifundia* spread from Italy all over the Roman Empire carrying serfdom throughout the known world. By A.D. 300 the small farmer had sunk through the stage of tenancy into that of *colonus*, a vassal tied to the land. Rome's power lapsed when her independent farm operators were debased into serfs. See Rudolf Sohn, *The Institutes: A Textbook of the History and System of Roman Private Law,* tr. by J. C. Ledlie, Oxford, The Clarendon Press, 1907, p. 45.

[20] "The Negro and Agricultural Development," *Annals of the American Academy of Political and Social Science,* XXXV (1910), 11. For an analysis of the results of large-scale agriculture in the West Indies, see Lowell Joseph Ragatz, *The Fall of the Planter Class in the British Caribbean, 1763–1833,* New York, D. Appleton-Century Company, 1928, p. 38.

trast with these areas of large holdings, those devoted to family farms, even though frequently far inferior in soil and transportation facilities, stand out clearly.

Economically, areas of large-scale agriculture seem to prosper greatly during periods of prosperity. On every hand there is evidence of wealth lavishly displayed. Symbolical of this are the large plantation homes of the ante-bellum South. (See Figure 80.) But when disaster strikes, the large establishments are the first to give way. Ruined upper classes and starving laborers then offer a sharp contrast to the small farm owners who more readily make the adjustment to radically changed conditions. Observed Stephen Powers immediately following the Civil War:

Down on the weary flats of South Carolina the Juggernaut car of the slave-lords crushed the masses utterly; but up among these good red hills of Georgia there lived many a ruddy farmer, above whose head its wheels rolled high and harmless.

Herein was the reason why the heart of Savannah was not so utterly eaten out by the war as was that of unhappy Charleston. It drew replenishment from a sounder middle class in the back country.[21]

Recently great wails have gone up because at last some observers have had called to their attention the fact that the agricultural ladder does not operate in those sections of the United States given over to the plantation system. A little reflection should convince such observers that it is impossible for the agricultural ladder to operate in a plantation area—for it to do so would in a single generation destroy the plantation system itself.

That the economic efficiency of large-scale agriculture, if there be such, is not translated into better living for the agricultural masses is excellently shown by a thorough comparative study of the levels of living of Negroes in the Mississippi delta and the hills of Mississippi. Despite the fact that the land in the delta is far superior to that of the red hills, the Negroes in the fertile plantation areas of the delta showed much lower levels of living than those on the poor lands in the hills where family farms have always been the rule.[22] Similar is the situation in other southern states; one of

[21] Stephen Powers, *Afoot and Alone, A Walk from Sea to Sea, by the Southern Route*, Hartford, Columbia Book Co., 1872, pp. 52–53.

[22] Dorothy Dickins, *Family Living on Poorer and Better Soil*, Mississippi AES Bulletin 320, State College, 1937, pp. 35–36.

FIGURE 80. Madewood—Formerly the Home of Thomas Pugh. Built in the decade before the Civil War, it is still in a fine state of preservation. (Photo by Vernon J. Parenton and Karl Brandt.)

the most recent of such reports comes from Missouri.[23] And on the basis of his extensive studies throughout the Latin American republics the eminent Chilean scholar, Moises Poblete Troncoso, has arrived at essentially the same conclusion. He states that "The existence of large holdings or *latifundium* is the principal obstacle to the improvement of conditions among agricultural workers." Not only has the dominance of large proprietors "been fatal for economic and social progress," but the large holding "is antisocial in the sense that it does not fulfill the function of producing sufficient food products for the subsistence of the people. Furthermore, the large agricultural proprietors have fostered undesirable living conditions for the agricultural workers in their employ; low wages, inadequate diet, and poor lodging have been characteristics of agricultural labor on the *latifundias* of the continent, all of which make for a low standard of living for the working people."[24] Equally striking is the conclusion of the noted authority, Dr. David Mitrany, with respect to the situation in eastern Europe. According to him, the breakup of the large estates in that part of the world, following World War I, resulted in a material improvement in the conditions of the peasants even though it greatly reduced exports.[25]

Large-scale agriculture always fails to develop well-rounded personalities in its workers. Large operations demand that the crops grown and the activities employed shall be those in which a high degree of standardization is possible and in which a fixed routine can be established. Otherwise it would be impossible to oversee the farm tasks adequately and for the manager or his assistants to instruct all the workers properly in each specific task to be performed. But this system leaves little to the initiative of the individuals. When one has learned a few simple tasks such as chopping cotton, there is little to do beyond repeating the process. Large operations necessitate the one-crop system in order that the laborer may be properly instructed and supervised, and the one-crop system keeps laborers from acquiring the innumerable skills and aptitudes that must be developed by the worker on a general

[23] Cf. Max R. White, Douglas Ensminger, and Cecil L. Gregory, *Rich Land— Poor People*, Farm Security Administration, Region III, Research Report 1, Indianapolis, 1938.

[24] Moises Poblete Troncoso, "Socio-Agricultural Legislation in the Latin-American Countries," *Rural Sociology*, V (1940), 9–10.

[25] See W. M. Macmillan, *Warning from the West Indies: A Tract for Africa and the Empire*, London, Faber and Faber Limited, 1936, pp. 160–161.

farm where farming enterprises are many and diversified and where in one man are combined the functions of entrepreneur, manager, and laborer.

Thus the tragedy of large-scale agriculture is that it cannot equip the oncoming generation with the proper habits, skills, and aptitudes to fit into any other scheme of operations. The ex-slaves, although politically free at a time when fertile lands were to be had for the taking, have remained for generations slaves to the pitiful paucity of agricultural skills bequeathed them by the plantation system.Maldistribution of land never contains within its own system the corrective forces to remake the situation.

Engendered by large-scale agriculture is the attitude that manual labor is degrading, that persons who work with their hands are to be despised as belonging to an inferior order of beings. Possession of the most highly skilled working techniques is a bar rather than an aid to social recognition and high social status. Useful only in a society dependent upon slave labor, such attitudes play havoc in a society of freemen. But upon almost all of Latin America the *hacienda,* the *estancia,* and the *fazenda* have left indelibly printed such attitudes, even to a greater degree than the plantation system has engraved them in the cultural pattern of the South.

A social effect not to be overlooked is the tendency for large-scale agriculture to develop and perpetuate a high degree of social stratification among the rural population. Sharply separated classes are a certain concomitant of concentration of landownership. On the one hand, the owners and operators of the *latifundia,* whether it be of the Roman type, the medieval manor, the *hacienda* of Spanish-speaking countries, or the American plantation, are set apart as a small class of the elite. But at the base of the social pyramid are the great masses of the rural population, living as a rule among conditions that are a sad commentary on the boasted culture of the region or nation. In America the plantation system produced Mount Vernon and all it stands for. Some of the homes built by southern planters were magnificent. But concentration of landownership has also produced the shacks that dot the landscape throughout the southern region. Granted that the lower strata of the population on these large units were recruited as slaves, the fact remains that the plantation system has kept the mass of these workers on a level that is but little advanced over slavery. On the other hand, the family-farm pattern of agriculture automatically goes a long way in insuring a wide distribution of income. At a time when economic problems are admittedly more those of distribution than of production, such an institution as the family farm deserves special consideration from state and national planning agencies.

Particularly important are the differing systems of social interaction that are generated by a system of large-scale agriculture and one in which family farms are the units. In large-scale agriculture domination and subordination are the warp and woof of social relationships; master and slave, lord and serf, *hacendado* and *peon*, planter and cropper, all of these and many other terms describe the predominant social relationship established by a system of large-scale agriculture.[26] In sharp contrast is the pattern of social relationships of the family-sized farm. Where all are on a fairly comparable economic and social level, interaction calls for coöperation.

The plantation system is also remarkable for its ability to perpetuate itself. The present areas of plantation farming in the South are largely the same as those of 150 years ago. Neither the Civil War, Reconstruction, the boll weevil, nor the great depression has been sufficient to destroy the tenacious three-way association between good land, the plantation, and the Negro. This means that there are potent self-perpetuating factors within the system itself.

In searching for the responsible factors in the situation, the writer has come to the conclusion that plantation areas remain in large holdings chiefly because there is no effective agency for bringing about a transition. The planter is not a land agent. Subdivision of lands is a job for the real-estate agent, not the planter. One can hardly censure a planter for his unwillingness to sell off part of his broad acreages to the small farmer desiring to purchase a farm.[27] Such a procedure would disrupt the enterprises on the plantation; it might also bring in a neighbor whose agricultural practices, livestock, etc., would prove a source of annoyance. In

[26] See chap. 21 for a more extended discussion of the social relationships in the plantation system.

[27] In the British West Indies, however, a few large landholders have found it profitable to deal in land at "retail rather than wholesale," i.e., to sell small parcels to the agricultural laborers. See Macmillan, *op. cit.*, p. 92. Throughout the highlands of Colombia in recent years many *hacendados* have been selling small acreages of the poorer lands on the margins of their holdings to the laborers who work on their estates.

any case, there are many plantations for sale, but as a general rule they are offered in their entirety. Even when the plantations get into the hands of insurance companies, banks, and even the Federal Land Bank, this policy is followed.

It follows that the demand for land is greatly restricted. One large holder can sell only to another. One with a plantation for sale cannot capitalize on the demands of the great mass of the people for land. And on the other hand, the cropper or tenant who attempts the purchase of a farm must go outside the plantation areas in order to do so. As a rule, then, he must go outside the fertile areas, usually to some poor piney woods section. There a few years may suffice for him to exhaust his meager resources and find his way back to the plantation sections. In any case, plantations and Negroes continue to occupy the best lands in the South; and the agricultural ladder in such areas has been aptly referred to as a treadmill.

Trends

There has been widespread a belief that the cotton plantation of ante-bellum days has completely disintegrated, that small farms have taken its place, and that large-scale agricultural operations no longer exist in the South. Data from the United States Census of Agriculture furnish abundant "proof" of such a trend. It is true that persons familiar with the southern region frequently express the belief that concentration of land is greater now than in 1860, but for the most part objective data for use in determining trends have been lacking.

Fortunately, events and agencies independent of the Bureau of the Census have intervened to make possible, for the first time since 1860, a fairly reliable inventory of the landholdings in some parts of the South. In those areas in which cotton is almost the sole crop, the 1934 Bankhead-Jones applications used in connection with the cotton-control program of the Agricultural Adjustment Administration constitute almost a complete coverage of the agricultural lands of a county. The Agricultural Adjustment Administration was forced to be realistic and to develop its own definitions of farm operator, farm tenant, farm, etc. For this reason it admitted to the category of farm operators only those "tenants" who exercised the managerial function, excluding the croppers and many other "non-managing tenants." From these records it is possible to make an inventory that can be related to the data in the Census of 1860. This gives for the first time since the Civil War an objective basis for determining trends in the concentration of landownership and operatorship. Probably fairly representative for much of the South is the situation in thirty-one cotton parishes of north Louisiana.

In the area now included in this section the acreage of farm land reported in the Census of 1860 was 6,008,757; summing the acreages reported on the 1934 Bankhead-Jones applications gave a total of 6,103,273, making a gain of 1.6 percent. Improved land in farms increased during the same period by 87.8 percent. Against this background of changes in total land in farms and improved lands in farms may be shown the changes in large holdings. Large holdings being defined as those of 1000 acres or more, the following changes were observed: In the area covered by the 31 parishes, there were 223 holdings of 1000 acres or more in 1860; in 1934 the corresponding number was 766, a gain of 244 percent. Thus, although the increase in the amount of land in farms was negligible, the number of large holdings was nearly two and one-half times as large in 1934 as in 1860.

The situation is more clearly revealed by the changes in five parishes whose boundaries did not change, and in which the plantation system has always been the dominant agricultural institution. These are East and West Feliciana, Concordia, Tensas, and Madison. The first two are the seat of one of the highest expressions of ante-bellum grandeur to be found in the South, and the last three all border on the Mississippi River and are known as delta parishes. In all these except East Feliciana the number of acres in farms declined between 1860 and 1934. In all except East and West Feliciana the improved lands also declined, and the increase in West Feliciana was only some 4000 acres and in East Feliciana some 25,000 acres. Nevertheless, the number of large holdings increased as follows: in Concordia, from 25 to 44; East Feliciana, from 12 to 42; in Madison from 23 to 49; in Tensas from 30 to 67; and in West Feliciana from 20 to 44.[28] Assertions that the plantations of the South have been broken up and replaced by

[28] These data are taken from an unpublished manuscript by T. Lynn Smith and C. L. Folse.

small farming units must rest upon better evidence than census data if they are to have validity.

Land Reforms

Rarely are fundamental land reforms the result of either a carefully planned program or a slow evolutionary process. As a rule they come quickly through violence, as one of the ingredients in a deep-seated revolution. Happy should be the society in which extreme concentration of land can be prevented or overcome without the necessity of undergoing the untold agonies that accompany revolution.[29] Naturally the question arises, What can a democratic society do by peaceful and just methods to bring about and maintain a widespread distribution of farm ownership, to strengthen and preserve the family-farm institution?

Attacks upon this problem are of two kinds: (1) measures to prevent further concentration of landownership and (2) ways of bringing about a wider distribution of the lands where concentration has already occurred. To give added security to the families already in possession of their farms is of fundamental significance, especially at present, for most of the forces operative in modern society are destroying rather than strengthening the family-farm institution. Among the more important forces now undermining the family-farm system may be listed the following: (1) The mechanization of agriculture. This makes the farm family dependent upon industry even for the power used in cultivation and harvest. This dependence means less security. Home-grown work stock and feed are being replaced by tractors, gas, and oil. (2) Commercialization of agriculture. As M. L. Wilson has said so aptly:

Agriculture has felt profoundly the influence of the new commercial age, and its most perfect response to the new world of technology, of economic specialization and interdependence is the completely commercialized, fully mechanized, highly specialized farm operated as a business and with no standards except market efficiency. In its extreme forms, exclusive susceptibility to economic and technological trends has led to such phenomena as suit-case farming. . . . The fully

---

[29] For a discussion of these, see P. A. Sorokin, *The Sociology of Revolution,* Philadelphia, J. B. Lippincott Company, 1925, pp. 58–116.

mechanized and wholly commercialized farm of today represents complete surrender to economic and technological forces.[30]

And (3) the general property tax as a basis for state and local revenue. This kind of taxation bears unduly heavily upon the man with visible assets in the shape of farm lands, machinery, and livestock. It is doubly vicious in that it taxes the things with which a man makes a living, and not the results of his endeavors. To many farm families the tax burden is the most difficult of all obligations to meet, the cause of daily worry and anxiety, and the factor that eventually brings about dispossession from their homes. The land tax is particularly hard on the small farmer because, as numerous studies have shown, his lands are assessed much higher, relative to their real value, than are larger holdings.[31]

The entailing of estates and the role of primogeniture in inheritance of landed property have had much to do with the concentration of land. Fortunately, this pair have been of less importance in the United States than in most of the nations of the world. But even in the American colonies and states the legislation devised to destroy entails and primogeniture was never completely successful.[32] Probably of vastly greater importance than the survivals in law has been the cultural lag through which a disproportionately large share of the property has passed into the hands of the oldest male child.

A graduated land tax is one way of overcoming the disadvantages under which the small farmer is laboring and of offering greater security to those in the family-farm system. The homestead exemption is a practical type of a graduated land tax. Such an exemption, of from $7500 to $10,000 at present values, would remove many of the disabilities under which the farm family is laboring and add greatly to its security in tenure. For a large number of such families it would eliminate their most pressing need for cash and thus remove one of the greatest stimuli forcing increased commercialization of agriculture and decreased self-sufficiency of the farm.

[30] M. L. Wilson, *Economic Agriculture and the Rural and General Social Welfare,* a paper presented to the International Conference of Agricultural Economists, McDonald College, Ste. Anne de Bellevue, Quebec, Canada, August 22, 1938, (mimeographed).

[31] Cf. R. L. Thompson and Bushrod W. Allin, *Louisiana Farm Taxes,* Louisiana AES Bulletin 231, Part 2, Baton Rouge, 1933, p. 20. See also the bibliography there.

[32] For a careful study of this point, see Morris, *op. cit.,* pp. 92 ff.

In many parts of the rural South another state or federal agency also seems to be necessary if a more widespread distribution of farm ownership is to be achieved. As pointed out above, plantation areas of 150 years ago are still the plantation areas of today. An agency established for the purpose of purchasing plantations, subdividing them, and offering them for resale in 40-, 80-, or 160-acre tracts on a long-term basis should do much to broaden the distribution of farm ownership throughout the rural South. Such an agency would do well to avoid the extreme degree of paternalism which was largely responsible for the poor showing of the activity programs of the 1930's and to confine itself to buying and selling land.

14

SYSTEMS OF AGRICULTURE

The integrated set of ideas, culture traits, skills, techniques, practices, prejudices, and habits employed by the members of a given society for extracting a living from the soil constitutes another of the basic relationships between man and the land. As in the case with those discussed in the preceding chapters, this part of the social order also is highly institutionalized. For the most part among the world's agriculturists the accepted methods of tillage, cultivation, caring for livestock, taking the harvest, and transportation are highly standardized on the local or community level; and generally the value systems of the community are oriented so as to help preserve the existing ways of coöperating with nature in the growing of plants and raising of livestock. For want of a more satisfactory term this fundamental part of the cultural heritage and social organization of a given people is designated its *system of agriculture*. This term was chosen rather than "agricultural techniques," the most suitable alternative, in order that the complexity, systematic arrangement, and organic unity of the cultural complex in action could be stressed more forcibly.

The system of agriculture must be defined broadly enough to include all of the lore, practical skills, "know-how," and scientific knowledge about agriculture, stock raising, and farm transportation. Thus that of a primitive community may have as central elements the digging stick mainpulated by the women of the tribe and a set of religious or magical practices designed to promote fertility; that of the most modern farming community may involve a highly intricate combination of tested practices assembled from many parts of the world, well-established scientific principles, and mechanical and other engineering skills which were inconceivable when the operator of one of the farms was a boy in the same locality.

Historically, the acquisition of the fund of knowledge which enables the modern farmer to multiply the gifts of nature, to bring forth plant and animal products in abundance, is mankind's greatest accomplishment. Only to the extent that mastery over the natural processes multiplied the amount of food and fiber that one man could produce were human energies available for the other activities that have brought us to the atomic age. Geographically, the present distribution of various systems of agriculture is probably the most reliable indicator of the basic reasons for the tremendous differences in levels and standards of living to be found throughout the world. Politically, socially, and economically one of the principal tasks confronting the human race in the second half of the twentieth century is to bring the agricultural systems in the so-called "backward" or "underdeveloped" countries up nearer the high levels already achieved in many parts of the United States, Canada, northwestern Europe, Australia, and New Zealand. Point Four programs may be known by other names in the decades which lie ahead, but efforts to improve the basic agricultural systems in many parts of the world are likely to be for many years one of the chief ways of attacking the hunger, poverty, misery, and disease which are the lot of the bulk of mankind.

Agricultural Systems and Levels of Living[1]

One who travels throughout the world, even in a cursory manner, is certain to observe that the standards and levels of living vary greatly from one place to another. In most of Asia, for example, he will note that the lot of the common man is almost inconceivably low. In Europe, too, he will find that the peoples of northwestern Europe enjoy much larger amounts of goods and services than do those of the southern and southeastern parts of the continent. In the New World he will soon generalize correctly that the plane of living in the United States and Canada is much above that prevailing in the countries which lie to the south and east of the Rio Grande. In the United States itself he will see that on the average the level of living of those who dwell to the north of the

[1] The analysis presented in this section is drawn largely from T. Lynn Smith, "Agricultural Systems and Standards of Living," *Inter-American Economic Affairs*, III (1949), 15–28; and T. Lynn Smith, "Sistemas Agricolas," *Revista Brasileira de Geografia*, IX (1947), 159–184.

Ohio is higher than that of the people who live south of that historic stream; and in Brazil, the country which occupies half of the South American continent, he will find undeniable proof that people living in the southern states of Rio Grande do Sul, Santa Catarina, Paraná, and São Paulo have much higher levels and standards of living than those in the more northerly sections of that great country.

Naturally, since the differences have been evident to many people, a great many explanations of the phenomenon have been advanced. The one of these that has enjoyed by far the most popularity is, of course, that which attributes the basic reason for the differences to heredity or to racial factors. According to this line of reasoning, it would seem, the level of living enjoyed by a given people is fairly indicative of its inherent biological capacities. Certain peoples who have high levels of living do so because they are "superior," and those who have low levels of living must therefore be "inferior." More recently industrialization has been seized upon by many as the principal cause or explanation of the variations. Overlooked almost entirely is the fact that such differences existed long before the industrial revolution, and high levels of living are attributed to a high development of industrialization while low levels are thought to result from the lack of it. The present writer accepts neither of these explanations as the important ones, and advances the truly cultural hypothesis that differences in the basic agricultural systems practiced by various peoples are the real key to an understanding of the way in which the widely varying levels and standards of living were generated and perpetuated.

As has been indicated elsewhere,[2] the analysis of the level of living among any people may be resolved into a consideration of the following three factors: (1) the quantity and quality of the natural resources available for exploitation by man, (2) the output per worker, and (3) the manner of distributing the results of the productive process among those who have had a part in it.

Natural resources in and of themselves are of no import until man's cultural heritage has reached a stage which enables them to be utilized. For all we know certain groups of Eskimos in the arctic regions, Indians in the heart of South America, or tribes in Assam may be occupying lands rich in ores yielding uranium. But if left

---

[2] T. Lynn Smith, *Brazil: People and Institutions*, Baton Rouge, Louisiana State University Press, 1946, p. 345.

to themselves there is small possibility that such groups would ever develop their cultures to the point at which these treasures would form a significant part of the natural resources at their disposal. Nor were the great iron resources of Venezuela or Brazil of any consequence to the natives whom the Portuguese, Spaniards, French, Dutch, and English encountered along the shores of the New World. The cultural heritages of those Indians did not include a knowledge of iron and how to get it, although their need for such a metal was very great. They were as avid in borrowing it from the white men, in order to make sharp and durable points for their arrows and spears, as are modern industrialists to develop the mines, build the railroads, construct the ports, and establish the smelters which are essential before those natural resources can add to the sinews of contemporary civilization. Any inventory of natural resources is almost impossible to make because man's developing cultural heritage constantly is changing the facts of life with respect to what is and what is not to be included as a resource. Every country contains vast amounts of natural resources which in effect become available for use only as man's cultural heritage accumulates.

The output per worker is a more serious matter for those interested in the levels and standards of living in any part of the world. It is precisely here that the agricultural system in use has such a tremendous bearing upon the living conditions among mankind. In countries such as Argentina, Brazil, the United States, and Soviet Russia, where the pressure of population upon resources is much less than in China, India, or most of Europe, the productivity per worker is largely determined by the extent to which labor is used in the process of production. If human labor is expended lavishly, that is, if it is combined with relatively small inputs of capital and management, the output per man can only be small. It cannot compare favorably with the production per man-hour or man-mouth in a place where each person makes considerable use of tools, implements, machinery, and power in the work he performs.

If, as has long been true throughout the southern part of the United States, the average farm worker uses relatively little power and equipment and even the hand tools which are employed are crude, gross, and ill adapted to the tasks to be performed, production per man is certain to be low. Until the basic manner of extracting products from the soil is improved, levels of living can hardly be expected to rise substantially. They certainly will not rival those in the parts of the nation in which hand tools are depended upon to a very limited extent, the tools in use are much more highly perfected, and especially where generous inputs of power and expensive farm machinery are combined with the labor of the average farmer.[3] If, as is the case throughout large parts of

[3] The necessity for detailed and comprehensive study of this part of the cultural heritage in the various regions of the United States is suggested by the keen observations of a New York farmer, Frederick Law Olmsted, who also was the designer of Central Park in New York City, on the occasion of one of his winter visits to the south. "But, here, I am shown tools that no man in his senses, with us, would allow a laborer, to whom he was paying wages, to be encumbered with; and the excessive weight and clumsiness of which, I would judge, would make work at least ten percent greater than those ordinarily used with us. And I am assured that, in the careless and clumsy way they must be used by the slaves, anything lighter or less rude could not be furnished them with good economy, and that such tools as we constantly give our laborers, and find our profit in giving them, would not last out a day in a Virginia cornfield—much lighter and more free from stones though it be than ours." *A Journey in the Seaboard Slave States, With Remarks on Their Economy,* New York, Dix & Edwards, 1856, pp. 46–47.

From the Old Dominion Olmsted continued on down the Atlantic coast to South Carolina, where in the neighborhood of Charleston he recorded:

"I saw women working again, in large gangs, with men. In one case they were distributing manure—ditch scrapings it appeared to be—and the mode of operation was this: the manure had been already carted into heaps upon the ground; a number of the women were carrying it from the heap in baskets, on their heads, and one in her apron, and spreading it with their hands between the ridges on which the cotton grew last year; the rest followed with great, long-handled, heavy, clumsy hoes, and pulled down the ridges over the manure, and so made new ridges for the next planting. I asked a young planter who continued with me a good part of the day, why they did not use plows. He said this was rather rough land, and a plow wouldn't work it in very well. It was light soil, and smooth enough for a parade ground. The fact is, in certain parts of South Carolina, a plow is yet an almost unknown instrument of tillage." *Ibid,* p. 397.

It was also near this center of trade and culture that he conversed with a farmer who described ". . . as a novelty, a plow, with 'a sort of a wing, like on one side,' that pushed off, and turned over a slice of the ground; from which it appeared that he had, until recently, never seen a mould-board; the common plows of this country being constructed on the same principles as those of the Chinese, and only rooting the ground like a hog or a mole—not cleaving and turning. He had never heard of working a plow with more than one horse." *Ibid,* p. 402.

Extracts from the writings of earlier visitors to the southern part of the United States are no less eloquent in their descriptions of basic deficiencies in the systems of farming the land. Almost 100 years before Olmsted wrote, a "Lady of Quality" from Scotland had been rudely shocked by the relatively crude methods employed by North Carolina farmers in their efforts to extract a living from the soil. For example, after visiting the section near Wilmington she recorded in her diary that "every instrument of husbandry was unknown," not only plows "but all the machinery used with success at home." Only the hoe was employed for the planting and tilling of the corn and "to accomplish this a good number of Negroes follow each other's tail the day long"; and it "will take twenty at

the American tropics, those of Africa, and those of the western Pacific, man's only aids in his struggle with nature consist of the ax and fire, the output per worker is bound to be small. Or if, as is generally true throughout the densely inhabited parts of Asia, hoe culture is the rule, merely supplemented here and there by a few poorly designed, crudely manufactured, and awkwardly drawn farm implements, the production of a few bushels of rice may require the expenditure of tremendous amounts of human time and energy. In all these cases the problem of production is fundamental, and until there is a greater return per worker the average levels and standards of living must remain low. On the other hand, where a system of agriculture prevails in which each worker makes use of plenty of land, efficient tools and implements, and large amounts of power—where capital is combined liberally with labor —there results a much greater production per worker. Under such circumstances, providing there is anything like an equitable system of distribution, the levels and standards of living can be very high.

The role of management also is of fundamental importance, as is stressed in Chapter 13, which treats "The Size of Holdings." If each person engaged in the cultivation of the soil is a thinking, deciding, acting agent, performing for himself the managerial functions of the agricultural enterprise (as is the case on the typical farm in the midwestern part of the United States or in the forms which blanket northwestern Europe), the rural level of living is thereby greatly increased. It compares most favorably with the situation in the areas of large estates, Indonesian plantations, southern plantations, Spanish American *haciendas*, Brazilian *fazendas*, and other types of latifundia in all parts of the earth.

---

least to do as much work as two horses with a man and a boy would perform." The perceptive lady also observed correctly that "here the wheel-plough would answer finely," since the ground was flat, the soil light, and there was "not a stone to be met with in a thousand acres." She realized that at first the settlers were obliged to plant amid the roots and stumps and that the hoe was the best way of handling the first crops, but she deplored the cultural lag which maintained the old "manner of dressing their fields, the same absurd method continuing every where." As one is tempted to observe when visiting many "underdeveloped" countries at the present time, she states flatly that "if horses were hard to come at or unfitted, there might be some excuse" but the fact is quite different. "They have them in plenty, and strong animals they are and fit for the hardest labour." Evangeline Walker Andrews and Charles McLean Andrews (eds.), *Journal of a Lady of Quality; Being the Narrative of a Journey from Scotland to the West Indies, North Carolina, and Portugal, in the Years 1774 to 1776*, New Haven, Yale University Press, 1934, pp. 163–164.

Where the men who perform the manual labor also participate actively and intelligently in the management of the enterprises, tremendous amounts of human energy are not knowingly and needlessly expended in the production process. Such a combination of skills in the same person also greatly simplifies the equitable distribution of the product. These facts, plus the additional one that the worker receives a return for managerial activities in addition to his laborer's wage, do much to insure a relatively high level of living. On the other hand, in all types of large-scale agricultural activities there is a tendency for managerial activities to be used sparingly, while labor is used lavishly. Large amounts of human energy are wasted. The laborers, who are the breadwinners for almost 100 percent of the families, can at best receive no more than the meager return attributable to their own poorly utilized toil; and as a rule the nature of the distribution process in areas dominated by the large estate makes it impossible for them to obtain more than the minimum necessary to meet the most primary of their creature needs. In those countries where the absence of a general property tax enables the monopolization of rural real estate to reach its maximum, makes it possible for land to become an asylum for capital, such latifundian degradation reaches its maximum.[4] In these cases a most inefficient combination of the economic factors of production, along with the failure of the mass of the workers to receive any return for managerial activities, makes it inevitable that the level and standard of living will be very low.

A Classification of Agricultural Systems

One of the most widely used reference books, a comprehensive work prepared with the needs of elementary- and secondary-school students especially in mind, asserts that the farmer today can care for 750 acres of land as easily as George Washington's father could cultivate fifty acres. The eminent authorities who prepared the materials for these volumes further state that the primitive husbandman would have required an equivalent amount of

[4] For a few typical examples as observed by the author, see T. Lynn Smith, "The Cultural Setting of Agricultural Extension Work in Colombia," *Rural Sociology*, X (1945), 235–246; T. Lynn Smith, "Notes on the Population and Rural Social Organization in El Salvador," *Rural Sociology*, X (1945), 359–379; and T. Lynn Smith, Justo Diaz Rodriguez, and Luis Roberto Garcia, *Tabio: A Study in Rural Social Organization*, Washington, Office of Foreign Agricultural Relations, 1945, pp. 44–45.

effort to cultivate merely one acre.[5] For present purposes it is not necessary to debate as to whether the ratios involved are exactly 50 to 750 and 1 to 750; one could allow for a tremendous margin of error in the estimates and still the point would be crystal clear. The improvements in man's ways of extracting a living from the soil, that is, in his systems of agriculture, have been tremendous. With much reason one might maintain that only by means of such improvements was it possible for energy and thought to be devoted to nonagricultural activities; and that in the last analysis the development of science and philosophy, of commerce and industry, and of what we know as modern civilization was made possible only through the discovery and application of better agricultural techniques.

There is little need of elaborating in detail the proposition that historically and geographically the variations in the ways of extracting a living from the soil are very great. It is well to mention, however, that some five thousand years ago the peoples of Egypt and Mesopotamia already possessed systems of tillage vastly superior to those used in many parts of the world in the early years of the atomic age. By the time the Sumerians and Egyptians had perfected writing as a means of communication and record keeping, the accomplishment which marked the dawn of the historical period, they were enjoying the benefits of rather highly developed systems of agriculture. They made abundant use of the plow, wheeled vehicles, hitching apparatus, animal power, and irrigation in producing and transporting the food crops on which their civilizations depended. It may be that the agricultural arts never attained any substantially higher level of perfection until hundreds of years after Columbus sailed to the New World. But although historically the origin and development of most of the basic traits in the more developed systems of agriculture are shrouded in mystery, the recent revolutionary developments in agricultural technology, animal industry, and rural transportation are thoroughly documented.

Geographically one can easily encounter the most diverse methods of wresting products from nature, from the most simple conceivable to the highly complex modern mechanized systems

<hr>

[5] *Compton's Pictured Encyclopedia and Fact-Index*, Chicago, F. E. Compton & Company, 1944, I, 47.

of farming. Properly classified, these may even be suggestive of the lines of cultural evolution through which man increased his control over nature, or coöperation with her, in the ages before recorded history began. From this point of view each of the distinct systems of agriculture described below may be thought of as a stage in the history of civilization, since in the long run no doubt the lines of development were from the simple to the more complex. However, it should not be assumed that any given people passed through all these stages in sequential order.

Tentatively, since the present author is introducing and developing a subject not previously treated in rural sociology texts, the various systems of agriculture are classified, for purposes of discussion and additional study, into the following six types: (1) river bank; (2) fire agriculture; (3) hoe culture; (4) rudimentary plow culture; (5) advanced plow culture; and (6) mechanized farming. Each of these will be described and discussed in turn.

River Bank Plantings

Since this is the most simple and presumably the first system of agriculture, it is well to begin by raising a few specific questions relative to the transition from a collecting economy to one based on agriculture. In spite of all that has been written upon the subject, the early phases of man's life as an agriculturist do not seem to be very clear. Precisely what was involved in the transition to an agricultural stage of existence from the collecting economy which is generally presumed to have preceded it? And how were pastoral activities related to the two? Is it fair to assume, as most writers seem to have done, that agriculture commenced with tillage by means of the primitive digging stick or a crude hoe? "A stick was the first hand tool used to scratch the surface of the ground before planting, and a forked stick, held in the ground by the plowman while the oxen dragged it ahead, was the first plow" is the way this entire subject is disposed of in the popular source to which reference has been made.[6] But from whence all the "know-how" these statements take for granted? The saving and planting of seeds, the idea of tillage, the yoking of oxen should hardly be assumed to be spontaneous or instinctive activities of mankind. Surely more elementary culture traits than these were involved in

[6] *Ibid.*

the epoch which marked the transition from a collecting economy to agriculture.

Probably the first farming was only a slight transition from the collecting stage which preceded it, and no doubt it was the woman who became the first agriculturist. It seems likely that she first interfered in the processes of nature by thinning out competing plants from among those wild ones from which she had come to expect a gift of seeds or tubers. But this practice alone hardly could be classed as farming. However, when she got and applied the idea of taking some of the seeds and depositing them in a spot where they could sprout, take root, and grow, she had begun her long history as an agriculturist. The fact that one crop season probably followed immediately upon the other, so that it was not too great a strain to forgo the pleasures of consumption, possibly was an important factor in the transition. The soft, mellow loam deposits left on the banks by a receding stream probably were among the first places she selected for her plantings. At least, very early primitive peoples probably learned that merely by saving seeds and pressing them into such spongy surface with the foot they could greatly multiply the gifts of nature. In any case, such a system of farming seems to be the simplest possible, since no tools whatsoever are needed, not even the digging stick.

This elementary system of agriculture, which we denominate as the river bank type, is still widely used throughout the great Amazon Basin in South America and in much of the Orinoco Valley as well.[7] In that area alone hundreds of thousands of persons are largely dependent upon this simple process for their daily

[7] Cf. Smith, *Brazil*, p. 104; Smith, "Sistemas Agricolas," p. 162; Smith, "Agricultural Systems and Standards of Living," p. 19; United States Department of Agriculture Extension Service and Office of Foreign Agricultural Relations, *Conference Report on Extension Experiences Around the World*, Washington, U.S. Department of Agriculture, 1951, pp. 149–150; and Henry Walter Bates, *The Naturalist on the River Amazonas*, London, John Murray, 1892, pp. 282–283. In the course of some of the "dull and dreary evenings" he spent at Javita, a small village on the Orinoco near the passage which links it with the Amazon system, Alfred Russell Wallace amused himself by describing in blank verse the life of the Indians of the area. Their system of agriculture called forth the following lines:

> "The women dig the mandiocca root,
> And with much labour make of it their bread.
> These plant the young shoots in the fertile earth—
> Earth all untill'd, to which the plough, or spade,
> Or rake, or harrow, are alike unknown."

Travels on the Amazon, London, Ward Lock & Co., 1911, p. 177.

bread. It may still be in use in other parts of the world, although documentation is lacking. Furthermore, there is at least some reason for supposing that the early development and perfection of agricultural methods in the valleys of the Nile, the Tigris, and the Euphrates were facilitated by the advantages these locations offered for these first beginnings of agriculture.[8]

Where the river bank type of agriculture prevails, transportation on the farm is limited to the back or head of woman herself, and transportation to the market, if it exists at all, is by means of some kind of boat, canoe, or raft.

Fire Agriculture

Possibly, at least in some places, tillage with the digging stick or the hoe may have developed directly out of the favored situations in which nature's rivers did a thorough job of preparing beds for seeds. It is even possible that the first combination of agricultural and stock-raising enterprises was one in which, as the river's waters receded, animals were employed to tread the broadcast seeds into the muddy surface of the land. But in many parts of the earth another system of agriculture developed, one which is still employed by millions of persons, and one to which we have given the name *fire agriculture*.[9]

Soft, pliable portions of the earth's surface are also left where a fire has encountered, in a dried condition, the highly concentrated results of centuries of abundant plant growth. Such a newly burned-over area in a virgin forest is almost entirely lacking in the many plants or weeds that might compete with those planted. Hence it is merely a step from the point when mankind depends

[8] Maspero used the present tense in describing agricultural operations in the Nile Valley ("As soon as the water of the Nile retires, the ground is sown without previous preparation, and the grain, falling straight into the mud, grows as vigorously as in the best-ploughed furrows"), although no doubt his reference is to ancient procedures. Gaston Maspero, *The Dawn of Civilization, Egypt and Chaldea*, London, Society for Promoting Christian Knowledge, 5th ed., 1910, p. 66. Cf. A. Bothwell Gosse, *The Civilization of the Ancient Egyptians*, London, T. C. and E. C. Jack, 1915, p. 28.

[9] For a detailed description and discussion of this way of extracting products from the soil, see Smith, *Brazil*, chap. 3. Many anthropologists have applied the name "slashing and burning" to these processes. In Brazil, where it is the chief reliance of several million rural inhabitants, the system is known as *derrubadas e quemadas;* and "a very favourite method of cultivation, among natives in the east at any rate," in Ceylon it is called *chena*, in Malaya *ladang*, and in India *jhuming*. J. C. Willis, *Agriculture in the Tropics*, Cambridge, The University Press, 1909, p. 1. Cf. U.S. Department of Agriculture, *Extension Experiences Around the World*, p. 149, *passim*.

upon nature's rivers to prepare the soil for the seeds to that in which fire may be relied upon for the same purpose. Tremendous areas in Central and South America, Africa, Asia, and Oceania are still occupied by peoples who have not passed beyond this elementary and destructive stage of agricultural existence. The word "destructive" is used advisedly since to make use of this method of

FIGURE 81. Fire Agriculture as Practiced in Brazil: The Seedbed Is Now Ready for Planting, and the Seeds Will Be Dibbled in with the Aid of the Big Toe, a Planting Stick, or, More Rarely, a Crude Hoe. (Courtesy of Herbert K. Ferguson.)

producing a crop annually a section of virgin forest or second growth which has been standing for decades must be destroyed. Willis' statement that "vast areas of good forest land have been ruined in southern Asia by this destructive practice"[10] is fully in line with the author's personal observations throughout immense sections of the American tropics.

Fire agriculture is a complex of agricultural practices in which the preparation of the soil for planting consists of clearing out the undergrowth from a patch of forest by means of the cutlass or

[10] *Op. cit.*, p. 2.

machete, felling the larger trees with an axe, permitting the tangled mass of fallen timber and brush to dry for a while, and then firing the entire lot. This part of the process is performed during the dry season, so that when the rains begin there is a tract of cleared and spongy surface awaiting the seeds. (See Figures 81 and 82.) In many areas no tools whatsoever are used in the plant-

Figure 82. The Transition from Fire Agriculture to Hoe Culture in Brazil: Land on Which Rice Was Produced a Few Years Previously by the System of Fire Agriculture Is Now Planted to Young Coffee Trees Which Will Be Cultivated with the Hoe. (Courtesy of Herbert K. Ferguson.)

ing process, the openings for the seeds being made by a few brushes of the big toe and the loose dirt filled in on top of them by a sidewise movement of the foot. Elsewhere, a digging stick or even a crude hoe may be used to open and fill the small holes in which the seeds are deposited. No hoeing or other cultivation is performed while the crops are growing, although sometimes competing shoots and suckers are cut away with the aid of the machete. Frequently some of the unburned limbs and branches are used to construct a rude fence about the clearing in order to keep animals out of the growing crops. Two or even three crops may be grown in quick succession, after which the land is abandoned to grow up to second growth while the farmer repeats the process in another part of the forest. In the American tropics as in the Far East the old clearing "grows up in scrubby jungle, and may again be chena-ed after 8–50 years."[11]

In the parts of the world in which fire agriculture remains as the standard means of producing food crops, farm and farm-to-market transportation have hardly advanced to the point at which the wheel and animal traction help relieve men and women of

a   **b**

FIGURE 83.   The Highly Developed Digging Stick Employed by the Indians of Andean Countries. (After Guaman Poma, a Peruvian artist and writer of the sixteenth century, as reproduced in Bulletin 143 of the Bureau of American Ethnology, 1946, II, 213–214.)

their burdens. Human beings themselves are the principal beasts of burden, although those living near the waterways may make use of boats and canoes for transporting products over the longer distances. The use of pack animals also may be an integral part of this system of agriculture.

Fire agriculture, of course, requires tremendous inputs of hu-

[11] *Ibid.*, p. 2. Cf. Julian H. Steward (ed.), *Handbook of South American Indians,* Bureau of American Ethnology Bulletin 143, Washington, Government Printing Office, 1948, III, 825, *passim.*

man labor for the production of a few pecks of corn or beans or a small heap of tubers. However, it continues to be the sole reliance of millions of people throughout the equatorial portions of the earth's surface for extracting a living from the soil.

Hoe Culture

Once it has been established through trial and error that soft, spongy surfaces are favorable to the growth of seeds, the stage has

FIGURE 84.   Modern Peruvian Indians Using the Digging Stick Portrayed in Figure 83. (Courtesy of Dr. M. Kuczynski-Godard.)

been set for man to take another basic step in the evolution of his agricultural systems. Men and women of many tribes throughout the world hit upon the idea of employing sharp sticks for stirring the soil. Possibly the idea of such tillage first came from the employment of sticks in the collection of tubers, but the use of the digging stick is not a complicated development. In some cases only hand grips were depended upon, while among many peoples the sticks selected and shaped were ones in which the foot as well as the hand could be used in the application of human energy in the preparation of the seedbed or in the taking of a harvest of root crops. (See Figures 83 and 84.) Once such tillage was established,

FIGURE 85. Hoe Culture as Practiced by the Indians of Florida. (From a sixteenth-century drawing by Le Moyne as engraved by De Bry.)

only the principle of fertilization was needed to make possible a permanent agriculture and a sedentary life.[12]

From the digging stick came the hoe, which continues to be the chief implement used by the bulk of the world's agriculturists. This development involved the fastening of a blade of bone or

FIGURE 86. Cleaning the Weeds from a Field of Rice in Colombia: Illustrating the Lavish Use of Labor on Large Estates Which Rely upon Hoe Culture. (Courtesy of Kenneth Wernimont.)

other sharp and durable material to the base of the digging stick and then substituting a pull for a thrust in its manipulation.[13] (See Figure 85.) Probably this fundamental invention was made independently over and over again by peoples separated geographically and historically, although hundreds of the smaller and less advanced groupings of mankind are still limited in their agricultural activities to those that can be accomplished merely by the

[12] The way in which such knowledge was acquired is not obvious, but every schoolboy in the United States knows that the American Indians of the eastern woodlands placed a fish in each hill of corn. This type of fertilization appears, however, to have had a very limited distribution. Cf. Lyman Carrier, *The Beginnings of Agriculture in America,* New York, McGraw-Hill Book Company, 1923, pp. 93–99.

[13] M. E. Seebohm, *The Evolution of the English Farm,* Cambridge, Harvard University Press, 1927, p. 41, thinks the first hoe was "doubtless an axe-blade turned in its socket broadwise," but this description can hardly account for the shell and other primitive hoes possessed by hundreds of peoples who never knew bronze or other metal axes.

digging stick. In any case hoe culture rivals elementary plow culture, in which it also competes for dominance, in the extent to
which it is relied upon by the world's agriculturists. At a time when
the human race is far along on the problem of domesticating the

Figure 87.   Harvesting Wheat in Colombia. (Courtesy of Kenneth Wernimont.)

atom, hundreds of millions of the world's agriculturists know and
use no less energy-consuming methods of extracting a living from
the soil than hoe culture.[14] (See Figure 86.) It would be well if it
were recognized frankly, especially by those who talk glibly about
Point Four Programs and the like, that their basic economic activi-

[14] "For simple tillage of the ground, the most common tool in the more equatorial countries is probably the large hoe. . . ." Willis, *op. cit.*, p. 25. This generalization is confirmed through ample personal observation throughout the American tropics, where, except for the extensive areas given over to the even more
rudimentary agricultural systems, hoe culture continues to reign supreme. Even
throughout much of Europe and the nonequatorial portions of Asia hoe culture
has by no means given way completely to the systems of agriculture in which
there is a less lavish expenditure of human energy. It is also well to recall that
the hoe continues to be the chief reliance throughout the United States in the
production of all garden and truck crops; and that tobacco farming, the growing
of corn and cotton throughout much of the southern region, the culture of sugar
cane and sugar beets, and even the cultivation of potatoes in many parts of the
nation still depend heavily upon the man with the hoe.

ties are at a level far below that of the Egyptians and Sumerians at the dawn of history.

In those sections of the world in which hoe culture remains supreme, the sickle is the principal device used in harvesting grain crops. (See Figure 87.) There, too, transportation on the farm and the movement of products from farm to market likewise require the expenditure of a maximum amount of human effort. Men and women themselves continue to be the chief beasts of burden, although pack animals or small water craft may be used to a limited extent.

Rudimentary Plow Culture

Before mankind had perfected an alphabet which enabled it to make written records, it had developed and widely diffused a rudimentary plow for use in tilling the soil. Quite probably the same inventive peoples were responsible for both, although the actual origins are obscured by the darkness of prehistoric times. Probably the first plow was merely a digging stick so selected or so fashioned that two persons could coöperate in its manipulation, one pulling and the other pushing; or it may have been an adaptation of the hoe. By the dawn of history, however, the crude wooden plow, with metal point and drawn by oxen, had already become the chief reliance of agricultural peoples in Egypt, Mesopotamia, and probably several other of the cradles of civilization.[15] These early plows, like their modern counterparts in many parts of the world, were highly inefficient. They merely rooted the soil instead of lightly cutting and neatly turning it. The fact that animal traction was used in the pulling of the instrument was a tremendous gain, a revolutionary achievement, even though the holding of the crude plow itself and the management of the oxen required the participation of several persons in the tillage activities. Lumbering oxen, with their jerky movements, have yet to be hitched efficiently to modern turning plows, and their use in combination with the old rooting variety leaves even more to be desired.

Rarely, if ever, were horses hitched to the rudimentary plows of the ancient world, and the same is true in the second half of the twentieth century. Throughout most of Asia, southern and eastern

[15] For one of the many excellent treatises on the origin of the plow, see E. B. Tylor, "On the Origin of the Plough, and Wheel-Carriage," *Journal of the Anthropological Institute of Great Britain and Ireland*, X (1881), 74–82.

Europe, and many of the Spanish American countries, the crude wooden plows commonly used are drawn either by oxen (Figure 88) or, in the more humid parts of Asia, by the water buffalo. In the ancient civilizations and those of the Mediterranean which succeeded them, it would seem, the possession and use of horses

FIGURE 88.   Rudimentary Plow Culture as Practiced in Colombia. (Courtesy of Kenneth Wernimont.)

were limited largely to the members of the upper classes.[16] They were used extensively by the members of the elite for riding and for hitching (with breast strap only) to chariots, especially in activities connected with war, but they probably were far beyond the reach of the menial classes who tilled the soil.

Rudimentary plow culture with the crudely hitched and inefficient animal traction connected with it is the agricultural system still used by the majority of the earth's agriculturists. Its preëminent position in China and India alone would be sufficient to make this generalization valid, but the statement is reinforced by the importance of this elementary mode of tilling the soil in Oceania, southern and eastern Europe, and much of Latin America.

The methods of harvesting the crops and threshing them also remain essentially the same in this system of agriculture as they

16 "Horses were fit chattels only for kings in the palmy days of Egypt. . . ." L. W. Ellis and Edward A. Rumely, *Power and the Plow*, Garden City and New York, Doubleday, Page & Co., 1911, p. 25.

were when the dawn of history first revealed its presence in Egypt and Mesopotamia. Then as now the wheat, rice, and other grains from which man makes his bread were harvested by hand with the use of the sickle. Then as now they were threshed merely by grasping a handful of straw and beating the heads upon the ground, by the use of the flail, or by driving animals over the straw spread out on the threshing floor.

Transportation on the farm and from farm to market made somewhat less rigorous demands upon human energy in the stage of rudimentary plow culture than in the stages which preceded it. The use of the wheel seems to be an integral part of this complex. By the time man's material culture had advanced to the point at which he was able to employ draft animals to pull a crude plow, he also seems to have attained a knowledge of the wheel and its use in a rude cart. Hence the two-wheeled cart drawn by oxen today is widely used by the world's agriculturists. Slow, crude, and inefficient as it is, nevertheless its development and use had done much to relieve men and women from primary roles as beasts of burden. (See Figure 89.)

Advanced Plow Culture

Before mankind could advance beyond the level of rudimentary plow culture, a stage had to be set in which several fundamental conditions could all be met at the same time and place. Northwestern Europe was the scene of the early basic inventions and discoveries involved in this change, although many of the more revolutionary improvements eventually were made in the United States. Let us consider briefly the things which were required for the development of an agricultural system markedly superior to that of the Egyptians, that relied upon by the Greeks and Romans, or that which continues to be used by the bulk of mankind.

In the first place a better source of farm power than that provided by the ox or the water buffalo was necessary. This depended upon the use of an animal with a smoother gait so that the force could be applied more evenly and steadily. The horse, of course, was admirably fitted for this role, but for him to be given it his use had to spread into regions where his position in relation to the class structure was not so firmly established. Naturally, this condition was fulfilled among the Germanic tribes of northwestern

FIGURE 89. Brazilian Oxcart. (From a drawing by Percy Lau, courtesy of the Instituto Brasileiro de Geografia e Estatística.)

Europe who were in contact with but not entirely dominated by the Romans.[17] Eventually, after the use of horses as draft animals became established, through breeding types highly adapted to heavy farm work were produced, also in this part of Europe.[18] These, of course, differed tremendously from the horses the Romans had used for their chariots or the Arabian breeds, famed for their speed and smooth-riding qualities, used by the pastoral peoples of western Asia.

The basic improvement of the system of agriculture also involved the perfection of hitching equipment. This was essential in order to secure a more efficient application of the animal power expended. Types adapted to the physiques of horses were especially needed, so that they could be used to pull farm implements and move farm vehicles. The old harnesses used by the Egyptians, Greeks, and Romans for hitching horses to their chariots definitely were inadequate. They depended upon the breast strap; and so harnessed any horse that threw his full weight forward in order to pull a heavy load would quickly have his wind cut off. Therefore, the perfection of a horse collar was of critical importance.[19] The writer has not been able to determine fully the history of the invention and perfection of this fundamental device, but certainly its more important applications took place in northwestern Europe.[20] Possibly the hitching of horses to sleighs and sleds furnished the daily stimulus to thought which resulted in the lucky improvision, but that cannot as yet be definitely established. In any case the perfection of a collar which made possible the use of horses as draft animals gave the countries of northwestern Europe, and the new ones such as the United States, Canada, Australia, New Zealand, and South Africa, which received their basic cultural heritages from them, a tremendous advantage over other sections of the world in the production and transportation of basic

[17] "As late as the tenth century, farmers in England were forbidden, by law, to harness the horse to the plow." *Ibid.* Such a law would hardly have been issued had the old Roman mores with respect to the horse and his use been in full power. Here we have indisputable evidence that the transition was taking place and a similar change doubtless was going on across the channel on the Continent.

[18] Most of this production did not take place until the eighteenth century. Cf. Seebohm, *op. cit.* pp. 296–297.

[19] It may be that the decline and abolition of slavery were due largely to the perfection of the horse collar and other parts of the harness for horses and mules.

[20] Charles Parain, "The Evolution of Agricultural Techniques," in J. H. Clapham and Eileen Power (eds.), *The Cambridge Economic History*, Cambridge, The University Press, 1941, I, 134, thinks the "stiff collar" may have come from northeast Asia between the fifth and the eighth centuries A.D.

agricultural commodities. As suggested above, this initial advantage and its cumulative effects do much to explain current differences in levels and standards of living throughout the world.[21]

The invention and perfection of a turning plow was a third development prerequisite to the emergence of a system of agriculture vastly improved over the ancient plow culture as practiced by the Egyptians and their successors. This, too, came about in northwestern Europe, and its beginnings seem to have come in Roman times.[22] The attachment of two wheels to the beam of the plow first took much of the burden of holding the instrument from the plowman. By the fifteenth century this plow had acquired a moldboard (of wood) and was coming to resemble the mental image which flashes into the mind of the North American farm boy when the word "plow" is mentioned. Probably this development took place in Flanders, which at that time was "an active center of agricultural improvement."[23]

It is hardly an accident that the English colonies in North America and the independent nation which they became was the location in which many of the more fundamental developments took place in the use of the horse as a draft animal, the further improvement of harnesses and hitching equipment, and the perfection of the turning plow. The shortage of labor for hire, the frontier society with its stimulation to change and adjustment, and the self-direction and individual responsibility of the farmers helped create a social situation in which the search for the new and the better became a thing of great necessity and merit.

By the time the United States became an independent nation, the evolution of the plow was near the place in which metal could be used for some of the parts other than the point. Thomas Jefferson, himself, was the agricultural scientist who worked out the mathematics of the turning plow; and the first steel plow that would scour in the prairie soils of the midwestern states was made from the blade of an old sawmill by John Deere in 1837. (See Figure 90.) These accomplishments are only two of the more important ones that came out of a feverish half-century of effort in

[21] See also Smith, "Agricultural Systems and Standards of Living," on this point.
[22] Cf. Parain, *op. cit.*, I, 139–141. Pliny located the origin of the wheeled plow in the country to the south of the Upper Danube. Vergil, born in Cisalpine Gaul, also knew such a plow. It is to be stressed, however, that, although some of the Romans knew of plows of improved types, the old Mediterranean *araire*, shaped along Egyptian lines, ruled supreme throughout the heartland of the Empire.
[23] *Ibid.*

this country to improve agricultural implements, an epoch that opened shortly after the United States had adopted its Constitution and resumed the activities of peacetime.[24] Others that might be mentioned include the development of early types of reapers and mowing machines, the manufacture of early and crude threshing machines, and the fairly successful efforts to develop grain

FIGURE 90.   Replica of the Steel Turning Plow Made by John Deere in 1837. (Courtesy of the J. I. Case Company.)

drills and corn planters.[25] By mid-century the old era definitely was drawing to a close. In the words of the anonymous writer who prepared the text for the 1900 Census of Agriculture: "The year 1900 practically marks the close of the period in which the only farm implements and machinery, other than the wagon, cart, and cotton gin, were those, which, for want of a better designation, may be called implements of hand production. The old cast-iron plows were in general use. Grass was mowed with the sythe, and grain was cut with the sickle or cradle and threshed with the

---

[24] For summaries of the more important events connected with the improvement of the plow, see R. L. Ardrey, *American Agricultural Implements*, Chicago, published by the author, 1894, pp. 5–20; and Percy Wells Bidwell and John T. Falconer, *History of Agriculture in the Northern United States, 1620–1860*, Washington, The Carnegie Institution of Washington, 1925, pp. 208–210 and 282–286.

[25] Cf. Ardrey, *op. cit., passim.*

flail."[26] Especially in the Ohio and the upper Mississippi valleys the farmers of this country were well on the way to attaining that system of agriculture to which we have given the name "advanced plow culture."

The fundamental improvements mentioned above were accompanied or quickly succeeded by others. The second half of the nineteenth century saw the perfection of the mowing machine and the development of the mechanical binder as an integral part of the grain harvester. All along the agricultural front in the United States and Canada, aided by the exchange of ideas and machines between the American countries, those of western Europe, and Australia and New Zealand, headway was made in the perfection of all the traits needed in a highly efficient system of agriculture. By the opening of the twentieth century, in the areas in which the work of advancing agricultural technology had been pursued most assiduously, advanced plow culture with animal traction had pretty well reached its acme of excellence. Henceforth most of the improvements made were those involved in or dependent upon the substitution of mechanical power for draft animals.

As exemplified by the practices in the midwestern and far western parts of the United States and other areas in which agricultural methods were most advanced at the opening of the twentieth century, the major features of advanced plow culture may be summarized as follows:

1. The basic instrument used in tillage was the sulky steel plow. (See Figure 91.) It was mathematically designed to cut and turn, rather than to root and tear, as had been the case with its predecessors. Finely balanced and adjustable, it could be drawn with a minimum of effort by the three or four horses commonly used for the purpose.

2. Along with the plow went a host of other pieces of horse- or mule-drawn equipment, the exact ones depending upon the crops grown in the locality. Among these may be named the mowing machine, the reaper with its mechanical binder, the corn planter, a wide variety of grain drills, the cotton planter, drag and disk harrows, and cultivators of many kinds for use in the tillage of row crops.

[26] *Twelfth Census of the United States . . . 1900*, "Agriculture," Part I, Washington, United States Census Office, 1902, p. xxix.

3. Well-established breeds of horses were developed specifically for draft purposes and trained to perform many types of work. (See Figure 92.)

4. Harnesses and hitching equipment included the all-important horse collar, cleverly designed and skillfully made and ad-

FIGURE 91. The Basic Complex (Horses as Draft Animals, Well-Balanced Hitching Equipment, the Horse Collar, and the Steel Turning Plow) Which Helped Raise the Levels of Living of American Farmers to Among the Highest in the World. (Photo by courtesy of the J. I. Case Company.)

justed to the end of getting the most efficient use of horsepower in the pulling of plows, wagons, and the host of other farm implements and vehicles.

5. The development of highly perfected four-wheeled farm wagons (Figure 93) had enabled transportation on the farm and that from farm to market to keep pace in efficiency with the tremendous advances that had been made in preparing the seedbed, planting the crop, cultivating, and harvesting.

6. Threshing machines, cotton gins, potato sorters, hay der-

FIGURE 92.   Digging Potatoes in Maine. (Photo by Jack Delano from the Farm Security Administration Collection in the Library of Congress.)

FIGURE 93.   This Combination (Horses as Draft Animals, Horse Collars, Harness, and the Four-Wheeled Farm Wagon) Played a Fundamental Role in the Development and Maintenance of the American Standard of Living. (Photo made on a dairy farm in Vermont by Jack Delano for the Farm Security Administration Collection now in the Library of Congress.)

ricks and bailers, and many other types of equipment were used in cleaning the crops and preparing them for storage or for the market. Many of these devices were powered by animal traction and some of them by steam engines. All of them greatly multiplied the strength of men's arms for the tasks of producing and processing the food, feed, and fiber upon which twentieth-century civilization relies.

By 1910 the advanced plow culture system of agriculture had pretty well reached its acme of perfection in certain parts of the United States, and the spectacular improvements to come were to be largely in terms of the mechanization of agricultural production. Between then and 1920 the use of horses and mules as sources of farm power reached its maximum and began to decline, whereas the number of tractors on farms began to move upward at a dizzy pace. Therefore, the year 1910 is the significant one for taking stock of rural America as it was on the eve of the epoch of mechanized farming.

According to the 1910 Census of Agriculture a total of 12,-659,203 persons of ten years of age or over were gainfully employed in agricultural pursuits. On the farms of the nation was a total of 17,430,418 mature horses and 3,787,316 mature mules, or in a very literal sense an average of 167.6 horse (and mule) power for every 100 persons engaged in the cultivation of the soil. Of course at that time, since the "gasoline buggy" was merely beginning to appear in the rural districts, these horses and mules had to provide the farm families with transportation for all purposes, in addition to furnishing the power for the farm implements and vehicles. Along with the horses and mules the nation's farmers in 1910 had farm implements and machinery valued at $1,265,150,-000, or almost exactly $100 of such investment per person employed in farming.[27] Thus by 1910, on the average, each person working in American agriculture had a considerable amount of animal power and equipment to combine with his labor in the process of extracting products from the soil.

But the situation varied widely from one part of the nation to another and these differences should not be passed by without comment. (See Figures 94 and 95.) Whereas the farmers of the corn belt and those in the western parts of the country had de-

---

[27] This figure, of course, is only a fraction of the real investment the farmers had in machinery and equipment.

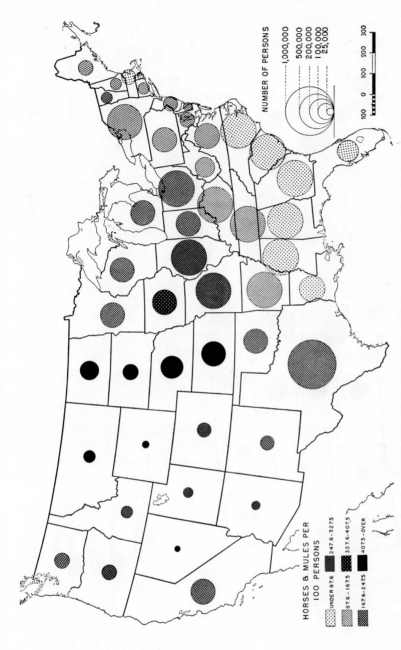

NUMBER OF PERSONS

1,000,000
500,000
200,000
100,000
25,000

HORSES & MULES PER
100 PERSONS

UNDER 87.6
87.6 - 167.5
167.6 - 247.5
247.6 - 327.5
327.6 - 407.5
407.5 - OVER

FIGURE 94. Number of Horses and Mules per 100 Persons Ten Years of Age and Over Engaged in Agriculture, 1910.

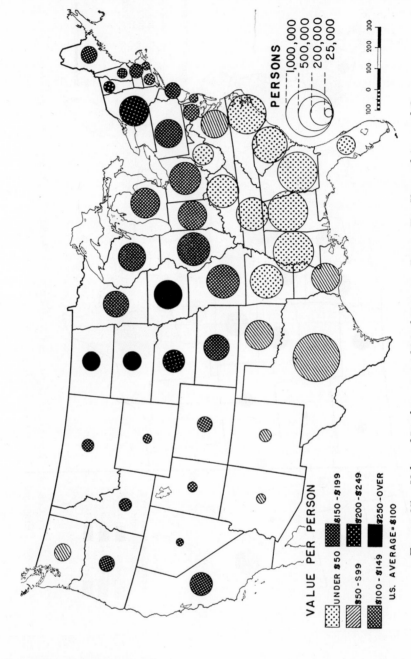

PERSONS

1,000,000
500,000
200,000
25,000

300
200
100
0
100

VALUE PER PERSON

UNDER $50
$50-$99
$100-$149
$150-$199
$200-$249
$250-OVER

U.S. AVERAGE = $100

FIGURE 95.   Value of Implements and Machinery per Person Ten Years of Age and Over
Engaged in Agriculture, 1910.

veloped the use of draft animals and agricultural machinery to a high degree (Figure 96), the planters and other farm operators in the South continued to rely heavily upon hoe culture and at best an elementary form of plow culture. At a time when the average farm worker in the heart of the corn belt could unite his labor with that of three or four horses and make use of several hundred dollars' worth of implements and machinery, his fellow in the South

FIGURE 96.   Advanced Plow Culture in One of Its Extreme Phases. (Illustration from *Harper's Weekly.*)

had very little in the way of power and equipment to assist in the making and gathering of a crop. As the stage was being set for the mechanization of American agriculture, the advanced plow culture of the midwestern and western states might be symbolized by the picture of a farmer with a team of four or more horses hitched to a sulky plow, a grain harvester, or a combine. In the South, on the other hand, the more appropriate imagery would be that of a man with one mule hitched to the simple walking plow, although even that would be a somewhat optimistic view of the system of agriculture in general use throughout the region.

Mechanized Farming

In the second half of the twentieth century, agriculture in the more advanced sections of the United States, Canada, and a few other areas has reached the stage in which it should be classed as mechanized farming. In this system of agriculture the ordinary farm family makes use of a tremendous amount of the most finished products of modern science and engineering. Light, large, finely adjusted implements powered by tractors are the core elements in this complex. Brute force ranks low, mechanical and managerial skills high, among the qualities making for success on the part of the farm operator in the mechanized system of agriculture. In this most advanced stage of agricultural production the efforts of a few hundred thousand farmers contribute more toward feeding and clothing the world's population than do those of many millions of the toiling masses who know no system of agriculture other than an antiquated hoe culture or rudimentary plow culture.

In large part the farm implements used in mechanized farming are merely improved versions of those that had been perfected as a part of the evolution of advanced plow culture. They are larger, geared to higher speeds, subject to finer adjustments, and made of lighter and more durable metals. Many of the machines or instruments are adapted to much more specialized functions than was the case with their predecessors; and some of them such as the cotton picker and the sugar cane harvester perform operations for which the older, multi-purpose contraptions were entirely unsuited. In addition, such machines as the flame cultivator are based on entirely different principles of weed control, while the use of the airplane for dusting purposes is a radical departure from all the earlier methods of spreading insecticides. In all probability mechanized farming is still only in its beginning stages, and two decades from now, when it may be more highly perfected, the implements and machines in use may make the most advanced ones employed at present seem antiquated indeed. Only then may it be possible for us to see clearly the principal differentiating characteristics of mechanized farming.

The Mechanization of Agriculture in the United States

Late in the nineteenth century the steam engine was adapted rather successfully for use in plowing, especially in the breaking of new land; and it gained even wider acceptance in this country as the source of power for driving the threshing machines used for separating wheat, barley, oats, and other grains from the straw. Other than this, however, the mechanization of agriculture had to

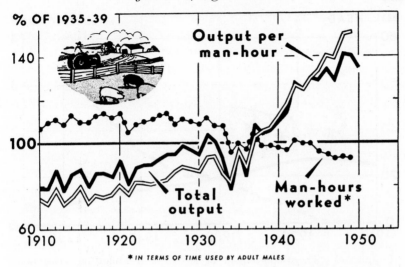

FIGURE 97.   The Increasing Productivity of Labor in American Agriculture. (Illustration from the Bureau of Agricultural Economics.)

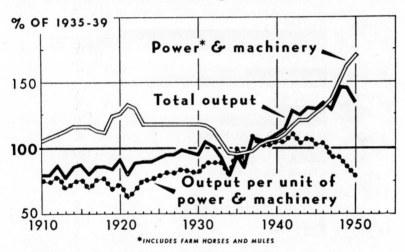

FIGURE 98.   The Increasing Production of American Farms Is Due to
Increased Use of Power and Machinery. (Illustration from the Bureau of
Agricultural Economics.)

await the coming of the twentieth century and the perfection of
the gasoline engine and the tractor. For all practical purposes the
real mechanization of agriculture in the United States got under
way about 1910.[28]

[28] First manufactured commercially in 1903, by 1910 tractors numbered about
1000 and in 1920, when they figured in the Census of Agriculture for the first

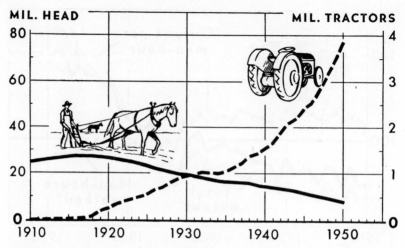

FIGURE 99. The Replacement of Horses and Mules by Tractors on American Farms. (Illustration from the Bureau of Agricultural Economics.)

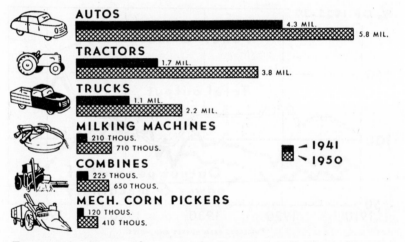

FIGURE 100. Recent Changes in the Equipment of American Farms. (Illustration from the Bureau of Agricultural Economics.)

In the United States the transition from the advanced plow culture system of agriculture, in which the use of draft animals, had reached its acme of perfection, to mechanized farming was a

time, there were some 246,000 on the nation's farms. Cf. Robert T. McMillan, "Effects of Mechanization on American Agriculture," *Scientific Monthly,* LXIX (1949), 23; and Martin R. Cooper, Glen T. Barton, and Albert P. Brodell, *Progress of Farm Mechanization,* U.S. Department of Agriculture, Miscellaneous Publication 630, Washington, 1947.

FIGURE 101. The Symbol of Mechanized Agriculture: Plowing by Tractor. (Courtesy of the J. I. Case Company.)

FIGURE 102. Highly Mechanized Agriculture: The Preparation of the Seed-bed. (Courtesy of the American Petroleum Institute.)

FIGURE 103.   Highly Mechanized Agriculture: Dusting to Control Insects.
(Courtesy of the American Petroleum Institute.)

gradual one. The process went on smoothly and gradually in an
evolutionary manner, although it did move rapidly. For the most
part the changes followed one another in strict sequence. In some
sections of the country, however, and particularly in the plantation
areas of the southern region, the changes took place in a revolutionary manner. On the estates which produce such a large part
of the nation's fiber it was only after 1933, and in many cases after
Pearl Harbor, that machines began to replace the old labor-de-
vouring processes which had typified cotton production since
slavery times. Then quickly and abruptly, and without many of
the intervening steps, a highly mechanized system of preparing
the soil, cultivating the crops, and taking the harvest was substituted for the antiquated system of hoe culture and elementary
plow culture which long had been relied upon in the area.

For the nation as a whole the major trends connected with the

FIGURE 104. Mechanical Cotton Picker at Work in Oklahoma Fields. (Photo by courtesy of the Oklahoma Agricultural Extension Service.)

FIGURE 105. Self-Propelled Combines Harvesting Grain in the Western Part of the United States. (Courtesy of the Minneapolis-Moline Company.)

rapid shift from advanced plow culture to mechanized farming is portrayed in Figures 97, 98, 99, and 100. The first of these, Figure 97, shows the tremendous increase, since 1910, in the output of our farms, although simultaneous input of human labor was decreasing to a marked extent. As a result the output per man-hour more than kept pace with the total output of the farms, and both of them more than doubled in the forty-year period 1910 to 1950. Figure 98 supplements this analysis by making it clear that the increased use of power and machinery was the factor which made man's labor more productive, and the change in the type of farm power and equipment is brought out by Figure 99. Between 1910 and 1920, the use of draft animals reached its maximum and began to decline. (The number of horses and mules on farms reached a peak of 26,723,000 in 1918, after which the decrease was rapid and continuous until there were only 7,463,000 in 1950.) Simultaneously the use of tractors and tractor-powered equipment began its spectacular rise. (From approximately 1000 tractors on farms in 1910 the number rose to 50,000 in 1917, after which the figure shot up to 3,825,000 by 1950.) Between the time the United States was plunged into war by the attack upon Pearl Harbor and 1950, the number of tractors on the nation's farms had far more than doubled, while the increase in tractor-drawn equipment such as combines and mechanical corn pickers was of even greater proportions. (See Figure 100.) Similar spectacular changes in the use of motor trucks, electric milking machines, and dozens of other modern labor-saving devices were also helping to revolutionize life and labor on the American farm. (See Figures 101, 102, 103, 104, and 105.)

15

SOCIAL DIFFERENTIATION

Social groups, or the forms of association, are the units or cells out of which society is constructed; and the study of social differentiation, or the nature and development of social groups, is of primary importance in the study of society. Together with the study of social interaction, or the processes and activities of social groups, it makes up the central core of sociology. Recognition of the importance of the social group as the primary determinant of personality is now widespread. In essence, an individual's personality is a reflection of the groups to which he belongs. The associations of which one is a member serve as the forms in which his personality is molded. It is legitimate to paraphrase an old saying as follows: "Tell me what groups you belong to and I will tell you what you are." As Sorokin has put it in his important study of social mobility: "In order to know a man's social position, his family status, the state of which he is a citizen, his nationality, his religious group, his occupational group, his political party, his economic status, his race and so on must be known."[1] It is also impossible to determine an individual's status in society without knowing the groups to which he belongs, for the chief frames of references in society are: "(1) The indication of a man's relations to specific groups, (2) the relation of these groups to each other within a population, and (3) the relation of this population to other populations included in the human universe."[2]

Nature of the Social Group

Definitions of the sociological or social group are legion, although many authors make extensive use of these terms without

[1] P. A. Sorokin, *Social Mobility*, New York, Harper & Brothers, 1927, p. 5.
[2] *Ibid.*

specifically defining them.[3] Of those who do attempt definitions of the group, almost everyone advances his own. Thus MacIver has defined a group as a collection of social beings "who enter into distinctive social relationships with one another."[4] Eubank thinks of a group as an entity comprised of two or more persons in "psychic interaction."[5] To these might be added a long list of others. In fact, the term "social group" has been used in so many senses that Eubank, in an attempt to classify the usages, was able to distinguish categories as follows:

1. Ethno-anthropological
2. General social
3. Those based on cultural levels
4. Those based on structure
5. Those based on function
6. Those based on the extent of the social contact
7. Those based on the nature of the bond which holds the group together[6]

An adequate definition of social group, it seems to the writer, must utilize at least three elements: (1) plurality of persons or social beings; (2) social interaction between these individuals; and (3) social solidarity or cohesion, sometimes designated the "we feeling" among the members. The concept of plurality or combination is inherent in all groups, social or otherwise, and cannot be dispensed with.

Also, almost all writers seem to agree that in order to have a genuine social group social interaction is indispensable.[7] If this element is lacking, the term refers to a mere statistical entity, such as an age group, i.e., persons of the same age, and has no functional reality, does not refer to a real functioning unity. This point

[3] See, for example, Dwight Sanderson, *The Rural Community: The Natural History of a Sociological Group*, Boston, Ginn and Company, 1932; E. A. Ross, *Outlines of Sociology*, New York, D. Appleton-Century Company, 1924; and John H. Kolb and Edmund deS. Brunner, *A Study of Rural Society*, Boston, Houghton Mifflin Company, 1935.

[4] R. M. MacIver, *Society: A Textbook of Sociology*, New York, R. Long and R. R. Smith, Inc., 1937, p. 13.

[5] E. E. Eubank, *The Concepts of Sociology*, Boston, D. C. Heath & Company, 1932, p. 163.

[6] *Ibid.*, pp. 160–163. For other discussions of group classification see Dwight Sanderson, "Group Description," *Social Forces*, XVI (1938), 309–319, and "A Preliminary Group Classification Based on Structure," *Social Forces*, XVII (1938), 196–201.

[7] Eubank, *op. cit.*, p. 160; and Henry Pratt Fairchild (ed.), *Dictionary of Sociology*, New York, Philosophical Library, Inc., 1944, p. 133.

deserves elaboration. The social process is one of interaction, mutual awareness, stimulation, and reaction. Individuals isolated on separate islands could never constitute a real social group. In the social process each member of the group is aware of the other members, is influenced by them; and his reactions are not what they would be if he were alone. In turn he serves as a stimulus to others. For this reason the behavior of the group is considerably different from the sum total of the behavior of the various individuals taken separately. Such a statement is not intended to maintain the possibility of a group mind, but merely to insist that a number of persons by mutually conditioning one another's behavior give rise to a product different from one created by the same individuals when they are not interacting with one another.

But it is also important to note that interaction by itself is not sufficient to bring about a social group, a fact which is not always brought out.[8] For example, soldiers of opposing armies in hand-to-hand combat, or two prize fighters in the ring, certainly cannot be termed a social group, although there are present social interaction, mutual awareness, and reaction to stimuli. These cases illustrate the general point that conflict situations destroy and do not produce social groups. Only when there is genuine unity or cohesion between the interacting individuals, i.e., social solidarity, or "we feeling," can a social group be said to exist. Hence, it is pertinent to inquire, How is this unity or solidarity attained?

The famous French sociologist, Durkheim, has produced one of the most penetrating analyses of this phenomenon. His work has been elaborated by Sorokin, Zimmerman, and Galpin in their *Systematic Source Book in Rural Sociology.*[9] Unfortunately these authorities have failed to give proper emphasis to what Durkheim styled the "organic" form of social solidarity, omitting it from consideration almost altogether. Durkheim rightly distinguished two types of social cohesion between members of the group, one type arising out of similarities among the members (like attracts like), which he designated *mechanistic* solidarity, and a second type dependent upon division of social labor, specialization, and the

[8] This fact is overlooked by a great many authorities. Even Eubank, who once seemed aware of it, failed to include it in his final definition of the group referred to above.

[9] P. A. Sorokin, Carle C. Zimmerman, and Charles J. Galpin, *A Systematic Source Book in Rural Sociology,* Minneapolis, University of Minnesota Press, 1930–1932, 3 vols.

resulting interdependence of parts, which he styled *organic* solidarity.[10] Ross drew much the same distinction when he maintained
that group members must be aware either of "essential common
traits" or of a "momentous common interest."[11]

According to Durkheim, simple primitive groups owe their
unity almost entirely to such a degree of homogeneity that the
member of a primitive tribe comes near being a duplicate of every
other person in the group. As social differentiation proceeds and
division of labor and function takes place, unity based on similarities is gradually replaced by solidarity growing out of the
mutual interdependence of the parts, each of which by itself lacks
self-sufficiency.

Durkheim demonstrated the importance of his classification by
correlating the type of solidarity with other social characteristics.
His analysis of the fundamental nature of crime and punishment
is especially illuminating. Thus he shows that in a society in which
mechanistic solidarity is strong (such societies are exemplified by
primitive peoples and many rural communities as well) everyone
sees reflected in his own personality all the essential characteristics
of the group. For this reason in such a society great stress is placed
on conformity; and the one who seeks to develop personal beliefs
and actions meets with strong discouragement. Departures from
the traditional mores are dealt with severely. An offense against
one member is an offense against the entire group. Restrictions are
many so that violations are numerous; these meet with immediate
and passionate repression and punishment. Departures from the
customary in public and religious affairs are put down with the
most rigorous measures.

On the other hand, says Durkheim, when organic solidarity
(division of social labor) is at the basis of social cohesion, the
nature of crime is quite different. An offense against one is not
an abuse that affects all. Some persons in society can play the role
of mere interested spectators. In extreme cases organic solidarity
may cause law enforcement to become a contest between the of-
fenders and the officers of the law, with a considerable part of
the population acting as mere bystanders.

Sorokin, Zimmerman, and Galpin have carried on the analysis

[10] See chap. 2, footnote 36, for the distinction between Durkheim's terms corrected for modern usage; also George Simpson, *Emile Durkheim on the Division
of Labor in Society*, New York, The Macmillan Company, 1933, *passim*.

[11] Ross, *op. cit.*, p. 389.

of group solidarity much more in detail. Unfortunately they seem to have been concerned entirely with the concept of mechanistic solidarity when they set forth a list of fourteen traits of similarity which, according to them, alone are efficient in developing and bringing about solidarity or cohesion between the members of a social group. The "efficient" ties or bonds in their list follow:

1. Kinship and community of blood (real or assumed [totemic])
2. Marriage
3. Similarity in religious and magical beliefs and rites
4. Similarity in native language and mores
5. Common possession and utilization of land
6. Territorial proximity
7. Common responsibility
8. Community of occupational interests
9. Community of economic interests
10. Subjection to the same lord
11. Attachment to the same social institution or social agency
12. Common defense
13. Mutual aid
14. Living, experiencing, and acting together[12]

According to Sorokin, Zimmerman, and Galpin, at least one of these ties must be operating before a real social group is possible. They further classify social groups on the basis of the number of common social bonds possessed, styling those groups united by only one tie as *elementary*, those possessing two or more efficient social ties as *cumulative*. By means of ingenious diagrams the differences between the two are clearly portrayed. These authors also demonstrate that the traits may cluster in varying degrees, that some groups are united by almost all of them, others by but few. Cumulation of social bonds is naturally great in many primitive communities of early times, and also among the simpler present-day peoples, groups who remain in such a relatively simple cultural status that they are referred to as our contemporary ancestors. Many rural communities have retained many of their cumulative characteristics, particularly in those countries which have retained a village form of settlement. In many such instances the locality bond is reinforced by so many other ties that it is valid to refer to them as cumulative communities. Urban groupings on the other hand tend to be elementary in nature. They are

[12] *Op. cit.*, I, 307–308.

largely associations with specific purposes or, as the authors of the *Source Book* put it, functional associations. Others have referred to such associations as interest groups. As social differentiation proceeds, the cumulative groupings tend more and more to disappear and to be replaced with these interest groupings or functional associations. Even in rural societies, such as the contemporary United States with its isolated farms, cumulative groupings become very weak. All in all, the analysis of Sorokin, Zimmerman, and Galpin is one of the most penetrating studies in the field.

But despite their interesting and important analysis, these authors neglect the important role played by specialization and the division of labor and the resulting mutual interdependence of individuals. Organic solidarity, or the cohesion arising out of the lack of self-sufficiency of the individual, plays an equally important role with mechanistic solidarity as a basis for social groupings, even in rural society, so that the decline of the cumulative community is not fully reflected in a loss of solidarity in social groupings. In fact, organic solidarity is the basis of the marriage group —neither man nor woman alone being sufficient to perform the all-important function of reproduction—and is thus indispensable in the family, the most fundamental group in society. Because it is present in the family the importance of organic solidarity is great in the rural as well as in the urban portions of society. To a considerable extent the decrease in mechanistic solidarity has been offset by an increase in organic solidarity of the rural group.

Thus in summary the concept social group seems to involve at least three elements: (1) plurality of social beings or persons; (2) social interaction between these individuals; and (3) social solidarity among the members, a unity which may be achieved as the result of bonds of similarity or as a result of the dependence arising from specialization and division of labor in all the social spheres from the biological to the economic.[13] As society has proceeded from its more simple primitive stages to its highly complex superurban expressions, mechanistic solidarity has become

[13] Ross has listed the following as factors which promote the "we feeling": crisis, harmony of interests, conversation, pleasuring together, and concerted rhythmic response. *Op. cit.*, p. 85. See also the very different but highly suggestive approach outlined by Charles P. Loomis in "The Nature of Rural Social Systems— A Typological Analysis," *Rural Sociology*, XV (1950), 156–174.

less important and organic solidarity more important in the cohesion of its social groupings.[14]

Primary and Secondary Groups

Guided by a wide variety of interests, scholars have developed numerous classifications of social groups. For many purposes the work of Charles H. Cooley is of paramount importance in this connection. Cooley was primarily interested in the intimacy of the relations between members of the group. He early stressed the important social role of the *primary* group, primary in the sense that it was the source of the individual's personality traits. By definition this is a form of relationship "characterized by intimate face-to-face association and co-operation." It is best represented by the family, the neighborhood, and the play groups. According to Cooley, human nature is largely determined through the social contacts obtained through membership in these three primary groups.[15]

To accompany Cooley's primary groups, other sociologists have completed a dichotomy by designating groups lacking in face-to-face relationships as *secondary*, or derivative.[16] These two categories represent one of the most fundamental classifications in sociology. As will be shown later, primary groups are of overwhelming significance in rural society, of much less relative importance in cities.

Locality Groups

Another important basis for classifying groups is that of the territory or area occupied by the members, for "man in his relationships with his fellows always divides the earth's surface up into areas of mutual aid, common living, and human association. In addition to the family, which is the smallest social grouping whose interests and activities converge in a definite locale, human societies are always segmented into neighborhood and community

---

[14] For a more detailed discussion of this long-continued trend, see T. Lynn Smith and Vernon J. Parenton, "Social Cohesion and Social Control," in Joseph S. Roucek (ed.), *Social Control*, New York, D. Van Nostrand Company, 1947, chap. 5.

[15] Charles H. Cooley, *Social Organization*, New York, Charles Scribner's Sons, 1925, pp. 23–26.

[16] Cf. L. L. Bernard, *Introduction to Social Psychology*, New York, Henry Holt & Company, 1926, p. 411; and W. A. Terpenning, *Village and Open-Country Neighborhoods*, New York, D. Appleton-Century Company, 1931, p. 3.

groups. Like the family, each of these occupies a definite part of the earth's surface and is an area of human association. The three together comprise the fundamental cells and tissues out of which the State and the Great Society are constituted. Even though the latter may disintegrate or fall into a state of anarchy, the smaller locality groups remain."[17] Thus locality groups form another important category of associational types, and, incidentally, one which is of particular importance in the study of rural sociology. Locality groups are characterized by having uppermost the factor of territorial proximity. Like the family and other primary groups, they are forms of association; but unlike primary groups, they have the territorial basis as a fundamental constituent. Within the category three important types of groups may be distinguished: neighborhoods, communities, and states. In rural sociology the roles of the neighborhoods and communities are of basic importance, although it should not be forgotten that the rural part is an indispensable portion of any state.

The Neighborhood

Neighborhoods are the smallest locality groups. They are small clusters of families. Such groupings are present to some extent in cities, but they are of fundamental importance in rural districts. The neighborhood has been well defined as the next group beyond the family which has sociological significance. Williams uses the term to refer to a number of families who are conscious of "intimate relations with one another."[18] Literally, it would seem to mean the area within which neighboring, i.e., mutual aid, is extended or takes place among families. Small localities in which country people live and know each other by their first names are neighborhoods. Within the territorial limits of the neighborhood, primary group relationships find their first expression outside the family.

In colonial days neighborhoods were the fundamental areas of association for rural people, who constituted the great bulk of the population. In those days neighborhoods were usually eco-

[17] T. Lynn Smith, "The Locality Group Structure of Brazil," *American Sociological Review*, IX (1944), 41. See also Frank D. Alexander and Lowry Nelson, *Rural Social Organization in Goodhue County, Minnesota*, Minnesota AES Bulletin 401, St. Paul, 1947, pp. 10–11; and Selz C. Mayo, "Testing Criteria of Rural Locality Groups," *Rural Sociology*, XIV (1949), 317–318.

[18] James M. Williams, *Our Rural Heritage*, New York, Alfred A. Knopf, Inc., 1925, p. 21.

nomically self-sufficient.[19] The families in the neighborhoods possessed so many traits in common that they constituted a cumulative social group of a high order of cohesion. Frequently, the families of a neighborhood were all related to one another. Nearly always they had known each other a lifetime. Differentiation along economic, religious, occupational, and educational lines was so slight as to be negligible. The folkways, mores, and traditional morals attained a high degree of homogeneity.

Revolutionary changes have occurred since colonial times, but within the United States neighborhoods still persist and are of great variety. Even today it is difficult for a family to be successful on the farm without the mutual aid of neighbors, even though, in the present-day organization of rural life, the function of neighborhoods has atrophied considerably from its dominant position in colonial days. But though neighborhood awareness has weakened, neighborhoods have not all disappeared.

Perhaps the best examples of neighborhoods are to be found where geographic barriers tend to segregate a small group of people. Small isolated mountain valleys, coves, and tiny islands often provide the physical setting in which the best examples of neighborhoods are produced. General observations throughout the nation are in line with the finding of an intensive study of Frederick County, Maryland, that "as the productivity of the land decreases, the number of neighborhoods increases."[20]

But neighborhoods have grown up and persisted without the presence of any marked physical barriers. As Galpin has pointed out, the social organization of farm settlements usually has been scaled down to the neighborhood.[21] In all parts of the nation, the families tributary to a local institution such as an open-country church, a crossroads store, a one-room school, or an organization such as grange, club, etc., constitute genuine neighborhoods. Thus, for example, thirty to forty families in an area of about five square miles may maintain a public school; and about this institution enough other activities may be polarized to make it a real neighborhood. Other neighborhood groups may be integrated about a

[19] *Ibid.*, pp. 21–23; cf. Sanderson, *The Rural Community*, p. 501; and N. L. Sims, *Elements of Rural Sociology*, New York, Thomas Y. Crowell Company, 1928, pp. 583–584.

[20] S. Earl Grigsby and Harold Hoffsommer, *Rural Social Organization of Frederick County, Maryland*, Maryland AES Bulletin A-51, College Park, 1949, p. 35.

[21] C. J. Galpin, *Rural Life*, New York, D. Appleton-Century Company, 1918, p. 97.

cotton gin, a general store, a cheese factory, a grain elevator, or an open-country church.

In a study of 140 village-centered rural communities located in all regions of the United States, made in 1924 by the Institute of Social and Religious Research, a total of 513 neighborhoods was discovered. Schools, churches, and trade service were the nuclei for most of these groupings, although social activities, industry, race, and family also were of importance. By 1930 a resurvey of these same communities showed a 16 percent decline, or a net loss of 84 neighborhoods.[22] This process was not arrested by the depression; and by 1936 the number decreased to 328, according to the results of the second resurvey.[23] Interestingly enough, the decline of the neighborhood during the years 1924 to 1936 was more pronounced in the South than elsewhere,[24] a situation undoubtedly due in no small measure to the fact that the incidence of the change from the old colonial and frontier neighborhood basis of organization got under way in this section of the country at a later date than in the other regions.

Prior to the institute's extensive researches, a number of important studies of the neighborhood were conducted in several states. The first of these was made in Dane County, Wisconsin, by John H. Kolb.[25] In essence, the methodology employed consisted of discovering the name given the locality in which the farmers lived. Each farm family was asked the question: "By what name is the country neighborhood called in which you live?" It was assumed that "when a family recognized some grouping as its own, and was willing to confess this name as it would its own family name, there was evidence of group consciousness and unity."[26] The possibility of true groups with no name was recognized, but the fact that the place name might be void of sociological meaning was not taken into account.

[22] E. deS. Brunner and J. H. Kolb, *Rural Social Trends*, New York, McGraw-Hill Book Company, 1933, pp. 67–72; see also E. deS. Brunner, *Village Communities*, New York, Doubleday, Doran & Company, 1928; and E. deS. Brunner, Gwendolyn S. Hughes, and Marjorie Patten, *American Agricultural Villages*, New York, Doubleday, Doran & Company, 1927.

[23] Edmund deS. Brunner and Irving Lorge, *Rural Trends in Depression Years*, New York, Columbia University Press, 1937, p. 93.

[24] *Ibid.*, p. 94.

[25] *Rural Primary Groups*, Wisconsin AES Research Bulletin 51, Madison, 1921. See John H. Kolb and Douglas G. Marshall, *Neighborhood-Community Relationships in Rural Society*, Wisconsin AES Research Bulletin 154, Madison, 1944, for a restudy of the neighborhoods in the same area.

[26] *Rural Primary Groups*, p. 6.

In Otsego County, New York, a study by Sanderson and Thompson revealed that neighborhoods continue to function as important social groupings, as many as five being found in one-half of a single township. Furthermore, 32 percent of the heads of families in these locality groups were intimately associated with one another, and 25 percent of the families were living on farms which had been first settled by their direct ancestors. The intimate acquaintance of these families with one another over a long period of years is indicated by the fact that over 40 percent of the farmers had been born on the farms they occupied.[27] Because of these and other data Sanderson has strongly contended that Sorokin, Zimmerman, and Galpin have overstressed the decline of cumulative groupings among American farmers.[28]

A survey of the neighborhoods in Boone County, Missouri, was made by E. L. Morgan with the assistance of Owen Howells. Using much the same technique as Kolb's, these students found in 1924 a total of fifty-nine neighborhoods in this county. Families were found to cluster about the district school more frequently than around any other agency. That the areas tributary to these schools represented genuine neighborhoods was evidenced by the fact that social contacts were largely confined to interaction with other families of the same locality.[29] A resurvey of the same area in 1931 found forty of the original neighborhoods and fifteen new ones.[30]

Another important early sounding into the neighborhood structure of the nation was conducted in Wake County, North Carolina, by Carl C. Taylor and Carle C. Zimmerman.[31] But these students came to the conclusion that integral sociological groups having a geographic basis were practically lacking. The study of these authors exposed the weakness of Kolb's methodology, without, however, demonstrating that neighborhoods were nonexistent.

[27] Dwight Sanderson and Warren S. Thompson, *The Social Areas of Otsego County, New York*, Cornell AES Bulletin 422, Ithaca, 1923, p. 14.

[28] Sanderson, *Rural Social and Economic Areas in Central New York*, Cornell AES Bulletin 614, Ithaca, 1934, p. 90; and "The Rural Community in the United States as an Elementary Group," *Rural Sociology*, I (1936), 142–150.

[29] E. L. Morgan and Owen Howells, *Rural Population Groups*, Missouri AES Research Bulletin 74, Columbia, 1925.

[30] Brunner and Kolb, *op. cit.*, p. 326.

[31] Carle C. Zimmerman and Carl C. Taylor, *Rural Organization: A Study of Primary Groups in Wake County, N.C.*, North Carolina AES Bulletin 245, Raleigh, 1922.

In the period following the Second World War many excellent community and county surveys have been carried on by rural sociologists throughout the United States. Almost without exception these studies show that the neighborhood still survives, but in a somewhat changed and weakened position as compared with that it enjoyed a quarter of a century ago. For example, a study of Hamilton County, Iowa, revealed that the county still "has 108 open-country neighborhoods, identified by the families living in them as locality groups. Most of these small groups of families depend mostly upon proximity to hold them together. Few if any are nearly as self-sufficient social units as they were in settlement days or one or two generations ago."[32] Another survey, in Seward County, Nebraska, found that "many farm families today are on intimate terms with families several miles away as well as with people on the next farm. They now choose their friends by similarity of interests as well as nearby residence. . . . A group of families living contiguously is not always as compact socially as it once was."[33] Likewise a Minnesota study featured the fact that neighborhoods were less important and village-centered communities more important than formerly;[34] one in Indiana concluded that "village-centered trade area communities, offering primary and secondary services, have substantially supplanted the small neighborhood groupings as meaningful areas of social togetherness";[35] and one in New York found that "rural neighborhoods are not so numerous as in earlier days."[36] In Missouri a sounding in one part of the state showed that "today, in many localities which once were centers for neighboring, there is little of the informal activity that once existed among families,"[37] while another, of a county "near the heart of the Missouri Ozarks," emphasized the extent to which the primary-group relationships of the neighborhood con-

[32] Paul J. Jehlik and Ray E. Wakeley, *Rural Organization in Process: A Case Study of Hamilton County, Iowa,* Iowa AES Research Bulletin 365, Ames, 1949, p. 136.

[33] A. H. Anderson, *A Study of Rural Communities and Organizations in Seward County, Nebraska,* Nebraska AES Bulletin 405, Lincoln, 1951, p. 11.

[34] Alexander and Nelson, *op. cit.,* p. 62.

[35] Paul J. Jehlik and J. Edwin Losey, *Rural Social Organization in Henry County, Indiana,* Indiana AES Bulletin 568, Lafayette, 1951, p. 57.

[36] Donald G. Hay and Robert A. Polson, *Rural Organizations in Oneida County, New York,* Cornell AES Bulletin 871, Ithaca, 1951, p. 5.

[37] Lawrence M. Hepple and Margaret L. Bright, *Social Changes in Shelby County, Missouri,* Missouri AES Research Bulletin 456, Columbia, 1950, p. 25.

tinued to fill the lives of the people.[38] Recent studies in the South
bear out the fact that the neighborhood still retains a considerable
part of its vitality in much of the region. Thus an article in *Rural
Sociology* reports that Rabun County, Georgia, still has a "pattern
of social organization that is typical of the mountain societies
throughout the Southern Highlands." It is that of a self-sufficing
folk, simple in manners, greatly attached to home and family, putting great store by kinship and visiting and "highly integrated
[into] neighborhoods that are centered around a rural church or
a one-room rural school."[39] In addition, a restudy of Wake County,
North Carolina, scene of the early survey by Taylor and Zimmerman, revealed that neighborhoods have persisted to a remarkable
degree. "About two-thirds of the [133] neighborhood areas as delineated in the earlier study were identified in the restudy with respect to both name and approximate location." In addition, the
fact that seventy-four other areas of primary-group relationships
were located raised some questions in the minds of the investigators relative to the adequacy of their methodology.[40]

In general the South is the most rural portion of the nation.
Therefore, it is not surprising that the neighborhood is more important in the South than in any other section of the United
States,[41] and that this region furnishes a large variety of neighborhood types. For example, in south Louisiana, where a native population of French descent and culture is of more than usual interest,
two good specimens of neighborhoods are to be found in the
"bayou settlement" and the brûlée. Both of these have unique geographic bases. Throughout Louisiana's low-lying alluvial sections
there are to be found many tiny fingerlike portions of higher lands.
These lie along the levees which were created by overflow from
the bayous, and many of them protrude far out into the swamps
and marshes. The fertile alluvial soils of these bayou banks are attractive to agriculturists, and the small line village settlements

[38] Ronald B. Almack and Lawrence M. Hepple, *Rural Social Organization in
Dent County, Missouri,* Missouri AES Research Bulletin 458, Columbia, 1950,
pp. 44–45, 49–51, and 59.
[39] Robert E. Galloway, "A Contrast in the Rural Social Organization of Rabun
County, Georgia and Franklin County, Washington," *Rural Sociology,* XIII (1948),
390.
[40] See Selz C. Mayo and Robert McD. Bobbitt, *Rural Organization: A Restudy
of Locality Groups in Wake County, North Carolina,* North Carolina AES Technical Bulletin 95, Raleigh, 1951, pp. 19–35.
[41] Cf. Sanderson, *The Rural Community,* p. 501.

along these natural levees constitute excellent examples of neigh-borhoods.[42] In the same sections, far out in remote swamp areas, other small portions of higher ground are frequent, and on these will be found settlements designated as brûlées, a name probably arising from the manner of clearing the land of trees. The settle-ments in these burned-over areas also constitute excellent exam-ples of neighborhoods. Several hundred thousand inhabitants residing in such settlements have preserved to this day their old patterns of mutual aid and helpfulness.

In the alluvial portions of the South where large-scale agricul-ture is the rule and where the three-way association of good land, the Negro, and the plantation is most evident, many plantation units make up genuine neighborhoods. (In fact, many of them so completely circumscribe the lives of the families of croppers and tenants residing on them—a school, a church, and a store are often integral portions of the plantation, and the Negroes have their own burial societies and other organizations—that they might rank as communities.)[43] A situation typical in this respect of large areas in the South was described by T. J. Woofter, Jr., in his valuable study of St. Helena Island in the South.[44] Another of the most important soundings made into the social life in southern plantation areas is represented by the work of Arthur Raper. So important was the neighborhood in Green and Macon counties, Georgia, that even the white planters lived in well-defined neighborhoods.[45]

A study of LaSalle Parish, Louisiana, one of the "hill" sections of the state, an area similar in most essentials to the upland por-tions of neighboring states, revealed the importance of the neigh-borhood in these small-farming upland areas where the bulk of the South's rural white population resides. In LaSalle Parish the popu-lation of small farmers was found to be unevenly distributed over the land. Farm families were clustered together in little groups along the beds of the small streams which flow through the area. Kinship seemed to be the most important basis for grouping, as

[42] For a survey of one of these "bayou settlements" somewhat intermediate be-tween a neighborhood and a community, see T. Lynn Smith, "An Analysis of Rural Social Organization Among the French-Speaking People of Southern Louisi-ana," *Journal of Farm Economics*, XVI (1934), 680–688.

[43] Cf. Charles S. Johnson, *Shadow of the Plantation*, Chicago, University of Chicago Press, 1934.

[44] T. J. Woofter, Jr., *Black Yeomanry*, New York, Henry Holt & Company, 1930, p. 8.

[45] Arthur Raper, *Preface to Peasantry*, Chapel Hill, University of North Carolina Press, 1936, p. 91.

many as four brothers and their families living in immediate proximity to one another. Frequently married sons and daughters built their homes in the immediate vicinity of the parental roof.[46]

Many factors have contributed to keep these small neighborhood groups of fundamental importance in the South. Among these the lack of facilities for communication is important. The retarded educational system also has been influential. But many other more obscure factors are involved. For example, because of the persistence of primitive modes of travel, the circuit system in church organization has prevailed and persisted much more in the South than in other portions of the country. It is true that the circuit rider has disappeared with the coming of the automobile, but even at the present time it is not unusual for one minister to preach to several congregations each Sunday. Attachment to these small, widely distributed local congregations does its part to assist in keeping locality groups small, i.e., in the neighborhood stage. In any case the neighborhood still performs a vital function in the social organization of rural life, serving as the nucleus in which much of the farm folks' social activities are organized.

The Community

Communities are also locality groups. In general they are larger than neighborhoods, although in many cases it is difficult to draw an exact dividing line between the two. As Sanderson has written:

Frequently it is difficult to say whether a given area is a community or a neighborhood, in the same way that it is not always possible to distinguish between a species and a variety of organisms. In some cases smaller communities are evidently being gradually absorbed into a larger community, thus being reduced to the status of neighborhoods. In a new country where neighborhood centers, or hamlets, are far apart, the reverse may be true, and they may be growing into communities. Again, some communities seem to have no one center, but may have two or three foci of interests, or the institutions may be scattered and no distinct community centers may exist.[47]

Communities are also more self-sufficient than neighborhoods. Today the neighborhood seems to be passing and the community ap-

[46] T. Lynn Smith and Martha Ray Fry, *The Population of a Selected "Cut-Over" Area in Louisiana*, Louisiana AES Bulletin 268, Baton Rouge, 1936, p. 6.
[47] *The Rural Community*, p. 485.

pears as the most important unit in the organization of rural life.

There are many difficulties in the way of a satisfactory definition of the community and especially the rural community. Abstractly, MacIver's definition of community may be the most satisfactory. He states: "Any circle of people who live together, who belong together, so that they share, not this or that particular interest, but a whole set of interests wide enough and complete enough to include their lives, is a community."[48] But it is frequently the case that the most logical definition of a concept is not the most useful one. On the basis of MacIver's definition, who can determine the territorial limits of any community? Who knows whether the locality, the county, the state, the section, the region, or even the nation can qualify as a community? For practical purposes another definition of community has proved most fruitful in the study of rural sociology. This is the one developed by C. J. Galpin. In order to grasp its significance, a hasty sketch of the background of its development is necessary.

In the United States prior to World War I some effort was made to determine the limits of the rural community. Several scholars set its boundaries in terms of the "team-haul." This was for the reason that farmers in horse-and-wagon days hauled their products to the center they found most convenient.[49] Later, when the town-country conflict was rampant, the farmer frequently was referred to as "the man without a community." To those who were familiar with the village settlement patterns so common in Europe and Asia, the prevalence of the scattered farmsteads in America obscured the real nature of rural locality groupings. The superficial observer, depending upon practical experience, was as likely to miss the nature of the American rural community as he was to identify the whale with the fishes instead of with the mammals. Under such circumstances it is not surprising that the political boundaries were established in a hit-and-miss fashion, with no consideration whatsoever of the natural groupings of rural society. Thus tax districts, school attendance areas, etc., were drawn in a very artificial and arbitrary manner. This procedure not only failed to capitalize on the actual group structure of society but helped to keep community and neighborhood groupings from becoming as closely knit and strong as they otherwise might have become. For-

[48] *Op. cit.*, pp. 9–10.

[49] Cf. Kenyon L. Butterfield, *The Farmer and the New Day*, New York, The Macmillan Company, 1919, p. 144.

tunately the trained observer at last came to look more closely than the superficial one had done: just as the whale came to be correctly classified with its fellow mammals, so the real nature of the American rural community came to be known. To Dr. C. J. Galpin belongs the distinction of being the first to see the real nature of our rural community, and of being the one to develop a practical method of delimiting its boundaries. Through his experiences as a rural schoolteacher, a resident on the "skims" of the Great Lakes cutover area, and an organizer for a milk-condensing plant in Walworth County, Wisconsin, Galpin learned that the farmer was not without his community. Later at the University of Wisconsin his studies developed an objective definition of community and formulated a relatively accurate method for determining its limits.[50] These proved to be of such fundamental importance that they merit careful consideration.

Walworth County in Wisconsin was the area used in Galpin's classic study. The objectives are clearly stated in the following words: "Each village or city was to be the center of information and the problem was how far out among the farm homes the village served any social purpose. From the point of view of the village, the problem was one of getting at the land area of village influence; from the point of view of the country man, it was learned that farms were connected with the same village."[51]

Large working maps of the country were prepared, assistants were appointed in each village, and merchants were interviewed and asked to indicate on the map the distance from which farmers came to the village to trade. Bankers, operators of milk stations, ministers, teachers, and others were approached with similar requests. This information provided rough sketches of the areas of influence of each village, and a portion of the map slightly larger than the indicated boundaries became the working map for each community. Printed forms were next prepared, one for each farmhouse as spotted on the map, to determine the following points of information: name of village; name of farmer; township; section; number of farms in section; which village the family depended upon for banking, dry goods, groceries, milk factory, high school, church, village newspaper, and village library.

[50] See C. J. Galpin, "My Drift into Rural Sociology," *Rural Sociology*, II (1937), 117–122.
[51] C. J. Galpin, *The Social Anatomy of an Agricultural Community*, Wisconsin AES Bulletin 34, Madison, 1915, p. 3.

When the data were secured for each of the farm homes, final maps of the country were prepared as follows:

The trade map was made first by merging the dry goods and grocery maps which nearly coincided. A large piece of corrugated paper board was placed upon a copy of the county base map. Each farm home trading at Elkhorn, for example, was marked and then a pin stuck in the spot. A thread was run around the outside of these pins, following from pin to pin so as to include the least amount of territory while enclosing every pin. This thread line became the boundary of the trade zone. After the trade zone of each of the twelve centers was marked out in this way, the common territory where zones overlap, with homes trading at more than one village, was colored alike and called neutral ground. Each community was given its own color. Then round, white seals were used to designate the homes that were found to use the same trade center. In like manner each set of maps was made in water colors.[52]

Twelve trade zones were discovered surrounding these twelve villages, running in irregular lines, paying no regard to some political boundaries and overlapping others. The survey also showed eleven banking zones, seven local newspaper zones, twelve milk zones, twelve church zones, nine high-school zones, and four library zones.

Galpin concluded:

It is difficult, if not impossible, to avoid the conclusion that the trade zone about one of these rather complete agricultural civic centers forms the boundary of an actual, if not legal, community, within which the apparent entanglement of human life is resolved into a fairly unitary system of interrelatedness. The fundamental community is a composite of many expanding and contracting feature communities possessing the characteristic pulsating instability of all real life.[53]

This objective method of delimiting the boundaries of a rural community has received widespread acceptance and use in rural social investigations. Very early a small publication giving detailed instructions for locating the rural community was included in the *Cornell Reading Course for the Farm*.[54] Subsequently a long series

---

[52] *Ibid.*, pp. 5–6.
[53] *Ibid.*, pp. 18–19.
[54] Dwight Sanderson, "Locating the Rural Community," *Cornell Country Life Series*, Ithaca, 1920.

of studies at Cornell used this concept of community and utilized similar methods for locating its boundaries.[55] Other studies were continued at Wisconsin. John H. Kolb mapped the boundaries of the neighborhoods of Dane County[56] and later located the service areas of villages and towns in Dane, Walworth, and Waupaca counties.[57] In the meantime investigators in other states were also employing the concept and technique. Zimmerman and Taylor studied both white and colored groupings of North Carolina;[58] in Missouri E. L. Morgan and Owen Howells mapped the primary population groups, both white and colored, church membership areas, trade areas, blacksmith areas, lodge membership areas, and banking areas for Boone County. Out of the blending of these various service areas there developed what they called the "fused community."[59] Three studies by A. E. Taylor and F. R. Yoder, made in the state of Washington, all plotted the areas of various communities and neighborhoods.[60] And the Institute of Social and Religious Research in its investigation of American agricultural villages mapped the areas of 140 villages located in almost all sections of the United States.[61]

Among the better of the studies are one of the rural communities of Chilton County, Alabama,[62] and another of those in Covington County, Mississippi.[63] In part, both of these were a response to

[55] Cf. Sanderson and Thompson, *op. cit.;* Gladys M. Kensler and Bruce L. Melvin, *A Partial Sociological Study of Dryden, New York,* Cornell AES Bulletin 504, Ithaca, 1930; Bruce L. Melvin, *The Sociology of a Village and Its Surrounding Territory,* Cornell AES Bulletin 523, Ithaca, 1931; Glenn A. Bakkum and Bruce L. Melvin, *Social Relationships of Slaterville Springs—Brooktondale Area, Tompkins County, New York,* Cornell AES Bulletin 501, Ithaca, 1930; and Ray E. Wakeley, *The Communities of Schuyler County, New York,* 1927, Cornell AES Bulletin 524, Ithaca, 1931.

[56] *Op. cit.*

[57] *Service Relations of Town and Country,* Wisconsin AES Research Bulletin 58, Madison, 1923; see also *Trends of Country Neighborhoods,* University of Wisconsin AES Research Bulletin 120, Madison, 1933.

[58] *Op. cit.*

[59] *Op. cit.*

[60] *Rural Social Organization in Whitman County,* Washington AES Bulletin 203, Pullman, 1926; *Rural Social Organization in Whatcom County,* Washington AES Bulletin 215, Pullman, 1927; and *Rural Social Organization in Clark County,* Washington AES Bulletin 225, Pullman, 1928.

[61] See Brunner, Hughes, and Patten, *op. cit.,* chap. 2.

[62] Irwin T. Sanders and Douglas Ensminger, *Alabama Rural Communities: A Study of Chilton County,* Alabama College Bulletin 136, Montevallo, 1940.

[63] Harold Hoffsommer and Herbert Pryor, *Neighborhoods and Communities in Covington County, Mississippi,* Washington, United States Department of Agriculture, 1941.

an increasing demand that the natural groupings of society be known and used in the organization of federal and state activity programs at the local level.[64]

This is a very encouraging trend, for rural America has suffered keenly from the lack of a strong, well-integrated, and clearly defined rural community. This deficiency has exercised a retarding influence in practically every important aspect of our economic and especially our social life. For example, the vast labyrinth of local government, the highly artificial nature of political boundaries, and the fact that rural government is the "dark continent" of American government are partly due to the indeterminate nature of the local community. In the field of education the schools have suffered from the same deficiency—there have been no sharply differentiated social boundaries that might be taken as the limits of school attendance and administrative units. Economic, recreational, and religious functions in rural areas have also been adversely affected by the confused nature of rural locality groupings.

All the factors responsible for our confused pattern of rural locality groupings have not been identified and measured. As yet there has been no thoroughgoing analysis of the evolution and present status of the American neighborhood and community. It seems apparent, however, that one important reason for the lack of clearly defined and well-integrated community and neighborhood units in rural America is due to the settlement pattern used in arranging the population on the land. Where scattered farmsteads are used, community lines are necessarily less distinct than where farmers' homes are clustered together as in the European farm village. But in part the nebulous state of American community outlines is due to the failure of governmental, educational, religious, economic, and other institutions to play their part in the development of distinct and integrated community units. Where attendance, taxation, and service districts are marked out in a haphazard manner without respect to social groupings, weak as these may be,

[64] In this connection, see Conrad Taeuber, "Some Recent Developments in Sociological Work in the Department of Agriculture," *American Sociological Review*, X (1945), 169–175; see also C. R. Hoffer and D. L. Gibson, *The Community Situation as It Affects Agricultural Extension Work*, Michigan AES Special Bulletin 312, East Lansing, 1941; John B. Holt, *Rural Neighborhoods and Communities of Lee County, Alabama, and Their Significance for Land-Use Planning*, Washington, United States Department of Agriculture, 1941; and Howard W. Beers, Robin M. Williams, John S. Page, and Douglas Ensminger, *Community Land-Use Planning Committees*, Kentucky AES Bulletin 417, Lexington, 1941.

the results are not conducive to the development of a stronger community consciousness and life.

Trends

The locality group structure of the United States is undergoing such definite changes that it seems safe to say that a more definite type of rural community is emerging. Social scientists who have been studying human relations in rural areas have built up a considerable amount of tested information relative to the changes that are occurring. In a comprehensive study[65] of the changes taking place when World War II broke out, the writer identified nine principal trends that were under way in rural America. These are as follows: (1) The rural community is expanding in size; (2) the neighborhood and the community as well are both losing exclusive claim to the loyalty and patronage of the individual farm family; (3) neighborhoods are not doomed to extinction but probably will find their principal role as an integral part of the enlarged community; (4) communities are developing complementary and supplementary relationships among themselves, are allowing the neighborhood to play a definite role, and are seeing the individual families participate in the activities of the great society in an extra-community capacity; (5) the family is gradually dividing its attachments and loyalty among the surrounding neighborhood, the encompassing community, and the centers of industry and trade whose influences envelop many rural communities; (6) cohesion within the community is rapidly shifting from the spontaneous type based on social similarities to a more consciously live-and-let-live type based on specialization and division of labor; (7) class differences are becoming more sharply defined and even more of the caste element is being observed; (8) social conflict is becoming more prevalent, but also more intermittent, less deep and cutting; and (9) old informal mutual-aid practices are giving way to types of coöperation based on contractual relationships.

A decade has passed since these generalizations were formulated, and many revolutionary changes have taken place in American society. Nevertheless, with the possible exception of (7), these

[65] Done as one of the reports in connection with a study of rural education by George A. Works and Simon A. Lesser, *Rural America Today*, Chicago, University of Chicago Press, 1942. A summary of this study was published in T. Lynn Smith, "The Role of the Community in American Rural Life," *Journal of Educational Sociology*, XIV (1941), 387–400.

propositions all seem to be as valid today as they were ten years ago. Class differences may be becoming more well defined, but the caste element, "the hardening of the social arteries," probably is not becoming any more pronounced in American rural society.

In the early decades of the atomic age the emerging rural community in the United States has the following indispensable characteristics:

1. It is a definite geographic area—it is a social group with a specific territorial basis. Galpin's method of determining the limits of this area seems most useful for the present.

2. It is also the social interaction of the people—persons, families, and other social groups in the area—including general assent to the proposition that the welfare of all the people in the area is inextricably tied up with the fortunes of the community as a whole.

3. Finally, it is a level of social relationships attained by pyramiding from the person to the family, from the family to the neighborhood, and from the neighborhood to the community.

16

SOCIAL STRATIFICATION

Social Classes and Castes

Although the terms "class" and "caste" are used frequently in sociological literature, their connotations are by no means universally agreed upon. It is certain, however, that there is in existence no Utopian society in which class lines are entirely obliterated; every known society is stratified to some extent. This is to say that some members of every society enjoy more rights and privileges, consume more goods and services, acquire more prestige and honor, receive more authority, and have more duties and obligations than other members of the same society. Society is divided into layers, some of which occupy a higher position than others.

It is a rather generally accepted practice to refer to these layers as social classes. Inequalities in wealth and income, therefore, are evidences of economic stratification; the existence of social ranks within a group, some members enjoying more authority and prestige, more honors and titles than others, is a proof of sociopolitical stratification; and a situation in which some occupations are preferred to others, in which some types of work are considered more honorable, dignified, refined, and uplifting than others, and in which those engaging in some activities have authority over those employed at other tasks is a demonstration of occupational stratification.[1] Used in the above sense, the term "class" means no more than a number of individuals in the same society whose economic, occupational, and political statuses are closely similar.[2] Under such circumstances social status refers to:

[1] Cf. P. A. Sorokin, *Social Mobility*, New York, Harper & Brothers, 1927, pp. 11–13; Sorokin's work is the classic study in this field. An important recent treatment of this subject is Paul K. Hatt, "Occupation and Social Stratification," *American Journal of Sociology*, LV (1950), 533–543.

[2] P. A. Sorokin and Carle C. Zimmerman, *Principles of Rural-Urban Sociology*, New York, Henry Holt & Company, 1929, p. 61.

. . . a hierarchic division of society into social classes which (1) differ both quantitatively and qualitatively in their social privileges and obligations. . . . (2) The material goods and services utilized by members of the classes considered not only differ quantitatively and qualitatively, but they are consumed by varying proportions of members of these classes. (3) Associated with these objective differences is a subjective differentiation in the characteristic degree of respect, prestige, and admiration expected by and accorded to members of the several classes. (4) The more pronounced the differentiation in the foregoing respects, the greater will be the tendency for differing class ideologies to appear in, and to be generally recognized as characteristic of, the thinking of the members of the several classes.[3]

For the author of this text the term "social class" has a very specific meaning. It denotes, to begin with, a number of individuals in a given society who have closely similar occupational, economic, and sociopolitical status, interests, and prestige. In addition, these persons must have become aware of the fact that they are on approximately the same social level, they must recognize that their well-being is intricately bound up with that of their fellows, and they must be willing to make common front with the others. In other words, along with similarity in social status, a class consciousness or solidarity is necessary before a genuine social class may be said to exist. The first part of this definition is not different from that discussed in the preceding paragraph, but the second deserves additional elaboration.

The consciousness of kind of the various social classes seems to be functionally related to the basic economic functions performed by their respective members. For simplicity in discussing this matter only three categories, namely, the upper, the middle, and the

---

[3] Edgar A. Schuler, "The Present Social Status of American Farm Tenants," *Rural Sociology*, III (1938), 21. P. A. Sorokin, *Social and Cultural Dynamics*, New York, American Book Company, 1937, III, 18–21, should be consulted about social privileges and obligations of the various classes; Faith M. Williams and Carle C. Zimmerman, *Studies of Family Living in the United States and Other Countries*, Miscellaneous Publication 223, United States Department of Agriculture, Washington, 1935, is an exhaustive bibliography on studies of living standards; and Carle C. Zimmerman, *Consumption and Standards of Living*, New York, D. Van Nostrand Company, 1936, is a monumental piece of analysis of this phase of social status. W. Lloyd Warner and Paul S. Lunt, *The Status System of a Modern Community*, New Haven, Yale University Press, 1942, and W. Lloyd Warner, Marchia Meeker, and Kenneth Eells, *Social Class in America*, Chicago, Science Research Associates, 1949, should be consulted by all interested in social stratification. The reading guide which constitutes Chapter 15 of the latter is particularly useful.

lower classes, will be used, although it is recognized that for many purposes more minute subdivisions are desirable. As a rule the members of the highest social class perform only one of the basic social functions, that of capitalist. Sometimes even that role is denied the members of the small aristocratic group who have a stranglehold upon the land and other natural resources in an extensive territory. In the "new" countries, however, such as the United States and Canada, the members of the upper class may engage to a considerable extent in managerial and entrepreneurial activities without serious loss of prestige. At the other extreme, manual labor is the great distinguishing feature of the lower class and the thing which brings its members to recognize their common interest and helps develop among them a strong bond of unity. The fact that his economic activity is limited almost exclusively to the performance of the labor function in production is largely responsible for the formation of the personality of the lower-class member.

Persons of middle-class status perform all three of the essential economic functions. This fact is evident from an analysis of the sources of the incomes of middle-class farmers, the operators of family-sized farms, who constitute the backbone of the middle class in most countries. Such a farmer is a capitalist on a small scale, although the investment is not large and it usually has been accumulated by thrift and self-denial. Part of his income is attributable to interest on the capital he has invested in land, buildings, livestock, machinery, and equipment. In addition, he himself is responsible for the managerial activities on the farm, and part of his income is earned in that manner. Finally, the typical middle-class operator of a family-sized farm devotes long and hard hours to tasks involving manual labor, and a part of his income is a return as wages for the work he has done. It is important to note that such a farmer does not think of work as bemeaning, but he also appreciates the contribution of management and capital. As a result he has a strong sense of solidarity with others who esteem the dignity of labor and work with their hands, who also exhibit proficiency in the planning and execution of various farming enterprises, and who carefully guard and add to the investments they have been able to make in land, buildings, livestock, and equipment. Collectively, such farmers cannot identify themselves with the owners of broad estates who rarely perform any of the managerial functions and never any of the manual labor on their land;

nor are they willing to accept as equals the landless ones who eke out an existence merely on what they may obtain by exchanging their labor for a cash wage or a share of the crop.

There are, however, other senses in which the term "class" is used. Ross, who has been widely followed, referred to social stratification as a "veritable social disease" which hinders the shifting of individuals, retards the rise of the talented, prevents the debasing of the incompetent, and in general shuts off the vertical social mobility of a society. He contended that there could be no social strata if it were not for inheritance of one kind or another.[4] Undoubtedly Ross included much more in the term "class" than is implied in the writings of other scholars. Probably it is more proper to apply the term "caste" to those class differences that are perpetuated by inheritance, and to reserve the term "class" to refer merely to similarity of position on the social pyramid.[5]

Some degree of class difference or social stratification seems to be an inseparable concomitant of social living. Plant and animal societies, the simplest primitive groups, great civilizations, and even organizations set up with the avowed purpose of eliminating class differences all consist of hierarchically superimposed layers.

The question naturally arises as to the causes of this universal phenomenon. They are of several sorts. In the first place there is a biological basis. Individuals at birth differ greatly from one another in native endowments. Some are born lacking the capacity to acquire human culture, and thus are condemned to a life of idiocy from the moment of birth. Imbeciles and morons have greater native capacities, but in their case, too, biological factors forever keep them below average. The masses of the population receive native equipment intermediate between that received by such unfortunates and that inherited by those who rank at the upper end of the scale. Only a few geniuses at the upper extreme are born with native equipment of the highest quality. These mental differences are paralleled by inequalities in physical endowments; the two combine to constitute the basis for those social classes that are universal in human society.

Differences in native endowments are greatly multiplied by education. The bright and the dull are more nearly equal before

[4] Cf. E. A. Ross, *Outlines of Sociology*, New York, D. Appleton-Century Company, 1933, p. 283.

[5] Cf. the articles on "caste" and "class" in *Encyclopaedia of the Social Sciences*, New York, The Macmillan Company, 1930.

a course of instruction than after it. Therefore the provision of equal educational opportunities for all children is more likely to promote social stratification than to decrease it. Strict equality, it would seem, might be attained only if educational opportunities were allocated in inverse proportion to native endowments; and this seems to be a proposition of which few would approve. For this reason, even within the smallest homogeneous group, class differences that develop out of original differences in ability and capacity are multiplied by variation in the extent to which education is received; social stratification, therefore, is likely to remain as an integral portion of every social structure.

A large share of the class and caste structure grows out of the mingling of races and the contacts of cultures. Peoples possessing superior culture—especially those material traits useful in warfare, a more efficient system of economic production and marketing, and a highly developed religious system—easily come to dominate peoples of inferior cultural attainments. Out of these contacts between unequals arise involved class differences and rigid caste patterns.[6]

Differences in the systems of stratification in rural and urban

[6] The slight differences which may be seized upon as a basis for discrimination, for placing oneself or one's group above others, and which generate classes in society are well illustrated by the following report of Stephen Powers, who traveled extensively in North Carolina and other southern states immediately following the Civil War:

"The first freedman I met, instead of assassinating me, grinned fearfully, when he discovered I was a Northern man. He wore but one shoe, and that was much dilapidated. His trowsers were sustained by a corn-husk belt, and he wore a government blouse, split all the way down the back, and kept to duty by a tow-string tied around his neck. Yet from his tattered breast fluttered a Union League badge, a bit of ribbon worth five cents, for which he said he expended a dollar. Said I to him:

" 'Uncle, do you enjoy "the feast of reason and the flow of soul" in the Union League?'

" 'No, sah; I can't say as we does, sah.'

" 'What stands between you and your soul's enjoyment, Uncle? Tell me about your troubles.'

"He glanced rather dubiously at his badge, as if he had a faint suspicion I might be poking fun at it; then he shifted his weight upon his other leg, as if to shift off the burden of conscience for telling the little family secret he was about to impart.

" 'Well, you see, sah, we was 'joying ourselves pretty sharp, and feelin' de lub ob de Union in de sperrit of de flesh, 'till dese hyur free niggers jined in. Dey was boun' for to rule de roost, and dey was all de time a kickin' up a fuss.'

" 'But you are all free negroes now.'

" 'But dese hyur is de old free niggers, I mean, afo' de wah. Dey calls us, sence de wah, Sherman's ash-cakes, and dey's all de time a kickin' up a fuss.' " *Afoot and Alone; A Walk from Sea to Sea,* Hartford, Columbian Book Company, 1872, pp. 21–22.

communities were discussed briefly in Chapter 2. The present chapter is concerned with the nature and extent of social stratification in rural areas.

The Class Structure of Rural America

The class structure of rural America is exceedingly complex; it is also little studied; and in the present stage of knowledge it is doubtful if any thoroughgoing analysis of classification is possible. Anything attempted is certain to contain grave defects. It is fairly certain, however, that there are upper, middle, and lower or disadvantaged groups in American agriculture.[7] But it should be recognized that these shade gradually into each other and that there are many social layers in each. In general, farm laborers, including the southern croppers, make up the bulk of the lower agricultural classes. Among the lower classes the hierarchy would no doubt place the migratory agricultural workers, those who follow the crops and have no fixed residence, no established status, at the bottom of the scale; permanent wage hands probably occupy at most times and in most places the middle stratum; and the sharecroppers rank at the top of these disadvantaged groups. The middle classes, most numerous in those areas given over exclusively to the family-farm system, are made up of farm operators, both owners and renters. A family's position is determined about as much by stability, permanency, and dependability as by the ownership of land. The upper agricultural classes consist almost entirely of large landholders, and only where a system of large estates long has been dominant is a genuine elite to be found. In the United States such a hereditary upper class in the rural areas is confined largely to the plantation South, the sections given over to "gentlemen's" estates on the Hudson, and areas monopolized by magnificent ranches in California and the other western states.

In all these cases a word of caution is necessary. The past history of a family as well as its present economic circumstances must be taken into account in determining social status. The "dead hand of the past" holds some families that have suffered severe economic reverses at a level quite inconsistent with present economic circumstances; likewise it makes it difficult for the newcomer, the upstart, and the climber to attain the social position commensurate

[7] See Carl C. Taylor, Helen W. Wheeler, and E. L. Kirkpatrick, *Disadvantaged Classes in American Agriculture*, Farm Security Administration and Bureau of Agricultural Economics Social Research Report VII, Washington, 1938.

with their economic resources.[8] A family's social status frequently is more closely correlated with its economic status of a quarter of a century in the past than with that of the present. As mentioned above, permanency, stability, dependability are important factors in establishing the social status of a rural family. The renter who moves frequently soon comes to rank at the base of the social pyramid with the farm laborers who also shift about frequently; the renter who remains on a farm decade after decade comes to attain a position similar to that of the landowners who are likewise strongly attached to specific tracts of land.

Factors Associated with Class Differences

Even though the class and caste structure of the rural part of the nation taken as a whole may be exceedingly complex, in a given community it is as a rule fairly simple and relatively easy to comprehend. No single community embraces all the variations. Some of the more important factors associated with the principal divergences are as follows: (1) the size of the holdings or the extent to which the ownership of the land is concentrated in the hands of a few or widely distributed among all the families of the community, (2) the importance of industrial-agricultural combinations, (3) the forms of land tenure, (4) the amount of shifting from farm to farm, and (5) the racial composition of the population. Since the significant social strata are those embodied in an actual community, no attempt will be made to evolve general classifications in which a given social stratum from one situation is properly placed with respect to quite different strata from other communities.[9] Instead, present purposes will be better served by an analysis that indicates how each of the above factors influences the social stratification of the various communities.

The size of holdings is basic in all considerations of rural social stratification. Only where there is great concentration of landownership is it possible to find a complete absence of the middle classes. Definitely a function of large-scale agriculture is the situation in which the social pyramid consists of a small number of the elite perched high on the social scale and the great mass of the

[8] Cf. Edgar A. Schuler, "Social and Economic Status in a Louisiana Hills Community," *Rural Sociology*, V (1940), 82–83.

[9] An attempt at such a classification will be found in P. A. Sorokin, Carle C. Zimmerman, and Charles J. Galpin, *A Systematic Source Book in Rural Sociology*, Minneapolis, University of Minnesota Press, 1930, I, 366.

population debased into a rural proletariat of landless agricultural laborers. The immense social chasm between these two classes is unbridged by the middle classes only where the concentration of landownership is great. Furthermore, it seems almost impossible to find a situation in which the concentration of landownership has proceeded far without finding society divided into the two classes, the elite and the poverty-stricken masses, separated by a great void. Under such circumstances the social strata become petrified into a strong caste system, vertical social mobility becomes so unimportant as to be negligible, and there comes to be little relationship between a person's inherent native ability and his position on the social scale. Accident of birth and inheritance dominate in determining for all time the position a person shall occupy in such a society. The tenancy system of Great Britain and the hypothetical agricultural coöperatives of the future seem to be the principal exceptions to the above generalizations.

In sharp contrast are the results of a wide distribution of landownership. Such a system makes almost impossible the rise of gross inequalities. To be sure, a family-farm system of agriculture knows social stratification, but this is in a form and degree that more closely correlates inherent native ability and social position. Vertical social mobility is not prohibited by the class structure, caste does not forever close the doors to ingress and egress from the different social strata, and a person's position in life is more dependent upon his own efforts and less dependent upon his ancestors.

Social stratification is also greatly influenced by the extent to which a community combines agricultural and industrial occupational pursuits for its members, and especially the extent to which part-time farming is combined with fairly regular industrial or commercial employment. Where there is much industrial employment, or large-scale development of rural homes for urban workers, the population tends to be fluid. The process of selection attracts and repels the extremes; ordinarily the lowest social strata gravitate into the nearby purely industrial areas, and the highly successful move to residential areas more in keeping with their newly acquired social positions. Under such a system the class differences in a community may be practically erased, and caste within the neighborhood can make but little headway.

Agricultural-industrial combinations affect social stratification in another way. They blur the lines of demarcation between occupational groups. People identify themselves with locality groupings rather than with occupational and economic strata. According to Paul H. Johnstone, part-time farming was an important factor in promoting community solidarity and retarding class divisions in New England settlements.[10]

The forms of land tenure are closely allied to differences in social status. In fact, it has been customary to think of owners, part-owners, tenants, and laborers as the typical hierarchy in rural America. Schuler has summarized the findings of fifty studies, all made since 1922, and reported the differences in status between owners and tenants. Supplementing with data from more than 2400 schedules secured from corn-belt and cotton-belt farmers, he concluded that "not only with regard to the consumption of certain goods, and participation in certain types of formally and informally organized social life, but in the prestige held, and in the social and economic ideologies expressed," there were significant differences between the tenure classes. But these class differences in the South where the plantation system was encountered were found to be different from those of the corn belt. White tenants in the South (the category included croppers) were found to be markedly lower in the social scale than white owners. But no such clear-cut differences were observed in the corn belt. Among southern Negroes there was also a clearly defined differentiation of tenants and owners. And pronounced racial differences were observed, not "only with respect to the consumption of goods and services, but especially with respect to attitudes, opinions, beliefs, and aspirations."[11]

It is an interesting commentary on our use of words that those rural Americans who shift most eventually become the shiftless. Among rural groups there is much truth to the old proverb, "A rolling stone gathers no moss." "Three moves is as good as a fire" is a more recent expression for the same idea. The frequency with which a farm family moves from one tract of land to another has much to do with its status in the community. Not infrequently this factor will outweigh differences in tenure status. Farm labor-

[10] "On the Identification of the Farmer," *Rural Sociology*, V (1940), 34.

[11] Schuler, "The Present Social Status of American Farm Tenants," *Rural Sociology*, III (1938), pp. 32–33; cf. the same author's study, *Social Status and Farm Tenure: Attitudes and Social Conditions of Corn Belt and Cotton Belt Farmers*, Farm Security Administration and Bureau of Agricultural Economics, Social Research Report IV, Washington, 1938.

ers who are stable come to attain much the same standing as their employers; the renter who moves about frequently is considered on the same level as casual farm laborers; and the renter who continues on the same place decade after decade is ranked with the farm owners.

Where two or more sharply differentiated racial elements make up the population of a community, class divisions among the members of the one racial group are likely to be paralleled by those in the other, while between the two races caste differences are pronounced. Southern rural communities have their upper-middle-, and lower-class Negroes, as well as clearly separated strata among the white population.[12] But historical and cultural factors, including slavery and the plantation system, have generated and perpetuated a strong caste system between the races; and this makes it difficult to scale the classes of the two racial groups properly in a single social pyramid.

Classes in the Midwest

A highly informative study describes social stratification in a small, homogeneous Iowa agricultural community.[13] With minor variations the situation reported in this small trade center and the surrounding trade basin is probably fairly well representative of the family-farm agricultural pattern of the Midwest. On first observation social classes seemed to be lacking in the community. The inhabitants maintained that there was no stratification, that previous class differences in which the Baptist aristocracy had been set apart from the others had disappeared. Nevertheless the study revealed clearly that the community was characterized by a definite class structure.

Perched at the top of the social and economic pyramid was the family of the local banker. The head of this family was the lord of the local community. In him were personified all those traits that lead many comparable villages to be characterized as "one-

---

[12] The influence of racial factors is of far-reaching importance in consideration of class and caste. For a given rural community the work by Hortense Powdermaker, *After Freedom*, New York, The Viking Press, 1939, is of importance.

[13] Earl H. Bell, "Social Stratification in a Small Community," *Scientific Monthly*, XXXVIII (1934), 157–164. Other studies of social stratification in the Midwest include Evon Z. Vogt, "Social Stratification in the Rural Middlewest: A Structural Analysis," *Rural Sociology*, XII (1947), 364–375; and James West (pseudonym for Carl Withers), *Plainville, U.S.A.*, New York, Columbia University Press, 1945.

man towns." He was intimately acquainted with everyone's business, financial standing, and personal affairs. For the entire community he was an inexhaustible source of advice and help. Farmers consulted him about the renting and buying of land, the purchase or sale of livestock, and the making of improvements on their places; merchants and other villagers first sought his advice before embarking on new undertakings; in all community disagreements he was the final arbiter; on matters of law he was the local adviser; all land deals were consummated in his presence and he himself drew up the final agreement; a letter from him was the last resort in collecting out-of-town debts. In times of stress and crisis all turned to him for aid and assistance. His business was banking; all the functions of local encyclopedia and agent were performed free of charge merely for the asking.

Next to the banker and his family ranked his business associates and their families. Nearness to the great man cast a sort of halo that added prestige to his employees from the cashier to the janitor. The fact that they worked in the bank meant that they had the approval of the local lord and this by itself was sufficient to place them on an enviable social plane.

The third stratum consisted of the "businessmen" and the members of their families. All operators of business establishments, regardless of the type, were included in this category. The barber and the blacksmith were considered businessmen fully as much as the hardware dealer. Thirty-six households were included in the businessmen class; but barred from the group were recent comers, "outsiders," who operated a grocery store, a meat market, a drug store, a café, a combined grocery and dry-goods establishment, and a produce house. Although the produce dealer was born and reared in the community, he did not belong to the business class because he had changed occupations frequently. The doctor and the dentist were also included with the business group, as was one of the railroad agents who had been stationed in the village for fifty years.

Landowners made up the next class or stratum. This group included active and retired farmers; as with the business group, stability and permanency were elements in determining status. The prestige of this group was nearly equal to that of the businessmen. Recent trends are toward a blending or fusion of these two strata.

Below the landowners came the group of farm renters, although the stable and permanent farm renter tended to enjoy the same recognition and prestige as the farm owner. The renter who moved frequently, on the other hand, tended to be debased in community opinion to a plane of equality with the farm laborer.

The class of occasional laborers made up one of the most distinct strata in the entire social and economic structure of the community. For the most part their employment was on the farm, but they were odd-job men, "jacks of all trades." Socially they mingled little if at all with the other classes. These casual laborers lacked the three great redeeming virtues of the community: permanent employment, stability, and industry. By the community at large they were considered to be afflicted with "laziness," and this was thought of as an innate, inherent biological characteristic. At the bottom of the class of occasional laborers were a few thought to be addicted to the habit of stealing. These persons lived in the poorest houses, had the least money and the most children, and were most frequently dependent upon the neighbors and the community for assistance and support. Tools, garden truck, automobile tires, and accessories became the objects of their attentions after a strong sentiment against chicken stealing crystallized in the community.

All these classes shaded imperceptibly into each other. Economic function and permanency and stability of the individuals were the principal differentiating criteria. Class lines were not institutionalized; children were largely free from class distinctions, unless undesirable parental traits were also clearly reflected in the offspring. In these cases the naughty children were taboo to those of many other families.

As indicated above, but minor variations are needed to make this analysis equally applicable to a large proportion of the purely agricultural communities of the Midwest and Far West. In such areas racial heterogeneity does not scramble the relationships. Owners of small department stores that have continued in the same family for several generations frequently occupy the position at the apex of the social pyramid.

Classes in the South

No analysis comparable to that by Dr. Bell is available for those parts of the country in which large-scale agriculture and a heterogeneous racial composition of the population dominate the rural scene. The most regrettable lack is an adequate recent study of class structure in the plantation areas of the South. However, for the period prior to the Civil War the history of the South is well documented; and more recently L. C. Gray included two chapters dealing with class structure in his monumental work on southern agriculture.[14] Gray attempted to characterize the principal social classes in southern agriculture in the period immediately preceding the Civil War. Although his analysis is defective in certain details, so constant are the social relations he has described that it has much value for the present. The following materials are based largely upon his work. According to Gray, the white population was differentiated into the following classes: (1) "poor whites," (2) highlanders, (3) commercial farmers, and (4) the planter aristocracy.[15] Among the Negroes the principal classes were: (1) the slaves and (2) the free Negroes. A favored few of the Negroes were employed domestically and enjoyed a much higher status than the field hands. Free Negroes were in a somewhat precarious position, but some of them attained large holdings of land and numerous slaves, and occupied a relatively high position.[16]

Gray begins by setting apart the "poor whites," who constituted the lowest social class, the base of the social pyramid. As late as 1860 life for them differed little from that of the pioneering stage. They lived on the fringes of the plantations and in the wastes. Rude log cabins, roughly furnished with homemade furniture, were their homes. Small patches of corn, rice, sweet potatoes, and garden truck furnished the greater portion of their foodstuffs. Some of them owned a few hogs, some kind of horse, and a rough cart. The men spent much of their time hunting, fishing, and idling, while the women and children did a large portion of the manual labor. Everyone possessed a rifle and every family owned a large number of "houn' dogs." The status of these white people was definitely inferior and recognized as such, and they were conscious of that fact. They were even looked down upon by the Negroes on the nearby plantations. Contemptuously called "dirt

[14] *History of Agriculture in the Southern United States to 1860,* Washington, The Carnegie Institution of Washington, 1933, 2 vols.

[15] *Ibid.,* I, 481–507.

[16] Guion Griffis Johnson, *A Social History of the Sea Islands,* Chapel Hill, University of North Carolina Press, 1930, pp. 130–131, gives interesting material on present-day social stratification among rural Negroes.

eaters," "clay eaters," "sand hillers," etc., they were a constant nuisance to the planters, who regarded them with suspicion and contempt. Outcasts from society, in competition with Negro slave labor, and handicapped by the stigma inevitably attached to manual labor in slave areas, their lot was a very unenviable one.[17]

Often confused with the "poor whites" are the mountain folk and the highlanders. Frequently they have been referred to as "hillbillies," "crackers," "red necks," etc. They have been and remain widespread throughout the entire southern region. In sharp contrast with the "poor whites," they were isolated geographically, not socially. They had little if any relationship with the plantation and few if any contacts with Negroes. Proud and independent, they did not suffer from social ostracism. Although they did manual labor, they suffered no social stigma on that account. Women worked in the fields with the men. Though they were largely a class of yeomen, nevertheless hunting and the collection of the free gifts of nature made important contributions to their domestic economy.[18]

The third class identified by Dr. Gray is that composed of commercial farmers in the lowlands and valleys. In all probability he draws too sharp a distinction between them and the uplanders. But according to his classification they occupy an intermediate place between the planters and the hill folk. Persons of this class were as a rule owners of a few slaves, with whom they were in friendly and intimate contact. Ordinarily they engaged in general farming, which was in sharp contrast to the practices of the planters, who concentrated on the production of the staples. This was a sturdy, independent, self-reliant, hospitable, sociable, and democratic class; they enjoyed more of the material comforts of life than any other class except the planters.

[17] Cf. William Gregg, "Domestic Industry—Manufactures at the South," *De-Bow's Review*, VIII (1850), 139–140; S. C. Hammond, "Progress of Southern Industry," *DeBow's Review*, VIII (1850), 519–520; George M. Weston, *Progress of Slavery in the United States*, Washington, 1857, pp. 39–42; Frederick Law Olmsted, *A Journey in the Seaboard Slave States*, New York, Mason Brothers, 1904, *passim;* Olmsted, *A Journey in the Back Country*, New York, G. P. Putnam's Sons, 1863, *passim;* and Frank L. and Harriet C. Owsley, "The Economic Basis of Society in the Late Ante-Bellum South," *The Journal of Southern History*, VI (1940), 24–25.

[18] The noted historian, Frank L. Owsley, and his many students have described this class, its way of life, and its social role in considerable detail. Owsley's *Plain Folk of the Old South*, Baton Rouge, Louisiana State University Press, 1949, does much to portray the yeomen of the Old South as they actually were. See also William E. Dodd, *The Cotton Kingdom*, New Haven, Yale University Press, 1921, pp. 19–20.

Best known of all southern agricultural classes is the planter aristocracy. This category was extremely heterogeneous. At the top of the scale stood a brilliant, cultured few who owned wide acreages of land and numerous slaves. Their homes were elegant in the extreme, and they frequently possessed both summer and winter dwellings. This upper crust were much away from home, absent at northern watering places or traveling. Their older children were sent north or to Europe for schooling, and private tutors were employed to instruct the younger ones. Music, literature, and all the social graces were highly cultivated. Some of their libraries were large in size and rich in content. To members of their own class they were hospitable in the extreme, and visiting formed one of the principal ways of spending the time. *Elegance* most completely describes their mode of living.

But the bulk of the planter class were of somewhat lower estate. They owned less land and fewer slaves. Except for the favored few, residence on the plantation was a necessity. Personal attention was given to the slaves and to agricultural enterprises, although as a rule an overseer was employed to assist with such details. Both the planter and his wife exercised a personal interest in the welfare of the slaves.[19]

Ranks or classes did not disappear from the South with the freeing of the slaves. Although greatly impoverished, many "old families" have retained their positions at the top of the social pyramid.[20] Likewise the channels of social circulation have remained for the most part closed to "no-account" white groups at the bottom of the hierarchy. Only during recent years does political ferment at the bottom of the social scale bid fair to upset the established scheme of social relationships.[21]

[19] For more details on this class, consult Thomas Perkins Abernethy, "Social Relations and Political Control in the Old Southwest," *The Mississippi Valley Historical Review*, XVI (1929), 532–534.

[20] Schuler has observed this tendency in a Louisiana "hills" community essentially similar to much of the upland portion of the South. Such a tendency, of course, makes the social position of a family correlate more closely with the economic position of its ancestors than with its own present economic status. See Edgar A. Schuler, "Social and Economic Status in a Louisiana Hills Community," *Rural Sociology*, V (1940), 82.

[21] Consult Vernon J. Parenton, "Notes on the Social Organization of a French Village in South Louisiana," *Social Forces*, XVII (1938), 79. The following observations from a report of a field worker in a north Louisiana plantation parish are informing concerning the present class structure:

"The Negro rural relief clients . . . are considered, by non-recipients of relief, to be socially and morally superior to the white clients on relief rolls. There is a current saying that the 'poor white trash from Arkansas has drifted down to Morehouse.' This class of white people is regarded as the dregs of society. When

The fact that social classes are readily discernible has been used by Gee and his students in their studies of qualitative selection in migration. Reuss has given the following statement concerning the manner in which the population was separated into the upper, middle, and lower classes:

It is difficult objectively to define the basis upon which such a separation is made. Yet, despite this seeming weakness, it is a technique valued by all who have thoroughly understood it. It is the sort of matter which one "senses" rather than brings into a definitive statement. The process involves both social and economic considerations, with family traditions and community worth as essential elements. For, whatever may or may not be the case elsewhere, in many sections of the South it is possible with a marked degree of exactitude to sort the population of the community into an upper, a middle, and a lower class. Each person's station is somehow known and recognized by everyone in the community, including the individual himself.[22]

With the assistance of a professional man who had practiced for forty years in Gee's native township in South Carolina, this authority graded the white families of the township as of both 1900 and 1930 into upper, middle, and lower classes. It is interesting to observe objective findings that are associated with the classes or layers so determined. The upper-class families were predominantly a landowning group, 74 percent of them owning land in 1900 and 91 percent in 1930. Less than half of the middle classes were landowners, 44 percent in 1900 and 42 percent in 1930. The lower classes were landless, only one family out of twenty-five owning land in 1900, and this was a small tract of only seventeen acres; only two out of fourteen owned land in 1930, although one of them owned 185 acres. The upper classes owned more land than the middle group, although there was much over-

---

a farm operator is in need of additional seasonal workers, he prefers to employ Negro workers rather than these whites. This attitude is openly discussed by the above class of white people and resentful remarks are frequently heard as to the attitude of white employers toward 'their own color.'

"The homes of these so-called poor whites are, on the whole, poorly kept, unsanitary hovels; the Negro rural relief clients, on the other hand, do appear to be making an effort to have their homes appear as attractive and well-preserved as their means permit. The morale of the 'poor whites' is broken; they are embittered and resentful—a people with whom it is difficult to work."

[22] Carl Frederick Reuss, "A Qualitative Study of Depopulation in a Remote Rural District: 1900–1930," *Rural Sociology*, II (1937), 67.

lapping. Thus the average landholding of the upper classes was 489 acres in 1900 and 356 in 1930, as compared with 264 in 1900 and 226 in 1930 among the middle classes. Landholdings of the upper classes ranged from twenty-two to 1826 acres in 1900 and from fifty to 2100 acres in 1930. Those of the middle classes ranged from 48 to 985 in 1900 and 50 to 742 in 1930. Assessed valuations of property, in which the assessed valuations averaged about 20 percent of the selling value, were $1678 and $1645 for the upper classes in 1900 and 1930, respectively, as compared with $669 and $611 for the middle classes.[23]

Gee and his students used this method in several areas in both Virginia and South Carolina. In each study the validity of the investigation was dependent upon an intimate knowledge of the community and the estate of everyone in it. There seems little reason to doubt that such an intimate knowledge was possessed by the investigators. In each study also the attempt was made to draw up a balance sheet showing what has happened to the population resident in the area in 1900, and the sources from which the populations of the different strata as of 1930 had been derived. But the possibility of shifting on the social scale was ignored. The upper-class membership in 1930 was accounted for by natural increase of population and migration, and not by allowing for the possibility that some of the members of one class or their children might have moved up or down the social pyramid. This basic assumption of the investigators itself is one of the strongest evidences for the proposition that the communities are rigidly stratified, the layers being more like castes than mere classes.[24]

On given plantations in the South the class structure is readily observable, the principal strata in ascending order usually being: wage hands; croppers, or half-hands; "share tenants," or three-fourths hands; renters; and operators. Superannuated couples or displaced families, allowed to continue living in a cabin on the plantation, frequently make up another class.[25]

[23] Wilson Gee, *The Qualitative Nature of Rural Depopulation in Santuc Township, South Carolina, 1900–1930*, South Carolina AES Bulletin 287, Clemson College, 1933, pp. 8–9.

[24] *Ibid.*, pp. 13–14; and Reuss, *op. cit.*, pp. 70–71.

[25] See T. J. Woofter, Jr., and others, *Landlord and Tenant on the Cotton Plantation*, Works Progress Administration Research Monograph V, Washington, 1936, pp. 9–10.

Trends in Social Stratification

What is happening to the class structure of rural America? Are the difficulties of passage from one level to another, up or down, relatively constant? Do the same proportions of the rural population remain in the upper, middle, and lower classes? Is there a tendency for the social pyramid to become more stratified, or is the leveling process at work? These and many other questions are of real significance for those who would anticipate what rural life in the nation is likely to be on the morrow.

There are at work many forces making for increased social stratification in rural society. As a rule they work smoothly and steadily; more social layers and greater differences between the layers come about in a gradual manner. The leveling process works much more spasmodically and convulsively. In general, increased social stratification results from social evolution; the leveling process works by revolution.[26]

Until recently trends in the rural areas of the United States seemed definitely to be in the direction of increased social stratification. It appeared that the middle classes were being thinned out and that a void was developing between the favored few at the top of the social scale and the less-privileged masses at the bottom. Our family-sized organization of farm life and the resulting middle-class mentality seemed doomed to extinction. Principally this was coming about through the reduction of many members of the middle class to the lower or laboring category of the farm population. Evidences of this tendency appeared to be the alarming increase of farm tenancy in the Middle West, the general increase in the size of farms, the mounting burden of farm-mortgage indebtedness, and the rapidly swelling army of displaced rural families who had turned to migratory agricultural labor as a way of life.

More recently, however, there seems to be considerable reason for doubting that such a development is under way at present. Temporarily at least the changes brought about by the national defense program, the Second World War, the boom times that accompanied reconversion, and the rearmament program precipitated by the Korean war seem to have reversed the trend toward greater social stratification in rural America. Millions of agricul-

[26] Sorokin, *Social Mobility*, p. 46.

tural workers, far more than the normal surplus of farm population, have been siphoned off to industrial and other employment
in the urban areas. But by greater use of power and machinery,
production on the farms has even been raised substantially,
greatly reducing the numerical importance of the lower agricultural classes, particularly in the South. In addition, in a period of
rapid inflation, mortgage indebtedness has not been a way station
on the road to bankruptcy as it frequently was a few decades ago,
but it usually has worked greatly to the advantage of the bor-
rower.[27] During the last decade hundreds of thousands of farm
operators have bought and paid for their farms in full; still other
hundreds of thousands have completed paying for farms purchased during the years preceding the outbreak of the Second
World War at a fraction of their money value today. Under the
circumstances prevailing from 1922 to 1940, a large part of them
would have found it impossible to avoid slipping down into the
category of farm laborers. But with the high prices of farm products and rapid inflation they have not merely paid for their farms
but also become thoroughly accustomed to the upper planes of
middle-class living and thoroughly embued with high standards
of living as well. At no time since the outbreak of the First World
War have the relative number and importance of the middle
classes in rural America ranked as high as at present.

[27] In 1940 the real-estate debt amounted to almost 20 percent of the value of
farm real estate in the United States, whereas by 1950 the corresponding figure
was less than 9 percent. Cf. Bureau of Agricultural Economics, *Agricultural Outlook Charts, 1951,* Washington, Government Printing Office, 1950, p. 30.

17

MARRIAGE AND THE FAMILY

Everywhere the family is the basic unit in the composition of society. As the most fundamental primary social group, it is the arena in which the major part of the individual's personality is formed. Strongly unified through the operation of the most basic social ties, cemented by both the organic and the mechanistic types of solidarity, it is the most closely knit social group in existence. The great influence of this highly cohesive group upon the individual, combined with the great number of such units, makes the family by far the most important form of social grouping known to mankind.

Historically the institution of marriage and the family group were features of the earliest civilizations of which we have record; they are to be observed among all savage tribes of the present.[1] Throughout all history the rural family has played a most significant role. The colonial family was the dominant social institution in the newly settled continent.[2] And at the present time the rural family remains strong and important. Today in America it is both the agency by which the bulk of the future population is produced and the crucible in which the majority of the citizens of the next generation are tested and molded.

Although the family as a group is everywhere recognizable, its forms and functions are by no means always and everywhere the same. Strictly speaking, the term *family* is used to designate a relatively permanent, socially sanctioned grouping of parents and children. It may also include relatives of the husband, the wife,

[1] Cf. Wilson D. Wallis, *An Introduction to Anthropology*, New York, Harper & Brothers, 1926, p. 348.

[2] See A. W. Calhoun, *A Social History of the American Family*, Cleveland, Arthur H. Clark Co., 1917–1919, 3 vols.

or both. In the establishment of a given family are involved: (1) the institution of marriage and (2) reproduction of the species. Because the human infant is helpless at birth and continues dependent upon others for many years, the relationships within a given family extend over a long period of time. To assist in clarifying the concept, several other observations may be made. Technically, married pairs do not constitute families until offspring result from the marriage. In societies where polygamy is practiced the family group may contain more than one wife or husband. If a marriage is terminated by death, divorce, or separation, the term "broken family" is properly applied to the remaining members of the group. "Household" is a term closely related to the family which sometimes may be used interchangeably with it but which has some specific connotations.

In a secondary sense the term "family" includes also kindred of both the father and the mother. Sometimes these relationships are close and definite, making a large, closely knit group. Such a grouping is referred to as a great family to distinguish it from the natural family usually thought of.

Since the foundation of a new family involves the institution of marriage, a brief consideration of the forms and conditions of matrimony may well precede other aspects of the subject.

Marriage

The institution of marriage is the central feature of all human societies. Ogburn contends that it is more intimately related to "that elusive thing we call happiness" than any other institution except possibly the church.[3] As previously mentioned, marriage is indispensable in the family grouping. But marriage must not be thought of as identical with sex relations, or even regularized sex relations. Marriage is a genuine social bond; it is sanctioned by the group; it establishes family relations, particularly with respect to the offspring.[4]

Classifications of marriages and marriage forms are abundant and each one has usefulness for special purposes. One who would understand his own society must be cognizant of the ways in

[3] E. R. Groves and William F. Ogburn, *American Marriage and Family Relationships*, New York, Henry Holt & Company, 1928, p. 125.

[4] Cf. John Lewis Gillin and John Philip Gillin, *Cultural Sociology*, New York, The Macmillan Company, 1948, p. 334; and Kimball Young, *An Introductory Sociology*, New York, American Book Company, 1934, p. 218.

which other people differ from his accepted patterns. Consideration of the various patterns of behavior with respect to marriage
is one of the best ways of realizing how readily one accepts the
cultural forms of his own particular group as "natural" and regards those of other groups as peculiar or queer. Furthermore,
even American marriage patterns are not entirely devoid of many
survivals of those customs we consider queer when reported
among strangers. The students of rural society must be familiar
with cultural norms in many social groups in order that they will
not consider variation from our standards in another culture a
mark of inferiority.

The first important variations in marriage forms arise out of
differences in the manner of securing a mate. Economics is usually involved in this, for only rarely in the history of the world has
marriage been separated from pecuniary consideration. Furthermore, marriage has almost always and everywhere been regarded
as a family and not an individual affair.[5] Rare indeed is the case in
which young people have been permitted to make their own mat-
rimonial arrangements; more prevalent has been the practice of
considering marriage as an arrangement between family groups.
Even yet much of this element prevails in rural areas. In many
societies girls have been regarded as an economic asset, have
been disposed of as property by the family, and have been received as property by the group into which they were married. So
important have been the economic arrangements that marriage
by exchange or marriage by purchase has been almost universal.
Child marriages, widespread throughout the world, are most frequently exchanges between families.

Even where child marriages are lacking, the case is rare in
which the group relinquishes claim to a maiden before adequate
compensation has been received. Although varieties of bargaining are by no means the equivalent of one another, marriage by
purchase has been much more widespread than marriage by exchange.[6] An important variation of marriage by purchase is the
case in which service has been substituted for an actual payment
of goods; this is a marriage form known to all those who are famil-

---

[5] James Hastings, *Encyclopedia of Religion and Ethics*, New York, Charles
Scribner's Sons, 1924, VIII, 469.
[6] Robert H. Lowie, *Primitive Society*, New York, Boni and Liveright, 1920,
p. 19.

iar with the stories of the Old Testament.[7] Other practices of the Hebrews that reveal the nature of the marriage forms are the *levirate,* a custom in which a brother was required to take as wife the widow of his deceased brother and count as his brother's the first child of the marriage,[8] and the feature of the Deuteronomic code which permitted only the husband to initiate a divorce.[9] Marriage by capture, another widely used method of securing a mate, also recognizes the economic value of women, but in this case prowess or cunning is used to avoid payment. In rural America marriage still remains much more of a family affair than is true in cities; there are still survivals of the economic considerations in marriage, but romantic love and its individualistic emphasis have undermined group importance even in the country.

Another fundamental classification of marriages may be made upon the basis of the number of parties to the contract. Marriages involving only one man and one woman are *monogamous;* those in which three or more people are concerned, *polygamous.* Polygamous unions may be subdivided into those cases in which one husband is united with two or more wives (*polygyny*), and those in which one wife is associated in marriage with two or more husbands (*polyandry*). Group marriage (several husbands and several wives banded together indiscriminately), sexual communism, and complete promiscuity in sexual matters are other more or less hypothetical possibilities in the way of marriage relationships. Monogamy as a marriage pattern is deeply imbedded in American rural culture. But Old Testament accounts and present-day practices in many important agricultural countries, especially in the Orient, indicate that monogamy is by no means a necessary rural trait.[10] Neither is it unalterably American. Current urban practices seem to be developing in this country a sort of progressive or "sequential" polygamy in which a woman has a succession of husbands, or a man a succession of wives, although only one at a time. Such progressive polygamy differs little in

[7] See especially the story of Jacob and Laban in Genesis 29:1–30.

[8] Deuteronomy 25:5 ff.; Genesis 38:7–11.

[9] Deuteronomy 24:1–4.

[10] Under the impetus of a strict and literal attempt to follow all Biblical practices and teachings, the practice of polygyny has also appeared in several American religious sects. The best-known example of these is the Latter-day Saints or Mormons, who began the practice prior to the death of Joseph Smith in 1844 and continued advocating it until 1890.

essentials from the temporary monogamy reported as typical of the lowest known societies.[11]

Marriages may also be classified according to several other criteria. From the standpoint of residence, marriage may be *patrilocal,* in which the couple resides in the husband's community or *matrilocal,* where it establishes residence in the wife's community. In rural America there seems to be some tendency toward patrilocal marriages, although the comparative absence of primogeniture makes them by no means the general rule.

The matter of a name is of great importance in the social world, and this is also intimately associated with marriage. Marriage forms in which the child takes the name of the father are properly called *patronymic;* those in which the child takes the mother's name, *matronymic.* Traditional American marriage patterns are *patronymic,* the wife and children taking the surname of the father. However, at present in certain ultrasophisticated urban groups there is a tendency to modify this traditional pattern in the direction of giving the child a new name formed by hyphenating the surnames of both parents.

The important questions of kinship and descent are also involved in the nature of the marriage relationship. A bilateral system, i.e., considering the children to be kin to the families of both parents, is by no means universal, although it is the accepted one in America. In many groups the child is considered a member of the mother's line of descent and is thought to bear no kinship to the father's kin. In other societies children are kin only to the father's side of the house. Unilateral systems in which the child is considered kin of the mother's kinfold are called *matrilineal;* those in which he is considered kin only to the father's people are called *patrilineal.* Rural America has of course a bilateral system of counting relationship, but in some communities the inheritance of property sometimes exhibits elements of the patrilineal system. Not always are daughters given an equal share with sons in the inheritance of family property. On the other hand, elements of the matrilineal system are not entirely lacking in rural America. The American Negro family, evolved in slavery and its aftermath, is an important element in rural life; particularly because the

[11] See Paul H. Landis, "Sequential Marriage," *Journal of Home Economics,* XLII (1950), 625–628; and Edward Westermarck, *The History of Human Marriage,* New York, The Allerton Book Company, 1922, III, 267 ff.

mother has served as the chief integrating force, what has been called the *mother family* arose. The nature, structure, and operation of this matrilineal system of marriage and family relationships deserve more attention than they have received from the sociologist.[12]

Marital Status

A number of pertinent points need to be kept in mind in discussing marital status or condition. First, few persons under fifteen are married, so it is customary to confine discussions of this subject to the population fifteen years of age and over. Second, the most widely accepted classification used in discussing marital condition consists of four categories: (1) single, (2) married, (3) widowed, and (4) divorced. Since "separation is the poor man's divorce," persons who are married but separated and living apart should form a fifth category; but unfortunately it is impossible to secure satisfactory data about such people. However, in 1940 the United States Census introduced into the summary tables for the nation, the states, and the cities of 100,000 or more, one subdivision of the married population. A person was classified as "married, spouse present" if that person's wife or husband resided in the same household, and as "married, spouse absent" if the wife or husband was living elsewhere at the time of the census. Thus, the second category includes, along with couples who have separated, immigrants whose mates have remained abroad, husbands and wives of those who are inmates of various institutions, and other married persons whose usual residence differs from that of their husbands or wives. Sailors, soldiers, men in labor camps, etc., help swell the numbers classed in the second category.[13]

Farm people, particularly farm females, live in the married state to a much greater extent than the urban population. Some may question such a statement if they refer to the reports of the 1940 Census. The census data show that among the population

---

[12] Cf. E. Franklin Frazier, "An Analysis of Statistics on Negro Illegitimacy in the United States," *Social Forces*, XI (1932) 249–257; E. Franklin Frazier, *The Negro Family in the United States*, Chicago, University of Chicago Press, 1939, *passim;* and Berta Asch and A. R. Mangus, *Farmers on Relief and Rehabilitation*, Works Progress Administration Research Monograph VIII, Washington, 1937, pp. 39–41.

[13] Cf. *Sixteenth Census of the United States: 1940*, Vol. IV, "Population, Characteristics by Age," Washington, Government Printing Office, 1943, p. 4.

fifteen years of age and over, 58.1 percent of the urban females were married as compared with 66.3 percent of the rural farm females, whereas only 58.3 percent of the rural farm males were married as compared with 61.8 percent of the urban males. But all such a criticism demonstrates is the necessity of standardizing the data for age before making the comparisons; for among males of every age group the percentage married was higher in the rural farm than among the urban population.[14] The census data also indicate that the single persons and divorced people are concentrated in the cities. Among the native white population of native parents and among Negroes, single persons of both sexes and practically every age group are more numerous in the urban population than in the rural farm group.[15] A similar uniformity prevails among the females of the foreign elements in the population (native white of foreign or mixed parentage and foreign-born whites). But males among the foreign elements exhibit a very interesting reversal of this uniformity: among these groups at all ages there are higher proportions of single persons in the farm population than in the urban. It would appear that the foreign-born male or even the male of foreign parentage is considerably handicapped by his cultural heritage and social barriers and is less able to secure a mate amid the keen rivalry created by the high sex ratio in the country than his countryman in the city, where males are at a premium.

Divorced of both sexes, of all ages, and of all the various race and nativity groups are much more prevalent in the city than in the country. In 1940, among the total population fifteen years of age and over, 1.4 percent of the urban males, 1.3 percent of the rural nonfarm males, and 0.8 of 1 percent of the rural farm males were divorced; for females the corresponding percentages were

---

[14] *Ibid., Table* 6, pp. 18–20. The same situation prevailed in 1930 and also in 1950. See *Abstract of the Fifteenth Census,* Washington, Government Printing Office, 1933, p. 241; and *1950 Census of Population: Preliminary Reports,* "General Characteristics of the Population of the United States: April 1, 1950," Series PC-7, No. 1, Washington, February 25, 1951.

[15] The only exceptions are among males aged twenty to thirty-five, where slightly higher proportions of the rural farm are single—an indication, no doubt, of a tendency for farm males to remain on the home farm with the parents for a considerable time. Also in this connection it should be remembered that at these ages the sex ratio among single persons is very high. This greatly handicaps the young farmer in finding a mate. For a more complete discussion of this subject, see T. Lynn Smith, *Population Analysis,* New York, McGraw-Hill Book Company, 1948, pp. 143–146.

2.1, 1.3, and 0.7. The data for 1950 available at the time this volume went to press do not show the divorced population separately from the widowed. However, among males fourteen years of age and over the percentages of widowers and divorced persons combined were 6.3, 6.1, and 4.7 in the urban, rural nonfarm and rural farm populations, respectively; and among the females the corresponding percentages were 15.6, 12.7, and 8.3.[16] These materials should make it evident that broken homes are not as prevalent on the farms as in the cities, their suburbs, and the villages.

There is also a strong tendency for widows to concentrate in the cities.[17] This situation is rather widespread throughout the nation, and it prevails among all race and nativity groups except Negroes. Since Negroes are a rural group primarily, care must be taken in making blanket comparisons of rural and urban populations on this score. Within the rural population, the heterogeneous lot in the catchall category styled nonfarm contains a much higher proportion of widows thirty-five years of age and over, indicating that many of this group gravitate to rural villages from the surrounding farms.[18]

Because Negroes are disproportionately numerous in the rural United States and especially the most rural part of the nation, the South, it is important to indicate the principal ways in which the marital status of this group is distinctive. The data make it clear that even today the marital and family mores of Negroes either are in a very undeveloped state or at least diverge widely from those of the white community. Single persons are much scarcer among Negroes than whites, a fact which is especially noticeable among the younger age groups. But although fewer Negroes are single and although they marry at a younger age than whites, the proportion of married among colored people is distinctively lower than among whites, a difference especially noticeable among females, but prevailing among males as well, at least in the cities. In this connection it should also be remembered that a great many of the marriages of Negroes, especially in the rural South, are of the common-law type. The most distinctive difference consists of

[16] "General Characteristics of the Population of the United States: April 1, 1950," p. 8.

[17] Smith, *Population Analysis*, p. 145; and T. Lynn Smith and Homer L. Hitt, *The People of Louisiana*, Baton Rouge, Louisiana State University Press, 1952, pp. 82–84.

[18] T. Lynn Smith, "Some Aspects of Village Demography," *Social Forces*, XX (1941), 16–23.

the very high proportion of widowed and divorced persons to be found in the Negro group.[19]

Family Functions

In all societies the family has been charged with the responsibility for performing certain necessary functions, essential for the well-being of society, that are carried on not at all or only partially by other agencies. The most important of the societal functions usually performed by the family may be listed as follows: (1) the reproduction of the species; (2) the sustenance, care, and rearing of the offspring, especially during infancy and the years of complete dependency; (3) the education and training of the young; (4) the induction of the new members of the race into the larger society, particularly in helping to establish their status in society's various groupings; (5) recreation; (6) protection of members from enemies and dangers, including the shielding of members from psychosocial isolation; and (7) the care of aged and other incapacitated members and relatives.[20]

The rural family has performed and continues to perform all these functions in a very successful manner. As has been indicated in Chapter 7, the rural family is the place of origin of a disproportionately large share of the oncoming generations. In the all-important function of reproduction the rural family has carried on while the urban family long failed to replace its members as they passed away.[21] The rural family has also been highly successful in sustaining, caring for, and rearing the infants entrusted to its care. In education and training, the apprentice system has operated in agriculture to give the oncoming generation the intimate knowledge and practical skills necessary in the multiple operations and details of farm production and family living.[22] Combined with the formal education received in the open-country and village schools,

[19] Cf. T. Lynn Smith, "A Demographic Study of the American Negro," *Social Forces*, XXIII (1945), 383.

[20] For other slightly different lists of family functions, see P. A. Sorokin, Carle C. Zimmerman, and Charles J. Galpin, *A Systematic Source Book in Rural Sociology*, Minneapolis, University of Minnesota Press, 1931, II, 4; and Dwight Sanderson and Robert G. Foster, *The Sociology of the Family*, Cornell Agricultural Experiment Station, Ithaca (mimeographed), 1929, p. 13.

[21] Walter C. McKain and N. L. Whetten have shown a positive correlation between homogeneity in fundamental traits in the married pair and fertility, in their article "Size of Family in Relation to Homogeneity of Parental Traits," *Rural Sociology*, I (1936), 20–27.

[22] Cf. N. L. Sims, *Elements of Rural Sociology*, New York, Thomas Y. Crowell Company, 1928, pp. 277–278.

handicapped though the rural communities have been in providing adequate educational facilities, this has probably given the farm youth a more well-rounded program of education than has been provided the young in most urban environments. At least there can be little doubt that the rural family has been more influential both quantitatively and qualitatively than the urban family in transmitting the cultural heritage of the group from one generation to another.

Concerning the function of inducting members of the family group into the larger society, it seems necessary to distinguish between the effects upon members of the rural family who have taken their places in rural society and those who have migrated to urban centers. With respect to the former it appears that the rural family has been highly efficient in determining the position of its members in the larger groups. So true has this been that rural society tends to have a distinctly caste nature, i.e., there is a strong tendency for the social position to be transmitted from one generation to another. But those members of rural families who have migrated to urban centers have been forced largely to shift for themselves. The rural family as a rule is able to wield little influence once the children have abandoned the rural community.

The rural family has also handled the recreational function in a highly satisfactory manner. Large houses and especially plenty of yard space have contributed to the maintenance of recreation as a family function, long after commercial entertainment supplies specialized recreational services to the individuals from the urban home. Even with the coming of the automobile and the village movie, there is still a great tendency for the family to engage as a unit in recreational activities. Family unions and picnics remain an important element in the rural life of most of the sections of the nation.[23] It need hardly be mentioned that the city is almost entirely lacking in a comparable activity.

Elaborate systems and personnel for law enforcement are lacking in rural areas. In a way they are hardly necessary, since the family accepts in a large measure the responsibility for the welfare of its members. In a very real sense every farmer's house is his castle. Quite aside from the century-old feuds which are still carried on in many of the rural sections of the nation, there still re-

[23] Cf. *ibid.*, p. 252; and Dwight Sanderson, "The Rural Family," *Journal of Home Economics*, XXIX (1937), 224, 227.

mains much of collective responsibility in rural areas. There is a tendency for the members of one family group to accept responsibility for the actions of its own members, on the one hand, and to fasten the responsibility for the behavior of another individual upon all the members of the family to which he belongs, on the other. Families find it necessary to exercise a strong control over their members because of this; but they protect individual members from encroachments by others, and they also shield a member from the wrath of his opponents. Family groupings also coöperate in protecting themselves from prowlers and strangers. All in all, such an informal system continues to this day to maintain a considerable degree of safety for person and property in the rural areas.[24]

Today it is recognized that many of the dangers against which the individual needs protection are mental rather than physical. The growing frequency of mental disorders is one of the greatest crises facing modern civilization. Durkheim in a penetrating analysis has shown the intimate association between mental strain, in the extreme form that results in suicide, and the degree of cohesion within the group. Individuals with membership in strong and closely knit family groups escape the dangers of suicide to a much greater extent than those lacking such a protective association.[25] Undoubtedly the strength of the rural family is the principal explanation of the escape of rural people from such perils to so much greater an extent than urban persons.

Finally the rural family has performed an excellent service in caring for aged and otherwise incapacitated members and relatives, with the result that specialized institutions for the care of such people have been largely lacking in rural areas.[26] Results of available studies indicate that about one rural family in every three or four has one or more grandparents living with the natural

[24] For the persistence of collective responsibility in rural areas, consult Helen Douglas-Irvine, *The Making of Rural Europe*, London, G. Allen & Unwin, Ltd., 1923, pp. 33–34; see also W. G. Sumner, *Folkways*, Boston, Ginn and Company, 1907, pp. 499–508.

[25] A translation of part of Durkheim's classical study, *Le Suicide*, is given in Sorokin, Zimmerman, and Galpin, *op. cit.*, III, 189–201.

[26] ". . . The rural family is a 'protective society' for the aged and also for helpless children. . . . [It] may be considered as an insurance institution." Charles P. Loomis, "The Study of the Life Cycle of Families," *Rural Sociology*, I (1936), 183–184. See also T. Lynn Smith, "The Aged in Rural Society," in Milton Derber, (ed.), *The Aged and Society*, Champaign, Illinois, Industrial Relations Research Association, 1950, pp. 40–53.

family, as compared with one family in twelve in urban areas.[27] Maiden aunts, adopted children, bachelor uncles, and persons incapacitated by one cause or another are met frequently in the rural household.

Family Types

Because so much has been written upon the subject of the family, one consults the literature hopeful of finding excellent identification and description of the principal types of family organization. This would seem to be one of the first aims and accomplishments of the scientific study of the family. But the search for meaningful classifications of families and careful descriptions of family types is almost in vain. In view of the basic importance of this primary, highly cumulative group this condition is, to say the least, disappointing.

Classifications of families are not entirely lacking. Mowrer has differentiated four types of family "patterns," namely, the paternal, maternal, equalitarian, and filio-centric.[28] But this is merely a classification of families on the basis of one characteristic—the seat of authority within the family grouping. According to Mowrer, ultimate authority resides with the father in the paternal type; this pattern is to be found among the immigrant groups. (Mowrer completely ignores the rural family, but probably he would include it in the paternal class.) In the maternal families, made up of the urban upper bourgeois who reside on the periphery of the city and commute to work, most of the authority is centered in the wife. In the residential areas of the city are found the other two types side by side. In the equalitarian family all members, including children, are equal in authority; in the filio-centric type, everything revolves about the child, especially the single child.

Another significant classification of family types is that by the French scholar Frédéric LePlay, made early in the nineteenth century and recently revived in this country by Zimmerman and Frampton. On the basis of extensive European researches, LePlay differentiated three major types of families as follows: (1) the patriarchal, (2) the unstable, and (3) the stem family. According to LePlay, the patriarchal family prevails in simple, virile societies.

[27] See the Minnesota study summarized in Sorokin, Zimmerman, and Galpin, *op. cit.*, II, 25.

[28] Ernest R. Mowrer, *The Family*, Chicago, University of Chicago Press, 1934, pp. 96–98.

Rural society is, of course, an excellent example of these. Such a type of organization almost completely engulfs the individual in the family group. Within the family is an intense spirit of self-preservation; all the individual members are strongly attached to one another and to the household. Family traditions are abundant and strong. Upon marriage, children do not separate entirely from the original unit, but settle near and continue to be subordinate in many respects to the father. This enlarged family, or *mesnie*, also embraced servants and workmen attached to the house. At the head was the *seigneur*, possessed of ultimate authority in all matters pertaining to the household and highly paternal and patronal in character.[29] Individual members may leave the group temporarily, but they continue under its influence, protected by it on the one hand, and dominated by it on the other. From the standpoint of personality, the individuality of the members is rather completely submerged in the group.

At the other extreme is the unstable family. The individual is the vital concern in this case. Attachments to the household and other members are weak and lack permanency. Traditions are few and puny, or entirely lacking. Such a family begins with the marriage of the parents, ends with their deaths. Found mostly in complex societies, this type of family gives free rein to the individuality of the members. But in times of disaster or catastrophe there is no strong, permanent group for the member to fall back upon.

The third family type, the stem family, combines part of the characteristics from each of the other two. LePlay used this term to designate a family that maintains, with part of its members, a group homestead; other of its members go elsewhere to make a living, but they continue to maintain contacts with and contribute to the support of the central cell. In case of misfortune, the member from afar is entitled to return and receive assistance from the main stem. This type of family fosters both the preservation of the past and the utilization of change.[30] It seems particularly fitted

[29] Cf. Frantz Funck-Brentano, *The Old Régime in France*, London, Longmans, Green & Company, 1929, pp. 5–6.

[30] See Carle C. Zimmerman and Merle E. Frampton, *Family and Society*, New York, D. Van Nostrand Company, 1935, pp. 97–99. More recently Zimmerman has proposed the classification of families into three types based in the amount of power, the extent of the field of action, and the degree of social control involved. These are the "trustee," "domestic," and "atomistic" varieties, respectively. The trustee family is the one with the greatest power, the widest range of action, and the most social control; the atomistic is the one with the least of all three; and the domestic type is intermediate in all respects. See Carle C. Zimmerman, *Family and Civilization*, New York, Harper & Brothers, 1947, p. 125.

for situations in which overpopulated rural areas regularly contribute migrants to other areas, particularly to cities.

Undoubtedly both the patriarchal and the stem family types are widespread in rural America; but their importance, their relative positions in different regions, and their true significance in rural culture must wait more detailed studies than are now available.

Characteristics of the Rural Family

As compared with the urban family the rural family has several outstanding characteristics. (1) As indicated in an earlier section, the rural family performs the various functions of the family much more thoroughly and completely than does the urban group. (2) As a union of husband and wife, parents and children, the rural family is much more closely integrated and more permanent than the urban family. Statistics of divorce and desertion leave no room for doubt that marriage ties are more permanent in the country than in the city. In addition, the rural family retains its children under the parental eye and supervision to a much greater extent than is possible in the city; it also retains the children under the parental roof for a considerably longer time than can the urban family. Not only do rural children remain at home longer than urban children before marriage, but frequently rural families retain the children in the old homestead even after they have married, a thing practically unknown in cities until the more recent developments growing out of the great depression. (3) The rural family fuses its members into one organic whole, obliterating the individual personalities to a much greater extent than does the urban family, on account of the highly cumulative nature of the rural familial group, the interdependence engendered by division of labor within the group, the long-continued and constant nature of the association, and the comparative weakness of competing institutions. In comparison with other social institutions, the role of the family is much more important in the country than in the city.[31]

Taylor has indicated that the great extent to which familism is characteristic of rural areas has both advantages and disadvantages. On the positive side he mentions that the close daily contact between parents and children deepens their regard and af-

---

[31] Cf. Carl C. Taylor, *Rural Sociology*, New York, Harper & Brothers, 1933, pp. 269–270; and Sorokin, Zimmerman, and Galpin, *op. cit.*, II, 5–17.

fection for one another, constantly subjects the children to the traditional moral integrity of the farm family, and keeps constantly before the children's eyes the social ethics and acceptable behavior patterns of the family. But, on the negative side, the following must be recognized: (1) The family is somewhat of a closed corporation, altruistic with respect to members but selfish with regard to outsiders; (2) limited contacts make for narrow and inflexible views and practices; (3) the nature of the family associations promotes clannishness; and (4) the personalities of the individuals are kept near the same level.[32]

Considerable disagreement would inevitably arise out of any attempt to evaluate the negative and positive results of a highly integrated family organization. There can be little doubt, however, that the development of a high degree of familism has been and continues to be an outstanding feature of agricultural societies, that familism persists most unabated in the most rural areas of the nation and particularly in the South and West, and that the family continues to be by far the most important group in rural society.

The Life Cycle of the Farm Family

As is the case with other social groups, the family too has a a life history. Students of rural life have made a good beginning at determining the nature of the cycle through which the farm family passes in the course of its life history. Sorokin, Zimmerman, and Galpin have traced the sequences of the farm family with respect to the composition of the family in its relationship to the agricultural operations and the material well-being of the family group. They distinguish four stages, as follows: (1) In the first stage, the young married couple is just starting as an independent group. Ordinarily at first the holdings of land are limited, although sufficient for the two. As a result, since both are capable of work and are not burdened by dependents, their economic well-being is comparatively good. (2) The second stage begins when children are born to the couple. Now it is necessary to feed more mouths; on the average the result is an increase in the size of the farm. But all in all, this second stage is the hardest period in the entire cycle. The couple is forced to exert more energy and to restrict consumption in order to care for and nourish young, completely dependent

[32] Taylor, *op. cit.*, pp. 270–271.

children. (3) When the children come to adulthood and self-sufficiency the family enters the third stage of the cycle. Abundant
labor forces now make it possible to place still larger acreages
under cultivation, and the farm is likely to be enlarged still more.
Children are able to pay their own way. Some help on the farm;
others work away from home for wages and send part of the proceeds back. All members are now producers and none are wholly
dependent. By and large this is the easiest and most prosperous
period in the cycle. (4) In the fourth and final stage, old age over-
takes the parents, and at the same time the children separate from
the original group and establish families of their own. The deple-
tion of the labor forces causes the land holdings to be decreased.
For many parents this is a period of increasing hardship. The
lower production of the aged pair makes them more dependent
for support as consumers upon the son or sons who have remained
with them.[33] The center of attention soon passes from the old
group to one of its newer offshoots.

Recent Changes in the Family

Changes from the rural family of colonial days early began in
the growing urban centers of the nation. More recently many of
the city's influences have been diffused to the country with the
result that the rural family is now undergoing decided changes.
To some this is an encouraging thing since they maintain that "the
traditional American pioneer type of family" is unworkable in
modern society and will become even more inadequate as time
passes.[34] This contention that family changes must keep pace with
changes in the material culture is popular at the present time.
Some there are, however, who fail to agree that changes in the
family necessarily accompany urbanization or changes in the material culture.[35] Probably this contention does not receive the at-

[33] See Sorokin, Zimmerman, and Galpin, *op. cit.*, II, 30–33; Loomis, *op. cit.*,
pp. 180–199; and Loomis, *The Growth of the Farm Family in Relation to Its
Activities*, North Carolina AES Bulletin 298, Raleigh, 1934. Cf. E. L. Kirkpatrick,
Rosalind Tough, and May L. Cowles, *The Life Cycle of the Farm Family*, Wisconsin AES Research Bulletin 121, Madison, 1934, pp. 28–32; and Allan Beegle
and C. P. Loomis, "Life Cycles of Farm, Rural-Nonfarm, and Urban Families in
the United States as Derived from Census Materials," *Rural Sociology*, XIII
(1948), 70–74.

[34] E. B. Reuter and Jesse R. Runner, *The Family*, New York, McGraw-Hill
Book Company, 1931, p. 8.

[35] Zimmerman and Frampton, *op. cit.*, pp. 43–50, *passim*. Here will be found
the theories of the famous student of the family, Frédéric LePlay.

tention it deserves. Although rarely noted in discussions on the subject, this second position is strongly supported by experience of the most highly urbanized group the world has ever known. This group is, of course, the Jews. Holding tenaciously to a patriarchal form of family organization, the Jews have nevertheless for centuries been city dwellers. What is more important, they not only have survived but have multiplied in the city, a truly phenomenal experience. The strong organization of the Jewish family is the only factor readily at hand to explain why the Jewish people have been able to maintain themselves in an urban environment when practically all others have failed.[36] As Ross has well said: "No other physiques can so well withstand the toxins of urban congestion."[37] The fact that urbanity is not necessarily inimical to a patriarchal type of family organization similar in many ways to our own colonial type is shown also by the marked success of the Spanish American family. Almost always confined to the cities of the Latin American countries, this group has persisted for centuries. The success of the Jews and the Spanish Americans and the conspicuous failure of the modern American family even to maintain members suggest that only the possession of strong family organization enables a society to cope successfully with the perplexing problems of urbanization.

In a basic study William F. Ogburn has outlined the principal current changes in the American family. A thorough student, Ogburn, unlike most contemporary writers on the family, was careful to take account of rural-urban differences; as a result his findings are much more significant than the usual run of conclusions. His analysis yielded two principal generalizations: (1) that the institutional functions of the family are declining and (2) that the importance of the family in the formation of character, the provision of social contacts—in short, what Ogburn calls the "affectual function"—has been increased.[38]

Consider first the decline in the functions of the family. In early America when all was rural, the colonial home was a workshop. Since then, and especially during the last fifty years, some

[36] See Hastings, *op. cit.*, V, "Family (Jewish)," for a discussion of the perpetuation of the Jewish family forms from pastoral Biblical times in the crowded ghettos of medieval cities.

[37] E. A. Ross, *The Old World in the New*, New York, D. Appleton-Century Company, 1914, p. 145.

[38] In *Recent Social Trends*, New York, McGraw-Hill Book Company, 1933, I, 661–663.

economic functions such as metalworking, spinning, and weaving have been given up almost entirely even by the rural families. Other functions such as baking, laundering, and canning have lost much ground. Ogburn cites data secured from Hildegarde Kneeland of the United States Bureau of Home Economics, showing that in 1930 two-thirds of the farm families depended entirely upon baker's bread, as compared with nine-tenths of the urban families. Similarly, 12 percent of the farm families have part or all of the laundry done outside the home, as compared with 67 percent of the city families. These and similar changes in the economic functions of the family are reflected in the shift of occupations from the home and the increased employment of women outside the home.[39] Churning, shoemaking, sugar making, cheese making, soap making, etc., are other economic functions once performed within the family group, now largely transferred to specialized agencies.

As with the economic function, so with many of the others. Much of the protective function has been passed to the state, as in the case of health, provision for the aged, care of the feeble-minded and insane, and the police power. In all of these, however, Ogburn indicates that the rural family still continues to function to a considerable extent.[40] Religious, recreational, and educational functions also have atrophied in recent years, especially in the cities. Even the matter of the importance of family status itself is thought to have declined. One's place in society is no longer so dependent upon his family. This change Ogburn calls the individualization of the family members; and he maintains that increased individuality of the wife has been especially pronounced.[41]

Along with the changes in functions recently have occurred important changes in family organization. These may be summarized as follows: (1) Until recently there has been some increase in marriage, especially early marriage; (2) the size of the household has been decreasing, very little on the farms, over one-fifth in the great metropolitan cities; (3) the size of the family has also decreased, but much less on farms than in cities; (4) families are becoming more diversified, especially in the cities where broken families, homes without children, immigrant families, Negro families, families in rooming-house areas, etc., make for a

[39] *Ibid.*, pp. 664–672.
[40] *Ibid.*, pp. 672–673.
[41] *Ibid.*, pp. 677–679.

motley assortment; and (5) family disorganization is ever becoming quantitatively greater and more perplexing. Homes broken by the death of father or mother, families disrupted by desertion especially in low-income families, and divorce (greatly on the increase) among the middle and upper classes are bringing strongly to the fore the problem of family disorganization.[42]

For his second proposition, the increase in the affectional function, Ogburn admits there is little evidence, reasons for the most part deductively.[43] In disagreement with Ogburn, the writer, also deductively, views affection largely as the net product of interaction, and believes that it too is weakened by the sloughing off of family functions and the increased disorganization of the modern family. Since neither of these has occurred to such an extent in the rural family, it seems probable that the constellation of functions there gives greater coherence and unity, a greater sum total of affection than is exhibited by the urban grouping.

[42] *Ibid.*, pp. 680–696.
[43] *Ibid.*, pp. 696–702.

18

RURAL EDUCATION AND EDUCATIONAL
INSTITUTIONS

Education ranks among the major tasks, educational progress among the chief hopes of society. Education is the name applied to the process whereby the socially approved part of the cultural heritage is transmitted from one generation to the next, and the process whereby newly acquired knowledge is diffused among the members of society. For performing these functions society has made use of a large number of institutions. Throughout the ages, the family has been by far the most important educational agency.[1] It still retains many of its educational functions in the rural America of today, especially the function of transmitting the cultural elements that have to do with adjustment to the everyday routine of farm life and activities.

To a considerable extent in rural communities there is a distinct division of labor between the family and the school in the educational sphere. Schools tend to give instruction in urban lore and activities, the family to instill in the children knowledge and skills directly related to everyday life on the farm. Today, however, the school is looked upon as the principal educational institution and it properly deserves a high place among the institutions of society. In addition to the family and the school, the educational process in rural areas goes on by means of the church, newspapers, and magazines, the radio, television, the movies, libraries, and a host of other associations, organizations, and agencies. One of the most vital factors in the rural educational system of the present

[1] Until very recently, in most countries, the school has been for use by children from the "better classes," "for gentlemen's children only." Cf., for example, N. S. B. and Ethel C. Gras, *The Economic and Social History of an English Village*, Cambridge, Harvard University Press, 1930, p. 61.

day is the agricultural extension service of the various colleges of agriculture, and the 9650 county, home, and club agents who are distributed throughout practically every county in the United States.

Educational Status

Because the rudiments of an education, especially the ability to read, write, and calculate, today are among the basic necessities of life, educational status is another important characteristic in the composition of a population. The illiterate person is shut off from many important current-day sources of information and advice, is unable to participate in many of the ordinary phases of everyday life, is handicapped in his contributions to the well-being of society, and is more at the mercy of unscrupulous associates than is the individual who knows how to read and write.

A survey of the relevant data reveals clearly that the benefits of the American educational system have not been extended to people in rural communities in the same degree as has been enjoyed by residents of urban centers. Thus in the population ten years of age and over, 4,000,000 persons (4.3 percent) were illiterate in 1930. Among the urban population the proportion was only 3.2 percent, as compared with 6.9 in the rural farm and 4.8 percent in the rural nonfarm populations. Furthermore, illiteracy was concentrated more in the younger ages in the rural farm population than in the urban. For example, only 0.3 of 1 percent of the urban children ten to fourteen years of age and 0.6 of 1 percent of those fifteen to nineteen years of age were illiterate in 1930, as compared with 2.5 and 4.0 percent, respectively, among the corresponding rural farm groups. For native whites these percentages were 0.2 and 0.3 in the urban, 1.0 and 1.5 in the rural farm population. But among Negroes they were 1.2 and 2.9 in the urban population and 7.8 and 12.9 in the rural farm group. Even in 1930, one Negro youth out of every eight was unable to read or write enough to be classed as literate in the census, a very minor accomplishment indeed![2]

Even more revealing are the data on educational status, materials that were gathered for the first time in the Census of 1940. This information makes possible a much more satisfactory com-

---

[2] Data from *Abstract of the Fifteenth Census of the United States,* Washington, Government Printing Office, 1933, Table 140, p. 277.

parison of the extent to which the urban and rural populations have received the benefits of formal schooling. (See Figures 106 and 107.) In every state of the Union the native white population of the urban centers has received more formal education than the rural farm population, although in Rhode Island, Connecticut, New York, New Jersey, Ohio, and Kansas the differences are so slight that the two categories fall in the same class interval. The rural nonfarm population also consistently ranks above the rural farm population in this respect. These rural-urban differences are greatest in the South, because of the sharp contrast between the very low educational status of farm people and the high educational status of urban people in the region. In the Far West, differences are also pronounced because even the high educational status of the farm population is considerably excelled by that of the urban people. These rural-urban differences are least throughout the densely populated section from Kansas to Rhode Island.

Among southern Negroes the low educational status of those living on farms is matched by that of those who live in urban centers. Northern Negroes, who are concentrated in the cities, make a good showing in comparison with their southern fellows but stand very poorly in comparison with their white neighbors.

Finally, the early releases of data from the seventeenth census makes it clear that the same sort of rural-urban differences in educational status prevailed in 1950. At the time of our latest census, April 1, 1950, the median years of schooling for the population aged twenty-five years and over in the United States had risen to 9.3, one full year higher than the 1940 level. Among the urban, rural nonfarm, and rural farm populations the medians were 10.0, 8.9, and 8.4 years, respectively. In the early tabulations the data were not separated by race and residence simultaneously, but the median number of years of schooling among the white population was 9.7 and that among the nonwhite was 7.0.[3]

Rural Schools

What Should the Schools Provide?

This important question has been answered in a clear, concise, logical, and adequate way by the Advisory Committee on Educa-

[3] Data are from the *1950 Census of Population, Preliminary Reports*, "Educational Attainment of the Population 25 Years Old and Over, for the United States: 1950," Series PC-7, No. 6, Washington, May 13, 1952.

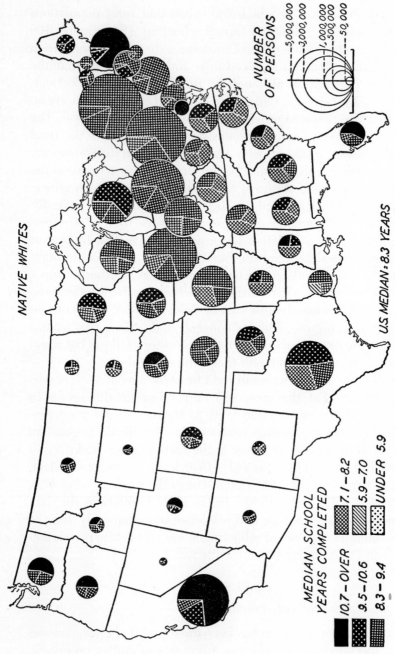

NATIVE WHITES

NUMBER OF PERSONS

MEDIAN SCHOOL YEARS COMPLETED

10.7 – OVER
9.5 – 10.6
8.3 – 9.4
7.1 – 8.2
5.9 – 7.0
UNDER 5.9

U.S. MEDIAN = 8.3 YEARS

Figure 106. Variation in the Amount of Formal Schooling Received by the Native White Population Aged Twenty-Five Years and Over, 1940, by Residence. (Starting at 12:00 o'clock on the circles and reading clockwise, the segments represent the urban, rural nonfarm, and rural farm populations, respectively.)

NEGROES

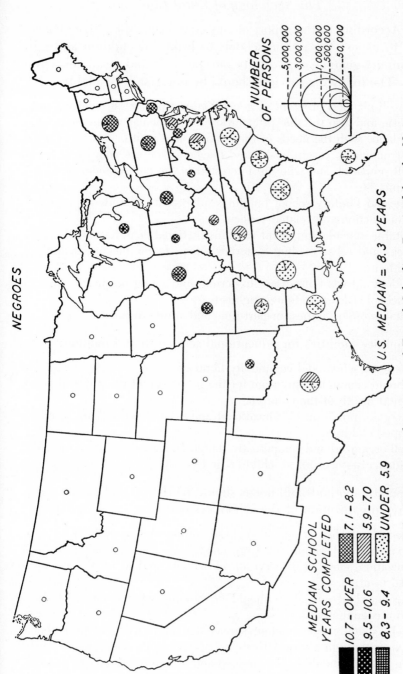

FIGURE 107. Variation in the Amount of Formal Schooling Received by the Negro Population Aged Twenty-Five Years and Over, 1940, by Residence. (Starting at 12:00 o'clock on the circles and reading clockwise, the segments represent the urban, rural nonfarm, and rural farm populations, respectively.)

tion. According to the report of this committee, the citizen has a right to expect the public schools to bring his children and his community genuine opportunities for personal and social development. The following services should be universally available:

1. A well-planned program of general education for all children and youth, and also suitable preparation for particular vocations in accordance with the needs of the children and youth.
2. Instruction by carefully selected teachers who are competent and well prepared, and who are interested in the development of community life.
3. Safe and sanitary school buildings adapted to a modern program of instruction and related services.
4. Suitable school equipment and instructional materials, including books and other reading materials adequate for the needs of the children.
5. Student aid when necessary to permit able young people to remain in school at least up to age eighteen.
6. Suitable opportunities for part-time and adult education.

Community facilities for educational service should include:

1. Adequate school and community libraries.
2. A broad community program for the protection of the physical and mental health of the children.
3. Adequate provision of educational and related services for handicapped children.
4. Well-organized and competently staffed educational and vocational guidance services for all children and youth.[4]

Democratic methods and needs should be the basis of the administrative organization of the school system:

1. The school district or other local administrative unit, whether urban or rural, should be large enough to permit economical organization, effective supervision of schools, and a broad base for local taxation.
2. The board of education should be broadly representative of the entire community.
3. There should be competent supervision of instruction and other services through a staff with supervisory capacity and social vision.
4. The teachers should be encouraged and given opportunity to participate actively and intelligently in the development of educational

[4] *Report of the Advisory Committee on Education,* House Doc. 529, 75th Congress, 3d Session, Washington, 1938, p. 11.

and administrative policies for the school system; they should also be encouraged to participate in community activities appropriate for public servants.

5. There should be definite cooperative arrangements for the coordination of the work of the schools with that of other community agencies concerned with the health, education, welfare, and guidance of children and youth.
6. In rural areas, the school system should be as efficiently organized and as well supported as in urban areas; so far as feasible school attendance areas should follow community lines.
7. Where separate schools are maintained for Negroes, they should be as well adapted to the needs of their pupils as are the schools for white children and youth.[5]

According to the committee, this catalogue of needs and standards is not a visionary ideal but a practical program for a country as rich, as democratic, and as convinced of the value of universal education as is the United States.

As the minimum objectives for a modern educational program the writer suggests the following:

1. The school should transmit all the essential knowledge and develop the basic skills which are presupposed by modern systems of communication and transportation. This means drill and plenty of it on the three R's (reading, writing, calculation, and speech).

2. The school should arouse and nurture in the student the wants and desires which will make for a full life and a well-rounded personality in the community of which he is a part. Especially if the family is settled into a routine existence, the school must instill new wants and desires in the developing child.

3. The school is obligated to instruct in the skills and technique whereby means to satisfy the new wants and desires may be attained. This process of creating new wants and desires and developing the skills whereby they may be satisfied is education in the truest sense of the word.

Magnitude of the Task

That the high birth rates in rural areas and rural-urban migration put a disproportionately large share of the burden of rearing and educating the oncoming generations upon the rural popula-

[5] *Ibid.,* pp. 11–12.

tion, and especially upon the farm population, is now fairly well known. Many states have recognized this fact and have provided systems of equalization whereby state funds are distributed to the counties least able to support schools. Some of them also allocate state educational funds to the counties in proportion to the number of children of school age, a procedure which helps to equalize opportunities for education. More recently a fuller understanding of the magnitude, nature, and significance of rural-urban migration has brought about a considerable demand that educational opportunities also be equalized as between states. With birth rates, death rates, and migration what they are today, a significant portion of the urban population must depend upon the rural school for a large part of its training. The result of inadequate rural educational facilities is immediately reflected in the mental equipment of the city population.

The magnitude of the task confronting rural areas in the provision of educational services is shown by the following data from the 1950 Census. Almost one-half (47 percent) of the 25,602,000 persons aged five to fourteen, inclusive, resided in rural territory, although only 36 percent of the total population was rural. For every 100 rural persons aged twenty to forty-five there were sixty-six children in the ages five to fourteen, inclusive; the corresponding number in urban areas was only thirty-six. These inequalities also have significance for the different ethnic stocks and races represented in the national population. Owing to the regional and residential distribution of the principal race and nativity groups, the "old Americans," both white and colored, are more largely concentrated in rural areas, where schools are poor, than in urban areas, where facilities are better. The rural population in 1940 included 50 percent of native white children aged five to fourteen, inclusive, and 60 percent of the Negroes, but only 17 percent of the foreign-born white children were living in rural areas. If the children of the "old American stock" are to have equal educational opportunities with immigrants and their children, rural schools must not be allowed to lag behind the urban.

The magnitude of the task confronting the rural schools of the nation is indicated not only by the numbers of children residing in rural areas but by the enrollment in these rural schools. In spite of the fact that many rural children attend schools that are located in urban centers,[6] the enrollment in rural public day schools in 1935–1936 was 13,116,399, as compared with 13,250,699 in urban day schools.[7] Three years later, in 1939–1940, the enrollment in rural public schools was 12,123,995, compared with 13,309,547 in urban public schools.[8] In the more recent issues of the *Biennial Survey of Education in the United States* the difficult task of presenting the data separately for rural and urban schools has been abandoned.

Inequalities in Educational Opportunity

For a nation that prides itself upon its democracy and in which the population is so highly mobile, the inequalities in educational opportunities within the states and among the various regions and states are unbelievably great. In Iowa estimates have shown that the most prosperous school district had 275 times as much wealth per child as the poorest district. "In a number of States, the most able local units could provide $100 or more per child for every $1

[6] The data on this point are far from satisfactory. Floyd Jordan, *The Social Composition of Secondary Schools in the Southern States*, Nashville, George Peabody College for Teachers, 1933, p. 48, reported that 3.5 percent of the high-school students in eleven southern cities were children of fathers who, at the time of the study, were actively engaged in agriculture. The investigation of the situation in Louisiana is even more revealing. Omitting the schools in Orleans and Jefferson parishes, we find that 22.3 percent of all high-school and 11.6 percent of all elementary students attending urban high schools were transported by bus; almost without exception they came from rural areas. See M. B. Smith, *A Sociological Analysis of Rural Education in Louisiana*, University, Louisiana State University Press, 1938, pp. 90, 100. In Michigan four-fifths of the farm boys and girls receive their elementary education in 6000 one-room neighborhood schools. Those who attend high school do so "as nonresident, tuition pupils at schools located in some 533 villages and cities." J. F. Thaden and Eben Mumford, *High School Communities in Michigan*, Michigan AES Special Bulletin 289, East Lansing, 1938, p. 34. This study presents no data as to the residences of high-school students, but "Saginaw high school serves all or a majority of the tuition pupils from 63 school districts, Traverse City high school serves 58 districts, Battle Creek 57, Hastings and Cold Water each 55, and Midland 53." *Ibid.*, p. 24. The total number of tuition pupils in 1933 was about 37,000 in approximately 6700 school districts. Of these, the children from over 2500 districts attended school in urban centers. These data were compiled from *ibid.*, pp. 12, 25. The rather obvious fact that rural children attending urban high schools must be corrected for before valid comparisons of the proportions of rural and urban children in school can be made seems to have escaped most of those who have compiled data on the subject. See, for example, W. H. Gaumitz, *Availability of Public-School Education in Rural Communities*, Bulletin 34, 1930, U.S. Office of Education, Washington, 1931, p. 5.

[7] David T. Blose and Henry F. Alves, *Statistics of State School Systems, 1935–36*, Washington, Government Printing Office, 1938, p. 50.

[8] United States Office of Education, *Statistical Summary of Education, 1941–1942*, Washington, Government Printing Office, 1944, p. 14.

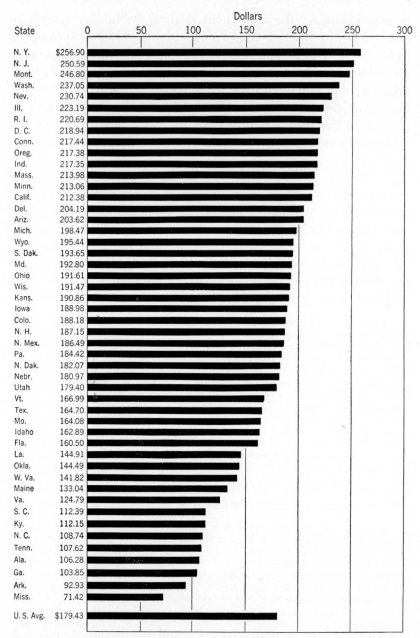

FIGURE 108. Current Expenditure per Pupil in Average Daily Attendance in Full-Time Public Elementary and Secondary Day Schools (Exclusive of Community Services), by State, 1947–1948. (Reproduced from the *Biennial Survey of Education in the United States,* Washington, Government Printing Office, 1950, p. 22.)

provided by the least able units."[9] In 1934 nearly one-fifth (404) of Montana's school districts had taxable valuations of less than $1500 per child, while 393 districts had taxable valuations of over $6000 per child; much of this variation was due to the method of allocating public utility taxable valuations.[10] Between the states there are also great differences in educational opportunity. As measured by expenditures per pupil, a useful but by no means perfect index, these differences in educational opportunity are indicated in Figure 108. Most of the variations are accounted for by differences in the proportions of rural and urban population: the low incomes of the agricultural areas, coupled with their large proportions of children, make the task of maintaining adequate rural schools almost impossible. Says the Advisory Committee on Education:

The problem of inequality of educational opportunities is to a large extent a problem in rural-urban differences in educational load and economic resources. If the rural and urban population were distributed among the States substantially in the same proportions, inequalities of educational opportunity could be minimized through the operation of equalization funds in the various States. The urban population, however, is concentrated in a relatively small number of States; more than half of the States are predominantly rural.[11]

The great differences in educational opportunities may not fairly be attributed to lack of effort in the states with the least adequate school facilities. On the contrary, in general the states having the poorest facilities are the ones putting forth the greatest efforts. (See Figures 109 and 110.) To quote again the Advisory Committee on Education:

Although the levels of expenditure cover a wide range, they do not differ as widely as do the levels of financial ability. The States of more than average financial ability are, in general, making less than average effort to support education, while the States of less than average ability are with few exceptions making considerably greater than average effort to support education.

It is to the credit of States of low financial ability that with few exceptions they rank at the top in the percentage of their income devoted

---

[9] *Report of the Advisory Committee on Education*, p. 13.
[10] Roland R. Renne, "Rural Educational Institutions and Social Lag," *Rural Sociology*, I (1936), 310.
[11] *Op. cit.*, p. 17.

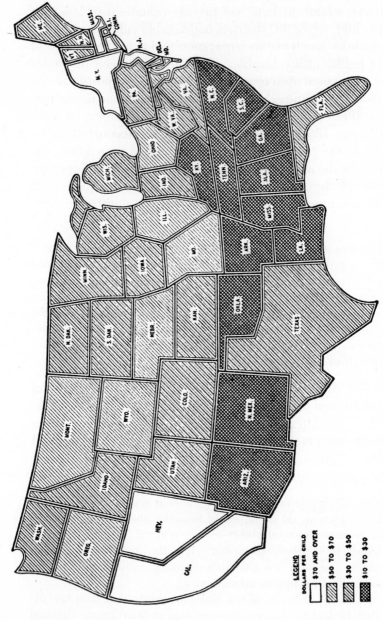

FIGURE 109. Revenue Available for the Education of Each Child Five to Seventeen Years of Age If Each State Made Average Effort to Educate Its Children at Average Cost, 1935. (Reproduced from the *Report of the Advisory Committee on Education*, Washington, 1938, p. 20.)

FIGURE 110. The Percentage of the Total Annual Personal Income in Each State That Is Spent for Public Schools, 1948. (Based on data published in the New York *Times*, September 17, 1950, by Benjamin Fine.)

to schools. Nevertheless, they rank at the bottom with respect to the quality of the schooling provided. Although the States having the least ability to support education tend to make the greatest effort in proportion to ability, even with such effort they are unable to support education at anything like the level attained, with less than average effort, by the more able States.[12]

Status of Rural Schools

Because of their small size and because they seem a particular group, certain definite problems are characteristic of rural schools.[13] Among these are a low pupil-teacher ratio, numerous subjects per teacher, inadequate plant and equipment, rapid turnover of teachers, narrow and limited curriculum largely determined by the textbooks, undue persistence of formalism and traditionalism, instruction that suffers from lack of supplementary material, ill-suited methods and techniques, poor organization, lack of adaptation to the environment of the pupils, and failure to devote primary attention to the immediate needs of all the children.[14] The quantitative data necessary for an adequate understanding of the structure and functioning of the rural schools of the nation are sadly lacking. The *Biennial Survey of Education* for 1934–1935 reports that "the collection of adequate educational statistics for rural areas is practically impossible,"[15] and the 1940–1942 *Survey* is not much more encouraging. The later issues, as mentioned above, abandoned the attempt altogether; but in November, 1951, the Office of Education published a special study[16] of the situation in the thirty-six states for which somewhat comparable materials could be assembled. Since these 1947–1948 data are the latest comprehensive materials on the subject they deserve summarizing in some detail.

The smallness of so many rural schools makes the average number of pupils in daily attendance per teacher in rural areas only twenty-two, as compared with twenty-five in the urban schools. In spite of the greater than the average effort put forth by rural

[12] *Ibid.*, pp. 19–20.

[13] Cf. W. H. Gaumitz, *The Smallness of America's Rural High Schools*, Bulletin 13, 1930, U.S. Office of Education, Washington, 1930.

[14] See the report prepared by C. L. Barrow, *A Suggested Program for the Training of Principals for Small High Schools*, Baton Rouge, State Department of Education, 1938, pp. 8–9.

[15] Blose and Alves, *op. cit.*, p. 50.

[16] Rose Marie Smith, *Education in Rural and City School Systems: Some Statistical Indices for 1947–48*, Circular 329, Washington, 1951.

sections to maintain more adequate schools, in 1947–1948 the rural term averaged only 172 days, whereas the urban term averaged 183 days; rural teachers received an average of only $2086 per year, as compared with an average salary of $3174 in urban districts; and the per pupil expenditure for maintaining public schools was only $282 in rural territory, as compared with $352 in urban areas. In spite of the great obstacles to regular attendance confronting the rural child, daily attendance in rural schools averaged 87 percent, as compared with 86 in the cities; and rural children attended an average of 148 days in the school year, as compared with 157 for urban children.

As might be expected, there are great regional variations in the school facilities available in the rural areas. Some states—Massachusetts, Washington, Connecticut, and Rhode Island—paid their rural schoolteachers an average of more than $3000 per term, while Mississippi paid only $1148, Arkansas $1415, Missouri $1447, North Dakota $1552, and Maine $1558.

The number of pupils in average daily attendance per teacher is very significant for a given school. But in a state the average is too greatly affected by the presence or absence of sparsely populated areas with one-room schools for such an index to have much significance. However, South Dakota and Nebraska have very low ratios of pupils to teacher, 13.3 and 13.6, respectively, whereas Mississippi (29.4), Rhode Island (27.1), and Arkansas (26.6) have the highest.

The length of the school term is one of the most significant items of information pertaining to the rural school situation. As indicated above, the rural school term averages much less than that of urban schools, or 172 days compared with 183 days. But here again the variations from state to state are very great. Some of the states (Massachusetts, Indiana, Connecticut, New Jersey, New Mexico, Pennsylvania, Delaware, and Maine) maintain rural school terms fully nine months in duration. Others, such as Mississippi, Kansas, and Wyoming, despite the admittedly greater effort put forth, did not average eight months in 1947–1948.

But in all the foregoing comparisons no attention is given to the important factor of race. This is because the data were not compiled in a manner to make possible separate comparisons for whites and Negroes. Were these data available, the situation would appear even more disquieting. Rural inequalities in educational opportunities of the races are even greater than the urban; and in a general comparison the Advisory Committee on Education reported as follows: "In most of the States where there are separate schools for Negroes, the schools for white children are far below the national average, yet Negro schools are only about half as well supported as white schools."[17] Because of the concentration of Negroes in the rural areas, particularly in plantation sections, the racial factor is an element that serves to pull the rural

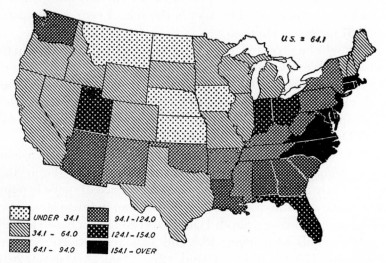

FIGURE 111. Average Number of Students per Rural School Building, by States, 1939–1940. (Source of data: Blose and Alves, *Statistics of State School Systems, 1939–40* and *1941–42.*)

average down. For example, in 1939–1940 in the seventeen states and the District of Columbia having dual educational systems the school terms averaged 170 days for whites and only 157 for Negroes; the average days in attendance were 144 for white children and only 128 days for Negro children.[18] In this connection it should be remembered that education of the masses is hardly considered an asset where caste is strong and agriculture is large scale.[19]

The small size of the rural school is frequently cited as one of the principal defects of the rural educational system and as a fac-

[17] *Op. cit.*, p. 7.
[18] *Statistical Summary of Education, 1941–42*, Table 28, p. 29.
[19] Cf. Charles S. Johnson, *Shadow of the Plantation*, Chicago, University of Chicago Press, 1934, p. 129.

tor that does much to make rural schooling unsatisfactory. Therefore, some data bearing on this subject are of considerable interest and importance. In 1939–1940 there were a total of 189,062 school buildings in the rural United States. In attendance at each of these schools was an average of 64.1 pupils, this index ranging from 25.4 in Montana and 25.7 in Kansas to 339.4 in New Jersey and 667 in Virginia. The South stands above the nation's average generally in pupils per rural school building; the lowest averages are to be found in the Midwest and Northwest. (See Figure 111.)

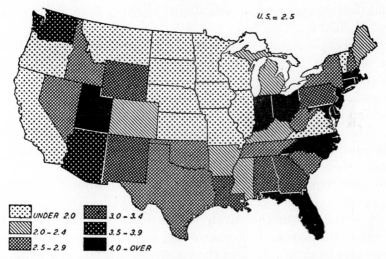

FIGURE 112. Average Number of Teachers per Rural School Building by States, 1939–1940. (Source of data: Blose and Alves, *Statistics of State School Systems, 1939–40* and *1941–42*.)

Another useful index of school size is the ratio of teachers per school building. Teaching positions in rural schools averaged 2.5 per building, as compared with 11.1 in urban schools. This figure was highest in Virginia (22.0), New Jersey (16.3), and Rhode Island (12.9); it was lowest in the Northwest: 1.4 in Montana, 1.5 in Iowa, Kansas, and South Dakota, and 1.6 in California, North Dakota, and Wisconsin. (See Figure 112.) Teachers per school in the South average well above the national average, indicating that excessively small schools are not the source of the region's educational difficulties.[20]

[20] These data are from Blose and Alves, *Statistics of State School Systems, 1939–40* and *1941–42*, Table 46, pp. 124–125.

The Rural School Curriculum

Educators are by no means in agreement as to the fundamental objectives of the public school, rural or urban. Some contend that a democratic society should supply to all children, in city and country, similar educational opportunities. It is insisted that "the large objectives of education do not differ because of location or economic conditions either of the parents of the children concerned or of the communities in which they chance to be reared and attend school. . . . Rural children cannot safely be satisfied with less comprehensive educational offerings than are essential for all children. . . ."[21]

Others place more stress upon the values of vocational training in education, urging that such instruction "fits youth for useful employment, providing training in the technique of the various occupations as well as in related subjects . . . which are useful to men and women both as workers and citizens."[22]

The curriculum that serves as such a tremendous social force in the rural communities of the nation represents a compromise between these different points of view. Under the pressure of college entrance requirements it has been, in the past, strongly propelled in the direction of a general classical type of educational offering, despite the fact that relatively few of the rural children ever entered institutions of higher learning. But the recent years have seen greater emphasis upon the vocational aspects, an attempt to make education more practical.

Consolidation of Schools

For solving all the rural school's ills the formula most frequently resorted to has been consolidation of schools. Unfortunately, critical examination and study of the results and implications of consolidation are largely lacking. Neither have the advocates of consolidation always been careful to indicate the sense in which the phrase is used, and the connotations have been many and varied. Marion B. Smith, after a thorough study of the literature, concluded as follows:

[21] Katherine M. Cook, *Review of Conditions and Development in Education in Rural and Other Sparsely Settled Areas*, Washington, Government Printing Office, 1937, p. 1.

[22] Carl A. Jessen, *Trends in Secondary Education*, Washington, Government Printing Office, 1937, p. 18.

From the time of the Committee of Twelve [National Educational Association, *Report of the Committee of Twelve on Rural Schools,* Chicago, 1897] to the present, investigators in the problems of the rural schools have found much ground for complaint. In the main there has been general agreement in the interpretation of the various studies of rural education. It has been agreed that certain weaknesses are characteristic of rural schools, and it has been generally agreed that these weaknesses can be corrected or relieved by increasing the size of the schools through consolidation of small schools, and through the redirection of educational activity.[23]

The same writer has pointed out the general agreement in the claims of educators and sociologists with respect to the merits of the consolidated school and has summarized the asserted benefits as follows:

1. The consolidated school would furnish better-equipped teachers and a more adequate supervision and administration for the schools.
2. More adequate school plants, located on school grounds more centrally situated, and more suitable for school purposes, would be erected.
3. The school term would be lengthened.
4. The consolidated school would serve as a natural social center for the area.
5. A widened acquaintance group would be formed by the children.
6. The plan should hasten provisions for the extension of work to high school level.
7. An inevitable tendency to increase the school attendance and the services of agriculture colleges and normal schools would result.
8. A better program of studies could be provided, based on the social needs of the children and the nature of their mental and physical growth.
9. The consolidated school furnishes the number of pupils necessary to supply wholesome competition and stimulus in school work, to carry through adequate grading, to develop group and project work, and to organize many socially significant types of extracurricular activities.
10. Education of the adults of the community would be fostered.
11. The health of the children would be safeguarded.
12. Improvement of roads would result because of the necessity of transporting the children to school.[24]

[23] *Op. cit.,* p. 17.
[24] *Ibid.,* pp. 15–16.

It seems impossible to evaluate the advantages of school consolidation without rigidly defining just what the term includes in
specific instances. The maintenance of public schools for the children of one family at a cost of $300 to $400 per pupil per year, as
is reported from isolated sections in Wisconsin, calls for the elimination of some schools in the interest of the general social welfare.
Whether consolidation of schools is the solution is another question. Control of settlement may be the better way.[25] On the other
hand, few persons would wholeheartedly endorse a condition in
which all the schools in a county had been consolidated into a few
units with almost complete disregard of community interests. Especially should such a practice call for analysis if: "In the consolidation program in the state it has been a common practice to transport the children from rural districts to urban centers or centers
having urban characteristics. Of those who are transported to
school approximately 25 percent of the elementary school and 39
percent of the high school pupils are transported to centers of population of 1000 inhabitants or more."[26]

Probably the soundest recommendation regarding consolidation of schools is as follows: Schools should be consolidated within
the community, but they should not be consolidated away from
the community.[27] In other words, school consolidation should accompany but not anticipate the expansion of the community area,
and the first few grades might well be handled on a different basis
from the upper grades. The ignoring of community interests and
boundaries in the consolidation of schools might well result in a
form of educational absenteeism fully as vicious as absentee landownership.[28] On the other hand, centralizing the rural schools of
a given community may do much to erase neighborhood differences, to eliminate village-country friction, to integrate community activities, and to stimulate larger and more inclusive social
community groupings. But if more than one village or community

[25] George S. Wehrwein and J. A. Baker, "The Cost of Isolated Settlement in
Northern Wisconsin," *Rural Sociology*, II (1937), 255, 262–263; cf. John E.
Mason, "Private and Public Costs of Isolated Settlement in the Cut-Over Area of
Minnesota," *Rural Sociology*, V (1940), 219–220.

[26] M. B. Smith, *op. cit.*, p. 37.

[27] This principle is recognized in the quotation above from the *Report of the
Advisory Committee on Education*, p. 12.

[28] On this point, consult M. B. Smith, "Rural Consolidated Schools and Educational Absenteeism in Louisiana," *Journal of Educational Sociology*, XII (1938),
93–100.

is included in the centralized school district, the results are by no means so promising.[29]

In order that those defending and those opposing school consolidation may be discussing the same phenomena, the nature and extent of the unions referred to should always be stated explicitly. It is one thing to combine the schools of one small rural community, but it is a different thing to consolidate the schools into units of the size commonly found in the South, where consolidation of schools is in a much more advanced position. The situation is not confined to one state, and the consolidations have proceeded in accordance with what was accepted as the most advanced educational theory. A publication of George Peabody College for Teachers, where a large share of southern educational leaders are trained, gives a local unit of 1600 pupils and 46 teaching units as "the minimum size of a satisfactory local unit of school administration."[30]

The writer strongly advocates the use of society's natural groups as the basis for delineating school attendance areas.[31] He thinks that the hierarchy of social relationships, which pyramids from the person to the family, the family to the neighborhood, and the neighborhood to the community, is of great significance for rural education. These various groupings constitute natural attendance areas; and their culmination, the community, is a logical unit for school administrative purposes. This point may be elaborated further. So far society has thought it best to leave the child with the parents for the first six years, making the family the first educational attendance area. So efficient is the rural family in performing its educational functions, so multiple the ideas, tasks, skills involved in farm work and farm living that it seems wise to continue this practice. From six to nine or six to twelve, however, the

[29] See Eugene T. Stromberg, *The Influence of the Central Rural School on Community Organization*, Cornell AES Bulletin 699, Ithaca, New York, 1938, pp. 3, 38–39.

[30] Howard A. Dawson, *Satisfactory Local School Units*, George Peabody College for Teachers, Field Study 7, Nashville, Tennessee, 1934, p. 82; Harry A. Little, *Potential Economies in the Reorganization of Local School Attendance Units*, Teachers College, Columbia University Contributions to Education 628, New York, 1934, p. 65, analyzes consolidation and its possible effects in terms of a minimum daily attendance of 290 pupils in the elementary grades and 726 students in the high school.

[31] See T. Lynn Smith, "The Role of the Community in American Rural Life," *Journal of Educational Sociology*, XIV (1941), 387–400. Cf. Dwight Sanderson, "The Relation of the School to the Sociological Status of the Rural Community," *ibid.*, XIV (1941), 401–410.

child should begin in a gradual manner to participate in the larger society and to secure the elements of a formal education. So that the transition may not be too abrupt and that the child may continue to benefit most from family influences, his first school years should be spent in a small school in close proximity to the home. The neighborhood is the natural unit best suited to serve as an attendance area for a school including the first three to six grades. As the child becomes more mature and advanced, as he becomes more sturdy physically, and as his social contacts increasingly occur outside the family circle, he may very well be assembled with his fellows from his own and other neighborhoods in a school serving the entire community. Here he can continue, amid surroundings more removed from his home environment and more in contact with the larger world, with the completion of his elementary and the securing of his high-school education.

By proceeding in this manner educational programs could capitalize on the natural social units of rural America. Beyond the elementary schools rooted in the neighborhood, the community can logically serve as a focal point for the educational activities of advanced elementary and high-school levels. Just as the community supplements and complements the neighborhoods in economic, political, and other social spheres, making life more complete by offering types of service which would be impractical on a neighborhood basis, in the educational realm the community can find its plane of greatest service as a focal point for more advanced educational activities.

Furthermore, from the standpoint of social relationships in general, schools planned in such a manner that their boundaries of influence coincide with those of locality groups will play a great part in increasing the elements of neighborliness and community in the rural areas. They draw strength from neighborhood and community units, but also feed back into these locality groups the strength-giving elements of social interaction and the example of successful working together for the attainment of common purposes.

The Agricultural Extension Service

Outranked in importance as a rural educational agency only by the family and the school is the Agricultural Extension Service. This service represents the coöperative effort of the United States

Department of Agriculture, the state agricultural colleges, county governments, and in some states the local farmers' organizations. The program varies from state to state, depending to a considerable extent upon the breadth of view of the director and his chief advisers. Unfortunate is the state with a technician as the director of extension. But in every state very important work is being done, and in some states the accomplishments are especially outstanding. Extension work in the South does not suffer in comparison with that in the North, as do most other aspects of education.

Growing out of the work of the early agricultural societies, the activities of farmers' institutes which were sponsored by the state departments of agriculture and state land-grant colleges, and the early extension services established by various agricultural colleges,[32] the Agricultural Extension Service was organized on its present basis under the Smith-Lever Act of 1914. The period of World War I was one of tremendous expansion. Then came a brief financial recession, after which the work continued to develop with little interruption until the great depression. For a time in 1933 the activities of the service were threatened with serious curtailment, but eventually it was given the enormous task of administering the crop-control programs put into operation under the provisions of the Agricultural Adjustment Act. The tremendous demands of these new responsibilities offered, for a time, a serious threat to the usual educational activities of the extension service, but gradually the time and energy going into educational work have resumed their former importance. Even during World War II they were carried on without serious setbacks.

Organization

The organization of the Agricultural Extension Service is detailed and complete. In Washington the service is an integral portion of the United States Department of Agriculture and is headed by a director, his assistant director, and a business manager. Surrounding them are division chiefs, field agents, extension spe-

[32] Edmund deS. Brunner and E. Hsin Pao Yang, *Rural America and the Extension Service,* New York, Teachers College of Columbia University, 1949, pp. 2–16. Cf. Clarence B. Smith and Meredith Chester Wilson, *The Agricultural Extension System of the United States,* New York, John Wiley & Sons, Inc., 1930, pp. 28–30. For a recent comprehensive summary of the present status of extension services throughout the world, see Edmund deS. Brunner, Irwin T. Sanders, and Douglas Ensminger (eds.), *Farmers of the World,* New York, Columbia University Press, 1945.

cialists, extension economists, agriculturists, home economists, administrative officers, editors, etc., making a considerable staff of persons in positions of responsibility. In each of the states a division of agricultural extension is one of the important divisions of the state college of agriculture and is headed either by the dean of the college of agriculture, with an assistant or associate director actively in charge, or by a director of extension who is responsible to the dean. The agents in the various counties are responsible through district agents to the state director of extension.

Agents of the Agricultural Extension Service are of several types: (1) county agricultural agents and their assistants; (2) county home demonstration agents; and (3) county club agents or assistants in charge of club work. In the southern states these categories are further divided on the basis of race. According to the reports for June 30, 1950, a total of 9650 agents were employed as of that date. Of these 5245, including 379 Negroes, were county agents or assistant county agents; 2428 (389 Negroes) were home agents; and 838 were club agents. Of the latter 107 were Negroes. As late as 1937 there was only one Negro club agent in the United States. By 1950 every one of the 3106 agricultural counties in the nation was served by one or more agents, although in some cases one man or woman was responsible for the work in two counties.[33]

Objectives and Activities

The nature of the Agricultural Extension Service is better explained by a brief statement of objectives and a short summary of activities. Broadly speaking, the Agricultural Extension Service has the objective of better lives for farm people. To accomplish this an effort is made to increase the farm income, promote better homes and higher planes of living, develop rural leadership, strengthen community life, increase appreciation of rural life among farm youth, diffuse knowledge among the general public concerning the place of agriculture in national life, and expand the mental and educational horizons of rural people.[34]

[33] Data are from M. L. Wilson, *Report of Cooperative Extension Work in Agriculture and Home Economics, 1950,* Washington, Government Printing Office, 1952, pp. 45–47.

[34] Cf. Smith and Wilson, *op. cit.,* pp. 5–6; William E. Cole and Hugh Price Crowe, *Recent Trends in Rural Planning,* New York, Prentice-Hall, Inc., 1937, pp. 366–369; and Brunner and Yang, *op. cit.,* chaps. 7 and 8.

Accomplishments and Needs

The Agricultural Extension Service, in some states at least, deserves a great deal of credit for the thorough job it is doing. Introducing improved farm practices, stimulating coöperation, laying the groundwork for a more diversified agriculture, contributing to added consumption and security through improved practices in producing, preparing, and preserving home food supplies, improving nutritional practices and dietary habits, stimulating a fuller social life and greater opportunity for social contacts within the rural neighborhood and community, and promoting boys' and girls' club work are a few of the important ways in which this service raises the quality of rural living.

But there still remains much to be done. Criticism is often heard that only farmers of the upper social and economic strata are reached through the regular extension channels. Whether the criticism is valid or not, the fact remains that there are millions of agriculturists, especially in such tenure categories as wage worker, sharecropper, and "share tenant," who lack many of the basic skills needed in efficient and well-rounded production, satisfying and health-maintaining consumption, and security-providing saving. If these people are to be reached at all, such agencies as the Agricultural Extension Service and the Farm Security Administration must do the work. Particularly necessary is a vast amount of the simplest and most elementary educational work among Negroes of the agricultural South. Without assistance through such channels it seems impossible for the masses of this race ever to attain the aptitudes and skills, the attitudes and motivation that will enable them to become self-reliant, independent, self-supporting, and efficient members of society.[35]

Other Educational Agencies

Rural Libraries

The library is the repository for the knowledge of the ages. In an urbanocracy such as the present-day United States, most of these storehouses of information are located in cities and are prac-

[35] Cf. Maurice E. Thomasson, *A Study of Special Kinds of Education for Rural Negroes*, Charlotte, N.C., 1936, pp. 97–98.

tically inaccessible to the rural population. The disadvantages rural people are under with respect to securing access to books are strikingly demonstrated by the results of a recent study. For the year 1933 it was estimated that only 7.9 percent of the urban population was without library service, as compared with 73.7 percent of the rural population.[36] Were differences in number and quality of books taken into account, the chasm would be even greater. Furthermore, this is a national average, obtained by blending data for states like Delaware, Massachusetts, New Hampshire, Connecticut, Wyoming, and California, where over 90 percent of the rural population reside in public library districts, with data for West Virginia, Arkansas, Florida, Illinois, Oklahoma, Missouri, North Dakota, Washington, Texas, Virginia, and Georgia, where less than 10 percent of the rural population reside in such districts.[37]

As is true of so many other rural problems, the lack of library facilities is most acute in the South. Books are lacking from private homes, community libraries are few and as a rule poorly equipped, and even the colleges and universities are without first-rate library facilities. In no small measure this lack of library facilities must be attributed to the plantation system and the high degree of social stratification which it generated. For generations southern society accumulated books, magazines, newspapers, etc., not as public possessions housed in public buildings, cared for by public attendants, but in the private libraries of the planter class. Some of these collections were magnificent. But it is not wise for society to depend upon such an organization for storing the accumulated records of ages. The libraries being private possessions, not only was their use largely restricted to a few of the elite, but the fortunes of the libraries themselves depended upon the fortunes of the family. In a few years silver fish and termites destroy the accumulation of generations. Adequate library service must be institutionalized, a movement, fortunately, which is now developing rapidly in the South.

The task of providing library service for the millions of rural people now lacking it is America's greatest library problem. The county library movement apparently is making little headway. Al-

[36] Louis R. Wilson, *The Geography of Reading*, Chicago, American Library Association and the University of Chicago Press, 1938, p. 29.
[37] *Ibid.*, Table 6, p. 28.

though started around 1900, by 1935 only 230 counties were spending as much as $1000 annually for library service. Perhaps the pooling of efforts by two or more counties, a village and its trade area, etc., may provide the way out.[38]

The Rural Newspaper

The small-town weekly newspaper is of considerable importance in rural America. Occasionally an editor is a ne'er-do-well, but more usually he proves a vital element in the town. Gee describes the threefold function of rural newspapers as follows: (1) The country newspaper keeps people informed of happenings in the local community; (2) it wields an important force in promoting or retarding community activities; and (3) it constitutes an invaluable historical source.[39] In 1952 weekly newspapers were published in 8812 towns and villages.[40] There is little room for doubt that the local newspaper forms an important item in the reading material of rural folk.

No recent thoroughgoing study of the nature and function of the rural newspaper is available. Some time ago Taylor, in a study of 243 North Carolina and Missouri weeklies, showed that an overwhelming preponderance of space was given to local items, particularly to village or town events.[41] Shortly after, Willey showed that Connecticut weeklies gave very incomplete coverage of locally important news, and that editorials were lacking or inconsequential.[42] But both of these studies were made several decades ago and neither should be considered typical for the rural America of their time, much less that of today. One recent study does reveal that editors of North Carolina weeklies make little use of the

[38] *Ibid.*, p. 32. For a detailed study of county libraries in the South, see Louis R. Wilson and Edward A. Wight, *County Library Service in the South*, Chicago, University of Chicago Press, 1935. Other significant studies of rural library services are Paul M. Houser and Robert E. Galloway, "Use and Acceptance of Public Library Services in a Rural Area," *Rural Sociology*, XIV (1949), 233–243; and Gus Turbeville and Edgar A. Schuler, "Reading and Reading Interests of Housewives in a Rural County: A Comparison of County Library Users and Non-Library Users in Families of Leaders and a Cross Section Sample in Lenawee County, Michigan, 1946–1947," *Rural Sociology*, XIV (1949), 220–232.

[39] Wilson Gee, *The Social Economics of Agriculture*, New York, The Macmillan Company, 1932, pp. 657–658.

[40] *Directory of Newspapers and Periodicals*, Philadelphia, N. W. Ayer & Son, 1952, p. 7.

[41] Carl C. Taylor, "The Country Newspaper as a Town-Country Agency," *Proceedings of the Fourth Country Life Conference*, Chicago, 1921 pp. 44–45.

[42] Malcolm M. Willey, *The Country Newspaper*, Chapel Hill, University of North Carolina Press, 1926.

mass of free clip-sheets, news releases, mats and other publicity materials sent them by government agencies and special interest groups.[43] Meanwhile nearly 10,000 towns and villages continue supporting and reading the small weeklies.

The Radio

The radio is another of the agencies of communication that is of tremendous educational significance. It ranks with the automobile, the telephone, and rural free delivery in potency as an agency for erasing the physical isolation of rural people. Rural people have available the same radio offerings as city people, and because of fewer competing attractions these have greater values for rural people than for others. The radio also has opened a channel whereby the services of the United States Department of Agriculture and the agricultural colleges are more readily available to farmers.[44] It must also be recognized that the radio is one of the principal channels through which urban culture traits are diffused to the rural areas.[45]

According to data gathered in the Census of 1940, 60.2 percent of the nation's rural farm families own radios. This is a very poor showing in comparison with rural nonfarm and urban areas, where 79.0 and 91.9 percent, respectively, of the occupied dwelling units are equipped with radios. By 1945, however, the percentage of farm families with radios had risen to 72.8. Among farm families ownership of radios is, of course, much higher among whites than Negroes and other nonwhites. It also seems to be closely associated with urban influences, being high on the west coast and in New England and the Northeast generally, and low in the South.[46] (See Figure 113.) In recent years television sets are being acquired by thousands of farm families, including those of many "tenants" and sharecroppers in the South, but as yet there are no comprehensive data on that subject.

[43] George L. Abernathy and C. Brooks Anderson, "The Use of Publicity Materials in North Carolina Weeklies," *Rural Sociology*, XIV (1949), 336–344.

[44] Cf. Edmund deS. Brunner, *Radio and the Farmer*, New York, The Radio Institute of the Audible Arts, 1935, pp. 5–8.

[45] F. Howard Forsyth's article, "The Radio and Rural Research," *Rural Sociology*, IV (1939), 67–77, is interesting in this connection. It also includes references to other studies on the subject.

[46] Data from the *Sixteenth Census of the United States: 1940*, "Housing," Vol. II, Part 1, Washington, Government Printing Office, 1943, Table 55, p. 96; and *United States Census of Agriculture: 1945*, Vol. II, Washington, Government Printing Office, 1947, p. 308.

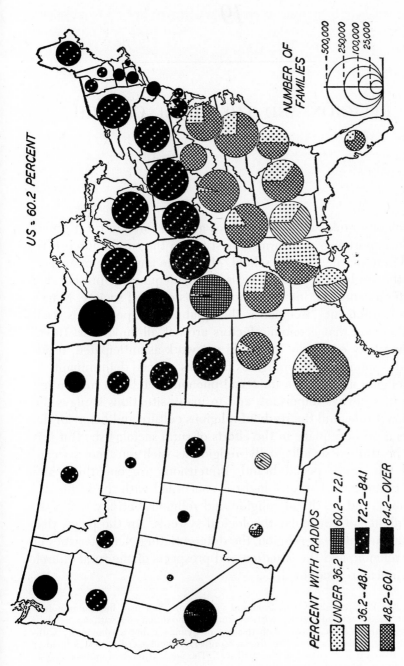

US = 60.2 PERCENT

NUMBER OF FAMILIES

500,000
250,000
100,000
25,000

PERCENT WITH RADIOS

UNDER 36.2

36.2–48.1

48.2–60.1

60.2–72.1

72.2–84.1

84.2–OVER

FIGURE 113. Percentages of Farm Families with Radios, by States, 1940. (Starting at 12:00 o'clock on the circles and reading clockwise, the segments represent Negro farm families and white farm families, respectively.)

19

RELIGION AND THE RURAL CHURCH

Religion ranks with education as a social force in rural America; in importance as a farmers' institution the rural church is rivaled only by the country school. More than any other phenomenon, the study of religion reveals the inadequacy of present-day unilateral economic interpretations of history and society. Marx's famous statement, "Religion is the opiate of the people," is itself an admission that economic factors are not all-important. In explaining why economic forces do not work as anticipated, it admits the potency of the religious factor as a social determinant.

Religion as such is a universal phenomenon;[1] as a motivating force it is always important, and in many situations it plays the dominant role; and the study of religious culture and behavior deserves a primary place in the efforts of rural sociologists. But if it is to be studied sociologically, religion as such must not be confused with any special brand. Pretensions are one thing and validity another. The sociologist is concerned with the forms, expressions, and results of religion and religious activity, not with the validity of particular theological systems.[2] In the pages that follow, the nature of religion, the differentiating characteristics of rural religion, and the situation and prospects of the rural church in America are examined.

[1] Wrote Plutarch nearly two thousand years ago: "You may find communities without walls; without letters; without kings; without money; with no need of coinage; without acquaintance with theatres or gymnasia; but a community without holy rite, without a God, that uses not prayer, without sacrifice to win good or avert evil—no man ever saw or ever will see." The work of modern anthropologists fully supports Plutarch's generalization.

[2] Cf. Wilson D. Wallis, *An Introduction to Anthropology*, New York, Harper & Brothers, 1926, p. 284.

Religion

The Concept

It is clear that the term "religion" refers to certain particular types of data such as beliefs, practices, feelings, emotions, moods, and attitudes. But it is not easy to draw a line between what is religious and what is secular or nonreligious. To some the idea of religion is inseparably connected with the idea of supernatural beings; Tylor, the eminent British social anthropologist, suggested as a minimum definition of religion "the belief in spiritual beings."[3] J. G. Frazer thought of religion as the conciliation or propitiation of supernatural powers which are believed to have power over nature and human life.[4] Both of these eminent authorities make the idea of divinity the core of religion. But there are many observances that rank as religious phenomena even though no supernatural beings or gods are involved. Furthermore, if the idea of deity is used as a criterion, the great religious system of Buddhism does not qualify as a religion. Other thinkers have stressed the element of mystery. Thus Herbert Spencer thought religion consisted essentially of the "belief in the omnipresence of something which is inscrutable";[5] and Max Müller defined it as "a struggle to conceive the inconceivable, to utter the unutterable, a longing after the infinite."[6] But Durkheim correctly indicates that the element of mystery is not a primitive conception, that the idea of the supernatural is possible only after the concept of natural has been evolved, and that associations or sequences which would seem miraculous to a person familiar with modern thought and science may be commonplace to the man of primitive culture.[7]

Holiness or *mana* is the great concept of religion,[8] and awe is the chief religious attitude or emotion. The idea of holiness presupposes the division of the universe into two parts, the *sacred* and the *secular* or profane. This way of dividing the universe into two domains and the attributing of holiness or mana to the per-

[3] E. B. Tylor, *Primitive Culture,* London, Henry Holt & Company, 1871, I, 424.
[4] Cf. *The Golden Bough,* London, Macmillan & Co., Ltd., 1912, I, 222.
[5] *First Principles,* New York, D. Appleton & Company, 1899, p. 37.
[6] *Introduction to the Science of Religion,* London, Longmans, Green & Co., Ltd., 1873, p. 18.
[7] Emile Durkheim, *Elementary Forms of Religious Life,* London, Macmillan & Co., Ltd., 1915, pp. 28–29.
[8] See the articles on "Holiness" in James Hastings, *Encyclopedia of Religion and Ethics,* New York, Charles Scribner's Sons, 1925.

sons, objects, rites, etc., making up the realm of the sacred seems to be the most distinguishing feature of all religious thinking.[9]

Holiness or mana is not an easy conception to define. All groups have the same general idea, but specific connotations differ widely. Its expressions have been much more objectively analyzed among primitive groups than among the great religions of the present day. Since the Melanesian word *mana* has been widely used as a name for the general concept, it is of interest to consider the meaning the Melanesians attached to it. Bishop Codrington has most clearly expressed its meaning in the following sentences:

> There is a belief in a force altogether distinct from physical power, which acts in all kinds of ways for good and evil, and which it is of the greatest advantage to possess or control. This is Mana. . . . I think I know what our people mean by it. . . . It is a power or influence, not physical, and in a way supernatural; but it shows itself in physical force, or in any kind of power or excellence which a man possesses. This mana is not fixed in anything, and it can be conveyed in almost anything. . . . All Melanesian religion consists, in fact, in getting this mana for one's self, or getting it used for one's benefit.[10]

In general some of the more important connotations of the concept may be listed as follows: invisible, powerful, all-pervasive, mysterious, wonder-working, supernatural, contagious, dangerous to those not accustomed to it or not specifically set apart to handle it, beneficial if properly used and detrimental if improperly handled, forbidden to the uninitiated.[11] Taken together, these are quite sufficient to give rise to a condition or feeling of awe on the part of the individual.

The realm of the sacred is extensive, and the variety of things that may be set apart as holy or possessing mana is very great. They include, in addition to objects, both beliefs or states of opinion, and rites or modes of action. Among the ancient Hebrews, from whom a large part of modern rural religious culture has been derived, the realm of the sacred included in addition to the deities both true and false: places or spots, mountains, stones, springs, trees, the apparatus of worship, certain animals, times and seasons,

---

[9] Cf. Durkheim, *op. cit.*, p. 37.

[10] Robert H. Codrington, *The Melanesians*, Oxford, The Clarendon Press, 1891, p. 118, n. 1.

[11] R. R. Marett's *The Threshold of Religion*, London, Methuen & Co., 1909, is the classical study in this field.

numbers, many operations and processes (rites, prayers, vows, even war), the name of deity, and persons (priests, kings, and an entire ethnic and cultural group).

But mysterious, wonder-working powers are attributed to states of action, objects, and beliefs that are not accepted as religious. The whole realm of the magical must somehow be set apart from the domain of the religious. Durkheim has made this differentiation on the basis of individual versus group participation and benefit. Magic is individual; although distribution is universal, it does not serve as a unifying force among its adherents. "There is no Church of magic." Emphasizing the group and social aspects of religion as contrasted with the individualistic nature of magic, Durkheim arrived at his famous definition, which holds that religion consists of "a unified system of beliefs and practices relative to sacred things," and that these beliefs and practices bind together all those who adhere to them into a single moral community (a church).[12] It is important to note that this definition combines two of the most widespread and accepted sociological theories of the origin of religion: the one which would derive religion solely from the idea of mana,[13] and that which holds religion to be an expression of the social life of the community.[14]

Rural Religious Culture

In the last analysis practically all great religions and most of the present-day denominations and sects have been developed in a rural environment. For this reason the chief differentiating characteristics of rural religious belief and practice are to be sought in the traditionalism of the country as opposed to the internationalism and cosmopolitanism of the city. Through what is known as cultural lag, many religious traits and practices persist in rural areas long after they have been abandoned or transformed in urban centers.[15] As compared with other cultural elements, traits per-

[12] *Op. cit.*, p. 47.

[13] Cf. Marett, *op. cit.*

[14] Probably exposition is the best in W. Robertson Smith, *The Religion of the Semites*, London, Black, 1894; Jane Harrison, *Themis*, Cambridge, 1912, is an elaboration of this thesis; and Frazer, *op. cit.* VII, VIII, marshals all the evidence in favor of this position. For a brief elementary summary of theories regarding the origin of religion, see Bertram C. A. Windle, *Religions: Past and Present*, New York, D. Appleton-Century Company, 1927, pp. 26–40; or Allan Menzies, *History of Religion*, New York, Charles Scribner's Sons, 1927, pp. 8–17.

[15] J. G. Frazer's *Folklore in the Old Testament*, London, Macmillan & Co., Ltd., 1919, is a veritable mine of information on this subject.

taining to religion usually change much more slowly; and in the rural areas these changes are slowest of all. History is filled with examples of this fact. So tenaciously did the peasants of the Roman Empire cling to their old religious beliefs and practices and so strenuously did they resist the spread of Christianity that the name of their countryman, *paganus* (pagan), became synonymous with unbeliever.[16] Similarly, the religious conservatism of English countrymen, dwellers on the heaths, added the word *heathen* to the English language.[17] Moreover, many items still remain in the realm of the unknown and inspire an attitude of awe in the country long after they have passed into the realm of the known among those acquainted with modern science. The belief that persons suffering from insanity were possessed of evil spirits[18] still finds expression in hexing and voodoo practices that persist in some rural areas. Then again, cases can still be found in which rural people drive the "devil" from the churn by means of a poker long after the relationship between temperature and successful buttermaking is well known. Even with the present knowledge of meteorology readily available, persons who would not think of praying for an eclipse of the sun devoutly offer prayers for rain, quite naturally principally in rural areas.

Rural religion is filled with agricultural symbolism and imagery. It must be so, if it is to be understood by the farmer. Sermons, songs, and even the sacred literature will contain numerous examples, analogies, and references to words involving agricultural processes such as field, vineyard, sowing, reaping, sickle, harvesting, shepherd, honey, fruit, tree, cow, lamb, etc. As urban influences become dominant in any given religious group, there is a tendency to slough off this agricultural coloration.[19]

In rural religion there is a close association between the secular and the spiritual planes of life, or more properly the religious element may be said to permeate almost all activities of rural life. Religious rites and ceremonies are associated with rising, retiring, meals, seasons such as harvest time, and ofttimes with preparing

[16] Cf. Charles Guignebert, *Christianity, Past and Present*, New York, The Macmillan Company, 1927, pp. 175–176.

[17] Arthur M. Schlesinger, *The Rise of the City*, New York, The Macmillan Company, 1933, p. 79.

[18] Matthew 8:28–34.

[19] For a modern example, the case of Mormonism, see P. A. Sorokin, Carle C. Zimmerman, and Charles J. Galpin, *A Systematic Source Book in Rural Sociology*, Minneapolis, University of Minnesota Press, 1931, II, 440–444.

the ground and planting. Prayers contain invocations for assistance in the daily round of activities, favorable weather, safeguarding of family members, and many other aspects of daily living. In the deterministic, mechanistic atmosphere of the city most of this association is lost.

Faith in spiritual beings and in their power to aid and injure man is an important cornerstone of rural religion. In this respect the rural man's faith is similar to that of many of his city fellows, but his belief is more universal and probably more intense.

At a time when a literal acceptance and interpretation of the Bible as the word of God and a handbook for guidance in everyday affairs is rapidly disappearing in the cities, the American countryman's old-fashioned adherence to these traditional beliefs appears as a sharp contrast. The same is true of the farmer's greater adherence to the strict puritanical moral code of the Old Testament. As a matter of fact, the greatest modern stronghold of puritanism seems to be in the rural South.[20]

The traditional belief in an anthropomorphic personal God, who is constantly concerning himself with the details of life on earth, prevails in wide parts of the countryside long after the more sophisticated urban classes have abandoned it in favor of a more impersonal, all-pervasive, noninterfering, unembodied force in the universe.

Finally, the uncompromising doctrine of salvation by one means only, a philosophic absolutism, prevails in rural areas long after more compromising "tolerant" doctrines are widespread in the city.

Religious Affiliations

Church affiliation, i.e., the religious denomination or sect to which people belong or adhere, is among the most important aspects of the sociological study of religion and the church. In view of this fact, many will regard it as inexcusable that the decennial Census of Population fails to give information concerning the religious affiliations of the people, data comparable to those secured on residence, race, marital condition, age, sex, occupation, literacy, etc., data which would be comparable to those secured in the pop-

[20] Cf. N. L. Sims, *Elements of Rural Sociology*, New York, Thomas Y. Crowell Company, 1928, p. 328. For the strength of puritanism in the South, see Holland Thompson, *The New South*, New Haven, Yale University Press, 1920, p. 217.

ulation censuses of the vast majority of the civilized nations of the world. Prior to 1900 it was said that no census had called for information concerning religious affiliation because of three factors: (1) Census enumerators have a limited time in which to query the people; (2) the schedules were already long; and (3) the First Amendment to the Constitution restrains Congress from making any "law respecting an establishment of religion, or prohibiting the free exercise thereof," and this has been interpreted as forbidding the inclusion of questions about religion on the census schedules.[21]

In the permanent Census Act of 1902, Congress did provide for the regular collection, every ten years, of data concerning the religious affiliations of the population.[22] Unfortunately, however, this has not been done as a part of the regular Census of Population, and has been entirely divorced from the decennial Population Census. Not only is the procedure followed clumsy, incomplete in results, much more expensive than need be, and unable to secure comparability from denomination to denomination, but it fails to give a complete inventory of the religious affiliations or preferences of the population.[23]

In spite of these weaknesses, the results do have some value. They constitute the only comprehensive information we have on the important topic of religious affiliations. Care should be taken not to use the results as indicative of the extent of church membership in the United States, or as showing the comparative degrees of church membership in the different sections of the country or in the rural and urban populations. The data are very incomplete, and they are probably more complete for one denomination than for another, one region than another, and probably even more complete for one residential group than for another. Again there is no consistency from one denomination to another in the extent to which young children are included in the membership reports. But these data do provide some indication of the relative strength of the various denominations and, more important for our purpose, of the relative importance of the rural

[21] Cf. H. K. Carroll, *The Religious Forces of the United States,* New York, The Christian Literature Co., 1893, p. xiii.

[22] *Religious Bodies: 1926,* Washington, Government Printing Office, 1930, I, 3.

[23] For a discussion of the inadequacy of the data gathered in the Census of Religious Bodies, see T. Lynn Smith and Homer L. Hitt, *The People of Louisiana,* Baton Rouge, Louisiana State University Press, 1952, pp. 128–130.

and urban populations in the constituencies of each of the denominations.

The first impression one gets from studying the Census of Religious Bodies is that the variety of religion in the United States is very great. At the turn of the century Carroll wrote as follows: "There are churches small and churches great, churches white and churches black, churches high and low, orthodox and heterodox, Christian and pagan, Catholic and Protestant, Liberal and Conservative, Calvinistic and Arminian, native and foreign, Trinitarian and Unitarian."[24] A quarter of a century later the 1936 report, the last that has been published, listed 256 denominations, 183 of which were grouped into 24 families and 73 returned (classified) as separate denominations. In 1936 there were listed 21 different kinds of Baptists, 20 branches of Lutherans, 21 varieties of Methodists, 10 types of Presbyterians, and 17 kinds of Mennonite bodies.

Eight denominations reported more than 400,000 members in rural areas, the Roman Catholic Church leading with nearly 3,900,000 rural adherents. Rural Roman Catholics were widely scattered, forming an important group in nearly every state except a few of those in the deep South but being most numerous in the states of Pennsylvania (315,443), Louisiana (305,212), and Wisconsin (270,047). Rural members of the Negro Baptist denomination totaled 1,909,555 and were, of course, most numerous in the South, being found in greatest numbers in Georgia, Alabama, and Mississippi, where the rural memberships were 297,957, 250,035, and 239,369, respectively.[25] To one interested in the northward migration of the Negroes, the fact that Illinois cities reported 133,906 Negro Baptists, Ohio cities 99,720, and Pennsylvania cities 90,334 is of considerable interest. The Southern Baptist Convention ranked third, reporting a total of 1,676,184 rural members. Of these, 211,696 were in North Carolina, 182,332 in Texas, and 163,-382 in Georgia. The fact that the 1926 Census reported 311,801 rural members of this denomination in Georgia raises serious questions about the accuracy of the counts. Two Methodist bodies—the Methodist Episcopal Church and the Methodist Episcopal Church, South—ranked fourth and fifth, reporting 1,452,751 and

---

[24] *Op. cit.*, p. xiv.
[25] There is a saying in rural areas of the South which goes somewhat as follows: "If you find a Negro who isn't a Baptist, somebody has been tinkering with him."

1,112,257 rural members, respectively. The former had the largest number of rural members in Ohio, Pennsylvania, and Illinois, respectively; the latter in Texas, North Carolina, and Virginia. The Northwest is the stronghold of the Lutheran bodies. One of these, the Evangelical Synod of Missouri, Ohio, and Other States, reported 488,140 rural members, with Minnesota, Wisconsin, and Illinois containing the largest numbers. The rural strength of the Presbyterian Church in the United States of America (reporting 460,764 rural members) lies in the northeastern part of the nation, Pennsylvania containing the largest number, followed by New York and Ohio. The reported rural membership of the Disciples of Christ fell from 625,680 in 1926 to 453,064 in 1936. The rural adherents of this denomination are most numerous in Indiana, Missouri, and Kentucky.

It is believed that denominations reporting more than 100,000 but less than half a million rural members should also receive some individual attention. These are sixteen in number. Taking them in the order in which they are listed in *Religious Bodies: 1936*, we begin with the Northern Baptist Convention. Rural members of this denomination, who total 364,722, are most numerous in the Middle Atlantic, East North Central, and West North Central States, although West Virginia contains the largest number of any single state. The denomination known as the Churches of Christ, 177,002 strong in rural areas, has its strength in the western part of the southern region and is particularly strong in Texas and Tennessee. The Congregational and Christian Churches' 342,642 rural members are mostly scattered through the tier of states from New England to North Dakota. The bulk of 273,683 rural members of the Evangelical and Reformed Church live in Pennsylvania, although Ohio, Illinois, and Wisconsin contain sizable contingents. Most of the 285,361 rural members of the Church of Jesus Christ of Latter-day Saints (Mormon) are located in the Great Basin and the immediately surrounding states. Ohio and Iowa contain the largest contingents of the 272,509 rural members of the American Lutheran Church. Almost one-half of the rural membership (117,516) of the Evangelical Lutheran Augustana Synod of North America live in Minnesota, and the adjacent states contain most of the others. Also concentrated in the Northwest is the rural membership of the Norwegian Lutheran Church of America, its 361,456 rural members being congregated for the most part in the states of Minnesota, Wisconsin, and the Dakotas. The Evangelical Lutheran Joint Synod of Wisconsin and Other States, with 116,481 rural members, is important in Wisconsin and Minnesota. More than one-half of the 386,591 rural members of the United Lutheran Church in America live in Pennsylvania. The African Methodist Episcopal Church is strongest in the lower South in the band of states extending from North Carolina to Texas. The concentration is in the eastern portion of this section, Georgia alone containing 63,686 of the 207,160 rural members reported. Another colored Methodist group, the African Methodist Episcopal Zion Church, having almost as many rural members (200,188), is strongest in the states from North Carolina to Mississippi, with North Carolina having the largest number, followed by Alabama. The Colored Methodist Episcopal Church, which has a total rural membership of 154,945, is most influential in the states from Georgia to Texas, Alabama and Mississippi having the largest numbers affiliated with this denomination.

The major southern branch of Presbyterianism, the Presbyterian Church in the United States, has a total of 155,572 rural members, with its strength centering in North Carolina and Virginia; it is of importance as far west as Texas and as far north as Missouri. The Protestant Episcopal Church reports 268,990 rural members, most of whom reside along the Atlantic coast from Massachusetts south to Virginia. The strength of this group centers in New York and Connecticut. The Church of the United Brethren in Christ, reporting a membership of 198,396 in rural areas, has its greatest strength in Pennsylvania, Ohio, and Indiana.

Ninety-seven of the denominations listed in the Census of Religious Bodies reported 10,000 or more members. In order to show the relative importance of each of these, Table 5 was prepared. For each of the denominations separately it gives the number of members reported in 1936, together with the percentage of those who were classified as residents of rural areas. Most of the smaller denominations which are omitted from this table are of local importance only, and a large proportion of them are almost entirely urban in membership.

It is of considerable interest to know which of the denominations is most important in the various states. In this respect the Roman Catholic Church far outshadows the other denominations. Thus, although only 19.4 percent of the members of the Roman

TABLE 5. Total Membership Reported and Percentage of Members Residing in Rural Areas for All Denominations Reporting 10,000 or More Members, 1936

Denomination	Membership	Percent Rural
All Denominations	55,872,366	30.6
United Baptists	27,000	96.8
Free Will Baptists	76,643	91.7
Regular Baptists	17,186	90.5
General Baptists	36,573	87.1
Mennonite Church	46,301	86.1
American Baptist Association	115,022	84.2
Primitive Baptists	69,157	84.2
Finnish Apostolic Lutheran Church of America	16,293	82.1
General Conference of the Mennonite Church of North America	26,535	80.3
Church of the United Brethren in Christ (Old Constitution)	15,401	73.6
Cumberland Presbyterian Church	49,975	71.6
Federated Churches	88,411	70.6
Norwegian Lutheran Church of America	516,400	70.0
Lutheran Free Church	47,140	68.0
Colored Cumberland Presbyterian Church	10,668	66.6
United Free Will Baptist Church (Colored)	19,616	65.5
Church of the Brethren (Conservative Dunkers)	153,516	63.4
Methodist Protestant Church	148,288	63.0
Southern Baptist Convention	2,700,155	62.1
General Eldership of the Churches of God in North America	30,820	59.8
Wesleyan Methodist Connection (or Church) of America	22,017	59.8
Church of God	44,818	58.6
Colored Primitive Baptists	43,897	58.0
(Tomlinson) Church of God	18,351	57.7
Colored Methodist Episcopal Church	269,915	57.4
Society of Friends (Orthodox)	75,652	57.4
Churches of Christ	309,551	57.2
The General Synod of the Associate Reformed Presbyterian Church	21,981	55.5
Danish Evangelical Lutheran Church in America	16,057	55.3
United Danish Evangelical Lutheran Church in America	33,531	55.0
American Lutheran Church	499,899	54.5
Advent Christian Church	26,258	54.4
Methodist Episcopal Church, South	2,061,683	53.9
Church of the United Brethren in Christ	376,905	52.6
Society of Friends (Hicksite)	14,680	52.4
Pentecostal Holiness Church	12,955	52.1

TABLE 5. Total Membership Reported and Percentage of Members
Residing in Rural Areas (*Continued*)

Denomination	Membership	Percent Rural
The Brethren Church (Progressive Dunkers)	30,636	50.8
Negro Baptists	3,782,464	50.5
Evangelical Lutheran Joint Synod of Wisconsin and Other States	235,402	49.5
African Methodist Episcopal Zion Church	414,244	48.6
Finnish Evangelical Lutheran Church of America	21,466	47.8
Christian Reformed Church	107,993	46.2
Independent Churches	40,276	46.2
Evangelical Church	212,446	44.4
Church of Jesus Christ of Latter-day Saints	678,217	42.1
African Methodist Episcopal Church	493,357	42.0
Methodist Episcopal Church	3,509,763	41.4
Evangelical Lutheran Synod of Missouri, Ohio, and Other States	1,192,553	40.9
Pilgrim Holiness Church	20,124	39.7
Disciples of Christ	1,196,315	37.9
Evangelical and Reformed Church	723,877	37.8
Assemblies of God, General Council	148,043	37.3
Free Methodist Church of North America	37,587	37.3
Reformed Church in America	184,536	36.2
Evangelical Lutheran Augustana Synod of North America	327,472	35.9
Congregational and Christian Churches	976,388	35.1
Presbyterian Church in the United States	449,045	34.6
Moravian Church in America	30,904	33.2
Church of God (Headquarters, Anderson, Ind.)	56,911	31.2
Buddhist Mission of North America	14,388	30.5
United Presbyterian Church of North America	170,967	30.4
Evangelical Congregational Church	23,894	30.0
United Lutheran Church in America	1,286,612	30.0
Reorganized Church of Jesus Christ of Latter-day Saints	93,470	29.6
Pentecostal Assemblies of Jesus Christ	16,070	29.0
Church of the Nazarene	136,227	28.9
Seventh-day Adventist Denomination	133,254	27.6
Northern Baptist Convention	1,329,044	27.4
Presbyterian Church in the United States of America	1,797,927	25.6
General Association of Regular Baptist Churches in the United States of America	22,345	24.9
Church of God in Christ	31,564	24.5
Evangelical Mission Convenant Church of America	43,981	24.5
Primitive Methodist Church in the United States of America	12,395	19.6
Roman Catholic Church	19,914,937	19.4

TABLE 5. Total Membership Reported and Percentage of Members Residing in Rural Areas (*Continued*)

Denomination	Membership	Percent Rural
Universalist Church	45,853	19.0
The Christian and Missionary Alliance	32,145	18.9
International Church of the Foursquare Gospel	16,147	18.4
Salvation Army	103,038	16.3
Protestant Episcopal Church	1,735,335	15.5
Russian Orthodox Church	89,510	15.4
Plymouth Brethren II	15,684	14.8
Slovak Evangelical Lutheran Synod of the United States of America	18,910	14.3
Unitarians	59,228	14.0
Ukrainian Orthodox Church of America	11,480	10.4
North American Old Roman Catholic Church	14,985	8.9
National Spiritualist Association	11,266	7.8
Polish National Catholic Church of America	63,366	7.5
Rumanian Orthodox Church	15,090	6.9
Church of God and Saints of Christ	37,084	5.6
Church of Christ, Scientist	268,915	3.5
Greek Orthodox Church (Hellenic)	189,368	1.5
Independent Negro Churches	12,337	0.9
Jewish Congregations	4,641,184	0.9
Serbian Orthodox Church	20,020	0.9
Church of Armenia in America	18,787	0.8
Syrian Antiochian Orthodox Church	18,451	0.4
Progressive Spiritual Church	11,347	0.0

Source of the data: U.S. Bureau of the Census, *Religious Bodies: 1936*, Washington, Government Printing Office, 1941, I.

Catholic Church reside in rural areas, the members of this denomination outnumber those of any other one sect in the rural parts of twenty-nine states, namely, Maine, New Hampshire, Vermont, Massachusetts, Rhode Island, Connecticut, New York, New Jersey, Pennsylvania, Illinois, Michigan, Wisconsin, Minnesota, Iowa, Missouri, North Dakota, South Dakota, Nebraska, Kansas, Maryland, Louisiana, Texas, Montana, Colorado, New Mexico, Arizona, Washington, Oregon, and California. Southern Baptists lead in the rural parts of four states (North Carolina, Kentucky, Tennessee, and Oklahoma), and Negro Baptists in seven others (Virginia, South Carolina, Georgia, Florida, Alabama, Mississippi, and Arkansas). The Methodist Episcopal Church has more members than any other denomination in the rural areas of Ohio, Indiana, and Delaware. Northern Baptists head the list in West Virginia. And in the rural portions of the four remaining states, Idaho, Wyoming, Utah, and Nevada, the Latter-day Saints (Mormons) outnumber the members of any other denomination.

The comparisons have more meaning if some of the denominational fragmentation is ignored and various kinds of Baptists are considered as one group, the many types of Lutherans as another, and so on for the other large religious bodies. On this basis, in 1936 Baptists were the largest religious group in rural America, their number being 4,312,602; they comprised 25.2 percent of the total. Roman Catholics came second, numbering 3,873,173 and constituting 22.7 percent of all. Methodists were a close third, rural Methodists totaling 3,270,030, or 19.1 percent of all. Lutherans, with 1,846,501 rural members, 10.8 percent of the total, were fourth, followed by Presbyterians (729,288, or 4.3 percent), the Disciples (453,064, or 2.7 percent), members of the Congregational and Christian Churches (342,642, or 2.0 percent), and Latter-day Saints (313,439, or 1.8 percent) in the order named.

Such a system of grouping is also useful in determining the faith of greatest numerical strength in the various states of the nation. Even on this basis, in 1936 Roman Catholics were most numerous among rural church members in twenty-two states, namely, Maine, New Hampshire, Vermont, Massachusetts, Rhode Island, Connecticut, New York, New Jersey, Pennsylvania, Illinois, Michigan, Wisconsin, Iowa, Kansas, Louisiana, Montana, Colorado, New Mexico, Arizona, Washington, Oregon, and California. Baptists led in fourteen states—Missouri, Virginia, West Virginia, North Carolina, South Carolina, Georgia, Florida, Kentucky, Tennessee, Alabama, Mississippi, Arkansas, Oklahoma, and Texas. Methodists were more numerous than the members of any of the other faiths in the rural parts of Ohio, Indiana, Delaware, and Maryland; Lutherans in Minnesota, North Dakota, South Dakota, and Nebraska; and Latter-day Saints in Idaho, Wyoming, Utah, and Nevada. (See Figure 114.)

For many persons, interest centers in the relative importance of Catholics and Protestants. On the whole, such a comparison is partially vitiated by the inclusion, in the reports, of most children of Catholic parents and the omission of many Protestant children. Nevertheless, from this standpoint a tabulation indicates that in

1936 Catholics comprised a majority of the rural church membership in nine states, namely, Maine, Vermont, Massachusetts, Rhode Island, Connecticut, Louisiana, New Mexico, Arizona, and California. Protestants were in the majority in the remainder of the states.

A corollary to the well-established principle that foreign-born population elements are concentrated in the cities, native-born in the rural parts of a country is Sorokin's hypothesis that persons affiliated with the established or native churches will be found in largest proportions in the rural districts, adherents of the non-native religious bodies in the cities.[26] If it can be established, this is a sociological principle of first-rate importance. The data in Table 5 would seem to be in agreement with such a hypothesis. Four Baptist denominations head the list in proportions of rural residents among the entire church membership, and two others rank sixth and seventh, respectively.[27] Descendants of Penn's Mennonite colonists, the United Brethren who stemmed from the Mennonites of Pennsylvania, the spiritual descendants of the transmontane Presbyterians who in 1810 established the Cumberland Presbyterian Church in Dickson County, Tennessee, also rank high in the list.[28] The preference of certain northern European groups for the open country is reflected in the situation in the Finnish Apostolic Lutheran Church, the Norwegian Lutheran Church of America, and the Lutheran Free Church. The Methodist Protestant Church, some of the Dunker groups, the Wesleyan Methodist and the Methodist Episcopal Church, South, the Southern Baptist Convention, the Friends, and the Negro Baptists are important denominational groups having a large proportion of their members in rural areas. At the other end of the scale one observes the numerous Jewish group, of whose more than four million members

[26] Cf. Pitirim Sorokin and Carle C. Zimmerman, *Principles of Rural-Urban Sociology*, New York, Henry Holt & Company, 1929, pp. 420–423.

[27] The first Baptist church in America was founded in 1639 by Roger Williams at Providence, Rhode Island. Members of this sect multiplied to about 15,000 communicants at the time of the Revolution. They participated with great zeal in the struggle with Great Britain, won much favor, and grew very rapidly, numbering over 65,000 in 1792, of whom more than 20,000 were in Virginia. Cf. Daniel Dorchester, *Christianity in the United States*, New York, Hunt & Eaton, 1889, pp. 267, 283; and John Hayward, *The Book of Religions*, Boston, Albert Colby and Company, 1860, p. 189. The Baptist faith is certainly entitled to be considered a "native" religion.

[28] The Scotch-Irish Presbyterians were archrebels in the revolutionary period. See Dorchester, *op. cit.*, p. 270.

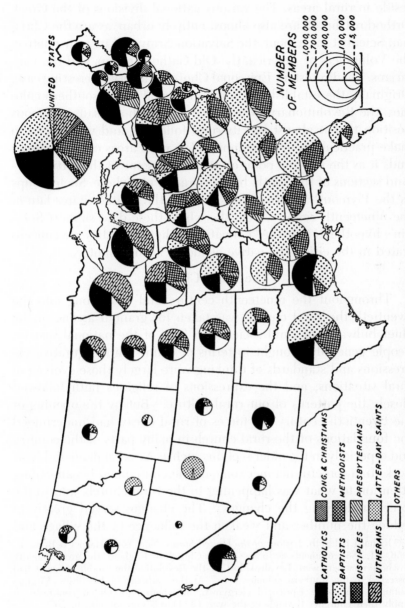

NUMBER
OF MEMBERS

1,000,000
700,000
400,000
100,000
15,000

CATHOLICS

BAPTISTS

DISCIPLES

LUTHERANS

CONG. & CHRISTIANS

METHODISTS

PRESBYTERIANS

LATTER-DAY SAINTS

OTHERS

FIGURE 114. Religious Affiliation of the Rural Church Membership, 1936, by States.

(most of them relative newcomers to America) less than 1 percent reside in rural areas. The various national divisions of the Greek Orthodox Church are also almost entirely urban, as are the Christian Scientist movement, the Salvation Army and its near relative, the Volunteers of America, the Old Catholic group, and the Unitarians. The Protestant Episcopal Church is a very interesting case. Originally the established church in several of the southern colonies, the Revolutionary War placed it in such a disadvantageous position that it almost lost its rural following and was forced to make practically a new beginning.[29] In rural areas one sometimes finds it as the rallying point of planters in some of the fertile lowland sections of the South, but very rarely elsewhere. Such groups as the Plymouth Brethren first came to the United States late in the nineteenth century.[30] On the whole these data support Sorokin's hypothesis that the "nonnative" religious bodies are concentrated in the cities, the native elements in the country.

The Rural Church

Throughout the nineteenth century and well along into the twentieth the rural church was taken for granted as one of the chief bulwarks of rural society—in fact, of the national society. People generally thought in terms of country life; figurative expressions and standards of thinking were largely those evolved in rural situations; and the expressions of religious faith followed closely the patterns of our rural culture.[31] But by the opening of the twentieth century the forces of rural decay had undermined the foundations of the rural church in many parts of the country and especially in the older sections such as New England and New York. In a forceful manner some of the churchmen began calling attention to what was happening to the rural church, and to the forces underlying the changes.[32] The changes served greatly to reduce the number and weaken the influence of the village and

[29] Richard Hildreth, *History of the United States*, New York, Harper & Brothers, 1856, III, 383, comments as follows: "The Church of England, the great majority of whose members were Loyalists, lost by the Revolution the establishment it had possessed in the southern colonies. . . ." At the outbreak of hostilities, Virginia contained ninety-one Episcopal clergymen, of whom only fifteen continued to supply their churches throughout the war. Cf. Dorchester, *op. cit.*, p. 267.

[30] The facts presented in this paragraph were drawn largely from *Religious Bodies: 1926*, II, *passim*.

[31] Cf. Warren H. Wilson, *The Farmer's Church*, New York, D. Appleton-Century Company, 1925, pp. 8–9.

[32] Cf. William DeWitt Hyde, "Impending Paganism in New England," *The Forum*, XIII (1892), 519–528; and especially Wilbert L. Anderson, *The Country Town*, New York, Baker & Taylor Company, 1906.

open-country churches of the nation, effects that were made even more pronounced when the automobile and good roads came to disrupt further the old patterns of rural organization and life. Even at that, however, studies in several states show that the church continues to have the widest distribution of membership of any organization in the rural community and that it still functions as the strongest motivating force in the rural districts.[33]

Number and Distribution of Rural Churches

Data from the 1936 Census of Religious Bodies indicate that there were only 128,097 rural churches in the United States. Undoubtedly, this is a very short count, even more erroneous than the preceding enumerations. Thus the 1926 Census found a total of 175,000 churches in the open country and villages of the United States. Furthermore, the 1937 *Handbook* of the Southern Baptist Convention, a denomination whose strength is concentrated in the most rural part of the nation, gives a total of 24,671 churches and 4,482,315 members, compared with the 13,815 churches and 2,700,155 members reported in the 1936 Census of Religious Bodies. Probably the number of rural churches in the United States is not far short of 200,000.

For the most part, these rural churches are distributed over the nation in proportion to population. But this is not strictly the case. Kolb and Brunner have observed that density of population tends to be associated with the number of churches, the general rule being the greater the density of population the larger the number of churches per 1000 population.[34] However, the reason may be that the Rocky Mountain region, where settlement is relatively recent, had only one church for each 1219 persons, as compared with one church for each 317 persons in the South. Such a proposition receives support from the data gathered in the 1936 survey of 140 villages, which indicate that the number of churches in the Far West made a net gain of one-third, while in all other sections the rural churches were decreasing in number.[35]

[33] Cf. Donald G. Hay and Robert A. Polson, *Rural Organizations in Oneida County, New York*, Cornell AES Bulletin 871, Ithaca, 1951, p. 20; and Selz C. Mayo, "The Country Church—No. 1 Rural Influence," *Research and Farming* (Raleigh), VII (Oct., 1949), p. 3.

[34] John H. Kolb and Edmund deS. Brunner, *A Study of Rural Society*, Boston, Houghton Mifflin Company, rev. ed., 1940, p. 495.

[35] Edmund deS. Brunner and Irving Lorge, *Rural Trends in Depression Years*, New York, Columbia University Press, 1937, p. 300. In 1936 Roman Catholic churches in rural areas averaged 382 members, a figure approached only by the

There are also other important factors affecting the distribution of rural churches. Among these may be listed the following: (1) The balance between Protestants and Catholics in the rural population is one factor. Catholic churches in rural areas average more than double the membership of rural Protestant churches for whites.[36] The more important the Catholic church in rural areas, the larger the rural parish. (2) The greater the rivalry among Protestant churches, the more rural churches per 1000 population. In extreme cases more than ten church congregations will be found in a single rural village of less than 2500 inhabitants. (3) Where society is still in the neighborhood stage, churches will be relatively numerous. This situation does much to explain the large number of churches to be found in the South relative to the population of the area. (4) Density of population exercises an important influence upon the number of churches. A sparse population makes it difficult to establish a church, duplication of effort is eliminated, and interdenominational strife may be reduced to a minimum. However, large areas may be entirely without church services. And, on the other hand, where density of population is high, division along denominational lines is facilitated, and the areas lacking church facilities are reduced to a minimum. (5) Where the traditional cultural pattern is deeply rooted and maintained, as in the South, churches tend to be relatively numerous. As was mentioned above, part of this situation is due to the retention of the neighborhood pattern of locality groupings. (6) Biracial composition of population, where the races worship separately as in the South, and cultural diversity, where each foreign-language group maintains services in its native tongue as in the

---

Latter-day Saints, with 346 members per rural church. Comparable averages for the rural churches of other large denominations are as follows: Northern Baptist Convention, 100; Southern Baptist Convention, 140; Negro Baptists, 123; Churches of Christ, 61; Congregational and Christian Churches, 100; Disciples of Christ, 122; Evangelical and Reformed Church, 156; American Lutheran Church, 206; Evangelical Lutheran Augustana Synod of North America, 181; Norwegian Lutheran Church of America, 175; Evangelical Lutheran Synod of Missouri, Ohio, and Other States, 202; United Lutheran Church in America, 204; African Methodist Episcopal Church, 70; African Methodist Episcopal Zion Church, 139; Methodist Episcopal Church, 106; Methodist Episcopal Church, South, 114; Presbyterian Church in the United States, 77; Presbyterian Church in the United States of America, 100; and the Protestant Episcopal Church, 98. *Census of Religious Bodies: 1936*, I, 86–97, Table 13.

[36] Brunner and Lorge, *op. cit.*, p. 303. See also Wilson Gee, *The Social Economics of Agriculture*, New York, The Macmillan Company, 1942, pp. 652–657.

Northwest, have much to do with increasing the number of churches per 1000 population.[37]

The Program of the Rural Church

Practically every rural church is part of a denominational body. For this reason its program is partially controlled by denominational policy. To some extent also, direct supervision is given to the local congregations by the denominational bodies, but the greater part of the responsibility for the local program is left in the hands of the local minister. This state of affairs in itself often creates a severe problem in rural churches, for less than one open-country church out of ten and only two out of five village churches have a full-time resident minister.[38] That this may be a conservative estimate is indicated by a thorough study in Missouri, where a well-distributed sample of 3000 churches revealed that only one out of five of all rural churches employed a full-time pastor. In the open country only one church out of ten conducted more than three half-time services, and 15 percent of all churches in the open country were either abandoned or on the verge of abandonment.[39] (See Figure 115.) It is also suggested by a survey of 1084 rural churches in the Bluegrass and Mountain sections of Kentucky in which it was found that one-half of the ministers were part-time workers and that only one-fifth of the churches had full-time ministers.[40]

Preaching constitutes the principal item in the rural church program. When the minister is nonresident there may be little else. Every effort is made to hold one service a Sunday, but where the circuit system still persists the minister may make his rounds only every two weeks or once a month. The relation between size of community and the regularity of preaching services is clearly shown in Figure 116.

In many ways the Sunday School is the most elemental part of the rural church. Such an organization is frequently maintained for the children even in localities where there is no regular preaching service. In the communities included in Brunner's 1930 study,

[37] Cf. C. Horace Hamilton and John M. Ellison, *The Negro Church in Rural Virginia*, Virginia AES Bulletin 273, Blacksburg, 1930, pp. 8–14.
[38] Kolb and Brunner, *op. cit.*, p. 505.
[39] Melvin W. Sneed and Douglas Ensminger, *The Rural Church in Missouri*, Missouri AES Research Bulletin 225, Columbia, 1935, pp. 22, 33.
[40] Harold F. Kaufman, *Rural Churches in Kentucky, 1947*, Kentucky AES Bulletin 530, Lexington, 1949, p. 47.

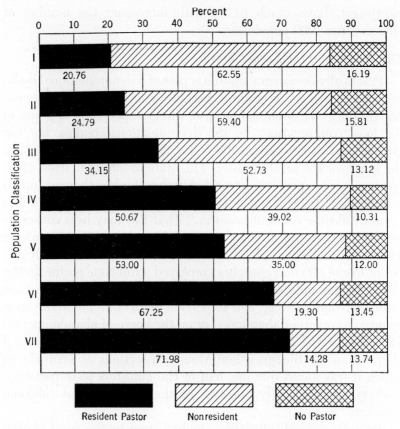

FIGURE 115. Availability of Pastors in 2561 Rural Churches in Missouri, 1934. (After Melvin W. Sneed and Douglas Ensminger, *The Rural Church in Missouri*, Missouri AES Research Bulletin 225, Columbia, 1935, p. 29.)

The key to the population classification is as follows: I—open country; II—under 200; III—200–400; IV—400–600; V—600–1000; VI—1000–1500; VII—1500–2500.

92 percent of the village and 86 percent of the open-country churches maintained a Sunday School.[41]

Trends

Trends in the number, distribution, size, functions, support, attendance, etc., of the rural church are of significance for all those interested in what rural life is becoming and likely to become in the future. The studies by Brunner and his associates

[41] Kolb and Brunner, *op. cit.*, p. 505.

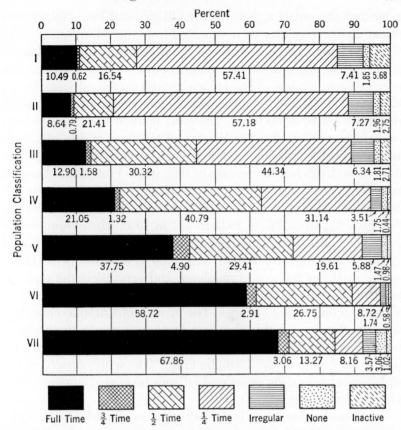

FIGURE 116. Frequency of Preaching Services in 2561 Rural Churches in Missouri, 1934. (After Melvin W. Sneed and Douglas Ensminger, *The Rural Church in Missouri*, Missouri AES Research Bulletin 225, Columbia, 1935, p. 21.)

The key to the population classification is as follows: I—open country; II—under 200; III—200–400; IV—400–600; V—600–1000; VI—1000–1500; VII—1500–2500.

again are the most important sources of data bearing on these questions. In the 140 village-centered communities which were studied in 1924, 1930, and again in 1936 the following significant changes were observed:

1. The number of rural churches declined. The decrease, to be sure, was very slight in the villages, but it was much more marked in the open country. The significant losses were confined to white Protestant churches, although in the South the white Protestant churches of the open country made a considerable

gain; and the greatest gains in the villages and losses in the surrounding open country were reported from the Far West.[42]

2. Although there were fewer rural churches in 1936 than in
1924 or 1930, the number of members per church was larger. The
average membership of the village church increased from 148 in
1924 to 171 in 1936; in the open country the corresponding
changes were from 80 to 93. The most marked increases, in both
categories, were in the Far West, and the most stable situations
in the Middle Atlantic and Southern States. Negro churches
showed no tendency to increase in size; white Protestant churches
increased considerably, the average rising from 140 to 163; but
the Catholic churches gained most markedly, the average membership growing from 287 in 1924 to 377 in 1936. The closing out of
the smaller and weaker churches, the return to religion stimulated
by the depression, which many regarded as a punishment visited
on the earth for the sins of mankind, and very likely the replacement of one ethnic stock by another are probably the most important factors in the changes. The growth of Catholic churches,
in particular, is probably due in a large measure to the replacement of older ethnic stocks, Protestant in religion, by more recent
immigrant groups of the Catholic faith.[43] The writer observed this
replacement occurring in several villages he visited in connection
with the 1930 survey.[44]

3. Church attendance is declining rather steadily. In 1924 the
average monthly attendance per person was estimated at 1.2, but
by 1936 this index had declined to .96. On the basis of resident
membership, monthly church attendance in 1924 was 3.9 per
member, compared with only 2.8 in 1936. Brunner and Lorge estimate the decrease at 20 percent for the last six years of the period,
and indicate that the loss was observed in all regions but was most
severe in the Middle West. They also attribute the loss in attendance to the churches' inability to compete with other social attractions, pointing out that attendance is better when the weather is
bad than on clear days, and maintaining that small competing
churches staffed by poorly trained ministers are not in a favorable
competitive position. In the attendance of village churches, a
marked increase in the proportion coming from the open country

[42] Brunner and Lorge, *op. cit.*, p. 300.
[43] *Ibid.*, pp. 301–302.
[44] See also John H. Kolb and C. J. Bornman, *Rural Religious Organization,*
Wisconsin AES Research Bulletin 60, Madison, 1924, pp. 12–38.

was observed. Thus in 1924, 31.6 percent of the attendance of village churches was made up of persons from the open country; by 1936 this figure was increased to 38.2. Combined with the more rapid closing of open-country churches, it indicates a growing tendency for the religious functions of the rural community to be centered in the village or trade center. Nevertheless, the increased attendance of people from the open country at village churches was not sufficient to offset the losses due to the closing of open-country churches. This fact leads to the generalization that the killing range of the village church exceeds its service range.[45]

[45] Brunner and Lorge, *op. cit.*, pp. 302–305; cf. Sneed and Ensminger, *op. cit.*, pp. 12–20. See also William G. Mather, Jr., *The Rural Churches of Allegheny County*, Cornell AES Bulletin 587, Ithaca, 1933; S. Earl Grigsby and Harold Hoffsommer, *Rural Social Organization of Frederick County, Maryland*, Maryland AES Bulletin A51, College Park, 1949, pp. 62–65; Lawrence M. Hepple and Margaret L. Bright, *Social Changes in Shelby County, Missouri*, Missouri AES Research Bulletin 456, Columbia, 1950, pp. 34–35; and Ronald B. Almack and Lawrence M. Hepple, *Rural Social Organization in Dent County, Missouri*, Missouri AES Research Bulletin 458, Columbia, 1950, pp. 42–44.

20

RURAL POLITICAL INSTITUTIONS AND GOVERNMENT

The farmer and rural folk generally are concerned with two rather separate aspects of political activity and governmental service. The first has to do with local activities, services, functions, and controls. The second pertains to the formal and functional relationships of the locality to the larger governmental units such as the state or province and the nation, with respect both to the administrative, legislative, and judicial machinery set up to relate the individual cells of the national structure and to the effect of local political activity upon the state and national life.

The Characteristics of Rural Local Government

Local government, always predominantly rural, is always basic in national structure. Old sayings in Russia, China, India, and elsewhere have it that when one knows the village he knows the empire. The importance of local governmental processes and structure is due in part to the slowness with which they change. Brunner and Kolb found that local government in the United States had changed less than any of the other institutions in our rural society.[1] This great resistance to change is undoubtedly one factor that makes for a high degree of similarity in the local governmental activity and organization in various countries, in different sections of the same country, and in the same area at different times.

Sorokin, Zimmerman, and Galpin have stressed the highly familistic nature of rural local government and have listed its chief

[1] Edmund deS. Brunner and John H. Kolb, *Rural Social Trends*, New York, McGraw-Hill Book Company, 1933, p. 285; cf. Edmund deS. Brunner and Irving Lorge, *Rural Trends in Depression Years*, New York, Columbia University Press, 1937, p. 285.

characteristics as follows: (1) Local governmental units insist upon and generally enjoy a high degree of autonomy,[2] whether the central authority is a monarchy, oligarchy, republic, or democracy. (2) Local government is highly informal, is based largely upon the mores. (3) The stability of local government is very great, and seems to remain fairly constant although surrounded on every hand by change. Brunner and Kolb, analyzing the situation in 1932–1933, declared momentous changes in local government to be imminent, but five years later Brunner and Lorge[3] reported that rural government had changed little if at all. After all, most frequently there is little to be gained through leadership in rural local governmental affairs; more often the holding of office is an economic liability rather than an asset. Furthermore, leadership in rural political affairs is most often vested in those who control the land—a class usually opposed to any changes likely to interfere with its continued control and use of the land. (4) There is little or no specialized political leadership in rural areas. Political leaders are the same as the leaders in other fields of activity. Landowners, members of prominent families, and natural leaders of all types are usually vested with the role of political leaders as well. Prominent families almost automatically supply the bulk of the leaders in all fields of activity including the political.[4] (5) Rule by discretion prevails in rural areas.[5] Few are the formal laws and ordinances; strong are the mores. Taxation, the execution of justice (often through extralegal associations, vigilante committees, etc.), and the maintenance of roads and schools are central functions of the local unit. Such is the analysis by the authors of the *Systematic Source Book*. In conclusion they

[2] P. A. Sorokin, Carle C. Zimmerman, and Charles J. Galpin, *Systematic Source Book in Rural Sociology*, Minneapolis, University of Minnesota Press, 1931, II, 540–545. Cf. Wilson Gee, *The Social Economics of Agriculture*, New York, The Macmillan Company, rev. ed., 1942, pp. 540–543.

[3] *Op. cit.*, p. 285. See also Karl A. Bosworth, *Tennessee Valley County: Rural Government in the Hill County of Alabama*, University, Alabama, Bureau of Public Administration, 1941, p. 114, in which the following conclusion was reached: "Tennessee Valley Authority operations have done much to the face of the country but have influenced its governmental institutions and practices but little."

[4] Cf. M. Ostrogorski, *Democracy and the Organization of Political Parties*, London, Macmillan & Co., Ltd., 1902, p. 11.

[5] Cf. Warren H. Wilson, *The Farmer's Church*, New York, D. Appleton-Century Company, 1925, p. 6, relative to this point. Wilson indicates correctly that the farmer is relatively unconcerned about civic processes, does not fear the policeman, and "administers his social life by homemade processes."

indicate that as a result of the growing complexity of society and the submersion of the local community in the larger political world, this informal government based on the mores is weakened, and that centralized government in which the state assumes control of rural affairs takes its place.

Relationship of Farmers to the State and Nation

In most countries of the world there is a definitely organized agrarian party having as its chief objective the political promotion of the welfare of the farming classes. Immediately following the First World War these parties sprang into prominence in the "green rising" that swept Europe.[6] The American farmer in his relations to his national government has lacked a national agrarian party. The nearest thing to one was the Democratic party of the South before the Civil War. It is also true that the Democratic party in the South has been largely agrarian in sympathy and objectives, although stripped of its strength by the War and Reconstruction, as has the Republican party in the Midwest. But the biparty system of the United States has rather effectively set the farmers of one section of the country against those of other sections.

Although a national agrarian party is lacking in the United States, farmers have by no means failed to make their influence felt through organized political activity. Time after time insurgency has spread like wildfire through the farm belts of the nation to make itself felt upon the policies of the administration in power.[7] (Figure 117.) Almost from the first the small western farmer has been in opposition to the conservative classes along the eastern seaboard. Andrew Jackson owed his election in 1828 in no small measure to the revolt of the western farmers against the political domination of the East. The Granger[8] and the Greenback movements in the seventies, the Farmers' Alliance and the Popu-

---

[6] For accounts of the agrarian parties in Russia, Czechoslovakia, Bulgaria, Rumania, Switzerland, Estonia, Greece, Sweden, Yugoslavia, Finland, and Latvia, see Sorokin, Zimmerman, and Galpin, *op. cit.*, II, 618–674; cf. William B. Bizzell, *The Green Rising*, New York, The Macmillan Company, 1926.

[7] Carl C. Taylor, "The Farmers' Movement and Large Farmers' Organizations," in Carl C. Taylor, et al., *Rural Life in the United States*, New York, Alfred A. Knopf, Inc., 1949, pp. 510–521, is the most adequate short survey of this subject.

[8] For a standard work on this, consult Solon J. Buck, *The Granger Movement*, Cambridge, Harvard University Press, 1913.

FIGURE 117. Revolt in the Farm Belt. (From *Harper's Weekly*.)

list[9] movement in the eighties, the Non-Partisan League[10] (originally a farmers' movement) during the period of World War I, the Farm Bureau Movement,[11] the activities of the Farmer-Labor party in the Northwest, and the Farmers' Holiday Movement in the Midwest during the depths of the last great depression—these are but a few of the activities of organized agriculturists which have marked our history. To the activities of the Grange, still one of the leading farm organizations, is due much of the railroad regulation, the establishment of state boards of agriculture, federal appropriations for agricultural colleges, compulsory education, federal development of water transportation, the establishment of the United States Department of Agriculture, improvement of the services of the United States Weather Bureau, and national standardization of weights and measures.[12] Although other movements such as the Farmers' Alliance have not persisted and have not left many tangible results, in many ways they have created greater upheavals politically than the Grange. Formed by combining the Louisiana Farmers' Union, the Arkansas Agricultural Wheel, and the Texas Farmers' Alliance, and coöperating with the Northwestern Alliance, the total membership of the Alliance approximated two million farmers in the period around 1890. In several southern states the Alliance took over the control of the Democratic party, controlled the legislatures of eight states, elected governors of four states, and sent more than forty Representatives to Congress.[13]

The Grange and the Farmers' Alliance together must be credited with placing the Secretary of Agriculture in the cabinet, effecting considerable railroad regulation, and bringing about the creation of the Interstate Commerce Commission. In addition

---

[9] See especially John D. Hicks, *The Populist Revolt*, Minneapolis, University of Minnesota Press, 1931; and Frank L. McVey, *The Populist Movement*, New York, American Economic Association, 1896, I, No. 3; cf. Alex M. Arnett, *Populist Movement in Georgia*, New York, Columbia University Press, 1922; John B. Clark, *Populism in Alabama*, Auburn, Auburn Printing Co., 1927; William DuBose Sheldon, *Populism in the Old Dominion: Virginia Farm Politics, 1885–1900*, Princeton, Princeton University Press, 1935; and H. C. Nixon. "The Populist Movement in Iowa," *Iowa Journal of History and Politics* (March, 1926).

[10] Andrew A. Bruce, *Non-Partisan League*, New York, The Macmillan Company, 1921, is a rather detailed treatment of this development.

[11] Cf. O. M. Kile, *The Farm Bureau Movement*, New York, The Macmillan Company, 1921.

[12] Carl C. Taylor, *Rural Sociology*, New York, Harper & Brothers, 1933, pp. 625–630.

[13] *Ibid.*, pp. 628–629; see also Robert L. Hunt, *A History of Farmer Movements in the Southwest, 1873–1925*, College Station, Texas A. and M. College Press, 1935.

their programs of activity had much to do with the creation of the rural free delivery service for farmers, and reform in the handling of the public domain.[14]

Political Processes in Rural Areas

The rural environment, both physical and man-made, should have tangible effects upon the political and governmental activities of rural people. Although difficult to measure, rural political campaigns, especially in the South, have a distinctly recreational flavor, a phenomenon that is not exemplified solely by the 1938 "Pass the biscuits, pappy" campaign in Texas, and the election of the composer of "You Are My Sunshine" as governor of Louisiana in 1944. Political gatherings are one of the principal occasions for large assemblies of rural people, and those attending expect a good show. More objective data, however, can be secured concerning other important rural political phenomena. Consider, for example, rural participation in voting, voting the straight ticket versus ticket splitting, the popularity of nontraditional political doctrines and parties, and the nature of agrarian extremest movements as aspects of the problem to receive consideration in this section.

Participation in Voting

Does the farmer exercise the privilege of the ballot as frequently as does the city man? Reasoning deductively and knowing the physical barriers between the rural person and the polls, some students have concluded that the farmer is less prone to utilize the privilege of voting than is his city cousin.[15] This is the basis for a claim that political life increases with urbanization.

Studies in the United States, far from supporting the idea advanced by Thompson that rural areas are deficient in voting, give rise to exactly the opposite conclusions. Thus the fundamental work of Titus, who studied voting in the state of California during the quarter-century 1900–1926, came to the conclusion that "the larger the city the smaller the vote relative to the voting population."[16] This principle received further confirmation from other

[14] Taylor, *Rural Sociology*, pp. 632–633.

[15] See, for example, J. G. Thompson, *Urbanization*, New York, E. P. Dutton & Co., 1927, p. 323.

[16] Charles H. Titus, "Voting in California," *Southwestern Political and Social Science Quarterly*, VIII, IX, and X (1928–1929).

studies in California, Nevada, Utah, Wyoming, Montana, Minnesota, Ohio, New York, Washington, South Carolina, Tennessee, and Kansas.[17] The uniformity was observed in the votes cast for presidential electors, Congressmen, governors, and state legislators.[18] Manny's results in New England agree that the open-country population voted in as large proportions as the inhabitants of urban centers.[19] Sorokin, Zimmerman, and Galpin have summarized studies from all over the world to show that this American tendency is also true elsewhere, and that in all probability the farmer is more likely to take advantage of his privilege to vote than is the average city man.[20] Probably fairly representative, the data indicate clearly that rural people, in spite of the disadvantage of physical isolation, exercise the privilege of the ballot in as large proportions as urbanites, who are much more accessible to the polls.

Ticket Splitting

The available evidence makes it apparent that farmers are more likely to vote the straight ticket than are people in the cities.[21] The indication is that farmers cling to traditional party platforms and creeds to a much greater extent than urban folk. Recent (1938 to 1950) elections are of great interest and deserve careful analysis because of the apparent rural-urban differentiation in the balloting.

Radicalism and Revolution

The experience of the United States amply demonstrates that the farmer is by no means always and everywhere staid and conservative. Probably over long periods of time he is less revolutionary than the city man, but frequently the farmers of the United States have been radical in the extreme.[22] There also seem to be about rural radicalism some peculiar aspects that differentiate it

[17] Charles H. Titus, *Voting Behavior in the United States*, Publications of the University of California at Los Angeles in the Social Sciences, V (1935), 27, 41, 68.

[18] *Ibid.*, pp. 28–29.

[19] Theodore B. Manny, *Attitudes Towards Rural Government*, United States Department of Agriculture, Washington (mimeographed), 1929, p. 7.

[20] *Op. cit.*, II, pp. 551–555.

[21] See particularly the thoroughgoing study by A. C. Millspaugh, "Irregular Voting in the United States," *Political Science Quarterly*, XXXIII (1918), 230–254; cf. Sorokin, Zimmerman, and Galpin, *op. cit.*, II, 555–556.

[22] Cf. Stuart A. Rice, *Quantitative Methods in Politics*, New York, Alfred A. Knopf, Inc., 1928, pp. 170–172.

from that of the city. The most important of these hinges about the control and operation of the land. Whenever any large proportion of the rural population is lacking lands of its own to cultivate, or whenever any significant number of owner-operators are threatened with dispossession, revolt is likely to flare up in the farm belts of the nation. The "Farmer's Holiday" movement which swept like wildfire through the Midwest and made its influence felt in the South during 1932–1933 is an excellent example of revolt among the farmers. Elemental in the extreme, without a clearly defined program and objectives, seeking by all means to prevent the dispossession of farm operators, the movement clearly typifies radicalism among farmers.

Measures Favored by the Farming Classes

Farmers' interests do not coincide exactly with those of any one urban class. As a result, farmers sometimes vote with one of the cities' classes, sometimes with another, now with the laborers, at another time with the employers. In general farmers have opposed such measures as wage and hour limitation,[23] the softening of the criminal code, pensions for occupational groups such as schoolteachers, increases in taxation, the modification of election laws to bring about stronger popular rule, and workmen's compensation. On the other hand they have supported such things as the prohibition amendment, regulation of banks and corporations (especially railroads), and measures designed to promote honesty in governmental affairs.[24] Thus the agriculturists sometimes unite for political purposes with the cities' laboring classes, sometimes with the middle classes, and at other times with the upper capitalistic classes of the urban centers. In view of this, the successful organization of a farmer-labor party on a national scale seems hardly feasible. On the other hand, a strong agrarian bloc in all political parties seems most likely to advance the welfare of the rural groups.

[23] Even the Non-Partisan League in North Dakota, which granted most of the other demands of labor, refused to sanction the eight-hour day for fear that it might be contagious and later be extended to labor in agriculture. Bruce, *op. cit.*, pp. 4–5.

[24] Sorokin, Zimmerman, and Galpin, *op. cit.*, II, 566–568; for special studies, see especially William F. Ogburn and Delvin Peterson, "Political Thought of Social Classes," *Political Science Quarterly*, XXXI (1916), 330 ff.; and Stuart A. Rice, *Farmers and Workers in American Politics*, Columbia University Studies in History, Economics, and Public Law, CXIII, New York, 1924, *passim*.

Evolution of Local Government in Rural America

The American farmers' local governmental institutions are a product of centuries of social evolution. For the most part their origins go back to the Old World and especially to England, where the prototypes of American political organization were developing hundreds of years before the discovery of America.[25] In the colonization of North America a considerable variety of local governmental units were transplanted to the New World where, in the face of radically different conditions from those of the mother countries, they rapidly underwent fundamental changes. In the compact group settlements of New England, Old World patterns evolved into the township system or type of local government. But in the southern colonies a quite different system developed. Here, where widely separated large plantations were dominant in governmental affairs, the county was developed as the basic unit of local government. In the middle colonies somewhat of a compromise system came into being, a form of local government that utilized both the township and the county. For example, in Pennsylvania, although towns were established as local governmental units, they were of little importance; their machinery and functions of government "were vague and indefinite." In New York, however, where the system of local government embraced both townships and counties, the townships had important functions and were definitely recognized as part of the county organization. New England left her imprint firmly upon the pattern of local government in New York.[26]

As the fringes of settlement pressed westward across the continent, the local governmental and political institutions from the older states diffused with them, following to a considerable extent parallel lines of latitude. Even in the face of radically contrasting situations in the new settlements, the primary factor determining the nature of rural governmental units in the new states was the type of unit the settlers had been accustomed to in the localities from which they came. The student of cultural lags could find excellent examples in this field. Kentucky and Tennessee adopted

[25] Those of Louisiana, however, derive largely from France, while Spain has left her imprint on the government of Texas and other southwestern states.

[26] For a discussion of local government in the colonies, see John A. Fairlie and Charles M. Kneier, *County Government and Administration*, New York, D. Appleton-Century Company, 1930, pp. 13–22.

as a matter of course the county system similar to that of Virginia.[27] North of Ohio the development was not so unchallenged. The state of Ohio, built somewhat along Pennsylvania governmental lines, became an arena of struggle between the two competing systems of local government, township and county. Constitutionally both townships and counties were established, but the townships never realized the important position they occupied in the New England states, and were more the equivalent of those in Pennsylvania. The checkerboard pattern of land division, coupled with homestead requirements necessitating residence on isolated farmsteads, made of the townships an artificial unit and prevented the township system from gaining the political significance it enjoyed in the older states. In Ohio the county became the focal point of local government.[28]

Indiana governmental institutions were fashioned largely on the Ohio model, as were those of Illinois. In the latter case, a considerable early influx of settlers from south of the Ohio River strengthened the county still further as the unit of local government. Michigan, originally organized along lines similar to Ohio, later revivified the townships with an influx of settlers from New York and developed a dual system involving both townships and counties as functional realities—a form of local governmental organization similar to that of New York. Wisconsin early felt the influence of Illinois on its local political institutions, but the pattern finally evolved leaned more heavily upon Michigan and New York.[29]

West of the Mississippi both townships and counties were established in Iowa, Minnesota, and Kansas; but in these states the dual system resembled that of Ohio and Indiana, i.e., the county was the fundamental unit, and the township possessed little definite purpose or function. In the South (including the states of Florida and Texas) and in California, the county system became the dominant pattern. But it was in the settlement of the West and Far West that the county reached its height in importance as a local governmental unit. All the new states were

[27] *Ibid.*, p. 24.
[28] *Ibid.*, p. 25.
[29] *Ibid.*, pp. 27–29; cf. Arthur W. Bromage, *American County Government*, New York, Sears Publishing Company, 1933, chap. 3; and Luke M. Smith, "Territorial Variables in American Local Government," *Social Forces*, XXVII (1949), 350–358.

divided into counties as the basic units; only a few of them established townships, and even there township government made little
headway.

In summary, the evolution of local governmental units in
America passed through a number of distinct phases: (1) the
introduction of governmental patterns into the colonies from the
mother countries, especially England; (2) radical changes in them
to adapt them to the new environment, remodelings which gave
rise to the township system in New England, the county system in
the South, and a mixed type in the middle colonies; and (3) the
diffusion of these patterns with the settlement of the West, settlers
from a given state establishing in their new surroundings the local
governmental units to which they had been accustomed in the
older states. In this diffusion, the mixed system, with the township
as an important integral part of the county, as in New York, spread
into Michigan and on into Wisconsin, but never succeeded in
crossing the Mississippi. The mixed system, with counties as the
dominant unit but including townships as in Ohio, spread westward through Illinois, Missouri, Kansas, and through Nebraska
and the Dakotas. The county system of the South, in which subdivisions of the county were mostly election districts and nothing
else, spread westward throughout the entire southern area and
was adopted in all the far western states, where it reached the
peak of its development.

The Structure of Local Governmental Units of the United States

Functions

The rural population of the United States has always looked to
the state and local governmental units for the performance of a
number of functions thought to be essential to the welfare of the
people on the land. Many of these societal functions carried on by
the government are of local significance only, and responsibility
for them has been centered in the county or township unit. This is
in reality local self-government.[30] Others, and probably the larger
share of the governmental functions performed by local units, are
in reality state functions which are delegated to the local divisions.

Local government in the United States is one vast labyrinth.

[30] See Kirk H. Porter, *County and Township Government in the United States*,
New York, The Macmillan Company, 1929, pp. 16–20.

Estimates place the number of local governmental units (most of which are rural) in the forty-eight states at between 150,000 and 200,000. This total includes some 3000 counties, 16,500 incorporated centers, and a host of townships, school districts, and special fire, water, lighting, drainage, irrigation, and other kinds of districts. In 1929 these local governmental units spent a total of over thirteen billions of dollars, as compared with two billions by state governments and four billions by the federal government.[31]

Throughout the entire United States the principal unit of rural local government is the county.[32] It is a subdivision of the commonwealth; the state itself is responsible for the establishment of the county.[33] Although other local governmental units such as New England towns and midwestern townships prevail, the county is far more important. The nature of the county is complex. It is at once an administrative agency and a quasi corporation. Deriving their privileges from the state, counties possess in general only those powers which have been expressly delegated to them by the state constitution or specifically granted to them by the state legislature.[34]

Among the functions usually performed by the county are the following: (1) the administration of justice; (2) the administration of corrections and charities; (3) the administration of health measures and programs; (4) the administration of education; (5) the administration of highways and roads; (6) the administration of revenues; and (7) the making and preserving of records. Recent developments have increased the importance of the county unit in agricultural extension work that is undertaken in coöperation with the state colleges of agriculture and the federal government, and in the administration of the Agricultural Adjustment programs. In fact, more and more federal activities are being organized on a county basis, although not as county functions.[35]

The nature of the county's conventional governmental functions is fairly well known. The administration of justice involves the exercise of the police power, coroners' inquests in cases of sudden death or where foul play is suspected, the prosecution of

[31] Cf. Bromage, *op. cit.*, pp. 3–4.
[32] Called a parish in Louisiana.
[33] John A. Fairlie, *Local Government in Counties, Towns and Villages*, New York, D. Appleton-Century Company, 1914, p. 57.
[34] Fairlie and Kneier, *op. cit.*, p. 221.
[35] Cf. B. L. Hummel, "County Organization for Program Planning in Virginia," *Rural Sociology*, I (1936), 90–93.

crime, and the provision of courts of justice. Activities in connection with corrections and charities on a county basis include the maintenance of county jails, provision of relief for the poor, and specialized welfare work. With the advent of state and national unemployment relief programs in 1932, and more recently the Social Security programs of aid to dependent children, aid to the needy blind, and old-age assistance, these welfare activities of the counties have assumed a role of first-rate importance. Health administration involves taking proper precautions to insure sanitation and providing hospitals, county nurses, and county physicians. In recent years the state, acting largely through the counties, has greatly broadened the public health facilities available to the rural population. Counties are also a basic unit in the provision of educational services to the population. Traditionally, as measured by the proportion of the total budget used for these purposes, the educational functions have been among the most important functions of the county.[36] Consolidation of schools and recently the provision of state aid to counties have still more increased the importance of the county in educational administration. The local governmental unit was for a long time almost the only agency concerned with roads and highways. Recent developments have taken the matter of roads and highways entirely out of the neighborhood stage or, as some would say, the "horse and buggy stage." State highway systems now crisscross practically every county in the United States, and the national government with its federal aid programs has also assumed a major share of the responsibility for roads and highways. The county has performed an essential function in its administration of revenues. It is on the one hand the unit in which the state revenues are collected; and it may, with the authority of the constitution or the legislature, levy, collect, and disburse tax money for the performance of local governmental services. The keeping of records such as deeds, mortgages, marriage registers, etc., is also a vital function of the county. Finally, many counties have performed essential services in connection with military organization, recreation, public service enterprises (irrigation, levees, drainage, etc.), and a host of miscellaneous activities. With all this it would be futile to think that the func-

---

[36] Herman G. James, *Local Government in the United States*, New York, D. Appleton-Century Company, 1921, p. 209; cf. Carl F. Reuss, *County Government in Washington*, Washington AES Bulletin 400, Pullman, 1941, pp. 7–13.

tions of the county are now fixed for all time. For example, just what functions adhere in the county as a result of the recent planning in agriculture will be an important development to observe.

Organization

The organization of county governments follows no set pattern, conforms to no general principles; but nearly every state has a system of its own. In every state there is provision for some elective county board that is responsible for the management of county affairs. Only rarely are the legislative, judicial, and executive functions clearly separated from one another. Nor is there any consistent practice of making executives responsible to a representative body. In county government there is no single officer who is the chief official of the county, corresponding to the mayor of a town or city. Furthermore, the county board or council which levies taxes and determines administrative policy has very limited legislative powers. Other officers, elective or appointive, exercise various functions and are largely independent of the board, council, or commissioners. Sometimes one officer will perform judicial as well as administrative functions.[37] An impartial report from Virginia says: "In our study of Virginia county government we were particularly impressed by the scattered, disjointed, and irresponsible type of organization that exists in all the counties. . . . The present county government has no responsible head; it is without a chief administrative officer and the board of supervisors controls through appointment only a small part of the county administration. Authority for carrying on the administrative work of the county . . . rests with many individuals. The voters of the county have very little power in the determination of county policies."[38] Fairlie and Kneier say that practically the same statements hold for county government throughout the United States.[39]

Many in title and duties are the officials charged with performing the social functions that American rural society has vested in its county units. With great variation in responsibilities and name, each state except Rhode Island has provided some sort of county board. These are variously designated as the county com-

[37] Fairlie and Kneier, *op. cit.*, p. 107.
[38] Report on *County Government in Virginia*, prepared by the New York Bureau of Municipal Research, Richmond, 1928, pp. 5–6.
[39] *Op. cit.*, p. 108.

missioners, county court, fiscal court, board of supervisors, board of chosen freeholders, board of revenue, and police jury. Whatever the name, these boards are of two chief types: (1) those composed of representatives from local subordinate governmental divisions, and (2) those chosen on a county-wide basis. Where the first type is employed, the board of supervisors may be small, consisting of as few as three members, but it may also be and usually is large, numbering as many as fifty. The second type usually results in a small board of from three to seven members.[40] The powers of these boards vary widely but include the right to levy taxes, borrow money, construct roads and bridges, build public buildings such as poorhouses, hospitals, asylums, etc., grant relief to widows and the poor, maintain public schools, spend moneys for public health and sanitation, and provide for the salaries and expenditures of other county officers. In some states the boards are granted powers by the legislature permitting them to make and enforce ordinances, particularly with respect to public protection, sanitation, and other local affairs.[41]

There is further variation in the county officers. Officials concerned with the judicial functions of the county include the county judge, the clerk of court, the attorney, the sheriff, and the coroner. Finance officers usually consist of the assessor, the tax collector (sometimes a special officer, sometimes the sheriff as in Louisiana) or treasurer, and the auditor. Important indeed are the clerical officers of the county, including the clerk and the recorder (sometimes these two offices are combined), and the surveyor. Other important county officers include the superintendent of education, the county health officers, and the directors of relief and public welfare.[42]

County government is frequently severely criticized, has suffered from a bad reputation, and has been referred to as the "dark continent in the field of American Government." Specific proposals for its improvement usually include: (1) adapting county governments to the needs of the various counties; (2) limiting the size of the county board, making it uniformly small; (3) abolishing some county offices, consolidating others, filling some offices by appointment, and making terms of office longer; (4) develop-

[40] James, *op. cit.*, p. 132.
[41] *Ibid.*, pp. 135–136.
[42] For descriptions of the duties of these officers in the various states, see *ibid.*, pp. 139–185.

ing a real county executive, and centralizing the executive functions in him; (5) thoroughly revising the county's finances by adopting accepted accounting and budgeting practices, eliminating the fee system of payment in favor of definite salaries; and (6) concentrating in the county functions now exercised by the townships, and transferring some county functions to the state.[43]

Towns and Townships

All the states include smaller areas within the counties with various administrative and political purposes. Each county is divided into towns,[44] townships, districts, wards, etc., which jointly make up the county. Centers of population of any size are usually incorporated as villages, towns, boroughs, or cities. In New England the towns continue to exercise most of the specific functions of local government, services elsewhere rendered by the counties, while the county serves principally as the agency for bringing state services to the local districts.[45] Towns also serve to tie up the open country with the urban unit.

From New York to North Dakota the township is important as the subdivision of the county. In these states, and particularly those west of Ohio, the geographic or congressional township of the land surveys has frequently been utilized as the organized civil township. When organized, these townships are corporate and political bodies. They serve as districts for local governmental affairs, and as agencies for county and state business. In New York, Michigan, and Wisconsin they perform many of the essential governmental functions elsewhere performed by the county. In the other Middle States their roles are of considerably less importance.[46] (See Figure 118.)

There are those who are greatly impressed with the importance of active participation in the transactions of local government. They insist that the absence of such governmental institutions as

[43] Cf. Helen M. Rocca, *County Government*, League of Women Voters, Washington, 1932, p. 50; *Proceedings of the First Conference for Better County Government in New York State*, Schenectady, H. S. Gilbertson, 1914, pp. 3–4, *passim;* and Paul W. Wager, *County Government and Administration in North Carolina*, Chapel Hill, University of North Carolina Press, 1928, pp. 393–423.

[44] As used in New England, "town" refers to a unit of local government within the county, and not to an incorporated population center intermediate between the village and the city.

[45] Fairlie, *op. cit.*, pp. 141–163.

[46] *Ibid.*, pp. 164–185.

the New England town and its town meeting in most of rural America is a serious deficiency in rural organization. For example, Sanderson has written as follows:

Thus over the larger part of the United States there is no adequate local government whatsoever, a fact which has a most unfortunate effect in preventing the mass of the rural population from having any personal experience in the affairs of the government, so essential to their intelligent exercise of the suffrage in affairs of county, state, and nation.[47]

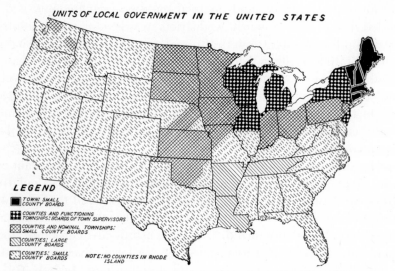

FIGURE 118.   The Units of Local Government in the United States.

Some lifelong students of local government, on the other hand, point out that even the New England type of local self-government has its serious deficiencies, especially in coping with modern conditions. For example, Fairlie and Kneier present survey data to show that only from one-fifth to one-eighth of all qualified voters attend the business meetings. They indicate that a small clique frequently determines all fundamental matters beforehand in a caucus and then uses the meeting merely as a formality. Paul Wager contends that frequently the town meeting has degenerated "into little more than a caucus of political wardheelers."[48] This of

[47] Dwight Sanderson, *The Rural Community*, Boston, Ginn and Company, 1932, p. 520.
[48] See his address, "Can Local Self-Government Be Preserved?" in *Rural Government: Proceedings of the Fourteenth American Country Life Conference*, Chicago, 1932, p. 54.

course undermines the real purpose and value of the town meeting. Fairlie and Kneier also indicate that the influx of foreign-born possessed of different cultural standards and practices, the spread of industrialization, and the rapid growth of population have made the old system too complex and unsatisfactory.[49] They might have mentioned also that many of the functions once performed by the town meeting are now obsolete. Today the local area is not empowered to determine who shall live within its borders, or to require bonds of the friends and relatives of new residents in order to insure that they will not become charges of the local unit. The management of communal property is no longer a proposition requiring deliberation. The individual property owner is now responsible for state taxes; they are no longer levied in a lump sum upon the town. Neither is it necessary to levy a specific rate to take care of the minister's salary, etc., as was the case in the early town of New England. Nor are the representatives elected by those present at the town meeting accepted as members of the state legislatures. In fact, if one goes through the list of functions of the early town meeting he finds that the great majority of them are entirely obsolete.[50] Those who, for sentimental reasons, set forth the New England town as the ideal prototype of what local self-government should be would do well to consider the degree to which it was merely the agency for the enforcement of "blue laws" that have long since been relegated to the discard.[51]

One study has shown that this town type of local government sometimes offers a convenient manner by which voters of the area can hire themselves as town officials, levy taxes upon nonresidents' property, abandon work, and live in comparative comfort on the proceeds of their unproductive political positions.[52]

Trends

Current trends in local governmental structure are definitely in the direction of greater centralization, especially of more state control over local activities. This greater concentration of power in the state has accompanied the addition of new functions to the

[49] *Op. cit.*, pp. 431–433; cf. Bromage, *op. cit.*, p. 7.

[50] For a discussion of the early town-meeting functions, see Porter, *op. cit.*, pp. 30–38.

[51] Cf. Bromage, *op. cit.*, p. 19.

[52] Carle C. Zimmerman, John H. Useem, and Lyman H. Ziegler, "Littleville: A Parasitic Community During the Depression," *Rural Sociology*, I (1936), 54–72.

activities of local governmental units. Since 1915 the fields of health, recreation, and education (including vocational agricultural teaching) have been developed in the various counties of the United States. Almost without exception these new functions have been added under provisions for state support and supervision. The report of the committee appointed by President Hoover to study social trends estimated that between 1915 and 1929 in four states (New York, Ohio, Wisconsin, and California) county expenditures had increased 205 percent, or, allowing for the fall in the purchasing power of the dollar, 80 percent. Although no state from the South is included, the results are still of considerable significance. Expenditures for public schools showed the greatest increase, 270 percent; those for highways were next, 245 percent; then came those for public welfare, 180 percent. In 1929 education took a larger portion of the county budget in these four states than any other function; highways ranked second; and the two together accounted for more than one-half of the total expenditures. Expenditures for recreation, health and sanitation, and protection increased more rapidly than the total budget, while governmental functions, charities and corrections, and miscellaneous expenditures were below the average increase.[53]

Suggested Reforms

Students of rural government seem to be pretty thoroughly in accord concerning certain reforms of local government thought to be necessary and desirable. In the first place the elimination of many townships, small villages, and other rather unnecessary and useless local governmental units is urged. Second is recommended the elimination of many county units through consolidation. It is urged that the county is a relic of the "horse and buggy days"; that it is commensurate in size with the distance it was possible to travel twice in one day by means of horse and buggy between the morning and evening chores on the farm; and that it is now out of keeping with our modern means of rapid communication and transportation as exemplified by the telephone, telegraph, automobile, and hard-surfaced roads. Formerly, it is pointed out, the county was larger than the trade areas or trade basins of the largest

[53] President's Research Committee on Social Trends, *Recent Social Trends*, New York, McGraw-Hill Book Company, 1933, II, 1317–1323. See also W. F. Kumlein, *Basic Trends of Social Change in South Dakota: VII. Local Government*, South Dakota AES Bulletin 347, Brookings, 1941.

centers serving farmers directly; now the county is frequently only a fraction of the trading territory of a given city which farmers go to for trading purposes.[54] Third, it is pointed out that it would be highly advantageous to reduce the number of overlapping special districts which have been created for one purpose or another and to make these coincide as much as possible with the enlarged county boundaries. Finally, it seems fairly well agreed that the small county board is superior to the large one, that it should be given more power (perhaps a county mayor), and that greater centralization of authority should be established in the county through the reduction of the number of county officials who would have to stand for election.[55]

[54] Bromage, *op. cit.*, pp. 266–268; cf. Frank O. Lowden, "The Problems of Rural Government," and Paul W. Wager, "Can Local Self-Government Be Preserved in Our Rural Areas?" in *Rural Government: Proceedings of the Fourteenth American Country Life Association*, Chicago, 1932, pp. 1–9; 54–60; George H. Hansen, *Influence of the History of County Boundaries on a Proposal to Redistrict the State of Utah in Keeping with Natural Boundaries*, Provo, Utah, 1936; T. N. Hurd, *Local Government in Tompkins County*, New York, Cornell AES Bulletin 657, Ithaca, 1936; and Gee, *op. cit.*, pp. 552–554.

[55] Bromage, *op. cit.*, pp. 269–283.

PART FOUR

Social Processes in Rural Society

The study of social processes has not been given the attention due it in the field of rural sociology. Competition is the basic social process. It may be aggravated into open conflict, *or differences may be harmonized and efforts pooled through co-operation. The contacts of cultures and races may result in mutual* adaptation *or* accommodation, *one may* assimilate *the other, or a blending of the two* (acculturation) *may be the net result. Society and all the elements that go to make it up are never in a state of rest. Social mobility is one of the most important of all the social processes.*

21

COMPETITION AND CONFLICT IN RURAL SOCIETY

The basic social processes are opposition and coöperation. Out of these all the other processes operative in society seem to arise. Opposition in turn may be subdivided into two principal types: *competition* and *conflict*. E. C. Hayes has stated well the distinction between the two as follows: "In competition the direct aim is the success of the actor, indirectly it may result in the failure of the competitor, but in conflict the direct result of the action of one person is to impede, prevent, or destroy the act of another."[1]

Opposition in general is rooted in scarcity, selfishness, egocentrism—all the elements that make for what Darwin called the "struggle for existence." If the struggle is indirect and impersonal it is termed competition; if it is direct and personal it is more properly called conflict. In competition, attention is concentrated on reaching the desired end and accomplishing the wished-for objective; there need be no thought of destroying or thwarting the rival. In conflict, on the other hand, the opponents are in one another's presence, each aware that the other stands in his way. Competition as a process is relatively continuous; conflict is intermittent—it may smolder for years and then break forth violently.[2]

Opposition grows out of a clash of interests; it arises whenever one member thinks he can gain more from the other than he is forced to give. Through hatred opposition may develop into

[1] "Some Social Relations Related," *American Journal of Sociology*, XXXI (1925), 338.
[2] Cf. Kimball Young, *Introductory Sociology*, New York, American Book Company, 1934, pp. 418–419; Robert E. Park and Ernest W. Burgess, *An Introduction to the Science of Sociology*, Chicago, University of Chicago Press, 1921, chap. 9; and Lowry Nelson, *Rural Sociology*, New York, American Book Company, 1948, pp. 150–151.

chronic conflict and lose all the elements of calculated objectives. A case in point is the animosity between white laborers and the Orientals in California or between northern organized wage earners and the recent Negro migrants from the South. But opposition has its wholesome aspects too. The right to oppose is essential to the preservation of society. Freedom of speech, freedom of press, and a sizable minority party are essential for the preservation of any social order. Frequently, strong opposition is a most important solidifying force; a foreign war is often resorted to by the nation that is torn by internal dissension.[3]

Competition

Competition arises and finds expression in practically every field of social activity. Rare is the person who at some period in his life is not involved in intense competition for a job, for a mate, and for status and prestige. With many such striving is chronic. Most attention has been centered upon the struggle for existence, and there can be no doubt that economic competition is of primary importance. But there are many other interests which develop competitive relationships. Racial and cultural groups struggle to outdo one another, sometimes in economic spheres, frequently along other lines. Practically every institution develops some competitive relationships with other similar institutions. Probably in no situation is the solidarity of a small community more evident than where an athletic team from the local high school is engaging that of a neighboring community in a contest. Children and adults alike identify themselves with the local team, enthusiasm and emotion run high, and both communities turn out en masse to witness the contest and to cheer their own representatives.[4]

Within a community the most intense rivalry and competition may characterize the relationships between two or more church congregations of different denominations generation after genera-

[3] The most thorough sociological study of competition is Jesse Bernard, *American Community Behavior*, New York, The Dryden Press, Inc., 1949, chaps. 5, 7, 8, 9, 10, 11, and 12. See also E. A. Ross, *The Outlines of Sociology*, New York, D. Appleton-Century Company, 1933, pp. 155–160.

[4] A field worker's notes from surveys of midwestern villages are revealing in this connection. One report states: "The school basketball team plays other county teams; its closest rival is B—— the town which lost the county seat. Last year B—— beat L—— in basketball. The winning team in its elation said, 'Now we're just waiting to come over and get the court house back.' The community carries a strong enthusiasm and spirit of conflict into its sports, and feels keenly the loss of a game."

tion. Or it may be that the competition is between two leading families or clans within the community or neighborhood. Between such kinship groups the struggle for status goes on without end. Hardly any small community where primary group relationships reign supreme is without a family or clan feud of a mild, bloodless nature. In some of the more isolated rural sections these differences develop into violent conflicts and express themselves as full-grown blood feuds persisting from generation to generation. For purposes of classification, therefore, the major forms of competition may be designated as (1) economic; (2) racial and cultural; and (3) institutional.[5] In the twentieth century revolutionary changes in the methods of communication and transportation have created intense competition between rural trade centers, largely economic, partially institutional, which deserves separate analysis.

Economic Competition

In rural society economic competition lacks many of the essentials that make it "the life of trade" in the commercial centers. The town or village merchant is forced into severe competition with his fellows for the patronage of the customers in the community trade area. But among farmers a comparable situation is almost entirely lacking. Only in the supplying of the limited local demand for vegetables, milk, wood, etc., is one farmer likely to see a danger or challenge in the marketing activities of any other individual farmer. After all, each agriculturist produces but an infinitesimal portion of any one of the major crops. What one's neighbor does is of small consequence in the total situation. There is little chance of individual gain or loss through the variations in the production of his immediate neighbors. Accordingly, rather than to engage in competitive practices designed to secure for himself the benefits that might go to his neighbors, the farmer is more strongly impelled to enter with them into mutual-aid activities for the purpose of increasing the welfare of all. However, if any part of the community's resources are common property, then intense competition and rivalry may result as individuals seek to exploit community resources for private ends.[6]

Competition adds much to the zest of farming, to the improve-

[5] Cf. Kimball Young, *op. cit.*, pp. 351–360.
[6] Cf. Lowry Nelson, "Early Landholding Practices in Utah," *Journal of Farm Economics*, IX (1927), 352–355.

ment of farm practices, and to the tone of social life in the agricultural community. In mild forms it brings about much good-natured
rivalry as to who will be first to finish haying, whose exhibits
will place first at the county fair, whose cows give the most milk,
whose chickens will produce the most eggs, whose land will produce the most bushels of wheat or the largest number of pounds
of cotton per acre, and numerous other contests of a similar nature.
The question of whose horse can trot or run the fastest is the cause
of keen competition in a large part of the farming communities of
the nation. Closely associated is intense rivalry among farmers in
the rural art of horse trading.

But economic competition among farmers has its more serious
side also; this has to do mostly with the ownership and control of
land. The old formula, "To raise more wheat, to get more money,
to buy more land, to raise more wheat," needs only to have the
name of the commodity changed in order to make it applicable
in every part of the nation. Despite complaints of being "land
poor," the ownership and control of land are still the major devices
for securing social status in rural areas.

The struggle for land is, of course, as old as permanent settlements themselves. The recorded history of the United States is
filled with episodes of "land-grabbing," sometimes resulting in
scandal; probably equally important, although largely unrecorded,
is the practice of squatting on unsettled lands. Lacking any systematic pattern of periodic subdivision of lands, such as that practiced by the Hebrews, in some parts of the United States those
concerned with the aggregation and subdivision of estates have
dealt with large units, as in the plantation districts of the South
or in California; in other sections, such as the Middle West, where
family-size units have predominated, the stakes have been smaller.
Until recently the local miser and moneylender have had almost
a monopoly on the business of granting loans to unsuspecting vic-
tims, lulling them into a sense of false security by leniency concerning the payments on principal and interest during prosperous
times and relentlessly foreclosing and dispossessing them when
times became hard and no succor was to be had. By the middle of
the twentieth century, however, corporations, insurance companies, and the federal government had revolutionized the system
of long-term farm credit.

Racial and Cultural Competition

Racial and cultural competition in rural areas is usually rather local in character. Often it is community against community, with racial and cultural differences intensifying the rivalry. Frequently, too, this type of competition finds expression in the struggle for land. One finds, especially in the northern states, community after community from which the "old American" stock has been "crowded out" by more recent arrivals from Europe. In the South, where landownership is less widely distributed, the competition assumes a rivalry for a limited number of places as sharecroppers on plantations. Although there are many exceptions, it seems that planters as a rule prefer Negroes to whites as croppers and that consequently the colored man, in this repect at least, has an advantage over his white competitor. Frequently whites of this economic class are embittered because the planters prefer Negroes to persons of their own color and race. On the Pacific coast competition for land has been a frequent cause of conflict between the Japanese and the members of the white race.

Institutional Competition

Institutional competition may occur in the rural community between any two institutions of the same type or even between institutions of different types. Church competes with church,[7] but the local religious organizations must also compete with the moving-picture theater, the school, and even the family and its radio, automobile, and televison set. When hard pressed by a competitor the institution may resort to several tactics: (1) It may seek the destruction of the competitor. For example, many sermons attack the movies, the automobile, and the radio. Sometimes ancient "blue laws" are dug up and invoked to prevent the operation of movies on Sundays. (2) It may withdraw from competition. A religious denomination may claim special protection from the state, a school may exploit the sentimental attachments of the alumni, a political party may exclude competitors from the ballot, and a business may resort to various subterfuges. (3) It may borrow from competitors, commonly known as "stealing the other

[7] For typical data about this, see N. L. Sims, *A Hoosier Village*, New York, Longmans, Green & Company, 1912, pp. 88–89; and Nelson, *Rural Sociology*, pp. 154–155.

fellow's thunder," more scientifically as "constrained adaptation." And (4) the institution may elude competitors by developing a highly specialized program catering to particular tastes.[8]

Competition Between Rural Trade Centers

Before the coming of the automobile and good roads the trade centers catering to farmer trade were in a stage of relative equilibrium. Lack of rapid means of communication, travel, and transportation made it essential that the retail outlets in close proximity to the farm should handle practically all the goods that the farmer's standard of living demanded. The farmer could not go great distances to trade, even for "Sunday clothes" and other goods that he was especially particular about. But the coming of the rural free delivery, followed shortly by the automobile, revolutionized the trading relationships of the farmer and the farm trade center. These new forces struck at one of the most limiting factors in farm life—the time it takes to go to town. The farmer's opportunities for choosing were greatly multiplied and the result was an intense competition between the existing trade centers. Galpin likened the situation that developed to a long-distance race in which the contestants were the farm trade centers, life itself the prize.[9]

The competition between trade centers has been observed by many students and has played an important part in the thinking about rural life. In the twenties the idea that rural villages were on their way to extinction gained widespread acceptance. Gillette is probably quoted more than anyone else on the question of village decline,[10] but the hypothesis of village decline has had other supporters. Hoagland[11] early maintained that a "process of elimination" was going on among villages; Walter Burr[12] insisted that the smaller villages were doomed, and saw in this another example of the "survival of the fittest"; the Ratcliffes[13] supported Gillette;

[8] Cf. Ross, *op. cit.*, p. 183.

[9] Charles J. Galpin, *Rural Life*, New York, D. Appleton-Century Company, 1920, p. 91.

[10] John M. Gillette, *Rural Sociology*, New York, The Macmillan Company, 1923, p. 466.

[11] H. E. Hoagland, "The Movement of Rural Population in Illinois," *Journal of Political Economy*, XX (1912), 917.

[12] Walter Burr, *Small Towns: An Estimate of Their Trade and Culture*, New York, The Macmillan Company, 1929, p. 125.

[13] S. C. and Agnes Ratcliffe, "Village Population Changes," *American Journal of Sociology*, XXXVII (1932), 760–767.

and Lively[14] concluded that the small trade center was declining.

Others analyzed in more detail the nature of the changes that were being brought about by the competitive process. H. Bruce Price and C. R. Hoffer[15] concluded that small trade centers were disappearing because their functions were being seized upon and performed by the larger centers. They insisted that the fates were against the small town and that slowly but surely a new type of trade center was developing in rural regions. According to them, the advantages formerly held by the small center, because of its proximity to the farms, had been overcome by the influence of the automobile. This assertion is similar to the statement published by a large advertising agency,[16] contending that the rural population had fallen under the influence of the automobile to such an extent that an increasing percentage of the market each year was reached through a smaller number of retail outlets in fewer trade centers. And Carl C. Taylor maintained that the automobile, by enlarging the community, was "slowly eliminating many of the smaller social and business centers."[17]

As mentioned above, Galpin saw as the end product of this competition between trade centers the emergence of a new type of farmers' town, the rurban community. Elsewhere he indicated that some 5000 of these would replace the haphazard system then existent that involved some 25,000 incomplete service centers.[18] L. H. Bailey earlier advanced the same idea. In 1908 he thought we were entering a new day, the epoch of the city; the surrounding country would be coördinated about it. Highways, rural free delivery service, telephones, and trolley lines were listed as the responsible factors.[19] J. B. Reynolds,[20] president of an agricultural college in Ontario, also viewed the decline of the village as inevitable. He contended that the present economic conditions required fewer farm trade centers than formerly; just as the amalgamation

[14] C. E. Lively, "The Small Trade Center Declines," *Rural America* (March, 1932), pp. 5–6.

[15] *Services of Rural Trade Centers in the Distribution of Farm Supplies*, Minnesota AES Bulletin 249, St. Paul, 1928, pp. 47–49.

[16] Critchfield and Company, *A New Market Analysis*, New York, no date, but internal evidence shows that it was published after 1925.

[17] *Rural Sociology*, New York, Harper & Brothers, 1926, p. 153.

[18] C. J. Galpin, *Rural Social Problems*, New York, D. Appleton-Century Company, 1924, p. 75.

[19] *The State and the Farmer*, New York, The Macmillan Company, 1908, p. 17.

[20] "City and Country," *Proceedings of the Fifth National Country Life Association*, Chicago, 1923, p. 103.

of industry closed the small factories, the mail-order houses were closing village stores; and the farmer's automobile was now passing through the village on its way to town. Flour mills, and the shops of the carpenter, the wagon maker, the blacksmith, and the tailor are only a memory in rural districts. Dwight Sanderson, too, indicated that a new community type was emerging as a result of the automobile. Schools, churches, granges, lodges, and stores were centering in the village.[21] Out of the competition between villages Yoder[22] concluded that a larger community, including both the people of the town and those from the surrounding area, was being built up. This he called the rurban community and credited Galpin with the concept. He also added that a distinctive feature of American farm life was its reorganization about country towns as centers both economic and social. The nature of the social structure evolved through the processes of competition and accommodation will be treated below. Here it is sufficient to indicate that the competition between trade centers has been one of the most significant social forces at work in rural America in the twentieth century.

Conflict

Social conflict finds expression in practically all the avenues of social life. Kimball Young has classified the principal types as follows: (1) industrial, (2) racial, (3) religious, (4) political, (5) inter-community and intra-community, (6) inter-class and intra-class, (7) sex and age conflict, and (8) conflict of intellectual and moral principles.[23] All of these are more or less important in rural areas, but the following three types of conflict seem to outrank all others in significance: (1) town-country conflict, (2) class struggle, and (3) inter-family and inter-clan strife. Religious and political differences are largely included within these three. Racial strife in rural areas has been of importance historically, especially in the South in the period of reconstruction. Following this period relations between the races in the South were stabilized and took on a form of caste organization. As a result of this adaptation there

[21] *Op. cit.*, pp. 41, 50; and *The Rural Community*, Boston, Ginn and Company, 1932, pp. 564–565.

[22] Fred R. Yoder, *An Introduction to Agricultural Economics*, New York, Thomas Y. Crowell Company, 1929, p. 37.

[23] *Op. cit.*, p. 419. For the recent most penetrating analysis of social conflict, see Jesse Bernard, "Where Is the Modern Sociology of Conflict?" *American Journal of Sociology*, LVI (1950), 11–16. See also Nelson, *Rural Sociology*, pp. 159–165.

has been in the region relatively little racial struggle for the last fifty years. In the North, where no adjustment has been reached and no pattern of race relationships has been developed, race conflict is still considerable. To quote Young, "Race riots mark the breakdown of a former accommodation or indicate a failure to arrive at some working arrangement which will meet a present crisis."[24] But with the migration of the Negro to the North and the Far West, this has become exclusively an urban matter and hence is of little concern in the present volume. Also an urban phenomenon is most of the race conflict that has come about in the South during and following World War II.

Town-Country Conflict

Throughout all ages the unlikeness of town and country has bred misunderstanding and hostility. The ever-present latent antagonism between the farmers of the open country and the tradesmen of the village frequently flares up into open conflict. Fundamental, of course, is the clash of economic interests between the two: the farmer's interests are those of both the primary producer and the ultimate consumer; the villager and townsman are primarily interested in the middleman's profit. The fact that the division of labor has made the village merchant and the open-country farmer mutually dependent upon each other frequently does not receive proper consideration. Many farmers think of townsmen as parasitic upon the country, and many villagers fail to appreciate how intimately their own welfare is related to that of the people on the land. When open strife bursts forth, the farmer succeeds in making felt his importance in the village by going elsewhere to trade, but at the same time has impressed upon himself through the medium of added costs and inconvenience the usefulness of the village.

Sharp cleavages between villagers and countrymen seem to be much more pronounced in the Midwest, where they have exhibited themselves in such phenomena as the Granger Movement, the Non-Partisan League, and the Farmers' Holiday, than in the South. Part of this cleavage is undoubtedly due to the fact that much of the farming land in the South is controlled, and its operation supervised, by a class of merchant-farmers residing in the village or town, who go regularly to the plantations to oversee the

[24] *Op. cit.*, p. 425.

farming operations being carried on in the fields. There also seems to be a tendency for conflict to appear more frequently as the size of the village increases—the larger the village the more likely that there will be open hostility between its residents and the farmers in the surrounding area.[25] Strife also seems to be more prevalent in those communities where the village folk are most hesitant about admitting farmers to membership in their social organizations.[26]

The genesis, nature, and course of many typical conflicts have been described by Brunner and his associates. For example, in one village

. . . some hitching posts were removed and in another the village government connived at the removal of a low watering trough which had stood for years at the intersection of two main streets and which had become an obstacle to automobiles driven rapidly through the center of the village. Even though a majority of the farmers did oper- ate cars these acts were interpreted by all as unfriendly to the rural interests. The farmers protested, but the villagers did not take their protests seriously. The farmers emphasized them by taking their trade to near-by towns. Then the protests were taken seriously, and hitching post and watering trough were duly restored after bitter contests. The embattled farmers, however, argued that if the village had not been unfriendly to them the removal of these conveniences would never have been attempted. If they were to meet an unfriendly attitude in these villages why should they deal there? Trade was slow in returning, and the villagers in turn became aggrieved at the failure of the farmers to respond to their surrender. In neither of these cases had the village authorities consulted with farm leaders as to the im- portance of the conveniences. The actions taken were exclusively from the village point of view. Probably it was this tacit assumption on the part of the village that it could act for the total community that the farmer resented, even though he admitted, the right of the incor- porated village to govern itself.

A similar difficulty arose in another community over the action of a local telephone company, the stock of which was largely owned in the village. This company operated several lines into the country. Originally there was no toll charge for any subscriber who desired to talk to any point of the system. Later a regulation was put into effect whereby a small charge was made if a country subscriber desired to

[25] Cf. Edmund deS. Brunner, Gwendolyn S. Hughes, and Marjorie Patten, *American Agricultural Villages,* New York, Doubleday, Doran & Company, 1927, pp. 96–97.
[26] *Ibid.,* pp. 106–107.

call any one on another rural line. Thus, the farmer could call only villagers or those on his own line free of charge, but the villager could reach any point on the system without charge. The farmers organized their own company as a result and boycotted the village stores for months.[27]

Conflicts over schools and school policy are a fruitful source of village-open-country cleavage.

One village decided that its own school district was too small. A citizen, with the consent of the village council and school board, circulated a petition which proposed to add some twelve square miles to the village school district. This territory was so plotted that no existing country schools were included. Thus each of the country school districts lost taxable property but, according to the plan, would have had to continue to support its own school. This would have meant an increase in taxes of some 60 per cent. Annexation to the village school district meant a similar increase to the farmers located within the twelve square miles. It was expected that in view of this equalization in taxation the outlying districts would close their schools and petition for consolidation. The rural school districts turned down the proposition. The case was brought to the County Common School Committee. Its decision was in favor of annexing the territory for reasons of greater efficiency and because a majority favored it, the majority being made up of villagers. This decision was sustained by the State Superintendent of Education, reversed by a Circuit Court, but confirmed by the Supreme Court of the state. The farmers secured the passage of a bill in the legislature dissolving this new district. The case is in the Circuit Court again and authorities say it must finally go to the Supreme Court. During all this time the farmers were first in, then out, and then in the proposed enlarged district. Now part of them are out and the rest are trying to get out. The court is called upon to interpret the detail of the law. Trade dropped off at the village stores very markedly and where before, according to all accounts, an unsually happy situation had existed between village and country, strife was the order of the day.

Incredible as it may seem, this move was initiated by the village without any prior consultation with leaders among the farmers. The petition dwelt on the benefits of consolidation and compared the situation in this community unfavorably with that in others, but made no effort to show the farmer that he would benefit in proportion to his increased taxation. The question of transportation for grade pupils—a live issue with country people—was not mentioned. In-

[27] *Ibid.*, pp. 98–99.

stead of answering natural questions and meeting objections, the village resorted to legal means to gain its ends. There was considerable open-country sentiment at the time in favor of a union high school but instead of discovering and capitalizing this, village leaders from the outset sought to include all grades. Farmers charge that this was because the village had been ordered by the state to build a new school, the cost of which they wanted the farmers to help bear. For whatever reason, the total disregard of the country by the village will cost it heavily for years to come.[28]

Perhaps as old as the village itself is the farmer's suspicion that the village merchant exploits while he serves. Not infrequently detailed comparison of prices item by item is exhibited by farmers to prove that the village merchant charges prices exorbitant in comparison with those of some not far-distant town. To this the merchant answers that the farmer's insistence upon credit forces him to charge higher prices for goods. Conflict arising out of the agriculturist's suspicion of the villager's motives is excellently illustrated in the following case:

. . . In the town the privately owned creamery and condensery took a real interest in its patrons, employed an agricultural agent to help them with their problems and frequently loaned them money when they could not obtain it from the banks. One of the two banks also catered to the farm trade and employed one man to assist its farm patrons and look after their business. In this community the state college of agriculture established a "cost route." For three years it employed an expert to keep careful records on costs of milk production under specific conditions upon some two dozen carefully selected farms. Toward the end of this period the agent began to arrive at tentative conclusions. The farmers were keenly interested; so were the creamery and the bank. These two institutions decided to invite all the farmers and their wives from these selected farms to a dinner in the village hotel at which the state college of agriculture's expert could present his conclusions and plans could be laid for improving the dairy farming of the community. Creamery, bank and expert united in a letter of invitation. The effect was electric. Two or three farmers refused to cooperate further with the experts. More refused to come to the dinner. "If the bank and the creamery are setting us up to a dinner they're going to get it back out of us somehow," was the usual statement to the amazed expert as he visited their farms. The expert's two years of constant contact with these farmers had not

[28] *Ibid.*, pp. 102–103.

built up sufficient confidence in his integrity and that of the college of agriculture to prevent this explosion. The dinner was finally held, but not all the farmers came, and those who had withdrawn refused to return, thereby crippling the total experiment by just that much.[29]

Some years ago the Improvement Club in C——, a village of some 1500 people in a midwestern state, sought ways and means of improving the relationships between the village and the surrounding territory. Among other things a questionnaire was prepared addressed "To Our Customers and Those Interested in C—— and the Surrounding Community." At the head of the questionnaire was the statement: "The C—— Improvement Club has prepared and sent out this questionnaire to the people of C—— and the surrounding country with the hope that through the replies received, it may see ways to better C—— as a market and community center. We hope you will take a little time right now to fill out the blanks and return them in the addressed envelope. . . ." Many of those in the trade area complied with the request, but others wrote personal letters stating their grievances. These letters throw considerable light upon the subject of town-country conflict. One of the most lucid reads as follows:

C—— Improvement Club

The more I think about the questionnaire you sent me the more I want to answer it on my own paper.

The first question I think of is do you buy from mail order houses and why?

When I order from mail order houses I get quality goods for less money than I can buy for at C——. Delivered to my door. I do not need to carry it half way to P—— or R——to my car. Why do I park half way to P—— or R——? Because nearly every business man or clerk Park their car in front of the store. But if I am tired worn out from my days labor I can carry my groceries to my car wherever I can find a place to park.

The same thing on band concert night. The business men park their cars close to the band stand in the after noon. So I can come in and park where I can.

As to the hospital, I do not question Dr. B——'s Equipment, his ability, but I do question his sociability.

A friendly good morning means a great deal to a customer.

One who has lived in D—— township for
over 30 years.

[29] *Ibid.*, p. 106.

The extent of the village-country conflict in the United States is not known accurately. Some data for the period 1924 to 1936 indicate that in about one-half of the agricultural communities in the United States the situation was no better than a watchful neutrality, and that in at least one out of ten it was a case of open active conflict,[30] but there have been no recent comprehensive studies of the subject.

Causes of Town-Country Conflict.

So prevalent is village-open-country conflict, so far-reaching are its consequences, that a detailed analysis of the factors that bring it to pass is of fundamental social importance. Some decades ago Brunner, Hughes, and Patten tabulated the active causes of friction between the village and country as follows: inadvertent acts, 17; prices, 17; school administration, 10; farmers' coöperatives, 8; credit and banking, 8; industry, 4; politics, 4; total, 68.[31] Cases involving inadvertent acts and conflicts over schools have been given in the preceding pages. Depending upon the time and the place, the other bases enumerated are equally capable of fanning the smoldering town-country antagonism.

Taylor, in the light of his intensive studies of the psychology of

[30] Edmund deS. Brunner and Irving Lorge, *Rural Trends in Depression Years,* New York, Columbia University Press, 1937, p. 89. This takes no account of lines of cleavage within the community along other lines than the town-country division. Conflicts cutting across village-open-country lines are also frequent. The question of Sunday movies has split community after community. Some villages included in Brunner's sample voted on this question no fewer than three times in a single year. Conflicts between communities are also important. Out of the twelve villages visited by the writer in the course of his duties as a field worker on Brunner's 1930 survey, there was hardly a case in which the dispute over the location of the county seat was not remembered as a fruitful source of social conflict. In one Indiana village a miniature war broke out when deputies came to transfer county records from the old county seat to the new. The natives got out the old town cannon "Black Betty," fired upon the building in which the deputies were assembled, and forced them to leave without the records—this in spite of the fact that the courts had awarded the county seat to the opposing village. The state militia finally effected the transfer of the documents, but the old residents still remember the fight and exhibit much antipathy to the neighboring center, now grown into a small city. See Sims, *op. cit.,* pp. 87–89, for the bases of the "strong and persistent prejudices, bigotry, and jealousy" that stirred another Indiana village from 1860 to 1910. Following the union of the Methodist Episcopal Church and the Methodist Episcopal Church, South, in 1939, conflict between those favoring the merger ("the Unificationists") and those opposed ("the Anti's") burst out in many rural communities in the South. For a description of the struggle in one South Carolina village, see Gus Turbeville, "Religious Schism in the Methodist Church: A Sociological Analysis of the Pine Grove Case," *Rural Sociology,* XIV (1949), 29–39.

[31] *Op. cit.,* p. 98.

farmers' movements, has given an excellent analysis of the factors which make for town-country conflict.[32] Condensed and modified somewhat, his analysis is as follows:

1. Differences in occupations create different modes of thinking. The farmer has acquired his skills and techniques rather unconsciously through a long period of apprenticeship under the tutelage of other members of the farm family. He fails to sense that his own skill depends to any extent upon training, much less to realize that skill and special aptitudes are necessary for the successful operation of a village store. The failure of farmers' coöperatives as a result of poor management because of the farmer's unwillingness to secure the services of a highly skilled manager is all too well known. Furthermore, the farmer secures such a large proportion of his living from the farm without direct money cost that he is unable to judge correctly the value of a dollar for the person residing in the village or town. The agriculturist thinks that the villager is growing rich at the expense of the farmer with whom he deals.

Neither does the villager understand the farmer and his psychology. Utterly dependent upon the exchange system, selling and buying on a profit-and-loss basis, the village merchant does not understand the farmer's suspicion of price dealings or the parsimonious element in his nature. Little realizing or appreciating the great multiplicity of aptitudes and skills called into play by the farmer's everyday work, the villager even underrates the mentality of the cultivator.

2. The apparent differences between rural and town standards of living are very real. The countryman observes the short working hours in the town, sees the villager wearing "Sunday clothes" every day, passes by the fine homes, churches, and schools in the incorporated center. He realizes all too keenly that the townsman has the services of electric lights, paved streets and sidewalks, municipal water supply, sewage disposal systems, etc., most of which the farmer lacks. Idle town children at play attract his attention; his own children have no such freedom from toil. The farmer rebels mentally against his own living conditions and blames them upon the townsman "either by some peculiar psychology of his own, or by imputing them to an unjust economic distribution." The townsman or villager, in turn, knows that the farmer lives without

[32] *Op. cit.* (1933 ed.), pp. 612–616.

most of the modern conveniences that have become the townsman's necessities; he takes their absence as proof of the farmer's
inferiority, and blames the countryman for his lack of urbanity,
culture, and polished manners. This attitude of superiority is resented by the farmer even more than his own lack of facilities and
gives rise to added suspicion, misunderstanding, and conflict.

3. Townspeople tend to identify themselves with the city population and the graces of city life; they affect urban manners in
their dealings with the people from the hinterland, consider themselves urbane, polished, "metropolitan and even cosmopolitan,"
and display their accomplishments freely in the course of their
contacts with farmers and "particularly in social affairs." The
farmer senses that after all the village is more similar to the open
country than to the metropolitan center and resents the "city airs"
of one from the nearby trade center.

4. The farmer deals with those particular village and town
classes in whose hands is concentrated the wealth of the centers,
and he is likely to consider them as representative of all villages.
Farmers have little reason to deal with section workers and other
unskilled laboring groups of the town. Through his identification
of all townsmen with the banking and merchant classes, the agriculturist is strengthened in his conviction that the country is being
robbed to support the fine homes and relatively high standards of
living of the townsmen.

5. Industrial elements in the town, even though small, have
only a remote connection with agriculture. Frequently factory
workers, railroad shop laborers, etc., regard all farmers as potential
"scabs" eagerly awaiting an opportunity to pounce upon their jobs.
If the center is very large, such groups consider that the farmer has
an easy time of it, because his food comes from the farm, his house
rent is taken care of, and his fuel can be secured on the place.

6. Although the institutional facilities of farmers are usually
deficient in material equipment, all the institutions and the values
they represent are strongly woven into the farmer's life. For this
reason he is easily disgusted with the obvious commercialism of
the tradesman, distrusts the merchant's ultimate interests and values, and rather generally is irritated at what he regards as the
town's one-sided, shallow ways of doing things.

7. In many ways the villager is merely a middleman between
the farmer and the economic interests of far-distant centers of

trade and industry. He is the local representative of distant interests highly obnoxious to the farmer. Farm distrust of "Wall Street" and "big business" is notorious. The townsman is the intermediary between the two. Furthermore, he must use accepted business techniques in dealing with the city business establishment, and also is likely to put them into practice with his farmer customers. The farmer's notes are discounted at central banks, designated prices are relayed to him from the cities, and even city wage scales are charged when his car must go to the village garage. The farmer follows different practices in dealing with his neighbor on the farm, and resents the fact that he must adopt new ways on dealing with the villager. He may know the village mechanic as a local boy unsuccessful on the farm and resent the "outrageous" charge for labor. "Furthermore, there is little doubt that many small-town merchants and bankers have used the pressure of city dealers and banks as a means of increasing their own profits at the expense of the farmer who is ignorant of actual conditions."[33]

8. Class consciousness and organization among farmers have resulted in their attempts to coöperate in supplying many of the necessary services. This kind of action strikes immediately at the villager's economic basis of subsistence. Vested interests in the villages, towns, and cities have struck vigorously with all the power at their command at these attempts of the farmer to enter commercial and political arenas.[34] Many of the farmer's political and commercial endeavors have failed, a fact which he attributes in a large measure to the opposition of the townsmen. Out of these attempts have come additional suspicion and hostility toward the town.

Town-country conflict, rooted in the factors described above, also is accentuated by the fact that the village is the arena in which much rural-urban conflict goes on. The village pulpit is the sounding board from which much modernistic religious thinking is let loose in the rural community, the village school is the place in which ideas of "progressive" education are tried out, and the village garage is the medium by which city standards of wages and

---

[33] *Ibid.*, p. 615.

[34] At the time he was chairman of the Federal Farm Board, Alexander Legge said to the members of the United States Chamber of Commerce, "Too many of your members were for the principle of co-operation only so long as it didn't work." American Cotton Co-operative Association, *Co-operative Handbook for 1931*, New Orleans, 1931, p. 43.

hours clash head-on with the farmers' radically different beliefs on these matters.[35]

Class Conflict in Rural Society

Class conflict, while probably less intensive in the country than in the city, is nevertheless a fundamental form of rural social conflict. But the bases of conflict in the country differ from those in the city. Urban class struggle savors of socialism and communism in the sense that collective ownership or state control of the agencies of production is one of the goals. Rural class struggle, on the other hand, very definitely has the objective of decentralization of control. Class struggle among agriculturists is nearly always a struggle of the masses for land. Growing out of the maldistribution of land, it can logically be designated as a function of large-scale agriculture. The family-farm system of farming lacks the elements necessary for class struggle. Where it prevails, farm laborers are few as compared with farm operators; the few laborers themselves are mainly young men, sons of farm owners, themselves beginning to climb toward farm ownership. In family-farm areas the agricultural ladder is in operation, functioning as a social elevator to lift persons from the status of farm laborers, through the various grades of tenants, into the ownership and possession of the land they till. In such sections there is little that savors of the closed class system, little to array the classes against one another.

But the situation is very different where there is concentration of ownership in the hands of a few. In this case the great mass of cultivators lack the security that comes with ownership of the soil. Vertical mobility is practically impossible; only a few can ever hope for the ownership of land; and the great masses are doomed to the permanent status of farm laborers. Inevitably this situation means a closed class system. It contains all the elements necessary for class struggle.

Perhaps the most intense and far-reaching present-day class struggle among agriculturists is to be found in the Mexican revolution, the struggle of the masses for the lands once owned by their ancestors. For centuries the large estate (hacienda) has been the dominant institution of Mexico and many other Latin American countries. In the Mexico of 1910 it was by far the most conspicu-

[35] Cf. T. Lynn Smith, "The Role of the Village in American Rural Society," *Rural Sociology*, VII (1942), 19–21.

ous feature of the land system. At the close of the Diaz regime, haciendas controlled the agriculture of the nation, set the pattern of social relations, and dominated the political life of Mexico. Many of these haciendas were of unbelievable extent. It is estimated that there were more than 300 containing above 25,000 acres each; 116 with at least 62,500 acres; 51 of 75,000 acres or more in area; and at least 11 containing 250,000 acres apiece.[36] But such excessive concentration of landownership necessarily meant that the bulk of the rural people would be landless. Most of the people in a dominantly rural nation were almost entirely deprived of property rights in the land. In some of the more important agricultural states such as Oaxaca only one head of a family out of 500 possessed individual property, and in none of the states except relatively unimportant Baja California did as many as 10 percent of the heads of families possess land. With such maldistribution of land, it is no accident that "lands for the people" was the only slogan that awakened a ready response, that this cry became the watchword of the revolution.[37]

Early successful revolutionary leaders were slow to sense the importance of the ground swell of agrarian discontent, to realize the intensity of the peasants' demand for lands. The great agrarian leader was Zapata. In rebellion even before Madero led the successful uprising against Diaz, Zapata was fired with only one idea —the return of the land to the cultivators. In the Madero revolution his power was great; but when Madero refused the immediate restoration of lands to the peasants, he turned against the popular chief, returned to his native mountains, again took up arms with the vow that he would never lay them down until he and his peasant following were again in possession of their village lands.[38] Only a month after the election of Madero as president, Zapata put forth the famous Plan of Ayala, ordering his followers to use armed might in seizing and holding lands. The uncompromising nature of his proposals is clearly seen in the following extract: ". . . we insert that all lands, mountains, waters, which have been usurped by the *hacendados científcos* or *caciques,* under the shadow of tyranny and venal justice be immediately passed into the possession

[36] George M. McBride, *Land Systems of Mexico,* American Geographical Society Research Series 12, New York, 1923, p. 25.

[37] *Ibid.,* pp. 154–157.

[38] Cf. Frank Tannenbaum, *The Mexican Agrarian Revolution,* New York, The Macmillan Company, 1929, pp. 159–160.

of the villages or citizens who have their titles to these properties
of which they have been deprived by the bad faith of our oppres-
sors and to maintain these at all costs with arms in their hands.
. . ."[39] Although Zapata never became president, and died fighting for his ideal, his influence has been of the highest significance
in the Mexican revolution. *Agrarismo* and *Zapatismo* became almost synonymous. Today he has already gone far on the road to
deification, is considered a superman, a symbol of agrarianism in
its highest forms.[40]

All in all, the Mexican revolution is one of the most significant
agrarian movements of the twentieth century. Simpson in the following terse sentences has summarized the struggle for land
among the agricultural classes of Mexico:

> . . . Just when the seeds of land monopoly were first planted in
> Mexican soil we do not know. But by the time of the Conquest they
> had already sunk their roots in the earth and produced the first crop
> of vested interests. To these native growths were grafted ancient and
> hardy plants brought by the Spaniards from the old world and for
> three hundred years they were watered with greed and nourished
> with rapacity. The result was one of the most luxuriant harvests of
> the weeds of special privilege the world has ever seen. In 1810 the
> people rose in arms determined to clear the land, to pull up root and
> branch the noxious plants which threatened their ejidos, indeed, their
> very existence. But to no avail. The roots were too deep, the branches
> too thick. In 1857, there was a great laying about with legal imple-
> ments. But again with little result, for the weeds had become a sturdy
> forest and the feeble instruments of the Reform turned in the hands
> of those who tried to wield them. Then came the thirty years' rule of
> Porfirio Diaz—concessions, land grabbing, spoliation, fraud, and lo,
> the forest was a vast tropical jungle in whose tangled depths there
> dwelt a race of slaves—sunless, airless, landless, and hopeless. The
> ejidos gone forever or gasping for breath; the hacienda triumphant
> and master of all it surveyed.

Thus the story from "in the beginning" down to the year 1910. In
that fateful year a spark was struck, a fire was lighted. Suddenly the
whole rotting jungle of privilege and preferment was a mass of rag-
ing flames. For almost a decade the holocaust of revolution. . . . Then,

---

[39] *Ibid.*, p. 160.
[40] See Eyler N. Simpson, *The Ejido: Mexico's Way Out*, Chapel Hill, University of North Carolina Press, 1937, p. 52; and Nathan L. Whetten, *Rural Mexico*,
Chicago, University of Chicago Press, 1948, pp. 111–13 and 122–123.

at last, the fires burnt out, the land swept clean and bare. Reform. Reconstruction. Rebirth of the ejidos. Thus the story from 1910 on.[41]

Concerted mass efforts to obtain a decentralization of land holdings have not developed to any great extent in the United States. The widespread distribution of family-sized farms and the predominant middle-class mentality of our rural population are, of course, the factors responsible. However, in areas where large estates are the rule, such as parts of California and the plantation sections of the South, most of the elements needed for violent and vicious struggle have been present, and sporadic outbursts of aggravated conflict have seized the headlines. Labor strikes in California's "factories in the field" may be expected to recur from time to time, and the same is likely in Florida's citrus districts and in other parts of the nation where landless workers supply the lion's share of the labor used in agricultural production. However, with the rapid mechanization of agriculture in the cotton plantation areas there would seem to be less danger of a repetition of the serious disorders which plagued some of them in the 1930's. Then the activities of the Sharecroppers' Union of Alabama,[42] and the work of the Southern Tenant Farmers' Union in Arkansas and other southern states were widely publicized. Class conflict was a feature of all of these. Says a statement by one of the leaders of the Southern Tenant Farmers' Union concerning the conflict in eastern Arkansas:

While violence of one type or another has been continuously poured out upon the membership of the union from its early beginning, it was in March 1935 that a "reign of terror" ripped into the country like a hurricane. For two and a half months violence raged throughout northeastern Arkansas and in neighboring states until it looked at times as if the union would be completely smashed. Meetings were banned and broken up; members were falsely accused,

[41] Simpson, *op. cit.*, pp. 41–42. Although they have not as yet gone as far as in Mexico, there is much discontent at the bottom of the rural social pyramids of Argentina, Peru, Brazil, Colombia, and many other Latin American republics. See, for example, T. Lynn Smith, "The Cultural Setting of Agricultural Extension Work in Colombia," *Rural Sociology*, X (1945), 235–246; T. Lynn Smith, "Notes on Population and Rural Social Organization in El Salvador," *Rural Sociology*, X (1945), 378–379; and T. Lynn Smith, "Some Observations on Land Tenure in Colombia," *Foreign Agriculture*, XVI (1952), 119–123.

[42] For the background and activity of this organization, consult John Beecher, "The Share Cropper's Union in Alabama," *Social Forces*, XIII (1934), 124–132.

arrested and jailed, convicted on trumped-up charges and thrown into prison; relief was shut off; union members were evicted from the land by the hundreds; homes were riddled with bullets from machine guns; churches were burned and schoolhouses stuffed with hay and floors removed; highways were patrolled night and day by armed vigilantes looking for the leaders; organizers were beaten, mobbed and murdered until the entire country was terrorized.

. . . .

The reign of terror resulted in bloodshed but not in slavish submission of the workers to the tyranny and exploitation of the plantation overlords. The union fought for its life as few dreamed that it could. At the end it counted its dead, its injured, its wrecked and blighted lives by the scores but emerged from the struggle a powerful, well organized and fighting union which, if it continues along the road it has thus far traversed, may have a significant influence upon the future of American history.[43]

Family and Clan Conflict

The strength of the individual family unit and its cohesion or clannishness with other units related by blood remain as major social assets of the rural community. But the strength of the individual units or combination of units also leads to rivalry, strife, and conflict with other family groups. Familism cements the relationships among all members of the in-group, but it also fans the flames of conflict between the members of rival families or clans. Sharply divided communities are scattered from ocean to ocean, and one can hardly find a divided community in which the line of cleavage fails to follow family lines closely. As Ross has well said: "When life is rather simple, grudges are cherished and handed down from fathers to sons as precious heirlooms."[44]

The blood feuds among our Appalachian mountaineers are, of course, universally known. But a feud is merely an extreme form of conflict between families, and interfamily conflicts of milder forms are omnipresent. In the feud, arms are employed by each group in an effort to exterminate the other or drive its members from the territory. Feuds spread like wildfire to all blood relatives, to those related by marriage, and even to the friends of the fami-

[43] Howard Kester, *Revolt Among the Sharecroppers*, New York, Covici Friede, Inc., 1936, pp. 82, 85; see also the Federal Council of the Churches of Christ in America, *Information Service*, XV (June 27, 1936).
[44] *Op. cit.*, p. 156.

lies concerned. One may lie dormant for a generation, its cause forgotten, and then flare up suddenly with renewed vigor.[45]

That feuds also linger in areas far removed from the Appalachians is not so well publicized. And the fact that such feuds are, after all, closely related (differing mainly in degree) to the rivalry between the best families of our own "Main Street" or "Littletown" rarely receives the recognition it deserves.

[45] See Horace Kephart, *Our Southern Highlanders*, New York, Outing Publishing Company, 1913, p. 337.

22

COÖPERATION IN RURAL AREAS

Coöperation may be defined as working together for the attainment of common or similar objectives. Like competition it is a form of striving; but coöperation is the striving with others, whereas competition is the striving against others.[1] All large permanent groups, other than those resulting from conquest and held together by force, are forms of coöperation. Society itself is the example par excellence of coöperation. Among the social processes coöperation is entitled to a position in the front rank.[2]

The motivation of coöperation is not well understood. May and Doob could do no better than to indicate that there are discrepancies between the "levels of achievement and those of aspiration, or between what the individual now is or has and what he would like to be or have . . . *motivation* is a function of these discrepancies."[3] But although little is known concerning the motivation, it is

[1] Cf. Mark A. May and Leonard W. Doob, *Competition and Cooperation,* Social Science Research Council Bulletin 25, New York, 1937, p. 8.

[2] Not all writers use coöperation in this sense. To some there seems to be no distinction between coöperation and the coöperative movement based on Rochdale principles. Thus Edward W. Bemis opened his monograph on coöperation in New England with the statement: "Cooperation in New England, if we except profit-sharing in the fisheries, begun in the year 1842–7 [sic] when organized labor first became a power in Massachusetts. . . ." *Cooperation in New England,* Johns Hopkins University Studies in History and Political Science, Sixth Series, VI, Baltimore, 1888, p. 17. The sociologist uses the term "coöperation" in a much broader sense than does the calculating person who thinks of coöperation as a device for saving a cent per pound on his purchases of bacon, flour, etc., or the social reformer who would use the lure of economic savings to cement the penurious into a powerful phalanx to be used for political purposes. A more recent general work on coöperation accepts mutual-aid activities as types of coöperation and shows how the American farmer laid the foundations of coöperation in the United States. John Daniels, *Cooperation: An American Way,* New York, Covici Friede, Inc., 1938, pp. 109–147.

[3] *Loc. cit.*

evident that the stimuli which result in coöperation are many and varied. The pooling of men's efforts for the purpose of fighting others is universal both geographically and historically.[4] Men everywhere also seem to have found it necessary to unite in the establishment of tribunals for the purpose of hearing and settling disputes within the group. As ancient as the earliest traditions of the Hebrews is the construction of public works as an incentive to coöperation.[5] Concrete evidences of coöperative effort in other early civilizations are the irrigation ditches and reservoirs for controlling the water of the Nile, the Euphrates, and the Ganges. Coöperation manifests itself among all peoples in their economic and other social activities.[6]

Types of Coöperation

Coöperation may be divided into a variety of types depending upon the purposes of the investigator. The careful student of human society cannot afford to neglect the phenomena of *symbiosis* or *commensalism*. These are the terms used by the naturalist in referring to situations in which plants and animals of different species live together in harmony and mutual helpfulness, directing their energies not so much against one another as against an unfriendly environment. This is certainly one form of coöperation; and it has a human counterpart in the mutual aid that members of small neighborhood groups such as early pioneering settlements gave to one another.

Among human beings, however, coöperative activities range through all degrees, from such rather unconscious spontaneous reactions as are exemplified in all the pioneering practices of neighboring and mutual aid, to the calculated contractual form of united effort typified by the farmers' coöperative marketing associations, purchase associations, or credit unions. In primary groups unconscious mutual aid is widespread; but as social differentiation proceeds, mutual aid tends to be replaced by coöperative activities based more on deliberate conscious efforts. Finally, in highly differentiated and heterogeneous societies such as industrialized

---

[4] For a valuable study of coöperation among contemporary primitive groups, see Margaret Mead, *Cooperation and Competition Among Primitive Peoples,* New York, McGraw-Hill Book Company, 1937.

[5] Genesis 11:1–9.

[6] Cf. E. A. Ross, *Outlines of Sociology,* New York, D. Appleton-Century Company, 1933, pp. 243–245.

states, organized governmental police powers evolve and enforce all sorts of activities for the public good. Ross has called this "compulsory cooperation."

Perhaps, for purposes of analysis, coöperative effort may best be considered as being *contractual* or *non-contractual*. With competitive coöperation which grows out of social differentiation and the development of impersonal relations, these varieties of coöperation include the principal modes of working together in human society.

Non-Contractual Coöperation

This term refers to all those mutual-aid practices whereby neighbor assists neighbor in the accomplishment of desired ends without any specific contractual agreement concerning the mode, method, time, or amount of payment.[7] Rooted in primary group relationships, coöperation of this type enjoyed widespread favor because people in general accepted favors only with the tacit understanding that they would return them. Such coöperation has been called a "habitual relation of mutual helpfulness between neighbours."[8] It includes all the pioneer practices such as barn-raisings, house-raisings, husking bees, distribution of game and other foodstuffs to neighbors, and quilting parties; under this heading also are classed community or neighborhood cultivation of the fields of a widow or disabled neighbor, donations of feed to the farmer whose haystacks have burned, assisting a neighbor to cut his grain before the frost, etc.[9] No unique case was it when the early settler in the piney woods of Mississippi had cut and squared enough trees for the construction of a cabin that "there came to him men out of the pathless depths of the woods, summoned by some mysterious telegraphy, and they 'raise.' "[10] It was always so—coöperation of a very efficient type.

---

[7] The classic work on this subject is P. Kropotkin, *Mutual Aid: A Factor in Evolution,* New York, McClure, Phillips & Co., 1902; cf. E. T. Hiller, *Principles of Sociology,* New York, Harper & Brothers, 1933, pp. 162–181; and W. A. Terpenning, *Village and Open-Country Neighborhoods,* New York, D. Appleton-Century Company, 1931, pp. 4–6.

[8] James M. Williams, *Our Rural Heritage,* New York, Alfred A. Knopf, Inc., 1925, p. 96.

[9] Cf. Martha Collins Bayne, *County at Large,* Poughkeepsie, New York, 1937, pp. 53–56.

[10] Stephen Powers, *Afoot and Alone: A Walk from Sea to Sea by the Southern Route,* Hartford, Columbia Book Co., 1872, p. 80.

Monette wrote as follows concerning mutual aid in the pioneer primary groups:

> Did a neighbor wish to erect a cabin, or to roll his logs, or to gather his harvest, each man was a willing hand, and in turn received aid from others. At such places an idler or an indifferent spectator dared not approach, or the contempt of the hardy pioneers settled upon him. Did any contract a debt, it was paid in labor or by the exchange of commodities; and the force of the moral sense, sustained by public sentiment, was a stronger guarantee than all the forms of law, which often serves as a protection against honest demands. Did a man want a bushel of salt, he received it in exchange for a cow and calf. So equal was the distribution of their scanty wealth, that no one envied that of his neighbor; if any were in want, they freely received from those who could give.[11]

Despite the recent commercialization of agriculture there still remain deeply graven in the patterns of rural culture many of these practices of mutual aid and neighboring.[12] Even today, the average farmer still can count upon a considerable amount of help from his fellows in time of sickness, death, the burning of his house or barn, and similar catastrophes. But the onslaught of urban mores and the disintegration of the cumulative community make it ever more difficult to maintain these informal, mutual-aid patterns of coöperation. Where secondary contacts prevail, favors are not returned and mutual-aid advances are accepted as donations or charity. When the neighbor becomes only the one living near and nothing more, coöperation to be successful must be of a contractual nature.

Contractual Coöperation

This type of coöperation operates through a formally constituted organization, by means of definitely specified rules and upon a strict give-and-take basis. As noted above, there is some tendency today to restrict the use of the word "coöperation" to this formally

[11] John W. Monette, *History of the Discovery and Settlement of the Valley of the Mississippi*, New York, Harper & Brothers, 1846, II, 16.

[12] See *ibid.*, especially chaps. 7 and 8. For an excellent discussion of non-contractual coöperation in a great rural civilization, Brazil, see J. V. Freitas Marcondes, "Mutirão or Mutual Aid," *Rural Sociology*, XIII (1948), 374–384; and for specific examples of this type of coöperation in the United States see Robert L. Skrabanek, "Forms of Cooperation and Mutual Aid in a Czech-American Rural Community," *The Southwestern Social Science Quarterly*, XXX (1950), 183–187.

organized type of association. Unlike mutual aid, coöperation of this type is not spontaneous but must be promoted. It need not be personal at all but may be highly impersonal. Neither is it limited to a relatively small homogeneous group living in a restricted area. Contractual coöperation is the type which Robert Owen, around the year 1820, advanced as the basis for a new social order that would differ radically from the existing system of *laissez faire*.[13] Owen conceived of coöperation as a device whereby the profit motive might be harnessed to serve the cause of general welfare. His life was filled with one venture after another designed to demonstrate the validity of his doctrines. Several coöperative communities in the United States were established under the direct personal sponsorship of Owen, and many others have a definite relationship to his projects.[14] Among the rural population coöperation of this contractual type is a fairly recent development. It has also been confined largely to the economic field, with some attempts in the political and religious areas.

Competitive Coöperation

This kind of coöperation arises out of the impersonal relations that develop as society differentiates and turns from a mechanistic to an organic basis for its social cohesion. Park and Burgess indicate its fundamental nature in the following: ". . . Competition invariably tends to create an impersonal social order in which each individual, being free to pursue his own profit, and, in a sense, compelled to do so, makes every other individual a means to that end. In doing so, however, he inevitably contributes through the mutual exchange of services so established to the common welfare."[15]

Coöperation in the Economic Field

The economic contacts of the farmer with nonfarm groups arise out of problems of credit, the purchasing of equipment and sup-

[13] See especially his *A New View of Society*, London, 1818. For a good biography of Owen, see Frank Podmore's *Robert Owen*, translated by Ernest F. Row, New York, D. Appleton-Century Company, 1907, 2 vols.

[14] See Charles Gide, *Communist and Co-operative Colonies*, New York, Thomas Y. Crowell Company, 1928, pp. 120–154; cf. Charles Nordhoff, *The Communistic Societies of the United States*, New York, Harper & Brothers, 1875; Podmore, *op. cit.*, I, 285–324.

[15] Robert E. Park and Ernest R. Burgess, *Introduction to the Science of Sociology*, Chicago, University of Chicago Press, 1921, p. 507; cf. Hiller, *op. cit.*, pp. 212–226.

plies, and the marketing of farm produce. Accordingly, where the farmer has been concerned, contractual coöperation has been quite largely confined to credit coöperation, coöperative buying, and coöperative marketing.

Coöperative Associations

The development of the coöperative associations for performing the economic functions of marketing, purchasing, and credit makes an interesting chapter in the history of rural America. Such associations have given the farmer tremendous leverage in dealing with other groups. Indeed, so important have they been that there is, as was mentioned above, a definite tendency to restrict the term "coöperation" to this specialized contractual form, instead of allowing it its full rich connotations. In general, coöperative associations differ from the corporation or stock company in three respects: (1) such associations usually adhere to the rule "one man, one vote," irrespective of the amount of funds invested; (2) their fundamental purpose is more efficient service rather than the securing of profits; and (3) earnings or savings are prorated to members and patrons according to the amount of business transacted with the association.[16]

Among farmers economic coöperation of the contractual type had its American beginnings before the Civil War. The local association was, of course, the first to appear, since neighbors have always found it advantageous to work together. A coöperative cheese factory is reported in Wisconsin as early as 1841.[17] Coöperative ventures for the irrigation of arid lands began among the Mormons as soon as the first members of the group arrived in the Great Basin (1847). This group utilized the principle that labor should "constitute the basis of stock" in each of their coöperative ventures in irrigation.[18] Local coöperative livestock shipping associations (driving associations at first), coöperative elevators, wool pools, ginning associations, and assembling plants for fruits, vegetables, poultry, etc., were early developments.[19] For a time

[16] Cf. Dwight Sanderson, *The Farmer and His Community*, New York, Harcourt, Brace & Company, 1922, p. 78.

[17] See B. H. Hibbard, "Agricultural Co-operation," *Encyclopaedia of the Social Sciences*, New York, The Macmillan Company, 1930.

[18] Charles Hillman Brough, *Irrigation in Utah*, Baltimore, Johns Hopkins Press, 1898, pp. 7–21.

[19] Cf. R. H. Ellsworth, *Statistics of Farmers' Co-operative Business Organizations, 1920–1935*, Farm Credit Administration, Bulletin 6, Washington, 1936, pp. 2–3.

they were largely confined to a neighborhood basis—a handful of neighbors here and there who united their efforts in the establishment of a cheese factory, the operation of a wheat elevator, the operation of a creamery, etc. Some of these coöperative associations were little more than the old informal, mutual-aid practices placed upon a contractual basis.[20] These early ventures in contractual economic coöperation received great impetus in the disturbed conditions and deflation that followed the Civil War. During the early seventies a wave of coöperative agitation swept the country. It was diffused among the laboring classes in the cities through the efforts of the Knights of Labor.[21] Among farmers, coöperative undertakings of the contractual type were enthusiastically sponsored by the Patrons of Husbandry, better known as Grangers.[22] Both of these efforts were largely unsuccessful, at least from the immediate point of view, and interest in coöperative associations lagged during the closing years of the nineteenth century.[23]

Following the turn of the twentieth century the coöperative movement took on new life, gained momentum, underwent fundamental changes in outlook and objectives, and developed into a large-scale undertaking. In part this was one phase of a revitalized outlook on rural life fostered by Theodore Roosevelt, and especially by the report[24] of the Country Life Commission which he appointed. Among farmers much of the development was due to the activities of two great new farmers' organizations—the Farmers Educational and Co-operative Union and the American Society of Equity.[25] Still later the American Farm Bureau became one of the most important of the large farm organizations.[26] All these or-

[20] As, for example, the coöperative butchery among the Acadians of southwest Louisiana. See T. Lynn Smith and Lauren C. Post, "The Country Butchery: A Co-operative Institution," *Rural Sociology*, II (1937), 335–337.

[21] Cf. George E. McNeill, *The Labor Movement: The Problem of Today*, Boston, A. M. Bridgman & Co., 1887, pp. 141–171, 397–410.

[22] Ellsworth, *op. cit.*, p. 7.

[23] Cf. Albert Sonnichsen, "Cooperation: United States and Canada," *Encyclopaedia of the Social Sciences*, IV, 393–394.

[24] First published as *Senate Doc. No. 705*, 60th Congress, 2nd Session. Republished, New York, 1911, and Chapel Hill, University of North Carolina Press, 1944.

[25] For excellent short accounts of these, the Grange, and other important farmers' movements, see B. H. Hibbard, *Marketing Agricultural Products*, New York, D. Appleton-Century Company, 1921. For the type of appeal made to the farmers, see Clarence Poe, *How Farmers Co-operate and Double Profits*, New York, Orange Judd Co., 1915.

[26] See Ralph Russell, "Membership of the American Farm Bureau Federation, 1926–1935," *Rural Sociology*, II (1937), 29–35. For representative careful studies of the history, organization, and activities of the Farm Bureau in several states,

ganizations set about the establishment of local coöperatives, consumers' societies, and selling agencies. The Equity, which later gave way to the Equity Union, went into the broader field of developing and operating central plants for the processing of farm products. Its creameries soon came to manufacture three million pounds of butter in a single year. Both organizations also set up local livestock shipping associations, later combining them with central exchanges for livestock. Both also ventured into the field of the coöperative purchase of farm equipment and supplies.[27] The movement, which took on new life in the early years of the twentieth century, attained its most rapid expansion in 1920, when more than 1800 farmers' coöperative marketing associations were formed in a single year, and crested in 1929–1930, when 10,546 associations were in operation. Thereafter, the number fell steadily to only 7159 in 1947–1948. Coöperative purchasing associations increased rapidly from 1913 to 1921 and then gained numbers rather steadily to 1947–1948.[28]

Real successes in large-scale coöperative ventures have not been numerous and have been largely confined to a few crops, particularly fruit, dairy products, and grain. (See Figure 119.) Coöperative marketing of cotton, the crop on which such a large percentage of the farm population is dependent, has been beset by all manner of pitfalls and can hardly be said to have enjoyed any significant measure of success,[29] although fifteen large-scale coöperative associations handled 13.8 percent of all ginnings in 1933–1934, 17.5 percent in 1934–1935, and 12.5 percent in 1935–1936.[30] Perhaps the most outstanding of all farm coöperatives are those of the California citrus growers. In spite of the general rule that co-

see E. D. Tetreau, *The Objectives and Activities of the California Farm Bureau,* California Bulletin 563, Berkeley, 1933, and W. A. Anderson, *Farmers in the Farm Bureau,* Cornell AES Rural Sociology Mimeographed Bulletin 4, Ithaca, 1941.

[27] See Hibbard's article in the *Encyclopaedia of the Social Sciences* which was referred to above; cf. G. Harold Powell, *Cooperation in Agriculture,* New York, The Macmillan Company, 1913, *passim.*

[28] Ellsworth, *op. cit.,* p. 7; and Grace Wanstall, *Statistics of Farmers' Marketing and Purchasing Cooperatives, 1947–48,* Miscellaneous Report 137, Farm Credit Administration, Washington, 1950, Table 2, p. 5. See also Ward W. Fetrow and R. H. Ellsworth, *Agricultural Cooperation in the United States,* Bulletin 54, Farm Credit Administration, Washington, 1947, *passim.*

[29] Robert H. Montgomery's *The Co-operative Pattern in Cotton,* New York, The Macmillan Company, 1929, is both a vivid description of the dismal failure of the Southern Cotton Association and the Southern States Cotton Corporation and a brilliant plea for a workable coöperative pattern for cotton production and marketing.

[30] Ellsworth, *op. cit.,* p. 23.

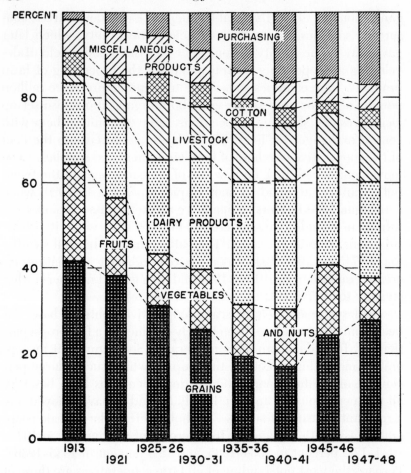

FIGURE 119. The Changing Importance of the Various Commodity Groups in the Business Done by Farmers' Coöperatives, 1913–1948. (Reproduced from Wanstall, *Statistics of Farmers' Marketing and Purchasing Cooperatives, 1947–48,* Miscellaneous Report 137, Farm Credit Administration, Washington, 1950.)

operatives handling fruits and vegetables have a high mortality rate, the California association, by federating small locals into a powerful state organization, growing a special crop, and spreading over a large enough area to control the bulk of the supply, may be said to have attained a high degree of success.

The situation at the present time leaves little doubt that the coöperative associations are among the most important of farmers' organizations. The best data available indicate that such associations among farmers numbered 5424 in 1915, increased to 12,000 in 1929–1930, and then fell off to 10,135 in 1947–1948. In the meantime the volume of business grew from $635,839,000 in 1915 to $2,500,000,000 in 1929–1930, fell to $1,340,000,000 in 1932–1933, rose steadily to $2,280,000,000 in 1941–1942, and then shot up to $8,635,000,000 in 1947–1948. Reported membership increased from 651,186 in 1915 to 3,100,000 in 1929–1930, and to 5,890,000 in 1947–1948.[31] However, there are many duplications in these figures so that the number of persons in coöperatives is considerably less. As a matter of fact, in the Census of 1940, only 1,364,402 farm operators reported that they had done business with coöperatives during the preceding year.[32] However, in 1936 Brunner's field workers discovered about 50 percent more coöperatives in the 150 villages in his sample than were reported to the Farm Credit Administration by its correspondents, for these communities.[33] Although part of this inconsistency was probably due to differences of definition, the discrepancies are of considerable significance. Therefore it was a notable achievement when in 1937 the Farm Credit Administration made a door-to-door count of farmers' coöperatives. At that time 10,752 "farmer-owned and farmer-controlled co-operative associations" marketing "everything from onions to oranges" and purchasing practically every kind of supply and equipment for the farm were discovered.

Of the 10,752 associations, more than one-half (52 percent) were over fifteen years old, and 19 percent had been in operation twenty-five years or longer. Only 18 percent were newcomers, i.e., in operation less than six years. See Figure 120 for information on the distribution of the associations. The amount of business for the year 1936 amounted to $2,700,000,000, netting $38,686,000, of which $25,380,000 was returned to the members as a patronage dividend and the remainder was added to working capital. Citrus fruit marketing coöperatives returned the largest amount of dividends to members ($6,043,000), and associations dealing with petroleum products ranked second, returning $4,294,000, or $7 per member.[34] In addition, reported by the survey were approximately

[31] Wanstall, *op. cit.*, pp. 4–7.
[32] *Census of Agriculture: 1940*, Vol. III, chap. 6, p. 2.
[33] See Edmund deS. Brunner and Irving Lorge, *Rural Trends in Depression Years*, New York, Columbia University Press, 1937, p. 58.
[34] "Agricultural Co-operative Associations in the United States," *Farm Credit Quarterly*, III (1938), 3–9; cf. "Co-operative Purchasing by Farmers, 1936," *Monthly Labor Review*, XLVII (1938), 804–805.

2500 mutual irrigation companies and 1900 farmers' mutual fire insurance companies.

Regionally farmers' coöperative activities have been and remain highly concentrated in the Middle West, especially in Minnesota, Wisconsin, and Iowa. They are particularly scarce in the South. (See Figure 121.)

Credit for productive purposes, including the purchase of land, the construction and repair of buildings, the raising of crops and

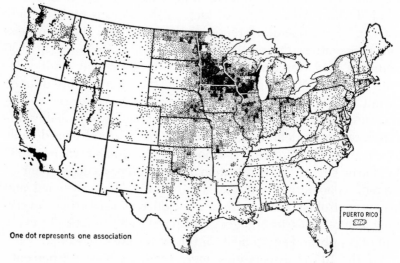

One dot represents one association

FIGURE 120.   Distribution of Farmers' Marketing and Purchasing Associations, 1937. (Reproduced from *Farm Credit Quarterly*, III [September, 1938], 3.)

livestock, and the purchasing of supplies and equipment, is one of the farmer's most pressing needs. Generally speaking, coöperatives until very recently had made little progress in this field, although agricultural credit unions have been among the most successful types of coöperation among the farmers in other lands.[35] In the 1930's under the supervision of the Farm Credit Administration there was established a comprehensive system, with governmental assistance, for extending credit to farmers. This has changed the farm credit situation completely. In 1936 there were in operation approximately 5000 farm-loan associations (all with farmers as

[35] See the articles on coöperation in the *Encyclopaedia of the Social Sciences,* particularly those of Augé-Laribé, Ernest Grünfeld, and A. N. Antsiferof, describing the credit coöperatives of France, Italy, and Russia.

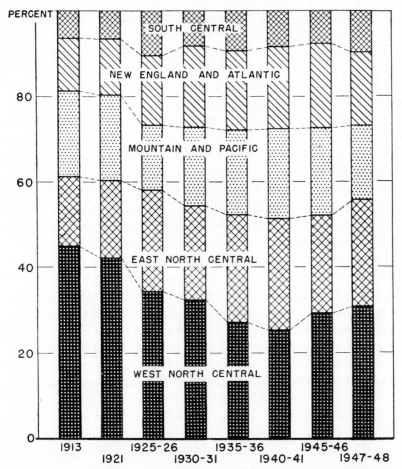

PERCENT

SOUTH CENTRAL

NEW ENGLAND AND ATLANTIC

80

MOUNTAIN AND PACIFIC

60

EAST NORTH CENTRAL

40

20

WEST NORTH CENTRAL

0

1913 1925-26 1935-36 1945-46
1921 1930-31 1940-41 1947-48

FIGURE 121. The Regional Distribution of Business Done by Farmers' Coöperatives, 1913 to 1948. (Reproduced from Wanstall, *Statistics of Farmers' Marketing and Purchasing Cooperatives, 1947–48*, Miscellaneous Report 137, Farm Credit Administration, Washington, 1950.)

members and officers and all forming an integral portion of the Farm Credit Administration) from which agriculturists could borrow for uses in connection with lands and buildings. On June 30, 1950, there were 502 active production-credit associations from which farmers could secure loans for use in the production of crops and livestock. These enrolled a total of 460,936 members, and during the preceding twelve months had made 282,693 loans totaling $967,737,941. Less successful had been the work of the farm-loan associations organized by the Administration. Many of these got into severe financial difficulties and were either reorganized or closed. Thus their number was reduced from 5034 on December 1, 1935, to 1216 on June 30, 1950. There are also thirteen banks for coöperatives, including one central bank and member banks in twelve regions, engaged in providing loans to assist farm coöperatives in marketing and purchasing activities. On June 30, 1950, these banks had outsanding loans of $244,605,580 to 1318 coöperatives.[36] The extent to which all of these are genuine farmers' coöperatives is perhaps somewhat questionable, but there can be little doubt that the present system of governmental credit to farmers is by all odds the most satisfactory that there has ever been. It is significant that of all the New Deal agencies the Farm Credit Administration has come in for the least criticism both from farmers and from the middlemen in the towns and villages.[37]

DISADVANTAGES OF COÖPERATIVE ASSOCIATIONS. Frequently overlooked by the advocates of coöperative associations among farmers is the fact that there are some disadvantages to coöperative undertakings of the contractual nature. (1) The formation of coöperatives fosters specialization. This simplifies the life of the farmer in many respects, eliminates many of the activities he formerly engaged in, decreases many of his skills, and in general makes life more monotonous and dull. (2) When specialization is highly developed, many by-products go to waste, a situation which is practically impossible on the general farm. (3) Coöperative associations have a tendency to drain the best food and produce out of the community and to leave the unsalable portions for domestic consumption. And (4) every advance in specialization makes the farmer more dependent upon the fluctuations of the business cycle, reduces his ability to provide for his own future, and diminishes the security that comes from producing a considerable part of his living on the farm.[38] Even though these may not outweigh the advantages derived from coöperative associations, they are the unlooked-for results which must be considered in evaluating the benefits of the associations.

[36] *Annual Report of the Farm Credit Administration, 1949–50*, Washington, Government Printing Office, 1951, pp. 4, 6, 9, 19, and 30.

[37] See Brunner and Lorge, *op. cit.*, pp. 33, 36.

[38] Cf. Helen Douglas-Irvine, *The Making of Rural Europe*, London, G. Allen & Unwin, Ltd., 1923, pp. 196–198; and Edwin V. O'Hara, *The Church and the Country Community*, New York, The Macmillan Company, 1927, pp. 86–88.

Conditions and Factors in Coöperation

For New York State, J. M. Williams has analyzed in some detail the conditions that were essential for the organization of the Dairymen's League, a rather typical farmers' coöperative. Since much the same factors were operative in the formation of farmers' coöperatives elsewhere, his analysis is of considerable importance. According to Williams, general conditions that resulted in the formation of the League were as follows: (1) The growth of cities brought about the concentration in limited areas of millions of consumers, not themselves producers of milk and milk products, and absolutely dependent upon the surrounding territory for supplies of milk and dairy products; (2) New York farmers by the early part of the twentieth century had become a highly homogeneous group; (3) most New York farmers, about 75 percent, owned their farms; (4) important improvements took place in the means of transportation and communication, and the most important of these was the development of the auto truck; (5) isolation had diminished with the development of communication and transportation and especially the diffusion of the Ford car into rural areas; this made possible interaction between farmers living miles apart. The like-mindedness achieved by more intimate association greatly strengthened the solidarity of the group.

In addition to these general resulting conditions were special effects of psychological import. (1) Farmers were keen to sense the need for some collective action; (2) back of them was a long historic struggle in coöperative ventures; (3) previous attempts, even though they had ended in failure, had done much to develop in the oncoming generation persons much more skilled than their predecessors in such arts of leadership as were necessitated by organizations like the League; (4) important changes in the farmer's attitude toward custom had taken place; the technological changes in the methods of production, which had been truly revolutionary, had created a different attitude toward other heritages from the past; (5) other groups, both laborers in the cities and farm groups elsewhere, apparently were making a success of coöperation; (6) the principle of collective bargaining had gained acceptance and was no longer regarded as something foreign and to be shunned; and (7) there was the culmination of a long series of grievances against the middleman in general and the dealer in farm produce in particular.

With these conditions existing, the farmer came to realize that each by himself was powerless. He joined the coöperative out of self-interest to benefit himself, realizing that his interests were opposed to those of the produce dealer, identical with those of other farmers. He believed, too, that the other farmers were being bled by the middlemen. This sense of injustice was one of the great factors in inducing farmers to join the coöperative.[39]

It is interesting to compare Williams' analysis of the conditions making for coöperation in New York State with that by Dr. E. C. Branson of the factors underlying coöperation among Danish farmers. Dr. Branson concluded that coöperation among the farmers of Denmark was successful because of: (1) extreme poverty and comradeship in poverty in the beginning; (2) the eradication of illiteracy and the wide diffusion of knowledge; (3) a high density of population achieved through the village form of settlement; (4) a geographic location convenient to one hundred million consumers; (5) nearly 100 percent of farm ownership; (6) "organization from the bottom up"; (7) modest beginnings by small groups with meager capital; (8) reliance upon self-help, asking nothing from the state that the farmers through coöperative efforts could do for themselves; and (9) the assistance of the state in the provision of transportation and terminal facilities.[40]

Coöperation as a Culture Pattern

Because farmers have such a deep-seated tradition of assisting one another by mutual-aid activities, contractual coöperative ventures, once they demonstrate their practicability, are likely to spread rapidly from one enterprise to another until they form the warp and woof of community structure. Hoffer has given an excellent account of the development and diffusion of contractual coöperation as a cultural pattern in a Michigan community. Howell, the community studied, is a small town of 3615, a county seat, and the nucleus of an open-country trade area containing 4745 people. As in most rural communities, the population had a long history of

[39] James M. Williams, *The Expansion of Rural Life*, New York, Alfred A. Knopf, Inc., 1926, pp. 172–181.

[40] E. C. Branson, *Farm Life Abroad*, Chapel Hill, University of North Carolina Press, 1924, pp. 209–219; cf. Frederic C. Howe, *Denmark: The Cooperative Way*, New York, Coward-McCann, Inc., 1936, pp. 45–49.

mutual-aid activities. Shortly after 1890 contractual coöperation emerged in the formation of a county Holstein-Friesian Association. Factors responsible for the organization of this association were: (1) the establishment of a milk condensary in the town and (2) the enthusiasm, energy, and foresight of one man in the community who imported Holstein cattle. It should be observed that both of these happenings represent sharp breaks with tradition. The background of this coöperative suggests a close relationship between the emergence of new opportunities and problems and the genesis of new types of social relationships. The association flourished and by 1936 had 300 members. At the meetings of the association proposals for a great many other types of coöperative activity arose and were discussed. Out of them came eventually the employment of a county agricultural agent, the formation of a coöperative association for purchasing feed, the establishment of a mutual fire insurance company, the organization of a county Farm Bureau, and the institution of a "Black and White" field day. Like a chemical reaction the coöperative pattern spread from one activity to another. In 1917 a farmers' coöperative association was formed for the purchase of farm supplies and equipment, and later it also added petroleum products to the list of commodities handled; in 1922 a dairy herd improvement association was set up; and in 1936 a coöperative county veterinary service was established. Furthermore, the coöperative pattern also overspread the economic field and reached out into other fields of activity. In connection with the community hospital, the library, the establishment of the vocational agricultural course in the high school, and in the field of town-country relations, attitudes of coöperation came to be much more in evidence than those of conflict. "The idea of co-operation, separate and apart from any specific instance of co-operative activity, has permeated the community. . . . Each successful venture in co-operative activity in one phase of community life makes easier and more probable its development in other phases." [41]

The Xaverian movement in eastern Nova Scotia is another excellent example of the development and diffusion of a cultural pattern built around the central core of contractual coöperation. There some 200,000 farmers, fishermen, and other rural folk of

[41] C. R. Hoffer, "Co-operation as a Culture Pattern Within a Community," *Rural Sociology,* III (1938), 157–158.

Scotch, French, Irish, and English ancestory are utilizing coöperative associations in practically every aspect of life. Their business
enterprises include seventy savings banks, a parent store and four
branches, a bakery, a milk pasteurizing plant, and a tailoring establishment. They include also coöperative lobster canning factories,
sawmills, and a wide variety of community industries. In a very
real sense all of these are the direct outgrowth of the study clubs
sponsored by the diocesan college, St. Francis Xavier, and led by
men who "realized that God gave the earth and the fullness
thereof for all men and that He gave men an intellect with which
to exploit these for their needs."[42] Furthermore, the coöperative activities were not confined to economic questions but included libraries and educational activities in the most real sense of the
words. The college study clubs, in which the whole movement
rooted, are the training fields for democratic citizenship of the
highest type.[43]

One of the more commendable activities of the Farm Security
Administration is the assistance it has rendered in the organization
and financing of farmers' coöperative associations. This work was
particularly important during the severe distress prevailing in the
thirties, but many of the projects were undertaken after the outbreak of World War II.[44]

The experience of Howell in Michigan, Antigonish in Nova
Scotia, and thousands of other communities throughout the world
amply demonstrates the keenness of perception, the validity of
generalization shown by Sir Horace Plunkett when he wrote:

Gradually the [cooperative] Society becomes the most important
institution in the district, the most important in a social as well as an
economic sense. The members feel a pride in its material expansion.
They accumulate large profits, which in time become a sort of communal fund. In some cases this is used for the erection of village halls
where social entertainments, concerts and dances are held, lectures
delivered and libraries stored. Finally, the Association assumes the
character of a rural commune, where, instead of the old basis of com-

[42] See Peter A. Nearing, "The Xavierian Movement," *Rural Sociology*, II (1937),
76–77.

[43] Cf. George M. Boyle, "Nova Scotia: An Experiment in Education," *Yearbook
of Agricultural Co-operation*, London, Horace Plunkett Foundation, 1935, pp.
140–144.

[44] Cf. Joe J. King, "Rural Cooperative Self-Help Activities in the Pacific Northwest," *American Sociological Review*, VIII (1943), 706–710.

mune, the joint ownership of land, a new basis for union is found in the voluntary communism of effort.[45]

Religious Coöperation

The church, as one of the principal nuclei of social groupings, has always played an important role in coöperation of all types. Furthermore, religious motives, polarized about the church, have been the moving force in many forms of coöperation.[46] With the disintegration of the cumulative community and the substitution of organic solidarity for cohesion based upon similarities, there occurs a great change in the entire pattern of social relationships. Especially are the relationships or associations with nonmembers of the intimate group subject to change. Mingling with and coming to know persons with widely differing cultural heritages, sharply contrasting social characteristics, and diametrically opposed mores is one of the most effective ways of developing tolerance and broad-mindedness. As a rule none of the traits of a traditional culture pattern are more tenaciously clung to than those customs and traditions associated with religion and the church. For years leaders of the various Protestant denominations have lamented the serious "overchurching" of the rural community as evidenced by the presence of from six to ten small struggling congregations in a single rural village, have deplored the lack of more coöperative relations between them. For this reason the emergence of various coöperative tendencies among various church groups in rural areas is a matter of no slight consequence. Coöperative efforts are in evidence in many lines, including the following: (1) In many communities the local pastors of all denominations have formed a council for the purpose of discussing common aims and problems; (2) pastors on invitation exchange pulpits on stated occasions;

[45] Sir Horace Plunkett, *The Country Life Movement in the United States,* New York, The Macmillan Company, 1910, pp. 128–129. For another important study of the coöperative movement in a given community and the way in which it spread from one field of activity to another, see Karel Galla, *Sociology of the Cooperative Movement in the Czechoslovak Village,* Praha, Spolek Pece o Blaho Venkova, 1936. Consult also, for modern accomplishments through coöperation, Marquis W. Childs, *Sweden: The Middle Way,* New Haven, Yale University Press, 1938.

[46] Especially have coöperative movements among Negroes been generated and nourished in the religious circle. See W. E. Burghardt Du Bois, *Economic Coöperation Among Negro Americans,* Atlanta University Publication 12, Atlanta, 1907. For a portion of the life history of a rural Negro consumer coöperative, see John Hope II, "Rochdale Cooperation Among Negroes," *Phylon,* I (1940), 48–51.

(3) union meetings are held periodically in many communities, with leaders and lay members of several denominations coöperating; and (4) there has been a definite tendency toward the development of union churches in rural areas. The latter deserves more than mention.

In the United States the movement for union of local churches had made little headway before 1890. At this time the depopulation of many rural areas and the decline of the village in some sections of the country created many pressing problems for the rural institutions serving the population of these sections. The earliest federated church reported was in a declining Massachusetts community, the union having occurred in 1887.[47] For twenty-five years the movement made little progress and overchurching continued as a vexing problem in many rural communities. Following the year 1912, however, the movement made rapid headway and by 1924 the surveys of the Institute of Social and Religious Research discovered almost one thousand united churches in the villages and open-country areas of the North and West. But they found not a single one in the South. The united churches discovered by the Institute were of four types: (1) 312 federated churches, in which each congregation kept its affiliation with the denominational body; (2) 137 undenominational churches, where the congregations uniting severed all denominational ties; (3) 491 denominational united churches, a category designed to fit those cases in which one of the congregations retained denominational ties and the members of the other congregations accepted them; and (4) 37 affiliated churches, so called because loose and vague ties were retained with one or more of the parent denominations. That these united churches were promoted by overchurching is evidenced by the fact that they were largely confined to the smaller villages, the number in towns being almost insignificant. Seven out of eight of the congregations entering formal unions with those of other denominations were either Northern Baptist, Congregational, Methodist Episcopal, or Presbyterian of the U. S. A. Scattered congregations from twelve other denominations also entered the unions, but this number included no foreign-language denominations, no Catholic, Hebrew, or Christian Science congregations.

[47] Elizabeth R. Hooker, *United Churches*, New York, Doubleday, Doran & Company, 1926, p. 25.

However, individual members of the united churches included representatives from at least fifty different faiths.[48]

Important as the movement toward united churches has been in specific communities, recent trends do not seem to justify the belief that it will solve the problems of the rural church in America. Brunner reports that of 400 churches passing out of existence in the 140 village communities of his sample between 1924 and 1936, less than 10 percent were closed as a result of coöperative efforts. Other forces were making a slow reduction in the number of churches per community (the average declined from 10 in 1924 to 9.5 in 1936) and in the number of churches per 1000 population, which was 3.3 in 1924 and 2.4 in 1936.[49] United churches made up 2.1 percent of all churches in the villages in 1936, as compared with 1.3 in 1924.[50]

[48] See Edmund deS. Brunner, *Village Communities*, New York, Doubleday, Doran & Company, 1928, pp. 76–79; cf. Hooker, *op. cit.*, pp. 27–31, and Ralph A. Felton, *Local Church Cooperation in Rural Communities*, New York, Home Missions Council, 1940.

[49] Brunner and Lorge, *op. cit.*, p. 323.

[50] *Ibid.*, p. 328.

23

ACCOMMODATION, ASSIMILATION, AND ACCULTURATION IN RURAL AREAS

All life is a process of adaptation and adjustment. Society itself is a vast arena in which groups and individuals are constantly adjusting themselves to one another, to the physical environment, and to the man-made environment or culture. Sociologists utilize a wide variety of terms in reference to the processes of adaptation and adjustment, terms that are not always precisely defined, rarely differentiated adequately from one another, and frequently highly ambiguous. It is no easy task to determine the exact meaning of even the commonest terms. Although sociologists are far from agreement on terms or definitions, at least three concepts seem to be in use in analyzing the processes of adaptation and adjustment. These are: (1) accommodation; (2) assimilation; and (3) acculturation.

Adjustment, according to Ernest W. Burgess, is of two types: one brought about by biological variation and selection, called adaptation; and the second due to social adjustments, called accommodation. This second variety of adjustment must be defined broadly enough to include social adjustment or accommodation between the man-made and the natural environments. Conflict and accommodation are closely related, the latter either growing out of the former or being the social adjustment between groups who otherwise might come into active conflict. Accommodation groups are many and varied, some of the principal varieties being castes and classes, denominations, clubs, and nations. In contrast are the conflict groups, including such organizations as gangs, sects, and nationalities.[1] The process of accommodation refers to

[1] This term being used to mean a consciously organized, culturally homogeneous minority within a nation. Cf. Robert E. Park, "Racial Assimilation in Secondary Groups," *American Journal of Sociology*, XIX (1913–1914), 606–623.

the manner by which a group achieves adjustment with its social milieu and is typified by the transition from gang to club, sect to denomination, nationality to nation. The ultimate result of accommodation is social organization, whereas out of conflict comes political order, and from competition comes a state of equilibrium. Stages in the process of accommodation are domination, toleration, compromise, conciliation, and conversion. A special form of accommodation, *modus vivendi*, occurs when groups in conflict agree to disagree on certain fundamental questions but to carry on together certain undisputed functions.[2]

The nature of the process of accommodation may also be stated in a slightly different way. If competition becomes immediate, direct, and personal, or if radically different cultures and races come into intimate contact with one another, conflicts are almost sure to arise. But such conflicts are of necessity short-lived or intermittent—men cannot fight all the time. Individuals, groups, and cultures, even though deadly antagonistic to one another, must discover some means of compromise, if only for short breathing spells. Accommodation is properly used to refer to the process by which such differences are resolved. Therefore it is a rather conscious organization of social relationships to the end of reducing conflict, disciplining competition, and establishing a working agreement that will enable divergent personalities, groups, and cultures to go about their varied activities. Each person or group retains its own characteristic traits, and each adjusts to a situation in which others are permitted the same privilege.

But conflict is not inevitable in the contact of one group, race, or culture with another; some contacts are extremely fleeting, and accommodation is not the only process of adjustment that arises from social and cultural contact. Not infrequently contacts are peaceable; members intermarry, groups fuse, and cultures blend with each other. To these processes are given the names *assimilation* and *acculturation;* the distinction between the two is seldom if ever clear. As used by social scientists, assimilation is usually restricted rather rigidly to social aspects, biological crossing or intermarriage being referred to as amalgamation. Nevertheless, assimilation, in the popular mind,[3] seems to carry the connotation

---

[2] See Ernest W. Burgess, "Accommodation," *Encyclopaedia of the Social Sciences,* I, New York, The Macmillan Company, 1930.

[3] Some scholars, too, are not careful to rule out the biological implication. Thus Sarah E. Simons refers to assimilation as the "adjustment between races," indicates

of biological mixing, so much so that many scholars have prefixed the term with *social* or *cultural* to insure the sense in which it was used.[4] And Park points out that although the Negro's culture is almost exclusively derived from his white fellows, the Negro is not assimilated.[5] According to Park, assimilation is more of a political than a cultural concept, is the abstract term that includes the verbs *Americanize, Anglicize, Germanize,* etc. It is the process by which peoples of diverse racial stocks and heterogeneous cultural heritages, when circumstances place them in a common territory, achieve enough social solidarity to maintain a national existence. He also points out that the process operates gradually and is not open to observation and measurement, and that we speak of an immigrant as being assimilated when he has lost the marks of the alien and has acquired enough of the language and ritual to enable him to get along in the country.[6]

But even if assimilation were expanded to include both biological fusing, or amalgamation, and the psychosocial process, all the difficulties with the term would not disappear. Miscegenation coupled with complete acceptance of the cultural heritage still does not guarantee assimilation, if Park's contention that the Negro is not assimilated will stand—and most scholars will agree that it will. There are today in the United States millions of persons more white than black who have completely, both individually and as a group, accepted the cultural heritage of the white Americans. Racially they stand close to the members of the white group; culturally they are practically identical; but, nevertheless, sociologically they stand with the Negroes. Moreover, a rather complete acceptance of the cultural heritage may occur without miscegenation or intermarriage—many persons of Chinese or Japanese descent born in this country have acquired the American cultural heritage and completely lost that of Asia, without in any sense undergoing a racial change. But in spite of these diffi-

---

that intermarriage is one of the assimilating forces, and presents the following analogy: "Figuratively speaking, it [assimilation] is the process by which the aggregation of peoples is changed from a mere mechanical mixture into a chemical compound." "Social Assimilation," *American Journal of Sociology,* VI (1910), 790–822.

[4] See Henry Pratt Fairchild, (ed.), *Dictionary of Sociology,* New York, Philosophical Library, Inc., 1944, p. 276; and Kimball Young, *An Introductory Sociology,* New York, American Book Company, 1934, p. 452.

[5] Robert E. Park, "Assimilation, Social," *Encyclopaedia of the Social Sciences.*

[6] *Ibid.*

culties, assimilation, viewed as a complete fusion of personalities and physical features, is more thoroughgoing when it is accomplished in the primary group, and particularly in the family where the child's cultural and physical equipment is a fusion and blend-ing of those of both parents.[7]

Acculturation is a third term used in referring to adaptation or adjustment at the social or cultural level. This concept has made its way into sociology from the field of cultural anthropology, where it has had a long and interesting history.[8] Usages of the term vary, but Herskovits and the Subcommittee on Acculturation of the Social Science Research Council, of which he is a member, use it to denote the process by means of which cultural elements are transferred from one group to another. He also differentiates it from diffusion by limiting its use to those instances of transference that may be checked through the use of verified historical facts.[9] Herskovits and other anthropologists have applied the term *assimilation* to the process by which cultural synthesis is achieved, and *acculturation* to the results of cultural contact.

Sociologists in general use the term in a rather different sense. Among them acculturation is used as a rule to designate the ways in which persons or groups acquire new culture traits and incorporate them into their accustomed pattern of living.[10] Unlike assimilation, acculturation thus used includes the acquisition by the individual of the cultural heritage of the group. It is not synonymous with education, because one may know about things or practices in great detail and never adopt them as his own, and may also be unaware of many of the behavior patterns that are most characteristic of his particular group.[11] Not until one adopts

[7] For basic treatments of these social processes of accommodation and assimilation, see Robert E. Park and Ernest W. Burgess, *Introduction to the Science of Sociology*, Chicago, University of Chicago Press, 1921, pp. 662–671, 734–741; Young, *op. cit.*, pp. 452–454, 495–498; C. A. Dawson and Warner E. Gettys, *An Introduction to Sociology*, New York, Ronald Press Company, 1935, pp. 300–309; and Howard Woolston, "The Process of Assimilation," *Social Forces*, XXIII (1945), 416–424.

[8] A recent study, *Acculturation*, by Melville J. Herskovits (New York, J. J. Augustin, 1938), traces in some detail the evolution of this term in anthropology. See especially pp. 2–23.

[9] *Ibid.*, pp. 14–15. Cf. Fairchild, *op. cit.*, p. 3.

[10] See Earle E. Eubank, *The Concepts of Sociology*, Boston, D. C. Heath & Company, 1932, pp. 371–372; and Fairchild, *op. cit.*

[11] Furthermore, education probably must be limited to include only the transmission of the socially accepted portions of the cultural heritage.

as his own and incorporates into his daily pattern of life the new culture traits is he acculturated. Following this line of analysis further, some sociologists have used acculturation to designate the process of adjusting to culture, and have introduced the compound, reacculturation, to refer to the process that occurs when a person who is acculturated into one cultural heritage moves to another culture area and adjusts himself to the man-made environment of the group residing there.[12] It should be evident from the above that although the term "acculturation" overlaps in many respects the concept of assimilation, the two are by no means identical. Acculturation has the distinct advantage of lacking biological connotations. It also fills a distinct need for a term to designate the process by which the person acquires the cultural heritage of the group into which he is born.

Accommodation

The forms of accommodation are many and varied. If one were to analyze them in detail, he would have a minute description of the processes which have crystallized to form a large part of the social organization or structure of any particular society. Only a few of the principal forms that are especially significant in the study of rural society are included in the following pages.

Subordination and superordination seem almost inevitable concomitants of accommodation. Social interaction on terms of absolute equality is inconceivable, especially if a large number of persons is concerned. The result would be not society but babel. Always when human beings mingle with one another the phenomena of subordination and superordination appear. Various animal studies are especially suggestive in this connection, but unfortunately, as in so many other respects, more is known about the animals than about man.

Place twelve strange hens together in a barnyard and shortly, after much fighting, there will emerge a perfect pattern of domination and subordination. Before one hen the remaining eleven will give way. One of these, although running from the first, will in turn cause all the others to give way before her. Another hen will run from two of the flock but dominate the remaining nine.

[12] Cf. Wilson D. Wallis and M. M. Willey, *Readings in Sociology*, New York, Appleton-Century-Crofts, Inc., 1930, p. 52.

And so will run the pattern until the twelfth hen is bossed by the entire flock and will give way in all disputes. This example from animal sociology is suggestive concerning the nature of the process of accommodation, especially in the form of domination, or superordination, and subordination.

Although adequate analyses of the forms of accommodation in the family, the neighborhood, and the community are lacking, it would seem that these would provide a most fruitful field for the study of this important social process. In a number of rural families personally known to the writer whom he has observed intimately over a long period of time, the pattern of subordination and superordination is as follows. In situations where the entire membership of the family is present and participating, the function of authority and the obligation and responsibility for directing the activities of and for stimulating and disciplining the other members of the group rest with the father. In his absence both the authority and the responsibility rest upon the mother. When the children are left by themselves with the care of the farm work, the oldest child or the oldest boy receives the mantle of authority to direct the activities of the younger children and is charged with the responsibility of carrying forward the work of the farmstead. In the absence of the oldest son, the responsibility and authority move down the scale to the second oldest child, and so on through the entire membership, until only the youngest member is relieved of the responsibility of directing the work of brothers and sisters. Even he may be charged with the obligation of directing the hired help in the absence of other members of the family group.

Slavery and its aftermath represent some of the most significant forms of accommodation in the rural areas of the nation. In the beginning, of course, this accommodation was imposed by force. The slave has three distinguishing characteristics, slavery three indispensable elements. The slave is: (1) the property of another, (2) at the base of the pyramid socially and politically, and (3) a compulsory laborer.[13] Park has set forth a vivid picture of the manner in which the institution of slavery operated to accommodate whites and Negroes of the ante-bellum South to one

---

[13] See extracts from H. J. Nieboer, *Slavery as an Industrial System,* The Hague, 1910, quoted in Park and Burgess, *op. cit.,* pp. 674–677.

another; he has also described the confusion that arose when the established patterns of paternalistic relationships were disturbed.[14] But the elimination of slavery did not destroy the customary forms of accommodation between the Negro farm laborers and the white planters of the rural South. The system of share-cropping has perpetuated many of the most essential features of the old pattern of accommodation.

Viewed from the standpoint of the number of rural persons affected, or of the persistence of the structural pattern, the share-cropping wage system in vogue in the cotton states is perhaps the most important of all the processes of accommodation to be found in rural America. Year after year, from immediately after the Civil War and the freeing of the slaves until the present time, the system has provided a working arrangement between the planters and the laborers of the southern states. In the truest sense of the word it provides a general basis whereby the planter and the laboring classes accommodate themselves to the efforts of the others.[15] Through the process of accommodation provided by share-cropping, millions of laborers, white and Negro, together with the southern planters, annually produce the nation's most important commercial crop.

The origin of the channels through which these particular processes flow goes back to the years immediately following the Civil War. When the slaves received their freedom, it spelled, of course, the disruption of the previous form of accommodation characteristic of the system of slavery.[16] Alfred H. Stone, who knows the intimate details of the plantation complex from a lifetime of personal experience, has pointed out in the following paragraph the chief differences between the races under slavery and in freedom in the problem of accommodation:

> The Civil War did not destroy the old plantation system. It merely altered the legal status of one of its elements. The Negro in the mass remained economically untouched by the gift of freedom, in so far as any free agency of his own was concerned. Where before, his labor had been bought with his body, now it was his labor alone which came to be trafficked in. The latter was a cheaper transaction than the former, and required less capital. It therefore was engaged in by a

[14] Park and Burgess, *op. cit.*, pp. 623–631.

[15] Eubank (*op. cit.*, p. 292) should be consulted with reference to such accommodational action.

[16] Cf. Park and Burgess, *op. cit.*, pp. 667–668, 674–681, and 761–762.

greater number of people. Formerly, a high order of intelligence was required to handle successfully a plantation on a large scale, involving as it did the care of the physical well-being of its labor, as well as the financing of its operations. Now, the main requirement came to be a small line of credit with a local merchant, and the ability to get together enough Negroes to make a crop for a single year. The best test of success in "making money out of Negroes" ceased to be the capacity to keep down sickness among them, to feed and clothe them properly, to keep them contented even though not free, to work them to the best advantage, having always in view the fact that life was the only limit to their tenure of service. It came to be, instead, the ability to secure their labor at the lowest price, to give them the least for the most work, to keep them satisfied, not by a full stomach but by the cajolery of promises never intended to be kept, and the unction of words which an antebellum planter would have scorned to utter. Booker Washington has repeated over and over again the phrase that before the war the Negro was "worked," but that now he has learned to work himself. The truth is that the Negro has been "worked," as the word is used in the vernacular of the street, to a vastly greater extent since he has been free than ever he was as a slave.[17]

Immediately following the Civil War great were the problems of accommodation facing the landowners of the dismantled South and the Negroes who drifted back to their accustomed haunts after their first brief experience of freedom and individual self-responsibility. The first working arrangement attempted was well known in other sections of the country, namely, the payment of cash wages for labor. But for a number of reasons this proved unsatisfactory and was abandoned after a brief period of trial.[18]

[17] Alfred H. Stone, "The Negro and Agricultural Development," *Annals of the American Academy of Political and Social Science,* XXXV (1910), 13–14.

[18] Almost as soon as the war was over, observers began reporting attempts to establish new patterns to provide for the processes of accommodation. Wrote Henry Latham in 1867: "One of our three negroes was a field-hand; the owner was to have half the produce, and the field-hand half; the labourer to keep himself, and find his own clothes, shoes, and tools. This is a very general arrangement; which will result in the master having to make advances, after which the negro will be greatly tempted to decline to work." *Black and White: A Journal of a Three Months' Tour in the United States,* London, Macmillan & Co., Ltd., 1867, p. 127. In another paragraph he wrote: "There seemed at first to be insuperable difficulties in the way of organizing free labour. Its practice was not understood by the labourer, nor its theory by the master. It seemed to be impossible to adjust the rate of wages equitably, and there was no money in the country to pay them with. . . . Contracts were made by the division of the crop between the employers and the labourers; this necessitated advances by the employer to enable the

Robert Preston Brooks, in his excellent study, *The Agrarian Revolution in Georgia, 1865–1912,*[19] has given thorough analysis of the evolution of the system of sharecropping as a substitute for slavery in the South. He outlines the developments as follows: (1) At first among the Negroes the belief was widespread that the plantations would be carved up into parcels and presented to the ex-slaves as Christmas gifts in December, 1865. (2) To cope with the Negroes' newly secured liberty to move, strict vagrancy laws were passed—the county court was empowered to bind out the vagrant for a twelve-months' period. (3) The plantation organization, then as now, required close supervision of all the details of operation; those engaged in cotton planting never had the slightest idea of abandoning this feature. (4) As early as 1865 the cash-wage system was under fire: wages fixed by the Freedmen's Bureau were relatively high, money was practically nonexistent, the planter could not demand steady work from his hands, and the evidence concerning the general unreliability of the wage hands was overwhelming. (5) By 1867 labor was extremely scarce and the planters were forced to make terms with the Negroes; however, even in 1869 a convention of planters agreed that the old wage system was superior to the newer sharecropping that was being adopted. (6) Brought into the arena at the same time were the Negro's dislike of close supervision, the great demand for labor, and the scarcity of cash. (7) The crop lien, which at first was a device whereby the planter received advances from the merchant by pledging his crop as security, came into being; later it was adopted between planter and cropper also. (8) Some merchants attempted to combine planting with their mercantile enterprises, and there arose a tendency for the Negroes to abandon the strict planter-regulated plantations for the looser merchant-regulated farming arrangements; here the phenomena of absenteeism came into full play. (9) The lien laws, however, proved to be effective agencies in transforming the system: the planters refused to assign their liens to merchants, and instead procured supplies, furnished their laborers, and deferred settlement until the end of the year; the laborer or cropper received the value of the crop he

---

labourer to live; and this resulted in the labourer disappearing as soon as he got tired of work. If they worked together until the crop was got in, disputes often arose over the division of the profits." (P. 271.)

[19] University of Wisconsin Historical Series III, 1, Madison, 1914.

produced less the advances he had secured; both were willing to give up money payments, the planter because he was alarmed at the fall in the price of cotton and the laborer because he was dismayed at the drop in wages; the planter did not give up his right of supervision, but it was relaxed. (10) The workers on the plantation were all placed under supervision; the others became renters.[20]

The essential relationships in the share system as established and perpetuated to this day are approximately as Brooks has described them:

Under the share system, the landlord supplies everything necessary to make the crop, except the manual labor, and the owner and tenant are in a sense co-partners in the undertaking. Since the landlord has undertaken all the risk, he claims the right of complete control over the tenant and the crop, just as in the case of the day laborer. It is this supervision that the darkies resent.[21]

But in some respects the nature of the accommodative process is even more clearly portrayed by Thompson:

The ordinary arrangement of share tenancy under which the negro in the cotton belt now works provides that the landowner shall furnish a cabin in which the family may live and an acre or two for a garden. In addition, working stock, implements, and seeds are supplied by the owner of the land. Both tenant and owner share the cost of fertilizers if any are used, and divide equally the expenses of preparing the crop for market and the proceeds of the sale. This arrangement means, of course, that the capitalist takes the laborer into a real partnership. Both embark in a venture the deferred results of which are dependent chiefly upon the industry and good faith of the laborer. By a seeming paradox it is only the laborer's unreliability which gives him such an opportunity, for if he were more dependable, the landowner would prefer in most cases to pay wages and take the whole of the crop. Because the average negro laborer cannot be depended upon to be faithful, he is given a greater opportunity, contrary to all ordinary moral maxims.[22]

[20] *Ibid.*, pp. 13–63.
[21] *Ibid.*, p. 53. For other important readings on the origin of sharecropping, see U. B. Phillips and James David Glunt, *Florida Plantation Records*, St. Louis, Historical Society, 1927, pp. 36–38, 191–193, 581–582; and Charles H. Otken, *The Ills of the South*, New York, G. P. Putnam's Sons, 1894, pp. 35–37.
[22] Holland Thompson, *The New South*, New Haven, Yale University Press, 1920, p. 67. A detailed outline of the variations in cropping arrangements that are encountered in the South will be found in E. A. Boeger and E. A. Goldenweiser,

The genesis of some of the most controversial aspects of the system, such as bookkeeping by the planters, is detailed in the interesting account of Frances Butler Leigh:

On Wednesday, when my father returned, he reported that he had found the negroes all on the place, not only those who were there five years ago, but many who were sold three years before that. Seven had worked their way back from the up country. They received him very affectionately, and made an agreement with him to work for one half of the crop, which agreement is remained to be seen if they would keep.

. . . .

My father was quite encouraged at first, the people seemed so willing to work and said so much about their intention of doing so; but not many days after they started he became quite disheartened, saying that half the hands left the fields at one o'clock and the rest by three o'clock, and this just at our busiest time. Half a day's work will keep them from starving, but won't raise a crop. Our contract with them is for half the crop; that is, one half to be divided among them, according to each man's rate of work, we letting them have in the meantime necessary food, clothing, and money for their present wants (as they have not a penny) which is to be deducted from whatever is due to them at the end of the year.

. . . .

This we found the best arrangement to make with them, for if we paid them wages, the first five dollars they made would have seemed like so large a sum to them, that they would have imagined their fortunes made and refused to work any more. But even this arrangement had its objections, for they told us, when they missed working two or three days a week, that they were losers by it as well as ourselves, half the crop being theirs. But they could not see that this sort of work would not raise any crop at all, and that such should be the result was quite beyond their comprehension. They were quite convinced that if six days' work would raise a whole crop, three days' work would raise half a one, with which they as partners were satisfied, and so it seemed as if we should have to be too.

. . . .

A Study of the Tenant Systems of Farming in the Yazoo-Mississippi Delta, U.S.D.A. Bulletin 337, Washington, 1916; summarized in Charles S. Johnson, Edwin R. Embree, and W. W. Alexander, *The Collapse of Cotton Tenancy,* Chapel Hill, University of North Carolina Press, 1935, p. 74, and in Arthur Raper, *Preface to Peasantry,* Chapel Hill, University of North Carolina Press, 1936, pp. 146–147.

Night after night, when the day's work was over, I sat up till two and three o'clock in the morning, going over and over the long line of figures, and by degrees got them pretty straight. I might have saved myself the trouble. Not one negro understood it a bit, but all were quite convinced they had been cheated, most of them thinking that each man was entitled to half the crop. I was so anxious they should understand and see they had been fairly dealt with, that I went over and over again each man's account with him, and would begin, "Well, Jack, (or Quash, or Nero, as the case might be), you got on such a date ten yards of homespun from your master." "Yes, missus, massa gave me dat." "Then on such and such a day you had ten dollars." "Yes, missus, dat so." And so on to the end of their debits, all of which they acknowledged as just at once. (I have thought since they were not clever enough to conceive the idea of disputing that part of the business.) When all these items were named and agreed to, I read the total amount, and then turned to the work account. And here the trouble began, every man insisting that he had not missed one day in the whole two years, and had done full work each day. So after endless discussions, which always ended just where they began, I paid them the money due them; which was always received with the same remark, "Well, well, work for massa two whole years, and only get dis much." Finding that their faith in my father's justice never wavered, I repeated and repeated and repeated, "But I am paying you from your master's own books and accounts." But the answer was always the same, "No, no, missus, massa not treat us so." Neither, oddly enough, did they seem to think I wished to cheat them, but that I was powerless to help matters, one man saying to me one day, "You see, missus, a woman ain't much 'count.'" I learnt very soon how useless all attempts at "making them sensible" (as they themselves express it) were, and after a time, used to pay them their wages and tell them to be off, without allowing any of the lengthy arguments and discourses over their payments they wished to indulge in, often more, I think, with an idea of asserting their independence and dignity, than from any real belief that they were not properly paid.

· · · · · · ·

From the first, the fixed notion in their minds has been that liberty meant idleness, and they must be forced to work until they become intelligent enough to know the value of labour. As for starving them into this, that is impossible, too, for it is a well-known fact that you can't starve a negro. At this moment there are about a dozen on Butler's Island who do not work, consequently get no wages and no food, and I see no difference whatever in their condition and those who get twelve dollars a month and full rations. They all raise a little corn and sweet potatoes, and with their facilities for catching fish and oysters, and shooting wild game, they have as much to eat as they want, and now are quite satisfied with that, not yet having learned to want things that money alone can give.[23]

As early as 1869 there was much discussion of the relative merits of cash wages and sharecropping as forms of accommodative relationships between the planters and their work hands. One of the most interesting studies of the problem is that conducted by Loring & Atkinson, Cotton Brokers and Agents of Boston, Massachusetts. This firm circulated widely throughout the South a questionnaire asking for information concerning these conditions and practices. Theirs was an attempt to secure "information which should do something to turn *Emmigration and Capital* to the cotton belt of our country."[24] The materials secured are of the highest interest, and the conclusions of great significance. Loring and Atkinson report two "systems of employing laborers at the South, by share and by wages."[25] From the replies of their correspondents they concluded that both systems have advantages and disadvantages. For the share system these are listed as follows:

1. It stimulates industry by giving the laborer an interest and pride in the crop. It has been found by experience that comparatively a small part of the laborers are influenced by these stimulants, but with this small class they certainly have a positive existence.
2. It is regarded by the laborer as a higher form of contract, and is, therefore, more likely to secure labor, especially in undesirable localities.
3. It gives the laborer a motive to protect the crop.
4. It does not subject the farmer to loss from a failure of, or a decline in, value of his crop.
5. It secures laborers for the year, with less likelihood of his breaking the contract, a thing he sometimes likes to do when the hard work begins.
Some of the disadvantages of the share system are—
1. The difficulty of discharging hands when they become inefficient or refractory.

. . . .

[23] Frances Butler Leigh, *Ten Years on a Georgia Plantation Since the War*, London, R. Bentley & Son, 1883, pp. 14, 25–27, 74–77, 124–125.
[24] F. W. Loring and C. F. Atkinson, *Cotton Culture and the South Considered with Reference to Emigration*, Boston, A. Williams & Co., 1869.
[25] *Ibid.*, p. 25.

2. The great difficulty of carrying on the general work of the farm, the tendency being to drift into a mere system of cropping, the most pernicious of all systems under which the laborer of a country has ever been employed—a system that leads to idleness on the part of the laborer for a large part of the year, to indolence and indifference on the part of the farm owner, to decay and ruin in the farm, and a general decline in the productive resources of the country.

3. The annoyance and perplexity of harvesting and dividing the crop, requiring the gin-house to be subdivided, and leading to a great loss of time in ginning and packing the crop. Also, settlements are often unsatisfactory at present, on account of the ignorance of the negro, and his tendency to suspect unfair dealing.

4. The disadvantage of having the laborers dictate methods of cultivation according to their own notions, which are seldom right ones.[26]

They likewise indicate the following advantages of the wage system:

1. It gives the farmer control over the labor, he having the power to discharge.

2. It stimulates industry and enterprise in the farmer. Profits go into his pockets, losses come on his shoulders.

3. It leads to economy in labor, causing the farmer to reduce the laborers to the smallest number consistent with the execution of the work, substituting mule labor and labor-saving machines for hand labor, both tending to *make labor more abundant.*

4. It enables the farmer to carry out a general system of improvement on his farm; to keep the fences, ditches, roads and buildings all in proper repair, and to pay due attention to other crops than cotton, all of which is impossible under the present share system.

5. It necessitates close personal attention from the farmer, *forcing* thriftiness upon him and preventing indolence, for the very essence of the system lies in constant and active supervision.[27]

Few students of society, acquainted as they are with the gradualness of social and cultural evolution, are surprised that the cropper system, whose resemblances were much nearer to the old slave system than those of the cash-wage system, should be the pattern of accommodation to persist in the cotton belt. In any case the plantation system has come down to the present time

[26] *Ibid.,* pp. 28–30.
[27] *Ibid.,* p. 30.

with only minor changes from the prewar plantation. A basic report from the Federal Emergency Relief Administration has summarized the developments and situation:

> On the plantations that had withstood the reconstruction period following the Civil War, the cropper system displaced the old slave system. For a satisfactory share of the harvest, the landlord would agree to "furnish" the cropper while he cultivated the crop. The "furnish" consisted of living quarters, foodstuff and equipment. The cropper and his family furnished the labor. . . . After the harvest the cropper would be paid for his portion of the crop less the value of his "furnish." . . . While the cropper system offered ample opportunity for the landlords to be fair, and some croppers may have profited under the system, in general, the cropper's independence was only nominal. Obviously, the system was merely a variation of the old slave relationship and kept the cropper on the margin of economic existence. This marginal existence, with its pseudo-economic freedom along with the owner's spirit of the landed aristocracy, emphasized whatever deficiencies appeared in the cropper class, fostered an attitude of dependence and suppressed initiative.[28]

Probably biased in favor of the wage system and ignorant of the psychosocial equipment of the ex-slave, Loring and Atkinson were unable to find any noteworthy disadvantages to cash wages except that "the wage system labors under the *temporary* disadvantage that the freedman prefers a share, and having complete control, he prevents its use."[29] Temporary disadvantage or not, the fact remains that just as in 1869 sharecropping was "the system in most general use,"[30] so it has remained until the present time. Only recently has the rapid mechanization of cotton production given promise of disrupting the sharecropping arrangements that have been in vogue for more than three-quarters of a century.

One of the principal elements in sharecropping as an accommodative process is that of supervision; neglect of this element probably leads to more misunderstanding of the plantation complex than any other single thing. Brannen in his classic study has developed the chief aspects of the system of supervision em-

---

[28] P. G. Beck and M. C. Forster, *Six Rural Problem Areas: Relief—Resources—Rehabilitation*, Federal Emergency Relief Administration Research Monograph I, Washington, 1935, pp. 21–22.

[29] *Op. cit.*, p. 30. Italics are my own.

[30] *Ibid.*, p. 33; cf. Charles Nordhoff, *The Cotton States in the Spring and Summer of 1875*, New York, D. Appleton & Company, 1876, p. 21.

ployed.[31] According to him, the amount of supervision that the management of the plantation will exercise is usually understood in advance, and it "often amounts to the control of the cropper's or tenant's crop and the direction of the worker's farming activities by the landlord or manager." More than two-thirds of the plantations included in his study reported close supervision, 30 percent reported general supervision, and only 2 percent reported no supervision. On closely supervised plantations the landlord determines the holidays, and these amount to two or three days a year. Saturday afternoons and Sundays are rest periods. Funerals are also an occasion for holidays. The management controls the work stock, although frequently the hands are allowed to use them for going to town and even for work off the plantation. As a rule each cropper is assigned a mule for the year, although some plantations pool the livestock and distribute them weekly. Implements, too, are usually allotted for the season, but several families may have to share a common piece of equipment. "One wagon often accommodates from three to six croppers." The assignment of plots to croppers is largely in the hands of the landlord, and as a rule each cropper works separately, although at certain seasons of the year all the workers may be concentrated into a gang. Daily rounds are made by the plantation manager for the purpose of instructing the workers in the details of the cultivation process, inspecting the lands, crops, etc.[32]

Another basic study sponsored by the Federal Emergency Relief Administration and conducted in Alabama inquired into the nature of the accommodative relationships between the landlords and the families on their places. This report supplies a rather detailed analysis and data concerning the prevailing relationships between the landlords and croppers with respect to the maintenance of the families by the landlords, indebtedness of croppers to the landlords, and the influence of the federal relief program

[31] C. O. Brannen, *The Relation of Land Tenure to Plantation Organization,* U.S. Department of Agriculture Bulletin 1269, Washington, 1924.

[32] *Ibid.,* pp. 42–43. Brooks in 1914 wrote as follows: "At the present time, an unsupervised 'cropper,' as share tenants have come to be known, is almost never met with. The supervision of his operations is as close as the planter can make it, the right of control being based on the fact that the owner furnishes all the capital necessary to make the crop. Few men would now think of entrusting such capital to uncontrolled negroes, and such evidence as is to be found tends to show that this practice of supervision dates back to the inception of the share system." *Op. cit.,* p. 48.

upon the established pattern of relationships. According to this study, the conventional attitude of both landlord and cropper was that the former was expected to take care of the latter whenever he needed it. "On both sides the relationship was paternalistic. The landlords as a group did not wish this relationship disturbed and the tenants had developed psychological attitudes which made dependence a normal condition."[33] Two-fifths of the families (this includes only those receiving relief at the time) were indebted to their landlords "with debts of more than one year's standing." Ninety percent of the landlords expressed "the opinion that share-cropping was a satisfactory arrangement for both landlords and tenants."[34] There was a decided tendency "among landlords to shift the responsibility of maintaining their tenants to governmental agencies," but "the conventional belief that the care of tenants was the landlord's function apparently persisted much as in the past. It is obviously basic to the sharecropping system."[35]

The intimate details of the relationship between planter and sharecropper are clearly set forth in the following letter. A Negro sharecropper appeals to his former employer for help as follows:

———, La.
Dec. 9. 1938

M.r.———

Dear Sir while seting down thanking of my troubles i throught that i would rite you a fure lines to ask you please sir come out here and let me talk to you M.r. if please get me out i will do any thing that you wont me to do i tell you what i will to i will Make a crop in 39 and it will Be yourse all i wants is a living and if you dont Believe it you come out here and i will go to M.r.———[sheriff] and sing a contract with you and you know that i mean what i say M.r.———i feel Mity Bad in here and for the next thing my family is sufering an i wonts to Be where i can take cure of them—i have never Bend in Jail But twiste in my life and it is Bend a long time ago. M.r. you know every since i Bend with you aint had a Minute trouBle with me i Never Sased you one Minute They say that i got Drunk and went around to Mister ——— ——— and curst him and if i did M.r. ——— i cant RememBer it But i wont say that i dident But i will say if i had of Knew that i did wouldent did it for nothing and that what they arrested Me for and Mister ——— if you

[33] Harold C. Hoffsommer, *Landlord-Tenant Relations and Relief in Alabama*, Federal Emergency Relief Administration, Washington (mimeographed), 1935, p. i.
[34] *Ibid.*
[35] *Ibid.*, p. 2.

come and get me out i will promous you that i wont leave home to come Near town Mister i wont Neve give you No More trouBle with me please sir and i Mean rain or shine coal or Hot i will work Just to Be out of here and i mean i will do any thing you say so plase sire come at once from——[36]

It is important to note, however, that World War II brought about some changes which are greatly reducing the importance of sharecropping as a type of accommodation. With the outbreak of war the planters who had followed the letter and spirit of the Agricultural Adjustment Administration's regulations found themselves seriously handicapped in comparison with their fellows who had pursued their own individual self-interests. In other words, the planter who did not mechanize his production and continued through the thirties to maintain his quota of sharecroppers found himself very badly off in comparison with his neighbor who ignored regulations and substituted power and machinery for the labor of families of sharecroppers. With the coming of the war, the workers deserted the plantations for higher-paying jobs in the war plants, and many of the planters who had held off were forced to change their system of production at a time when it was almost impossible to secure the necessary machinery and equipment. Out of this situation has come a firm resolve on the part of many never again to place themselves so completely at the mercy of labor—just as quickly as machinery is available to mechanize production as far as possible.[37]

Another of the most interesting and significant processes of accommodation now under way in rural America is that going on between farmers' trade centers of various types. The time was when every trade center, from the general store at the crossroads to the large wholesale and retail center, was striving to be a complete service center for all the farmers tributary to it. Every village and hamlet, from those that grew around essential services to those artificially propagated by the coming of the railroad, had visions of growing and developing into a large metropolis. Many village policies were framed with this as the basic consideration, not the question of most efficiently and satisfactorily filling the immediate need of the farmers of its trade basin. The merchants

[36] The writer is indebted to Dr. E. A. Schuler for permission to use this document.

[37] Cf. Alvin L. Bertrand, "The Social Processes and Mechanization of Southern Agricultural Systems," *Rural Sociology*, XIII (1948), 31–39.

in a given village, instead of concerning themselves with the type of service they were best fitted to render, frequently banded together and subsidized highly uneconomic specialized retail units, such as shoe stores, to persuade them to locate in the village. Before the coming of the automobile and hard-surfaced roads, the internal structure of farm trade centers showed little tendency toward specialization; every trading place from the open-country store up was in serious competition with every other.

Galpin early observed the intense competition between existing trade centers, sensed the importance of the automobile and good roads in the competitive process, and reflected upon the changes that were to occur. According to him, when the cross-roads post office was replaced by the rural free delivery route, a decline occurred in the hamlet. Farmers began to relate themselves to larger and larger towns. Hamlets and villages were started on an endurance test for their lives. The coming of the automobile made it still more difficult for the small and inefficient centers to survive, until "we can watch the phenomenon of the passing of the hoe-farmers' hamlet and the rise of the machine-farmer's business center." And ". . . sooner or later the slow process of greater business economy will, if the present tendencies continue, relate each farmstead quite definitely to a single, complete, retail business center."[38] Thus it is evident that Galpin conceived the competition between trade centers as a bitter struggle that would end only when large numbers of them had been entirely eliminated. Out of this conflict he envisioned the time when there should emerge "five thousand up-to-date farmers' towns, replacing twenty-five thousand present incomplete centers of trade. . . . Five thousand terminal towns, 'terminal' in the sense that a town is at the end of a railway journey for goods, each town met by a complete highway system of a community character connecting it with the twelve hundred farm houses belonging to it!"[39] Galpin looked forward to the day when a planned system of highways would make supreme these farmers' towns or rurban communities.

Since Dr. Galpin wrote, however, nearly thirty years have passed and still the competition between trade centers has not

---

[38] Charles J. Galpin, *Rural Life*, New York, D. Appleton-Century Company, 1920, p. 91.

[39] Charles J. Galpin, *Rural Social Problems*, New York, D. Appleton-Century Company, 1924, p. 75.

brought about the looked-for results. Instead, careful analyses indicate that a process of accommodation has given rise to a quite different situation, preserved the great mass of the small trade centers, created new ones, and in general is making rural trading facilities much more of a differentiated system, rather than simplifying them as Galpin predicted. A detailed study of all trade centers in Louisiana from 1910 to 1931 indicates that the process of accommodation developed in the following manner in that state:

The manner in which the distribution of trade centers within the State has changed since 1901 is an outstanding example of the changes in general. There has been a tendency for centers of various sizes to distribute themselves more uniformly with regard to the area, population and resources of the State. Or the changes seem to be in the direction of a more efficient pattern of rural organization. This redistribution of centers in conjunction with improved methods of communication and transportation, has placed each family in frequent contact with several trade centers, which means that the loyalty of the farm family is divided among several centers instead of being confined to one. This, too, makes for heterogeneity in the locality group and decreases the differences between various locality groups.

From 1901 to 1931 important alterations took place in the internal structures of the trade centers. A fundamental tendency towards specialization and division of labor between trade centers was found to be under way. Analysis of the existing situation in 1931 showed that, despite much overlapping, the small centers were specializing in certain types of services, medium-sized centers in others, and the largest centers in still others. Analysis of changes since 1901 showed that this division of labor had become much more evident during the thirty-year period. In general small centers nearest the farms are ceasing the attempt to provide all services and concentrating their efforts upon certain types of enterprises for which their location gives them a comparative advantage. The types of enterprises offered by the smallest centers are: those which are most undifferentiated, those satisfying the most immediate needs, those most closely connected with agricultural production and those which process farm products. As centers became larger, these types became relatively less important, and more highly specialized types made their appearance. This has an immediate influence upon the behavior of the farm family. Small centers near the farm are resorted to for securing services which meet many of the most pressing needs; larger centers at a greater distance, for services satisfying other less immediate needs; and even the largest centers at considerable distance, for supplying some of the least press-ing needs of the farm family.

The manner in which centers are now distributed, and the internal changes they have been undergoing lead to the belief that small centers are not doomed to extinction. Probably part of the small centers, those which are poorly situated with respect to modern arteries of communication and transportation, will continue to decline and disappear; but others more favorably located will continue to serve many of the pressing and basic needs of the population im-mediately surrounding them. If leaders in small elementary trade centers correctly visualize the role the small trade centers are fitted to play and make the corresponding adjustments, the shock of present and future changes can be made less severe.[40]

On the basis of detailed studies in seven New York counties, Sanderson has generalized his results in a chart which supports in all essentials the conclusions outlined above. (See Figure 122.)

More recently a resurvey of Wake County, North Carolina, found that "particular trade centers, regardless of the number of services available, no longer have exclusive claim to serving the needs of rural people. Propinquity is not now a compelling force in the relationship between the people in the open country and a specific trade center."[41]

A study of the settlement of the Great Plains and of the sub-sequent cultural evolution in the area also gives a great deal of insight into the process of accommodation. In this case the more important aspects of the adjustment are those involved in the ac-

---

[40] T. Lynn Smith, *Farm Trade Centers in Louisiana, 1901 to 1931*, Louisiana AES Bulletin 234, Baton Rouge, 1933, pp. 54–55. Cf. Carle C. Zimmerman, *Farm Trade Centers in Minnesota, 1905–29*, Minnesota AES Bulletin 269, St. Paul, 1930, p. 20; Paul H. Landis, *South Dakota Town-Country Trade Relations, 1901–1931*, South Dakota AES Bulletin 274, Brookings, 1932, p. 43; Paul H. Landis, *The Growth and Decline of South Dakota Trade Centers, 1901–1933*, South Dakota AES Bulletin 279, Brookings, 1933, pp. 37–38; Harold C. Hoffsommer, *Relation of Cities and Larger Villages to Changes in Rural Trade and Social Areas in Wayne County, New York*, Cornell AES Bulletin 582, Ithaca, 1934, pp. 60–61; Dwight Sanderson, *Rural Social and Economic Areas in Central New York*, Cornell AES Bulletin 614, Ithaca, 1934, p. 95; and John H. Kolb and R. A. Polson, *Trends in Town-Country Relations*, Wisconsin AES Research Bulletin 117, Madison, 1933, pp. 20–31.

[41] Selz C. Mayo and Robert McD. Bobbitt, *Rural Organization: A Restudy of Locality Groups in Wake County, North Carolina*, North Carolina AES Technical Bulletin 95, Raleigh, 1951, p. 40. See also Paul J. Jehlik and Ray E. Wakeley, *Rural Organization in Process: A Case Study of Hamilton County, Iowa*, Iowa AES Research Bulletin 365, Ames, 1949, pp. 141–164; and Charles R. Hoffer, "The Changing Ecological Pattern in Rural Life," *Rural Sociology*, XIII (1948), 176–180.

commodation of social institutions to physiographic features that are radically different from those in which the institutions were generated and by which they were conditioned. No aspect of cultural evolution is more interesting, and few cases of accommodation have been more important to social welfare than those

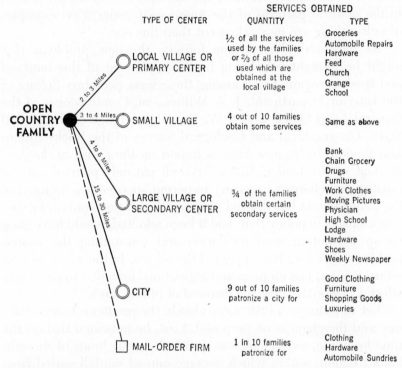

TYPE OF CENTER	SERVICES OBTAINED	
	QUANTITY	TYPE
LOCAL VILLAGE OR PRIMARY CENTER	½ of all the services used by the families or ⅔ of all those used which are obtained at the local village	Groceries Automobile Repairs Hardware Feed Church Grange School
SMALL VILLAGE	4 out of 10 families obtain some services	Same as above
LARGE VILLAGE OR SECONDARY CENTER	¾ of the families obtain certain secondary services	Bank Chain Grocery Drugs Furniture Work Clothes Moving Pictures Physician High School Lodge Hardware Shoes Weekly Newspaper
CITY	9 out of 10 families patronize a city for	Good Clothing Furniture Shopping Goods Luxuries
MAIL-ORDER FIRM	1 in 10 families patronize for	Clothing Hardware Automobile Sundries

FIGURE 122. "Diagram of the Relations to Service Centers of an Average Open-Country Family Living Within the Service Areas of a Medium-Sized Village." (Reproduced from Dwight Sanderson, *Rural Social and Economic Areas in Central New York*, Cornell AES Bulletin 614, Ithaca, 1934, p. 95.)

involved in the most satisfactory use of the resources of the plains states.

Prior to the settlement of the Great Plains in the latter half of the nineteenth century, American institutions had evolved in a natural environment whose predominant features were (1) a humid climate, (2) forested lands, and (3) gently rolling to hilly terrain. As the frontier edged forward through the semihumid fringe of the plains and onto the plains proper, these natural features gave way to a world that was semiarid, treeless, and relatively flat. Although a foresighted few recognized that existing institutions were inadequate to cope with the problems of settlement and successful living in this radically different milieu, they were like voices "crying in the wilderness." The processes of settlement went rapidly on along the lines previously deeply graved in the cultural patterns of the American frontier. Few examples of cultural lag are more clear-cut than this one.

As indicated above, some foresaw the new problems that might be brought into being by the settlement of this semiarid and treeless region. Chief among these were Secretary Schurz of the Interior Department; J. A. Williamson, Commissioner of the General Land Office; and J. W. Powell, in charge of the United States Geographical and Geological Survey of the Rocky Mountain Region. In his now famous *Report on the Lands of the Arid Regions of the United States*,[42] Powell not only pointed out the institutional changes necessary to permit successful settlement of the plains region but drafted proposed legislation containing specific changes in policy that, had it been adopted, would have gone far in promoting accommodation and forestalling the serious problems that long have plagued the region. In the words of Secretary Schurz, Powell proposed legislation "intended to carry into effect a new system for the disposal of public lands."[43]

Let us examine a little more closely the problems Powell foresaw and the changes he proposed. First, he indicated that, at the time he wrote, settlement was approaching the limits of the sub-humid region, within which average annual rainfall varied from twenty to twenty-eight inches. West of the isohyetal line of twenty inches of rainfall, roughly delineated by the 100th meridian (which forms the eastern boundary of the Texas Panhandle and divides the Dakotas into nearly equal parts) successful agriculture is possible only by means of irrigation. Adequate water being unavailable through most of the vast area, Powell thought that the land should be devoted almost exclusively to grazing— "pasturage farms," in his own terminology. In his estimation these pasturage farms needed to be many times the size of the conventional 160-acre homesteads, and he recommended 2560 acres as a

[42] House of Representatives, Executive Document No. 73, 45th Congress, 2nd Session, Washington, Government Printing Office, 1878.
[43] *Ibid.*, p. iv.

minimum size. He also thought that they should each include or be operated in connection with a small irrigated tract not to exceed twenty acres in size. In order that the limited water supply should not be monopolized by a few, it was recommended that the established system of regular land surveys and apportionments be abandoned, that the surveys be made to conform to topographic features, and especially that the amount of water front be limited. To provide for the adequate functioning of schools, churches, and other institutions, and to facilitate social intercourse, he recommended the grouping of farmhouses. Powell seems to have envisioned a line village settlement pattern, with the houses strung along the watercourses on twenty-acre irrigated plots. To fence the vast sparsely sodded areas was thought far too costly, and as a consequence there was recommended the development of communal regulations to govern the grazing of herds.

The texts of the two bills recommended for Congressional action are also informative. The first of these bills related to irrigation districts and included the following provisions: (1) Nine or more persons should be entitled to form an irrigation district, and adopt any bylaws, not in conflict with more general statutes, for the division and use of the water and the land; (2) any area containing as much as 320 acres susceptible of irrigation should be classed as irrigable; (3) each irrigation district should constitute a continuous tract of land and no person should possess more than eighty acres in it; and (4) the right to the water should inhere in and be inseparable from the land.

The second of the proposed bills dealt with pasturage districts and included the following provisions: (1) Nine or more persons should be empowered to form a pasturage district and to adopt any bylaws, not in conflict with more general regulations, for controlling the use of the water and pasture in the district; (2) each person should be entitled to 2560 acres of land all in one piece, except that as much as twenty acres of the total might be a separate piece of irrigable land; and (3) all lands in those parts of the United States in which irrigation is necessary for successful agriculture, except those irrigable tracts of 320 acres or more and timbered tracts, should be classed as pasture lands and be open to settlement only under the provisions of this act.

As is well known, no such modifications in our land policy as those proposed by Powell were ever put into general effect. Land

policies generated in and adapted to humid regions were continued when settlement overspread the plains. The wide expanses
of the arid, treeless plains were homesteaded in small tracts, and
a large part of them put under the plow.

But experience in the years since Powell wrote has thoroughly
substantiated his conclusion that most of these lands were better
suited for grazing than for the plow and that basic changes in
land policies were essential. Almost before the ink was dry on
the Powell report, the region had become a problem area. As he
was writing, there was a rapid influx of settlers into the western
plains. In the decade 1880 to 1890 population gains took place
amounting to 299 percent in the Dakotas, 265 percent in Montana,
201 percent in Wyoming, 135 percent in Nebraska, and 113 percent in Colorado.[44] But in the next decade drought was intense
and the area staged a dress rehearsal of the tragic "dust bowl"
era that was to come in the 1930's. Say Taeuber and Taylor: "Numerous homesteads were abandoned, and many persons who had
settled only recently in western Nebraska, western Kansas, Montana, Wyoming, Colorado, and New Mexico shifted to other parts.
The western sections of Kansas and Nebraska and the drier portions of other States suffered net losses in 114 counties, and some
areas were abandoned altogether. This was the time when the
population of Omaha, Nebraska, declined from 140,000 to 103,-
000."[45]

Depopulation and bitter experience promoted the process of
accommodation; but as the effects of the first disaster became
more remote, people again flocked onto the lands west of the
100th meridian. The First World War and the high prices for
wheat brought tremendous acreages of the arid lands under plow,
and with the destruction of the buffalo grass the stage was rapidly
set for the "dust bowl" disaster of the thirties.

The above data should not be interpreted to mean that the
process of accommodation was not working. Fundamental
changes were operating to bring about a more satisfactory adjustment of people and institutions to the natural environment. Indeed, it is unlikely that the process of accommodation has ever
moved more rapidly than it did in the plains states during the

[44] Conrad Taeuber and Carl C. Taylor, *The People of the Drought States*, Research Bulletin, Works Progress Administration, Washington, 1937, p. 15.
[45] *Ibid.*, p. 17.

last century. But the necessary adjustments were very great. Webb, in his suggestive work on *The Great Plains*,[46] describes many aspects of the accommodation process. He emphasizes the importance of a few inventions upon culture and adjustment in the region. For example, he attributes much importance to the influence of the invention and diffusion of the six-shooter, first in wresting the plains from the Indians and later in modifying the legal patterns inherited from the East. He also gives the particulars concerning the invention of the barbed-wire fence, and treats in detail the role of barbed wire in the settlement of the treeless plains. This new cultural trait made it economically possible to graze livestock without the benefit of the free range, and also enabled the agriculturist to protect his crops from the free-ranging cattle. Without economical fencing the shift from grazing to agriculture would have been impossible. Therefore, one might defend the thesis that the invention of barbed wire brought calamity to the people of the plains. The third invention stressed by Webb as being of great importance in accommodating to the plains environment is the windmill. He shows how this freed settlement from the necessity of confining itself to the immediate proximity of streams and springs and permitted it to spread over the entire area. Other aspects of the necessary adjustment included the enlarging of the homestead unit and the revision of land and water laws. But the process of accommodation was also affecting land policy. Under pressure from the West, Congress reversed the previous trend toward smaller homesteads and increased them to sizes more adaptable to plains situations. Unfortunately it did not carry through to the full extent Powell's recommendations mentioned above. Gradually the lawmakers revised the land and water laws to recognize the value and necessity of timber culture and of grazing; revised statutes came to place more emphasis on water and less on land; and there were also changes in water laws and riparian rights.

But the accommodation process must still make much headway before the inhabitants of the Great Plains will have a culture adjusted to the environment. Recurrent droughts will probably continue to plague the people of the region. However, since World War II a succession of wet years and high prices for wheat seem

[46] Walter Prescott Webb, *The Great Plains*, Boston, Houghton Mifflin Company, 1936, *passim.*

to have caused many people to forget the hardships and depopulation of 1930 to 1940. In view of this fact the findings of a recent study in North Dakota are particularly significant. "Since 1930, North Dakota has lost one-third of its farm population, declines in the 53 counties ranging from 20 to 50 percent. Generally, the losses were greater to the westward where settlement was most sparse. . . . Basically, the declines in population have made for a better balance between people and the land. Differences in living levels between the various parts of the state seem to have narrowed. Farms are becoming better adapted to climatic and technological conditions."[47]

Assimilation

Not only does the southern system of sharecropping represent one of the most important processes of accommodation now operating in rural America, but the incorporation of hundreds of thousands of whites in the pattern offers one of the most significant examples of assimilation. This appears to have reached its maximum around 1930 or 1935, when the number of croppers was the largest on record and the geographic dispersion of the sharecropping system the greatest. According to the 1935 Census data, the number of colored sharecroppers in the southern states totaled 368,408, and the number of white only slightly less, 347,848.[48] Quantitatively, sharecropping was almost as prevalent among whites as Negroes. Geographically, whites disseminated the cropping culture pattern much more widely than the Negroes.

The evidence also seems to indicate that the whites have been so thoroughly incorporated into the system that in many respects the outlook and status of the white sharecropper are not very different from those of his Negro fellow. Charles S. Johnson has written as follows: "What stands out starkly now is the fact that the changing tides of cotton farming have finally and fatally reduced white and black tenants alike to a status but a step removed from feudalism."[49] At the present time a given plantation may shift suddenly from Negro to white labor, or vice versa; families of one race

[47] A. H. Anderson, *Changes in Farm Population and Rural Life in Four North Dakota Counties,* North Dakota AES Bulletin 375, Fargo, 1952, p. 3. Cf. the report of the National Resources Planning Board entitled *Northern Great Plains,* Washington, Government Printing Office, 1940.

[48] *U.S. Census of Agriculture, 1935,* Washington, Government Printing Office, 1937, III, 126.

[49] See *Problems of the Cotton Economy,* Proceedings of the Southern Social Science Research Conference held in New Orleans, 1935, Dallas, Texas, 1936, p. 46.

move into cabins recently vacated by those of the other, and on the same terms; women and children of the white race work in the fields as do the Negroes; and many plantations depend entirely upon white people for labor.[50] Hoffsommer reports from Alabama that the landlords believed it to be their obligation to take care of the sharecroppers, and the croppers expected aid from the planters whenever "they got into a tight place," and that this attitude of dependence was found in a slightly higher proportion of the white than of the Negro household.[51] On the basis of his intensive study of two Georgia counties, Raper reports that there is a tendency for "tenure types of the two races to parallel each other in the same area,"[52] and he also states that "the white and Negro tenants [croppers], competing within the system . . . are now the common heirs to its impositions."[53] So thoroughly have the whites been assimilated into the sharecropping system that the stereotype of the "childlike" cropper, improvident and laboring regularly only because of hunger, now fits them as well as the Negroes. Likewise the cropper's basic assumption that there is "nothin' but a livin' in it" for him finds as ready acceptance by the white man as by the Negro. A concrete case is described by Raper:

A white tenant, with wife and three young children, has $75 cash in hand upon settlement, $65 of which he used to make an initial payment on a second-hand automobile priced to him at $116. At the end of the first week the car was in need of repairs. Three years later the car—with no tires, top broken, and most of the upholstering gone—still stood back of the cabin, and was the prized toy of the children of the Negro tenant family which had moved in when the white family moved to another plantation three miles away. . . .

This white tenant's foolish expenditure was made in spite of his landlord's effort to get him to use his money on his family. The tenant listened to the landlord politely enough, but he wanted an automobile, and it was his own money and he would spend it as he liked.[54]

Acculturation

Studies on the blendings of culture are only in their beginning stages. In the analysis of culture contacts between primitive

---

[50] Cf. Albert Bushnell Hart, *The Southern South*, New York, D. Appleton-Century Company, 1910, p. 45.

[51] *Landlord-Tenant Relations* . . . , p. 2.

[52] *Op. cit.*, p. 150.

[53] *Ibid.*, p. 157.

[54] *Ibid.*, p. 161. See also Arthur Raper and Ira De A. Reid, *Sharecroppers All*, Chapel Hill, University of North Carolina Press, 1941, *passim*.

groups the cultural anthropologists have made a creditable beginning, but much less is known concerning the nature of the cultural
fusions occurring among more advanced civilizations. Despite the
fact that rural America has long been a great crucible in which
the most heterogeneous cultural elements have been blended into
something of a cultural unity, the details of this process are still
unknown. In this field, as in so many others, the questions that can
be asked are of much greater significance than those that can be
answered.

Several beginnings have been made in the kind of analysis essential before the workings of the process of acculturation among
the rural social groupings of America can be understood. Fundamental to all is a study of social origins, and fortunately this has
not been entirely neglected. In tracing the history of American
agriculture, for example, the contributions of the American Indian
have been noted. It is well known that the cultivation of maize,
Irish potatoes, sweet potatoes, beans, squash, tomatoes, pine-
apples, tobacco, peanuts, several varieties of cotton, and many
other plants was among the cultural practices of the aborigines of
this hemisphere.[55] It has also been pointed out that the Indian's
agricultural methods were made part and parcel of the farm practices of the colonists.[56] For example, "Planting corn, potatoes,
beans and other plants of New World origin in hills and then
heaping the earth about their stalks during cultivation is still a fundamental process in our present-day farming. . . ."[57] From the
Indians also came the methods of preparing many foods for consumption.[58] An important field for research would be a thorough
analysis of the elements in contemporary agricultural systems, indicating both material and nonmaterial elements borrowed from
the Indians; those brought here by the first colonists; those derived from various ethnic and cultural groups migrating since the

[55] Cf. W. E. Safford, "Our Heritage from the American Indians," *Smithsonian
Institution Annual Report for 1926*, Washington, 1927, pp. 405–410.

[56] Cf. Lyman Carrier, *The Beginnings of Agriculture in America*, New York,
McGraw-Hill Book Company, 1923, pp. 93–101.

[57] Everett E. Edwards, *Agriculture of the American Indians*, United States Department of Agriculture, Library Biographical Contributions 23 (Edition 2),
mimeographed, Washington, 1933, p. ix. See also O. F. Cook, "The Debt of Agriculture to Tropical America," *Smithsonian Institution Annual Report for 1931*,
Washington, 1932, pp. 491–501.

[58] Cf. Alexander F. Chamberlain, "The Contributions of the American Indian
to Civilization," *Proceedings of the American Antiquarian Society*, XVI (1904),
91–126.

Revolution; and those invented or discovered on this continent since the arrival of the white man. Until this has been made, little understanding of the basic factors in agricultural progress and change can be secured. Similar investigations are needed with respect to food habits and many other phases of our culture. In the absence of such thoroughgoing studies it is doubtful, even, if the cultural differences between the various regions can be properly evaluated. To what extent are the agricultural practices of the Midwest the product of a cultural blending of the best ideas, skills, techniques of Europe grafted on the old Indian and colonial stock? Do those of the South represent primarily an evolution of the cross between Indian and colonial sources? Had immigration been lacking, would the agricultural techniques of the United States be as far advanced as they are? What is the correct role of agricultural experimentation in the growth and diffusion of agricultural skills?

The great variety and wealth of ideas and skills brought to this country by immigrants have seldom received much attention. The ordinary researches of the historian are not sufficient on this point. Other studies such as the one by John P. Johansen of South Dakota State College are greatly needed.[59] Quite properly he points out the naïveté of considering the process by which the immigrant stock—with all its material objects, customs, social organization, etc.—becomes merged with the larger community as one-sided. "The process is two-sided or many-sided; it is mutual and not one-sided in nature."[60] Because all the phases of culture are affected, as well as individual persons, he indicates that the process is more properly referred to as acculturation than assimilation. With data for immigrant churches, he makes a good beginning in outlining the workings of the process of acculturation in the state of South Dakota.[61]

More recently Douglas G. Marshall has contributed an important analysis of the process of acculturation among the Norwegians, Poles, Welsh, and other ethnic groups in rural Minnesota. As might be expected, the groups with values approximating those of the established community were readily accepted, while some of the other ethnic groups experienced more difficulty. Eventually,

[59] *Immigrant Settlements and Social Organization in South Dakota,* South Dakota AES Bulletin 313, Brookings, 1937.
[60] *Ibid.,* p. 52.
[61] *Ibid.,* pp. 52–61; see also John and Ruth Hill Useem, "Minority-Group Pattern in Prairie Society," *American Journal of Sociology,* L (1945), 377–385.

however, all who remained were "infected" by the patterns prevailing among the dominant group. But acculturation was not a one-way process: "Not only does the value system of the Polish and Norwegian change because of his associations with the Welsh, but so does that of the Welsh." The results of the study seem in line with the remark of the late George S. Wehrwein that "it takes three generations of a family to own a piece of land and four generations to erase their more obvious old world characteristics."[62]

From Oklahoma comes a significant study of acculturation in rural areas.[63] There, where the New South converges with the West, has occurred a blending of the Indian cultures of many tribes with those of French, Spanish, and Anglo-American heritage. Adding still further to the racial and cultural mixture was a goodly proportion of Negroes. Duncan has made a good beginning at breaking the resulting culture pattern down into the component parts from which it has been derived, thus promoting a better understanding and appreciation of the product.

New Mexico also offers an excellent laboratory for the study of acculturation in rural areas. This territory, acquired from Mexico following the Mexican War, contains large rural elements that have never been incorporated into the dominant cultural pattern. Stephen Powers early called attention to the fact that extraneous ethnic elements were rapidly incorporated thoroughly into the Spanish American culture,[64] but careful studies of acculturation in

[62] "Nationality and the Emerging Culture," *Rural Sociology*, XIII (1948), 41–47. For studies of communities in which the process of acculturation has gone on more slowly, see Oscar F. Hoffman, "Culture Changes in a Rural Wisconsin Ethnic Island," *Rural Sociology*, XIV (1949), 39–50; R. L. Skrabanek and Vernon J. Parenton, "Social Life in a Czech-American Rural Community," *Rural Sociology*, XV (1950), 220–231; and Robert L. Skrabanek, "The Influence of Cultural Backgrounds on Farming Practices in a Czech-American Rural Community," *Southwestern Social Science Quarterly*, XXXI (1950), 258–266.

[63] O. D. Duncan, "The Fusion of White, Negro, and Indian Cultures at the Converging of the New South and the West," *Southwestern Social Science Quarterly*, XIV (1934), 357–369.

[64] *Afoot and Alone; A Walk from Sea to Sea by the Southern Route*, Hartford, Columbia Book Company, 1872, pp. 180–181. Powers wrote as follows:

"Ah! Brother Jonathan and Mr. John Bull, what becomes of your proud theory of the 'extirpating Saxon' in these frontier villages? Whose language do these little mongrel jackanapes, these young Mexican Partheniae, speak—yours, or that of the renowned Sancho Panza? Perhaps you don't understand bad Spanish. Do these poor Mexican girls learn English? or do their paramours rather learn Spanish? It is wonderful how the language of those grand old hidalgos, even when spoken by these mongrels, holds its own against the sharp and thrifty incursions of Americans. Even so is it in Tyrol, where the indolent and sunny children of Italy, though almost incomparably inferior in moral stamina and intellectual vigor

the area are only now getting under way. Sanchez has pointed out the inherent difficulties in the way of acculturation as two: (1) If the Spanish American lives in the village home of his ancestors, he is practically isolated from the social and economic contacts through which he might improve his condition, and he is inaccessible both physically and culturally to public agencies which might assist in the incorporation. (2) If he leaves his ancestral community to work in the sheep camps, in fruit and truck crops or cotton, he is unable to establish roots in the new community and remains on "the other side of the tracks" as one of "society's stepchildren."[65] Fortunately, this blending of cultures in the Spanish Southwest is now receiving deserved attention in a series of excellent studies.[66]

The writer and one of his colleagues have attempted limited studies of acculturation in Louisiana. The following brief abstract gives the essential results of one study:

The current obscurity enveloping the social process of acculturation challenges the analytical and descriptive skill of the sociologist. Louisiana, settled by a gradual infiltration of numerous and diverse European stocks, as well as a variety of distinct African types, offers an unexcelled laboratory for a study of this phenomenon. Of particular interest in this respect is the extent to which the white elements in this extremely heterogeneous mass have been absorbed into the French (mainly Acadian) culture of South Louisiana. Deiler [*The Settlement of the German Coast of Louisiana and the Creoles of German Descent*, Philadelphia, 1909], in a pioneering study of acculturation, demonstrated beyond all doubt the Germanic origin of many well-known Louisiana "French" family names. The assimilation of the Spanish and Anglo-Saxons by this virile group was even more significant, since it took place in spite of official efforts to accomplish the opposite. A social survey conducted in 1934 in two Louisiana parishes having a large Acadian population revealed entire households of various ethnic elements other than French who nevertheless claimed French descent and spoke French by preference. This transformation of the heterogeneous diversity of ethnic elements into the homo-

---

to the Germans, see their language steadily gaining. My brave and 'enterprising' countrymen, know you not that these wretched villagers, living in the Apache's land, are indebted for their very existence to the presence of less than a dozen of you? and yet you learn their language, and not they yours!"

[65] George I. Sanchez, *Forgotten People: A Study of New Mexicans*, Albuquerque, University of New Mexico Press, 1940, pp. 37–40, *passim*.

[66] See particularly Olen E. Leonard and Charles P. Loomis, *Culture of a Contemporary Rural Community: El Cerrito, New Mexico*, United States Department of Agriculture, Rural Life Studies 1, Washington, 1941.

geneous Acadian ethnic and cultural unity resulted largely from the presence of the following factors: (1) the intermarriage of the Acadian and French maidens with the masculine newcomers; (2) the dominance of the Acadian mother in child-rearing; (3) the influence of the Catholic priest; (4) the *esprit de corps* of the French-speaking people which engendered imitation; and finally (5), the way of life of the Acadians.[67]

But it should be repeated that much more study and research are necessary before the operation and results of the process of acculturation will be thoroughly understood.[68]

[67] T. Lynn Smith and Vernon J. Parenton, "Acculturation Among the Louisiana French," *American Journal of Sociology*, XLIV (1938), 355.

[68] North Americans will gain considerable insight into the basic nature of the process from a careful reading of José Arthur Rios, "Assimilation of Emigrants from the Old South in Brazil," *Social Forces*, XXVI (1947), 145–152.

24

SOCIAL MOBILITY

The shifting of persons or culture traits from one social group or class to another is properly referred to as social mobility. Movement from group to group without respect to vertical or class differences is known as *horizontal* mobility; and the shifting of traits or persons up or down the social scale, as *vertical* mobility. Social climbing or sinking may occur within the group on the part of the individual member, or it may take place through the whole group's gaining or losing status in the general society. A given change may include mobility of both types, and frequently the breaking of old group ties and the establishment of new ones are associated with changes of both a horizontal and a vertical nature. Migration, the movement of persons or traits in physical space, is associated with but not synonymous with social mobility. Nomadic tribes constantly on the move may exhibit little or no social mobility, and the social mobility that does exist is not a function of migration. But in sedentary societies the movement of a person from one territory to another is nearly always accompanied by the disruption of old group relationships and the establishment of new ones.[1]

General Characteristics and Effects of Social Mobility

Social mobility may occur in connection with any of the wide variety of social groups that become differentiated from one another in the course of social evolution. Particularly significant are those forms of mobility involving the increase or decrease of wealth and income; the gain or loss of prestige, power, privilege,

[1] P. A. Sorokin's *Social Mobility*, New York, Harper & Brothers, 1927, is the classic work on this subject. For the nature and forms of social mobility, see especially pp. 133–136. Cf. W. Lloyd Warner, Marchia Meeker, and Kenneth Eells, *Social Class in America*, Chicago, Science Research Associates, 1949, pp. 23–25.

and authority; and the shifting from one occupational group to another.

Some societies are highly mobile, others quite immobile. No society is known in which the various social classes or social strata have been entirely closed to members from the other layers, nor is any society known in which there have been absolutely no obstacles connected with shifts from one class or group to another. Sorokin in his valuable study of social mobility discovered no evidence of a perpetual trend of increase or decrease in mobility of the vertical type, but found this phenomenon to vary from place to place, group to group, and time to time. In a given society there appears to be a rhythmic variation from mobile periods to immobile periods. Mobility seems to be greater in the so-called democracies than in the autocracies, but there are many exceptions to the rule.[2] In vertical mobility, or the shifting up or down the social pyramid, a wide variety of social institutions serve as channels of circulation; many agencies may play the role of staircase or elevator. Important among these are the army, the church, the school, governmental hierarchies or bureaucracies, political parties, professional societies, economic organizations such as corporations, and the family. Their importance as channels of vertical social circulation, as agencies for lifting some persons up the social scale and debasing others, varies from time to time, place to place, and society to society; but some of them are always functioning to shift persons from one social class to another.[3] However, the rising and sinking of persons in the social scale is not a matter of chance. The same social institutions that serve as channels of vertical circulation also serve as agencies of testing and selection; these agencies sort and grade the persons in the population and tend to place them in a social class commensurate with their abilities. It is a fact of fundamental importance that the church, the school, the family, and the occupational institutions are not only agencies for passing on the cultural heritage from one generation to another but also agencies of selection and distribution, testing grounds that are largely responsible for the types of persons who rise or sink in a given society. If the institutions perform their functions well, the distribution of persons within the social classes will be equitable and in accordance with the capacities of the individuals; if they

[2] Sorokin, *op. cit.*, p. 160.
[3] *Ibid.*, pp. 164–180.

fail to perform efficiently the tasks of testing, selecting, and distributing the members of society throughout the social classes in an equitable manner, men located in positions for which they are not fitted can weaken or even destroy society itself.[4]

The factors of vertical mobility are many, but three seem to be primary. (1) Differential fertility of the social classes has the net result of creating a vacuum in the higher social layers and bringing about the rise of persons from the middle and lower classes to fill the vacancies created by the failure of the upper classes to reproduce themselves. (2) Biological variation continually endows some children with more ability than their parents, some children with less, so that the offspring are not suited for positions in society exactly corresponding to those occupied by their parents. These discrepancies cause some sinking and some rising on the social scale. (3) Every change of the cultural base, or man-made environment, affects the populations of the various social strata. In times of disorder—strikes, revolution, or war—a particular type of personality may arise rapidly which in times of peace might remain undisturbed in an inferior position.[5] Ulysses S. Grant, who rose to the command of the Union armies during the Civil War, was not very successful as a citizen before the war, not particularly brilliant in the Presidency with which he was rewarded after the conflict was over. The skilled artisan in the handicraft stage of society degenerates into the jack-of-all-trades under the factory system.

Effects of Mobility

The process of social mobility has significant and far-reaching effects upon the general nature of the great society, the personality of the individuals making it up, the system of social organization, and the nature of the other social processes. The general effects of social mobility are discussed immediately; those more peculiar to to rural society are given at the end of the chapter.

Intense vertical mobility that is generated through a progressive wasting of the upper classes of society, if long continued, ultimately leads to the disintegration of society itself. It may be that under such circumstances the city will progressively drain the superior elements of the population from the country, and the upper

[4] *Ibid.*, pp. 207–208.
[5] *Ibid.*, p. 373.

classes draw off the best elements from the middle and lower classes. Ultimately such a trend means the diminution of the best ethnic elements, the derivation of the entire population from the least fit portions of the population, the exhaustion of the elite, and the decay of the nation.[6] The effects of mobility on the personalities of society's members are more immediate. With an increase in mobility follow: (1) more plastic and versatile individual behavior; (2) less narrow-mindedness, intolerance, and provincialism; (3) more intellectuality, more superficiality, more mental strain, and more mental disease; (4) increased skepticism, misoneism, cynicism, psychosocial isolation and loneliness, and the search for sensual pleasures; and (5) the disintegration of the traditional mores.[7] The effects of mobility upon the other social processes and upon social organization are also pronounced. Normally mobility facilitates the distribution of individuals in an equitable manner among the social classes. It contributes to economic prosperity and rapid social change. It contributes to the disintegration of a given cultural pattern. Social mobility makes for complexity in social relationships and generally disrupts the lines of social cleavage between the various groups and classes. And finally it makes for an increase in individualism, usually followed by intensive efforts to develop on a contractual basis collectivism of a cosmopolitan type.[8]

Social Mobility in Rural Society

In Chapter 2 significant variations in social mobility were indicated as among the important factors differentiating the rural world from the urban. Quantitatively the differences are pronounced, mobility in rural areas being considerably less than in cities. Less divorce and separation, the tendency for the rural family to retain children within the parental home for longer periods than the urban family, and many other elements are evidences of lower interfamily mobility in the country than in the city. Occupationally, farm classes are recruited almost entirely from children of farmers, while the city in order to survive must necessarily recruit its newcomers from the rural areas; urban people shift occupations constantly; and in general occupational mobility is far greater in urban areas than in the open country.

[6] *Ibid.*, pp. 493–504.
[7] *Ibid.*, pp. 508–528.
[8] *Ibid.*, pp. 530–545.

Some of the factors contributing to the lower vertical mobility of the farming population have been noted in Chapted 2. Other factors making for less mobility, both vertical and horizontal, in rural areas are as follows: (1) The caste element is still prevalent in rural society, and this creates difficulties in the way of moving from one social stratum to another; (2) rural groups are comparatively few, with the result that there is little opportunity for changing from one group to another; (3) primary-group controls still continue as important factors in rural society and these serve to hamper the individual in his movement from group to group if not class to class; (4) the patriarchal element continues strong in rural society, and the vesting of control in the hands of the elders makes for less experimentation with the new, and consequently less shifting from group to group, than where the opposition to change is not so great; and (5) familism is still important in rural areas; the personality of the rural person is submerged in the group, with the result that the tempo of individual change is considerably slower than where family considerations are of less importance.

From the qualitative standpoint, too, there are probably important differences between social mobility in the country and in the city. It seems highly probable that a change from group to group or from class to class represents a much greater break with custom in the country than in the city.

It should also be indicated that there are wide variations in mobility among the various social classes of the open country. The planter class and the family-farm class, being relatively stable territorially, are also strongly attached to local institutions and shift but little from one social group to another. But this is not the case among the important cropper class, so near the bottom of the social pyramid in the South. Excessive territorial mobility is always mentioned as one of the outstanding characteristics of this group; it need only be noted that movement in space inevitably means the severing of ties with local institutions as often as the moves occur. Because croppers move about the first of January, in some plantation areas the rural schools have a turnover of 50 percent or more of their pupils in the middle of the school year. Corresponding changes occur in all the groups to which croppers are admitted; but, unfortunately, comprehensive studies of this and most other aspects of horizontal social mobility among rural people are still to be made.

Some of the most significant shifts, quantitatively and qualitatively, in the group affiliations of American farmers recently have been in the political field. Traditionally, the farmers of the northern states have been a tower of strength in the Republican party. In the elections of 1932 and 1936, however, they were to be found largely in the Democratic ranks. But the tide shifted, and in the 1940 and 1944 elections there seemed to be a tremendous swing of rural votes to the Republican column. However, in 1948 and 1950 they seemed to be once more strongly in the Democratic fold; and in 1952 they once more voted Republican. The fact to note is the wholesale shift from party to party in these elections.

Vertical Mobility

Long-continued interest in farm tenancy and farm ownership has given us studies of vertical social mobility among farmers that are very informing. It seems fair to say that this is one of the most adequately studied aspects of rural sociology. So fundamental are the differences in the patterns of social mobility in family-farm and plantation areas that the two may best be considered separately.

The Agricultural Ladder

The family-farm system of agriculture generates a distinct type of vertical mobility. This is present in all parts of the United States, but it is best illustrated in regions that are blanketed with family farms. Particularly significant for study are such areas when rapidly fluctuating land values do not endanger the operator's equity in the land and bring about corporation farming, chain farming, and various other types of absentee ownership. In family-farm areas the social pyramid is relatively low and flat, social classes are few, caste is unimportant, and a majority of the population occupies successively the various social strata in the pyramid. For analytical purposes it is important to seek the time and region in which this type of mobility may be observed in its purest form. Such was the situation in the midwestern states during the closing years of the nineteenth century and the opening decade of the twentieth. Students of land tenure early referred to the vertical mobility present in the system as "climbing the agricultural ladder." Generally speaking, the young farmer on his way to ownership began work as an unpaid laborer on the home farm and remained until the age of nineteen; then he probably hired out to neighboring farmers for a cash wage; after a brief interval in this category, or the second rung of the agricultural ladder, the young farmer amassed sufficient savings to purchase a team and equipment and advanced to the third rung of the ladder, the tenant or independent renter stage. Eventually farm ownership was attained by all but a small proportion.

The situation prevailing in such a system was early depicted clearly in the works of W. J. Spillman, Henry C. Taylor, and many others. Spillman analyzed the farming histories of 2112 owners in the states of Illinois, Iowa, Kansas, Nebraska, and Minnesota. One-fifth of all had passed through all four stages, occupied all four rungs of the agricultural ladder: starting as unpaid laborers on the home farm, they had been successively hired men, tenants, and owners. Thirteen percent of all had skipped the tenant stage but passed through the other three; 32 percent missed the hired-man stage, going directly from the home farm to the tenant category; and 34 percent passed directly to ownership from the category of unpaid laborers on the home farms. This last group of course contained that considerable number of farmers who had attained their land by inheritance.

Farmers passing through the hired-man stage left home at the average age of nineteen; those skipping the hired-man rung averaged twenty-three at the time of leaving home; and those passing directly to ownership from laboring on the home farm averaged 26.5 years upon attaining ownership. The farm owners who had started without capital worked from four to six years as hired men and from four to ten years as tenants, before beginning the purchase of farms of their own.[9] So general was the ascending current of vertical mobility that in 1900, even though 39.3 percent of all farm operators were tenants, only 10 percent of those who had attained the age of sixty-five years remained in the tenant category. And in the surrounding states the residuum remaining in the tenant category was even smaller: 8.6 percent in Iowa, 7.6 in Indiana, and 4.1 in Wisconsin.[10]

Since 1890 the Bureau of the Census has been collecting and

[9] W. J. Spillman, "The Agricultural Ladder," *American Economic Review Supplement*, IX (1919), 170–179.

[10] Henry C. Taylor, *Agricultural Economics*, New York, The Macmillan Company, 1923, p. 266. For the report of an interesting analysis of the social circumstances associated with establishing a foothold as a farm operator in one Iowa area, see Robert A. Rohwer, "Social Relations in Beginning as a Farm Operator in an Area of Prosperous, Commercial Farming," *Rural Sociology*, XIV (1949), 325–335.

tabulating data to show the tenure status of farm operators classified according to age. These materials constitute a great fund of information that may be used in a study of the operation of the agricultural ladder.[11] Unfortunately the farm labor stage is missing from these tabulations, and the data also suffer from the weakness common to practically all agricultural statistics for the South, in that one category of laborers (sharecroppers) is mixed in with the farm operators. In spite of this, however, the data are our most important source of information concerning vertical social mobility in the farming population of the United States.

A particularly significant analysis is to note the decreasing proportion of tenants, or the increasing proportion of owners, as the age of operators increases. This can be shown graphically as in Figure 123, an illustration that gives data for the United States and for the South, with information for the races placed in separate categories. Significant indeed is the small proportion of the white farm operators of the United States who remain in the category of tenants after age sixty-five is attained. Even in the South it is surprisingly low. Among Negroes the situation is different, owing in part to their closer association with the plantation system, but probably largely to the fact that the same government that forced their freedom abandoned practically all responsibility for inculcating in them the habits, skills, techniques, etc., essential to climbing the agricultural ladder or, indeed, to decent independent living at any level. Such training in the arts of advancement as they have received has been largely at the hands of the very communities that were economically strangled by their emancipation, the war, and the reconstruction period.

The time required to pass from one rung of the agricultural ladder to another varies widely from time to time and place to place. In the black lands of Texas in the period before 1889 an average of 7.1 years was required to attain tenancy, and an average of 16.1 years of agricultural experience preceded ownership; between 1889 and 1899, the corresponding averages changed to 4.9 and 13; in the next decade they fell to 2.2 and 9.4; and by 1909–1919 they were only 1.3 and 4.3, respectively.[12]

[11] These materials have been used rather extensively. One of the most thoroughgoing analyses is to be found in E. A. Goldenweiser and Leon E. Truesdell, *Farm Tenancy in the United States*, 1920 Census Monographs IV, Washington, 1924, pp. 83–116.

[12] J. T. Sanders, *Farm Ownership and Tenancy in the Black Prairie of Texas*, U.S. Department of Agriculture Bulletin 1068, Washington, 1922, p. 37.

The above remarks and data should not be interpreted to mean that one-way traffic is the general rule on the agricultural ladder. Many reverses of direction occur, and it is likely that slipping back is accentuated in times of severe financial depression. Such rever-

PERCENT OF OWNERS AMONG ALL FARM OPERA- TORS BY AGE

SOUTH

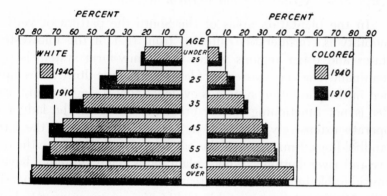

UNITED STATES

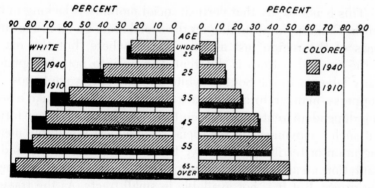

FIGURE 123. The Agricultural Ladder in the United States and the South, 1910 and 1940.

sals, however, were not confined to the last great depression. For example, a 1922 study of 368 farmers on the black prairies of Texas showed that the following proportions of the following tenure groups had suffered one or more reverses, dropped one or more rungs on the agricultural ladder: croppers, 60 percent; share tenants, 29.8 percent; part owners, 19.2 percent; and owner-operators, 14.5 percent.[13] Williams' studies in South Carolina open up another important aspect of vertical social mobility that deserves intensive study. In his sample of 2000 South Carolina farm families he discovered that the children of owners start on the lower rungs of the agricultural ladder and ascend step by step, but that rare was the case in which a child of a tenant rose out of the tenant class.[14]

Large-Scale Agriculture and Vertical Mobility

In the plantation areas of the South the pattern of vertical mobility is considerably different from that of the midwestern states and other regions where the family-farm system is predominant. The very existence of large-scale agriculture as exemplified in the plantation system is evidence that the agricultural ladder is not functioning to any great extent. Were the ladder to operate extensively, it would in a short time destroy the large landholdings. Furthermore, the patterns of mobility set in the deltas and river bottoms, where plantations reign supreme, have a considerable influence in the areas of small holdings in the nearby hills. Other states too, notably California, are given over to large estates and include vast areas in which the agricultural ladder functions weakly.

This is not to say that vertical social mobility is lacking in the South. Climbing and sinking on the social scale go on in the rural areas of the region just as they do elsewhere, but the nature of the general pattern is different. Contrary to popular opinion, many laborers in the South—white and colored, wage hands and croppers—manage to accumulate enough capital to make a start as independent renters and even to begin the purchase of farms. But such a movement in the social scale almost inevitably means migration or territorial mobility. There is of course much land in plantation areas for sale; sometimes it may be had at extremely low prices. But it is not available in small tracts. As the traveler Charles Nordhoff wrote of the South in 1875: "Nobody, except a land-speculator, likes to sell land; especially where it has been his home. And these people are not land-speculators."[15] The planter

[13] *Ibid.*, p. 34.
[14] B. O. Williams, "Mobility and Farm Tenancy," *Journal of Land and Public Utility Economics*, XIV (1938), 207–208.
[15] *The Cotton States in the Spring and Summer of 1875*, New York, D. Appleton and Company, 1876, p. 71.

would have to possess the skills and techniques of the real-estate dealer to subdivide and sell his lands to small holders successfully. Furthermore, even if he were willing to attempt this, the task of getting sufficient purchasers for his entire acreages at one time would be far beyond his capacities. To sell off parts of the plantation year after year would mean a continual readjustment of plantation operations. Most planters, wisely from their own standpoint, either sell the plantation in its entirety or keep it all. Governmental agencies such as the Federal Land Bank pursue the same course. The net result is, with the plantation system monopolizing the best land in the South as it does,[16] that it is practically impossible for those ascending the agricultural ladder to attain the status of either independent renter or owner in the good land areas. Renters and owner-operators, both white and Negro, appear in "the out-of-the-way, or neglected tracts, in the nooks and corners between the creeks. . . ."[17] Reported Frances Butler Leigh in 1883:

Notwithstanding their dissatisfaction at the settlement, six thousand dollars was paid out among them, many getting as much as two or three hundred apiece. The result was that a number of them left me and bought land of their own, and at one time it seemed doubtful if I should have hands at all left to work. The land they bought, and paid forty, fifty dollars and even more for an acre, was either within the town limits, for which they got no titles, and from which they were soon turned off, or out in the pine woods, where the land was so poor they could not raise a peck of corn to the acre. These lands were sold to them by a common class of men, principally small shopkeepers and

[16] M. B. Hammond, *The Cotton Industry*, New York, 1897, pp. 62–63, indicated this correlation and analyzed some of the factors which tended to fasten this system to the South. Says he: "The inevitable tendency of cotton culture under slavery to seek out the most fertile lands in the South, kept these lands out of the hands of the non-slave holders, and rendered competition in cotton growing by white labor on the small farms almost impossible. In the Southwest, the great cotton producing country, De Bow, 'Industrial Resources,' II:106, says: 'The non-slave holders possess generally but very small means, and the land which they possess is almost universally poor and so sterile that a scanty subsistence is all that can be derived from it cultivation, and the more fertile soil being in the hands of the slave holders, must ever remain out of the power of those who have none.' To have worked as a hired laborer on the large plantation, cultivating cotton alongside of the negro slave, was too much of a social disgrace for the self-respecting white man in the South to undergo. To 'work like a nigger!' the southern way of expressing contempt for the white man who was obliged to earn his living in this way, proved a hindrance which not only prevented the 'poor whites' in the South from rising in the scale of life, but repelled European immigrants from the southern shores."

[17] Arthur Raper, *Preface to Peasantry*, Chapel Hill, University of North Carolina Press, 1936, p. 129; cf. pp. 105–106.

Jews (the gentlemen refusing to sell their land to the Negroes, al-though they occasionally rented it to them), and most frightfully cheated the poor people were. But they had got their land, and were building their little log cabins on it, fully believing that they were to live on their property and incomes the rest of their lives, like gentle-men.[18]

Since Mrs. Leigh wrote, the situation has changed but little. The plantation has continued to blanket the most productive soils; the independent renter and the owner-operator have no part in such a system;[19] and those ascending the agricultural ladder have to abandon the districts in which the plantation continues for the poor piney woods area or the areas of disintegrating plantations if they are to set themselves up as farm operators. Annually, families which have acquired a little livestock and capital while working under close supervision as croppers on the plantation move from the plantation to nearby piney woods areas in the hills and bargain to rent or purchase a farm. Some of them stay, eking out a meager existence on the poor soils of such areas for the remainder of their days. Probably a larger number, however, soon dissipate their meager resources, lose their livestock, equipment, and even the payments they have put into their land, and make their way back to the plantations to begin again as sharecroppers. A considerable degree of social mobility of the vertical type is exhibited in these cases, but unfortunately positions on the top rung of the agricul-tural ladder (farm ownership) are almost impossible to achieve and retain.

Within the plantation system, too, there are established pat-terns of vertical mobility. Brooks'has described one of the impor-tant cycles as follows:

The history of the normal negro agricultural laborer is about as fol-lows. He begins as a youth working for wages. As soon as he has a family that can be utilized for field work he becomes a share tenant.

[18] *Ten Years on a Georgia Plantation Since the War*, London, R. Bentley & Son, 1883, pp. 78–79.

[19] The presence of any considerable number of renters on a plantation is an in-dication that that particular unit is in its last stage of decay. When the land comes into the possession of an owner who lacks the ability or the will to engage in entrepreneurial activities, a host of renters is likely to appear. Former laborers from the estate and those nearby give the owner a share of the produce in ex-change for the privilege of farming selected portions of the estate. See Raper, *op. cit.;* and W. M. Macmillan, *Warning from the West Indies*, London, Faber and Faber Limited, 1936, pp. 74–75, 100–101.

Under the semi-compulsion of this system, he makes good profits, and, if he has any capacity for saving, can in a short time buy a mule and a few tools, and set up as a renter. So great has been the competition for laborers and so completely have the negroes had the upper hand in the matter, that negro wage earners and share hands have in many instances been able to achieve an independent position even without the inconvenience of having to save the small amount necessary to stock a renter's farm. In thousands of cases where there was not the slightest reason to anticipate success from the venture, landlords have been forced to sell to negroes on credit tools and work animals or to rent the equipment along with the land, and to set up laborers as renters. Being, in the mass, of low grade efficiency, the cash tenant begins getting in debt the first year; after two or three years everything he has is taken for debt, and he returns to his former position of day laborer or share tenant.[20]

Brooks adds in a footnote:

The following extract from the report on a Brooks County plantation gives a typical case of negro experience as a renter. "Anthony Moore, a splendid worker, had a farm on this plantation, twenty acres in cotton and fifteen in corn, in 1905. He made thirteen bales of cotton and a large quantity of corn (working as a share tenant). The attached original account (a sheet torn from the plantation ledger) shows the large amount of cash this negro got during the year, as well as other advances, and the credits of cotton, half of the bale being credited in each case. He settled up the entire account and had corn and meal extra, not to mention the $100 in cash which he got just prior to the final settlement. This negro abandoned the place the following year, because the landlord would not rent to him and he had enough to buy a mule. He rented a farm from Mr. ——, another Brooks County planter, and wound up his first year $70 in debt and nothing to show for the year's work. His former employer was interested to see how the case would turn out, as this was a good negro, as far as his application to work was concerned. The next year the deficit was taken up by another planter, named ——. At the end of that year, he was worse off than at the end of the former year. The negro came to Mr. ——, the original employer, last Sunday and told him of his troubles. Mr. —— expects him to go back to work as a cropper, but has no doubt that as soon as he pays out of debt and saves enough to buy an animal he will again resort to renting. His observation is that after an unusually good crop year, it is very difficult to get labor for the

[20] Robert Preston Brooks, *The Agrarian Revolution in Georgia, 1865–1912*, University of Wisconsin Historical Series III, Madison, 1914, pp. 60–61.

following year. The negroes have all made money and do not want to work again as croppers, that is, practically day laborers receiving their pay at the end of the year."[21]

Other studies have contributed much to the data and understanding of mobility in the South. Some of the most important

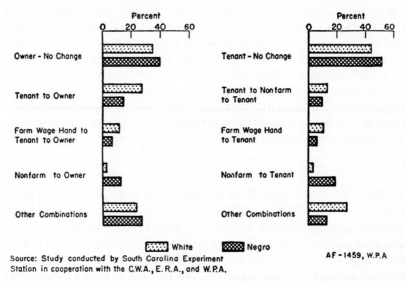

FIGURE 124. Occupational History of 1830 South Carolina Farmers, by 1933 Tenure and by Color. (Reproduced from T. J. Woofter, et al., *Land-lord and Tenant on the Cotton Plantation*, Works Progress Administration Research Monograph V, Washington, 1936, p. 120.)

studies are those by B. O. Williams. For 1830 South Carolina farmers, of whom 1046 were whites and 744 Negroes, Williams traced the entire occupational history, noting both changes in residence and changes in status. White farm owners in the group numbered 515, and it is interesting to note that 39 percent of them entered agriculture as owners; Negro farmers totaled 162, and 22 percent of them began as owners. Of the 531 white tenants (including sharecroppers), 69 percent had been in the tenant category only; among 622 Negro tenants, the corresponding percentage was 78. Interestingly enough, the hired-hand stage was practically lacking, a fact, however, that is largely vitiated because the sharecroppers were included with the farm operators. Figure 124, reproduced from Williams' study, shows the various changes in detail and makes evident the fact that the agricultural ladder in South

[21] *Ibid.*, p. 61.

Carolina is by no means the simple affair found by the studies in the Midwest a generation ago. It indicates, however, that considerable vertical mobility, both ascending and descending, is to be found in the South.

Hoffsommer's Alabama study, although limited to households on relief, contributes some facts of interest concerning the vertical mobility of white and Negro families in the South. Included in the sample were 982 families (698 white and 284 Negro), of whom 618 were classed at the time of the study as croppers, 182 as renters, and 182 as owners. Nearly three-fourths of the croppers first entered agriculture as croppers, and the proportion was only slightly higher among Negroes than among whites. Sixty percent of the renters entered agriculture as renters, and there was no significant difference between the races in this respect. And 79 percent of the owners began their farming experience as owners; the proportion for Negroes (77 percent) was not significantly below that for whites. Among these Alabama families, descending the ladder had been about as common as ascending: 11 percent of the white croppers and 6 percent of the Negro croppers had once been owners, and 18 percent of the white renters and 9 percent of the Negroes had begun farming as owners, but only 8 percent of the white owners and 4 percent of the Negro owners had begun at the bottom of the ladder as croppers; however, 23 percent of the white and 30 percent of the Negro renters had begun farming as croppers.[22]

Perhaps the most significant study of vertical mobility on the cotton plantation, and one that brings out the inevitable tendency of large-scale agriculture to promote endless rising and falling on the lower rungs of the agricultural ladder, is Alfred H. Stone's "A Plantation Experiment." It deserves rather extensive quotation.

[It was to] . . . the desire and hope of building up some such "assured tenantry" that our experiment largely owed its inception. Its salient features were: uniformity of tenant system, all land being rented at a fixed cash rental; the sale of stock, implements, and wagons to tenants upon exceptionally favorable terms; the excercise of proper supervision over the crop; the use of a contract defining in detail the undertakings of each party; the handling and disposition of the gathered crop by the plantation management. Let there be no mis-

[22] H. C. Hoffsommer, *Landlord-Tenant Relationships and Relief in Alabama,* Federal Emergency Relief Administration, Washington (mimeographed), 1935, p. 29.

understanding of the motives behind all this. There was nothing phil-
anthropic about it. It was a business proposition, pure and simple,
but certainly one with two sides to it. The plan was to select a number
of negro families, offer them the best terms and most advantageous
tenant relation, and so handle them and their affairs as to make them
reach a condition approaching as nearly as possible that of independence. The hope was that, having accomplished this purpose, we would
thereby also have in large measure solved the labor problem, having
attached to the plantation by ties of self-interest a sufficient number
of these independent renters to make us in turn measurably independent of the general labor situation. The problem before us was to
place in the hands of these people the means of acquiring something
for themselves, and then, in every instance of deficient individual initiative, by proper supervision to make them acquire it.[23]

After six years of operation the following results were detailed:

 . . . We brought to the plantation, at the close of the season of
1898, 30 new families, and began the first year, 1899, with a total of
58. On 1064 acres of cotton land we made but 459 bales of 500 pounds
average, a family average of 7.9 bales. The average price received
was 7.50 cents per pound; and the entire crop, cotton and seed,
brought $21,633.88, or a family average of $373.51. Of the families on
the place, 26, or 44.8 percent., left at the end of the year. We moved
in 27 families, and, with the 59 which the addition gave us, cultivated
1048 acres of cotton in 1900. The crop was 817 bales, or 13.8 per
family. It sold at an everage price of 9.94 cents, and with its seed
brought $47,541.66. This was an average cash product value of
$805.79 per family. The number of families who left the place at the
close of the year was 13, or 22 percent. of the total. We secured 15
new ones, and had on the place 61 families in 1901. We had this year
in cotton 1348 acres, and raised 1270 bales, 20.8 to the family. At an
average price of 7.90 cents for the cotton this crop, including seed,
realized $60,724.04, being $995.77 per family. We lost 16 families this
year, 26.2 percent. of the whole force, and moved in 24 new squads,
which gave us 69 for 1902. The latter year we raised 1131 bales of cotton on 1341 acres. Seed and cotton brought $54,593.26, the average
price for the latter being 8.08 cents per pound. The average product of
cotton was 16.4 bales per family, the average value of cotton and seed
$791.20. At the end of the year we lost 17 families, 24.6 percent. of the
total, and moved in 23 for the following year. This gave us 75 squads
for 1903. We cultivated 1392 acres of cotton, and raised 741 bales,

 [23] Alfred H. Stone, "A Plantation Experiment," *Quarterly Journal of Economics,*
XIX (1904), 271–272.

9.8 to the family. This brought 11.77 cents per pound, the cotton and seed selling for $53,527.73, or an average of $713.70 per family. At the close of the season 31 families, 41.3 percent. of our working force, left the plantation.[24]

The single planter is helpless in the face of the cultural pattern of habitual migration established as slavery's aftermath.

. . . From 1899 to 1903, leaving out of consideration the 30 new families brought in at the beginning of the former year, we moved in 124 families. In the same period we lost 103. Of the 79 families on the place in 1904 but 8 were with us in 1899. Of the 103 who have left, some with little, some with much, not one has become an owner of land. Most have simply continued as tenants elsewhere. Many have lost what they carried away, and have become share-hands on other plantations. Some have dropped into the ranks of day laborers. A few have drifted into towns. Let me illustrate one of these removals. In December, 1900, we moved in a crew of 7 people. They all represented themselves as working hands, though one of the men was over sixty-five, with a wife past sixty. Their entire outfit consisted of a horse, worth a liberal valuation of $50, and $58 worth of miscellaneous and indescribable household effects. In December, 1903, while riding over the place one day, my attention was arrested by a procession slowly approaching me. It consisted partly of two wagons, one buggy, two mules, one horse, three cows, two calves, and five dogs,—the property of this same crew of seven. In addition they had with them outside wagons enough to assist them in hauling away 285 bushels of corn, $190 worth of household effects (including a sewing-machine for each woman and a gun for each man), and a half-dozen crates of hogs and several of poultry. During the three years they had paid rent and accounts amounting to $4168.96, had received in cash $747.85, and had cash paid for help in their crops to the amount of $393.90. Their accounts, of course, included a variety of purchases in addition to their living expenses. They carried away $1100 worth of personal property. They left to get rid of the supervision incident to plantation management, and removed a short distance to the property of a non-resident, and secured their advances from a merchant. In November last I learned that the head of the squad had applied to a neighboring planter for a location for 1905, and wanted the latter to lift a debt of $1000 for him. (Since the above was put in print this squad has returned to us to make a crop the present year. It surrendered all it had, save household effects, to its merchant, and in addition we advanced

[24] *Ibid.*, pp. 272–273.

$75 to cover a balance. It begins where it started before, with nothing, and this time will work on shares.)[25]

Stone's experiment throws a great deal of light upon the process of vertical mobility in both its ascending and descending aspects. In addition it reveals much concerning the territorial mobility of the cotton laborers. At the end of six years the experiment was abandoned. Says Stone:

. . . We demonstrated our ability to make independent, property owning families out of poverty-stricken material. These families in turn demonstrated the fact of their independence by severing relations with us almost as promptly as we put them on their feet. After the termination of three years we had begun to feel reasonably certain that even the most practical appeal we could make to radically improved material welfare would be generally overcome by an apparently instinctive desire to "move." After the experience of five years we were quite satisfied of our entire incapacity to make the average plantation negro realize the remotest causal relation between stability and prosperity.[26]

Effects of Rural Social Mobility

Among agriculturists, as elsewhere, every change in social or physical space has a double aspect. On the one hand it shatters existing social bonds, and on the other it means the establishment of new ones. Mobility, vertical and horizontal, as well as territorial, shatters the social relationships and social structure in the old groups and causes significant modifications in the arrangements of the new. In these ways mobility exerts important influences upon the nature and structure of rural society. Sorokin, Zimmerman, and Galpin have listed its more important results for rural society as follows: (1) Mobility tends to mix thoroughly all the ethnic and cultural elements in a society. Accordingly, the more mobile a society, the greater the admixture, and the more heterogeneous it will be in racial stocks, nationalities, mores, religious beliefs, and cultural traits generally. (2) Mobility tends to eliminate unique and distinctive features from any particular group. Previous local patterns tend to be replaced by those of a more general nature. Within the community social differences are increased, but the community itself comes to resemble more closely other communi-

[25] *Ibid.*, pp. 275–276.
[26] *Ibid.*, p. 274.

ties in the general society. (3) The more mobile the population, the more plastic the behavior of the population, the larger the social vista, the less the prevalence of narrow-mindedness, and the slighter the dependence upon tradition. Also the more mobile the population, the greater the disintegration of the traditional mores and the greater the incidence of criminality and antisocial behavior. (4) As mobility increases, rural institutions lose their traditional character and force, become less stable or more flexible, and are likely to lose much of their hold upon the population. A mobile population is likely to be less concerned about the maintenance and support of schools, churches, and other institutions than a more stable group. As a result they are likely to be less intense in their attachment or loyalty to the local community, more broad-minded or cosmopolitan. (5) As mobility increases in the rural community, social contacts become less intimate, more formal and more superficial, psychosocial isolation increases, and social relationships take on a higher degree of anonymity. The pattern of social interaction approaches that of the city. (6) The shifting of individuals from group to group and class to class is accompanied by a confusion in the patterns of solidarity and antagonism. Lines of cleavage become confused and blurred; the social world becomes much more intricate.[27]

[27] P. A. Sorokin, Carle C. Zimmerman, and C. J. Galpin, *A Systematic Source Book in Rural Sociology*, Minneapolis, University of Minnesota Press, 1930, I, 504–506.

PART FIVE

Conclusion

25

CONCLUSION

The Factors in Human Behavior

Sociology and all social science in the last analysis is an attempt to explain human behavior, to get at the fundamental bases of personality, to account for the social relationships that prevail among men. All the conditions or factors underlying and influencing human behavior may be reduced to three large categories: (1) innate or biological factors, including the psychological; (2) geographic factors; and (3) cultural factors. The first set includes everything with which man is equipped at birth, the original nature of man, and only that; the second embraces all the multifarious elements of the natural environment; and the third pertains to that portion of the environment which man himself has produced and which he passes on from one generation to another.

In their attempts to explain the specific manner in which men act or fail to act, many writers resort to "human nature" as an "open sesame." Certain patterns of behavior or forms of social organization are held to be contrary to human nature, and others in accord with it. Indeed, the term is used as though human nature were something immutable, constant, as if the primary determinants of human behavior were all biological. Such a position is untenable. If generalites are not accepted and an attempt is made to isolate specific biological factors that might be used as explanations, little success attends the effort. Formerly writers endowed the human being with a long list of instincts. In recent years psychologists have greatly reduced the number of inherited behavior traits and patterns attributed to man. They have also abandoned the hypothesis of instincts, or the inheritance of complicated patterns of behavior, in favor of less differentiated original tendencies

597

or impulses. But few if any of these instinctive tendencies, drives, organic desires, or preponent reflexes are peculiar to man. This is certainly the case with respect to those most frequently mentioned, i.e., those involved in feeding, drinking, vocalization, bodily elimination, rest and sleep, muscular activity, sexual activity, the avoidance of stimuli that result in pain, and the tendency to seek repetition of pleasurable sensations. Because these tendencies are not limited to man, they should be used only with great caution as the differentiating characteristics of human nature. Even upright posture and the opposition of thumb and forefinger are not peculiar to the human species. Indeed, except for a more complex and more plastic nervous system, it is difficult to find any distinctively human features that might be utilized for establishing the specific biological basis of human nature. A biological basis there must be; but the range of potential behavior patterns is tremendous, the behaviors specifically determined by biological structures are few, and they are not unique with man.

Neither are geographic influences of much worth in explaining human nature. Granted that they have played a role in the past,[1] as man has ascended the scale of civilization the influences of geography on his behavior become less and less determinative.

The fundamental determinants of human nature seem to be cultural. It appears to be true that man alone possesses the unique biological constitution that enables him to develop and perpetuate cultural phenomena. But this may be only a slight variation, merely a matter of degree, from the biological equipment of other animal species. The possession and use of culture, on the other hand, are a difference of kind; they create a tremendous chasm between man and the remainder of the animal kingdom. He alone is a culture-making, culture-preserving, and culture-transmitting animal. Because of the material and nonmaterial man-made environment with which he has surrounded himself, man lives in a very different world from that inhabited by the other animals. Even when he adopts other species through domestication so that they

---

[1] Frederick J. Turner's observation, ". . . At the frontier the environment is at first too strong for the man," properly qualifies this phrase. But it also emphasizes the extreme circumstances required in order for geographic factors to become operative in shaping human nature. See his "The Significance of the Frontier in American History," *Annual Report of the American Historical Association for the Year 1893*, Washington, Government Printing Office, 1894, p. 201.

become adapted to and even dependent upon man's cultural world, they never come to have a share in it. Were it not for man, who serves as a culture carrier, it would all perish in a single generation.

Implicit throughout this book are the propositions that the cultural factors are the primary determinants of human nature and human behavior; that the cultural heritage can be modified and changed; and that what is called human nature will change along with these modifications in the social framework or structure. Farmers differ from townsfolk largely because of the differences in the cultural influences impinging upon them. Specific cultural forms such as the way the population is arranged on the land, the nature and distribution of property rights in land, the group bonds, the class and caste structure, the nature and strength of domestic, educational, religious, and governmental institutions—all of these are the molds in which human nature is set. Even granting an as yet undetermined biological basis, the possession of culture is the primary thing that makes man human; the differences in the cultural heritages of various groups are the primary determinants of the diversity in mankind. Human nature changes as the institutional pattern and other cultural elements are changed. More detailed and specific knowledge concerning the particular manner in which cultural forces operate offers the chief hope for a more complete predictability of human behavior.

Cultural Change in Rural Areas

The cultural heritage of a group or society is constantly changing in magnitude, content, and structure. New traits are being added, old ones sloughed off, and new combinations are being made of the existent traits. Only a small part of the change is due to the loss of arts or traits or to the conscious abandonment of knowledge once obtained. Fundamentally cultural change is cumulative. The persistence of old forms and the addition of new ones make the process of cultural change largely one of growth and differentiation of the cultural base. Through resistance to change or through pure cultural inertia many old forms persist long after their usefulness is past; by and large, however, culture traits persist because they possess utility. Even though a material object in which the trait is objectified may wear out, be lost, or be destroyed, the knowledge of how to duplicate the object remains, and utility calls forth new copies of the old.[2]

The possession of a rich cultural heritage by itself is no proof of the genius of a people; nor is the absence of such a heritage evidence of biological inferiority. The size and complexity of the cultural heritage are largely a function of the system of social contacts. A given group or society may add traits to its cultural base through invention and discovery, diffusion and borrowing. Invention is the successful combination of two or more previously existing traits or complexes into a new functioning unity. The larger the base and the more complex its structure, the greater the opportunities for new combinations or inventions. When man through science develops a systematic method of interrogating nature, inventions are greatly multiplied. Discovery refers to the obtaining of a bit of knowledge in the first place. It is largely a fortuitous procedure, the result of lucky coincidences or accidents. Discovery added the knowledge of edible plants and animals to the cultural heritage. Borrowing of culture traits refers to the conscious adoption of the traits of another group or culture. Diffusion of culture denotes the tendency of traits to spread from one group to another, sometimes in the face of active opposition on the part of the receivers.

The mechanics of cultural change in rural areas have been almost completely remade during recent years. Most important of all is the fact that in the present century the system of communication and transportation has been thoroughly revolutionized. With these developments has come a complete change in the patterns of interaction within the community, as well as in the system of contacts between communities. These innovations mean that social change in rural areas is radically different from what it was fifty or even twenty years ago. Under the pattern which prevailed until recently, rural people necessarily had to depend for additions to their culture almost entirely upon their own personal inventive ingenuity and skill. Even if new devices and ideas were discovered, practically all the social and economic channels that would facilitate their rapid diffusion were lacking. The result was a static type of rural society. Changes have been so slow, innovations so rare as to be strange and regarded with suspicion. Stagnation is the

[2] Cf. William F. Ogburn, *Social Changes*, New York, The Viking Press, 1922, pp. 74–75.

inevitable result of lack of social contacts and social interaction.

Today rural people are in constant communication with one another and with the townsfolk and city people. The telephone, the telegraph, the radio, television, the automobile and good roads, the airplane, differentiation of contacts with social and service centers, the decline of the cumulative community and the rise of special-interest groups, the agricultural extension service—all of these and many other forces contribute to the increased tempo of change in rural areas. The locality group is now more able to learn of and adopt the improved practices of other groups; the farm family can more quickly utilize the invention of another farmer in a distant part of the nation; in brief, the changed systems of social interaction and communication make possible a much more rapid diffusion among farm people of rural inventions and discoveries, a process that has been greatly retarded by the segmented nature of rural society. It also makes readily available to rural people all urban cultural phenomena.

The net result of all this is to reduce greatly the rural-urban cultural differences. The greatest factor is, of course, the rapid diffusion of urban traits to rural areas. However, with the improved methods of communication between farm families, diffusion within strictly rural territory of traits specifically germane to rural life is likely to increase. Furthermore, future developments may mean a greater ruralization of the city and a lesser urbanization of the country. The generalization of Sorokin and Zimmerman that the city is the innovator, the country the preserver of culture traits may be less true in the future than it has been in the past. But between city and country present trends seem to indicate a progressive erasure of differences, a greater standardization, a more homogeneous society. The country promises to be less a balance wheel and more a dynamo.

The Future of the Agricultural Classes

The welfare of the American farmer is now fully as dependent upon the nature of state and national policies for agriculture as it is upon the individual efforts of the farm family itself.[3] The tariff, the general property tax, the commercialization of agriculture, specialization by enterprises and tasks, the Federal Farm Board,

[3] Cf. T. Lynn Smith and Ralph W. Roberts, "Sources and Distribution of the Farm Population in Relation to Farm Benefit Payments," *Journal of Farm Economics,* XXIII (1941), 607–618.

"seed loans," drought relief, the Agricultural Adjustment Administration, the Office of Price Administration, and finally the Production and Marketing Administration have all had a part in bringing this situation about. The well-being of the people on the land demands that national and state policies be such that these people will obtain a fair share of the national opportunity and income. In the last analysis, only comprehensive development of rural sociological fact and theory, including the increase of knowledge concerning farm production and consumption, rural government, rural education, and rural-urban relations, can form the basis upon which such a sound state and national policy can be founded.

The most promising places to begin are with the tariff, the general property tax, the extension of public health to rural areas, the framing of a national educational policy, an extensive program of adult education, the strengthening of the rural community by making it the functional unit in all activity programs, and a thorough renovation of the relations of the population to the land.

Exercises and Suggested Readings

CHAPTER 1: INTRODUCTION

QUESTIONS

1. What forces playing upon present-day rural society are bringing about the most important changes?
2. What are the essentials of the scientific method? Can this method be applied in the study of rural social relationships? If so, what will the resulting body of knowledge—the fact and theory—be called?
3. Precisely how does rural sociology differ from general sociology?
4. If sociology were defined as "the philosophy of history," would it be valid to refer to it as a science? Why or why not?
5. What are the respective roles of induction and deduction in the scientific method? What part does hypothesis play?

SUGGESTED READINGS

Landis, Paul H., *Rural Life in Process,* New York, McGraw-Hill Book Company, 1948, chap. 1.

Loomis, Charles P., and Beegle, J. Allan, *Rural Social Systems,* New York, Prentice-Hall, Inc., 1950, chap. 1.

Nelson, Lowry, *Rural Sociology,* New York, American Book Company, 1948, chap. 1.

Taylor, Carl C., "Rural Life and Rural Sociology," in Carl C. Taylor, et al., *Rural Life in the United States,* New York, Alfred A. Knopf, Inc., 1949, chap. 1.

CHAPTER 2: THE RURAL WORLD

QUESTIONS

1. In what manner are the social advantages imputed to the rural way of life by the philosophy of agrarianism related to the fundamental differences between the rural and urban worlds?
2. Define in your own words the terms *rural* and *urban*.
3. In what significant ways does the rural world differ from the urban? What relationship do these differences have to the institutions, behavior patterns, and personalities of rural and urban people?

4. Is it desirable to develop more part-time farming and rural homes for urban workers? Why?
5. Contrast the systems of social interaction among rural and urban groups.
6. How are the facts of urban heterogeneity and rural homogeneity related to the other essential rural-urban differences?

SUGGESTED READINGS

Nelson, Lowry, *Rural Sociology,* New York, American Book Company, 1948, chap. 2.

Sorokin, P. A., and Zimmerman, Carle C., *Principles of Rural-Urban Sociology,* New York, Henry Holt & Company, 1929, chap. 2.

Sorokin, P. A., Zimmerman, Carle C., and Galpin, Charles J., *A Systematic Source Book in Rural Sociology,* Minneapolis, University of Minnesota Press, 1930, I, chap. 4.

Urbanism Committee of the National Resources Committee, *Our Cities: Their Rôle in the National Economy,* Washington, Government Printing Office, 1937, pp. 1–70.

CHAPTER 3: THE NUMBER, ORIGIN, DISTRIBUTION, AND IMPORTANCE OF THE RURAL POPULATION

QUESTIONS

1. How many people are there in your home county? What is their racial distribution? Urban, rural farm, and rural nonfarm distribution? When was your county settled? Where did the early settlers come from? What important influxes of population have taken place since?
2. Between 1930 and 1935 there was a tendency for the farm population to concentrate on the poorer soils of the nation. Is this trend likely to continue indefinitely? Why or why not?
3. To what extent are rural Americans "old Americans"? Explain.
4. What effect has the absence of immigration of Europeans to the South had upon the agricultural skills, techniques, and attitudes in the region?
5. Suppose the Congress of the United States appropriates an additional $100,000,000 to be distributed among the states for agricultural research and teaching. What difference, if any, will it make to your state whether the money is divided in proportion to the sizes of the rural populations or in proportion to the numbers in the rural farm populations?

SUGGESTED READINGS

Kolb, John H., and Brunner, Edmund deS., *A Study of Rural Society,* Boston, Houghton Mifflin Company, 1952, chap. 4.

Nelson, Lowry, *Rural Sociology,* New York, American Book Company, 1948, chap. 6.

Smith, T. Lynn, *Brazil: People and Institutions,* Baton Rouge, Louisiana State University Press, 1946, chap. 5.

Smith, T. Lynn, *Population Analysis,* New York, McGraw-Hill Book Company, 1948, chap. 2.

CHAPTER 4: COMPOSITION OF THE POPULATION

QUESTIONS

1. Discuss the social implications of the differences in the age and sex distributions of rural and urban populations.
2. During the last ten years what changes have occurred in the composition of the population in your county or your community?
3. How will the following factors affect the profile of the age and sex pyramid: (a) a rapid fall in the birth rate? (b) a considerable influx of immigrants? (c) an extensive emigration? (d) (for the rural pyramid) a migration to cities?
4. Why does the curve of sex ratios by age resemble an S? Of what significance is this fact?
5. Is any particular significance to be attached to the fact that in the years following World War I the sex ratio at birth was around 106? Explain.

SUGGESTED READINGS

Hagoood, Margaret Jarman, "Rural Population Characteristics," in Carl C. Taylor, et al., *Rural Life in the United States,* New York, Alfred A. Knopf, Inc., 1949, chap. 12.

Smith, T. Lynn, and Hitt, Homer L., *The People of Louisiana,* Baton Rouge, Louisiana State University Press, 1952, chaps. 4, 5, 6, and 7.

CHAPTER 5: PHYSICAL CHARACTERISTICS AND HEALTH

QUESTIONS

1. State in your own words the principle known as Livi's Law. Using pigmentation as an example, illustrate how this principle operates.

2. What is meant by "race"? Are there any pure races?
3. Since doctors, nurses, hospitals, and almost all modern health and sanitation facilities are concentrated in urban areas, how do you account for the comparatively good showing of rural areas with respect to health indexes?
4. What should be the next steps in a national health program?

SUGGESTED READINGS

Ensminger, Douglas, and Longmore, T. Wilson, "Rural Health," in Carl C. Taylor, et al., *Rural Life in the United States,* New York, Alfred A. Knopf, Inc., 1949, chap. 9.

Interbureau Committee on Post-War Programs, *Better Health for Rural America,* Washington, Government Printing Office, 1945.

Landis, Paul H., *Rural Life in Process,* New York, McGraw-Hill Book Company, 1948, chap. 31.

Mott, Frederick D., and Roemer, Milton I., *Rural Health and Medical Care,* New York, McGraw-Hill Book Company, 1948, chaps. 5, 6, 7, 8, and 13.

Nelson, Lowry, *Rural Sociology,* New York, American Book Company, 1948, chap. 25.

CHAPTER 6: PSYCHOLOGICAL CHARACTERISTICS AND MENTAL HEALTH

QUESTIONS

1. What evidences of urbanization of attitudes have you observed in a given rural community?
2. Compare the experience worlds of rural and urban people.
3. What is the effect of isolation upon insanity among farm women?
4. The country furnishes relatively few people to institutions for mental defectives. Does this fact mean that rural people are more intelligent than urban? Explain.
5. Are farmers individualistic? Explain.

SUGGESTED READINGS

Kolb, John H., and Brunner, Edmund deS., *A Study of Rural Society,* Boston, Houghton Mifflin Company, 1952, chap. 5.

Landis, Paul H., *Rural Life in Process,* New York, McGraw-Hill Book Company, 1948, chap. 9.

National Resources Committee, *The Problems of a Changing Population,* Washington, Government Printing Office, 1938, pp. 157–165.

Taylor, Carl C., "Farm People's Attitudes and Opinions," in Carl C.

Taylor, et al., *Rural Life in the United States,* New York, Alfred A. Knopf, Inc., 1948, chap. 28.

CHAPTER 7: FERTILITY

QUESTIONS

1. What are the advantages and disadvantages of the *birth rate* and the *fertility ratio* as indexes of human fertility in the United States?
2. Of what social significance is the following principle: The country is the producer of population, the city the consumer.
3. Where are the peaks of population fertility in the United States? What factors explain the high fertility in these areas?
4. How do recent trends in the birth rate compare in the rural and urban parts of the United States?
5. In what ways and to what extent were the influences of war reflected in the rural birth rate in the United States in 1936? 1945? and 1947?

SUGGESTED READINGS

Hagood, Margaret Jarman, "Dynamics of Rural Population," in Carl C. Taylor, et al., *Rural Life in the United States,* New York, Alfred A. Knopf, Inc., 1949, pp. 233–239.

Landis, Paul H., *Rural Life in Process,* New York, McGraw-Hill Book Company, 1948, chap. 4.

Nelson, Lowry, *Rural Sociology,* New York, American Book Company, 1948, pp. 106–114.

Smith, T. Lynn, *Brazil: People and Institutions,* Baton Rouge, Louisiana State University Press, 1946, chap. 8.

Smith, T. Lynn, and Hitt, Homer L., *The People of Louisiana,* Baton Rouge, Louisiana State University Press, 1952, chap. 11.

CHAPTER 8: MORTALITY

QUESTIONS

1. What accounts for the recent "prolongation of life" that has occured in the United States?
2. Why is the infant mortality rate a valuable index of social well-being?
3. What factors are most important in explaining rural-urban differences in mortality?
4. Why must death rates be corrected for age and sex differences before valid comparisons are possible?

5. What will be the trend of the crude death rate in the United States during the period 1950 to 1960?
6. Are the life tables a good index for use in comparisons of longevity in different parts of the nation? Explain.

SUGGESTED READINGS

McMahan, C. A., "Rural-Urban Differences in Longevity," in T. Lynn Smith and C. A. McMahan, *The Sociology of Urban Life: A Textbook with Readings*, New York, The Dryden Press, Inc., 1951, pp. 280–289.

National Resources Committee, *The Problems of a Changing Population*, Washington, Government Printing Office, 1938, pp. 166–192.

Smith, T. Lynn, *Brazil: People and Institutions*, Baton Rouge, Louisiana State University Press, 1946, chap. 9.

Smith, T. Lynn, and Hitt, Homer L., *The People of Louisiana*, Baton Rouge, Louisiana State University Press, 1952, chap. 12.

CHAPTER 9: MIGRATION

QUESTIONS

1. Trace the moves made by your family (either the father's or mother's side) as far back as you can. Give the motives for each major change in location.
2. What significance, if any, does a knowledge of rural-urban migration have for a national educational policy?
3. Discuss the comparative role of migration and natural increase in the growth of city populations.
4. The following index has been used by Goodrich and others as a measure of migration: To the population of a county in 1920 was added the computed natural increase between 1920 and 1930; from the sum was subtracted the population in 1930; and the remainder was said to represent migration between 1920 and 1930. Is this a valid index of migration? Why or why not?
5. In what respects is rural-urban migration selective?
6. How does the social significance of migration compare in sedentary and nomadic societies?

SUGGESTED READINGS

Landis, Paul H., *Rural Life in Process*, New York, McGraw-Hill Book Company, 1948, chaps. 13, 14, and 15.

Nelson, Lowry, *Rural Sociology*, New York, American Book Company, 1948, chap. 7.

President's Commission on Migratory Labor, *Migratory Labor in American Agriculture*, Washington, Government Printing Office, 1951.

Smith, T. Lynn, *Brazil: People and Institutions*, Baton Rouge, Louisiana State University Press, 1946, chap. 11.

Smith, T. Lynn, and Hitt, Homer L., *The People of Louisiana*, Baton Rouge, Louisiana State University Press, 1952, chap. 13.

CHAPTER 10: FORM OF SETTLEMENT

QUESTIONS

1. What are the advantages and disadvantages of each principal settlement type?
2. Of what importance is the village form of settlement in the social organization of rural America?
3. Why did New England largely abandon village settlements? Why did the postwar southern cotton plantation give up its village settlement pattern?
4. The French people of south Louisiana are said to be gregarious. Did they settle in line villages because of this gregariousness or are they gregarious because they settled in line villages? Would an infant from one of these families, if taken at birth and reared in an Iowa farm family, be more or less gregarious than his foster brothers and sisters?
5. In Brazil's great Amazon Valley are millions of unsettled acres. The health of the population is the principal limiting factor in all colonization projects. If you were in charge of a program for bringing settlers into the area, what form of settlement would you use? Why?

SUGGESTED READINGS

Landis, Paul H., *Rural Life in Process*, New York, McGraw-Hill Book Company, 1948, chap. 2.

Loomis, Charles P., and Beegle, J. Allan, *Rural Social Systems*, New York, Prentice-Hall, Inc., 1950, chap. 7.

Nelson, Lowry, *Rural Sociology*, New York, American Book Company, 1948, chap. 4.

Smith, T. Lynn, *Brazil: People and Institutions*, Baton Rouge, Louisiana State University Press, 1946, chap. 13.

Whetten, Nathan L., *Rural Mexico*, Chicago, University of Chicago Press, 1948, chap. 4.

CHAPTER 11: LAND DIVISION

QUESTIONS

1. If the village form of settlement is in vogue, what are the fundamental issues involved in determining the most satisfactory system of land division?
2. What is the distribution in the United States of each of the principal types of land division?
3. What principles should govern the division of lands on resettlement projects?
4. Give a detailed description of the manner in which the lands of your home county are divided. Trace the development of this pattern.

SUGGESTED READINGS

Donaldson, Thomas, *The Public Domain*, Washington, Government Printing Office, 1884, pp. 575–605.

Leonard, Olen E., *The Role of the Land Grant in the Social Organization and Social Processes of a Spanish-American Village in New Mexico*, Ann Arbor, Michigan, Edwards Brothers, Inc., 1948, chap. 5.

Nelson, Lowry, *Rural Cuba*, Minneapolis, University of Minnesota Press, 1950, chap. 6.

Smith, T. Lynn, *Brazil: People and Institutions*, Baton Rouge, Louisiana State University Press, 1946, chap. 14.

CHAPTER 12: LAND TENURE

QUESTIONS

1. Can the lack of tenancy sometimes be more detrimental than its presence? Cite cases substantiating your point of view.
2. Is the southern cropper a renter? Explain. If not, can you justify classifying him as a tenant? Explain.
3. What are the causes and results of farm tenancy?
4. Why cannot the proportion of landowning farmers in the United States be determined accurately? What census fact is more important than this?
5. What changes are needed in the system of renting lands in your county?

SUGGESTED READINGS

Harris, Marshall, and Ackerman, Joseph, "The Farm Tenure System in the United States," in Joseph Ackerman and Marshall Harris (eds.), *Family Farm Policy*, Chicago, University of Chicago Press, 1947, chap. 2.

Hoffsommer, Harold (ed.), *The Social and Economic Significance of Land Tenure in the Southwestern States*, Chapel Hill, University of North Carolina Press, 1950, *passim*.

Loomis, Charles P., and Beegle, J. Allan, *Rural Social Systems*, New York, Prentice-Hall, Inc., 1950, chap. 9.

Nelson, Lowry, *Rural Sociology*, New York, American Book Company, 1948, chap. 13.

Raper, Arthur F., and Taylor, Carl C., "Land Owners and Tenants," in Carl C. Taylor, et al., *Rural Life in the United States*, New York, Alfred A. Knopf, Inc., 1949, chap. 15.

Smith, T. Lynn, *Brazil: People and Institutions*, Baton Rouge, Louisiana State University Press, 1946, chap. 15.

Taylor, Carl C., *Rural Sociology*, New York, Harper & Brothers, 1933, chap. 11.

Taylor, Carl C., Wheeler, Helen W., and Kirkpatrick, E. L., *Disadvantaged Classes in American Agriculture*, Washington, United States Department of Agriculture, 1938, chaps. 2 and 3.

U.S. Bureau of the Census and Bureau of Agricultural Economics, *Graphic Summary of Farm Tenure in the United States*, Washington, Government Printing Office, 1948.

CHAPTER 13: THE SIZE OF HOLDINGS

QUESTIONS

1. To what extent have modern scholars confused the problems of land tenure with those of size of holdings?
2. What part has the plantation system played in bringing about the social and economic ills besetting the southern region?
3. How can the security of the farmer who tills his own land be increased?
4. Why do census reports show the South to be blanketed with small farms?

SUGGESTED READINGS

Ackerman, Joseph, and Harris, Marshall (eds.), *Family Farm Policy*, Chicago, University of Chicago Press, 1950, chap. 3.

Brannen, C. O., *Relation of Land Tenure to Plantation Organization,* U.S.D.A. Department Bulletin 1269, Washington, 1924, pp. 1–67.

Smith, T. Lynn, *Brazil: People and Institutions,* Baton Rouge, Louisiana State University Press, 1946, chap. 16.

Sorokin, P. A., Zimmerman, Carle C., and Galpin, Charles J., *A Systematic Source Book in Rural Sociology,* Minneapolis, University of Minnesota Press, 1931, I, chap. 11.

Woofter, T. J., Jr., et al., *Landlord and Tenant on the Cotton Plantation,* Works Progress Administration Research Monograph V, Washington, 1936, pp. 1–106.

CHAPTER 14: SYSTEMS OF AGRICULTURE

QUESTIONS

1. Of what significance is the study of the "systems of agriculture" in connection with the so-called Point Four programs of the United States government?
2. Describe the mechanization of agriculture in a county with which you are familiar over the last twenty-five years.
3. Why have countries such as Peru, Guatemala, and Mexico made such little use of horses for draft purposes, the steel plow, and the ordinary farm wagon?
4. How may a collecting economy be distinguished from an agricultural economy?
5. In what parts of the United States is the mechanization of agriculture now going on the most rapidly?

SUGGESTED READINGS

Cooper, Martin R., Barton, Glen T., and Brodell, Albert P., *Progress of Farm Mechanization,* Washington, United States Department of Agriculture, Miscellaneous Publication 630, 1947.

McMillan, Robert T., "Effects of Mechanization on American Agriculture," *Scientific Monthly,* LXIX (1949).

Smith, T. Lynn, "Agricultural Systems and Standards of Living," *Inter-American Economic Affairs,* III (1949).

Smith, T. Lynn, *Brazil: People and Institutions,* Baton Rouge, Louisiana State University Press, 1946, chap. 3.

CHAPTER 15: SOCIAL DIFFERENTIATION

QUESTIONS

1. Trace in detail the origin, growth, and recent changes in a rural neighborhood with which you are intimately acquainted.

2. What factors are now operating to integrate and what to disintegrate rural neighborhoods?
3. What is a rural community and how would you determine its limits?
4. Contrast the meaning of the term "neighbor" in the "cumulative community" and in the locality wherein "special-interest groups" are the principal forms of social grouping.
5. Trace the emergence and growth of some urban community with which you are acquainted.

SUGGESTED READINGS

Ensminger, Douglas, "Rural Neighborhoods and Communities," in Carl C. Taylor, et al., *Rural Life in the United States,* New York, Alfred A. Knopf, Inc., 1949, chap. 4.

Hayes, Wayland J., *The Small Community Looks Ahead,* New York, Harcourt, Brace and Company, 1947, chap. 1.

Loomis, Charles P., and Beegle, J. Allan, *Rural Social Systems,* New York, Prentice-Hall, Inc., 1950, chap. 6.

Nelson, Lowry, *Rural Sociology,* New York, American Book Company, 1948, chap. 5.

Smith, T. Lynn, *Brazil: People and Institutions,* Baton Rouge, Louisiana State University Press, 1946, chap. 18.

CHAPTER 16: SOCIAL STRATIFICATION

QUESTIONS

1. Describe the principal social layers or classes in a rural community with which you are intimately acquainted.
2. Of what significance nationally is the recent rapid increase in the proportion of owner-operators of farms?
3. What is the relationship between concentration of landownership and rural social stratification?
4. To what extent is a caste system in accord with American tradition and ideals?
5. Does public education reduce social stratification? Explain.

SUGGESTED READINGS

Kaufman, Harold F., *Prestige Classes in a New York Rural Community,* Cornell AES Memoir 260, Ithaca, New York, 1944.

Landis, Paul H., *Rural Life in Process,* New York, McGraw-Hill Book Company, 1948, chap. 18.

Loomis, Charles P., and Beegle, J. Allan, *Rural Social Systems,* New York, Prentice-Hall, Inc., 1950, chaps. 10 and 11.

Nelson, Lowry, *Rural Cuba*, Minneapolis, University of Minnesota Press, 1950, chaps. 8 and 9.

Nelson, Lowry, *Rural Sociology*, New York, American Book Company, 1948, chap. 11.

Raper, Arthur F., "Rural Social Differentials," in Carl C. Taylor, et al., *Rural Life in the United States*, New York, Alfred A. Knopf, Inc., 1949, chap. 18.

CHAPTER 17: MARRIAGE AND THE FAMILY

QUESTIONS

1. Evaluate Burgess' definition of the family as "a unity of interacting personalities."
2. How does the life cycle of farm families differ from that of village and city families?
3. What are the current trends in rural family organization?
4. What are the bases of affection in the family?
5. Discuss the validity of Confucius' contention that as the family is, society will be.
6. What are the principal functions of the family?

SUGGESTED READINGS

Landis, Paul H., *Rural Life in Process*, New York, McGraw-Hill Book Company, 1948, chap. 21.

Loomis, Charles P., and Beegle, J. Allan, *Rural Social Systems*, New York, Prentice-Hall, Inc., 1950, chap. 2.

Nelson, Lowry, *Rural Sociology*, New York, American Book Company, 1948, chap. 15.

Sanderson, Dwight, *Rural Sociology and Rural Social Organization*, New York, John Wiley & Sons, Inc., 1942, chap. 10.

Smith, T. Lynn, *Brazil: People and Institutions*, Baton Rouge, Louisiana State University Press, 1946, chap. 19.

CHAPTER 18: RURAL EDUCATION AND EDUCATIONAL INSTITUTIONS

QUESTIONS

1. To what extent are the schools in your county consolidated? What principles should govern further consolidation?
2. Should the Agricultural Extension Service extend its program to include all rural people? Why or why not?

3. In the high school that serves the rural community with which you are most intimately acquainted, how adequately is the curriculum serving the needs of the local people? What changes would you recommend?
4. Is it desirable to have a national department of education headed by a member of the President's cabinet? Why or why not?
5. What are the pros and cons with respect to federal aid for rural education?
6. Using the data from the 1950 Census, compare the educational status of the urban, rural nonfarm, and rural farm populations. Divide the materials according to race before making the comparisons.

SUGGESTED READINGS

Hatch, Spencer D., *Up from Poverty in Rural India,* Bombay, Oxford University Press, 1938, chaps. 7–9.

Landis, Paul H., *Rural Life in Process,* New York, McGraw-Hill Book Company, 1948, chap. 22.

Loomis, Charles P., and Beegle, J. Allan, *Rural Social Systems,* New York, Prentice-Hall, Inc., 1950, chaps. 14–16.

Nelson, Lowry, *Rural Sociology,* New York, American Book Company, 1948, chaps. 19–21.

Sanderson, Dwight, *Rural Sociology and Rural Social Organization,* New York, John Wiley & Sons, Inc., 1942, chap. 16.

Smith, T. Lynn, *Brazil: People and Institutions,* Baton Rouge, Louisiana State University Press, 1946, chap. 20.

CHAPTER 19: RELIGION AND THE RURAL CHURCH

QUESTIONS

1. What is the origin of the term *pagan? heathen?* Of what significance are these facts in the study of rural religious attitudes?
2. Analyze the program of a rural church congregation well known to you. How would you modify this program?
3. In what ways does Livi's Law contribute to an understanding of differences in rural and urban religious phenomena?
4. What are the prospects for the united church in rural areas?
5. If, as is claimed in this book, the church organization in the South is still in the neighborhood stage, what changes do you anticipate in the immediate future?
6. What are the principal distinctive features of rural religious culture?

SUGGESTED READINGS

Kolb, John H., and Brunner, Edmund deS., *A Study of Rural Society*, Boston, Houghton Mifflin Company, 1952, chap. 20.

Landis, Paul H., *Rural Life in Process*, New York, McGraw-Hill Book Company, 1948, chap. 23.

Sanderson, Dwight, *Rural Sociology and Rural Social Organization*, New York, John Wiley & Sons, Inc., 1942, chap. 15.

Smith, T. Lynn, *Brazil: People and Institutions*, Baton Rouge, Louisiana State University Press, 1946, chap. 21.

Sorokin, P. A., and Zimmerman, Carle C., *Principles of Rural-Urban Sociology*, New York, Henry Holt & Company, 1929, chap. 18.

CHAPTER 20: RURAL POLITICAL INSTITUTIONS AND GOVERNMENT

QUESTIONS

1. What are the essential features of rural local government in your home county? Enumerate the functions of the county's governing board.
2. What is the nature of agricultural radicalism?
3. Compare rural and urban groups with respect to participation in voting.
4. What are the prospects for a national agrarian party? Would the welfare of the agricultural classes be more advanced by such a party or by an agrarian block from the southern and western states?

SUGGESTED READINGS

Ensminger, Douglas, and Longmore, T. Wilson, "Rural Local Government," in Carl C. Taylor, et al., *Rural Life in the United States*, New York, Alfred A. Knopf, Inc., 1949, chap. 8.

Loomis, Charles P., and Beegle, J. Allan, *Rural Social Systems*, New York, Prentice-Hall, Inc., 1950, chaps. 17–19.

Nelson, Lowry, *Rural Sociology*, New York, American Book Company, 1948, chaps. 22–23.

Smith, T. Lynn, *Brazil: People and Institutions*, Baton Rouge, Louisiana State University Press, 1946, chap. 22.

Taylor, Carl C., "The Farmers' Movement and Large Farmers' Organizations," in Carl C. Taylor, et al., *Rural Life in the United States*, New York, Alfred A. Knopf, Inc., 1949, chap. 29.

CHAPTER 21: COMPETITION AND CONFLICT IN RURAL SOCIETY

QUESTIONS

1. What types of retail establishments are leaving and which remaining in typical agricultural villages? Give your explanation.
2. To what extent are the trade centers of your home county complementary to one another, to what extent are they competitive? Explain.
3. Describe the nature of town-country relations in a community well known to you.
4. To what extent is interdenominational strife a factor in the religious life of a rural community with which you are intimately acquainted?

SUGGESTED READINGS

Nelson, Lowry, *Rural Sociology,* New York, American Book Company, 1948, chap. 8.

Sanderson, Dwight, *Rural Social and Economic Areas in Central New York,* Cornell Bulletin 614, Ithaca, 1934.

Sanderson, Dwight, *Rural Sociology and Rural Social Organization,* New York, John Wiley & Sons, Inc., 1942, chap. 26.

Taylor, Carl C., *Rural Sociology,* New York, Harper & Brothers, 1933, chap. 26.

CHAPTER 22: COÖPERATION IN RURAL AREAS

QUESTIONS

1. What are the nature and extent of coöperation among the farmers in a rural community with which you are intimately acquainted?
2. Would it be possible and desirable to develop a coöperative movement similar to the one in Denmark, among the farmers of the United States?
3. Is it possible to secure the economic advantages of large-scale agriculture without incurring the social disadvantage of tenancy? Discuss.
4. What can be done to promote coöperation of the contractual type among farmers?

SUGGESTED READINGS

Hatch, D. Spencer, *Up from Poverty in Rural India,* Bombay, Oxford University Press, 1938, chap. 10.

Hoffer, C. R., "Co-operation as a Culture Pattern Within a Community," *Rural Sociology*, III (1938), 153–158.

Kolb, John H., and Brunner, Edmund deS., *A Study of Rural Society*, Boston, Houghton Mifflin Company, 1952, chap. 9.

Nelson, Lowry, *Rural Sociology*, New York, American Book Company, 1948, chap. 9.

Sanderson, Dwight, and Polson, Robert A., *Rural Community Organization*, New York, John Wiley & Sons, Inc., 1939, chap. 4.

CHAPTER 23: ACCOMMODATION, ASSIMILATION, AND ACCULTURATION IN RURAL AREAS

QUESTIONS

1. How does education differ from propaganda? From acculturation?
2. Is the American Negro assimilated? Acculturated? Explain.
3. Describe the nature and extent of town-country accommodation in your home county.
4. From your own observation, present facts to illustrate the two-sided nature of acculturation.
5. Is sharecropping or cash wages the better type of accommodation between planter and laborer in the cotton South? Explain.

SUGGESTED READINGS

Landis, Paul H., *Rural Life in Process*, New York, McGraw-Hill Book Company, 1948, chaps. 16 and 17.

Nelson, Lowry, *Rural Sociology*, New York, American Book Company, 1948, chap. 10.

CHAPTER 24: SOCIAL MOBILITY

QUESTIONS

1. A farm boy marries a ten-cent-store heiress, accepts a lucrative white-collar job in his father-in-law's organization, and makes his home in the city. Discuss the various forms of mobility involved.
2. List the principal factors that account for the high vertical social mobility in the cities. Explain how each of these operates.
3. What are the principal social effects of mobility?
4. What are the established facts relative to the selectivity of rural-urban migration?
5. Over a period of three generations is it possible for the "agricultural ladder" to operate in a plantation area? Explain.

SUGGESTED READINGS

Landis, Paul H., *Rural Life in Process*, New York, McGraw-Hill Book Company, 1948, chap. 12.

Nelson, Lowry, *Rural Sociology*, New York, American Book Company, 1948, chap. 12.

Sorokin, P. A., Zimmerman, Carle C., and Galpin, Charles J., *A Systematic Source Book in Rural Sociology*, Minneapolis, University of Minnesota Press, 1930, I, chap. 8.

CHAPTER 25: CONCLUSION

QUESTIONS

1. Contrast the roles of the city and the country in the formation and preservation of national culture.
2. Sketch the most recent trends in rural-urban differentiation.
3. Describe in some detail the most important social or cultural changes now occurring in a community with which you are intimately acquainted.
4. What would result if lack of contact produced a "pure" race or culture?
5. Who are our "contemporary ancestors"?
6. What role should rural sociology play in national planning?

SUGGESTED READINGS

Kolb, John H., and Brunner, Edmund deS., *A Study of Rural Society*, Boston, Houghton Mifflin Company, 1952, chap. 26.

Landis, Paul H., *Rural Life in Process*, New York, McGraw-Hill Book Company, 1948, chap. 32.

Nelson, Lowry, *Rural Sociology*, New York, American Book Company, 1948, chap. 26.

Taylor, Carl C., "Significant Trends and Direction of Change," in Carl C. Taylor, et al., *Rural Life in the United States*, New York, Alfred A. Knopf, Inc., 1949, chap. 30.

Bibliography

Abernathy, George L., and Anderson, C. Brooks, "The Use of Publicity Materials in North Carolina Weeklies," *Rural Sociology*, XIV (1949).

Abernethy, Thomas Perkins, *From Frontier to Plantation in Tennessee*, Chapel Hill, University of North Carolina Press, 1932.

Abernethy, Thomas Perkins, "Social Relations and Political Control in the Old Southwest," *Mississippi Valley Historical Review*, XVI (1929–1930).

Abstract of the Fifteenth Census of the United States, Washington, Government Printing Office, 1933.

Ackerman, Joseph, and Harris, Marshall, *Family Farm Policy*, Chicago, University of Chicago Press, 1947.

Adams, Herbert B., *The Germanic Origin of New England Towns*, Baltimore, Johns Hopkins Press, 1882.

Adams, Herbert B., *Village Communities of Cape Anne and Salem*, Johns Hopkins University Studies in Historical and Political Science, First Series, IX–X, Baltimore, 1883.

Adams, Thomas, *Rural Planning and Development*, Ottawa, Commission of Conservation, 1917.

"Agricultural Co-operative Associations in the United States," *Farm Credit Quarterly*, III (September, 1938).

Alexander, Frank D., and Nelson, Lowry, *Rural Social Organization in Goodhue County, Minnesota*, Minnesota Agricultural Experiment Station Bulletin 401, St. Paul, 1947.

Allin, Bushrod, and Parsons, K. H., "Changes in the School Census Since 1920," *Land Policy Review*, I (1935).

Almack, Ronald B., *The Rural Health Facilities of Lewis County, Missouri*, Missouri Agricultural Experiment Station Research Bulletin 365, Columbia, 1943.

Almack, Ronald B., and Hepple, Lawrence M., *Rural Social Organization in Dent County, Missouri*, Missouri Agricultural Experiment Station Research Bulletin 458, Columbia, 1950.

Ammon, Otto, *Die natürliche Auslese beim Menschen*, Jena, G. Fischer, 1893.

Anderson, A. H., *Changes in Farm Population and Rural Life in Four*

North Dakota Counties, North Dakota Agricultural Experiment Station Bulletin 375, Fargo, 1952.

Anderson, A. H., *A Study of Rural Communities and Organizations in Seward County, Nebraska,* Nebraska Agricultural Experiment Station Bulletin 405, Lincoln, 1951.

Anderson, C. Arnold, and Smith, T. Lynn, *Research in the Social Psychology of Rural Life,* Social Science Research Bulletin 17, New York, Social Science Research Council, 1933.

Anderson, Henry S., "The Little Landers' Land Colonies: A Unique Agricultural Experiment in California," *Agricultural History,* V (1931).

Anderson, W. A., *Farmers in the Farm Bureau,* Cornell University Agricultural Experiment Station, Rural Sociology Mimeographed Bulletin 4, Ithaca, 1941.

Anderson, W. A., *Mobility of Rural Families,* Cornell University Agricultural Experiment Station Bulletin 607, Ithaca, 1934.

Anderson, W. A., *The Transmission of Farming as an Occupation,* Cornell University Agricultural Experiment Station Bulletin 768, Ithaca, 1941.

Anderson, W. A., and Loomis, Charles P., *Migration of Sons and Daughters of White Farmers in Wake County, 1929,* North Carolina Agricultural Experiment Station Bulletin 275, Raleigh, 1930.

Anderson, Wilbert L., *The Country Town,* New York, Baker & Taylor Co., 1906.

Andrews, Charles M., *The River Towns of Connecticut,* Johns Hopkins University Studies in Historical and Political Science, Seventh Series, VII–IX, Baltimore, 1889.

Andrews, Evangeline Walker, and Andrews, Charles McLean (eds.), *Journal of a Lady of Quality; Being the Narrative of a Journey from Scotland to the West Indies, North Carolina, and Portugal, in the Years 1774 to 1776,* New Haven, Yale University Press, 1934.

Ardrey, R. L., *American Agricultural Implements,* Chicago, published by the author, 1894.

Arnett, Alex M., *Populist Movement in Georgia,* New York, Columbia University Press, 1922.

Ashley, A. W., "Meitzen's Siedelung und Agrarwesen der Germanen," *Political Science Quarterly,* XIII (1898).

Atwater, R. M., *Public Health in Cattaraugus County,* Olean, New York, The Commonwealth Fund, 1929.

Aurousseau, M., "The Distribution of the Population: A Constructive Problem," *Geographical Review,* XI (1921).

Bailey, L. H., *The State and the Farmer,* New York, The Macmillan Company, 1908.

Baker, O. E., "The Effect of Recent Public Policies on the Future Population Prospect," *Rural Sociology,* II (1937).

Bakkum, Glenn A., and Melvin, Bruce L., *Social Relationships of Slaterville Springs—Brooktondale Area, Tompkins County,* Cornell Agricultural Experiment Station Bulletin 501, Ithaca, 1930.

Ballagh, James Curtis, "Introduction to Southern Economic History— The Land System," *American Historical Association Annual Report for the Year 1897,* Washington, 1898.

Ballagh, James Curtin, "Southern Economic History: Tariff and Public Lands," *American Historical Association Annual Report for the Year 1898,* Washington, 1899.

Bancroft, Herbert Howe, *History of California,* San Francisco, The History Company, 1890.

Barnes, C. P., "Economies of the Long-Lot Farm," *Geographical Review,* XXV (1935).

Barrow, C. L., *A Suggested Program for the Training of Principals for Small High Schools,* Baton Rouge, Louisiana State Department of Education, 1938.

Bates, Henry Walter, *The Naturalist on the River Amazonas,* London, John Murray, 1892.

Baxter, J. H., *Medical and Anthropological Statistics of the Provost-Marshal General's Bureau,* Washington, Government Printing Office, 1875.

Bayne, Martha Collins, *County at Large,* Poughkeepsie, New York, The Women's City and Country Club with Vassar College, 1937.

Beck, P. G., and Forster, M. C., *Six Rural Problem Areas: Relief—Resources—Rehabilitation,* Federal Emergency Relief Administration Research Monograph I, Washington, 1935.

Beecher, John, "The Share Cropper's Union in Alabama," *Social Forces,* XIII (1934).

Beegle, Allan, and Loomis, C. P., "Life Cycles of Farm, Rural-Nonfarm, and Urban Families in the United States as Derived from Census Materials," *Rural Sociology,* XIII (1948).

Beers, Howard W., Williams, Robin M., Page, John S., and Ensminger, Douglas, *Community Land-Use Planning Committees,* Kentucky Agricultural Experiment Station Bulletin 417, Lexington, 1941.

Belcher, John C., and King, Morton B., Jr., *Mississippi's People,* Oxford, University of Mississippi, 1950.

Bell, Earl H., "Social Stratification in a Small Community," *Scientific Monthly,* XXXVIII (1934).

Bemis, Edward W., *Cooperation in New England,* Johns Hopkins University Studies in History and Political Science, Sixth Series, VI, Baltimore, 1888.

Bernard, Jesse, *American Community Behavior,* New York, The Dryden Press, Inc., 1949.

Bernard, Jesse, "Where Is the Modern Sociology of Conflict?" *American Journal of Sociology,* LVI (1950).

Bernard, L. L., *Introduction to Social Psychology,* New York, Henry Holt & Company, 1926.

Bernard, L. L., "Research Problems in the Psychology of Rural Life," *Journal of Social Forces,* III (1925).

Bernard, L. L., "A Theory of Rural Attitudes," *American Journal of Sociology,* XXII (1917).

Bertrand, Alvin L., "The Social Processes and Mechanization of Southern Agricultural Systems," *Rural Sociology,* XIII (1948).

Bidwell, Percy W., and Falconer, John I., *History of Agriculture in the Northern United States, 1620–1860,* Washington, The Carnegie Institute of Washington, 1925.

Biesanz, John, "Social Forces Retarding Development of Panama's Agriculture," *Rural Sociology,* XV (1950).

Binns, Bernard O., *The Consolidation of Fragmented Agricultural Holdings,* FAO Agricultural Studies II, Washington, Food and Agriculture Organization of the United Nations, 1950.

Birkbeck, Morris, *Notes on a Journey in America,* Philadelphia, Caleb Richardson, 1817.

Bizzell, William B., *The Green Rising,* New York, The Macmillan Company, 1926.

Black, John D., *Introduction to Production Economics,* New York, Henry Holt & Company, 1926.

Blackmar, Frank W., *Spanish Institutions of the Southwest,* Baltimore, Johns Hopkins University Press, 1891.

Blanchard, Raoul, "Flanders," *Geographical Review,* IV (1917).

Blose, David T., and Alves, Henry F., *Statistics of State School Systems, 1939–1936,* Washington, Government Printing Office, 1938.

Blose, David T., and Alves, Henry F., *Statistics of State School Systems, 1939–40 and 1941–42,* Washington, Government Printing Office, 1944.

Boeger, E. A., and Goldenweiser, E. A., *A Study of the Tenant Systems of Farming in the Yazoo-Mississippi Delta,* U.S. Department of Agriculture Bulletin 337, Washington, 1916.

Bohlen, Joe M., and Wakeley, Ray E., "Intentions to Migrate and Actual Migration of High School Graduates," *Rural Sociology,* XV (1950).

Bosworth, Karl A., *Tennessee Valley County: Rural Government in the Hill Country of Alabama,* University, Alabama Bureau of Public Administration, 1941.

Boyle, George M., "Nova Scotia: An Experiment in Education," *Yearbook of Agricultural Co-operation,* London, Horace Plunkett Foundation, 1935.

Brackenridge, H. M., *Views of Louisiana Together with a Journal of a Voyage up the Missouri River in 1811,* Pittsburgh, Cramer, Spear, and Eichbaum, 1814.

Brandt, Karl, "The English System of Regulating Landlord-Tenant Relations," *Journal of the American Society of Farm Managers and Rural Appraisers,* II (1938).

Brandt, Karl, "Fallacious Census Terminology and Its Consequences in Agriculture," *Social Research,* V (1938).

Brannen, C. O., *The Relation of Land Tenure to Plantation Organization,* U.S. Department of Agriculture Bulletin 1269, Washington, 1924.

Branson, E. C., *Farm Life Abroad,* Chapel Hill, University of North Carolina Press, 1924.

Bremer, Fredrika, *The Homes of the New World; Impressions of America,* New York, Harper & Brothers, 1854.

British Association for the Advancement of Science, *A Handbook to Winnipeg and the Province of Manitoba,* Winnipeg, The Local Executive Committee, 1909.

Bromage, Arthur W., *American County Government,* New York, Sears Publishing Company, 1933.

Bromwell, William J., *History of Immigration to the United States,* New York, Redfield, 1856.

Brooks, Robert Preston, *The Agrarian Revolution in Georgia, 1865–1913,* University of Wisconsin Historical Series III, Madison, 1914.

Brough, Charles Hillman, *Irrigation in Utah,* Baltimore, Johns Hopkins Press, 1898.

Browne, Lewis, *This Believing World,* New York, The Macmillan Company, 1926.

Bruce, Andrew A., *Non-Partisan League,* New York, The Macmillan Company, 1921.

Bruce, Phillip A., *Economic History of Virginia in the 17th Century,* New York, The Macmillan Company, 1895.

Brunner, Edmund deS., *Community Organization and Adult Education: A Five Year Experiment,* Chapel Hill, University of North Carolina Press, 1942.

Brunner, Edmund deS., *Radio and the Farmer,* New York, The Radio Institute of the Audible Arts, 1935.

Brunner, Edmund deS., *Village Communities,* New York, Doubleday, Doran & Company, 1928.

Brunner, Edmund deS., Hughes, Gwendolyn S., and Patten, Marjorie,

American Agricultural Villages, New York, Doubleday, Doran & Company, 1927.

Brunner, Edmund deS., and Kolb, John H., *Rural Social Trends,* New York, McGraw-Hill Book Company, 1933.

Brunner, Edmund deS., and Lorge, Irving, *Rural Trends in Depression Years,* New York, Columbia University Press, 1937.

Brunner, Edmund deS., Sanders, Irwin T., and Ensminger, Douglas (eds.), *Farmers of the World,* New York, Columbia University Press, 1945.

Brunner, Edmund deS., and Smith, T. Lynn, "Village Growth and Decline, 1930–40," *Rural Sociology,* IX (1944).

Brunner, Edmund deS., and Yang, E. Hsin Pao, *Rural America and the Extension Service,* New York, Teachers College of Columbia University, 1949.

Buck, Solon J., *The Granger Movement,* Cambridge, Harvard University Press, 1913.

Bureau of Agricultural Economics, *Agricultural Outlook Charts, 1951,* Washington, Government Printing Office, 1950.

Bureau of the Census, "Birth and Death Registration in Mississippi with Special Reference to the County Registrar," *Vital Statistics— Special Reports,* IX (1940).

Bureau of the Census, "Educational Attainment of the Population 25 Years Old and Over, for the United States: 1950," *1950 Census of Population, Preliminary Reports,* Series PC-7, No. 6, Washington, May 13, 1952.

Bureau of the Census, *Fifteenth Census of the United States: 1930,* "Population," Vols. I, II, III, and IV, Washington, Government Printing Office, 1933.

Bureau of the Census, "General Characteristics of the Population of the United States: April 1, 1950," *1950 Census of Population, Preliminary Reports,* Series PC-7, No. 1, Washington, February 25, 1951.

Bureau of the Census, "Multiple-Unit Operations," *United States Census of Agriculture, 1945,* Washington, Government Printing Office, 1947.

Bureau of the Census, "Population of Standard Metropolitan Areas: April 1, 1950," *1950 Census of Population, Preliminary Counts,* Series PC-3, No. 3, Washington, November 5, 1950.

Bureau of the Census, "Population of the United States, Urban and Rural, by States, April 1, 1950," *1950 Census of Population, Preliminary Reports,* Series PC-3, No. 10, Washington, February 16, 1951.

Bureau of the Census, *Religious Bodies: 1926,* Washington, Government Printing Office, 1930, 2 vols.

Bureau of the Census, *Religious Bodies: 1936,* Washington, Government Printing Office, 1941, 2 vols.

Bureau of the Census, *Sixteenth Census of the United States: 1940,* "Agriculture," Vol. I, Washington, Government Printing Office, 1942.

Bureau of the Census, *Sixteenth Census of the United States: 1940,* "Population," Vols. I, II, III, and IV, Washington, Government Printing Office, 1942 and 1943.

Bureau of the Census, *Sixteenth Census of the United States: 1940,* "Population, Differential Fertility 1940 and 1910, Standardized Fertility Rates and Reproduction Rates," Washington, Government Printing Office, 1944.

Bureau of the Census, *Sixteenth Census of the United States: 1940,* "Population, Nativity and Parentage of the White Population, Mother Tongue," Washington, Government Printing Office, 1943.

Bureau of the Census and Bureau of Agricultural Economics, *Graphic Summary of Farm Tenure in the United States,* Washington, Government Printing Office, 1948.

Burr, Walter, *Small Towns: An Estimate of Their Trade and Culture,* New York, The Macmillan Company, 1929.

Burrus, John N., *Life Opportunities,* Oxford, University of Mississippi, 1951.

Butterfield, Kenyon L., *Chapters in Rural Progress,* Chicago, University of Chicago Press, 1908.

Butterfield, Kenyon L., *The Farmer and the New Day,* New York, The Macmillan Company, 1919.

Byrd, Mary, "Factors Influencing the Death Rates in Louisiana," M.A. thesis (unpublished), Louisiana State University, 1934.

Calhoun, A. W., *A Social History of the American Family,* Cleveland, The Arthur H. Clark Co., 1917–1919, 3 vols.

Carpenter, Niles, *Immigrants and Their Children, 1920,* Census Monographs VII, Washington, Government Printing Office, 1927.

Carrier, Lyman, *The Beginnings of Agriculture in America,* New York, McGraw-Hill Book Company, 1923.

Carroll, H. K., *The Religious Forces of the United States,* New York, The Christian Literature Company, 1893.

Chamberlain, Alexander F., "The Contributions of the American Indian to Civilization," *Proceedings of the American Antiquarian Society,* XVI (1904).

Channing, Edward, *Town and County Government in the English Colonies of North America,* Johns Hopkins University Studies in Historical and Political Science, Second Series, X, Baltimore, 1884.

Charlton, J. L., *Social Aspects of Farm Ownership and Tenancy in the Arkansas Ozarks*, Arkansas Agricultural Experiment Station Bulletin 471, Fayetteville, 1947.

Cheyney, Edward P., *An Introduction to the Industrial and Social History of England*, New York, The Macmillan Company, 1916.

Childs, Marquis W., *Sweden: The Middle Way*, New Haven, Yale University Press, 1938.

Clapham, J. H., and Power, Eileen (eds.), *The Agrarian Life of the Middle Ages*, first volume of *The Cambridge Economic History*, Cambridge, The University Press, 1941.

Clark, John B., *Populism in Alabama*, Auburn, Auburn Printing Co., 1927.

Cleland, Herdman, "The Black Belt of Alabama," *Geographical Review*, X (1920).

Codrington, Robert H., *The Melanesians*, Oxford, The Clarendon Press, 1891.

Cole, William E., and Crowe, Hugh Price, *Recent Trends in Rural Planning*, New York, Prentice-Hall, Inc., 1937.

Collins, Selwyn D., "The Incidence and Causes of Illness at Specific Ages," *Milbank Memorial Fund Quarterly*, XIII (1935).

Commons, John R., *Races and Immigrants in America*, New York, The Macmillan Company, 1907.

Compton's Pictured Encyclopedia and Fact-Index, Chicago, F. E. Compton & Company, 1944.

Cook, Katherine M., *Review of Conditions and Development in Education in Rural and Other Sparsely Settled Areas*, Washington, Government Printing Office, 1937.

Cook, O. F., "The Debt of Agriculture to Tropical America," *Smithsonian Institution Annual Report for 1931*, Washington, 1932.

Cooley, Charles H., *Social Organization*, New York, Charles Scribner's Sons, 1909.

Cooley, Thomas M., *Michigan: A History of Governments*, Boston, Houghton Mifflin Company, 1905.

Cooper, Martin R., Barton, Glen T., and Brodell, Albert P., *Progress of Farm Mechanization*, Miscellaneous Publication 630, Washington, U.S. Department of Agriculture, 1947.

Co-operative Handbook for 1931, New Orleans, American Cotton Co-operative Association, 1931.

Crane, Verner W., *The Southern Frontier, 1670–1732*, Durham, Duke University Press, 1928.

Crevenna, Theo R., *Materiales para el Estudio de la Clase Media en la America Latina*, Washington, Pan American Union, Vols. I–VI (mimeographed), 1950, 1951.

Critchfield and Company, *A New Market Analysis*, New York, Critchfield and Company, 1927.

Cross, William T., and Cross, Dorothy E., *Newcomers and Nomads in California*, Stanford University, Stanford University Press, 1937.

Dahlke, H. Otto, and Stonecipher, Harvey V., "A War-time Back-to-Land Movement of Old Age Groups," *Rural Sociology*, XI (1946).

Daniels, John, *Cooperation: An American Way*, New York, Covici Friede, Inc., 1938.

Davenport, Charles B., and Love, A. G., "Army Anthropology," *The Medical Department of the United States Army in the World War*, XV, Washington, 1921.

Davies, Vernon, and Belcher, John C., *Mississippi Life Tables by Sex, Race and Residence, 1940*, Jackson, Mississippi Commission on Hospital Care, 1948.

Davis, William T. (ed.), *Bradford's History of Plymouth Plantation, 1606–1646*, New York, Charles Scribner's Sons, 1908.

Dawson, C. A., and Gettys, Warner E., *An Introduction to Sociology*, New York, The Ronald Press Company, 1935.

Dawson, Howard A., *Satisfactory Local School Units*, George Peabody College for Teachers Field Study 7, Nashville, 1934.

DeBow, J. D. B., *Statistical View of the United States: A Compendium of the Seventh Census*, Washington, A.O.P. Nicholson, 1854.

de Kruif, Paul, *Microbe Hunters*, New York, Harcourt, Brace & Company, 1926.

Demangeon, A., "La géographie de l'habitat rural," *Annales de géographie*, XXXVI (1927).

Dennett, Daniel, *Louisiana as It Is*, New Orleans, Eureka Press, 1876.

Dickins, Dorothy, *Family Living on Poorer and Better Soils*, Mississippi Agricultural Experiment Station Bulletin 230, State College, 1937.

Directory of Newspapers and Periodicals, Philadelphia, N. W. Ayer & Son, 1952.

Dixon, R. B., *The Racial History of Mankind*, New York, Charles Scribner's Sons, 1923.

Documents of the First Session of the 6th Legislature of the State of Louisiana, Baton Rouge, Tom Bynum, 1862.

Dodd, W. E., *The Cotton Kingdom*, New Haven, Yale University Press, 1921.

Doddridge, Joseph, *Settlement of Western Country*, Bowling Green, Historical Publications Company, 1923.

Dodson, L. S., *Living Conditions and Population Migration in Four*

Appalachian Counties, U.S. Department of Agriculture, Farm Security Administration, Bureau of Agricultural Economics, Cooperating, Social Research Report III, Washington, October, 1937.

Donaldson, Thomas, *The Public Domain,* House Miscellaneous Document 45, 47th Congress, 2nd session, XIX, Washington, Government Printing Office, 1884.

Dorchester, Daniel, *Christianity in the United States,* New York, Hunt & Eaton, 1889.

Dorn, Harold F., "The Effect of Allocation of Non-Resident Deaths upon Official Mortality Statistics," *Journal of the American Statistical Association,* XXVII (1932).

Douglas-Irvine, Helen, *The Making of Rural Europe,* London, G. Allen & Unwin, Ltd., 1923.

Drachsler, Julius, *Democracy and Assimilation,* New York, The Macmillan Company, 1920.

Drake, Daniel, *Principal Diseases of the Interior Valley of North America,* Cincinnati, privately printed, 1850.

Dublin, Louis I., *Health and Wealth,* New York, Harper & Brothers, 1928.

Dublin, Louis I., and Lotka, Alfred J., *Length of Life,* New York, The Ronald Press Company, 1936.

DuBois, W. E. Burghardt, *Economic Co-operation Among Negro Americans,* Atlanta University Publication 6, Atlanta, 1907.

Duncan, O. D., "The Fusion of White, Negro, and Indian Cultures at the Converging of the New South and the West," *Southwestern Social Science Quarterly,* XIV (1934).

Duncan, O. D., "Relation of Tenure and Economic Status of Farmers to Church Membership," *Social Forces,* XI (1933).

Duncan, O. D., "A Sociological Approach to Farm Tenancy Research," *Rural Sociology,* V (1940).

Duncan O. D., *Some Social and Economic Aspects of the Problem of Rural Health in Oklahoma,* Oklahoma Agricultural Experiment Station Circular 78, Stillwater, 1931.

Duncan, O. D., *The Theory and Consequences of Mobility of Farm Population,* Oklahoma Agricultural Experiment Station Circular 88, Stillwater, 1940.

Duncan, O. D., and Sanders, J. T., *A Study of Certain Economic Factors in Relation to Social Life Among Oklahoma Cotton Farmers,* Oklahoma Agricultural Experiment Station Bulletin 211, Stillwater, 1933.

Durkheim, Emile, *Elementary Forms of Religious Life,* London, Macmillan & Co., Ltd., 1915.

Duval, Evelyn Millis, and Motz, Annabelle Bender, "Are Country Girls So Different?" *Rural Sociology*, X (1945).

Dwight, Timothy, *Travels in New England and New York*, London, W. Baynes and Son, 1823, 4 vols.

Edwards, Everett E., *Agriculture of the American Indians*, Washington, United States Department of Agriculture, Library Bibliographical Contributions 23 (mimeographed), 1933.

Egleston, Melville, *The Land System of New England Colonies*, Johns Hopkins University Studies in Historical and Political Science, Fourth Series, XI–XII, Baltimore, 1886.

Ellis, L. W., and Rumely, Edward A., *Power and the Plow*, New York, Doubleday, Page & Co., 1911.

Ellsworth, R. H., *Statistics of Farmers' Co-operative Business Organizations*, Farm Credit Administration Bulletin 6, Washington, 1936.

Elting, Irving, *Dutch Village Communities on the Hudson River*, Johns Hopkins University Studies in Historical and Political Science, Fourth Series, I, Baltimore, 1886.

Encyclopaedia of the Social Sciences, New York, The Macmillan Company, 1937, 8 vols.

An Estimate of the Amount of Disabling Illness in the Country as a Whole. U.S. Public Health Service, Sickness and Medical Care Series Bulletin 1, Washington, 1938.

Eubank, Earle E., *The Concepts of Sociology*, Boston, D. C. Heath & Company, 1932.

Fairchild, H. P. (ed.), *Dictionary of Sociology*, New York, Philosophical Library, Inc., 1944.

Fairchild, H. P., *Immigration*, New York, The Macmillan Company, 1925.

Fairlie, John A., *Local Government in Counties, Towns, and Villages*, New York, D. Appleton-Century Company, 1906.

Fairlie, John A., and Kneier, Charles M., *County Government and Administration*, New York, D. Appleton-Century Company, 1930.

Farm Tenancy, Message from the President of the United States Transmitting the Report of the Special Committee on Farm Tenancy, 75th Congress, 1st Session, House Document 149, Washington, 1937.

Faust, Albert Bernhardt, *The German Element in the United States*, Boston, Houghton Mifflin Company, 1909.

Federal Council of the Churches of Christ in America, *Information Service*, XV (June 27, 1936).

Feeble-Minded and Epileptics in Institutions: 1923, Washington, Government Printing Office, 1926.

Felton, Ralph A., *Local Church Cooperation in Rural Communities*, New York, Home Missions Council, 1940.

Fetrow, Ward W., and Ellsworth, R. H., *Agricultural Cooperation in the United States*, Bulletin 54, Washington, Farm Credit Administration, 1947.

Fisher, Sydney G., *The Quaker Colonies*, New Haven, Yale University Press, 1919.

The Five-Year Program of the Committee on the Cost of Medical Care, New York, Committee on the Cost of Medical Care, 1928.

Flint, Timothy, *The First White Man of the West, or the Life and Exploits of Col. Dan'l Boone*, Cincinnati, Applegate and Company, 1856.

Ford, Amelia Clewley, *Colonial Precedents of Our National Land System as It Existed in 1800*, University of Wisconsin History Series, II (1910), Bulletin 352.

Forstall, E. J., "French Colonial Records—Louisiana," *DeBow's Review*, I (1846).

Forsyth, F. Howard, "The Radio and Rural Research," *Rural Sociology*, IV (1939).

Frazer, J. G., *Folklore in the Old Testament*, London, Macmillan & Co., Ltd., 1919, 3 vols.

Frazer, J. G., *The Golden Bough*, London, Macmillan & Co., Ltd., 1925–1926, 12 vols.

Frazier, E. Franklin, "An Analysis of Statistics of Negro Illegitimacy in the United States," *Social Forces*, XI (1932).

Frazier, E. Franklin, *The Negro Family in the United States*, Chicago, University of Chicago Press, 1939.

Freeman, Ronald, and Hawley, Amos H., "Education and Occupation of Migrants in the Depression," *American Journal of Sociology*, LVI (1950).

Freitas Marcondes, J. V., "Mutirao or Mutual Aid," *Rural Sociology*, XIII (1948).

Frey, Fred C., "Factors Conditioning the Incidence of Migration Among Louisiana Negroes," *Southwestern Social Science Quarterly*, XV (1934).

Frey, Fred C., and Smith, T. Lynn, "The Influence of the AAA Cotton Program upon the Tenant, Cropper, and Laborer," *Rural Sociology*, I (1936).

Fries, Adelaide L. (ed.), *Records of the Moravians in North Carolina*, Raleigh, Raleigh, Edwards and Broughton, 1922.

Fry, C. Luther, *American Villagers*, New York, Doubleday, Doran & Company, 1920.

Fuller, Varden, and Tetreau, E. D., *Volume and Characteristics of Migration to Arizona, 1930–39*, Arizona Agricultural Experiment Station Bulletin 176, Tucson, 1941.

Funck-Brentano, Frantz, *The Old Regime in France*, New York, Longmans, Green & Company, 1929.

Galla, Karel, *Sociology of the Co-operative Movement in the Czechoslovak Village*, Praha, Spolek Pece o Blaho Venkova, 1936.

Galloway, Robert E., "A Contrast in the Rural Social Organization of Rabun County, Georgia and Franklin County, Washington," *Rural Sociology*, XIII (1948).

Galloway, Robert E., and Kaufman, Harold F., *Health Practices in Choctaw County* Mississippi State College, Sociology and Rural Life Series, No. 2 (mimeographed), 1950.

Galloway, Robert E., and Kaufman, Harold F., *Health Practices of Rural People in Lee County*, Mississippi State College, Sociology and Rural Life Series, No. 1 (mimeographed), 1950.

Galloway, Robert E., and Loftin, Marion T., *Health Practices of Rural Negroes in Bolivar County*, Mississippi State College, Sociology and Rural Life Series, No. 3 (mimeographed), 1951.

Galpin, Charles J., "The Development of the Science and Philosophy of American Rural Sociology," *Agricultural History*, XII (1938).

Galpin, Charles J., *My Drift into Rural Sociology*, University, Louisiana State University Press, 1938.

Galpin, Charles J., *Rural Life*, New York, D. Appleton-Century Company, 1918.

Galpin, Charles J., *Rural Social Problems*, New York, D. Appleton-Century Company, 1924.

Galpin, Charles J., *The Social Anatomy of an Agricultural Community*, Wisconsin Agricultural Experiment Station Bulletin 34, Madison, 1915.

Galpin, Charles J., and Manny, T. B., *Interstate Migrations Among the Native White Population as Indicated by Differences Between State of Birth and State of Residence*, U.S. Department of Agriculture, Bureau of Agricultural Economics, Washington, 1934.

Gaumitz, Walter H., *The Smallness of America's Rural High Schools*, U.S. Office of Education Bulletin 13, Washington, 1930.

Gee, Wilson, *The Qualitative Nature of Rural Depopulation in Santuc Township, South Carolina, 1900–30*, South Carolina Agricultural Experiment Station Bulletin 287, Clemson, 1933.

Gee, Wilson, "A Qualitative Study of Rural Depopulation in a Single Township, 1900–1910," *American Journal of Sociology*, XXXIX (1933).

Gee, Wilson, *Research in the Social Sciences*, New York, The Macmillan Company, 1929.

Gee, Wilson, *The Social Economics of Agriculture*, New York, The Macmillan Company, 1932.

Gee, Wilson, *The Social Economics of Agriculture,* New York, The Macmillan Company, 1942.

Genthe, Martha Krug, "Valley Towns of Connecticut," *Bulletin of the American Geographical Society of New York,* XXXIX (1921).

George, Henry, *Our Land and Land Policy,* New York, Doubleday, Doran & Company, 1911.

Gewehr, Wesley M., *The Great Awakening in Virginia, 1740–1790,* Durham, Duke University Press, 1930.

Gide, Charles, *Communist and Cooperative Colonies,* New York, Thomas Y. Crowell Company, 1928.

Gillette, John M., *Constructive Rural Sociology,* New York, Sturgis and Walton Company, 1913.

Gillette, John M., *Rural Sociology,* New York, The Macmillan Company, 1923.

Gillette, John M., *Rural Sociology,* New York, The Macmillan Company, 1928.

Gillette, John M., *Rural Sociology,* New York, The Macmillan Company, 1936.

Gillin, John Lewis, and Gillin, John Philip, *Cultural Sociology,* New York, The Macmillan Company, 1948.

Godkin, James, *The Land-War in Ireland,* London, Macmillan & Co., Ltd., 1870.

Goldenweiser, E. A., and Truesdell, Leon E., *Farm Tenancy in the United States,* 1920 Census Monographs IV, Washington, 1924.

Goldschmidt, Walter R., "Some Evidence on the Future Pattern of Rural Settlement," *Rural Sociology,* VIII (1943).

Goldstein, Marcus S., "Physical Status of Men Examined Through Selective Service in World War II," *Public Health Reports,* LXVI (1951).

Gomme, George Laurence, *The Village Community, with Special Reference to the Origin and Form of Its Survivals in Britain,* London, Walter Scott, Ltd., 1890.

Goodrich, Carter, and others, *Migration and Economic Opportunity,* Philadelphia, University of Pennsylvania Press, 1936.

Goodwin, Maud Wilder, *Dutch and English on the Hudson,* New Haven, Yale University Press, 1919.

Gosse, A. Bothwell, *The Civilization of the Ancient Egyptians,* London, T. C. and E. Jack, 1915.

Gould, B. A., *Investigations in the Military and Anthropological Statistics of American Soldiers,* Boston, Hurd and Houghton, 1869.

Grady, Henry, "Cotton and the South," *Harper's Magazine,* LXIII (1881).

Grant, Madison, *The Passing of the Great Race*, New York, Charles Scribner's Sons, 1916.

Gras, N. S. B., *An Introduction to Economic History*, New York, Harper & Brothers, 1922.

Gras, N. S. B., and Gras, Ethel C., *The Economic and Social History of an English Village*, Cambridge, Harvard University Press, 1930.

Gray, L. C., *History of Agriculture in the Southern United States to 1860*, Washington, The Carnegie Institution of Washington, 1933, 2 vols.

Gray, L. C., Stewart, Charles L., Turner, H. A., Sanders, J. T., and Spillman, W. J., "Farm Ownership and Tenancy," *Yearbook of the Department of Agriculture, 1923*, Washington, Government Printing Office, 1924.

Gregg, Alexander, *History of the Old Cheraws*, Columbia, S.C., The State Company, 1905.

Gregg, William, "Domestic Industry-Manufactures at the South," *De Bow's Review*, VIII (1850).

Grigsby, S. Earl, and Hoffsommer, Harold, *Cotton Plantation Laborers*, Louisiana Agricultural Experiment Station Bulletin 328, Baton Rouge, 1941.

Grigsby, S. Earl, and Hoffsommer, Harold, *Rural Social Organization of Frederick County, Maryland*, Maryland Agricultural Experiment Station Bulletin No. A-51, College Park, 1949.

Groves, E. R., and Ogburn, W. F., *American Marriage and Family Relationships*, New York, Henry Holt & Company, 1928.

Guignebert, Charles, *Christianity, Past and Present*, New York, The Macmillan Company, 1927.

Hall, Marshall, *Two-Fold Slavery of the United States*, London, A. Scott, 1854.

Hamilton, C. Horace, "The Annual Rate of Departure of Rural Youths from Their Parental Homes," *Rural Sociology*, I (1936).

Hamilton, C. Horace, *Rural-Urban Migration in North Carolina, 1920 to 1930*, North Carolina Agricultural Experiment Station Bulletin 295, Raleigh, 1934.

Hamilton, C. Horace, "Social Effects of Recent Trends in the Mechanization of Agriculture," *Rural Sociology*, IV (1939).

Hamilton, C. Horace, and Ellison, John M., *The Negro Church in Rural Virginia*, Virginia Agricultural Experiment Station Bulletin 273, Blacksburg, 1930.

Hamilton, C. Horace, Hobbs, S. H., and Stimson, R. T., *Medical Care Services in North Carolina: A Statistical and Graphic Summary Pre-*

pared for the Governor's Commission on Hospital and Medical Care, Raleigh, Department of Rural Sociology, North Carolina Agricultural Experiment Station, 1944.

Hammond, M. B., *The Cotton Industry,* New York, The Macmillan Company, 1901.

Hammond, S. C., "Progress of Southern Industry," *DeBow's Review,* VIII (1850).

Hankins, Frank H., *The Racial Basis of Civilization,* New York, Alfred A. Knopf, Inc., 1926.

Hansen, Georg, *Die drei Bevolkerungstuffen,* Munich, Lindauer, 1889.

Hardin, Charles M., *The Politics of Agriculture: Soil Conservation and the Struggle for Power in Rural America,* Glencoe, Illinois, The Free Press, 1952.

Harris, Marshall, *Agricultural Landlord-Tenant Relations in England and Wales,* Land Use Planning Publication 4, Resettlement Administration, Washington, 1936.

Harris, William H., *Louisiana Products, Resources and Attractions, with a Sketch of the Parishes,* New Orleans, New Orleans *Democrat,* 1881.

Harrison, Jane, *Themis,* New York, The Macmillan Company, 1927.

Hart, Albert Bushnell, *The Southern South,* New York, D. Appleton-Century Company, 1910.

Hart, Hornell N., *Selective Migration as a Factor in Child Welfare in the United States, with Special Reference to Iowa,* University of Iowa Studies, Iowa City, 1921.

Hastings, James, *Encyclopedia of Religion and Ethics,* New York, Charles Scribner's Sons, 1924.

Hatch, D. Spencer, *Up from Poverty in Rural India,* Bombay, Oxford University Press, 1938.

Hatt, Paul K., "Occupation and Social Stratification," *American Journal of Sociology,* LV (1950).

Hawthorne, H. B., *The Sociology of Rural Life,* New York, D. Appleton-Century Company, 1926.

Hay, Donald G., and Polson, Robert A., *Rural Social Organization in Oneida County, New York,* Cornell Agricultural Experiment Station Bulletin 871, Ithaca, 1951.

Hayes, A. W., *Rural Sociology,* New York, Longmans, Green & Company, 1929.

Hayes, E. C., "Some Social Relations Related," *American Journal of Sociology,* XXXI (1925).

Hayes, Wayland J., *The Small Community Looks Ahead,* New York, Harcourt, Brace and Company, 1947.

Hayward, John, *The Book of Religions,* Boston, Albert Colby and Company, 1860.

Helper, Hinton Rowan, *The Impending Crisis of the South: How to Meet It,* New York, Burdick Brothers, 1857.

Hepple, Lawrence M., and Bright, Margaret L., *Social Changes in Shelby County, Missouri,* Missouri Agricultural Experiment Station Research Bulletin 456, Columbia, 1950.

Herskovits, Melville J., *Acculturation,* New York, J. J. Augustin, 1938.

Hewes, Lawrence I., Jr., *Japanese Land Reform Program,* Natural Resources Section Report 127, Tokyo, General Headquarters, Supreme Commander for the Allied Powers, 1950.

Hibbard, B. H., *A History of the Public Land Policies,* New York, The Macmillan Company, 1924.

Hicks, John D., *The Populist Revolt,* Minneapolis, University of Minnesota Press, 1931.

Hildreth, Richard, *The History of the United States of America,* New York, Harper & Brothers, 1856.

Hill, Robert Tudor, *The Public Domain and Democracy,* New York, Columbia University Press, 1910.

Hitt, Homer L., *Recent Migration Into and Within the Upper Mississippi Delta of Louisiana,* Louisiana Agricultural Experiment Station Bulletin 364, Baton Rouge, 1943.

Hitt, Homer L., and Bertrand, Alvin L., *Social Aspects of Hospital Planning in Louisiana,* Baton Rouge, Department of Rural Sociology, Louisiana Agricultural Experiment Station and Health and Hospital Division, Office of the Governor, 1947.

Hitt, Homer L., and Bradford, Reed H., "The Relation of Residential Instability to Fertility," *Rural Sociology,* V (1940).

Hoagland, H. E., "The Movement of Rural Population to Illinois," *Journal of Political Economy,* XX (1912).

Hoffer, C. R., "The Changing Ecological Pattern in Rural Life," *Rural Sociology,* XIII (1948).

Hoffer, C. R., "Co-operation as a Culture Pattern Within a Community," *Rural Sociology,* III (1938).

Hoffer, C. R., and Gibson, D. L., *The Community Situation as It Affects Agricultural Extension Work,* Michigan Agricultural Experiment Station Special Bulletin 312, East Lansing, 1941.

Hoffer, Charles S., *Health and Health Services for Michigan Farm Families,* Michigan Agricultural Experiment Station Bulletin 352, East Lansing, 1948.

Hoffman, Charles S., "Drought and Depression Migration into Oregon 1930 to 1936," *Monthly Labor Review* (January, 1938).

Hoffman, Oscar F., "Culture Changes in a Rural Wisconsin Ethnic Island," *Rural Sociology,* XIV (1949).

Hoffsommer, H. S., *Landlord-Tenant Relations and Relief in Alabama,* Research Bulletin, Series II, No. 9, Federal Emergency Relief Administration, Washington, 1935.

Hoffsommer, H. S., *Relation of Cities and Larger Villages to Changes in Rural Trade and Social Areas in Wayne County, New York,* Cornell University Agricultural Experiment Station Bulletin 582, Ithaca, 1934.

Hoffsommer, H. S. (ed.), *The Social and Economic Significance of Land Tenure in the Southwestern States,* Chapel Hill, University of North Carolina Press, 1950.

Hoffsommer, H. S., and Pryor, Herbert, *Neighborhoods and Communities in Covington County, Mississippi,* Washington, United States Department of Agriculture, 1941.

Holmes, Roy H., *Rural Sociology,* New York, McGraw-Hill Book Company, 1932.

Holt, John B., *German Agricultural Policy, 1918–1934,* Chapel Hill, University of North Carolina Press, 1936.

Holt, John B., "Recent Changes in German Rural Life," *Rural Sociology,* II (1937).

Holt, John B., *Rural Neighborhoods and Communities of Lee County, Alabama, and Their Significance for Land Use Planning,* Washington, United States Department of Agriculture, 1941.

Hooker, Elizabeth R., *United Churches,* New York, Doubleday, Doran & Company, 1926.

Hope, John, II, "Rochdale Cooperation Among Negroes," *Phylon,* I (1940).

Houser, Paul M., and Galloway, Robert E., "Use and Acceptance of Public Library Services in a Rural Area," *Rural Sociology,* XIV (1949).

Howe, Frederic C., *Denmark: The Co-operative Way,* New York, Coward-McCann, Inc., 1936.

Howe, Henry, *Historical Collections of Ohio,* Cincinnati, E. Morgan, 1856.

Hulbert, Archer B. (Introduction by), *Washington and the West,* New York, D. Appleton-Century Company, 1905.

Hummel, B. L., "County Organization for Program Planning in Virginia," *Rural Sociology,* I (1936).

Hunt, Robert L., *A History of Farmer Movements in the Southwest, 1873–1925,* College Station, Texas A. & M. College Press, 1935.

Hyde, William DeWitt, "Impending Paganism in New England," *The Forum,* XIII (1892).

Hypes, J. L., *Population Mobility in Rural Connecticut,* Storrs Agricultural Experiment Station Bulletin 196, Storrs, 1934.

Illness and Medical Care in Relation to Economic Status, The National Health Survey, U.S. Public Health Service, Sickness and Medical Care Series Bulletin 2, Washington (mimeographed), 1938.

Interbureau Committee on Post-War Problems, *Better Health for Rural America: Plans of Action for Farm Communities,* Washington, Government Printing Office, 1945.

James, Herman G., *Local Government in the United States,* New York, D. Appleton-Century Company, 1921.

Jameson, J. Franklin, *Johnson's Wonder-Working Providence, 1628–1651,* New York, Charles Scribner's Sons, 1910.

Jefferson, Mark, *Peopling the Argentine Pampa,* New York, American Geographical Society, 1926.

Jehlik, Paul J., and Losey, J. Edwin, *Rural Social Organization in Henry County, Indiana,* Indiana Agricultural Experiment Station Bulletin 568, Lafayette, 1951.

Jehlik, Paul J., and Wakeley, Ray E., *Rural Organization in Process: A Case Study of Hamilton County, Iowa,* Research Bulletin 365, Ames, 1949.

Jernegan, Marcus W., *The American Colonies, 1492–1750,* New York, Longmans, Green & Company, 1929.

Jessen, Carl A., *Trends in Secondary Education,* Washington, Government Printing Office, 1937.

Johansen, John P., *Immigrant Settlements and Social Organization in South Dakota,* South Dakota Agricultural Experiment Station Bulletin 313, Brookings, 1937.

Johnson, Cecil, "The Distribution of Land in British West Florida," *Louisiana Historical Quarterly,* XVI (1933).

Johnson, Charles S., *Shadow of the Plantation,* Chicago, University of Chicago Press, 1934.

Johnson, Charles S., Embree, Edwin R., and Alexander, W. W., *The Collapse of Cotton Tenancy,* Chapel Hill, University of North Carolina Press, 1935.

Johnson, Guion Griffis, *A Social History of the Sea Islands,* Chapel Hill, University of North Carolina Press, 1930.

Johnson, John H., *Old Maryland Manors, with the Records of a Court Leet and a Court Baron,* Johns Hopkins University Studies in Historical and Political Science, First Series, VII, Baltimore, 1883.

Johnstone, Paul H., "On the Identification of the Farmer," *Rural Sociology,* V (1940).

Jordan, Floyd, *The Social Composition of Secondary Schools in the*

Southern States, Nashville, George Peabody College for Teachers, 1933.

Kaufman, Harold F., *Prestige Classes in a New York Rural Community*, Cornell Agricultural Experiment Station Memoir 260, Ithaca, 1944.

Kaufman, Harold F., *Rural Churches in Kentucky, 1947*, Kentucky Agricultural Experiment Station Bulletin 530, Lexington, 1949.

Kaufman, Harold F., *Use of Medical Services in Rural Missouri*, Missouri Agricultural Experiment Station Research Bulletin 400, Columbia, 1946.

Kemp, Louise, and Smith, T. Lynn, *Health and Mortality in Louisiana*, Louisiana Agricultural Experiment Station Bulletin 390, Baton Rouge, 1945.

Kensler, Gladys M., and Melvin, Bruce L., *A Partial Sociological Study of Dryden, New York*, Cornell University Agricultural Experiment Station Bulletin 504, Ithaca, 1930.

Kephart, Horace, *Our Southern Highlanders*, New York, Outing Publishing Company, 1913.

Kester, Howard, *Revolt Among the Sharecroppers*, New York, Covici Friede, Inc., 1936.

Kile, O. M., *The Farm Bureau Movement*, New York, The Macmillan Company, 1921.

Kirkland, Edward C., *A History of American Economic Life*, New York, Appleton-Century-Crofts, Inc., 1932.

Kirkpatrick, E. L., Tough, Rosalind, and Cowles, May L., *The Life Cycle of the Farm Family*, Wisconsin Agricultural Experiment Station Research Bulletin 121, Madison, 1934.

Kiser, Clyde V., "Birth Rates Among Rural Migrants in Cities," *Milbank Memorial Fund Quarterly*, XVI (1938).

Klein, Julius, *The Mesta: A Study in Spanish Economic History, 1273–1836*, Cambridge, Harvard University Press, 1920.

Kolb, John H., *Rural Primary Groups*, Wisconsin Agricultural Experiment Station Research Bulletin 51, Madison, 1921.

Kolb, John H., *Trends in Country Neighborhoods*, Wisconsin Agricultural Experiment Station Bulletin 51, Madison, 1921.

Kolb, John H., and Bornman, C. J., *Rural Religious Organizations*, Wisconsin Agricultural Experiment Station Research Bulletin 60, Madison, 1924.

Kolb, John H., and Brunner, Edmund deS., *A Study of Rural Society*, Boston, Houghton Mifflin Company, 1935.

Kolb, John H., and Brunner, Edmund deS., *A Study of Rural Society*, Boston, Houghton Mifflin Company, 1940.

Kolb, John H., and Brunner, Edmund deS., *A Study of Rural Society*, Boston, Houghton Mifflin Company, 1952.

Kolb, John H., and Marshall, Douglas G., *Neighborhood-Community Relationships in Rural Society,* Wisconsin Agricultural Experiment Station Research Bulletin 154, Madison, 1944.

Kolb, John H., and Polson, Robert A., *Trends in Town-Country Relations,* Wisconsin Agricultural Experiment Station Research Bulletin 117, Madison, 1933.

Kropotkin, P., *Mutual Aid: A Factor in Evolution,* New York, McClure, Phillips & Co., 1902.

Kumlein, W. F., *Basic Trends of Social Change in South Dakota, VII: Local Government,* South Dakota Agricultural Experiment Station Bulletin 347, Brookings, 1941.

Landis, Paul H., "The Development of Rural Sociology in the United States," *Sociology and Social Research,* XXII (1938).

Landis, Paul H., *The Growth and Decline of South Dakota Trade Centers, 1901–1933,* South Dakota Agricultural Experiment Station Bulletin 279, Brookings, 1933.

Landis, Paul H., "Personality Differences of Girls from Farm, Town, and City," *Rural Sociology,* XIV (1949).

Landis, Paul H., *Rural Life in Process,* New York, McGraw-Hill Book Company, 1940.

Landis, Paul H., *Rural Life in Process,* New York, McGraw-Hill Book Company, 1948.

Landis, Paul H., "Sequential Marriage," *Journal of Home Economics,* XLII (1950).

Landis, Paul H., *South Dakota Town-Country Trade Relations, 1901–1931,* South Dakota Agricultural Experiment Station Bulletin 274, Brookings, 1932.

Landis, Paul H., and Brooks, Melvin, *Farm Labor in the Yakima Valley,* Washington Agricultural Experiment Station Bulletin 343, Pullman, 1936.

Latham, Henry, *Black and White: A Journal of a Three Months' Tour in the United States,* London, Macmillan & Co., Ltd., 1867.

Laveleye, Emile de, *Primitive Property,* London, Macmillan & Co., Ltd., 1878.

Leigh, Frances Butler, *Ten Years on a Georgia Plantation Since the War,* London, R. Bentley & Son, 1883.

Leonard, Olen E., *Canton Chullpas: A Socioeconomic Study in the Cochabamba Valley of Bolivia,* Foreign Agriculture Report 27, Washington, Office of Foreign Agricultural Relations, 1948.

Leonard, Olen E., *Pichilingue: A Study of Rural Life in Coastal Ecuador,* Foreign Agriculture Report 17, Washington, Office of Foreign Agricultural Relations, 1947.

Leonard, Olen E., *The Role of the Land Grant in the Social Organiza-*

tion and Social Processes of a Spanish-American Village in New Mexico, Ann Arbor, Michigan, Edwards Brothers, Inc., 1948.

Leonard, Olen E., *Santa Cruz: A Socioeconomic Study of an Area in Bolivia*, Foreign Agriculture Report 31, Washington, Office of Foreign Agricultural Relations, 1948.

Leonard, Olen E., and Loomis, Charles P., *Culture of a Contemporary Rural Community: El Cerrito, New Mexico*, U.S. Department of Agriculture, Rural Life Studies 1, Washington, 1941.

Ligutti, Luigi G., and Rawe, John C., *Rural Roads to Security*, Milwaukee, Bruce Publishing Company, 1940.

Linder, Forrest E., and Grove, Robert D., *Vital Statistics Rates in the United States, 1900–1940*, Washington, Government Printing Office, 1943.

Lindstrom, David Edgar, *American Rural Life*, New York, The Ronald Press Company, 1948.

Little, Harry A., *Potential Economies in the Reorganization of Local School Attendance Units*, Teachers College, Columbia University Contributions to Education 628, New York, 1934.

Lively, C. E., "The Development of Research in Rural Migration in the United States," *Congrès International de la Population*, IV (1938).

Lively, C. E., "The Small Trade Center Declines," *Rural America* (March, 1932).

Lively, C. E., "Spatial Mobility of the Rural Population with Respect to Local Areas," *American Journal of Sociology*, XLIII (1937).

Lively, C. E., and Beck, P. G., *The Rural Health Facilities of Ross County, Ohio*, Ohio Agricultural Experiment Station Bulletin 412, Columbus, 1927.

Lively, C. E., and Foott, Frances, *Population Mobility in Selected Areas of Rural Ohio, 1928–1935*, Ohio Agricultural Experiment Station Bulletin 582, Columbus, 1937.

Livermore, Shaw, *Early Land Companies: Their Influence on Corporate Development*, New York, The Commonwealth Fund, 1939.

Lombroso, Cesare, *Crime, Its Causes and Remedies*, Boston, H. P. Horton, 1911.

Loomis, Charles P., *The Growth of the Farm Family in Relation to Its Activities*, North Carolina Agricultural Experiment Station Bulletin 208, Raleigh, 1934.

Loomis, Charles P., "The Nature of Rural Social Systems," *Rural Sociology*, XV (1950).

Loomis, Charles P., *Studies in Rural Social Organization*, East Lansing, Michigan State College Book Store, 1945.

Loomis, Charles P., "The Study of the Life Cycle of Families," *Rural Sociology,* I (1936).

Loomis, Charles P., "Trial Use of Public Opinion Survey Procedures in Determining Immigration and Colonization Policies for Bolivia, Ecuador, and Peru," *Social Forces,* XXVI (1947).

Loomis, Charles P., and Beegle, J. Allan, *Rural Social Systems,* New York, Prentice-Hall, Inc., 1950.

Loring, F. W., and Atkinson, C. F., *Cotton Culture and the South Considered with Reference to Emigration,* Boston, A. Williams & Co., 1869.

Love, Albert G., and Davenport, Charles B., *Defects Found in Drafted Men,* Washington, Government Printing Office, 1920.

Lowden, Frank O., "Can Local Self-Government Be Preserved in Our Rural Areas?" *Rural Government: Proceedings of the Fourteenth American Country Life Association,* Chicago, University of Chicago Press, 1932.

Lowie, Robert H., *Primitive Society,* New York, Boni and Liveright, 1920.

MacIver, R. M., *Society: A Textbook of Sociology,* New York, Farrar & Rinehart, Inc., 1937.

MacIver, R. M., *Society: Its Structure and Changes,* New York, R. Long and R. R. Smith, Inc., 1931.

Maclachlan, John M, and de Tamble, Forbes R., "Florida's Medical Care Resources," University of Florida *Economic Leaflets,* III, No. 6 (1944).

MacLear, Anne B., *Early New England Towns,* Columbia University Studies in Economics, History, and Public Law, New York, Longmans, Green & Company, 1908.

Macmillan, W. M., *Warning from the West Indies: A Tract for Africa and the Empire,* London, Faber and Faber Limited, 1936.

Maine, Sir Henry Sumner, *Village Communities in the East and West,* New York, Henry Holt & Company, 1889.

Maitland, F. W., *Domesday Book and Beyond,* Cambridge, The University Press, 1897.

Mangus, A. R., "Personality Adjustment of Rural and Urban Children," *American Sociological Review,* XIII (1948).

Mangus, A. R., and Woodward, R. H., *An Analysis of the Mental Health of Elementary School Children,* Hamilton, Ohio State Department of Public Welfare, The Ohio State University, and the Ohio Agricultural Experiment Station in coöperation with the Butler County Mental Hygiene Association (processed), 1949.

Mangus, A. R., and Woodward, R. H., *An Analysis of the Mental Health of High School Students,* Hamilton, Ohio State Department of Public Welfare, The Ohio State University, and the Ohio Agricultural Experiment Station in coöperation with the Butler County Mental Hygiene Association (processed), 1949.

Manny, Theodore B., *Attitudes Towards Rural Government,* United States Department of Agriculture, Washington, (mimeographed), 1929.

Manny, Theodore B., Allin, Bushrod W., and Bradley, Clifton J., *Farm Taxes and Local Government in Crittenden and Livingston Counties, Kentucky,* Kentucky Agricultural Experiment Station Bulletin 355, Lexington, 1934.

Marett, R. R., *The Threshold of Religion,* London, Methuen & Co., 1914.

Mason, John E., "Private and Public Costs of Isolated Settlement in the Cut-Over Area of Minnesota," *Rural Sociology,* V (1940).

Maspero, Gaston, *The Dawn of Civilization, Egypt and Chaldea,* London, Society for Promoting Christian Knowledge, 1910.

Mather, William G., Jr., *The Rural Churches of Allegheny County,* Cornell University Agricultural Experiment Station Bulletin 587, Ithaca, 1933.

May, Mark A., and Doob, Leonard W., *Competition and Co-operation,* Social Science Research Council Bulletin 25, New York, 1937.

Mayo, Selz C., "Testing Criteria of Rural Locality Groups," *Rural Sociology,* XIV (1949).

Mayo, Selz C., and Bobbitt, Robert McD., *Rural Organization: A Restudy of Locality Groups in Wake County, North Carolina,* North Carolina Agricultural Experiment Station Technical Bulletin 95, Raleigh, 1951.

Mayo, Selz C., and Fullerton, Kie Sebastian, *Medical Care in Green County,* North Carolina Agricultural Experiment Station Bulletin 363, Raleigh, 1948.

McBride, G. M., "The Agrarian Problem in Chile," *Geographical Review,* XX (1930).

McBride, G. M., *Chile: Land and Society,* American Geographical Society Research Series 19, New York, 1936.

McBride, G. M., *Land Systems of Mexico,* American Geographical Society Research Series 12, New York, 1923.

McCrady, Edward, *The History of South Carolina Under the Proprietory Government, 1670–1719,* New York, The Macmillan Company, 1897.

McKain, Walter C., and Whetten, N. L., "Size of Family in Relation to Homogeneity of Parental Traits," *Rural Sociology,* I (1936).

McKain, Walter C., Jr., and Baldwin, Elmer D., *Old Age and Retire-*

ment in Rural Connecticut, Storrs Agricultural Experiment Station Bulletin 278, Storrs, 1951.

McKinley, A. E., "The English and the Dutch Towns of New Netherlands," *American Historical Review,* VI (1901).

McMahan, C. A., *Georgia Life Tables by Sex, Race, and Residence,* Atlanta, Georgia Department of Public Health (mimeographed), 1950.

McMillan, Robert T., "Effects of Mechanization on American Agriculture," *Scientific Monthly,* LXIX (1949).

McMillan, Robert T., *Migration of Population in Five Oklahoma Townships,* Oklahoma Agricultural Experiment Station Bulletin B-271, Stillwater, 1943.

McMillan, Robert T., *Migration and Status of Open-Country Families in Oklahoma.* Oklahoma Agricultural Experiment Station Technical Bulletin T-19, Stillwater, 1943.

McNamara, Robert L., "Changes in the Characteristics and Number of Practicing Physicians in Rural Ohio in 1923–1942," *Rural Sociology,* IX (1944).

McNamara, Robert L., and Mitchell, John B., *Supply of Physicians in Selected Rural Areas,* Columbia, Department of Rural Sociology, University of Missouri (mimeographed), 1951.

McNeill, George E., *The Labor Movement: The Problem of Today,* Boston, A. M. Bridgman & Co., 1887.

McVey, Frank L., *The Populist Movement,* New York, American Economic Association, 1896, I.

Mead, Margaret, *Cooperation and Competition Among Primitive Peoples,* New York, McGraw-Hill Book Company, 1937.

Meitzen, A., *Siedelung und Agrarwesen der Westgermanen und Ostgermanen, der Kelten, Finnen, und Slaven,* Berlin, Besser, 1895.

Melvin, Bruce L., *The Sociology of a Village and Its Surrounding Territory,* Cornell University Agricultural Experiment Station Bulletin 523, Ithaca, 1931.

Mental Defectives and Epileptics in Institutions: 1935, Bureau of the Census, Washington, 1937.

Menzies, Allan, *History of Religion,* New York, Charles Scribner's Sons, 1927.

Metropolitan Life Insurance Company, *Statistical Bulletin,* XVI (1935) and XIX (1938).

Metzler, William H., and Sayin, Afife F., *The Agricultural Labor Force in The San Joaquin Valley, California, 1948,* Washington, U.S. Department of Agriculture coöperating with University of California Institute of Industrial Relations (mimeographed), 1950.

M'Greagor, John, *British America*, Edinburgh, W. Blackwood Publishing Company, 2nd ed., 1833.

Mikkelsen, Michael A., *The Bishop Hill Colony*, Johns Hopkins University Series in Historical and Political Science, Tenth Series, Baltimore, 1892.

Millspaugh, A. V., "Irregular Voting in the United States," *Political Science Quarterly*, XXXIII (1918).

Molyneaux, J. Lambert, "Differential Mortality in Texas," *American Sociological Review*, X (1945).

Molyneaux, J. Lambert, *Differential Mortality in Virginia*, Charlottesville, University of Virginia, 1947.

Monette, John W., *History of the Discovery and Settlement of the Valley of the Mississippi*, New York, Harper & Brothers, 1846, 2 vols.

Montgomery, Robert H., *The Co-operative Pattern in Cotton*, New York, The Macmillan Company, 1929.

Moore, Jane, *Cityward Migration: Swedish Data*, Chicago, University of Chicago Press, 1938.

Morgan, E. L., and Howells, Owen, *Rural Population Groups*, Missouri Agricultural Experiment Station Research Bulletin 74, Columbia, 1935.

Morris, Richard B., *Studies in the History of American Law*, New York, Columbia University Press, 1930.

Morrison, T. Maxwell, *Coopersburg Survey: Being a Study of the Community Around Coopersburg, Lehigh County, Pennsylvania*, Easton, Moravian Country Church Commission, 1914.

Mott, Frederick D., and Roemer, Milton I., *Rural Health and Medical Care*, New York, McGraw-Hill Book Company, 1948.

Mountin, J. W., Pennell, E. H., and Nicolay, Virginia, "Location and Movement of Physicians, 1923 and 1938: Age Distribution in Relation to County Characteristics," *Public Health Reports*, LVIII (1943).

Mowrer, Ernest R., *The Family, Its Organization and Disorganization*, Chicago, University of Chicago Press, 1932.

Müller, Max, *Introduction to the Science of Religion*, London, Longmans, Green & Co., Ltd., 1873.

Munch, Peter A., "Gard: The Norwegian Farm," *Rural Sociology*, XII (1947).

Munro, William Bennett, *The Seigneurs of Old Canada*, Toronto, Brook and Company, 1922.

Mustard, Harry S., *A Chapter of Child Health*, New York, The Commonwealth Fund, 1930.

Mustard, Harry S., *Cross-Sections of Rural Health Progress*, New York, The Commonwealth Fund, 1930.

National Catholic Rural Life Conference, *Manifesto on Rural Life,* Milwaukee, Bruce Publishing Company, 1939.

National Institute of Mental Health, *Patients in Mental Institutions, 1948,* Washington, Government Printing Office, 1951.

National Office of Vital Statistics, "Births by Person in Attendance: United States, Each Division and State, 1949," *Vital Statistics— Special Reports,* XXXVI (1951).

National Office of Vital Statistics, "Births by Race and by Urban and Rural Areas: United States, Each Division and State, 1949," *Vital Statistics—Special Reports,* XXXVI (1951).

National Office of Vital Statistics, "Deaths by Race and by Urban and Rural Areas: United States, Each Division and State, 1949," *Vital Statistics—Special Reports,* XXXVI (1952).

National Office of Vital Statistics, "Infant Mortality by Race and by Urban and Rural Areas," *Vital Statistics—Special Reports,* XXXV (1950).

National Office of Vital Statistics, *Preliminary Results of the 1950 Birth Registration Test,* Washington, Federal Security Agency (mimeographed), 1952.

National Office of Vital Statistics, "United States Abridged Life Tables, 1939: Urban and Rural by Regions, Color, and Sex," *Vital Statistics—Special Reports,* XXIII (1947).

National Resources Committee, *Our Cities: Their Role in the National Economy, Washington,* Government Printing Office, 1937.

National Resources Committee, "State Data," *Population Statistics,* Washington, Government Printing Office, 1937.

National Resources Committee, "Urban Data," *Population Statistics,* Washington, Government Printing Office, 1937.

National Resources Planning Board, *Northern Great Plains,* Washington, Government Printing Office, 1940.

Nearing, Peter A., "The Xavierian Movement," *Rural Sociology,* II (1937).

Nelson, Charles W., "Testing the Influence of Rural and Urban Environment on A. C. E. Intelligence Test Scores," *American Sociological Review,* VII (1942).

Nelson, Lowry, "Bauerndorfer im westen der Vereinigten Staaten," *Internationale Agrar-Rundschau,* II (1939).

Nelson, Lowry, "Early Landholding Practices in Utah," *Journal of Farm Economics,* IX (1927).

Nelson, Lowry, *The Mormon Village: A Study in Social Origins,* Brigham Young University Studies 3, Provo, 1930.

Nelson, Lowry, *Rural Cuba,* Minneapolis, University of Minnesota Press, 1950.

Nelson, Lowry, *Rural Sociology,* New York, American Book Company, 1948.

Nelson, Lowry, *Some Social and Economic Features of American Fork, Utah,* Brigham Young University Studies 4, Provo, 1933.

Nelson, Lowry, *The Utah Farm Village of Ephraim,* Brigham Young University Studies 2, Provo, 1928.

New York Bureau of Municipal Research, *Report on County Government in Virginia,* 1928.

Newsholme, Sir Arthur, *The Elements of Vital Statistics,* New York, D. Appleton-Century Company, 1924.

Nielson, N., *Medieval Agrarian Economy,* New York, Henry Holt & Company, 1936.

Nixon, H. C., *Forty Acres and Steel Mules,* Chapel Hill, University of North Carolina Press, 1938.

Nixon, H. C., "The Populist Movement in Iowa," *Iowa Journal of History and Politics* (March, 1926).

Nordhoff, Charles, *The Communistic Societies of the United States,* New York, Harper & Brothers, 1875.

Nordhoff, Charles, *The Cotton States in the Spring and Summer of 1875,* New York, D. Appleton & Co., 1876.

Notestein, Frank W., "Differential Fertility in the East North Central States," *Milbank Memorial Fund Quarterly,* XVI (1938).

O'Callaghan, E. B., *The Documentary History of the State of New York,* Albany, Weed, Parsons, & Co., 1850, 3 vols.

Ogburn, W. F., *Social Change,* New York, The Viking Press, 1922.

Ogburn, W. F., and Peterson, Delvin, "Political Thought of Social Classes," *Political Science Quarterly,* XXXI (1916).

O'Hara, Edwin V., *The Church and the Country Community,* New York, The Macmillan Company, 1927.

Olmsted, F. L., *A Journey in the Back Country,* New York, Mason Brothers, 1863.

Olmsted, F. L., *A Journey in the Seaboard Slave States,* New York, G. P. Putnam's Sons, 1904.

Olmsted, F. L., *A Journey in the Seaboard Slave States, with Remarks on Their Economy,* New York, Dix & Edwards, 1856.

Osgood, Herbert L., *The American Colonies in the 17th Century,* New York, The Macmillan Company, 1924.

Ostrogorski, M., *Democracy and the Organization of Political Parties,* London, Macmillan & Co., Ltd., 1902.

Otken, Charles H., *The Ills of the South,* New York, G. P. Putnam's Sons, 1894.

Owen, Robert, *A New View of Society,* London, Longman, Hurst, Rees, Orme, and Brown, 4th ed., 1818.

Owsley, Frank L., *Plain Folk of the Old South,* Baton Rouge, Louisiana State University Press, 1949.

Owsley, Frank L., and Owsley, Harriet C., "The Economic Basis of Society in the Late Ante-Bellum South," *Journal of Southern History,* VI (1940).

Parenton, Vernon J., "Notes on the Social Organization of a French Village in South Louisiana," *Social Forces,* XVII (1938).

Park, Robert E., "Racial Assimilation in Secondary Groups," *American Journal of Sociology,* XIX (1913–1914).

Park, Robert E., and Burgess, Ernest W., *Introduction to the Science of Sociology,* Chicago, University of Chicago Press, 1921.

Patients in Hospitals for Mental Disease: 1935, Washington, Government Printing Office, 1937.

Patterson, Cecil H., "The Relationship of Bernreuter Scores to Parent Behavior, Child Behavior, Urban-Rural Residence, and Other Background Factors in 100 Normal Adult Parents," *Journal of Social Psychology,* XXIV (1946).

Peake, Harold, *The English Village,* London, Benn Brothers, Ltd., 1922.

Peattie, Roderick, "The Isolation of the Lower St. Lawrence Valley," *Geographical Review,* V (1918).

Penn, William, "A Further Account of the Province of Pennsylvania, 1685," *Narratives of Early Pennsylvania, West New Jersey and Delaware, 1630–1707,* edited by Albert Cook Myers, New York, Charles Scribner's Sons, 1912.

Pennell, Elliot H., "Death of Nonresidents in Syracuse," *Quarterly Bulletin of the Milbank Memorial Fund,* X (1932).

Peters, W. E., *Ohio Lands and Their Subdivision,* Athens, privately printed, 1918.

Phillips, U. B., *American Negro Slavery,* New York, D. Appleton-Century Company, 1918.

Phillips, U. B., *A History of Transportation in the Eastern Cotton Belt to 1860,* New York, Columbia University Press, 1908.

Phillips, U. B., and Glunt, James David, *Florida Plantation Records,* St. Louis, Historical Society, 1927.

The Pioneer, Cincinnati, 1842.

Platt, Robert S., *Latin America: Countrysides and United Regions,* New York, McGraw-Hill Book Company, 1943.

Plunkett, Sir Horace, *The Country Life Movement in the United States,* New York, The Macmillan Company, 1910.

Poblete Troncoso, Moises, "Socio-Agricultural Legislation in the Latin American Countries," *Rural Sociology,* V (1940).

Podmore, Frank, *Robert Owen* (translated by Ernest F. Row), New York, D. Appleton and Company, 1907, 2 vols.

Poe, Clarence, *How Farmers Co-operate and Double Profits,* New York, Orange Judd Co., 1915.

Poincaré, H., *The Foundation of Science* (translated by G. B. Halsted), New York, The Science Press, 1929.

Porter, Kirk H., *County and Township Government in the United States,* New York, The Macmillan Company, 1929.

Powdermaker, Hortense, *After Freedom,* New York, The Viking Press, 1939.

Powell, George Harold, *Cooperation in Agriculture,* New York, The Macmillan Company, 1913.

Powell, J. W., *Report on the Lands of the Arid Regions of the United States,* House of Representatives, Executive Document No. 73, 45th Congress, 2nd Session, Washington, Government Printing Office, 1878.

Powers, Stephen, *Afoot and Alone: A Walk from Sea to Sea by the Southern Route,* Hartford, Columbia Book Co., 1872.

President's Commission on Migratory Labor, *Migratory Labor in Agriculture,* Washington, Government Printing Office, 1951.

President's Research Committee on Social Trends, *Recent Social Trends,* New York, McGraw-Hill Book Company, 1933.

Price, H. Bruce, and Hoffer, C. R., *Services of Rural Trade Centers in the Distribution of Farm Supplies,* Minnesota Agricultural Experiment Station Bulletin 249, St. Paul, 1928.

Price, Paul H., and Hitt, Homer L., *The Availability of Medical Personnel in Rural Louisiana,* Louisiana Agricultural Experiment Station Bulletin 459, Baton Rouge, 1951.

Priestley, Herbert I., *The Coming of the White Man, 1492–1848,* New York, The Macmillan Company, 1929.

"Problems of the Cotton Economy," *Proceedings of the Southern Social Science Research Conference,* New Orleans, 1935, Dallas, Southern Methodist University, 1936.

Proceedings of the Congress of the Scotch Irish Society in America, Nashville, 1896.

Proceedings of the First Conference for Better Government in New York State, Schenectady, H. S. Gilbertson, 1914.

Proudfit, S. V., *The Public Land System of the United States,* United States Department of Interior, Washington, 1923.

Purry, Peter, "Proposals," *Historical Collections of South Carolina,* New York, 1836.

Ragatz, Lowell Joseph, *The Fall of the Planter Class in the British Caribbean, 1763–1833,* New York, D. Appleton-Century Co., 1928.

Raper, Arthur, *The Japanese Village in Transition,* Tokyo, General Headquarters, Supreme Commander for the Allied Powers, Natural Resources Section Report 136, 1950.

Raper, Arthur, *Preface to Peasantry,* Chapel Hill, University of North Carolina Press, 1936.

Raper, Arthur, *Tenants of the Almighty,* New York, The Macmillan Company, 1943.

Raper, Arthur, and Reid, Ira De A., *Sharecroppers All,* Chapel Hill, University of North Carolina Press, 1941.

Ratcliffe, S. C., and Ratcliffe, Agnes, "Village Population Changes," *American Journal of Sociology,* XXXVII (1932).

Ravenstein, E. G., "On the Laws of Migration," *Journal of the Royal Statistical Society,* XLVII (1895).

Reid, Ira De A., "Negro Immigration to the United States," *Social Forces,* XVI (1938).

Renne, Roland R., "Rural Educational Institutions and Social Lag," *Rural Sociology,* I (1936).

Report of the Advisory Committee on Education, 75th Congress, 3rd Session, House Document 529, Washington, 1938.

"Report of the Agricultural Census Committee," *Journal of Farm Economics,* XXI (1939).

Report of the Commissioner of Agriculture for the Year 1866, Washington, Government Printing Office, 1867.

Report of the Country Life Commission, 60th Congress, 2nd Session, Senate Document 705, Washington, 1909.

Report of the National Resources Board, Washington, Government Printing Office, 1934.

Report of the Population of the United States at the Eleventh Census: 1890, Part I, Washington, Government Printing Office, 1895.

Reuss, Carl Frederick, *County Government in Washington,* Washington Agricultural Experiment Station Bulletin 400, Pullman, 1941.

Reuss, Carl Frederick, "A Qualitative Study of Depopulation in a Remote Rural District: 1900–1930," *Rural Sociology,* II (1937).

Reuter, E. B., and Runner, Jesse R., *The Family,* New York, McGraw-Hill Book Company, 1931.

Reynolds, J. B., "City and Country," *Proceedings of the Fifth National Country Life Association,* Chicago, 1923.

Rice, Stuart A., *Farmers and Workers in American Politics,* Columbia University Studies in History, Economics, and Public Law, CXIII, New York, 1924.

Rice, Stuart A., *Quantitative Methods in Politics,* New York, Alfred A. Knopf, Inc., 1928.

Richter, H., "Consolidation of Scattered Farm Holdings in Germany," *Foreign Agriculture*, II (1938).

Rife, Clarence White, "Land Tenure in New Netherland," *Essays in Colonial History*, New Haven, 1931.

Rios, José Arthur, "Assimilation of Emigrants from the Old South in Brazil," *Social Forces*, XXVI (1947).

Ripley, W. Z., *The Races of Europe*, New York, D. Appleton and Company, 1894.

Rister, Carl Coke, *Southern Plainsmen*, Norman, University of Oklahoma Press, 1938.

Roberts, H. Stephen, *History of Australian Land Settlement* (*1788–1920*), Melbourne: Macmillan & Co., Ltd., in association with Melbourne University Press, 1924.

Rocca, Helen M., *County Government*, Washington, National League of Women Voters, 1932.

Rohwer, Robert A., "Social Relations in Beginning as a Farm Operator in an Area of Prosperous, Commercial Farming," *Rural Sociology*, XIV (1949).

Roosevelt, Theodore, *The Winning of the West*, New York, The Current Literature Publishing Company, 1905, I.

Ross, E. A., *The Outlines of Sociology*, New York, D. Appleton-Century Company, 1924.

Ross, E. A., *The Outlines of Sociology*, New York, D. Appleton-Century Company, 1933.

Rusinow, Irving, *A Camera Report on El Cerrito, a Typical Spanish American Community in New Mexico*, U.S. Department of Agriculture, Miscellaneous Publication 479, Washington, 1942.

Russell, Ralph, "Membership of the American Farm Bureau Federation, 1926–1935," *Rural Sociology*, II (1937).

Ryan, Bryce, "Socio-Cultural Regions of Ceylon," *Rural Sociology*, XV (1950).

Safford, W. E., "Our Heritage from the American Indians," *Smithsonian Institution Annual Report for 1926*, Washington, 1927.

Sanchez, George I., *Forgotten People: A Study of New Mexicans*, Albuquerque, University of New Mexico Press, 1940.

Sand, René, *Health and Human Progress*, New York, The Macmillan Company, 1936.

Sanders, Irwin T., *Balkan Village*, Lexington, University of Kentucky Press, 1949.

Sanders, Irwin T., and Ensminger, Douglas, *Alabama Rural Communities: A Study of Chilton County*, Alabama College Bulletin 136, Montevallo, 1940.

Sanders, J. T., *Farm Ownership and Tenancy in the Black Prairie of*

Texas, U.S. Department of Agriculture Bulletin 1068, Washington, Government Printing Office, 1922.

Sanderson, Dwight, *The Farmer and His Community,* New York, Harcourt, Brace & Company, 1922.

Sanderson, Dwight, "Group Description," *Social Forces,* XVI (1938).

Sanderson, Dwight, *Locating the Rural Community,* Cornell Country Life Series, Ithaca, 1920.

Sanderson, Dwight, "A Preliminary Group Classification Based on Structure," *Social Forces,* XVII (1938).

Sanderson, Dwight, "The Relation of the School to the Sociological Status of the Rural Community," *Journal of Educational Sociology,* XIV (1941).

Sanderson, Dwight, *The Rural Community: The Natural History of a Sociological Group,* Boston, Ginn & Company, 1932.

Sanderson, Dwight, "The Rural Community in the United States as an Elementary Group," *Rural Sociology,* I (1936).

Sanderson, Dwight, "The Rural Family," *Journal of Home Economics,* XXIX (1937).

Sanderson, Dwight, *Rural Social and Economic Areas in Central New York,* Cornell University Agricultural Experiment Station Bulletin 614, Ithaca, 1934.

Sanderson, Dwight, *Rural Sociology and Rural Social Organization,* New York, John Wiley & Sons, Inc., 1942.

Sanderson, Dwight, *A Survey of Sickness in Rural Areas in Cortland County, New York,* Cornell University Agricultural Experiment Station Memoir 112, Ithaca, 1928.

Sanderson, Dwight, and Foster, Robert G., *The Sociology of the Family,* Cornell University Agricultural Experiment Station Mimeographed Bulletin 1, Ithaca, 1929.

Sanderson, Dwight, and Polson, Robert A., *Rural Community Organization,* New York, John Wiley & Sons, Inc., 1939.

Sanderson, Dwight, and Thompson, Warren S., *The Social Areas of Otsego County,* Cornell University Agricultural Experiment Station Bulletin 422, Ithaca, 1923.

Sato, Shosuke, *History of the Land Question in the United States,* Johns Hopkins University Studies in Historical and Political Science, Fourth Series, VII–IX, Baltimore, 1886.

Saunders, Lyle, and Leonard, Olen E., *The Wetback in the Lower Rio Grande Valley of Texas,* Inter-American Education Occasional Papers VII, Austin, University of Texas, 1951.

Schiavo, Giovanni, *The Italians in America Before the Civil War,* New York, The Vigo Press, 1934.

Schickele, Rainer, *Farm Tenure in Iowa,* Iowa Agricultural Experiment Station Bulletin 356, Ames, 1937.

Schlesinger, Arthur M., *The Rise of the City,* New York, The Macmillan Company, 1933.

Schuler, Edgar A., "The Present Social Status of American Farm Tenants," *Rural Sociology,* III (1938).

Schuler, Edgar A., "Social and Economic Status in a Louisiana Hills Community," *Rural Sociology,* V (1940).

Schuler, Edgar A., *Social Status and Farm Tenure: Attitudes and Social Conditions of Corn Belt and Cotton Belt Farmers,* U.S. Department of Agriculture, Social Research Report IV, Washington, 1938.

Schuler, Edgar A., Mayo, Selz C., and Makover, Henry B., "Measuring Needs for Medical Care: An Experiment in Method," *Rural Sociology,* XI (1946).

Schuler, Edgar A., and Turbeville, Gus, "Reading and Reading Interests of Housewives in a Rural County: A Comparison of County Library Users and Non-Library Users in Families of Leaders and a Cross Section Sample in Lenawee County, Michigan, 1946–1947," *Rural Sociology,* XIV (1949).

Schultz, Theodore W., "What Has Happened to the Agricultural Ladder?" *Farm Tenure in Iowa,* Part III, Iowa Agricultural Experiment Station Bulletin 357, Ames, 1937.

Scofield, Edna, "The Origin of Settlement Patterns in Rural New England," *Geographical Review,* XXVII (1938).

Scudder, S. H., *The Winnipeg Country, or Roughing It with an Eclipse Party,* New York, N. D. C. Hodges, 1890.

Seebohm, Frederic, *Customary Acres and Their Historical Importance,* New York, Longmans, Green & Company, 1914.

Seebohm, Frederic, *The English Village Community,* New York, Longmans, Green & Company, 1926.

Seebohm, M. E., *Evolution of the English Farm,* Cambridge, Harvard University Press, 1927.

Selective Service System, *Physical Examination of Selective Service Registrants,* Special Monograph 15, Washington, Government Printing Office, 1948.

Semple, Ellen Churchill, *American History and Its Geographic Conditions,* Boston, Houghton Mifflin Company, 1903.

Semple, Ellen Churchill, *Influence of the Geographic Environment on the Basis of Ratzel's System of Anthropo-Geography,* New York, Henry Holt & Company, 1911.

Semple, Ellen Churchill, "The Influence of the Geographic Environment on the Lower St. Lawrence," *Bulletin of the American Geographical Society,* XXXVI (1904).

Sewell, William H., and Fisher, Robert L., "Size of Farm Family in Relation to Homogeneity of Parental Traits," *Rural Sociology,* VIII (1943).

Shaw, Albert, *Cooperation in the Northwest,* Johns Hopkins Series in Historical and Political Science, Sixth Series, IV–VI, Baltimore, 1888.

Sheldon, William DuBose, *Populism in the Old Dominion: Virginia Farm Politics, 1885–1900,* Princeton, Princeton University Press, 1935.

Shepard, Eugene L., "Measurements of Certain Nonverbal Abilities of Urban and Rural Children," *Journal of Educational Psychology,* XXXI (1942).

Shepherd, William R., "The Land System of Provincial Pennsylvania," *Annual Report of the American Historical Association,* Washington, Government Printing Office, 1895.

Simons, Sarah E., "Social Assimilation," *American Journal of Sociology,* VI (1901).

Simpson, Eyler N., *The Ejido: Mexico's Way Out,* Chapel Hill, University of North Carolina Press, 1937.

Sims, N. L., *Elements of Rural Sociology,* New York, Thomas Y. Crowell Company, 1928.

Sims, N. L., *Elements of Rural Sociology,* New York, Thomas Y. Crowell Company, 1934.

Sims, N. L., *Elements of Rural Sociology,* New York, Thomas Y. Crowell Company, 1940.

Sims, N. L., *A Hoosier Village,* New York, Longmans, Green & Company, 1912.

Sims, N. L., *The Rural Community: Ancient and Modern,* New York, Charles Scribner's Sons, 1920.

Skinner, Constance Lindsay, *Pioneers of the Old Southwest,* New Haven, Yale University Press, 1921.

Skrabanek, Robert L., "Forms of Cooperation and Mutual Aid in a Czech-American Rural Community," *Southwestern Social Science Quarterly,* XXX (1950).

Skrabanek, Robert L., and Parenton, Vernon J., "Social Life in a Czech-American Rural Community," *Southwestern Social Science Quarterly,* XXXI (1950).

Small, A. W., and Vincent, George E., *An Introduction to the Study of Society,* New York, American Book Company, 1894.

Smith, Clarence B., and Wilson, Meredith Chester, *The Agricultural*

Extension System of the United States, New York, John Wiley & Sons, Inc., 1930.

Smith, J. M. Powis, *The Origin and History of Hebrew Law,* Chicago, University of Chicago Press, 1931.

Smith, Luke M., "Territorial Variables in American Local Government," *Social Forces,* XXVII (1949).

Smith, M. B., "Rural Consolidated Schools and Educational Absenteeism in Louisiana," *Journal of Educational Sociology,* XII (1938).

Smith, M. B., *A Sociological Analysis of Rural Education in Louisiana,* University, Louisiana State University Press, 1938.

Smith, Rose Marie, *Education in Rural and City School Systems: Some Statistical Indices for 1947–48,* Circular 329, Office of Education, Washington, 1951.

Smith, T. Lynn, "The Aged in Rural Society," in Milton Derber (ed.), *The Aged and Society,* Champaign, Illinois, Industrial Relations Research Association, 1950.

Smith, T. Lynn, "The Agricultural Population: Realism vs. Nominalism in the Census of Agriculture," *Journal of Farm Economics,* XX (1938).

Smith, T. Lynn, "Agricultural Systems and Standards of Living," *Inter-American Economic Affairs,* III (1949).

Smith, T. Lynn, "An Analysis of Rural Social Organization Among the French-Speaking People of Southern Louisiana," *Journal of Farm Economics,* XVI (1934).

Smith, T. Lynn, *Brazil: People and Institutions,* Baton Rouge, Louisiana State University Press, 1946.

Smith, T. Lynn, "Brazilian Land Surveys, Land Division, and Land Titles," *Rural Sociology,* IX (1944).

Smith, T. Lynn, "Characteristics of Migrants," *Southwestern Social Science Quarterly,* XXI (1941).

Smith, T. Lynn, "The Cultural Setting of Agricultural Extension Work in Colombia," *Rural Sociology,* X (1945).

Smith, T. Lynn, "The Demographic Basis of Old Age Assistance in the South," *Social Forces,* XVII (1939).

Smith, T. Lynn, "A Demographic Study of the American Negro," *Social Forces,* XXIII (1945).

Smith, T. Lynn, "Discussion," *Journal of Farm Economics,* XIX (1937).

Smith, T. Lynn, "Discussion," *Journal of Farm Economics,* XX (1938).

Smith, T. Lynn, *Farm Trade Centers in Louisiana, 1901–1931,* Louisiana Agricultural Experiment Station Bulletin 234, Baton Rouge, January, 1933.

Smith, T. Lynn, "The Locality Group Structure of Brazil," *American Sociological Review,* IX (1944).

Smith, T. Lynn, "The Migration of the Aged," in T. Lynn Smith (ed.), *The Problems of America's Aging Population,* Gainesville, University of Florida Press, 1951.

Smith, T. Lynn, "Notes on Population and Rural Social Organization in El Salvador," *Rural Sociology,* X (1945).

Smith, T. Lynn, *Population Analysis,* New York, McGraw-Hill Book Company, 1948.

Smith, T. Lynn, "The Role of the Community in American Rural Life," *Journal of Educational Sociology,* XIV (1941).

Smith, T. Lynn, "The Role of the Village in American Rural Society," *Rural Sociology,* VII (1942).

Smith, T. Lynn, "Rural-Urban Differences in the Completeness of Birth Registration," *Social Forces,* XIV (1936).

Smith, T. Lynn, "The Significance of Reported Trends in Louisiana Agriculture," *Southwestern Social Science Quarterly,* XXII (1941).

Smith, T. Lynn, "Sistemas Agricolas," *Revista Brasileira de Geografia,* IX (1947).

Smith, T. Lynn, "The Social Effects of Land Division in Relationship to a Program of Land Utilization," *Journal of Farm Economics,* XVII (1935).

Smith, T. Lynn, "Some Aspects of Village Demography," *Social Forces,* XX (1941).

Smith, T. Lynn, "Some Observations on Land Tenure in Colombia," *Foreign Agriculture,* XVI (1952).

Smith, T. Lynn, Diaz Rodriguez, Justo, and Garcia, Luis Roberto, *Tabio: Estudio de la Organizacion Social Rural,* Bogotá, Ministerio de la Economía Nacional, 1944.

Smith, T. Lynn, and Fry, Martha Ray, *The Population of a Selected "Cut-Over" Area in Louisiana,* Louisiana Agricultural Experiment Station Bulletin 268, Baton Rouge, 1936.

Smith, T. Lynn, and Hitt, Homer L., "The Misstatement of Women's Ages and the Vital Indices," *Metron,* XIII (1939).

Smith, T. Lynn, and Hitt, Homer L., *The People of Louisiana,* Baton Rouge, Louisiana State University Press, 1952.

Smith, T. Lynn, and McMahan, C. A., *The Sociology of Urban Life: A Textbook with Readings,* New York, The Dryden Press, Inc., 1951.

Smith, T. Lynn, and Parenton, Vernon J., "Acculturation Among the Louisiana French," *American Journal of Sociology,* XLIV (1938).

Smith, T. Lynn, and Parenton, Vernon J., "Social Cohesion and Social Control," in Joseph S. Roucek (ed.), *Social Control,* New York, D. Van Nostrand Company, 1945, chap. 5.

Smith, T. Lynn, and Post, Lauren C., "The Country Butchery: A Co-operative Institution," *Rural Sociology*, II (1937).

Smith, T. Lynn, and Roberts, Ralph W., "Sources and Distribution of the Farm Population in Relation to Farm Benefit Payments," *Journal of Farm Economics*, XXIII (1941).

Smith, W. H., *Canada: Past, Present, and Future*, Toronto, Thomas Maclear, 1851, I.

Smith, W. Robertson, *The Religion of the Semites*, London, Black, 1894.

Sneed, Melvin W., and Ensminger, Douglas, *The Rural Church in Missouri*, Missouri Agricultural Experiment Station Research Bulletin 225, Columbia, 1935.

Sohn, Rudolf, *The Institutes: A Textbook of the History and System of Roman Private Law* (translated by J. C. Ledlie), Oxford, The Clarendon Press, 1907.

Sorokin, P. A., *Contemporary Sociological Theories*, New York, Harper & Brothers, 1928.

Sorokin, P. A., *Social and Cultural Dynamics*, New York, American Book Company, 1937, 4 vols.

Sorokin, P. A., *Social Mobility*, New York, Harper & Brothers, 1927.

Sorokin, P. A., *The Sociology of Revolution*, Philadelphia, J. B. Lippincott Company, 1925.

Sorokin, P. A., and Zimmerman, Carle C., *Principles of Rural-Urban Sociology*, New York, Henry Holt & Company, 1929.

Sorokin, P. A., Zimmerman, Carle C., and Galpin, C. J., *A Systematic Source Book in Rural Sociology*, Minneapolis, University of Minnesota Press, 1930–1932, 3 vols.

Spencer, Herbert, *First Principles*, New York, D. Appleton and Company, 1899.

Spillman, W. J., "The Agricultural Ladder," *American Economic Review Supplement*, IX (1919).

Stanberry, V. B., *Migration into Oregon, 1930–1937*, Salem, Oregon State Planning Board (mimeographed), 1938.

Statistical Atlas of the United States, Washington, Government Printing Office, 1925.

Steward, Julian H. (ed.), *Handbook of South American Indians*, Bureau of American Ethnology Bulletin 143, Washington, Government Printing Office, 1948.

Stone, Alfred H., "The Negro and Agricultural Development," *Annals of the American Academy of Political and Social Science*, XXXV (1910).

Stone, Alfred H., "A Plantation Experiment," *Quarterly Journal of Economics*, XIX (1904).

Stone, Alfred H., "Some Problems of Southern Economic History," *American Historical Review*, XII (1908).

Stott, Leland H., "Parental Attitudes of Farm, Town and City Parents in Relation to Certain Personality Adjustments in Their Children," *Journal of Social Psychology*, XI (1940).

Stromberg, Eugene T., *The Influence of the Central Rural School on Community Organization*, Cornell University Agricultural Experiment Station Bulletin 699, Ithaca, 1938.

Sumner, W. G., *Folkways*, Boston, Ginn and Company, 1907.

Sutherland, Stella H., *Population Distribution in Colonial America*, New York, Columbia University Press, 1936.

Sydenstricker, Edgar, *Health and Environment*, New York, McGraw-Hill Book Company, 1933.

Sydenstricker, Edgar, "Physical Impairments and Occupational Class," *U.S. Public Health Reports*, XLV (1930).

Sydnor, Charles Sackett, *Slavery in Mississippi*, New York, D. Appleton-Century Company, 1933.

Taeuber, Conrad, "A Registration System as a Source of Data Concerning Internal Migration," *Rural Sociology*, I (1936).

Taeuber, Conrad, "Some Recent Developments in Sociological Work in the Department of Agriculture," *American Sociological Review*, X (1945).

Taeuber, Conrad, and Taylor, Carl C., *The People of the Drought States*, Washington, Works Progress Administration, 1937.

Tannenbaum, Frank, *The Mexican Agrarian Revolution*, New York, The Macmillan Company, 1929.

Tate, Leland B., *The Health and Medical-Care Situation in Rural Virginia*, Virginia Agricultural Experiment Station Bulletin 363, Blacksburg, 1944.

Taylor, A. E., and Yoder, F. R., *Rural Social Organization in Clark County*, Washington Agricultural Experiment Station Bulletin 225, Pullman, 1928.

Taylor, A. E., and Yoder, F. R., *Rural Social Organization in Whatcom County*, Washington Agricultural Experiment Station Bulletin 215, Pullman, 1927.

Taylor, A. E., and Yoder, F. R., *Rural Social Organization in Whitman County*, Washington Agricultural Experiment Station Bulletin 203, Pullman, 1926.

Taylor, Carl C., *Rural Life in Argentina*, Baton Rouge, Louisiana State University Press, 1948.

Taylor, Carl C., *Rural Sociology*, New York, Harper & Brothers, 1926.

Taylor, Carl C., *Rural Sociology*, New York, Harper & Brothers, 1933.

Taylor, Carl C., "The Country Newspaper as a Town-Country

Agency," *Proceedings of the Fourth Country Life Conference,* Chicago, 1921.

Taylor, Carl C., et al., *Rural Life in the United States.* New York: Alfred A. Knopf, Inc., 1949.

Taylor, Carl C., Wheeler, Helen W., and Kirkpatrick, E. L., *Disadvantaged Classes in American Agriculture,* U.S. Department of Agriculture, Farm Security Administration, and Bureau of Agricultural Economics coöperating, Social Research Report VIII, Washington, 1938.

Taylor, Henry C., *Agricultural Economics,* New York, The Macmillan Company, 1923.

Taylor, Henry C., *The Decline of Landowning Farmers in England,* Bulletin of the University of Wisconsin, Economics and Political Science Series, Madison, 1904.

Taylor, Paul S., "Migratory Farm Labor in the United States," *Monthly Labor Review,* XLIV (1937).

Taylor, Paul S., "Perspective on Housing Migratory Agricultural Laborers," *Land Economics,* XXVII (1951).

Taylor, Paul S., and Vasey, Tom, "Contemporary Background of California Farm Labor," *Rural Sociology,* I (1936).

Taylor, Paul S., and Vasey, Tom, "Historical Background of California Farm Labor," *Rural Sociology,* I (1936).

Teggart, Frederick J., *Theory of History,* New Haven, Yale University Press, 1925.

Terpenning, Walter A., *Village and Open-Country Neighborhoods,* New York, D. Appleton-Century Company, 1931.

Tetreau, E. D., *Arizona Farm Leases,* Arizona Agricultural Experiment Station Bulletin 179, Tucson, 1942.

Tetreau, E. D., *The Objectives and Activities of the California Farm Bureau,* California Agricultural Experiment Station Bulletin 563, Berkeley, 1933.

Thaden, J. F., "Characteristics of Persons Listed in *Rus,*" *Rural Sociology,* II (1937).

Thaden, J. F., *Distribution of Doctors of Medicine and Osteopaths in Michigan Communities,* Michigan Agricultural Experiment Station Special Bulletin 370, East Lansing, 1951.

Thaden, J. F., and Mumford, Eben, *High School Communities in Michigan,* Michigan Agricultural Experiment Station Special Bulletin 289, East Lansing, 1938.

Thomas, Dorothy Swaine, *Research Memorandum on Migration Differentials,* Social Science Research Council Bulletin 43, New York, Social Science Research Council, 1938.

Thomasson, Maurice E., *A Study of Special Kinds of Education for Rural Negroes,* Charlotte, N.C., privately printed, 1936.

Thompson, Edgar T., "The Climatic Theory of the Plantation," *Agricultural History,* XV (1941).

Thompson, Holland, *The New South,* New Haven, Yale University Press, 1920.

Thompson, J. G., *Urbanization,* New York, E. P. Dutton & Co., Inc., 1927.

Thompson, James W., "East German Colonization in the Middle Ages," *Annual Report of the American Historical Association, 1915,* Washington, Government Printing Office, 1917.

Thompson, R. L., and Allin, Bushrod, *Louisiana Farm Taxes,* Louisiana Agricultural Experiment Station Bulletin 231, Baton Rouge, 1933.

Thompson, Warren S., *Average Number of Children per Woman in Butler County, Ohio: 1930—A Study in Differential Fertility,* Washington, Bureau of the Census, 1941.

Thompson, Warren S., *Ratio of Children to Women, 1920,* Census Monograph XI, Washington, Government Printing Office, 1931.

Thompson, Warren S., *Research Memorandum on Internal Migration During the Depression,* Social Science Research Bulletin 30, New York, Social Science Research Council, 1937.

Thompson, Warren S., and Jackson, Nelle E., "Fertility in Rural Areas in Relation to Their Distance from Cities, 1930," *Rural Sociology,* V (1940).

Thompson, Warren S., and Whelpton, P. K., *Population Trends in the United States,* New York, McGraw-Hill Book Company, 1933.

Thornthwaite, C. Warren, *Internal Migration in the United States,* Philadelphia, University of Pennsylvania Press, 1934.

Thurnwald, Richard, *Economics in Primitive Communities,* New York, Oxford University Press, 1932.

Thwaites, Reuben Gold, "Flint's Letters from America, 1818–1820," in *Early Western Travels, 1748–1846,* Cleveland, Arthur H. Clark Co., 1904.

Timasheff, N. S., "Structural Changes in Rural Russia," *Rural Sociology,* II (1937).

Titus, Charles H., *Voting Behavior in the United States,* Publications of the University of California at Los Angeles in the Social Sciences, V (1935).

Titus, Charles H., "Voting in California," *Southwestern Political and Social Science Quarterly,* VII, IX, X (1928–1929).

Toennies, F., *Gemeinschaft und Gesellschaft,* Leipzig, Hans Bushe, 3rd ed., 1935.

Trask, John W., *Vital Statistics,* Supplement 12 to the *Public Health Reports,* Washington, 1914.

Treat, Payson Jackson, *The National Land System, 1785–1820,* New York, E. B. Treat and Company, 1910.

Treat, Payson Jackson, "Surveys of Land," *Cyclopedia of American Government,* New York, D. Appleton-Century Company, 1914.

Trewartha, Glenn T., "The Suwa Basin: A Specialized Sericulture District in the Japanese Alps," *Geographical Review,* XX (1930).

Turbeville, Gus, "Religious Schism in the Methodist Church: A Sociological Analysis of the Pine Grove Case," *Rural Sociology,* XIV (1949).

Turner, Frederick Jackson, *The Frontier in American History,* New York, Henry Holt & Company, 1921.

Turner, Frederick Jackson, "The Significance of the Frontier in American History," *Annual Report of the American Historical Association for 1893,* Washington, Government Printing Office, 1894.

Tylor, E. B., "On the Origin of the Plough, and Wheel-Carriage," *The Journal of the Anthropological Institute of Great Britain and Ireland,* X (1881).

Tylor, E. B., *Primitive Culture,* London, Henry Holt & Company, 1871.

United Nations, *Data on Urban and Rural Population in Recent Censuses,* Population Studies 8, Lake Success, United Nations, 1950.

United Nations, *Demographic Yearbook, 1948,* Lake Success, United Nations, 1949.

United States Census of Agriculture: 1935, Washington, Government Printing Office, 1936.

United States Census of Agriculture: 1945, II, Washington, Government Printing Office, 1947.

United States Census Office, *Twelfth Census of the United States . . . 1900,* "Agriculture," Part I, Washington, United States Census Office, 1902.

United States Department of Agriculture, Extension Service and Office of Foreign Agricultural Relations, *Conference Report on Extension Experiences Around the World,* Washington, United States Department of Agriculture, 1951.

United States Department of Labor, *Negro Migration in 1916–17,* Washington, Government Printing Office, 1919.

United States Office of Education, *Biennial Survey of Education in the United States—1946–48,* Washington, Government Printing Office, 1950.

United States Public Health Reports, XXIII, Washington, Government Printing Office, 1918.

United States Public Health Reports, XXXIX, Washington, Government Printing Office, 1924.

Urbanism Committee of the National Resources Committee, *Our Cities*, Washington, Government Printing Office, 1937.

Useem, John, and Useem, Ruth Hill, "Minority Group Pattern in Prairie Society," *American Journal of Sociology*, L (1945).

Vance, Rupert B., *Human Factors in Cotton Culture*, Chapel Hill, University of North Carolina Press, 1929.

Vance, Rupert B., *Regional Reconstruction: A Way Out for the South*, Chapel Hill, University of North Carolina Press, 1935.

Vance, Rupert B., *Research Memorandum on Population Redistribution in the United States*, Social Science Research Bulletin 42, New York, Social Science Research Council, 1938.

Vinogradoff, Paul, *The Growth of the Manor*, New York, The Macmillan Company, 1905.

Vogt, Evon Z., "Social Stratification in the Rural Middlewest: A Structural Analysis," *Rural Sociology*, XII (1947).

Wager, Paul, "Can Local Self-Government Be Preserved?" *Rural Government: Proceedings of the Fourteenth American Country Life Conference*, Chicago, University of Chicago Press, 1932.

Wager, Paul, *County Government and Administration in North Carolina*, Chapel Hill, University of North Carolina Press, 1928.

Wakefield, Richard, and Landis, Paul H., "Types of Migratory Farm Laborers and Their Movement into the Yakima Valley, Washington," *Rural Sociology*, III (1938).

Wakeley, Ray E., *The Communities of Schuyler County, New York, 1927*, Cornell University Agricultural Experiment Station Bulletin 524, Ithaca, 1931.

Wakeley, Ray E., *Differential Mobility Within the Rural Population in 18 Iowa Townships, 1928 to 1935*, Iowa Agricultural Experiment Station Bulletin 249, Ames, 1938.

Wallace, Alfred Russell, *Travels on the Amazon*, London, Ward Lock & Co., 1911.

Wallace, Henry A., "Farm Tenancy," Columbia Broadcasting Station broadcast, January 22, 1937.

Wallis, Wilson D., *An Introduction to Anthropology*, New York, Harper & Brothers, 1926.

Wallis, Wilson D., and Willey, M. M., *Readings in Sociology*, New York, Appleton-Century-Crofts, Inc., 1930.

Wanstall, Grace, *Statistics of Farmers' Marketing and Purchasing Cooperatives*, Washington, Farm Credit Administration, Miscellaneous 1947–48 Report 137, 1950.

Warne, Frank Julian, *The Tide of Immigration,* New York, D. Appleton-Century Company, 1916.

Warner, Estella Ford, and Smith, Geddes, *Children of the Covered Wagon,* New York, The Commonwealth Fund, 1930.

Warner, W. Lloyd, and Lunt, Paul S., *The Status System of a Modern Community,* New Haven, Yale University Press, 1942.

Warner, W. Lloyd, Meeker, Marchia, and Eells, Kenneth, *Social Class in America,* Chicago, Science Research Associates, 1949.

Webb, John N., *The Migratory Casual Worker,* Works Progress Administration Research Monograph VII, Washington, 1937.

Webb, Walter Prescott, *The Great Plains,* Boston, Houghton Mifflin Company, 1936.

Weber, A. F., *The Growth of Cities in the Nineteenth Century,* New York, Columbia University Press, 1899.

Weeden, William B., *Economic and Social History of New England, 1620–1789,* Boston, Houghton Mifflin Company, 1891.

Wehrwein, George S., and Baker, J. A., "The Cost of Isolated Settlement in Northern Wisconsin," *Rural Sociology,* II (1937).

West, James (pseudonym for Carl Withers), *Plainville, U. S. A.,* New York, Columbia University Press, 1945.

Westaway, F. W., *Scientific Method,* New York, Hillman-Curl, Inc., 1937.

Westermarck, Edward, *The History of Human Marriage,* New York, The Allerton Book Company, 1922.

Weston, George M., *Progress of Slavery in the United States,* Washington, the author, 1857.

Whelpton, P. K., "The Completeness of Birth Registration in the United States," *Journal of the American Statistical Association,* XXIX (1934).

Whetten, Nathan L., *Rural Mexico,* Chicago, University of Chicago Press, 1948.

Whipple, George C., *Vital Statistics,* New York, John Wiley & Sons, Inc., 1923.

White, Max R., Ensminger, Douglas, and Gregory, Cecil L., *Rich Land—Poor People,* Farm Security Administration Research Report I, Indianapolis, 1938.

White House Conference on Child Health and Protection, *The Adolescent in the Family,* New York, D. Appleton-Century Company, 1936.

Wiehl, Dorothy G., "The Correction of Infant Mortality Rates for Residence," *American Journal of Public Health,* XIX (1929).

Willcox, Walter F., *Introduction to the Vital Statistics of the United States, 1900 to 1930,* Washington, Government Printing Office, 1933.

Willcox, Walter F. (ed.), *Natural and Political Observations Made upon the Bills of Mortality by John Graunt*, Baltimore, Johns Hopkins University Press, 1939.

Willey, Malcolm M., *The Country Newspaper*, Chapel Hill, University of North Carolina Press, 1926.

Williams, B. O., "Mobility and Farm Tenancy," *Journal of Land and Public Utility Economics*, XIV (1938).

Williams, B. O., *Occupational Mobility Among Farmers*, South Carolina Agricultural Experiment Station Bulletin 296, Clemson, 1934.

Williams, Faith, and Zimmerman, Carle C., *Studies of Family Living in the United States and Other Countries*, United States Department of Agriculture, Washington, 1935.

Williams, James M., *The Expansion of Rural Life*, New York, Alfred A. Knopf, Inc., 1926.

Williams, James M., *Our Rural Heritage*, New York, Alfred A. Knopf, Inc., 1925.

Willis, J. C., *Agriculture in the Tropics*, Cambridge, The University Press, 1909.

Wilson, Isabella C., and Metzler, William H., *Sickness and Medical Care in an Ozark Area in Arkansas*, Arkansas Agricultural Experiment Station Bulletin 353, Fayetteville, 1938.

Wilson, Louis R., *The Geography of Reading*, Chicago, American Library Association and University of Chicago Press, 1938.

Wilson, Louis R., and Wight, Edward A., *County Library Service in the South*, Chicago, University of Chicago Press, 1935.

Wilson, M. L., *Economic Agriculture and the Rural and General Social Welfare*, paper given at the International Conference of Agricultural Economists, McDonald College, Ste. Anne de Bellevue, Quebec, Canada (mimeographed), August 22, 1938.

Wilson, M. L., *Report of Cooperative Extension Work in Agriculture and Home Economics, 1950*, Washington, Government Printing Office, 1952.

Wilson, Warren H., *The Farmer's Church*, New York, D. Appleton-Century Company, 1925.

Windle, C. A., *Religions: Past and Present*, New York, D. Appleton-Century Company, 1927.

Wolf, A., *Essentials of the Scientific Method*, New York, The Macmillan Company, 1930.

Woofter, T. J., Jr., *Black Yeomanry*, New York, Henry Holt & Company, 1930.

Woofter, T. J., Jr., *Negro Migration*, New York, W. D. Gray, 1920.

Woofter, T. J., Jr., and others, *Landlord and Tenant on the Cotton*

Plantation, Works Progress Administration Research Monograph V, Washington, 1936.

Woolston, Howard, "The Process of Assimilation," *Social Forces*, XXIII (1945).

Works, George A., and Lesser, Simon D., *Rural America Today: Its Schools and Community Life*, Chicago, University of Chicago Press, 1942.

Yarbrough, W. H., *Economic Aspects of Slavery in Relation to Southern and Southwestern Migration*, Nashville, George Peabody College for Teachers, 1932.

Yoder, Fred R., *An Introduction to Agricultural Economics*, New York, Thomas Y. Crowell Company, 1929.

Yoshpe, Harry B., *The Disposition of Loyalist Estates in the Southern District of the State of New York*, New York, Columbia University Press, 1939.

Young, E. C., *The Movement of Farm Population*, Cornell University Agricultural Experiment Station Bulletin 426, Ithaca, 1924.

Young, Kimball, *Introductory Sociology*, New York, American Book Company, 1934.

Zimmerman, Carle C., *The Changing Community*, New York, Harper & Brothers, 1938.

Zimmerman, Carle C., *Consumption and Standards of Living*, New York, D. Van Nostrand Company, 1936.

Zimmerman, Carle C., *Family and Civilization*, New York, Harper & Brothers, 1947.

Zimmerman, Carle C., "The Family Farm," *Rural Sociology*, XV (1950).

Zimmerman, Carle C., *Farm Trade Centers in Minnesota, 1905–29*, Minnesota Agricultural Experiment Station Bulletin 269, St. Paul, 1930.

Zimmerman, Carle C., and Frampton, Merle, *Family and Society*, New York, D. Van Nostrand Company, 1935.

Zimmerman, Carle C., and Taylor, Carl C., *Rural Organization: A Study of Primary Groups in Wake County, N. C.*, North Carolina Agricultural Experiment Station Bulletin 245, Raleigh, 1922.

Zimmerman, Carle C., Useem, John H., and Ziegler, Lyman H., "Littleville: A Parasitic Community During the Depression," *Rural Sociology*, I (1936).

AUTHOR AND SOURCE INDEX

SUBJECT INDEX

Accommodation, 542, 543, 546–568
  between trade centers, 559–562, 563
  forms of, 546–548
  in the Great Plains, 562–568
  sharecropping as, 548–559
Acculturation, 542, 543, 545–546, 569–574
Adjustment, 542, 543
African Methodist Episcopal Church, 461
African Methodist Episcopal Zion Church, 461
Age composition, 76–80
Agrarian reform, 13, 275–276, 321–323, 516–520
Agricultural Adjustment Administration, 319–320
Agricultural classes, future of, 601–602
Agricultural Extension Service, 445–447
Agricultural laborers, 182, 286, 330, 516
  See also Farm laborers
Agricultural ladder, 314, 580–584
Agriculture, origins of, 333
Alpine race, 89
American Farm Bureau, 480, 528
American Lutheran Church, 460
American Society of Equity, 528, 529
Ammom-Lapouge "laws," 88
Arabs, 73
Arithmetic mean, 8
Arkansas Agricultural Wheel, 480
Armenians, 73
Assimilation, 542, 543, 544–545, 546, 568–569
Attitudes, rural, 68
Austrians, 63

Bankhead-Jones Act, 320
Bare observation, 6
Biological factors, 597–598
Birth rate, 75, 126–127
  crude, 127, 128–129
  decline of, 139, 140
  nuptial, 127
  rural, 132, 143, 145

Birth rate—(*Continued*)
  specific, 127
  standardized, 127, 129
  urban, 132, 143, 145
Births, place of occurrence, 109–11
  underregistration of, 129–131

"Cabin" rights, 276
Caste, 385, 388, 389
Cavaliers, 55
Cephalic index, 87–88
Christian Science, 448
Church of Jesus Christ of Latter-day Saints (Mormon), 460
Church of the United Brethren, 461, 466
Churches of Christ, 460
Cities, growth of, 50
City, diversity in, 26–27
City and country, distinction between, 15–18
Classification, 7, 8, 9
Code of Hammurabi, 274–275
Colored Methodist Episcopal Church, 461
Communistic colonies, 231–232
Community, 367, 369, 377–384, 442, 443, 444
  "cumulative," 367
  rurban, 505, 506
Competition, 499, 500–506
  economic, 501–503
  institutional, 503–504
  racial and cultural, 503
  rural trade centers, 504–506, 560
Composition of population, 68–84, 409–412, 424–425, 457–468
  age, 76–80
  educational status, 424–425
  marital status, 409–412
  race and nativity, 69–76
  religious, 457–468
  sex, 80–84
Congregational and Christian Churches, 460, 465